The Complete Handbook of

Coaching

The Complete Handbook of
Coaching
Second Edition

Edited by

Elaine Cox | Tatiana Bachkirova | David Clutterbuck

Los Angeles | London | New Delhi
Singapore | Washington DC

Los Angeles | London | New Delhi
Singapore | Washington DC

SAGE Publications Ltd
1 Oliver's Yard
55 City Road
London EC1Y 1SP

SAGE Publications Inc.
2455 Teller Road
Thousand Oaks, California 91320

SAGE Publications India Pvt Ltd
B 1/I 1 Mohan Cooperative Industrial Area
Mathura Road
New Delhi 110 044

SAGE Publications Asia-Pacific Pte Ltd
3 Church Street
#10-04 Samsung Hub
Singapore 049483

Editor: Susannah Trefgarne
Editorial assistant: Laura Walmsley
Production editor: Sushant Nailwal
Copyeditor: Sunrise Setting Limited
Proofreader: David Hemsley
Indexer: Avril Ehrlich
Marketing manager: Tamara Navaratnam
Cover design: Lisa Harper
Typeset by: C&M Digitals (P) Ltd, Chennai, India
Printed and bound in Great Britain by Ashford Colour
Press Ltd

First edition published 2009. Reprinted 2010, 2011 and 2013.
This second edition published 2014

Library of Congress Control Number: 2013947175

British Library Cataloguing in Publication data

A catalogue record for this book is available from the British Library

ISBN 978-1-4462-7615-0
ISBN 978-1-4462-7616-7 (pbk)

Contents

About the Editors and Contributors

EDITORS

Elaine Cox is a principal lecturer and the leader of programmes for the International Centre for Coaching and Leadership Development at Oxford Brookes University in the UK, where she also directs the Doctor of Coaching and Mentoring Programme and supervises doctoral students. She is an experienced researcher, author and editor and has recently published *Coaching Understood* with Sage. She is also the founding editor of *The International Journal of Evidence Based Coaching & Mentoring*.

Tatiana Bachkirova is a Reader in Coaching Psychology at Oxford Brookes University, UK and a Visiting Professor at HSE, Moscow. She is a Chartered Occupational Psychologist recognized for her contribution to coaching psychology with the achievement award from the BPS in 2011. As an active researcher she has published many articles, book chapters and books including *Developmental Coaching: Working with the Self*. She is also a director of the annual *International Conference in Coaching Supervision*.

David Clutterbuck is Visiting Professor of coaching and mentoring at both Sheffield Hallam and Oxford Brookes Universities. Co-founder of the European Mentoring and Coaching Council and chair of the International Standards for Mentoring Programmes in Employment and a board member of the International Mentoring Association, he supervises coaches around the world. A regular amongst the list of HR Most Influentials, he is author or co-author of 55 books. He consults and lectures globally on coaching and mentoring.

CONTRIBUTORS

Geoffrey Abbott is Director of Executive Coaching at the Graduate School of Business, Queensland University of Technology. Geoff also delivers international coaching programs through his company (The Centre for International Business Coaching). He specializes in coaching in complex international environments and is a passionate advocate for action learning methodologies. Geoff is co-editor of *The Routledge Companion to International Business Coaching* (Moral and Abbott, 2011) and has numerous published articles and chapters on international coaching. Geoff is a member of the Global Advisory Board of the Association for Coaching. He is a regular presenter at coaching and related conferences and is active in promoting coaching in Central America.

Rona S. Beattie is Professor of Human Resource Development (HRD) in the Department of Business Management, Glasgow School for Business and Society, Glasgow Caledonian University, Scotland. Rona has published widely, presented many papers at international conferences and is a member of a number of journal editorial boards. Whilst her teaching and research interests are diverse including healthcare management, employee engagement, voluntary sector leadership, and HRM in public service organizations; her first and greatest research passion continues to be coaching, mentoring and the role of line managers as facilitators of learning, the latter the subject of her PhD. Rona is also a Chartered Fellow of the Chartered Institute of Personnel and Development (CIPD) and a Fellow of the Higher Education Academy (HEA) both in the UK.

Peter Bluckert is the founder of Peter Bluckert Consulting, an international leadership, team and organizational development consultancy. He was formerly the Managing Director and founder of PB Coaching, a leading corporate coaching firm. Author of several journal articles, a book chapter in *The Complete Handbook of Coaching* (Sage, 2014) on the Gestalt Approach to Coaching, and a coaching textbook *Psychological Dimensions of Executive Coaching*, he has delivered workshops, presentations and coaching to senior leaders in Europe, USA, South America, UAE, Asia, Africa and China. During a career spanning 30 years Peter has consulted to more than 250 UK and International organizations across a wide range of sectors. As a co-founder of the European Mentoring and Coaching Council (EMCC) and its first Chair of Standards and Ethics Committee he remains committed to the purpose of this work.

Ilona Boniwell is one of the world leaders in positive psychology, having founded the first Masters in Applied Positive Psychology (MAPP) in Europe. Currently, she teaches at l'Ecole Centrale Paris and consults businesses and educational institutions around the globe as a Director of Positran, a boutique consultancy dedicated to achieving transformation through positive psychology. Dr Boniwell wrote or edited six books and multiple scientific articles, founded the European Network of Positive Psychology, organized the first European Congress of Positive Psychology (2002) and was the first vice-chair of the International Positive Psychology Association (IPPA).

Diane Brennan is an executive coach and consultant, and works with individuals and organizations in healthcare, science and engineering. She holds a Masters in Business Administration, and the International Coach Federation (ICF) credential of Master Certified Coach. She served as President of ICF in 2008. Brennan is co-editor and contributing author of *The Handbook of Knowledge-Based Coaching: From Theory to Practice* (2011) and *The Philosophy and Practice of Coaching: Insights and Issues for a New Era* (2008). In addition to coaching, she has more than 20 years experience in senior leadership and clinical practice positions within private and publicly traded healthcare companies.

Andrew Buckley is founder of the mental wellbeing organization Kipepeo, and has been helping individuals and organizations to understand mental health since the mid-1990s. He is a psychotherapist, coach and co-author of *A Guide to Coaching and Mental Health: The Recognition and Management of Psychological Issues* (Routledge, 2006). Andrew is regularly invited to speak at conferences and events on the topic of managing mental-health issues and advocates a simple approach that looks for practical and effective means which will help all concerned.

Michael J. Cavanagh is Deputy Director of the Coaching Psychology Unit at the University of Sydney. A registered psychologist, he is the Australian co-ordinating editor for *International Coaching Psychology Review*. Michael has over 20 years experience in facilitating personal, group and organizational change. He has coached leaders and managers at all levels from a diverse range of public and private, national and multinational organizations. He is also the principal author of the *Standards Australia Handbook of Organisational Coaching* – one of the world's first ISO aligned national guidelines for the training of coaches and the provision of coaching services.

David B. Drake, PhD is Executive Director of Center for Narrative Coaching & Leadership in San Francisco. He founded the field of narrative coaching in 2002, leads workshops internationally and supports peer groups in various countries to advance the field and the community of practice (www.narrativecoaching.com). He also works with leaders, teams and change agents in organizations to develop a coaching mindset and apply it in real time to address real issues (www.narrativedesignlabs.com). These projects are based in his pioneering work on narrative design as a new integral theory of adult development. He is the author of 40 publications; Associate Editor for *Coaching: An International Journal of Theory, Research and Practice*; editor of *The Philosophy and Practice of Coaching* (Jossey-Bass, 2008); and author of *Coaching and Organizational Culture: A Narrative Perspective* (Routledge).

Nick Edgerton is an independent Chartered Psychologist providing coaching, counselling and Cognitive Behavioural Therapy (CBT) services from his practices near Woodbridge in Suffolk and Blackheath in London. His consultancy work has mainly been in the provision of coaching, counselling and interpersonal skills courses for public service organizations and the oil and gas industry. He has been Chair of the Counselling Psychology Section of the BPS and was Head of the Centre for Studies in Counselling at the Polytechnic of East London. He is currently developing and presenting courses at the Centre for Stress Management and Centre for Coaching in London.

Andrea D. Ellinger is Professor of Human Resource Development in the Department of Human Resource Development and Technology, College of Business and Technology at The University of Texas at Tyler. She is the current editor of *Human Resource Development Quarterly* and is the 2012 recipient of The Academy of Human Resource Development Outstanding Scholar of the Year Award. She serves on several editorial boards, including *Management Learning*, the *Journal of Workplace Learning* and the *International Journal of Evidence Based Coaching and Mentoring*, and is a Consulting Editor for *Adult Education Quarterly*. She has presented and published her scholarship nationally and internationally. Her research interests include informal learning in the workplace, evolving managerial roles, coaching, mentoring, organizational learning and the learning organization concept.

Annette Fillery-Travis is currently Coordinator for the Professional Doctorate at Middlesex University where she is a senior coach educator, researcher and author supervising a number of doctorate students in coaching. She has designed leadership programmes (as internal programmes and external Masters degrees) for public sector managers and school leaders, and manager coach training programmes across a range of sectors. She co-wrote *The Case for Coaching – Making Evidence-based Decisions on Coaching* (CIPD Publications, 2006), which remains a standard text and has worked for many of the coaching professional associations, including WABC and EMCC, where she is a member of the research committee.

Bob Garvey is a leading academic practitioner in mentoring and coaching. His work is regarded as deeply influential, groundbreaking, original and innovative in terms of both research and practice. In particular, his 'dimensions' framework has proved to be of both practical and theoretical use to communities in which mentoring and coaching take place. His research has directly influenced policy, practice and productivity in a range of organizations in all sectors – corporate, small business, public and the not-for-profit sector. Bob's work has benefited organizations by offering best practice guidance and skills practice; developing knowledge of mentoring and coaching processes and skills; increasing knowledge of scheme design and implementation and providing models and a language with which to discuss mentoring and coaching. He is a member of the European Mentoring and Coaching Council and the co-author of four best-selling books and numerous journal articles.

Anthony M. Grant is widely recognized as a key pioneer of Coaching Psychology and evidence-based approaches to coaching and has over 100 coaching-related publications. He is the Director of the Coaching Psychology Unit at Sydney University; a Visiting Professor at the International Centre for Coaching and Leadership Development, Oxford Brookes University, Oxford, UK; a Senior Fellow at the Melbourne School of Business, Melbourne University, Australia; and a Visiting Scholar at the Säid School of Business, Oxford University, Oxford, UK. In 2007, Anthony was awarded the British Psychological Society Award for outstanding professional and scientific contribution to Coaching Psychology and in 2009 he was awarded the 'Vision of Excellence Award' from Harvard University for his pioneering work in helping to develop a scientific foundation to coaching. Anthony has considerable coaching experience at senior levels with leading Australian and global corporations with well over 5,000 hours of executive coaching experience. He also plays loud (but not very good) blues guitar.

Bruce Grimley is a successful Coaching Psychologist and Neuro Linguistic Programming (NLP) trainer based in St Ives, Cambridgeshire. His company, Achieving Lives Ltd (www. achieving-lives.co.uk), has been established since 1995 and through coaching assists at both organizational and individual levels. Bruce's first book, published by Sage, looked at the theory and practice of NLP coaching from the perspective of a chartered psychologist and is the first of its kind. At present Bruce's PhD research is asking why NLP has not been accepted into the mainstream provision of services around the world and what barriers need to be overcome to ensure that the potential of NLP can be more readily achieved. Bruce is the UK President of both the International Association of NLP Institutes (www.nlp-institutes.net/index.php) and Coaching Institutes (www.coaching-institutes.net/index.php).

Robert G. Hamlin is Emeritus Professor and Chair of Human Resource Development (HRD) at the University of Wolverhampton, and also works as an independent management and organization development consultant, researcher and author. His research is focused mainly on perceived 'managerial and leadership effectiveness', 'managerial coaching effectiveness' and 'mentoring effectiveness' within public, private and third sector organizations within the UK and other countries around the globe. He is Honorary Treasurer of the University Forum for HRD and a distinguished Fellow of the Chartered Institute of Personnel and Development. He is author of *Universalistic Models of Managerial and Leadership Effectiveness* (VDM Verlag Dr. Muller, 2009), lead editor for *Organizational Change and Development: A Reflective Guide for Managers, Trainers and Developers* (FT Prentice Hall, 2001), and author or co-author of 21 book chapters and 35 peer-reviewed journal articles. He is a co-recipient of a 2014 ASTD Excellence in Research-to-Practice Award from the American Society of Training and Development, and of the 2013 IFTDO Research Excellence Award from the International Federation of Training and Development Organizations.

Peter Hawkins is Professor of Leadership at Henley Business School and Emeritus Chair and founder of Bath Consultancy Group and Honorary President of the Association for Professional Executive Coaching and Supervision (APECS). He is an international organizational consultant, executive coach and supervisor, and author of several books, including *Creating a Coaching Culture* (2012) *Leadership Team Coaching* (2011) and co-author of *Coaching, Mentoring an Organizational Consultancy: Supervision and Development* (Open University Press 2006 and 2013). Peter is leader of the Bath Consultancy Group training in Coaching Supervision and Systemic Team Coaching.

Bruce Hazen has extensive and diverse industry experience as an internal and external management coach and consultant, as a member of corporate staff as well as in line management. He is the President of Three Questions Consulting and coaches professionals regarding the interface where their skill and style come together to impel or impede success. He lectures on career management at the Oregon Health Sciences University and is the author of *Answering The Three Career Questions: Your Lifetime Career Management System* (2014) as well as a major contributor to the international business book (16 translations) on careers by Tim Clark, *Business Model You* (2012). He has a BS in Industrial and Labor Relations from Cornell University, with an emphasis in organizational behaviour and psychology. In addition, he holds an MS in Clinical Psychology.

Erika Jackson, BCC, PCC, MA, received an undergraduate degree in Psychology from Otterbein College and a Master's Degree in Labor and Human Resources from The Ohio State

University with a concentration in Adult Development and Learning. Erika is the VP, Training and Operations for Wellcoaches, responsible for the quality of programs, curriculum and operational systems. She was a contributor to the first textbook for health and wellness coaching, *The Coaching Psychology Manual*, and has been an active health and wellness coach for 12 years.

Peter Jackson is a professional coach, supervisor and academic. He teaches part-time on the Oxford Brookes University postgraduate programme in Coaching and Mentoring Practice and is currently carrying out doctoral research on physicality in coaching. He has publications in the areas of coaching approaches, coaching philosophy, professional and academic development of coaching practitioners and the physical and environmental influences on the coaching process.

Richard Jolly is a Director of the consulting firm, Stokes & Jolly (www.stokesjolly.com), who provide leadership coaching, top team facilitation, management development programmes and assessment selection services for a wide range of professional service and corporate clients. Richard is Adjunct Professor of Organisational Behaviour at London Business School, where he teaches several core modules and electives on the topics of leadership, change management and power and politics in organizations, as well as working on a diverse range of open and company-specific programmes, both in the UK and across Europe, the Middle East and Asia.

Stephen Joseph, PhD, is a professor in the School of Education at the University of Nottingham where he convenes the psychotherapy and counselling cluster. His interests are in positive psychology, psychological trauma and the person-centred approach. He is a senior practitioner member of the British Psychological Society register of psychologists specialising in psychotherapy, and registered with the Health and Care Professions Council as a counselling and health psychologist. He has published over 200 articles, chapters and books including *Positive Psychology in Practice* (Wiley, 2004), *Person-Centred Practice* (PCCS Books, 2007) and *What Doesn't Kill Us: A Guide to Overcoming Adversity and Moving Forward* (Piatkus, 2013).

Carol Kauffman, PhD ABPP is the Founder and Executive Director of the Institute of Coaching at Harvard Medical School where she is an Assistant Professor. In leadership development and coaching she works with multinational corporations partnering with Authentic Leadership Institute and Harvard Business School to help leaders raise the bar on themselves and their lives. In the UK she is Chief Supervisor Meyler Campbell Ltd,. based business coaching programme. Professor Kauffman was founding co-editor in chief of *Coaching: An International Journal of Theory, Research & Practice*. The Institute of Coaching has a Professional Association that has access to extensive educational materials in leadership, health, positive psychology and personal coaching.

Richard Ladyshewsky is a professor at the Curtin Graduate School of Business, Curtin University in Perth, Western Australia. His professional qualifications range from registered physiotherapist and healthcare administrator to educator in leadership and management development. His research interests centre around professional development and reasoning in the healthcare sector, leadership development in the higher education sector and more recently online learning and educational quality. He has developed a range of initiatives to promote leadership and learning in these sectors on a national and international level. He uses peer coaching as a central strategy to promote professional and leadership development, and publishes widely on this topic.

David A. Lane is Director of the Professional Development Foundation and Visiting Professor to Middlesex University and contributes to leading-edge research in coaching as well as supervising leading coaches undertaking doctoral research. He was Chair of the British Psychological Society (BPS) Register of Psychologists, specializing in psychotherapy, and convened the psychotherapy group of the European Federation of Psychologists Associations. His work with the European Mentoring and Coaching Council has been concerned with codes of conduct and standards and kite marking of coach training. Working with the Worldwide Association of Business Coaches, he has researched and developed the standards for the Certified Master Business Coach award. He was a member of the steering group for the Global Convention on Coaching. He was recognized by the British Psychological Society in 2010 for his Distinguished Contribution to Professional Psychology. His current interests as both a researcher and practicing coach include decision making under conditions of uncertainty and supervision practice.

Graham Lee is a Leadership Coach and Consultant. With a background in both business and psychoanalysis, he has championed the need to understand the psychology of leaders and their organizations in enabling change, as explored in his influential book, *Leadership Coaching* (CIPD, 2006).

Margaret Moore, MBA, a 17-year veteran of the biotechnology industry, founded the Wellcoaches School of Coaching for health professionals in 2002. Margaret is co-founder and co-director of the Institute of Coaching at McLean Hospital, a Harvard Medical School affiliate, and co-director of the annual Coaching in Leadership & Healthcare conference offered by Harvard Medical School. She co-leads the National Consortium for Credentialing Health & Wellness Coaches, which is developing national standards, certification and collaborative research. She co-authored the first coaching textbook in healthcare, the Coaching Psychology Manual published by Lippincott, Williams & Wilkins, and a Harvard Health Book titled *Organize Your Mind, Organize Your Life*.

Rosemary Napper is internationally qualified as a trainer and supervisor in the organizational and educational applications of transactional analysis, and is also accredited as a TA 'counsellor', which is the continental European designation for a coach. She is Director of TAworks in Oxford, where she provides five-year part-time training programmes in all applications of TA (www.TAworks.co.uk), she was also President of the International Transactional Analysis Association 2009–2010, and founder member of the International Association for Relational Transactional Analysis. Rosemary has an MA in Education and has written a number of articles and books. Additionally she is a partner with Crescere Institute in Brazil, providing coaching programmes, an electronic newletter and bi-annual coaching conferences.

Trudi Newton is a Teaching and Supervising Transactional Analyst, writer and consultant on learning, working internationally with educators to facilitate radical learning and community development. She has an active practice supervising accredited coaches in both the executive and life coaching fields. Over the last few years she has developed coach supervisor training programmes, one of which is the first such to be recognized by the International Coach Federation.

Stephen Palmer is Founder Director of the Centre for Coaching, London. Since 2001, he has been Visiting Professor of Work Based Learning and Stress Management at the Institute of Work Based Learning, Middlesex University. He is Executive Editor of Coaching: An International Journal of Theory, Research and Practice, UK Coordinating Editor of the International Coaching Psychology Review and co-editor of the Handbook of Coaching Psychology: A Guide for Practitioners (with Whybrow) (Routledge, 2007). He is Honorary President of the International Society for Coaching Psychology and Honorary Fellow of the Association for Coaching. He is an accredited executive coach and supervisor, and award winning Chartered Psychologist. In 2008 the British Psychological Society, Special Group in Coaching Psychology gave him the 'Lifetime Achievement Award in Recognition of Distinguished contribution to coaching psychology'.

John Rowan has been working with the transpersonal since the early eighties, and has been described as one of the founding fathers of transpersonal psychology in the UK. He is the author of a number of books, including *The Transpersonal: Spirituality in Psychotherapy and Counselling* (2nd ed., Routledge, 2005). He is on the editorial board of the *Journal of Humanistic Psychology*, the *Transpersonal Psychology Review* and the *Counselling Psychology Review*. He is a Fellow of the British Psychological Society (member of the Psychotherapy Section, the Counselling Psychology Division, the Special Group on Coaching Psychology and the Transpersonal Psychology Section) and a member of the Association for Coaching. His particular workshop interests are creativity, research, the dialogical self, AQAL and the transpersonal.

Alan Sieler is the Director of Newfield Institute, an international coach training, executive coaching and consulting company. Alan leads the Graduate Diploma of Ontological Coaching in Australia, Asia and South Africa. He has been an executive coach for more than 17 years, working with corporate clients from 15 countries. Alan's three volumes of *Coaching to the Human Soul* (Newfield, 2005, 2007 and 2013) sell to 30 countries and have been used in coaching, leadership and organizational change courses at universities in the United States, South Africa and Australia. Major organizations, such as Intel, Hewlett Packard and NASA, have also purchased copies of all volumes for their training departments.

Jordan Silberman began his career as a pianist, and studied at the Eastman School of Music. He has performed at Carnegie Hall in New York City, the Viper Room in Los Angeles and many places in between. Since changing paths in 2002, Jordan has authored and co-authored articles on healthcare communication, psychology, bioethics, pediatric palliative care and proteomics; served as a reviewer for a major health services research journal; chaired a psychology symposium in Hong Kong; completed two provisional patents; and finished three marathons. His first-authored research has been described in Prevention, Self, and Good Housekeeping magazines; co-authored work has been covered by the New York Times, NPR, CNN, and others. Jordan earned a Masters of Applied Positive Psychology at the University of Pennsylvania, where he was advised by Martin Seligman. He is currently a graduate student in the department of Department of Clinical and Social Sciences in Psychologyat the University of Rochester.

Nick Smith has been a part of Bath Consultancy Group for over 15 years. He is a senior faculty member of Bath Consultancy Group's international modular training programme on the Supervision of Coaches, Mentors and Consultants and supervises executive coaches in a number of organizations. He coaches senior leaders in organizations across public, private and third sectors, as well as working as part of BCG's organizational development consultancy. Nick is the co-author of *Coaching, Mentoring and Organizational Consultancy: Supervision and Development* (McGraw-Hill/Open University Press, 2nd ed., 2013).

Ernesto Spinelli has gained an international reputation as one of the leading contemporary trainers and theorists of existential analysis as applied to psychology and psychotherapy and coaching. He is a Fellow of the British Psychological Society (BPS) as well as a founding member of the BPS Special Group in Coaching Psychology, and accredited executive coach and coaching supervisor. Ernesto is also a consultant trainer, supervisor and faculty member of the i-coach Academy and Director of ES Associates, an organization dedicated to the advancement of coaching, facilitation, mediation and psychotherapy through specialist seminars and training programmes.

Nicole A. Steckler is Associate Professor of Management in the School of Medicine at Oregon Health and Science University. She holds a PhD in Organizational Behavior from Harvard University. Niki's expertise is in communication and collaboration across disciplines and organizational boundaries. She coaches academic leaders and healthcare professionals on increasing their leadership capabilities and reaching their career goals. Niki has won awards for her teaching excellence; she currently teaches graduate courses and professional development workshops on becoming an effective manager, influence and communication skills for leaders, and increasing individual and organizational resilience in healthcare contexts through practicing mindfulness and positivity.

Reinhard Stelter is Professor of Sports and Coaching Psychology and Head of the Coaching Psychology Unit, Department of Nutrition, Exercise and Sports, at the University of Copenhagen, Denmark, Visiting Professor at Copenhagen Business School and coach and lecturer at Copenhagen Coaching Center, offering an EMCC accredited master practitioner program. Reinhard holds a PhD in Psychology and is Honorary Vice-President and accredited member of the International Society for Coaching Psychology. He is a member of the Research Advisory Board, Institute of Coaching at Harvard Medical School, and author of the book *A Guide to Third Generation Coaching* (Springer), covering almost ten years of his theoretical, applied and research-based work. His major research interests are around identity, learning and coaching on phenomenological, social constructionist and narrative bases.

Dianne R. Stober is Managing Partner of C Cubed (Cognitive Change Concepts) and is a licensed clinical psychologist. C Cubed is a psychology consulting company bringing an innovative approach to psychology in the workplace, including a cutting-edge approach to mobile learning and micro-training. She works with clients on their leadership of safety and organizational culture within heavy industries. She has written a number of articles on coaching and is the co-editor of the *Evidence Based Coaching Handbook: Putting Best Practices to Work for Your Clients* (Wiley, 2006). Dianne has presented and facilitated on coaching internationally, including at the *American Psychological Association*, the *British Psychological Society*, the *Australian Evidence-based Coaching Conference* and the *Harvard Coaching and Positive Psychology Conference*, along with numerous conferences and presentations within her client organizations.

Jon Stokes is a Director of the consulting firm Stokes & Jolly (www.stokesjolly.com) who provide leadership coaching, top team facilitation, management development programmes and assessment selection services for a wide range of professional service and corporate clients. Jon is an Associate Fellow at Said Oxford University Business School, a member of Associate Faculty at Henley Business School and an Associate of the Institute for Government. He trained and worked as a clinical psychologist at the Tavistock Clinic in London for over 20 years, where he was Head of the Adult Psychotherapy Department. He founded and ran the Tavistock's Organisational Consultancy Service (TCS) for six years. He is a coach tutor at Meyler Campbell and an APECS accredited coach supervisor.

Sunny Stout-Rostron is an executive coach and consultant, with a wide range of experience in leadership and management development, business strategy and executive coaching. With over 25 years' international experience as an executive coach, Sunny has played a leading role in building the emerging profession of coaching. She is Executive Director of Sunny Stout-Rostron Associates, a Founding Fellow at the Institute of Coaching at Harvard, an Advisory Board Director with the Professional Development Foundation UK (PDF) and Founding President of COMENSA (Coaches and Mentors of South Africa). Sunny's books include: *Business Coaching International: Transforming Individuals and Organizations* (2009/2013), *Business Coaching Wisdom and Practice: Unlocking the Secrets of Business Coaching* (Knowres, 2009/2012) and *Accelerating Performance: Powerful New Techniques to Develop People* (Kogan Page, 2002).

Bob Tschannen-Moran is President of LifeTrek Coaching International, CEO of the Center for School Transformation, and has served on the faculty of Wellcoaches Corporation. Bob has co-authored two books on coaching, the *Lippincott Wellcoaches Coaching Psychology Manual* (2010) and *Evocative Coaching: Transforming Schools One Conversation at a Time* (2010), and publishes a weekly email newsletter, 'LifeTrek Provisions', with more than ten thousand subscribers in 152 countries. Bob received an undergraduate degree from Northwestern University, a Master of Divinity degree from Yale Divinity School, as well as coach certifications from Coach U, CoachVille,

Wellcoaches and FastTrack Coach Training Academy. He is also trained in the cognate practices of Appreciative Inquiry and Nonviolent Communication. Bob has served as President of ICF Greater Richmond and as President of the International Association of Coaching (IAC) Board of Governors.

Leni Wildflower is the Founder and original Director of Fielding Graduate University's Evidence Based Coaching certificate programmes. She holds a doctorate in Human and Organizational Systems and is credentialed by the International Coach Federation (ICF) as a Professional Certified Coach. Dr. Wildflower is a contributing author to the *Sage Handbook of Online Learning* (2009). In addition to her university work, she has worked for over 35 years as a consultant and executive coach in business and not-for-profit agencies. Her coaching related books include *The Handbook of Knowledge Based Coaching* (edited with Diane Brennan) and *The Hidden History of Coaching*.

Helen Williams is a qualified coaching psychologist specialising in solution-focused cognitive behavioural coaching. She is currently Director of Performance Coaching at Sten 10 Ltd, and an associate consultant at the Centre for Coaching. Helen is registered with the Health Professions Council, chartered with the British Psychological Society and a member of the Association for Coaching (MAC), International Society for Coaching Psychologists (MISCP) and BPS Special Group in Coaching Psychology (SGCP).

Foreword

The introductory chapter to this fascinating, timely and comprehensive text includes a full description of its structure and contents, so I will not repeat that here. Instead I will offer a more personal reaction to the volume and invite you, as the reader, to follow the same route.

I think that everyone who reads this book will have a different take on it. Just consider what the three most engaging chapters are for you – out of the 31 here – and this gives thousands of different possibilities, even before starting to take into account the different things that even two people who chose the same three chapters might take from them. So, I am not prioritising my three chapters as being the best or the most important in the book or recommending them to you above others. They just happened to chime with *my* preoccupations when I was writing this Foreword.

I was surprised and delighted by John Rowan's take on transpersonal coaching. In contrast to the rest of a field – the transpersonal – filled with hippies (the meadows before Longshaw Lodge in England's Peak District in autumn swarming with people in red bandanas hunting for magic mushrooms, is a metaphor that comes to mind), this chapter is full of sound sense and spirited defence of what is important. From the definition of the two types of transpersonal, through to the splendid distinction between 'letting go' and 'letting come', John Rowan is clear, undogmatic and pragmatic in how we ordinary coaches can deal with these heady but crucially important issues.

David Drake's chapter on narrative coaching addresses one of the areas that has been preoccupying me in the past year. His chapter explores how we position ourselves in our inner constructions and our outer interactions, and describes the back story of the narrative approach, with its roots in literary theory, humanism and psychology. He offers a strong and helpful challenge to the lingering behaviourism that hangs round some accounts of coaching like the miasma from a swamp. Drake is a suitable candidate to be the hero that comes to defeat the monster in the swamp – a Beowulf to challenge the Grendel of SMART goals and the Grendel's mother of performativity.

The chapter on psychological development in adulthood and coaching by Tatiana Bachkirova is underpinned by the idea that developmental trajectories can help coaches to address their clients' needs. Building on the theoretical work of authors such as Robert Kegan and including a different conceptualization of the self, Bachkirova develops a new approach to developmental coaching, one which includes a range of specific mechanisms for facilitating change in coaching. This chapter is central to the book because the perspective of the author here is *au fond*, grounded in adult learning.

If I am to integrate what I have learned from these three chapters it is about articulating the crucial agendas that Rowan points to, using the tools of developmental coaching explored by

Bachkirova, and deepening further my use of stories using frameworks from Drake as not only a tool of diagnosis but also as a means (for myself and for clients) of re-storying and restoring a life.

So, those are my three chapters. Remember, I am not recommending you to pay attention to those in particular – they are just mine at this particular moment in my development. I suggest that a reading of Section 1: Theoretical approaches – could lead you to choosing your own three perspectives and then you could seek to integrate them into your own practice.

However, for me, the real joy of this book, and it is impressive the extent to which it has been pulled off, is the integrative structure which separates perspectives and genres in a fruitful and intriguing way. As well as the theoretical perspectives section, there are a series of chapters addressing different contexts and genres and these are comprehensively integrated and cross referenced with the theoretical perspective chapters. It is rare in any book to have so comprehensive an interaction of different aspects of the authors' meta-model, and for a book of contributed chapters it is almost unprecedented. It is a testimony to the clear thinking and thorough briefing of the contributors, and it makes it very valuable to students and more experienced coaches wanting to articulate and develop their own approach – their signature presence. I remember hearing members of the Lindsays string quartet talking about their long collaboration with the composer Michael Tippett. They asked him about the source of his inspiration for themes and harmonies. However, he was much more interested in structure. I have the sense that the authors of this volume are preoccupied with structure too, and the result is that for us readers, we have a structure which can help us to make sense of what we read, and this structure also gives us tools and ways of thinking that can enrich our own structures in developing our practice.

Some areas of difference between perspectives and genres are exposed. Some perspectives are radically emancipatory: concerned with the development of human freedom, in which the agenda, the content and to an extent the process all best belong with the coachee/client. Other contributors acknowledge the coach as being in there in the process of change (coach as participant, not neutral observer); and this is a helpful challenge to those of us who see ourselves as emancipatory and learner centred. I found the arguments laid out chapter by chapter to be provocative and stimulating. So I enjoyed even the bits I disagreed with.

I like the mixture of those researching and commenting on the part of the field that is the focus of their chapter (e.g. Grant and Cavanagh on life coaching), in contrast with the chapters where the authors are passionate advocates for their method, for example, Sieler, who has invented his own brand of ontological coaching, or Clutterbuck who has presciently developed team coaching as a genre.

This is a great resource for coaches of all persuasions, it is the most comprehensive handbook that I know and it is one that I expect to cherish for a long time to come.

David Megginson, Sheffield Hallam University, 2013

Introduction

Tatiana Bachkirova, Elaine Cox and
David Clutterbuck

Coaching is a human development process that involves structured, focused interaction and the use of appropriate strategies, tools and techniques to promote desirable and sustainable change for the benefit of the coachee and potentially for other stakeholders. The use of coaching continues to grow. Across all economic sectors an increasing number of organizations are commissioning coaches to support their staff at different stages in their careers and individuals at various stages in their lives also seek the support of a coach. Coaching is recognized as a powerful vehicle for increasing performance, achieving results and optimizing personal effectiveness.

As the field has developed, models of coaching have begun to be applied in wider contexts, used with diverse client groups and with different media. Coaching practitioners come from a variety of professions and often from multi-disciplinary backgrounds. They constantly bring new dimensions to the field via the adaptation of concepts, ideas and practical tools developed in their 'home' traditions. It is possible to meet coaches whose philosophies and practices of coaching would have very little in common, although their aims and purposes may be similar.

In this book, we recognize that coaching is an applied field of practice that has intellectual roots in a range of disciplines: social psychology; learning theory; theories of human and organizational development; and existential and phenomenological philosophy, to name just a few. This diversity creates exciting opportunities for meaningful interaction and mutual enrichment but there is also the potential for confusion, particularly for novices in the field and for users of coaching. Questions that may be asked include: What is the difference between existential coaching and solution-focused coaching? What would a performance coach do differently from a developmental coach? Is it possible to compare psychodynamic coaching with life coaching? Could a Gestalt-trained coach be a good choice in career coaching? Until now, there were no resource books in the field that could help practitioners and other stakeholders to find comprehensive answers to these types of questions. In this book we aim to address this gap by clarifying not only the differences between the theoretical approaches to coaching but also the differences and links between these perspectives in relation to the genres and contexts of coaching.

In this introduction there are three sections. The first section discusses coaching in terms of its identity, definition and role in organizations. In the second section we discuss the knowledge base of coaching and identify adult learning theory as an important theoretical tradition underpinning coaching. In the third section we explain the matrix structure of the book and conclude with short summaries for each chapter.

I. THE IDENTITY OF COACHING

According to the Online Etymology Dictionary, the word 'coach' derives from a town called 'Kocs' in northern Hungary, where horse drawn carriages were made. The meaning of coach as an instructor or trainer is purportedly from around 1830, when it was Oxford University slang for a tutor who 'carried' a student through an exam; the term coaching was later applied in the 1800s to improving the performance of athletes.

In the twentieth century, coaching found its way into the workplace, where it was associated with a specific process of education for young recruits. The coach was typically a more experienced employee, often with managerial authority over them. He or she would typically demonstrate a task, instruct them to attempt the same task, observe their performance and provide feedback based either on their own experience, or a standardized perception of performance. Coach and coachee (usually called trainee or apprentice) would then discuss the feedback and plan how the coachee would approach the task differently next time. In essence, this form of coaching has much in common with instruction. Where instruction and coaching clearly differ in this model is the transition from assignment of task and extrinsic observation (by the coach) to self-managed experimentation and intrinsic observation (by the coachee). We have no reliable information that would allow us to identify what proportion of coaching today fits this approach.

The concept and application of coaching has since mushroomed into a panoply of models and approaches, many of which are more non-directive in nature. The distinction between directive and non-directive approaches is shown in Table 0.1.

Table 0.1 Transitions from traditional coaching

From	To
Coach requires expertise/knowledge of the task	Coach requires expertise/knowledge of the coaching process
Driven by the coach's agenda, or, at best, an agreed agenda	Driven by the coachee's agenda
Coachee performance (doing)	Coachee self-actualization (becoming)
Skills acquisition (building knowledge of the task)	Capability development (building insight and self-knowledge as stepping stones to more substantive change)
Meeting standards set by others	Meeting standards set by the coachee

A next step in identifying what coaching is would be to try to provide a definition of it. Coaching books invariably begin with some kind of definition that identifies coaching as a helping strategy, designed to enable people to reach their full potential. It appears, however, that these definitions are not definitive enough to distinguish coaching from its close neighbours – mentoring, counselling and consulting – as these other forms of helping all make similar claims.

Attempts to define coaching usually try to make it distinctive in terms of ultimate purpose (what it is for?), type of clients (who uses this service?), or process (how it is done?) or a combination of these. In relation to an ultimate purpose coaching is often described as aiming at individual development or 'enhancing well-being and performance' (Grant & Palmer, 2002). These definitions are difficult to dispute but they cannot differentiate coaching from counselling or mentoring or even training, because essentially their purposes are the same. The initial attempts (Grant, 2000) to define coaching as designed for the 'mentally healthy' clientele group are now seen as unsatisfactory for many practical and ethical reasons. Attempts to define coaching on the basis of a distinct process are similarly problematic. Not only do they include some characteristics that cannot distinguish coaching from other helping professions, they also include characteristics that are so specific or just desirable, that they cannot be attributed to all the various forms of coaching (Bachkirova, 2007).

We are aware, therefore, that creating a unique identity of coaching is still an unresolved problem. Nevertheless, we believe that readers should be able to see our position in relation to what coaching is. Our working definition is presented in the very first sentence of this introduction. It is not, of course, free from limitations, but we hope the reader will make use of it while reading this book.

Coaching is used in various contexts, sometimes unconnected with the world of work. However, the use of coaching within organizations has given an immense impetus for the development and growth of the field. Therefore we want to give particular attention to coaching in organizations and suggest the role categorization as a reflection of the pragmatic distinctions that we have observed in organizations:

Line manager as a coach. This is perhaps the most difficult and controversial coaching role. Many commentators express doubt as to whether line managers can ever give priority to the coachee's agenda and devote enough time and effort to coach at anything more than a basic level (Ferrar, 2006).

Coaching role model. Companies such as Kellogg Europe have equipped some of their senior line managers with relatively advanced levels of coaching skills. Their role is to be role models to other line managers for good coaching practice and to champion the cause of coaching within the organization.

The expert coach. Many organizations reward experienced employees at all levels for transferring knowledge and skills to others. It is a core part of effective knowledge management. The coaching skills required in this role are arguably too similar to instruction-giving and the agenda of the process is as questionable as it is for coaching by the line manager.

The internal coach. Internal coaches are trained as professional coaches and perform many of the same roles as an external coach. However, they may be constrained by authority structures within the organization (for example, in confronting more senior executives) and may find it difficult to take an independent perspective.

The performance coach is typically an external professional coach, who specializes in helping the coachee to focus on and achieve task-specific behavioural change over a relatively short period.

The developmental coach is usually an external professional coach, who focuses on the broader and possibly longer-term changes in the client as a professional which may include the crystallization of life purpose.

II. THE KNOWLEDGE BASE OF COACHING

Many different disciplines and areas of knowledge contribute to the emerging knowledge base of coaching. These include management, education, social sciences, philosophy and psychology. Within each of these established fields of knowledge there are various schools, traditions and approaches. They contain their own set of assumptions about human nature, how people grow and change and how this process can be facilitated. All of them potentially enrich the knowledge base of coaching. However, their diversity can be confusing, particularly for newcomers to the field. Within psychology, for example there are significant differences among existential and solution-focused traditions or between psychodynamic and transpersonal.

Coaches who were educated originally in different fields, and so were trained according to different traditions, may disagree profoundly on their philosophy and their practice of coaching. When adapted to coaching, each discipline and school of thought seems to have significantly different assumptions, not just about how to coach but even about what is worth exploring and what is not. The intention of this book is to reflect the diversity of the field and to illustrate how a multiplicity of approaches can enrich the knowledge base of coaching. We hope this will also help individual coaches to find their way through this diversity towards their own style of coaching.

At the same time we acknowledge that by introducing such diversity we are taking a risk of appearing over inclusive, particularly to those who, while valuing their own approach, take a very strong stand and reject other approaches. The following is therefore our attempt to make transparent our philosophy and main assumptions in relation to the knowledge base of coaching. An overview of the current literature and research on coaching increasingly shows that coaching has been described and explored in at least four major dimensions (Figure 0.1):

- 'I' – a first person perspective on the coaching process by the coach and/or coachee describing individual experiences of both parties involved
- 'We' – a second person perspective that emphasizes the relationship between the coach and the coachee, the role of language and culture in their interaction
- 'It' – more tangible elements of the coaching process, that are able to be observed by a third party and even measured if necessary, such as particular interventions and tools of coaching, specific behaviours and models
- 'Its' – the systems that are present as a background and an influencing force of the coaching process, such as sponsoring organizations and other social and professional groups.

These dimensions correspond to four quadrants described by Wilber (1996, 2000) as essential perspectives that are important to take into account if we want to understand any phenomenon or event that involves human beings. If we look now at various theoretical traditions that are applied to coaching we can see in what corner of this 'map' they would sit more comfortably and could claim their main influence. Individual coaches may also see where the weight of their coaching approach mainly lies, even if they treat as important all of these dimensions.

For example some coaching approaches in the 'It' corner tend to rely on outcome studies of coaching that are based on data that are observable and measurable. They are looking for effective techniques that can be reliably used in coaching interactions. Other approaches lean towards the 'I' corner, focusing on how individuals experience an event or process such as a

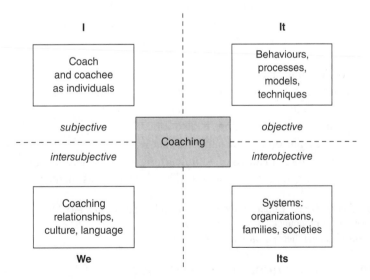

Figure 0.1   Four dimensions of coaching

coaching encounter. They are looking for individuals' feedback on interventions. Within this corner even standpoints such as the transpersonal are valuable as they can deepen understanding of what matters to people in coaching. Approaches that lean towards the 'We' corner emphasize the role of language in the way we interpret events and experiences and the historical and cultural perspectives that have an impact on these interpretations. They, and also those who defend a systemic approach to coaching from the 'Its' corner, are emphasizing how important is an awareness of the complexity of factors that influence the coaching process. They bring to our attention the fact that each approach represents a particular cultural and historical perspective and that such a position may differ significantly from country to country and may also change with further development of the coaching field.

Unfortunately, those who position themselves very strongly at some particular standpoint within this structure sometimes reject other perspectives and approaches, thus missing an important angle on the process of coaching. We, however, advocate the value of all dimensions and recommend questioning absolutist claims for the exclusivity of any of them. We believe that the approaches discussed in each chapter can illuminate a particular angle on coaching practice, being clear about their strengths and ensuring sufficient criticality at the same time. This should allow readers to explore each approach and decide which, if any, they want to integrate into their own personal model of coaching.

Adult learning theories and their relevance to coaching

In this book, we argue for 'inclusivity' and equality of approaches. However, we want at the same time to emphasize a particular theoretical tradition that in our view underpins coaching practice. Adult learning theory is not an approach that can be applied to coaching in the way that, for example, cognitive-behavioural theories or Gestalt principles can. Rather, it underpins all coaching practice. It is for this reason that we discuss adult learning theories in the introduction.

The definition of learning that we use is one of three outlined by Knowles, Holton and Swanson (2011: 11): 'the extension and clarification of meaning of one's experience'. This, it seems to us, is the implicit theme for our clients in any coaching encounter. The concept of change, which is at the heart of coaching, is also inherent in the concept of learning: any discernible change in behaviour or attitude suggests that learning has taken place.

The basic principles of three theories of adult learning are presented here in order to reinforce how they underpin the very nature of coaching. The three theories identified are:

A. Andragogy, the theory of adult learning introduced by Malcolm Knowles in the 1970s
B. Experiential learning as propounded by David Kolb (1984)
C. The transformative learning theory of Jack Mezirow (1990).

A. The assumptions and principles of andragogy

Andragogy is concerned with recognizing the inherent characteristics of adults as learners and using these to guide and support learning. Building on work by Lindeman in the 1920s, together with a variety of other theories from across a range of disciplines, Knowles (1978) devised a set of assumptions about adult learning that would contrast it distinctly with the traditional pedagogical approach to teaching children. These assumptions or principles have come to underpin our views about learning and development, and about adulthood. Knowles (1978; Knowles et al., 2011) identified a number of characteristics of adult learners that impact on the way in which they learn or approach learning. Since the 1970s these principles have been assimilated into the learning culture and are now discernible in coaching (Cox, 2006) as the following six main principles:

1. *Adults need to know.* Working with adults as collaborative partners for learning satisfies their need to know what they will be learning, as well as appealing to their self-concept as independent learners. Therefore, in coaching the agenda always belongs to the coachee, or is carefully negotiated so that ownership is theirs and they know the course of the learning.
2. *Adults are self-directed.* As a person matures, they become a more self-directed, autonomous human being (Knowles et al., 2011). However, it is recognized that not all adults have full personal autonomy in every situation: learners still exhibit different capabilities and preferences. Nevertheless, adult learning tends to be facilitated rather than directed: adults want to be treated as equals and shown respect both for what they know and how they prefer to learn. This also explains why specific feedback that is free of evaluative or judgemental opinions is a key feature of coaching (Cox, 2013).
3. *Adults have a wealth of prior experience.* A mature person accumulates a growing reservoir of experience that becomes an increasing resource for learning and coaches recognize that adults' experiences have a very important impact on their learning. However, as well as being a source of new learning, experience can also act as a gate-keeper, reinforcing mental models and schemas. Therefore, the unlearning process is as important as the learning process. The coach is very well placed to challenge coachees' existing assumptions in relation to new learning or new experiences, thus encouraging both learning and unlearning.
4. *Adults learn when they have a need to learn.* Adults generally become ready to learn when their life situation creates a need to know or understand, e.g. when they need to cope with a life situation or perform a task. The more the coach can anticipate and understand the client's life situation and respond to readiness for coaching, the more effective their role in coaching will be.
5. *Adults are relevancy-oriented.* Instead of being interested in knowledge for its own sake, adults frequently seek immediate application of what they learn and are oriented to problem-solving. They learn best when there is a need to address a pressing issue. For the coach, this suggests that the client may need to work on immediate problems, as well as longer-term, developmental issues.
6. *Adults are internally motivated.* Adults are generally more motivated towards learning that helps them to solve problems as they see them, or that results in 'internal payoffs' (Knowles et al., 2011: 202). This does not mean that external motivators, such as requests or encouragement from the line manager, do not have relevance, but rather internal needs and values are more powerful motivators. The coach's role then is to help provide the sense of connection between the client's needs and values, and the results of the coaching.

B. Experiential learning

The second learning theory that we identify as underpinning all coaching practice is the theory of experiential learning, first articulated in the philosophy of John Dewey (1910) and later operationalized by David Kolb (1984). Like coaching, experiential learning can be viewed as concerned with technique and process, rather than with content. In experiential learning theory, an immediate concrete experience is the basis for observation and reflection. The reflections are then assimilated into a 'theory' from which the implications for future action are deduced. The process can take place incidentally or intentionally. According to Kolb, experiential learning is best viewed as a process and should not be seen in terms of outcomes. It is a constructivist theory that suggests that 'ideas are not fixed and immutable elements of thought but are formed and re-formed through experience' (Kolb, 1984: 26). Learning is seen as a dialectic process that integrates experience, concepts and observations, in order to give direction to impulse. This would seem to us to be very much in tune with coaching as a process.

C. Transformative learning

Transformative learning involves a deep, fundamental revision to our beliefs, principles and feelings: it implies a shift of perception that has the potential to alter our understanding of ourselves and others, and our sense of possibilities (Mezirow, 1990). Transformative learning, as Mezirow explains, refers to the process by which we transform our 'taken-for-granted frames of reference (meaning perspectives, habits of mind, mind-sets) to make them more inclusive, discriminating, open, emotionally capable of change, and reflective so that they may generate beliefs and opinions that will prove more true or justified to guide action' (2000: 7). Meaning perspectives are notoriously difficult to change, but do need to be challenged if deep learning is to occur. Sometimes such a challenge occurs spontaneously through life events and is the focus of the client's opening agenda, but often, significant challenge is generated by the coach, in order to promote the required learning. The challenge, however generated, results in a 'disorienting dilemma'.

This dilemma is then followed by discussions of long held beliefs and values. This is one of the most important stages in a transformative coaching situation and involves the critical reflection on the nature and origin of the dilemma. Critical reflection, Mezirow argues, necessitates the suspension of judgement about the truth or falsity of ideas, until a better determination can be made (2000: 13). The final stage in the transformative process, following self-examination, is some kind of reorientation that results in deep learning and revised action.

These three adult learning theories provide examples of what we consider to be foundational theories for coaching practice. They are at the heart of all adult learning and development and consequently are at the heart of coaching practices.

III. DESIGN AND STRUCTURE OF THE BOOK

The book consists of three main sections. The chapters of the first two sections are presented in the matrix below (Table 0.2). The left-hand vertical column of the matrix represents theory-based approaches to coaching. The top horizontal line represents a variety of contexts and genres of coaching. The matrix illustrates the relationships between the theoretical traditions that coaches might adopt and the genres and contexts of coaching in which these theoretical traditions may be applied. For example, coaches who consider their approach to be cognitive-behavioural may practice as skills and performance coaches or deliver team coaching; a coach with a distinct person-centred orientation may work as a life coach or career coach. In the same way a transformational coach may be informed by the approach based on adult development theories, or an executive coach can be trained in a Gestalt tradition or as an existential coach.

One intention of the book is to make explicit the possible links between the theoretical traditions and the range of genres and contexts of coaching, in order to encourage thinking about how a tradition is used in practice. Each stars in the matrix indicate that an explicit link is made, whether by the authors of a theory-based chapter (vertical) or by the authors of a 'genres and context' chapter (horizontal). If in a particular junction there are two stars, this means that the authors of both theory-based chapter and context and genres chapter described their link to each other. The absence of the stars in other junctions does not mean that this particular combination is not possible – only that the authors were not explicit about it. In fact, we suggest that readers use the matrix to identify their own combinations or begin to question any links advocated.

Table 0.2 The matrix

Section I Theoretical traditions of coaching	Section II: Genres and contexts of coaching										
	Skills & performance	Developmental coaching	Transformational coaching	Executive & leadership	The manager as coach	Team coaching	Peer coaching	Life coaching	Health & wellness coaching	Career coaching	Cross-cultural coaching
The psychodynamic approach to coaching	*	*		**		*					**
Cognitive-behavioural coaching	*	**		**	**	**	**	**	**	**	**
The solution-focused approach to coaching	**	*		*	*	*	*	*			*
The person-centred approach to coaching	**	*		*		*	**	**		**	
The Gestalt approach to coaching		*	*	*	*	*					
Existential coaching		*		**				*		*	*
Ontological coaching			*						*		*
Narrative coaching	*	**								*	*
Cognitive development theories and coaching	*	**				**					*
The transpersonal approach to coaching	*	*						*		*	

(Continued)

Table 0.2 (Continued)

Section I Theoretical traditions of coaching	Section II: Genres and contexts of coaching										
	Skills & performance	Developmental coaching	Transformational coaching	Executive & leadership	The manager as coach	Team coaching	Peer coaching	Life coaching	Health & wellness coaching	Career coaching	Cross-cultural coaching
Positive psychology approach to coaching	**			*		*		**	*	*	*
Transactional analysis and coaching				*	*	*					*
The NLP approach to coaching	*			*	*	*				*	*

Section I

Coaching is no longer seen as an atheoretical enterprise that relies only on common sense and an eclectic combination of tools. A number of theory-based approaches in this section describe a coherent explanation of how learning and developmental change can take place and how they can be adapted for coaching. Elaborate theories usually include essential elements: main concepts and assumptions about human nature, core distinctive features, such as processes of change and methods and techniques of influencing. This structure was followed in each chapter for readers to be able to discern the most important elements and to compare theoretical approaches. It should be noted that the list of chapters in this section (Chapters 1–13) is not exhaustive in terms of all theoretical traditions in coaching; however, most well-known and influential ones are included.

1. The psychodynamic approach to coaching

Graham Lee opens this section with a chapter on the psychodynamic approach to coaching. He describes how this rich influential body of ideas can inform coaches in their pursuit for deepening their practice by contributing to awareness about the working of the unconscious. He explains the origin of such terminology as defence mechanisms, transference and countertransference with which coaches currently become more familiar, without knowing the background and nature of such phenomena. This chapter suggests that there is a significant layer in our coaching interactions which is mainly beyond our conscious grasp but may influence individual behaviour, teamwork or organizational dynamics.

2. Cognitive behavioural coaching

Helen Williams, *Stephen Palmer* and *Nick Edgerton* describe an approach to coaching that aims at enhancing the quality of a client's thinking with the help of skilful interventions by the coach in collaboration with the client. The approach emphasizes the importance of identifying realistic goals and facilitates self-awareness of underlying cognitive and emotional barriers to goal attainment. It aims to equip the client with more effective thinking and behavioural skills. The chapter illustrates the use of various methods in health coaching, in addition to other genres and contexts included in this Handbook.

3. The solution-focused approach to coaching

Michael Cavanagh and *Anthony Grant* describe an approach that is based on the premise that knowing how a problem arose does not necessarily tell one how to fix it. As a very different course of action, it aims at assisting the client to define a desired future state and to construct a pathway in both thinking and action that assists the client in achieving that state. The chapter describes how solutions can emerge through useful questions framed by the coach, questions that arise as the result of collaborative thinking and the coach's expertise in the coaching process.

4. The person-centred approach to coaching

Stephen Joseph presents a person-centred approach as the one that is based on the most important assumption: the actualizing tendency – a tendency of people to develop in a positive and constructive way when the appropriate conditions are present. He emphasizes that it is a biological tendency and not a moral imperative, and describes six conditions that the coach needs to provide for coaching to be person-centred. It is possible that many coaches, who describe their coaching as person-centred, may not fully appreciate the depth of the philosophical underpinnings of this approach.

5. The Gestalt approach to coaching

Peter Bluckert argues that the main principles of Gestalt, such as creative adjustment to a changing environment and a paradoxical theory of change, bring a significant contribution to the understanding and practice of coaching. When applied to the coaching process, this approach emphasizes the need for clients' moment-to-moment awareness in relation to their experience, external world and blocks to awareness. The chapter explains why Gestalt practitioners aim to be more faithful to an honouring of clients' own words, meanings and subjective experience and use their own subjective experience, when appropriate, as part of an authentic dialogue.

6. Existential coaching

Ernesto Spinelli introduces the reader to his version of existential coaching, based on three principles describing the human condition: relatedness, uncertainty and existential anxiety. He identifies the issue of traditional coaching that may be mainly aiming at speedy alteration, reduction or the removal of clients' concerns that bring them to coaching. Instead, the focus of existential coaching is primarily on a descriptive exploration of the clients' worldview from the context of their presenting concerns.

7. Ontological coaching

Alan Sieler describes ontological coaching as a way of working with individuals in their engagement in three inter-related spheres of human existence. These three spheres are language, emotions and physiology (body posture). The coach attempts to be a catalyst for change by triggering a shift in the coachee's 'way of being' to enable him or her to develop perceptions and behaviours that were previously unavailable.

8. Narrative coaching

David Drake makes a convincing case for an approach to coaching in which clients are seen as *narrators* and the coach helps them to identify new connections between their stories, their identities and their behaviours, using the narrative material in the session. Narrative coaches invite people to see their stories from different perspectives. Working experientially, contextually and transpersonally, the coach enables clients to generate new options and to create new stories of their lives in action.

9. Psychological development in adulthood and coaching

Tatiana Bachkirova invites the reader to explore an approach that is based on extensive research and theories of cognitive development. These theories suggest that developmental changes in meaning-making, worldviews and maturity of the ego occur in a logical sequence of stages throughout the life of the individual. She argues that learning about developmental trajectories allows coaches to be better equipped to understand the diverse needs of their clients.

10. The transpersonal approach to coaching

John Rowan gives an introduction to the approach which recognizes dimensions beyond the personal. He starts from clarifying the notion of the transpersonal by considering what it is usually confused with, such as religion, spirituality, New Age ideas and so on. Coaching from the transpersonal perspective is said to enhance awareness of the transpersonal dimension of life and to facilitate the experience of being connected to others in a way that provides feelings of completeness and joy. The chapter suggests several ways of engaging with various manifestations of the transpersonal, such as creativity.

11. The positive psychology approach to coaching

Ilona Boniwell, *Carol Kauffman* and *Jordan Silberman* describe an approach to coaching based on positive psychology as a discipline. The distinct feature of this approach is a consistent shifting of attention away from problems and weaknesses to opportunities and strengths. Coaches who are interested in this orientation will find good ground in this chapter for being selective about what to focus their attention on, in order to energize and pull people forward.

12. Transactional Analysis and coaching

Trudi Newton and *Rosemary Napper* describe this interactional approach to coaching as one that is based on several notions such as the ego states, life-scripts and interactional patterns. The chapter suggests several ways in which Transactional Analysis (TA) can inform coaching practice by providing a thinking framework and by offering accessible language that can be shared with clients for greater understanding of the motivations, interactions and coaching goals.

13. The NLP approach to coaching
Bruce Grimley presents this approach to coaching as one that assists clients in exploring their reality, which may both enable and hinder them. The Neuro-linguistic Programming (NLP) approach attempts to identify patterns that represent the way individuals construct their realities in order to control their inner experiences in various environmental contexts. The chapter gives an overview of a wide range of the NLP techniques that could be useful for coaches, such as matching and pacing; working with well-formed outcomes and anchoring.

Section II

Applied contexts, forms or types of coaching are referred to in this Handbook as genres and contexts. Genres are forms of coaching that identify the purpose of the coaching in their title, such as performance coaching, developmental coaching or transformational coaching, while contexts refer to the settings or subject matter of the coaching, such as in 'manager as coach' or 'life coaching'. Each draws on many additional cross-disciplinary theories that are applied in specific contexts, e.g. management, learning, career development and team building.

Section II (Chapters 14–25) of the Handbook examines the most common genres and contexts of coaching. All chapters set out the history and specific features of each context or genre and discuss the role of the coach and the relationship with the client. Each chapter also includes discussion on the relationship of the type of coaching with theoretical traditions and evaluates strengths and weaknesses.

14. Skills and performance coaching
Bob Tschannen-Moran describes the goals and tasks of skills and performance coaching (SPC), suggesting that the agenda for SPC is often determined through external, often organizational, requirements. The focus is on meeting a skills or performance need that may have been identified by the organization, rather than the client. Even so, as Bob makes clear, there is a vital need to link the learning need with the coachee's internal desires and ambitions; he argues that there can be no mastery of skills or performance without giving attention to mental, emotional and volitional frameworks, since it is these that govern our performance.

15. Developmental coaching
The integral theme introduced by Bob Tschannen-Moran is continued in Chapter 15, where *Elaine Cox* and *Peter Jackson* explore developmental coaching. In this chapter it is explicitly suggested that many of the different kinds of coaching (from either the theoretical or the contexts/genres dimensions) work towards helping the coachee to develop in some way: there is an element of client development and progress making in all forms of coaching. However, developmental coaching is built on a range of often unarticulated assumptions about individual

development and the holistic nature of change that may affect clients. The chapter discusses these assumptions as central to the coaching process and the role of the developmental coach.

16. Transformational coaching

Peter Hawkins and *Nick Smith* explain their conceptualization of transformational coaching, where the aim is to help coachees to make significant change in their life or work and to make that change speedily. Ideally, they say, this change can be discerned even before a client leaves the coaching room. The authors present the CLEAR process model for facilitating such change. Transformational coaching has applications across coaching contexts, particularly where the need for a meaningful change is pressing.

17. Executive and leadership coaching

Jon Stokes and *Richard Jolly* present an overview of the coaching provided at senior levels in organizations. They explain the challenges that face the executive or leader in relation to developing a strategic perspective, enabling others and balancing the competing forces and interests within the organization.

18. The manager as coach

Andrea Ellinger, *Rona Beattie* and *Robert Hamlin* look at the particular issues facing the manager who also acts as coach. They identify the need to clarify beliefs about managerial roles and capabilities and about learning processes and learners. In addition, the manager needs to have an awareness of where the opportunities for coaching lie in their everyday managerial work and also what constitute effective and ineffective coaching behaviours in this context. The authors draw on their own considerable research in this area to pull together the issues.

19. Team coaching

David Clutterbuck examines the issues surrounding team coaching. He describes his own definition of team coaching as 'a learning intervention designed to increase collective capability and performance of a group or team, through application of the coaching principles of assisted reflection, analysis and motivation for change'. The contrast in theoretical approach here is between short-term performance orientation and the concept of the team as a learning organism.

20. Peer coaching

Richard Ladyshewsky describes peer coaching, where emphasis is on reciprocal relationships between colleagues with similar experience and responsibility. The focus is generally on expanding or refining work-based skills and competencies. Rick pulls out a number of important issues that have a particular resonance in this context, including trust and confidentiality.

21. Life coaching

Anthony Grant and *Michael Cavanagh* introduce life coaching as a way of enhancing well-being in a whole life context, rather than as a strategy to increase functionality in the workplace. They describe it as a 'personal values-based, holistic approach to personal change and development', but note that, despite its popularity and potential to individuals and society, there is a comparative paucity of research into life coaching, which sometimes reflects on its status within the coaching community.

22. Health and wellness coaching

Margaret Moore and *Erika Jackson* focus on how coaching can be used to help people take better care of their health. They explain the different range of health and wellness issues that can benefit from coaching, contrasting the medical expert approach with the coaching approach. In the chapter they introduce some coaching mechanisms that can be used to enable sustained cognitive and behavioural change.

23. Career coaching

Bruce Hazen and *Nicole Steckler* describe the particular features and processes of coaching that are specifically designed to enhance career development. Career coaches, they explain, help with the establishment of a 'satisfying marriage of work and current identity where work fits the character, competencies, values and experiences of the coachee'. At the same time, career coaches also seek to gently disturb the current identity, then design and guide a range of experiments to try and refine or develop that identity to its next stage of actualization.

24. Cross-cultural coaching: a paradoxical perspective

Geoffrey Abbott discusses the nature and purpose of cross-cultural coaching, suggesting that the successful management of the differences that occur in cross-cultural contexts, consists of managing paradox. Abbott argues that cross-cultural coaching can encourage clients towards synergistic, inclusive approaches to conflicting and confusing challenges and should help them to find clarity and commonality, despite the complexity of their situations. Cross-cultural coaching should not marginalize culture and give attention to the 'problem' of cultural differences, rather, as Abbott argues, it should support a homogeneous quest for identification of similarities.

25. Mentoring in a coaching world

In the final chapter of this section, *Bob Garvey* talks about mentoring. He explains how mentoring has a longer tradition than coaching, but that both activities share many of the same practices, applications and values. He suggests that ultimately it depends on our choice of terminology and the meaning associated with that terminology: mentoring and coaching will mean different things to different people in different contexts. Bob suggests that mentoring is likely to be closely aligned with coaching: the choice of terminology is often based on sector or organizational preference, rather than a distinct divergence in the goals or tasks of practice.

Section III

Despite the expansion of coaching as a practice, the concept of coaching as a profession is still relatively new. Since 2000, a variety of bodies have been established that link coaches together and provide access to focused developmental opportunities. They embrace a number of important functions, such as creating standards, which although not enforced are indicators of good practice for coaches and other stakeholders. Collaborations between these bodies in Europe, for example, have created an emphasis on coaching supervision and it is now becoming increasingly difficult to practice at a senior level in employer organizations without evidence of both supervision and appropriate coaching qualifications. There seems to be, however, a long way to go in establishing coaching as a profession. Section III (Chapters 26–31) attempts to pull together the main strands of activity and the concerns that have to be addressed in the wider discussion around professionalization of coaching.

26. The future of coaching as a profession

David Lane, *Reinhard Stelter* and *Sunny Stout Rostron* examine the prerequisites for an occupation to become a profession and assess where coaching fits within these. They explore the question of whether coaching needs to be a profession and/or whether its being an occupation might suffice, offering a more pragmatic solution to the breadth of coaching philosophy and practice. They also draw a useful distinction between being a profession and acting professionally.

27. Coaching supervision

Peter Hawkins presents an overview of issues around coaching supervision, arguing that coaching without supervision is unethical, in that it exposes clients to potential dangers of which the coach may not be aware. As supervision is also an essential element of the coach's continuing professional development, an absence of supervision can impoverish the quality of reflection-on-practice.

28. Coaching and mental health

Michael Cavanagh and *Andrew Buckley* reinforce the issue of client safety by reviewing the relationship between coaching and mental health. The coach with a wide portfolio of clients will inevitably meet some clients whose needs extend into the psychotherapeutical. Recognizing these needs and responding appropriately is essential from several perspectives, including the well-being of the client, the reputation of the coach and the reputation of the coaching profession.

29. Continuing professional development for coaches

Diane Stober's review of the state of coach education identifies one of the main reasons for the inadequacy of ethical management, supervision practice and boundary management – the sheer confusion of competing training and qualification providers, each operating from a different and sometimes competing theoretical base and approach. While competence frameworks may help, the establishment of a common knowledge base appears to be a long way off. She argues that only with a substantially expanded evidence base will that knowledge base begin to solidify and that will require a significant shift in the focus of research away from proving that coaching adds value to investigating the dynamics of relationship effectiveness.

30. Ethics in coaching

Diane Brennan and *Leni Wildflower* address the issue of ethics, in the light of both the establishment of ethical codes within all the professional bodies and the increasing collaboration between bodies aimed at harmonizing those codes. Fortunately, the codes are for the most part remarkably similar in concept, even though the precise wording varies.

31. Research in coaching

In the final chapter of this section *Annette Fillery-Travis* and *Elaine Cox* discuss the developing evidence base for coaching. However, they uncover significant gaps in the research on coaching. This chapter considers those gaps and also explains how, as an applied field, coaching might eschew the researcher/practitioner dichotomy that is often created in professions when research begins to thrive. The chapter proposes that practitioners and researchers alike adopt a pragmatic approach. Pragmatists insist that truths be 'tested' against practice or action and ask that the evidence from application be 'mapped' back to relevant theoretical origins.

Suggestions for the reader

This book can be engaged with in different ways. Readers could begin with the chapters on theoretical approaches (Section I) and from there move linearly through the text. Alternatively, they may want to pinpoint their particular theoretical or practical approach and so choose a chapter from either Section I or Section II and pick up links from that first chapter in relation to which theory, genre or context to focus on next. Another way would be to use the matrix as a guide (Table 0.2) and to begin by reading chapters where the starred squares next to their approach are in alignment. Readers who approach the book in this way may find that there are links and associations with theories or practical applications that they had not previously considered.

The following questions may be useful to keep in mind while reading each chapter:

- How do you feel when you read the chapter? What resonates with you?
- What sort of evidence is most persuasive for you?
- What does your intuition tell you about why you align with the tradition/approach?
- What is your personal philosophy of change, development and coaching? What helps to formulate it better?
- How has this personal philosophy been enriched or challenged by what you have read?

REFERENCES

Bachkirova, T. (2007). Role of coaching psychology in defining boundaries between counselling and coaching. In S. Palmer & A. Whybrow (Eds), *Handbook of coaching psychology*. London: Routledge.

Cox, E. (2006). An adult learning approach to coaching. In D. Stober and A. Grant (Eds), *The handbook of evidence-based coaching*. Hoboken, NJ: John Wiley & Sons.

Cox, E. (2013). *Coaching understood: A pragmatic inquiry into the coaching process*. London: Sage.

Dewey, J. (1910). *How we think*. Lexington, MA: Heath.

Ferrar, P. (2006). The paradox of manager as coach: Does being a manager inhibit effective coaching? (Unpublished MA dissertation, Oxford Brookes University.) Oxford.

Grant, A. (2000). Coaching psychology comes of age. *PsychNews*, 4(4): 12–14.

Grant, A. & Palmer, S. (2002). Coaching psychology workshop. Annual conference of the Division of Counselling Psychology, British Psychological Society, Torquay, England. 18 May 2002.

Knowles, M. (1978). *The adult learner: A neglected species*. Houston, TX: Gulf.

Knowles, M., Holton, E., & Swanson, R. (2011). *The adult learner* (7th ed.). Oxford: Elsevier Butterworth-Heinemann.

Kolb, D. (1984). *Experiential learning: Experience as the source of learning and development*. Englewood Cliffs, NJ: Prentice Hall.

Mezirow, J. (1990). *Fostering critical reflection in adulthood: A guide to transformative and emancipatory learning*. San Francisco, CA: Jossey-Bass.

Mezirow, J. (2000). How critical reflection triggers transformative learning. In Mezirow, J. & Associates (Eds), *Learning as transformation*. San Francisco, CA: Jossey-Bass.

Wilber, K. (1996). *Eye to eye: The quest for the new paradigm*. Boston, MA and London: Shambhala.

Wilber, K. (2000). *Integral psychology*. Boston, MA: Shambhala.

Wilber, K. (2006). *Integral spirituality*. Boston, MA: Shambhala.

Theoretical Approaches

1

The Psychodynamic Approach to Coaching

Graham Lee

For more than 100 years, psychodynamic thinking has been an influential body of ideas about the workings of the human mind. This chapter describes the distinctive way these ideas can inform the activity of coaching, in particular showing how it provides a method for working with the unconscious factors underlying human behaviour.

The term psychodynamic refers to a broad lineage of models that focus on the role of unconscious processes in human behaviour and, more specifically, on the dynamic relationship between different parts of the mind. Since Freud's (1922) first description of psychoanalysis there have been many developments, some of them building on Freud's ideas and his emphasis on instinctual drives and others providing quite different formulations. Jung (1956) broke away to develop 'analytical psychology' in which prominence is given to the Self and the role of archetypes; Klein (1988) shifted the focus to the role of fantasy in the earliest stages of a child's development; Winnicott (1971) and many other object relations theorists (Greenberg & Mitchell, 1983) stressed the importance of the relationship between mother and baby in the shaping of mental life; and Bowlby (1988), for a long time disowned by much of the psycho-analytic community, researched the role of the caregiver in enabling the baby to form a safe attachment and his empirical approach sparked a rich vein of research into attachment theory (Goldberg, Muir, & Kerr, 1995). These are just some of the leading contributors to a constantly evolving field, which in some areas is now being validated by neuroscientific research into the role of non-conscious processes in emotional development (e.g. Solms, 1996; Schore, 2003; Siegel, 2010).

It is perhaps useful to highlight at the outset four key assumptions that underpin a psycho-dynamic approach to coaching. First, human behaviour is powerfully influenced by unconscious motives; this means that the coach is constantly curious about what might be implicit, hidden or a blind spot for the coachee. Second, much of human behaviour is unconsciously shaped by past experiences; this means that as part of coaching conversations the coach is likely to invite the coachee to talk about past experiences and to explore links or resonances between past and present situations. The third assumption is that different parts of the mind can be in conflict with each other; this means that the coach is curious about apparent inconsistencies in what the coachee says or does, and encourages the coachee to become aware of mixed or con-flictual feelings. The fourth assumption is that there can be unconscious communication between people; this means that the coach periodically brings attention to her or his own bodily sensations and emotions as possible clues about unconscious communications from the coachee (the countertransference). With these key assumptions in mind, we turn to explore in more detail the distinctive features of the psychodynamic approach, followed by a consideration of its methods, its applications and an evaluation of its strengths and limitations.

DISTINCTIVE FEATURES

Making the unconscious conscious

The primary task of a psychodynamic approach to coaching is to enable coachees to have more choice and freedom. Before coaching, the lack of freedom is represented by coachees having a relatively fixed sense of identity that has been unconsciously shaped by experience. The great potential of psychodynamic coaching is to make the unconscious conscious, to increase self-awareness, to understand the subtle ways in which coachees can limit themselves and so learn how to approach new challenges with more awareness and freedom. However, this may not be simple to achieve. Unconscious material is often emotionally-laden material – it has stayed out-of-awareness for a good reason. It can be psychologically painful to acknowledge and assimi-late. For this reason the coach needs to understand how to create a 'holding environment' for the coachee.

Creating a holding environment

The concept of the 'holding environment' (Winnicott, 1965) describes a physical and, perhaps more significantly, a psychological space in which coachees feel safe enough to be open with their thoughts and feelings; to be able to share their anxieties, frustrations, aspirations and deepest hopes. The metaphor of 'holding' comes from the idea of a mother's attuned response to, and handling of, her baby. In psychodynamic coaching, 'holding' takes the form of being sensitively attuned to the underlying emotional agenda of the coachee, and making choices about pace, focus and questioning that meet the coachee's readiness. The practical methods for creating a sense of holding are discussed further in the section on Methods and Techniques.

Unconscious emotional regulation

A contemporary psychodynamic perspective views the regulation of emotions (rather than instincts) as lying at the heart of much of human behaviour (Schore, 2003). As a result of previous relationships, particularly those with our parents or earliest caregivers, we develop distinctive but unconscious strategies for regulating our emotions and for building up a sense of self-identity. These early emotional habits tend to persist into adulthood because they become part of the developing brain's neuronal structure and brain chemistry (Gerhardt, 2004). These unconscious strategies are the engine of what Freud first described as 'the dynamic unconscious', an out-of-awareness part of the mind that shapes how we relate to ourselves and to others.

The goal of the coach is essentially to expand the coachee's capacity for emotional regulation, that is, to enable the coachee, through the trust and containment of the relationship with the coach, to revisit difficult emotional territory in a way that is contained, so that the need for defensive strategies is reduced, and in which thinking, rather than reacting, can take place. By creating a space in which feelings can be experienced and labelled in language, they become phenomena that can be looked at and understood. Such a reworking of inner emotional territory, from disconnected sensations of emotional distress that have to be instantly defended against, to meaningfully connected patterns of experience, is transformative because what was once unconscious has been brought into awareness.

Defence mechanisms

Defence mechanisms, such as repression, denial and projection, are specific examples of unconscious patterns of emotional regulation that operate to avoid or minimize emotions that are currently experienced as too difficult to tolerate. The particular form of our defences develops unconsciously in childhood and later, in situations where we perceive that others will not adequately regulate our emotions, or where our emotions will be perceived as socially unacceptable. For example, coachees in organizations often use intellectualization as a way of dealing with upsetting personnel issues, projection as a way of blaming another department for organizational failings and displacement as a way of keeping busy with unimportant details rather than tackling more important but anxiety provoking issues.

In coaching the goal is not so much to name specific defence mechanisms but to recognize when the coachee is enacting an unconscious strategy of emotional regulation; they are a clue that the coachee is in psychological territory that feels problematic or overwhelming. In time, with sufficient holding and with the development of a working alliance underpinned by trust and rapport, the coach is likely to gain some understanding of the underlying emotional agenda, and so gradually move towards exploring the nature of these feelings with the coachee, their origins, their development and their impact on current behaviour and performance.

Transference and countertransference

One of the primary tools for gaining access to the coachee's implicit and potentially limiting interpersonal strategies is through the dynamics of transference and countertransference.

Transference refers to the implicit assumptions that we make about others based on our past experiences. If a coachee has experienced frowns from a routinely disapproving parent, he/she may attribute to a frowning coach disapproval that was actually an expression of confusion. If a coachee has experienced a parents' preoccupation with time as somewhat rejecting, then the coachee may experience the coaches' strict management of session times as rejecting rather than appropriately bounded. Transference can refer to any piece of unconscious learning that is applied to a new context, but its impact is most tangible when the transference occurs in relation to the coach, for example with the coachee unconsciously behaving towards the coach as if he/she is the coachee's boss or colleague or parent. If the coach is vigilant as to how he or she is being perceived by and related to, the coachee, the coach can gain some understanding of how the coachee is unconsciously projecting ('transferring') an aspect of another person, or of themselves, onto the coach.

One of the ways that the coach may come to understand the transference – the coachee's unconscious projection of aspects of a past relationship onto the coach – is through the countertransference. Countertransference refers to the feelings, bodily sensations, thoughts and behaviours that can be unconsciously evoked in the coach by the coachee. This apparently mysterious transmission of unconscious feelings is understood in terms of a further mechanism: projective identification. Projective identification, a concept originally introduced by Klein (1988), is a process where the unconscious emotional experience of one person can be communicated to the unconscious of another. This is thought to occur through subtle nuances of behaviour, such as facial expressions and modulations in the pace, tone and rhythm of the voice that are processed rapidly, non-consciously, and non-verbally in parts of the human brain (possibly the mirror neurons; Iacoboni, 2009) that are also linked to our perception of bodily sensations (Schore, 2003). By tuning into bodily feelings and sensations, the coach can experience the coachee's non-conscious signals and so come to learn something about the coachee's disowned emotional state.

METHODS AND TECHNIQUES

There are a number of methods and techniques that are particularly characteristic of the coach working from a psychodynamic perspective. These are: establishing and maintaining a 'holding environment', eliciting personal stories, the use of silence, introspection, thinking and the 'good-enough' coach – and making links.

Establishing and maintaining a 'holding environment'

I have already described the importance of the psychological 'holding' that arises from the coach's attunement and responsiveness to the coachee. We can think of this attuned 'holding' as paradoxically offering the coachee both boundary and space; the boundary of appropriate challenge and clear expectations, and the space to follow impulses and to flow freely and creatively with associations and connecting ideas. Psychological holding needs to be matched and supported by certain practical conditions, such as setting up clear boundaries for coaching sessions, both in terms of time and space. The coaching should take place in a quiet, secluded room, away from distractions such as the possibility of colleagues gazing in through a glass window. It is also important for the coach to manage the boundary of time clearly and firmly, expecting to start and end at the agreed times.

A further aspect of 'holding' comes from setting clear expectations at the outset of coaching, including the idea that conversations will explore past experiences and the patterns of learning from those experiences that may be playing through in the present. Many coachees are relieved to be given permission to talk widely and fully about themselves and their lives, whilst others are initially uncomfortable or embarrassed about the idea of talking so personally. In my experience, this discomfort is often based on a concern that personal recollections may be upsetting and may evoke strong feelings of vulnerability. In such circumstances, it is useful to normalize the idea that visiting a full range of emotional experience is part and parcel of the coaching experience, and that exploring how much we can trust another person with our vulnerability is often an important learning edge.

Eliciting personal stories

Much of coaching is either concerned with what is happening in the present, or with what the coachee would like to happen in the future. However, in the psychodynamic approach we also want to explore the coachee's past experiences and possible links to their present circumstances. This can be achieved in two, complementary ways. First, by asking coachees in one of their early coaching sessions to give a detailed account of their life to date, starting with their childhood and their earliest relationships with siblings and parents, and continuing forward through the stages of education, career history and including key events in their personal lives. By inquiring into key reactions, responses and feelings at times of joy, achievement, challenge, difficulty, setback, loss, etc, we can gain a very rich picture of our coachees' lives and how their experiences may have shaped them. We can also note how they tell their story, what they gloss over and what they get caught by, as unconscious clues to possible areas of difficulty (see Holmes, 2001 and Lee & Roberts, 2010 for a discussion of narrative coherence).

In addition to a biographical account towards the beginning of a coaching assignment, the coach may also invite coachees to consider possible resonances between a current situation and something that happened in the past. For example, I may say to a coachee who is currently feeling very stuck and disempowered by a boss, 'if you cast your mind back, does this current situation remind you of any other situation from earlier in your life, perhaps in previous job roles, or at school, or perhaps even from your childhood?' If questions like this are asked in an open, exploratory way, as an invitation to think broadly and inquisitively, coachees develop an increasing sense of themselves as characters who are, at least to some extent, shaped by experience, and whose present-day beliefs and styles are often implicit, unconscious extensions of those earlier experiences.

The use of silence

Coachees commonly assume that a coaching session should be filled with conversation. However, if the coach and the coachee are to have time to reflect and to allow associations and links to emerge, it is important to foster the value of silences. There are a number of ways in which the coach can encourage the use of silence. First, the coach can model the possibility of silence in sessions by taking time to pause and reflect before speaking. In this way the coach demonstrates that unlike most day-to-day conversations, pausing and going inward to examine what is arising within, is a valid aspect of the work. Second, sometimes it is useful for the coach to ask the coachee how they feel about silences, and possibly to invite them to experiment with what it feels like to pause and reflect during sessions. Third, it can be useful to direct coachees towards introspection (see below), which usually involves a degree of silent reflection.

Introspection

Learning to introspect is important for the coachee because it provides the basis for self-knowledge and understanding. Some coachees will naturally turn inwards in response to a question, examining their inner worlds and weighing what is true for them. However, many coachees spend little time looking within themselves and may need to be supported in learning how to introspect. I have found it useful to teach coachees about the distinction between thoughts, emotions, bodily sensations and actions (these categories are used in cognitive behavioural coaching), and to ask them to describe what they are currently experiencing in each of these domains as a particular issue is discussed. In my experience it is particularly useful to spend time helping coachees to tune into their bodily sensations and emotions, because they can be quite disconnected from these domains of experience. Opening up these aspects of experience as territories for investigation can in itself be a source of revelation, showing how formerly out-of-awareness body signals and emotions are directly linked to particular thoughts and impulses to act.

Thinking and the good-enough coach

Working with the transference and the countertransference are challenging aspects of the psychodynamic approach, because disowned feelings of the coachee can be unconsciously projected onto the coach, and containing these feelings often challenges to the limit the coach's own capacity for emotional regulation. They can find themselves filled with feelings of anger, or disgust, or desire, or boredom, and with a blocked capacity for thinking. In my experience such disruptions to the coach's thinking are not uncommon (Bion, 1962). The goal for the coach – and I think coaching supervision can be invaluable here – is to find a way to reinstate the capacity to think. The coach needs to operate with a dual mode of attention, to attend to his/her own self-regulatory functioning and at the same time participate fully with the coachee in mutual exploration. The 'good-enough coach' – an adaptation of Winnicott's phrase, the 'good-enough mother' – is not someone who always gets this right – rather it is a coach who manages to return him/herself to a state of regulation, having temporarily been overwhelmed. It is probable that the coachee, at an unconscious level, perceives this two-stage process, the rupture in the holding environment and then the coach's return to a thinking state, and so gains an implicit, experiential knowledge that such feelings can be contained. Working at this level is undoubtedly demanding on the coach, but it lays the ground for a fundamental shift in the coachee's capacity to think about feelings and clears the way for making more explicit links, such as those between past experiences and their impact on the present.

Making links

In making links (or interpretations as they were described by Freud, 1905) the coach is helping coachees to develop a more integrated self-awareness and a more self-compassionate understanding of why they are the way they are. The naming of experiences – memories, thoughts, feelings, aspirations – and making links between different aspects of experience, enables them to be perceived and expressed as part of a more coherent sense of identity and personal narrative. One of the most powerful links that the psychodynamic approach seeks to make is between past and present. In my experience, coachees will often make links themselves, simply by being invited to explore possible past experiences that resonate with present situations. However, this is not always the case and so it is important for the coach to offer possible links or formulations in a very tentative way, inviting the coachee to 'try on' an interpretation of his or her behaviour, rather than immediately to accept it or dismiss it.

For example, a coachee had a reputation for being difficult and abrasive with his colleagues and his career was stalling as a consequence. After working with this man for some time and based on what he had shared with me about his early life and relationship with his father, I suggested to him that his difficulties with current colleagues were, in part, an unconscious re-run of his unresolved frustration with his father's lack of attention for him (a transference interpretation). He was initially quite dismissive of this interpretation and seemed to become annoyed with me as if I was his heartless and mis-attuned father. But, over several sessions, as we worked through this idea, he was increasingly able to acknowledge its relevance for him. By recognizing the unconscious agenda driving his behaviour, he was able to look at his current relationships more objectively and to discern ways in which he could influence and collaborate with his boss and colleagues more effectively.

APPLICATION

In this section I look at the psychodynamic approach in relation to five types of coaching: skills and performance coaching (SPC); developmental coaching; executive and leadership coaching; team coaching; and cross-cultural coaching.

Skills and performance coaching

Viewed as a method for optimizing performance in organizations, SPC has become an established management development intervention. On the face of it, the psychodynamic approach does not appear to be the most obvious fit in a context where the emphasis is on fulfilling certain behavioural competency standards. However, in many situations, behavioural change cannot be achieved without understanding the underlying issues blocking change.

I introduced the concept of ACE patterns (Lee, 2006), integrated patterns of Actions, Cognitions and Emotions, to make explicit the link between unconscious emotional issues and their impact on behaviour. For example, a junior manager who had not managed to improve her presentation skills, despite being sent on various skills-development workshops, received a single session of coaching with me. She described how she would freeze when in front of an audience. I asked her to describe this experience of freezing (the Action) in detail and then to look back through her history for times when she might have first had this experience. She reported that she would freeze like this when seeing her father's blank face as she sought his permission to do something and went on to describe her deep fear (Emotion) of his disapproval. The link that we made was that she was unconsciously projecting her father's disapproval onto the blank faces of the audience when she made a presentation and consequently froze with fear. By recognizing this link she could begin to approach presentations less dogged by her unconscious fear of her father's disapproval. This example illustrates that improving performance often requires coachees to increase their awareness of unconscious emotional blocks, and the psychodynamic approach provides an elegant method for making links and raising the coachee's self-awareness.

Developmental coaching

Developmental coaching is concerned with the development of the individual as a whole. While other types of coaching, such as performance or career coaching, are more focused on enabling the coach to develop in a specific area, development coaching has a broad remit encompassing a coachee's personal life as well as his/her work-life. Thus development coaching might explore such areas as overarching purpose, underpinning values, signature talents and strengths, key obstacles, career ambitions and personal/work relationships. The breadth of the approach means that developmental coaching is likely to draw on a range of theoretical traditions, including that of psychodynamic thinking.

One of the central goals of both developmental coaching and the psychodynamic approach to coaching is to increase awareness, since awareness of self and others is viewed as the foundation for making choices that are consistent with the purpose, values, ambitions and strengths of the coachee. The psychodynamic approach can be particularly useful in this context, because many people find that as life goes on they have gradually lost sight of their core passions and convictions; life has become a series of compromises, diluted ambitions, disillusioned hopes and opportunities avoided due to fear. For example, I worked with a senior manager in the pharmaceutical industry whose passion for healing, his core motivation for entering the industry, had been forgotten amid the daily challenge of meeting revenue and profit targets and managing a large sales force. Through an exploration of stories of people he found most inspiring he recalled how much he had enjoyed working in a health centre as a student. He also recalled that his father, a self-made businessman, had disapproved of his altruistic, 'softer' side and had strongly directed him towards a business career. He realized that his desire for his father's approval had unconsciously influenced his choices over many years. This psycho-dynamic awareness opened up a much wider exploration of his choices, less constrained by his unconscious desire to please his father.

Although developmental coaching, like psychodynamic coaching, is more focused on raising awareness than on achieving specific shifts in behaviour, an increase in awareness typically leads to a shift in how a coachee thinks and feels and these deeper shifts are often the key elements that underpin a more enduring shift in behaviour.

Executive and leadership coaching

In executive and leadership coaching, we are usually working with a population of managers who have already achieved a good deal of success in their careers, but whose future development requires them to shift perspective; for example, to augment their technical competence with a more strategic view, or to temper their driving leadership style with greater political awareness and effective influence skills. I have suggested (Lee, 2006) that if managers are to be successful leaders then they need to become authentic, in the sense that they consciously balance their personal needs and convictions with the needs and convictions of their colleagues, whether in their team or the wider organization. Drawing on attachment theory, I have suggested that we routinely come across leaders whose authenticity and consequent effectiveness is limited by their use of unconsciously defensive leadership styles, which I call defiant and compliant leadership. Defiant leadership arises where a manager denies his/her vulnerability or self-doubt by adopting a dominant and dogmatic style, which tends to evoke resistance and frustration in others. Compliant leadership arises where a manager avoids confrontation by too readily fitting in with the needs of others and so limiting his/her capacity for assertiveness and creativity.

The psychodynamic approach to coaching provides an opportunity for leaders to examine the relational assumptions that unconsciously underpin their leadership styles. The defiant leader, contained by the coach's attunement and resilience, finds a space to look at feelings that have long been banished from awareness, and so finds an opportunity to re-examine the need to be controlling of others. The compliant leader, invited to connect with hidden frustrations, learns to confront others in a useful way and so gains confidence in his/her ideas and their potential value to others. In this way, psychodynamic coaching can provide a rich learning environment for evoking authenticity and increased effectiveness in executives and leaders.

Team coaching

Just as individuals can adopt defensive strategies for managing feelings, groups can also behave in ways that defend against anxiety. Bion (1961) proposed three defensive strategies, called basic assumptions: fight/flight, dependency and pairing. For example, team members, anxious about how to solve a difficult issue, may become distracted and angry with senior management for putting them in this predicament (fight or flight). By blaming others they spare themselves the emotional challenge of taking responsibility and for integrating mixed feelings they may have about their capacity to solve the issue.

Another way the team may manage their anxiety is by idealizing one of the team members (or sometimes the coach) and then relying on them to resolve the challenge facing the team (dependency). While appropriate followership is useful, dependency means that there is a lack of shared initiative and responsibility within the team, and if the idealized leader is not successful, then dependency can turn to fight or flight in relation to the leader. A further defensive strategy, somewhat similar to dependency, is to rely on a pair within the team to solve the team's difficulties (pairing).

The goal in team coaching is to enable the team to manage itself in such a way that it can focus on its primary tasks, drawing usefully on the skills and talents of all of its members, managing differences effectively, operating with appropriate levels of self-disclosure, building creatively on the contributions of others and effectively managing the boundary with other parts of the organization. By noticing when the team is resorting to defensive strategies, the coach seeks to understand the nature of the anxiety underlying the defence, and from this awareness can decide on an appropriate intervention. This might involve naming the defence in some way, but if the team lacks the resilience to face this observation, then the coach might, for example, encourage the team to work on a simpler, more manageable task in order to reinstate its sense of effectiveness.

Cross-cultural coaching

In its emphasis on the impact of past experiences and the subtleties of context in shaping our behaviour at an unconscious level, the psychodynamic perspective brings important insights to cross-cultural coaching. It highlights the need for the coach to be vigilant to his or her own inevitable, implicit biases in relation to others. Transference, whether from the coach to the coachee, or vice versa, is an unconscious prediction or assumption about another person based on past learning, and in this sense it is a pre-judgement or prejudice. Such transferential prejudices are problematic if they remain out-of-awareness as implicit truths about others. In cross-cultural coaching, the coach needs to examine his/her own assumptions about the impact of a coachee's cultural origins, to explore his/her capacity to suspend judgement, and to cultivate understanding and a sense of empathy with the coachee's particular life conditions and circumstances. It is important to recognize that many cultural experiences are significantly different from our own and, depending on the kind of issues to be explored, some coachees will benefit from working with a coach who has direct knowledge or personal experience of their cultural background.

EVALUATING THE PSYCHODYNAMIC APPROACH

In this last section, I consider the strengths and limitations of the psychodynamic approach and finish by discussing the contexts in which this approach can be most usefully applied.

Strengths

The psychodynamic approach opens our minds to the possibility that there is substantially more going on below the surface of coaching interaction than can be seen on the surface. Whether it is in the hidden agendas of an organizational sponsor, the defences of a coachee or the diversionary games of a team, the psychodynamic approach provides an unparalleled resource for investigating and making sense of unconscious processes and their role in shaping, and often limiting, the achievement of goals.

Applied to the arena of coaching, this approach usefully emphasizes the importance of managing boundaries, since it is through an experience of 'holding' and safety that coachees can allow their defences to loosen. While coaching is necessarily more flexible than counselling or psychotherapy with regard to the regularity of sessions and the location of meetings, the psychodynamic approach encourages us to recognize that the containment provided by fixed start and end times, a consistent physical environment and explicit confidentiality all contribute to an experience of holding, and so make possible a deeper exploration of the coachee's ways of making meaning.

The coach informed by psychodynamic practice will also have a particular appreciation of the role of restraint and silence in one-to-one work. Viewed as a space for thinking more than doing, reflecting more than solving, coachees come to experience the coach's restraint as an invitation to go deeper into oneself, to ask the question 'why', to sit with the discomfort of not knowing, to tolerate distressing feelings and to discover the transformative potential of awareness.

The psychodynamic approach does, however, set a challenge to coaches to stretch their own developmental capacity for meaning-making, and undertaking one-to-one work with a psychodynamic practitioner is perhaps one of the most powerful ways of promoting that. The task for the coach is to be able to take a meta-perspective on their own implicit biases and defences, and through this process gain a more expansive awareness of self and others. It is the emotional resilience that comes from such self-awareness and integration that provides coachees with the profound experience of psychological containment, and so enables them to visit parts of themselves that have long been disowned.

Limitations

However, the depth of the psychodynamic approach is not always appropriate in coaching. Quite apart from whether coaches feel qualified to move towards unconscious territory, there are many coachees who neither want nor need this style of work. Coachees are often looking for relatively short engagements to help them think through a particular issue, and so favour approaches that focus on the present and the future, without needing to dig into patterns learned from the past. Where coachees have specific goals or a preference for pragmatic solutions, the psychoanalytic question 'why do you want that?' may be less useful than 'what do you want?' and 'how can you get it?'

Furthermore, the psychodynamic approach has the potential to be overly concerned with problems and so miss the value of focusing on a coachee's strengths. The positive psychology movement has arisen out of the concern that much of psychological theory has evolved from the clinical treatment of mental disturbance, which consequently views people as problems to be solved. Psychoanalytic theory must take some responsibility for this problem-centric bias and coaches drawing on the psychodynamic approach need to be cautious about pathologizing coachees. Valuing and building on strengths, appreciating what is working already and actively celebrating coachee's achievements are important aspects that can put the psychodynamic approach into a more balanced and constructively useful context.

Best use

The psychodynamic approach brings great depth and insight to the work of coaching, and as such is most appropriate for contexts where coachees are interested in exploring the roots of their meaning-making patterns, or where they feel stuck and are prepared to do what it takes to achieve an enduring shift. Leadership, developmental and team coaching, together with coaching supervision, are the areas that lend themselves most to the psychodynamic frame, and in all of these areas I have witnessed the profound effectiveness of the approach. Having said that, I would reiterate that the effectiveness of coaching often derives from the ability of the coach to flex his/her style, to draw on multiple approaches, and so respond usefully to the changing needs of coachees. The psychodynamic approach used within an integrative coaching framework is a potent method for evoking change.

FURTHER READING

Freud, S. (1960). *The psychopathology of everyday life*. London: Penguin. (Classic account of the unconscious in everyday life, such as the 'Freudian Slip'.)

Holmes, J. (2001). *The search for the secure base*. Hove. Brunner-Routledge. (A very accessible discussion of attachment theory in psychotherapy, including a discussion of narrative competence.)

Lee, G. (2006). *Leadership coaching: from personal insight to organisational performance*. London. CIPD. (My own pragmatic integration of the psychodynamic approach into coaching, based on work with senior leaders from the UK, Europe and the US.)

Winnicott, D. (1971). *Playing and reality*. London: Penguin. (By a ground-breaking psychoanalyst and paediatrician who writes very insightfully about the experience of working with children.)

DISCUSSION QUESTIONS

- To what extent is a psychodynamic approach to coaching relevant in a context where a person or organization is looking for tangible, behavioural change?
- From a psychodynamic point of view, what thoughts might be in your mind about a coachee arriving late for sessions and how might you address that in the work with the coachee?
- Imagine you find yourself feeling bored or distracted during a coaching session. Explore two or more hypotheses you might have about this, based on thoughts about the transference/countertransference dynamic?
- What would the psychodynamic perspective suggest as the possible, unconscious expressed feelings if a coachee is:

- o   Constantly friendly, positive and enthusiastic about the work.
- o   Constantly distant, sceptical and challenging.
- o   Filling the session with talk and giving you little opportunity to comment or ask questions.
- o   And for each of these, what might you say or do to deepen the coaching relationship?

REFERENCES

Bion, W. (1961). *Experiences in groups*. London: Tavistock.

Bion, W. (1962). *Learning from experience*. London: Heinemann.

Bowlby, J. (1988). *A secure base: Clinical applications of attachment theory*. London: Routledge.

Freud, S. (1922). *Introductory lectures on psychoanalysis*. London: George Allen & Unwin.

Gerhardt, S. (2004). *Why love matters: How affection shapes a baby's brain*. Hove: Brunner-Routledge.

Goldberg, S., Muir, R., & Kerr, J. (Eds) (1995). *Attachment theory: Social, developmental and clinical perspectives*. Hillsdale, NJ: Analytic Press.

Greenberg, J. & Mitchell, S. (1983). *Object relations in psychoanalytic theory*. Cambridge, MA: Harvard University Press.

Holmes, J. (2001). *The search for the secure base*. Hove. Brunner-Routledge.

Iacoboni, M. (2009) Imitation, empathy and mirror neurons. *Annual Review of Psychology, 60*: 653–70.

Jung, C.G. (1956). *Two essays on analytical psychology*. Cleveland, OH: Meridian.

Klein, M. (1988). *Love, guilt and reparation and other works 1921–1945*. London: Virago Press.

Lee, G. (2006). *Leadership coaching: From personal insight to organisational performance*. London: Chartered Institute of Personnel and Development.

Lee, G. & Roberts, I. (2010). Coaching for authentic leadership, in J. Passmore (Ed.), *Leadership coaching*. London: Kogan Page.

Schore, A.N. (2003). *Affect regulation and the repair of the self*. New York: Norton.

Siegel, D. (2010). *Mindsight: The new science of personal transformation*. New York: Random House.

Solms, M. (1996). Towards an anatomy of the unconscious. *Journal of Clinical Psychoanalysis, 5*: 331–67.

Winnicott, D. (1965). *The maturational processes and the facilitating environment*. London: Hogarth Press.

Winnicott, D. (1971). *Playing and reality*. London: Penguin.

2

Cognitive Behavioural Coaching

Helen Williams, Stephen Palmer and Nick Edgerton

This chapter focuses on the theory and practice of cognitive behavioural coaching (CBC). First, we endeavour to define and explain CBC, looking back on its history and acknowledging the main proponents of the tradition. Next, we look at the distinctive features that set CBC apart from other approaches, considering tasks and goals, essential processes, the role of the coach and their relationship with the client. The 'methods and techniques' section presents a range of models, tools and techniques that are both cognitive and behavioural in nature. Finally, we discuss the application of CBC across a range of coaching contexts before evaluating the approach and suggesting areas for further discussion. This chapter will not be describing the cognitive coaching developed by Costa and Garmston (2002) that has been applied to the teaching profession in the USA.

CBC has been defined as: 'An integrative approach which combines the use of cognitive, behavioural, imaginal and problem solving techniques and strategies within a cognitive behavioural framework to enable coachees to achieve their realistic goals' (Palmer & Szymanska, 2007: 86). CBC has largely developed since the 1990s, integrating theoretical concepts and strategies based on cognitive behavioural (Neenan & Palmer, 2001; Neenan & Dryden, 2002; Edgerton & Palmer, 2005; Palmer & Gyllensten, 2008), rational-emotive behavioural (DiMattia & Mennen, 1990; Neenan & Palmer, 2001; Anderson, 2002; Kodish 2002; Palmer & Gyllensten, 2008), problem (D'Zurilla, 1986; Palmer, 1997a, 1997b; Palmer, 2007, 2008) and solution-focused approaches and techniques (O'Hanlon, 1998; Palmer, 2008). Goal setting theory (Locke & Latham, 1990), social cognitive theory and self-efficacy may help to explain the effectiveness of CBC (Bandura, 1986)

CBC is based on the premise that 'the way you think about events profoundly influences the way you feel about them' (Neenan and Dryden, 2002: ix), which in turn impacts upon stress and performance. Aaron T. Beck (1976) described the existence of 'internal dialogue', the critical inner voice in our heads that impacts our self-esteem making us doubtful of our self-efficacy (competence) and self-worth. In the 1950s, Albert Ellis (see 1994) highlighted how emotional disturbance is caused not by the activating event, but by the mediating beliefs about the activating event.

Judith Beck (1995) describes three levels of cognitions: automatic thoughts; intermediate beliefs (attitudes, rules and assumptions); and core beliefs. Both intermediate and core beliefs generally develop in early childhood (Curwen, Palmer, & Ruddell, 2000). Unhelpful cognitive 'schema' can lead to negative automatic 'thoughts', preventing us from achieving our true potential. A number of common errors of processing, better known as cognitive distortions or 'thinking errors', have been identified (see Box 2.1 [Palmer & Szymanska, 2007: 99–100]).

DISTINCTIVE FEATURES

Tasks and goals

The main goals of CBC are to:

1. facilitate the client in achieving their realistic goals
2. facilitate self-awareness of underlying cognitive and emotional barriers to goal attainment
3. equip the individual with more effective thinking and behavioural skills
4. build internal resources, stability and self-acceptance in order to mobilize the individual to their choice of action
5. enable the client to become their own self-coach.

Self-awareness

In order to facilitate self-awareness of underlying cognitive and emotional barriers, the CBC coach invites the coaching client to explore the problem or issue they have difficulty with, to challenge the evidence for their current perspective on the situation and consider alternative perspectives they might generate. The questioning process used is referred to as 'Socratic' questioning, after the philosopher Socrates, and involves the coach asking a series of questions aimed at increasing awareness (Neenan & Palmer, 2001).

Box 2.1   Example thinking errors

- Mind reading/jumping to conclusions: jumping to foregone conclusion without the relevant information, e.g. 'If I don't work overtime I'll get sacked'
- All-or-nothing thinking: evaluating experiences on the basis of extremes such as 'excellent or 'awful', e.g. 'She always arrives late'

(Continued)

(Continued)

- Blame: not taking responsibility and blaming somebody or something else for the problem, e.g. 'It's all her fault. She should have reminded me to post the letter'
- Personalization: taking events personally, e.g. 'If our team presentation is rejected, it's my fault'
- Fortune-telling: assuming you always know what the future holds, e.g. 'I know I'll be made redundant next week'
- Emotional reasoning: mistaking feelings for facts, e.g. 'I feel so nervous, I know this merger will fall apart'
- Labelling: using labels or global ratings to describe yourself and others, e.g. 'I'm a total idiot' or 'As I failed my exam this proves I'm a complete failure'
- Demands: peppering your narrative with rigid or inflexible thinking such as 'shoulds' and 'musts': making demands of yourself and others, e.g. 'He should have made a better job of that project'
- Magnification or awfulizing: blowing events out of all proportion, e.g. 'That meeting was the worst I've ever attended. It was awful'
- Minimization: minimizing the part one plays in a situation, e.g. 'It must have been an easy exam as I got a good mark'
- Low frustration tolerance or 'I-can't-stand-it-itis': we lower our tolerance to frustrating or stressful situations by telling ourselves, e.g. 'I-can't-stand-it"
- Phoneyism: believing that you may get found out by significant others as a phoney or imposter, e.g. 'If I perform badly, they will see the real me – a total fraud'.

© Palmer & Szymanska, 2007. Note: Reproduced with permission

Thinking skills

Thinking skills have been defined as '*methods to help you modify your stress-inducing thinking*' (Palmer & Cooper, 2013:4). However, thinking skills also enhance performance, and increase coping and resilience. Thinking skills include inviting the coaching client to decide whether their idea or belief is logical, whether it is realistic or empirically correct (does the evidence support or refute it?) and whether the belief is helpful (McMahon, 2007; Palmer & Szymanska, 2007).

Further thinking skills are captured by the three Ps – Perspective, Persistence and Positive thinking. Coaching clients may gain a realistic perspective by considering the question 'If X were to be true, would it really be the end of the world?', and then deciding how bad a situation really is, as seldom are most situations really the end of the world. A 0–10 rating scale where 10 is very bad can be used to re-evaluate how bad the situation or problem seems. The coaching client may also learn to recognize self-imposed demands or rules, and to replace imperatives with preferences (Ellis & Blum, 1967; Palmer & Cooper, 2013). Given the length of time over which our core beliefs and thinking errors have become established, persistence with new more helpful ways of thinking is of great importance. Clients often reframe realistic and helpful thinking as positive thinking. Coping imagery assists clients in preparing for change (Palmer & Cooper, 2013) (see Section III).

Self-acceptance

Palmer and Cooper (2013: 85) described self-acceptance as holding the belief that 'I'm ok, just because I exist' and 'I can accept myself, warts and all, with a strong preference to improve myself, even though realistically I don't have to'. For coaching clients self-acceptance means never globally rating themselves (e.g. good, bad, weak, strong, success, failure), only rating aspects of the self, such as skills or skills deficits, as a global rating cannot capture the complexity and uniqueness of a human being (Lazarus, 1977; Palmer, 1997c). A student having just heard the news they did not pass their driving examination may conclude 'I failed my driving test therefore I am a total failure', while another student in the same scenario chooses to conclude 'I have failed my driving test, but I am ok. It just means I need to improve my driving skills and re-take the test next month'.

Essential processes and dynamics

The CBC approach has a distinct psychological management model at its core, which most coaching clients find easy to learn and adopt. The techniques and strategies are systematically applied depending upon the particular issue the client needs to address.

CBC is an active-direct approach in that goal-blocking thoughts, feelings and behaviours, and the links between, are identified, examined and then modified. The client is encouraged to put these changes into practice as soon as possible through a series of planned exposures and experiments.

The directness of CBC is in contrast to other approaches such as psychodynamic and person-centred coaching, with the Socratic challenges standing out in contrast to the empathic responses that are the hallmark of the person-centred approach (Joseph, 2006). Empathy is important in CBC; however, it is not emphasized as much as in the person-centred approach and is normally coupled with the direct challenges illustrated above. Person-centred approaches are likely to rely on the client eventually challenging him/herself but this can take time and may not occur spontaneously. The use of exposure or behavioural experimentation, combined with cognitive interventions, is another characteristic of CBC that contrasts with other approaches, such as psychodynamic and person-centred.

The dual systems approach underlying CBC enables coach and client to assess what needs to be addressed in coaching: the external, practical or goal-orientated behavioural aspects and/or the internal, psychological or cognitive aspects to a problem or issue (Neenan & Palmer, 2000). There is no need to focus on psychological aspects if a simple problem-solving model will suffice.

Role of the coach and relationship with a client

Neenan and Palmer describe how the cognitive behavioural approach 'is based on a collaborative relationship that helps individuals to focus on problem-solving in a structured and systematic way' (Neenan & Palmer, 2001: 17). Through Socratic questioning, active participation and discussion (Roberts & Billings, 1999) the coach supports and challenges the client to achieve heightened awareness, self-esteem, self-acceptance and mobility to act. Through the transfer of the knowledge and skills of CBC, the coach is able to facilitate the ultimate goal 'for individuals to become their own coach' (Neenan & Palmer, 2001).

It is important to establish a clear contract, both with the coaching client and, where relevant, the line manager or organizational sponsor. This type of 'triad' coaching contract typically includes agreement of objectives of coaching engagement, outcome measurements, feedback procedures and confidentiality, and is best agreed by all parties (McMahon, 2005). It is likely that a set number of coaching sessions or hours will be agreed so that each engagement is clear and purposeful. Lengths of sessions may vary from 30 to 120 minutes; often with a series of six to eight sessions over a time period of four to six months (see Palmer & Szymanska, 2007).

O'Broin and Palmer (2012: 67) highlight that the coach 'can experience coaching-interfering thoughts, feelings and behaviours'. These can hinder the development of a good working relationship. In addition to discussing these issues within supervision, the coach can also use cognitive behavioural self-coaching to tackle problems as they arise.

METHODS AND TECHNIQUES

Behavioural methods and techniques

The CBC coach may initially discuss the issues with the client and then help the coaching client to develop and prioritize their SMART goals, i.e. Specific, Measurable, Achievable, Realistic, Time-bound goal(s), and action plans (Locke & Latham, 1990; Schwalbe, 2005). There are a number of action-oriented coaching models used within CBC, for example Wasik's (1984) seven-step model and the PRACTICE model (Palmer, 2007, 2008, 2011; Palmer & Cooper, 2013).

PRACTICE is an acronym for a problem-solving and solution-focused model that has been used within coaching, counselling, psychotherapy and stress management (Palmer, 2007, 2008). The sequential steps of the PRACTICE model facilitate the coaching conversation and help orientate the client towards understanding the problem, developing realistic goals, selecting feasible solutions and their implementation, and finally reviewing progress. Table 2.1 provides an outline of each step in the model and summarizes key questions that may be used to facilitate discussion. Initially the 'P' represented a Problem. However, as illustrated in Table 2.1, in 2011 the PRACTICE model was further developed so that the 'P' was used more flexibly to meet the clients' needs, whether this be a Problem, a Presenting issue, the Purpose of coaching, a Preferred outcome/solution (Palmer, 2011) or Performance-related issue (Palmer & Cooper, 2013).

The early behaviour therapists Joseph Wolpe and Arnold Lazarus (Wolpe & Lazarus, 1966) developed a number of behavioural techniques to assist clients to relax, reduce anxiety and overcome phobias by using progressive relaxation and systematic desensitization. Although these are usually considered therapeutic interventions, a cognitive behavioural coach may use relaxation techniques and encourage clients to develop cognitive and behavioural coping

Table 2.1 PRACTICE model of coaching

Steps	Questions/statements/actions
1. Problem identification; or Presenting issue; or Purpose of coaching; or Performance-related issue; or a Preferred outcome/solution	What's the problem, issue or concern?
	What would you like to change?
	Any exceptions when it is not a problem?
	How will we know if the situation has improved?
	Any distortions? Or can the problem or issue be viewed differently?
2. Realistic, relevant goals developed (e.g. SMART goals)	What do you want to achieve?
	Let's develop SMART goals.
3. Alternative solutions generated	What are your options?
	Let's note them down.
4. Consideration of consequences	What could happen?
	How useful is each possible solution?
	Let's use a 'usefulness' rating scale for each solution where '0' is not useful at all and '10' is extremely useful.
5. Target most feasible solution(s)	What is/are the most feasible solution(s)?
6. Implementation of Chosen solution(s)	Let's implement the chosen solution by breaking it down into manageable steps.
	Now go and do it!
7. Evaluation	How successful was it?
	Use a success rating scale 0 to 10.
	What can be learnt?
	Can we finish coaching now or do you want to address or discuss another issue?

Source: adapted from Palmer (2007, 2008, 2011) (reproduced with permission)

strategies; and to experience in imagination and *in vivo* to anxiety triggering situations, such as giving presentations or chairing meetings, which would not normally be associated with clinical disorders. Personal experimentation is encouraged in a bid to help clients incorporate new and more functional ways of thinking and behaving. Wolpe and Lazarus also introduced the concept and practice of assertiveness training that continues as an important component of CBC. Behavioural relaxation techniques (Poppen, 1998) have an important role in CBC. Helping a client breathe well is one method used to help clients manage anxiety and panic tendencies in stressful or high-performance situations.

Cognitive methods and techniques

There are a range of different cognitive methods and techniques, a selection of which are covered in this section.

Coaching clients may be helped to recognize patterns of unhelpful thinking by first identifying Performance Interfering Thoughts (PITS) in order to generate alternative Performance Enhancing Thoughts (PETS) (Neenan & Palmer, 2001). Table 2.2 provides an example of the PITS/PETS activity for a coaching client with a fear of making presentations.

Table 2.2   Example of PITS and PETS for making a presentation

Performance Interfering Thoughts (PITS)	Performance Enhancing Thoughts (PETS)
It's going to go badly	It will be at least okay
I'm terrible at making presentations	Some have gone well, some less well but overall I'm reasonable at making presentations
Visions of being unable to speak and of being laughed at	Visions of making the presentation with a mistake or two, but overall going well
The audience will be bored	How do I know? I haven't even given the presentation yet!

The ABCDEF model (Ellis, Gordon, Neenan, & Palmer, 1997; Palmer, 2002, 2009) of the rational-emotive behaviour approach allows the coach to facilitate a review of the event that triggers psychological disturbance for the coaching client, in order to identify unhelpful thinking patterns and replace these with more constructive thoughts and behaviours (see Neenan & Dryden, 2002; Palmer & Szymanska, 2007).

The model is based on Albert Ellis's ABC model of emotional disturbance (Ellis et al., 1997), whereby an individual typically assumes a direct link between A, the Activating event or an Awareness of a problem or issue, and C, the emotional and/or behavioural and/or physical Consequence, when in actuality this relationship is mediated by B, the Beliefs and perceptions about the activating event. D is about Disputing or examining the beliefs, while E is about developing an Effective, new response or change in behaviour. The ABCDEF model also includes F, representing a Future focus on personal work goals and the learning from ABCDE – 'what the employee has learnt from the process to ensure that they are less likely to become stressed by a similar event in the future' (Palmer, 2002: 16). Figure 2.1 depicts an example of the ABCDEF model in use for a coaching client as part of a stress management and prevention programme.

The ABCDEF framework is a model of stress, performance, coping and resilience depending upon its application. In practice goals are developed early on in the process and this is often depicted as G-ABCDEF framework. The coaching client is often shown this model using an A4 landscape, five or six column form, noting down the client's problem, beliefs, consequences, modified beliefs, effective new approach and future focus.

The SPACE model was developed by Nick Edgerton (see Edgerton & Palmer, 2005). Its development was influenced by Multimodal Therapy (Lazarus, 1989) and the Five Aspect

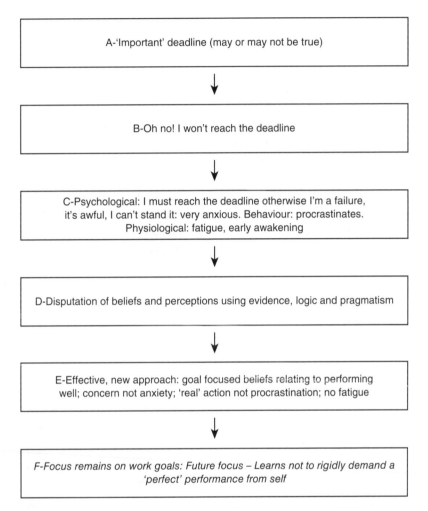

Figure 2.1 Client example using the ABCDEF model (© Stephen Palmer, 2002)

Model described by Dennis Greenberger and Christine Padesky (1995). SPACE is a cognitive behavioural framework revolving around a diagram designed to help individuals become aware of their dysfunctional patterns, and can be used to plan more effective ways of functioning. SPACE is an acronym for five key aspects of the model and incorporates a series of nested models of Actions, Cognitions and Emotions (ACE), and with the added dimensions of Physical/Physiological (PACE) and Social context (Edgerton & Palmer, 2005).

One of the benefits of the SPACE model comes through the deployment of multi-aspect intervention strategies. The coaching client is encouraged to review each of the five areas and to agree how and what they would choose to do differently in each area. Figures 2.2 and 2.3 provide examples of the SPACE model, depicting in turn both low- and high-performance states.

The CLARITY model is a more recent development and is intended as a cognitive behavioural model that allows coach and coachee to focus directly on imagery within the coaching conversation (Williams & Palmer, 2010). Lazarus described how 'through the proper use of mental imagery, one can achieve an immediate sense of self confidence, develop more energy and stamina, and tap one's own mind for numerous productive purposes' (Lazarus, 1984: 3). A range of imagery techniques are available including: Goal imagery (Palmer & Puri, 2006); Motivation imagery (Palmer & Neenan, 1998); Anger reducing imagery (Palmer & Puri, 2006); Coping imagery (Lazarus, 1984; Palmer & Puri, 2006); Relaxation imagery (Lazarus, 1982; Palmer, Cooper, & Thomas, 2003a); and Time projection imagery (Lazarus, 1984; Palmer & Cooper, 2013). The CLARITY acronym represents the seven steps of the model: Context, Life event/experience, Actions, Reactions, Images and identity, Thoughts/beliefs and Your future choices.

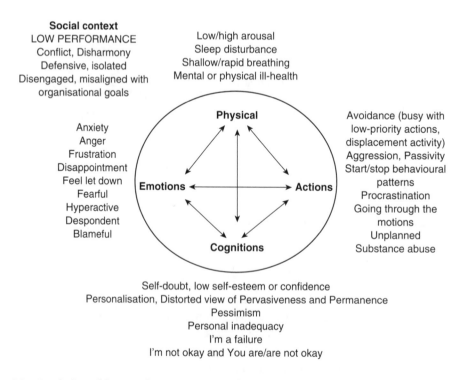

Figure 2.2   Depiction of low-performance state using the SPACE model

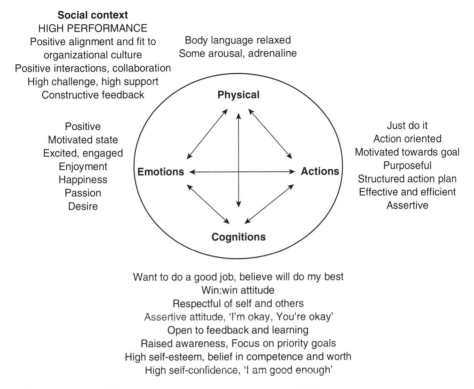

Social context
HIGH PERFORMANCE
Positive alignment and fit to
organizational culture
Positive interactions, collaboration
High challenge, high support
Constructive feedback

Body language relaxed
Some arousal, adrenaline

Physical

Positive
Motivated state
Excited, engaged
Enjoyment
Happiness
Passion
Desire

Emotions ←→ **Actions**

Just do it
Action oriented
Motivated towards goal
Purposeful
Structured action plan
Effective and efficient
Assertive

Cognitions

Want to do a good job, believe will do my best
Win:win attitude
Respectful of self and others
Assertive attitude, 'I'm okay, You're okay'
Open to feedback and learning
Raised awareness, Focus on priority goals
High self-esteem, belief in competence and worth
High self-confidence, 'I am good enough'

Figure 2.3   Depiction of high-performance state using the SPACE model

APPLICATION

CBC may be used in the majority of the contexts identified in the book's introduction. It can also be used for health coaching. Wherever a client is disturbing or limiting him/herself by unhelpful thinking, or engaging in self-defeating behaviours that undermine their performance, CBC can be a powerful coaching intervention.

Skills and performance coaching

In skills and performance contexts a client can easily begin to doubt him/herself, thinking: 'I'm not good enough', 'I'm about to fail' and/or 'any moment now my performance will collapse'. Imagery may include others criticizing them and showing disapproval, while anticipated emotions, such as shame and embarrassment, may be experienced and sooner or later their performance will falter or be impaired by avoidance or procrastination. CBC teaches the client to both recognize and correct these self-disturbances.

Life coaching

In life coaching, clients explore their life goals and review their progress against these goals. Often the limiting factor to progress is the client's self-limiting beliefs. The CBC approach would be to recognize that the client is thinking and behaving in ways that are self-defeating or limiting. The client would then be helped to see how they could think about themselves in ways that would enhance their confidence and self-esteem before deliberately engaging in personal experiments designed to develop and enhance confidence to take action towards achieving their life goals.

Developmental coaching

Developmental coaching for executives often focuses on professional and personal transformation within the context of the executive's job and organization (Sperry, 2004). CBC can provide insight into personal beliefs that influence the executive and their team and may block transformation. CBC can facilitate the adult's understanding of their emotions, helping them to comprehend the links between thoughts and emotions, and to learn how to express themselves emotionally and make requests of others in an appropriately assertive manner (Wolpe & Lazarus, 1966). Some researchers also assert that developmental coaching can address life transitions and generational issues, i.e. 'key turning points that many of us are likely to experience during the lifespan, with varying degrees of opportunity and challenge' (Palmer & Panchal, 2011: 4).

Executive and leadership coaching

Executives and leaders in organizations need to be or become skilful in managing their own psychological processes, to manage emotions such as anxiety, frustration and anger, and to maintain an appropriate level of self-confidence without becoming complacent, arrogant or narcissistic. They are more likely to be effective in their roles if they develop high levels of interpersonal, influencing and communication skills. CBC can be helpful in all of these processes as the client learns to become increasingly skilful in managing the interaction between their own actions, cognitions and emotions.

Business coaching

Business coaching goes beyond executive coaching in that it also assists the business owner or key person within a company to develop the business as well as themselves. Williams, Palmer and Wallace (2011) illustrate how the cognitive behavioural ABCDEF and PRACTICE models can be integrated in order to help the coachee address the practical problems that need addressing in the business as well as their own psychological blocks which are hindering progress. Ideally the business coach should be experienced in business development too.

Peer coaching

Peer coaching can come in many forms. For example, within teaching in the UK, peer coaching was set up by the National Union of Teachers on the Teacher2Teacher continuing professional development programme as a collaborative and normally formalized process between two peers to support each other (National Union of Teachers, 2008). It provides a structured framework to provide feedback on each other's work and includes suggestions on informed professional dialogue. This particular approach is on the more behavioural spectrum of coaching, but in other settings the cognitive skills could be introduced. As CBC is a pragmatic and transparent approach, peers can use the theory, models and techniques on each other within peer coaching.

Team coaching

CBC adapts very easily to group settings as it is both insight and skills-based with relatively easy to understand theory and models such as the G-ABCDEF, SPACE and PRACTICE as previously described. Depending upon the team concerned, it can be used to enhance performance and manage stress. The coach facilitates the group to look at both team and individual issues. Members can work in pairs when looking at their own particular issues. This has a secondary gain for the organization, as supervisors and managers start to learn how to use CBC skills and techniques on themselves, each other and subsequently their own team.

Career coaching

Career coaching can occur across the entire young person and adult spectrum of life. Often, people benefit from career coaching as they make transitions from school to college, from college to work, then from job to job or redundancy to a new career. These transitions are now more prevalent in modern society, as adults are less likely to remain in the same job or even career for a long period of time. The PRACTICE and SPACE models of CBC have been applied to career coaching, for example when a client has been hesitant to make the move from one job to another or to decide upon a new profession.

Coaching and managing

Managers can usefully incorporate coaching strategies and skills into their repertoire. If a manager learns how to apply CBC to him/herself, it puts them in a good place to begin to use the same principles and techniques with their team. If, for example, one of their team is continually late finishing assignments and the manager simply puts the pressure on, it could be counterproductive. A CBC analysis of what is happening might identify a perfectionist demand, either on the part of the manager, the team member or both. Once identified, these demands can be modified to preferential statements and softened to 'good enough', 'fit for purpose', contributing to a learning culture within the team.

Health and well-being coaching

Health coaching has been described as 'the practice of health education and health promotion within a coaching context, underpinned by psychological principles, to enhance the well-being of individuals and to facilitate the achievement of their health-related goals' (Palmer, Tubbs, & Whybrow, 2003b: 92). Health and well-being coaching is now being used within organizational and company settings to help employees tackle health-related issues such as weight control, nutrition, blood pressure, alcohol intake and smoking. This has enabled some American companies to prevent large rises in their annual staff health insurance premiums and demonstrates a noticeable return on investment.

CBC adapts very easily to the field of health coaching (Palmer et al., 2003b; Palmer, 2004). Motivational interviewing is used to engage and motivate clients to address their health-related issues (Miller & Rollnick, 1991). CBC techniques and strategies are often used to tackle psychological blocks to goal achievement by examining the client's Health Inhibiting Thinking (HITs) and then helping them to develop Health Enhancing Thinking (HETs) (Palmer, 2004; 2012a, 2012b).

The cross-cultural context

CBC is a flexible approach with a range of models and techniques that can be adapted to different languages and cultures. This can enhance cross-cultural work too which occurs in global organizations as well capital cities where there is a multicultural population. Great effort has been made by the founders of CBC to work with colleagues internationally to adapt the approach and models. For example, SPACE has been adapted to Portuguese in Brazil (Dias, Edgerton, & Palmer, 2010) and Polish (Syrek-Kosowska, Edgerton, & Palmer, 2010). PRACTICE has been adapted to Portuguese in Brazil (Dias, Gandos, Nardi, & Palmer, 2011), to Spanish (Sánchez-Mora García, Ballabriga, Celaya, Dalmau, & Palmer, 2012) and Danish (Spaten, Imer, & Palmer, 2012).

EVALUATION

While the responsibility for change rests at many levels (government, society, organizations and the individual), CBC offers support directly to the individual by equipping them with coping strategies and thinking skills to ready them to achieve their full potential. The applications of CBC are varied, from building confidence and being assertive to tackling blocks to performance such as procrastination, perfectionism and poor time management; reducing unhelpful emotional reactions such as excessive anger or anxiety; or helping to achieve broader life goals.

Palmer and Whybrow (see Palmer & Whybrow, 2007; Palmer, O'Riordan, & Whybrow, 2011) have researched the prevalence of coaching practices as used by practising coaching psychologists 2003 onwards by using online surveys. In 2011, 62.7% of coaching psychologists reported using the cognitive behavioural approach and it is the most regularly used approach (see Palmer et al., 2011). The next is Strengths coaching which is used by 50% and then Behavioural coaching used by 47.3% of coaching psychologists.

In 2001, Anthony Grant recommended that researchers investigate whether a 'combined cognitive-behavioural coaching approach [is] effective in helping adults reach "real life" such as establishing businesses or enhancing work performance' (Grant, 2001: 17). Over the last decade CBC has met this challenge, firmly establishing itself as a coaching practice recognized in its own right. Initially borrowing from the academic and applied research of Cognitive Behavioural Therapy (CBT), there is now a growing body of evidence to directly support the value and effectiveness of CBC.

Grant has conducted a controlled study comparing cognitive, behavioural and cognitive behavioural approaches to coaching for trainee accountants (Grant, 2001). The follow-up study found 'academic performance increases were maintained only for combined cognitive and behavioural program participants' (Grant, 2001: 1). In a further controlled study on the effects of a ten-week cognitive behavioural, solution-focused life coaching group programme, significant increases in goal striving, well-being and hope were found for those receiving coaching, with some of the effects being evident up to thirty weeks later (Green, Oades, & Grant 2006). A study of the efficacy of CBC for perfectionism and self-handicapping reported that perfectionism fell and the effect was still evident four weeks later; self-handicapping showed a significant reduction at four weeks (Kearns, Forbes, & Gardiner, 2007). Green, Grant, and Rynsaardt (2007) found that solution-focused CBC enhanced cognitive hardiness and hope, with significant decreases in depression, in high school students.

Grbcic developed a stress self-coaching manual for middle managers, based on the cognitive behavioural approach (Grbcic & Palmer, 2007). Significant changes were observed indicating intervention effectiveness regardless of the frequency of work stressors and lack of organizational support. No coach, trainer or counsellor was used to teach the self-help approach, highlighting how alternative media may be considered to transfer the benefits usually derived from an actual coach–client relationship.

As with all coaching models and techniques, CBC is only appropriate to use when the coach is CBC trained and is in receipt of supervision, when the coaching contract has been clearly established and the CBC methods explained in non-jargon terms to the coaching client, with their affirmation of interest to pursue this line of enquiry.

CBC will not be necessary where action-oriented models will suffice to generate the desired change in behaviour, and will not be appropriate where the coaching client expresses:

- a need to revisit and address the past, requiring a more psychodynamic approach
- a desire to focus on greater meaning and purpose, where an existential approach will be more aligned to their needs
- an explicit interest in positive psychology and coaching, which may be at odds with the CBC theoretical assumption that negative cognitions and emotions need to be explored in order to be addressed.

CBC is most likely to fail when the coaching client has a clinical disorder or is not accepting either the emotional responsibility for the problems they bring to coaching or the coaching responsibility for taking action (Palmer & Szymanska, 2007).

The following scenarios are examples of when a CBC approach may be of most benefit:

- when action models of coaching are not enough to bring about change
- when there is a cognitive or emotional block to achieving full potential
- when current levels of anxiety/avoidance are negatively impacting on performance
- when levels of stress are impacting upon mental and physical health.
- CBC provides clients with the conceptual tools to better understand themselves; it also provides vehicles for change through personal experimentation and exposure to situations that previously they may have avoided. Clients will still have to work hard and be vigilant to establish their new ways of thinking and behaving.

FURTHER READING

Neenan, M. & Palmer, S. (2012). *Cognitive behavioural coaching in practice: An evidence-based approach.* Hove: Routledge. (This book covers a wide range of key topics.)

Neenan, M. & Dryden, W. (2013). *Life coaching: A cognitive behavioural approach* (2nd ed.). Hove: Routledge. (This book provides a summary of cognitive behavioural models and significant challenges that may be addressed using CBC.)

Palmer, S. & Whybrow, A. (2007). *Handbook of coaching psychology: A guide for practitioners.* Hove: Routledge. (This Handbook includes a chapter on CBC offering a comprehensive outline of the founding theories, proponents and research of CBC, with descriptions of various CBC models and case examples.)

DISCUSSION QUESTIONS

- To what extent are issues presented in coaching typically cognitive, behavioural or both? How does this vary across coaching contexts?
- What role does imagery play in leading to and/or preventing coachees from achieving their goals?
- What do you view as the advantages and disadvantages of using CBC in cross-cultural settings?

REFERENCES

Anderson, J.P. (2002). Executive coaching and REBT: Some comments from the field. *Journal of Rational-Emotive and Cognitive-Behavior Therapy, 20*(3/4): 223–33.

Bandura, A. (1986). *Social foundations of thought and action: A social cognitive theory.* Englewood Cliffs, NJ: Prentice Hall.

Beck, A.T. (1976). *Cognitive therapy and the emotional disorders.* New York: New American Library.

Beck, J. (1995). *Cognitive therapy: Basics and beyond.* New York: Guilford Press.

Costa, A.L. & Garmston, R.J. (2002). *Cognitive coaching: A foundation for Renaissance schools.* Norwood, MA: Christopher-Gordon.

Curwen, B., Palmer, S., & Ruddell, P. (2000). *Brief cognitive behaviour therapy.* London: Sage.

Dias, G., Edgerton, N., & Palmer, S. (2010). From SPACE to FACES: The adaptation of the SPACE model of cognitive behavioural coaching and therapy to the Portuguese language. *Coaching Psychology International, 3*(1): 12–16.

DiMattia, D.J. & Mennen, S. (1990). *Rational effectiveness training: Increasing productivity at work.* New York: Institute for Rational-Emotive Therapy.

D'Zurilla, T.J. (1986). *Problem-solving therapy: A social competence approach to clinical intervention.* New York: Springer.

Edgerton, N. & Palmer, S. (2005). SPACE: A psychological model for use within cognitive behavioural coaching, therapy and stress management. *The Coaching Psychologist, 2*(2): 25–31.

Ellis, A. (1994). *Reason and emotion in psychotherapy* (rev. and updated). New York: Birch Lane Press.

Ellis, A. & Blum, M.L. (1967). Rational training: A new method of facilitating management labor relations. *Psychological Reports, 20*: 1267–84.

Ellis, A., Gordon, J., Neenan, M. & Palmer, S. (1997). *Stress counseling: A rational emotive behavior approach*. New York: Springer.

Grant, A.M. (2001). *Coaching for enhanced performance: Comparing cognitive and behavioural approaches to coaching*. Paper presented at the 3rd International Spearman Seminar, Extending intelligence: Enhancement and new constructs, Sydney. Retrieved 10 November 2008 from www.psych.usyd.edu.au/coach/CBT_BT_CT_Spearman_Conf_Paper.pdf.

Grbcic, S. & Palmer, S. (2007). A cognitive behavioural self-help approach to stress management and prevention at work: A randomized controlled trial. *The Rational Emotive Behaviour Therapist, 12*(1): 41–3.

Green, L.S., Oades, L.G., & Grant, A.M. (2006). Cognitive-behavioral, solution-focused life coaching: Enhancing goal striving, well-being and hope. *Journal of Positive Psychology, 1*(3): 142–9.

Green, S., Grant, A.M., & Rynsaardt, J. (2007). Evidence-based life coaching for senior high schools: Building hardiness and hope. *International Coaching Psychology Review, 2*(1): 24–32.

Greenberger, D. & Padesky, C.A. (1995). *Mind over mood*. New York: Guilford Press.

Joseph, S. (2006). Person centred, coaching psychology – a meta-theoretical perspective. *International Coaching Psychology Review, 1*(1): 47–54.

Kearns, H., Forbes, A., & Gardiner, M. (2007). A cognitive behavioural coaching intervention for the treatment of perfectionism and self-handicapping in a nonclinical population. *Behavioural Change, 24*(3): 157–72.

Kodish, S.P. (2002). Rational emotive behaviour coaching. *Journal of Rational-Emotive and Cognitive Behavior Therapy, 20*(3–4): 235–46.

Lazarus, A.A. (1977). Towards an egoless state of being. In A. Ellis and R. Grieger (Eds), *Handbook of rational-emotive therapy*. New York: Springer.

Lazarus, A.A. (1982). *Personal enrichment through imagery* (cassette recording). New York: BMA Audio Cassettes / Guilford Publications.

Lazarus, A.A. (1984). *In the mind's eye*. New York: Guilford Press.

Lazarus, A.A. (1989). *The practice of multimodal therapy*. Baltimore, MD: Johns Hopkins Paperbacks.

Locke, E.A. & Latham, G.P. (1990). *A theory of goal setting and task performance*. Englewood Cliffs, NJ: Prentice Hall.

McMahon, G. (2005). Behavioural contracting and confidentiality in organisational coaching. *Counselling at Work, Spring*: 1–3.

McMahon, G. (2007). Understanding cognitive behavioural coaching. *Training Journal, January*: 53–7.

Miller, W.R. & Rollnick, S. (1991). *Motivational interviewing*. London: Guilford Press.

National Union of Teachers (2008). *The A to Z of peer coaching*. Retrieved 12 September 2008 from www.teachers.org.uk/resources/pdf/A-Z-peer-coaching.pdf.

Neenan, M. & Dryden, W. (2002). *Life coaching: A cognitive behavioural approach*. Hove: Routledge.

Neenan, M. & Palmer, S. (2000). Problem focused counselling and psychotherapy. In S. Palmer (Ed.), *Introduction to counselling and psychotherapy: The essential guide*. London: Sage.

Neenan, M. & Palmer, S. (2001). Cognitive behavioural coaching. *Stress News, 13*(3): 15–18.

O'Broin, A. & Palmer, S. (2012). Enhancing the coaching alliance and relationship. In M. Neenan and S. Palmer (Eds), *Cognitive behavioural coaching in practice: An evidence based approach*. Hove: Routledge.

O'Hanlon, W. (1998). Possibility therapy: An inclusive, collaborative, solution-based model of psychotherapy. In M.F. Hoyt (Ed.), *The handbook of constructive therapies: Innovative approaches from leading practitioners*. San Francisco, CA: Jossey-Bass.

Palmer, S. (1997a). Problem focused stress counselling and stress management: An intrinsically brief integrative approach. Part 1. *Stress News, 9*(2): 7–12.

Palmer, S. (1997b). Problem focused stress counselling and stress management training: An intrinsically brief integrative approach. Part 2. *Stress News, 9*(3): 6–10.

Palmer, S. (1997c). Self-acceptance: Concept, techniques and interventions. *The Rational Emotive Behaviour Therapist, 4*(2): 4–30.

Palmer, S. (2002). Cognitive and organisational models of stress that are suitable for use within workplace stress management/prevention coaching, training and counselling settings. *The Rational Emotive Behaviour Therapist, 10*(1): 15–21.

Palmer, S. (2004). Health coaching: A developing field within health education. *Health Education Journal, 63*(2): 189–91.

Palmer, S. (2007). PRACTICE: A model suitable for coaching, counselling, psychotherapy and stress management. *The Coaching Psychologist, 3*(2): 71–7.

Palmer, S. (2008). The PRACTICE model of coaching. *Coaching Psychology International, 1*(1), 4–8.

Palmer, S. (2009). Rational coaching: A cognitive behavioural approach. *The Coaching Psychologist, 5*(1): 12–18.

Palmer, S. (2011). Revisiting the P in the PRACTICE coaching model. *The Coaching Psychologist, 7*(2): 156–158.

Palmer, S. (2012a) Health Coaching Toolkit Part 3. *Coaching at Work, 7*(5): 36–7.

Palmer, S. (2012b) Health Coaching Toolkit Part 4. *Coaching at Work, 7*(6): 38–9.

Palmer, S. & Cooper, C. (2013). *How to deal with stress* (3rd ed.). London: Kogan Page.

Palmer, S. & Gyllensten, K. (2008). How cognitive behavioural, rational emotive behavioural or multimodal coaching could prevent mental health problems, enhance performance and reduce work related stress. *The Journal of Rational Emotive and Cognitive Behavioural Therapy, 26*(1): 38–52.

Palmer, S. & Neenan, M. (1998). Double imagery procedure. *The Rational Emotive Behaviour Therapist, 6*(2): 89–92.

Palmer, S. & Panchal, S. (2011). Life transitions and generational perspectives. In S. Palmer and S. Panchal (Eds), *Developmental Coaching: Life Transitions and Generational Perspectives*. Hove: Routledge. pp 1–28.

Palmer, S. & Puri, A. (2006). *Coping with stress at university: A survival guide*. London: Sage.

Palmer, S. & Szymanska, K. (2007). Cognitive behavioural coaching: An integrative approach. In S. Palmer & A. Whybrow (Eds), *Handbook of coaching psychology: A guide for practitioners*. Hove: Routledge.

Palmer, S. & Whybrow, A. (2007). Coaching psychology: An introduction. In S. Palmer & A. Whybrow (Eds), *Handbook of coaching psychology: A guide for practitioners*. Hove: Routledge.

Palmer, S., Cooper, C., & Thomas, K. (2003a). *Creating a balance: Managing pressure*. London: British Library.

Palmer, S., Tubbs, I., & Whybrow, W. (2003b). Health coaching to facilitate the promotion of healthy behaviour and achievement of health-related goals. *International Journal of Health Promotion and Education, 41*(3): 91–3.

Palmer, S., O'Riordan, S., & Whybrow, A. (2011). *Coaching Psychology Past, Coaching Psychology Present, Coaching Psychology Future*. Keynote presentation at the BPS (British Psychological Society), SGCP 3rd European Coaching Psychology Conference, London, held on 13–14th December, 2011.

Poppen, R. (1998). *Behavioural relaxation training and assessment* (2nd ed.). London: Sage.

Roberts, T. & Billings, L. (1999). *The Paideia classroom: Teaching for understanding*. Larchmont, NY: Eye on Education.

Schwalbe, K. (2005). *Information technology project management* (4th ed.). Boston, MA: Course Technology.

Sánchez-Mora García, M., Ballabriga, J.J., Celaya, J.V., Dalmau, R.C., & Palmer, S. (2012). The PRACTICE Coaching model adapted to the Spanish language. From PRACTICE to IDEACIÓN. *Coaching Psychology International, 5*(1): 2–6.

Spaten, O.M., Imer, A., & Palmer, S. (2012). From PRACTICE to PRAKSIS – models in Danish coaching psychology. *Coaching Psychology International, 5*(1): 7–12.

Sperry, L. (2004). *Executive coaching: The essential guide for mental health professionals*. New York: Brunner-Routledge.

Syrek-Kosowska, A., Edgerton, N., & Palmer, S. (2010). From SPACE to SFERA: adaptation of the SPACE model of cognitive behavioural coaching and therapy to the Polish language. *Coaching Psychology International, 3*(2): 18–20.

Wasik, B. (1984). *Teaching parents effective problem solving: A handbook for professionals*. (Unpublished manuscript). Chapel Hill, NC: University of North Carolina.

Williams, H. & Palmer, S. (2010). CLARITY: A cognitive-behavioural coaching model. *Coaching Psychology International, 3*(2): 5–7.

Williams, H., Palmer, S., & Wallace, E. (2011). An integrative coaching approach for family business. In M. Shams & D.A. Lane (Eds), *Coaching in the family owned business: A path to growth*. London: Karnac. pp. 21–39.

Wolpe, J. & Lazarus, A.A. (1966). *Behavior therapy techniques*. New York: Pergamon.

3

The Solution-focused Approach To Coaching

Michael Cavanagh and Anthony Grant

All forms of coaching, in one way or another, seek to develop solutions to the issues brought forward by the client. What then is unique about solution-focused coaching? How does it differ from other forms of coaching? This chapter outlines the background and basic tenets of the solution-focused (SF) approach, and examines some core assumptions and processes underpinning it as a methodology for change.

The SF approach to coaching places primary emphasis on assisting the client to define a desired future state and to construct a pathway in both thinking and action that assists the client in achieving that state. It contrasts with other approaches by eschewing much of the problem state definition seen in other traditions. In so doing, the SF approach is situated squarely in a constructivist epistemology – maintaining that events and their meanings are actively constructed in dialogue rather than simply given to us in experience (O'Connell, 1998).

According to SF theorists, the act of spending large amounts of time and effort in articulating a strong definition of the client's problem, deconstructing the chain of cause and effect that led to the current state of affairs, or apportioning blame, is often a waste of time and energy. Indeed, SF theorists hold that it is often positively counterproductive (Jackson & McKergow, 2007). Knowing how a problem arose does not necessarily tell one how to fix it. Furthermore, proponents of the SF approach suggest that the very act of articulating a causal explanation may serve to constrain the coach and coachee into a frame of reference that limits potential solutions rather than uncovers them (de Shazer, 1994).

HISTORY OF THE SOLUTION-FOCUSED APPROACH

Like many of the recognized approaches to coaching, the SF approach has its roots in therapy. The foundational work in brief therapy, out of which the SF approach arose, was conducted by Gregory Bateson, John Wicklund and others at the Mental Research Institute in Palo Alto, California, in the 1960s (Jackson & McKergow, 2007). The SF approach as we have come to know it today was first articulated in the late 1970s and early 1980s by Steve de Shazer, Insoo Kim Berg and colleagues at the Brief Family Therapy Centre, in Milwaukee Wisconsin, USA. Since then, considerable work has been undertaken in articulating and developing the main tenets of the approach by a host of authors, both at the Brief Family Therapy Centre and at a range of locations around the world (O'Connell, 1998).

According to Berg and Szabo (2005), therapists and researchers at these centres had become dissatisfied with the traditional therapeutic approach, finding that the more clients talked about their problems the more entrenched they would get. Rather than analysing problems, developing diagnoses, uncovering root causes and prescribing treatment plans, based on *a priori* theoretical models of the issue, they began to simply ask questions that focused their clients' attention on building solutions. The key question in developing the approach was 'what works for the client?'

They found that a focus on solution talk, strengths and resources, rather than problem talk, was very effective for a large range of clients. Indeed, there is a growing body of research suggesting SF therapy can be effective for a wide array of problems, including couple counselling (Murray & Murray Jr, 2004), child and adolescent counselling (Corcoran & Stephenson, 2000; Lethem, 2002) and depression (Dahl, Bathel, & Carreon, 2000). There is also research that supports the use of SF coaching in personal coaching (Green, Grant, & Rynsaardt, 2007; Green, Oades, & Grant, 2006; Spence & Grant, 2007) and workplace coaching (Barrett, 2004).

DISTINCTIVE FEATURES

The SF approach is distinguished from more traditional models of psychological change (e.g. cognitive behavioural and psychodynamic coaching) by two fundamental philosophical assumptions.

First, as mentioned above, the SF approach adheres to a constructionist philosophy. It holds that it is the way in which the client (and coach) think and talk about events that constructs those events as problematic. The problem is not something given in reality, but constructed in the discourse between the client and others in the client's world.

Second, the SF approach sees the client as fundamentally capable of solving their problem. That is to say, they already have all they need to create the solution state (Berg & Szabo, 2005; de Shazer, 1988). This conceptualization of the client sees the person as whole and resourceful, rather than as dysfunctional and needy. When taken together these assumptions lead to several key tenets of SF approaches (O'Connell, 1998):

1. *Use of a non-pathological interpretive framework.* Problems are not indications of pathology or dysfunction. Rather they indicate a need to try different perspectives or behaviours.
2. *Client-based expertise.* The idea is that the client rather than the coach is the expert in their own life.

3. *Coaching is about facilitating solution construction.* The coach primarily facilitates the construction of solutions rather than trying to understand the aetiology of the problem.
4. *Focus on client resources.* The coach helps the client recognize and utilize existing resources.
5. *Clear, specific and personalized goal setting.* To assist the client in attaining their preferred future, the articulation of that future state should be clear and behaviourally detailed. Because problems and solutions are constructed by the client, coaching interventions should be tailored to each client.
6. *Action orientation.* There is a fundamental expectation on the coach's part that positive change both can, and will, occur, and that the work of change takes place primarily outside of the coaching session.
7. *Do what works and stop doing what does not work.* Allied to the commitment to an action orientation is a pragmatic focus on identifying what is working for the client and amplifying this. Similarly, if an attempt at problem resolution is not working, then stop and try something different.
8. *Change can happen in a short period of time.* Because the client is already whole, change does not require fixing the client. This stands in contrast to the assumption that change must be worked on over a long period of time.
9. *Enchantment.* Borrowed from the work of Milton Erikson, SF approaches suggest that the coaching process be designed and conducted in a way that is attractive and engaging for the client.

More recently, following a review of the SF literature, Visser (2012a) proposed and tested nine basic assumptions held by SF coaching practitioners (see Table 3.1). Visser (2012a) surveyed 134 practitioners and found significant correlations between these assumptions and the number of years of practice and intensity of use of SF approaches.

Table 3.1 Assumptions made by solution-focused practitioners (taken from Visser, 2012a)

Assumption		
About people	1.	People prefer to choose for themselves what they initiate and they want to control as much as possible what they do (need for autonomy).
	2.	People prefer to be competent, view themselves as competent and they are already competent to some extent (need for competence).
	3.	People want to have and build meaningful and caring relationships with other people and want to do things that make a positive difference to others (need for relatedness).
About change	1.	There is always already a beginning of the desired situation on which further progress can be built (existence of past success).
	2.	People change best by taking actions, one step at a time, and reflecting on and responding to the consequences of those actions so that an intelligible pattern eventually starts to form (stepwise change).
	3.	Positive behaviour descriptions, both in the future and in the past, irresistibly trigger positive behaviours (positive behaviour descriptions).
About helping	1.	Treating clients as cooperative, no matter how resistant they may appear, is the quickest and most promising way to encourage further cooperation (cooperativity).
	2.	Working within the client's frame of reference, without confrontation or blame and without imposing an expert view on the client is the quickest and most promising approach to help the client develop an ever more constructive, realistic and useful perspective (client perspective).
	3.	Focusing on identifying and amplifying what works, rather than on explanations in terms of personal characteristics and problem causes, is the quickest and most promising way to help clients make progress (focus on what works).

Core characteristics of the solution-focused approach

The SF approach was developed as a brief intervention. Brevity here is not about limiting the number or length of sessions. Rather, it reflects an intention to do only that which is necessary for the client to achieve movement forward (Berg & Szabo, 2005). Hence, the goals of SF coaching are often narrower or more limited than goals set in other traditions (Berg & Szabo, 2005). The SF approach does not seek to resolve past injuries, uncover and reduce defence mechanisms, rebuild cognitive schemas, or effect character change. Rather, it seeks to uncover with the client his/her own resourcefulness and bring this to bear in the service of the client's goals.

Once the goals have been identified, the SF practitioner seeks to assist the client in identifying the simplest and easiest path to achieving a result that is satisfactory for the client. For example, a coachee might identify that they would like a better relationship with their spouse. The coach would assist the coachee in identifying what a better relationship might look, sound and feel like – what sort of behaviours, feelings, thoughts and actions might be present in a better relationship. The coach would then work with the client to identify how much of this desired state needs to be present for the coaching to have been successful and the coachee to feel like they are on the way toward their solution.

Implicit in the above is the goal of building a capacity for self-directed learning in the coachee. This goal lies at the heart of the SF approach. Self-directed learning seeks to build self-efficacy and self-reliance through the process of discovering personalized solutions to problems, identifying solution steps that work for the individual, assessing effectiveness through feedback and then altering one's behaviour to maximize the effectiveness of one's attempts to reach the goal. Such a process seeks to elicit a curious, experiential and experimental mind-set. Once this learning capacity is activated in service of the client's goal, the expectation of the SF practitioner is that the client will continue to self-regulate and integrate these skills into other aspects of their life.

Self-regulation is thus an important part of the SF approach. Greene and Grant (2003) have graphically represented the process of self-regulation as a simple, iterative cycle of setting a goal, developing an action plan, acting, monitoring, and evaluating, and then changing what does not work and doing more of what works (see Figure 3.1). The coach's role is to facilitate the client's journey through this cycle while holding the client's focus on their goal/s.

METHODS AND TECHNIQUES

To enhance and facilitate the development of self-regulatory functioning in the client the SF approach seeks to enhance two types of change – change in the way in which the client views the problem and the development of behaviours consistent with solution attainment. In other words, the two main tasks of SF coaching are to 'change the viewing' and 'change the doing' (O'Hanlon & Beadle, 1996: 11). A useful metaphor for this is 'Taking a PEEP at some new MAPS'.

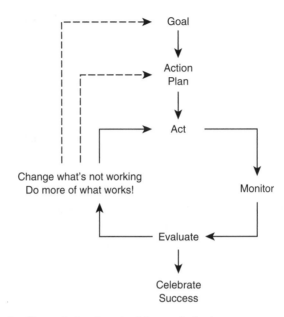

Figure 3.1   The cycle of self-regulation (used with permission)

1. Changing the viewing – PEEP

Changing the viewing is central to the SF approach. Clients, when they are focused on the problem or on all the reasons why the problem is difficult to solve, are by definition not looking toward the solution or the resources and steps needed to make the solution real. We know from experience and research that what you focus on grows. When we habitually focus our attention two psychological processes come into play – sensitization and amplification (Barsky, 1992).

Sensitization refers to the process whereby we learn to notice, or become sensitive to, a particular class of stimuli. For example, many parents become sensitized to the cry of their own child; or we might start to notice a particular model of car when we are considering purchasing one.

Amplification refers to the perceptual impact of what we notice. As we pay attention to a particular stimulus, it seems to grow in its importance or impact. Common examples include lying in bed listening to a tap drip or a dog bark. The more we attend to the sound the louder it gets. Of course, it is our perception of the sound that changes, not the volume of sound itself.

Changing the viewing shifts the perceptual cycles of sensitization and amplification from problem to solution. The more we become practised at focusing on solutions, the more solutions we notice and the more obvious they become. The acronym PEEP covers a wide range of techniques that can be used to change the way a problem is viewed:

> **P**referred outcome – move quickly to focusing on the preferred outcome rather than unpacking the problem. The miracle question (discussed below) is particularly useful here.
>
> **E**xceptions to the problem – uncover times when the problem does not exist, or when part of the solution is present.

Existing resources – focus on the resources already available to the client, rather than what is lacking.

Progress made so far – here the coach helps the client notice success rather than what is left to do. Scaling (discussed below) and complimenting the client are useful techniques to refocus on success.

The logic behind PEEP is that the first step in solving a problem is identifying the approach goal. Once the solution state has been clearly identified, the task then becomes to marshal the resources needed to achieve the chosen goal and build reality-based belief that the solution is possible (O'Hanlon & Beadle, 1996).

SF practitioners have developed dozens of techniques for assisting clients to change the viewing and identify resources. The following techniques are some of the more commonly used:

The Miracle Question. The miracle question is paradigmatic of the SF approach (Berg & Szabo, 2005). In the 'Miracle Question', in which the coach asks 'Imagine that you went to bed tonight, and when you woke up the problem had somehow magically disappeared, and the solution was present ... but you didn't know that the solution had arrived ... what is the first thing that you'd notice that would tell you that the solution was present?'

Scaling. Scaling is perhaps one of the most versatile of the SF techniques. It can be used to: (i) identify progress toward a goal – 'on a scale of 1 to 10 with ten representing the complete solution, and one representing the problem at its worst, where would you say you are now?'; (ii) clarify fuzzy goals – 'What does an 8 look like; how would you know you were at an 8?'; (iii) identify resources available to the client – 'so how come you are at a 4 now – what did you do to get that far?'; (iv) articulate small steps toward the goal – 'so what would be different if you were at a 5, or even a 4½?'.

Reframing. Reframing is another set of central SF tools. In this set of techniques the coach seeks to reframe the client's statements in a way that opens up possibilities and focuses the client on resources. Some examples include:

- Reframing problems to solutions:

    Client: 'I feel completely lost.'

    Coach: 'So, you'd like to get back a sense of direction and control?'

- Reframing problems to highlight hidden resources:

    Client: 'The tender was not successful and all the work I put in was completely wasted.'

    Coach: 'Sounds disappointing, but was it a complete waste – what did you learn from the experience?'

- Reframing using compliments:

    Client: 'It's far too expensive.'

    Coach: 'It's great that you are concerned about keeping on budget. How can we make it more affordable?'

- Reframing that highlights exceptions:

    Client: 'I really hate my work.'

    Coach: 'It sounds very unpleasant ... tell me, which parts of your job are less unpleasant for you?'

2. Changing the doing – MAPS

Changing the viewing is not enough. If the coaching conversation is to be more than an interesting exercise in how we perceive the world, it must result in action. Hence the second major task of SF coaching is to 'change the doing' (O'Hanlon & Beadle, 1996: 11). In this part of the coaching process, the task is to identify and support patterns of behaviour that enhance goal attainment. This may involve mapping the behavioural sequences present at times when the solution or part of it is present (O'Hanlon & Beadle, 1996). The client and coach then identify helpful patterns that can be replicated and these are practised in homework tasks.

Some techniques that can be useful in changing the doing can be represented by the acronym MAPS:

1. Multiple options – assisting the client to generate multiple options for action (O'Hanlon & Beadle, 1996).
2. Asking 'how' questions instead of 'why' questions.
3. Problems into possibilities – recognizing possibilities by turning presenting problems into springboards for solution construction (Jackson & McKergow, 2007).
4. Small SMART steps – generating initial actions that are achievable so as to build motivation and a history of success (Specific, Measureable Attractive, Realistic and Timebound).

The SF approach makes no prediction about what should be done. Rather, the coach and coachee work together to discover a pathway to success that works for the client, in their context. Hence, identifying what has worked in the past and experimenting with new possibilities are both important. This experimental mind-set is consistent with a scientist-practitioner model of coaching practice (Cavanagh & Grant, 2006).

The philosophical belief that the client is not broken also encourages the SF coach to change as little as possible (de Shazer, 2005). Hence small steps and active engagement in the feedback and evaluation process are important.

The solution-focused coaching engagement

From the client's perspective, the SF approach is often an attractive strengths-based intervention (Chou, 2007). By avoiding delving deeply into an examination of the client's problems, or searching for aetiological explanations in the client's psychological profile, clients are enabled to experience themselves as healthy and capable.

The principal challenge for the coach is taking on the mind-set needed for effective SF coaching. Do we really believe in the essential wholeness of the client? Holding the client in this way is not always easy, but it is vital to the SF enterprise – the quality of the working alliance significantly contributes to success (Horvath & Symonds, 1991).

The SF mind-set is a challenge for clients too. Some clients are able to clearly articulate what they want to achieve. They seem to fall naturally into solution talk. Other clients will more naturally move into problem talk and feel the need to explain the problem in detail. The coach's task is to help the client shift from a problem-focused to a SF mind-set as quickly as possible. Sometimes this shift occurs very quickly. However, with heavily problem-saturated clients the coach needs to exercise patience and sensitivity. It is important to meet such clients where they are – and gradually to help shift the conversation toward a more SF frame. Failure to empathically reflect the client's experience is likely to lead to a break in rapport.

As the coaching conversation unfolds, the coach works with the client to build up a picture of their preferred future through reflection and reframing. Scaling can be used to help the client judge their progress in relation to specific goals. As Grant (2006: 85) states: 'Scaling is nearly always an opportunity for the coach to give a compliment. Even if the clients say that they are at a 3 on a 10-point scale, the coach can respond – "well done – one third of the way there already"'.

Like many of the SF techniques, the giving of compliments and reframing must be done from a position of genuine positive regard and desire to really understand and move toward the client's goals. Without this fundamentally respectful stance, SF techniques can appear as superficial and manipulative.

Some SF authors suggest that a hallmark of the SF approach is the use of the miracle question, typically delivered in the first session (de Shazer 1988; O'Connell, 1998). However, we have found that it is often best to ask this question, once the client is ready to shift from an exploratory or deliberative mind-set to an implementational mind-set (Bayer & Gollwitzer, 2005; Oettingen & Gollwitzer, 2002). The deliberative mind-set is characterized by a careful exploration of the issue and potential goals (Carver & Scheier, 1998) and is therefore more likely to produce abstract problem-focused responses to the miracle question. The implementational mind-set, on the other hand, is focused on identifying means to change, and is therefore more behaviourally focused and detailed (Bayer & Gollwitzer, 2005). To ask the miracle question while the client is still exploring the problem can result in client confusion, a lack of engagement and even anger or resentment.

For some clients, the wording of the miracle question can be problematic. They experience talk of miracles as polyanna-ish. For such clients, more concrete variations of the miracle question may be useful – e.g., the 'Two Videos Question'. Here the client is asked to imagine two videos playing. One shows the problem as it is being enacted. The other shows the preferred outcome being enacted. The client's role is to simply describe the difference between the two.

These questions help the client describe their situation and the solution in concrete behavioural, emotional and relational terms – i.e. 'who is doing what, how and with whom and what impact does that have?' By describing the solution in this way, both the coach and client are usually able to identify do-able actions that will lead toward the goal.

The miracle question and its variants also help to build the client's capacity for mindfulness. These questions require the client to emotionally disengage from the problem so as to envisage a different future. This metacognitive distance helps to make visible a solution that cannot be seen when we are 'in' the problem – changing the viewing to change the doing!

Ending the coaching engagement

As mentioned above, the SF approach is designed to minimize intervention. For this reason, contracting for particular numbers of sessions is not entirely consistent with SF coaching. While the coach might ask at the beginning of the engagement about the client's expectation of the number of sessions needed, each session in the SF model is complete in itself (Berg & Szabo, 2005; O'Connell, 1998). Terminating the coaching engagement occurs when the client has met their goal, or feels satisfied that they can move toward it without the coach. Hence, SF coaching typically ends each session with a real question as to whether another session is needed: 'Do we need to meet again, or do you feel like you have done what you needed to do?'

APPLICATION

The SF approach is a methodology that is applicable in a wide range of coaching settings. Because it seeks to work with the client's goals and begins with the client's perspective, the application across settings is very similar. Nevertheless, it is worth noting some differences in emphasis found in different settings.

Skills and performance coaching

The psychological literature distinguishes between two types of development – horizontal development or assimilation, and vertical development or accommodation. Horizontal development occurs when a person is able to assimilate new information or new practices into their current worldview. Skills and performance coaching would typically fall into this category of development. In skills and performance coaching, the task is to focus on the development and application of specific knowledge skills and abilities in order to enhance workplace performance or achieve specific organizational targets (Standards Australia, 2011).

This focus on organizational goals and needs adds some complexity to SF coaching. In cases where there is congruence between what the organization and the coachee's goals goal setting within coaching is often straightforward. However, when there is a mismatch between the coachee's perceived needs and the organization's requirements, then goal clarification becomes critical.

A SF approach to this conundrum is to treat this apparent dilemma as a platform for more solutions (Jackson & McKergow, 2007). For example, the coach might bring the issue into the foreground as follows: 'I notice that you would like to achieve X, and at the same time, the organization is requiring that we work toward Y. I wonder is it possible for us to work toward both targets together, or is one more important for you? Perhaps there are other solutions possible?'

Skills and performance coaching often require the use of organizational metrics such as 360-degree feedback and other data driven performance measures. These metrics may encourage a focus on what is missing or undone, rather than what is positive about the client's performance. Here the SF coach's role is to help the client see measurement as feedback in service of their goals. Reframing of metrics as identifying progress and resources is also important.

Developmental coaching

Developmental coaching differs from skills and performance coaching in that it requires the coachee to form new ways of seeing the world so as to more effectively meet the challenge he/she is facing (Kegan, 1994; Standards Australia, 2011). In other words, it requires vertical development or accommodation. The curiosity and respectfulness that characterizes the SF approach is critical to the formation of more spacious meaning-making.

There is, however, an inherent tension in the developmental enterprise. The goal of constructing developmental solutions often requires the coach to challenge, at least implicitly, the current worldview of the coachee. For example, let us say a coachee has a goal of dealing with team conflict more effectively and they are considering an action plan that involves avoiding an aggressive team member. The SF coach might enquire into, and affirm, the client's positive intent, while asking the client to consider other perspectives and any possible unforeseen consequences of their course of action (Berg & Szabo, 2005) with a view to exploring more effective options.

Executive and leadership coaching

Executive and leadership coaching also hold some particular challenges for the SF coach. Typically, executive coaching involves a mix of skills, performance and development coaching. Unlike other areas of SF practice, executive coaching often involves the identification of a coherent personalized model of leadership and the competencies that support it.

A second area of difference is that leaders and executives often present in coaching with goals that need others to change behaviour. However, a basic assumption in the SF approach is that change is not something we can determine for others. When a client has a strong need to change another person's behaviour, the SF approach calls for questioning that assists the client in making their view of the situation explicit and tangible, exploring alternate views and identifying what the client can do to influence self-directed change in the other person, rather than repeating past unhelpful strategies like simply insisting that the other person change.

As in all SF coaching, clear identification of the desired outcome is important. Similarly, identifying positive intentions and providing support for trying new ways of seeing and dealing with the situation are likely to be useful. The coach might use a number of techniques to assist the client to focus on what is do-able and what works. For example, the coach might ask the client to recall conversations that seemed to be effective in helping the target person modify their behaviour, or enquire with the client as to what might be going on for the target person and how the client might check this out. Encouraging the client to experiment with different types of change conversations with the target person often leads to successful outcomes.

EVALUATION

Perhaps the greatest challenge facing the SF coach is to let go of causal problem-focused explanations as a foundation of practice. Given that most of us have had a lifelong education based on deterministic principles and scientific method, this is not always an easy task.

The lack of causal reasoning in the SF approach has led to claims that it is a superficial intervention (e.g. Ellis, 1997). Some authors have suggested that for coaching to be truly effective, a 'deeper' approach is necessary (e.g. Berglas, 2002; Kilburg, 2004). The idea that an approach is superficial or deep is interesting. The extended discussion of causes can take place with little or no positive change in the person's sense of self, worldview or behaviour. In what sense then is such an approach deemed to be 'deep'? Conversely, the construction of a preferred future and the identification of hitherto untapped personal resources can have profound impacts on the person's worldview and sense of self, and lead to significant behavioural change.

There are times when the SF approach is not appropriate. Some clients may have causal explanations that form a central and protected part of their worldview. Similarly, when clients have deeply felt needs to explore aetiology, attempting to impose a methodology that feels incongruent is likely to be counterproductive. While clients often respond favourably to a well-presented rationale for the SF approach, when they do not referral or use of an alternative methodology may be indicated. To force a SF perspective onto an unwilling client runs counter to the core principle of respect the client.

The SF approach has sometimes been called theory-free, maintaining that the imposition of external theories undermine the client's own expertise. The coach does not need any expert knowledge about the client's problems, beyond asking the right questions to unlock the client's own knowledge and solutions (e.g. de Shazer, 1988). However, this cannot truly be the case. In order for the coach to ask meaningful questions, the coach must have at least an implicit theory about the issue, and a theory about what kind of question will best help the client explore and articulate a solution. If the coach really had no expertise and no theory about how best to help a client, on what basis can they presume to help? (See Held, 1996 for a detailed discussion of these issues.)

Is the coach then the real expert in coaching? No – complexity theory teaches us that outcomes are an emergent property of the system and not the sole responsibility of any single part of the system (Lewin, 1993). As a complex adaptive system, the outcome of the coaching engagement emerges from the complex interaction of the coach *and* client together (Cavanagh, 2006). In other words, the solution is radically co-created by both client and coach.

When viewed from this perspective, expert-centric views of coaching which suggest that the coach 'adds value' either by imposing expert knowledge, or by their ability to view the client's system from a more objective perspective, are fundamentally flawed. Similarly, overly simplistic understandings which suggest that the client is the 'expert' in the coaching session are also distorted.

Nevertheless, the idea that the solution lies within the client, and the coach's role is merely to facilitate the client in discovering what they already have within them, is a useful metaphor for helping coaches develop an attitude of curiosity and facilitation. In that sense, the SF project requires the coach to take the beginner's mind. While the catch cry 'Ask, don't tell' is often used to encourage this attitude, experience shows that sometimes, no matter how long we ask, the solution does not emerge, because it is not 'in' the client.

This leads us to another more serious limitation of the SF method. As Einstein is oft quoted to have said, 'a problem cannot be solved with the same level of thinking that created it'. What counts as a solution is relative to the network of beliefs, assumptions and rules that make up a person's worldview (their 'level of thinking' or meaning-making). The belief that the client has the solution within them, assumes the client can readily rise above their current pattern of meaning-making to embrace a wider, more effective worldview. Experience and research suggest this is not always the case (see Kegan, 1994). For example, if one believes that businesses are only viable when growing, then the choice to shrink or limit long-term growth in one's business is unlikely to arise as a solution, even though this might best serve the goal of creating a more resilient organization.

Coaching is often sought to assist clients face challenges for which their current level of meaning-making produces only suboptimal solutions. As the rate of change, and complexity of issues, facing organizations increase, the need to challenge current perspectives and solutions will become an even more important part of the coach's role (Cavanagh & Lane, 2012). This task is not readily supported by the basic assumptions of the SF approach. Visser (2012b) has shown that many experienced SF coaches do tell and do challenge the solutions and goals formed by clients. The SF approach needs to find a way to recognize the critical role of the coach in the co-creation of goals.

Valuing the tensions

There is an important tension between the different expert knowledge bases brought to the session by the coach and client. The creativity of the SF approach relies on this tension; for it is out of the interaction between the two understandings that creative solutions are born. Hence, tension should not only be valued, but also actively sought, nurtured and, where necessary, managed (Stacey, 2000). Rush to closure on a goal stifles creativity. Too much tension between the understandings brought by coach and client is also counterproductive, and usually indicates one or other of the parties have stopped being open to alternate views. The great contribution of the SF approach is to provide a perspective and techniques that assist the coach to remain genuinely curious in their asking, and respectful and timely in their telling.

FURTHER READING

Greene, J. & Grant, A.M. (2003). *Solution-focused coaching: Managing people in a complex world.* London: Momentum Press. (An easy-to-read primer on SF coaching and management.)

O'Hanlon, B. & Beadle, S. (1999). *A guide to possibility land: Fifty-one methods for doing respectful brief therapy.* London: Norton & Co. (While written for therapy, this little book is a gold mine of SF methods which are readily translated to fit the coaching context.)

Berg, I. & Szabo, P. (2005). *Brief coaching for lasting solutions.* London: Norton & Co. (A practical overview from some of the pioneers of the approach. They describe a range of techniques illustrated with engaging case studies and examples.)

DISCUSSION QUESTIONS

- What is the coach's expertise in the SF approach?
- When is it OK to tell?
- How can I develop an SF mind-set?

REFERENCES

Barrett, F. (2004). Coaching for resilience. *Organization Development Journal, 22*(1): 93–6.

Barsky, A.J. (1992). Amplification, somatization, and the somatoform disorders. *Psychosomatics, 33*(1): 28–34.

Bayer, U. & Gollwitzer, P. (2005). Mindset effects on information search in self-evaluation. *European Journal of Social Psychology, 35*: 313–27.

Berg, I. & Szabo, P. (2005). *Brief coaching for lasting solutions*. London: Norton & Co.

Berglas, S. (2002). The very real dangers of executive coaching. *Harvard Business Review, June*: 87–92.

Carver, C.S. & Scheier, M.F. (1998). *On the self-regulation of behavior*. Cambridge: Cambridge University Press.

Cavanagh, M. & Lane, D. (2012). Coaching psychology coming of age: The challenges we face in the messy world of complexity. *International Coaching Psychology Review, 7,* 75–90.

Cavanagh, M. (2006). Coaching from a systemic perspective: A complex adaptive conversation. In D. Stober & A.M. Grant (Eds), *Evidence based coaching handbook* (pp. 313–54). New York: Wiley.

Cavanagh, M. & Grant, A. (2006). Coaching psychology and the scientist-practitioner model. In S. Corrie & D. Lane (Eds), *The modern scientist practitioner* (pp. 146–57). London: Routledge.

Chou, Yu-Chen. (2007). A study of the effects and therapeutic factors of a solution-focused parenting group. *Bulletin of Educational Psychology, 39*(1): 1–21.

Corcoran, J. & Stephenson, M. (2000). The effectiveness of solution-focused therapy with child behavior problems: A preliminary report. *Families in Society, 81*(5): 468–74.

Dahl, R., Bathel, D., & Carreon, C. (2000). The use of solution-focused therapy with an elderly population. *Journal of Systemic Therapies, 19*(4): 45–55.

de Shazer, S. (1988). *Clues: Investigating solutions in brief therapy*. New York: Norton & Co.

de Shazer, S. (1994). *Words were originally magic*. New York: Norton & Co.

de Shazer, S. (2005). *More than miracles: The state of the art of solution-focused therapy*. Binghamton, NY: Haworth Press.

Ellis, A. (1997). Response to Jeffrey T. Guterman's response to my critique of his article 'A social constructionist position for mental health counseling'. *Journal of Mental Health Counseling, 19*(1): 57–63.

Grant, A.M. (2006). Solution-focused coaching. In J. Passmore (Ed.), *Excellence in coaching: The industry guide* (Ch. 5). London: Kogan Page.

Greene, J. & Grant, A.M. (2003). *Solution-focused coaching: Managing people in a complex world*. London: Momentum Press.

Green, L., Oades, L., & Grant, A. (2006). Cognitive-behavioral, solution-focused life coaching: Enhancing goal striving, well-being and hope. *The Journal of Positive Psychology, 1*(3): 142–9.

Green, S., Grant, A., & Rynsaardt, J. (2007). Evidence-based life coaching for senior high school students: Building hardiness and hope. *International Coaching Psychology Review, 2*: 24–32.

Held, B.S. (1996). Solution-focused therapy and the postmodern: A critical analysis. In S.D. Miller, M.A. Hubble & B.L. Duncan (Eds), *Handbook of solution-focused brief therapy*. San Francisco, CA: Jossey-Bass.

Horvath, A.O. & Symonds, B. (1991). Relation between working alliance and outcome in psychotherapy: A meta-analysis. *Journal of Counseling Psychology, 38*(2): 139–49.

Jackson, P. & McKergow, M. (2007). *The solutions focus: Making coaching and change simple* (2nd ed.). Bristol: Nicholas Brealey Publishing.

Kegan, R. (1994) *In over our heads: The mental demands of modern life*. Cambridge, MA: Harvard University Press.

Kilburg, R.R. (2004). When shadows fall: Using psychodynamic approaches in executive coaching. *Consulting Psychology Journal: Practice & Research, 56*(4): 246–68.

Lethem, J. (2002). Brief solution-focused therapy. *Child & Adolescent Mental Health, 7*(4): 189–92.

Lewin, R. (1993) *Complexity: Life at the edge of chaos*. London: Phoenix.

Murray, C.E. & Murray, T.L., Jr (2004). Solution-focused premarital counseling: Helping couples build a vision for their marriage. *Journal of Marital & Family Therapy, 30*(3): 349–58.

O'Connell, B. (1998). *Solution-focused therapy*. London: Sage.

Oettingen, G. & Gollwitzer, P. (2002). Turning hope thoughts into goal-directed behavior. *Psychological Inquiry, 13*(4): 304–7.

O'Hanlon, B. & Beadle, S. (1996). *A field guide to possibility land: Possibility therapy methods*. London: BT Press.

Spence, G.B. & Grant, A.M. (2007). Professional and peer life coaching and the enhancement of goal striving and well-being: An exploratory study. *Journal of Positive Psychology, 2*(3): 185–94.

Stacey, R.D. (2000). *Strategic management and organisational dynamic* (3rd ed.). Harlow: Pearson Education.

Standards Australia. (2011). *Handbook coaching in organization*. Sydney, Australia: SAI Global Limited.

Visser, C.F. (2012a). *The solution-focused mindset: An empirical test of solution-focused assumptions*. Accessed online 15 November 2012 at www.solutionfocusedchange.com.

Visser, C.F. (2012b). *What solution-focused coaches do: An empirical test of an operationalization of solution-focused coach behaviors*. Accessed online 15 November 2012 at www.solutionfocusedchange.com.

4

The Person-centred Approach to Coaching

Stephen Joseph

INTRODUCTION TO THE PERSPECTIVE

The aim of this chapter is to provide an introduction to person-centred coaching. The chapter will help readers to identify and clarify the main concepts and assumptions about human nature and development underpinning the person-centred approach, its distinctive features, methods and techniques, and finally its applications.

The person-centred approach was originally developed by Carl Rogers during the 1940s and 1950s. Person-centred (or client-centred, as it was originally known) refers to the philosophical stance that people are their own best experts. The person-centred approach was seen as an alternative to the then dominant models in American psychology of behaviourism and psychoanalysis. Unlike these previous approaches, Rogers' emphasized the agency of the person and their ability to make conscious choices. As such the person-centred approach became aligned with the third force in psychology, that of humanistic psychology.

Today, Rogers is best remembered for his books *Client-centered therapy: Its current practice, implications and theory* (1951) and *On becoming a person: A therapist's view of psychotherapy* (1961), both of which have been reprinted numerous times and remain in print and widely read. The person-centred approach is now an established psychological tradition supported by over fifty years of research and theory (see Barrett-Lennard, 1998; Kirschenbaum, 2007; Patterson & Joseph, 2007). There has also been much theoretical and practical developments (see Sanders, 2004), ranging from the classical client-centred approach (Merry, 2004) with its principled role of going with the client at the client's pace, through to more process-directed approaches (Worsley, 2001, 2004) and motivational interviewing, which has its roots in the person-centred approach (Csillik, 2013; Passmore & Whybrow, 2008).

The theoretical foundation stone of the person-centred approach is the *actualizing tendency*. The actualizing tendency is defined as a universal human motivation resulting in growth, develpment and autonomy of the individual (Rogers, 1959, 1963). It is a biological tendency, not a moral imperative. The metaphor most often used to convey this theoretical principle is how an acorn has the potential to develop into an oak tree and, given the right nutrients from the soil, the right balance of sunlight and shade, it will grow to its fullest potential as an oak tree. But given a lack of nutrients from the soil, the wrong balance of sunlight and shade, its potential as an oak tree will be only partially fulfilled. The actualizing tendency is an aspect of a formative tendency present in all living systems to move towards an adaptive self-organizing function (Cornelius-White, 2007).

Evidence for the person-centred approach is underpinned by self-determination theory (SDT). SDT is a more contemporary but essentially synonymous theory of human motivation and personality functioning with a strong evidence base which underpins the person-centred approach. Developed over the past 30 years SDT emphasizes the central role of the individual's inner resources for personality development and behavioural self-regulation (Deci & Ryan, 2002; Ryan & Deci, 2002). In accord with person-centred theory, SDT views the person as an active growth-oriented organism, attempting to actualize his or her potentialities within the environment in which he or she functions. The organismic tendency toward actualization is seen as one pole of a dialectical interface, the other pole being the social environment which can be either facilitating or inhibiting of the person's synthesizing tendency (Ryan & Deci, 2002; Deci & Vansteenkiste, 2004; Vansteenkiste & Sheldon, 2006). Similarities between person-centred theory and SDT have been obscured by the differences in terminology and separate research trajectories, but on examination there are such close similarities between these approaches that the extensive research evidence from SDT can be read as providing evidence consistent with person-centred theory (Patterson & Joseph, 2007).

In short, the person-centred approach to helping is founded on the assumption that people are intrinsically motivated to grow and develop in the direction of becoming optimally functioning, when the right social environmental conditions are present:

> individuals have within themselves vast resources for self-understanding, and for altering their self-concepts, basic attitudes, and self-directed behaviour; these resources can be tapped if a definable climate of facilitative psychological attitudes can be provided. (Rogers, 1980: 115)

DISTINCTIVE FEATURES

Joseph and Murphy (2013) have conceptualized person-centred practice as at the centre of a Venn diagram consisting of three overlapping circles representing: (1) the meta-theory of the tendency towards actualization; (2) relational ways of helping; and (3) positive psychology with its emphasis on optimal functioning (see Figure 4.1). At the centre of these three overlapping circles is a

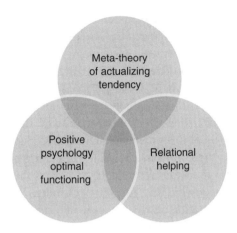

Figure 4.1

relationship-based approach grounded in the meta-theoretical approach that people are intrinsically motivated towards optimal positive psychological functioning. The person-centred approach refers to approaches to helping that are situated at the interface of these three circles. Other forms of coaching may also be relational and orientated towards positive functioning but what makes person-centred coaching unique is its grounding in the meta-theory of a tendency towards actualization. As a result of the meta-theory there are two distinctive features.

First, person-centred coaching is relationship based. While it is true that all coaching approaches could be described as relationship based the person-centred approach is based on a particular type of relationship in which the coach has an attitude of non-directivity. By adopting an attitude of non-directivity the coach endeavours to foster the client's self-determination (Grant, 2004). To do this, Rogers (1957a: 96) described six conditions that he held were necessary and sufficient for positive therapeutic change:

1. Two persons are in psychological contact.
2. The first, whom we shall call the client, is in a state of incongruence, being vulnerable or anxious.
3. The second person, whom we shall call the therapist, is congruent or integrated in the relationship.
4. The therapist experiences unconditional positive regard for the client.
5. The therapist experiences an empathic understanding of the client's internal frame of reference and endeavours to communicate this experience to the client.
6. The communication to the client of the therapist's empathic understanding and unconditional positive regard is to a minimal degree achieved.

The above relationships conditions were specifically formulated as a way of working that is consistent with the meta-theory. They describe a non-directive relationship in which it is the client who takes the lead. Non-directivity does not mean there is no direction; the therapist is non-directive because he or she is following the client's directions – hence the use of the term client-centred. As such, the essence of person-centred practice is that the task of the coach is always to follow the client's lead (Brodley, 2005; Joseph, 2003; Levitt, 2005; Schmid, 2005).

Second, originally aligned with humanistic psychology, contemporary person-centred practice is now recognized within the context of and as a precursor to the positive psychology movement (Hefferon & Boniwell, 2011; Joseph & Linley, 2006a). Like person-centred psychologists (Rogers, 1957b; Shlien, 2003), positive psychologists are interested in the 'good life', arguing that mainstream psychology has been overly concerned with distress and dysfunction at the expense of well-being and optimal functioning (Seligman & Csikszentmihalyi, 2000).

But as a result of the meta-theory of the actualizing tendency, the person-centred approach adopts a unified and holistic focus on both the negative and the positive aspects of human functioning (Joseph & Worsley, 2005; Joseph & Linley, 2006a). The person-centred approach does not make a distinction between people in terms of their level of psychological functioning, because the process of alleviating distress and dysfunction is the same as that for facilitating well-being and optimal functioning. Psychological functioning is defined in relation to the extent to which self-actualization is congruent with the actualizing tendency (Ford, 1991). When there is greater congruence, greater well-being and more optimal functioning result; but when there is less congruence, greater distress and dysfunction result (see Wilkins, 2005).

METHODS AND TECHNIQUES

The practice implication that follows from the idea of respecting the self-determination of the client is that reflective listening is central to what the coach does:

Client. I don't know, it's like we don't connect anymore, we don't talk, it's not like it was, she says that everything is ok and that she loves me, but I don't feel loved. I don't know what to do.

Coach. You feel stuck, not knowing, she says she loves you, but you don't feel loved. You look frightened as you say that.

Client. Do I? ... I suppose I am, I don't know what to do, if she leaves me, I'll ... I'll, I don't know ...

Coach. You feel frightened and when you think about this you are ... lost?

Client. Abandoned, I don't know if I could cope ...

Coach. You don't know if you could cope ...

Client. ... I know I could cope, but I don't want to go through that, I can't face it, but I know that I'll get through in the end (sighs) ... I can't carry on like this either, I can't cope with this ...

Coach You are really struggling to manage what's happening right now in your life, all the confusion ... you don't want to separate but you know that you will be able to get through it if you have to ... is that it?

Client Yes ... I've got to look after myself ...

In this short example of life coaching, the coach is staying with the client's agenda. The coach does not introduce new material, nor prompt the client about how to think about the content of what they say, or what direction to go in. In reflecting to the client that they seem frightened, the coach is following the lead of the client and in doing so helps the client to become more aware of how they are feeling. It is hard on paper, and with such a snapshot example, to convey the complexity and depth of the relationship that develops between the coach and the client (but see Worsley & Joseph, 2007). Reflective listening is not a passive process, it requires active attention to all that is said, and all that is not said, and it requires the coach to choose on the basis of their empathic understanding as well as their own congruence in that moment what to reflect on. Reflective listening, when skilfully done and in the context of an empathic, congruent, positively regarding and unconditional relationship encourages the client to verbalize further, to explore issues in more depth, to be challenged, to reach new insights and ultimately to be more equipped to make new choices in life.

But reflective listening is not the whole story. So long as it is the client's lead that is driving the session, the person-centred coach can draw on and offer to the client various cognitive behavioural, multimodel, solution-focused and systems theory techniques (see Kauffman & Scoular, 2004). Cognitive behavioural psychology, for example, offers a wealth of techniques that can be helpful to people in learning about themselves and in exploring the relationship between thoughts and feelings, and learning how what we say to ourselves can hold us back from achieving our goals (Neenan & Palmer, 2001). For example, the coach may think it appropriate to offer the suggestion that the client could explore their coping style, perhaps suggesting an appropriate self-help book on the topic, or suggesting to the client that they complete a psychometric test in order to gain insight into their coping style, but only within the context of not violating the principle of the self-determination of the client. Person-centred coaching refers not to what you do, but how you do it (Joseph & Linley, 2006b).

APPLICATION

Life coaching is probably the most obvious arena in which person-centred coaching is applied. Often, client's come knowing that they want to change the direction of their lives, but are struggling to hear their inner voice about the best way to move forward. The person-centred coach can help the person think through relationship choices, managing stressful situations and so on. Person-centred coaching is ideally suited for the exploration of values, beliefs and assumptions.

The person-centred approach does not prescribe what the client should do, because it is grounded in the meta-theoretical assumption that people have an inherent tendency toward growth, development and optimal functioning. The task of the coach is to trust the client to find his or her own direction in life and to maintain an empathic, congruent and positively regarding stance towards the other.

Thus it is that person-centred coaching emphasizes the successful formation of a collaborative relationship (Stober & Grant, 2006; O'Broin & Palmer, 2008) and the coaches' attributes – their authenticity, emotional literacy and so on, factors which are thought to be important in determining coaching effectiveness (Fillery-Travis & Lane, 2008), as with counselling and psychotherapy (Duncan & Miller, 2000; Wampold, 2001; Worsley & Joseph, 2007; Bozarth & Motomasa, 2005).

In practice, the person-centred coach strives to understand both the content of what the client is saying and the process they are working through, reflecting back their understanding to the client so that the client has a mirror to his or her experiencing in that moment (Joseph & Bryant-Jefferies, 2008). This helps the client to hear their own inner voice, to go deeper into their process and become aware of new material that was previously at the edge of their awareness. But at no point does the coach direct the client as to how they ought to be experiencing; his or her role is only to offer the relational conditions within which the client's own process will direct the session.

Life coaching is usually funded by the client him/herself. However, contracting is still important, particularly in relation to boundary issues and what should or should not be included in the coaching agenda. Also, as we have seen, attention needs to be paid to the role of influential others, the client's system and circles of influence. The main question faced by the person-centred coach is 'Whose agenda am I addressing?' It has to be the client's agenda and boundaries must be set clearly in place when the contract is with an organization. Issues could arise from lack of clarity in contracting or lack of alignment between client and organizational goals. Issues to be considered in relation to person-centred coaching include understanding the client system and particularly influential others who may undermine the coaching process. Confidentiality may also be an issue within an organization. Unless otherwise agreed, it would be usual for details of the coach–client relationship to remain confidential, and when such details are shared with the organization it would be at the agreement of the client, who would in most cases be given the opportunity to discuss the report and to agree with the coach that it provides a fair representation.

The person-centred approach is also well-suited to career coaching and coaching in higher education to help individuals discover what direction to take their working lives. Person-centred coaching is most suitable with clients who have or who are capable of obtaining the relevant information but are struggling to choose their direction. A further area of applicability is mentoring in which the person-centred approach serves to build up self-direction.

Again it must be emphasized that it is an approach to helping people grounded in the theoretical principle of the tendency towards actualization and a respect for the self-determination of the other. There are no contexts or populations with whom this approach is not applicable if one agrees with these fundamental theoretical assumptions. For example, the person-centred approach, because of its grounding in the idea of intrinsic motivation, is useful to developmental work in which the client is interested in making new decisions, understanding their values and beliefs, becoming authentic or discovering new purpose. This can be appropriate in an organizational context, although one issue of relevance to person-centred coaches is that because of their principled stance of non-directivity, and going with the client's direction, it becomes less appropriate when commissioned by organizations that have particular goals in mind for the client. The person-centred coach will always stay with the agenda of the client, and this can be problematic if they are employed by an organization whose goals are different from those of the client.

The same issue is pertinent in executive and leadership coaching where often the focus is on organizational performance. Insofar as the client is also focused on organizational aims, the person-centred coach will stay with that agenda, but they would not see it as their task to stay with that agenda if the client's agenda shifted. This may seem a disadvantage, and certainly it would be in terms of organizational performance requirements, such as learning new analytical and business skills. What can result, however, is that clients move away from their organizational agenda towards a more personal agenda in a way which is actually beneficial to them in terms of self-understanding and developing social and emotional skills, which in turn has a knock-on effect in terms of decision making and the ability to relate to others, which can benefit the organization.

Person-centred coaching is least appropriate to peer coaching, because of the need to adopt a consistent and clearly communicated attitude of principled non-directivity. Without appropriate experience and training in person-centred theory and practice it is difficult for colleagues to be able to work together effectively in this way. Reflections on current practice, and sharing experiences, can easily spill into advice giving, which although appropriate at times, needs to be done in the context of principled non-directivity. But some basic training grounded in person-centred constructs, such as reflective listening and empathic understanding, can be useful to increase the effectiveness of peer coaches using other approaches; but it would be misleading to call this person-centred as it lacks the full philosophical depth of the approach.

Person-centred coaches come from a variety of backgrounds and although some are able to offer skills and performance coaching related to their own expertise, generally person-centred coaching does not set out to achieve goals against set performance criteria. Where it can be particularly useful, however, is in the group learning context, in which experienced person-centred coaches can facilitate group interaction in such a way that the group members are better able to focus on identifying their goals and finding ways of working to achieve these, and to consider their shared values and discuss what is important to them.

But the skills of the person-centred coach are also applicable to a wide range of contexts. The person-centred approach refers to a philosophical *approach* to human relationships not a set of techniques. The person-centred approach can be applied to a range of contexts, from one-to-one settings, in small groups, in community settings, or as applied to social policy (Barrett-Lennard, 1998).

EVALUATION

The ideas associated with the person-centred movement underpin the practice of many coaches. Although coaching is a comparatively new professional movement, the development of coaching and the origin of many of the ideas can be traced back to the humanistic tradition of psychology

(Grant, 2008; Whybrow, 2008). Palmer and Whybrow (2006) found that the majority of coaching psychologists describe themselves as facilitational (67.9%) rather than instructional (17.4%), and that the person-centred approach is one of the most frequently mentioned influences on coaching practice.

Ask, don't tell

The most important influence of the person-centred approach seen across the contemporary field of coaching is how the self-determination of the client is the basis for most forms of coaching. While most coaches agree on the principle of self-determination, they differ on *how* they implement this idea. Most coaches would generally adopt an 'ask not tell' approach (Grant, 2008). The more one adopts an ask not tell approach the more their practice can be described as person-centred. Those who adopt an ask don't tell approach might be said to be informed by person-centred principles.

Listen, don't ask

But the motto of the person-centred coach is more likely to be 'listen, don't ask', as even asking can limit the self-determination of the client. Questions that arise in order to clarify the meaning of what the client has said are qualitatively different from questions that are to elicit information from the coach's frame of reference. Clarifying meaning is a form of listening that respects the self-determination of the client. Asking for information is not following the client's lead but requires the client to follow the coach's lead.

In terms of one-to-one practice, Carl Rogers introduced the term counselling but he might equally well have used the term coaching, because in person-centred practice these terms are interchangeable. The current use of these two terms reflects the prevalent medical model ideology (Joseph, 2006). The coaching profession has distinguished itself from psychological interventions that are aimed at fixing, remedying, or healing something that is pathological. However, counselling as it was originally envisaged by Carl Rogers was never aimed at fixing, remedying, or healing. The person-centred practitioner adheres to the same philosophical principle of respecting the self-determination of the other, whether they are practising as a coach or as a therapist. Unlike other therapeutic approaches, person-centred practice is not concerned with 'repairing' or 'curing' dysfunctionality, and never adopted the 'diagnostic' stance of the medical model in which the therapist is the expert. Like coaching, the focus of person-centred counselling has always been to facilitate the self-determination and full functioning of the client.

The development of different terminology, i.e. counselling versus coaching, to describe people at different points on the spectrum of psychological functioning, reflects the pervasive medical model conception that helping people in distress is different from helping people achieve well-being. It must be emphasized that the way in which professional organizations have developed to deal with people at different points on the spectrum ultimately reflects a social construction of human functioning grounded in a medical model and an illness ideology.

From the person-centred perspective there is no boundary between coaching and counselling. Thus, person-centred coaching is the same activity requiring the same theoretical base, the same skills and high level of personal development as required for person-centred counselling. There is no meaningful theoretical distinction from the perspective of the person-centred approach between the process of coaching and that of counselling. In essence both require principled non-directivity within the context of a facilitative relationship.

But this is not to say that an observer would not notice any difference between person-centred coaching and person-centred counselling. Quite simply, what terms we use will determine what clients we work with. If the public understanding is that counselling is about looking back in life at what has gone wrong, whereas coaching is about looking forward to what can go right, different people with different issues will be attracted to counselling than to coaching. Thus, although the task of the person-centred counsellor or coach is the same in either case – to stay with the person and to facilitate the person's process of self-determination – at the level of content the sessions would be different, simply because clients are more likely to bring different material to counselling compared to coaching.

On the other hand, it may be that it is the coach who uses the term coaching deliberately to provide a forum for clients who are embarrassed to meet with a counsellor. An example is that of police officers offered the opportunity of counselling in the aftermath of a critical incident. Few took up the opportunity. Following the next critical incident they were offered coaching which was taken up. What they were being offered was person-centred in both cases but the term coaching was less stigmatising than the term counselling. For person-centred practitioners, where the terminology is interchangeable, which term is used is likely to reflect contexts of employment.

Finally, the emergence of the coaching movement has served to reinvigorate interest in the person-centred approach. As mentioned previously, many coaching practitioners describe themselves as using a person-centred approach, and certainly the general ethos of the person-centred approach, that clients are the best experts on themselves, is one that is readily accepted by the coaching community. Grant (2008), for example, argues that coaching should be collaborative and client-centred. As discussed above the majority of coaches may emphasize the quality of the coach–client relationship as being important, but not all fully appreciate the philosophical underpinnings of the approach with its deliberate strategic approach to fostering self-determination.

FURTHER READING

Joseph, S. & Linley, P.A. (2006). *Positive therapy: A meta-theory for positive psychological practice*. London: Routledge. (In this book, we discuss the alternative meta-theoretical paradigm of person-centred theory and how it can provide the underpinning to positive psychology, therapy and coaching.)

Rogers, C.R. (1959). A theory of therapy, personality, and interpersonal relationships as developed in the client-centered framework. In S. Koch (Ed.), *Psychology: A study of a science: Formulations of the person and the social context* (Vol. 3, pp.184–256). New York: McGraw-Hill. (This is the most sophisticated theoretical statement of the person-centred tradition in which Rogers attempted to show how the approach was applicable to a range of contexts, setting out in detail the theoretical propositions that remain the core of the approach today.)

Rogers, C.R. (1980). *A way of being*. Boston, MA: Houghton Mifflin Co. (This book brings together some of Rogers's personal and philosophical writings. As such it provides a good introduction to the later writings of Rogers and the wider applications of the person-centred approach, including to contexts that we would today recognize as coaching.)

DISCUSSION QUESTIONS

- What is the defining feature of person-centred coaching?
- Is there a difference between counselling and coaching in the person-centred approach?
- What contexts of coaching is the person-centred approach most suitable for?

REFERENCES

Barrett-Lennard, G.T. (1998). *Carl Rogers' helping system: Journey and substance*. London: Sage.

Bozarth, J.D. & Motomasa, N. (2005). Searching for the core: The interface of client-centered principles with other therapies. In S. Joseph & R. Worsley (Eds), *Person-centred psychopathology: A positive psychology of mental health*. Ross-on-Wye: PCCS books.

Brodley, B.T. (2005). About the non-directive attitude. In B.E. Levitt (Ed.), *Embracing non-directivity: Reassessing person-centered theory and practice in the 21st century* (pp. 1–4). Ross-on-Wye: PCCS books.

Cornelius-White, J. H. D. (2007). The actualizing and formative tendencies: Prioritizing the motivational constructs of the person-centered approach. *Person-Centered and Experiential Psychotherapies, 6*, 129–140.

Csillik, A. S. (2013). Understanding motivational interviewing effectiveness: Contributions from Rogers' Client-Centered Approach. *The Humanistic Psychologist, 41*, 350–363.

Deci, E.L. & Ryan, R.M. (2002). Self-determination research: Reflections and future directions. In E.L. Deci & R.M. Ryan (Eds), *Handbook of self-determination research* (pp. 431–41). Rochester, NY: University of Rochester Press.

Deci, E.L. & Vansteenkiste, M. (2004). Self-determination theory and basic need satisfaction: Understanding human development in positive psychology. *Ricerchedi di psicologia: Special issue in positive psychology, 27*: 23–40.

Duncan, B. & Miller, S. (2000). *The heroic client: Doing client-directed, outcome informed therapy*. San Francisco, CA: Jossey-Bass.

Fillery-Travis, A. & Lane, D. (2008). Research: Does coaching work? In S. Palmer & A. Whybrow (Eds), *Handbook of coaching psychology: A guide for practitioners* (pp. 57–70). London: Routledge.

Ford, J.G. (1991). Rogerian self-actualization: A clarification of meaning. *Journal of Humanistic Psychology, 31*: 101–11.

Grant, A.M. (2008). Past, present, and future: The evolution of professional coaching and coaching psychology. In S. Palmer & A. Whybrow (Eds), *Handbook of coaching psychology: A guide for practitioners* (pp. 23–39). London: Routledge.

Grant, B. (2004). The imperative of ethical justification in psychotherapy: The special case of client-centered therapy. *Person-Centered and Experiential Psychotherapies, 3*: 152–65.

Hefferon, K. & Boniwell, I. (2011). *Positive psychology: Theory, Research and Applications*. Open University Press: Maidenhead.

Joseph, S. (2003). Client-centred psychotherapy: Why the client knows best. *The Psychologist, 16*: 304–7.

Joseph, S. (2006). Person-centred coaching psychology: A meta-theoretical perspective. *International Coaching Psychology Review, 1*: 47–55.

Joseph, S. & Bryant-Jefferies, R. (2008). Person-centred coaching psychology. In S. Palmer & A. Whybrow (Eds), *Handbook of coaching psychology: A guide for practitioners* (pp. 211–28). London: Routledge.

Joseph, S. & Linley, P.A. (2006a). Positive psychology versus the medical model. *American Psychologist, 61*: 332–3.

Joseph, S. & Linley, P.A. (2006b). *Positive therapy: A meta-theory for positive psychological practice*: London: Routledge.

Joseph, S. & Murphy, D. (2013). Person-centered approach, positive psychology and relational helping: Building bridges. *Journal of Humanistic Psychology, 53,* 26–51.

Joseph, S. & Worsley, R. (2005). A positive psychology of mental health: The person-centred perspective. In S. Joseph & R. Worsley (Eds), *Person-centred psychopathology: A positive psychology of mental health* (pp. 348–57). Ross-on-Wye: PCCS Books.

Kauffman, C. & Scoular, A. (2004). Toward a positive psychology of executive coaching. In P. A. Linley & S. Joseph (Eds), *Positive psychology in practice* (pp. 287–302). Hoboken, NJ: John Wiley & Sons.

Kirschenbaum, H. (2007). *The life and work of Carl Rogers.* Ross-on-Wye: PCCS Books.

Levitt, B.E. (Ed.). (2005). *Embracing non-directivity: Reassessing person-centered theory and practice in the 21st century.* Ross-on-Wye: PCCS Books.

Merry, T. (2004). *Classical client-centred therapy.* In P. Sanders, The tribes of the person-centred nation: An introduction to the schools of therapy related to the person-centred approach (pp. 21–44). Ross-on-Wye: PCCS Books.

Neenan, M. & Palmer, S. (2001). Cognitive behavioural coaching. *Stress News, 13*: 15–18.

O'Broin, A. & Palmer, S. (2008). Reappraising the coach-client relationship: The unassuming change agent in coaching. In S. Palmer & A. Whybrow (Eds), *Handbook of coaching psychology: A guide for practitioners* (pp. 295–324). London: Routledge.

Palmer, S. & Whybrow, A. (2006). The coaching psychology movement and its development within the British Psychological Society. *International CoachingPsychology Review, 1*: 5–11.

Passmore, J. & Whybrow, A. (2008). Motivational interviewing: A specific approach for coaching psychologists. In S. Palmer & A. Whybrow (Eds), *Handbook of coaching psychology: A guide for practitioners* (pp. 160–73). London: Routledge.

Patterson, T.G. & Joseph, S. (2007). Person-centered personality theory: Support from self-determination theory and positive psychology. *Journal of Humanistic Psychology, 47*: 117–39.

Rogers, C.R. (1951). *Client-centred therapy: Its current practice, implications and theory.* Boston, MA: Houghton Mifflin.

Rogers, C.R. (1957a). The necessary and sufficient conditions of therapeutic personality change. *Journal of Consulting Psychology, 21*: 95–103.

Rogers, C.R. (1957b). A therapist's view of the good life. *The Humanist, 17*: 291–300.

Rogers, C.R. (1959). A theory of therapy, personality, and interpersonal relationships as developed in the client-centered framework. In S. Koch (Ed.), *Psychology: A study of a Science: Formulations of the person and the social context* (Vol. 3, pp.184–256). New York: McGraw-Hill.

Rogers, C.R. (1961). *On becoming a person: A therapist's view of psychotheraphy.* Boston, MA: Houghton Mifflin.

Rogers, C.R. (1963). The actualizing tendency in relation to 'motives' and to consciousness. In M. R. Jones (Ed.), *Nebraska Symposium on Motivation* (Vol. 11, pp. 1–24). Lincoln, NE: University of Nebraska Press.

Rogers, C.R. (1980). *A way of being.* Boston, MA: Houghton Mifflin.

Ryan, R.M. & Deci, E.L. (2002). *An overview of self-determination theory: An organismic dialectical perspective.* In E.L. Deci & R.M. Ryan (Eds), *Handbook of self-determination research* (pp. 3–33). Rochester, NY: University of Rochester Press.

Sanders, P. (2004). *The tribes of the person-centred nation: An introduction to the schools of therapy related to the person-centred approach.* Ross-on-Wye: PCCS Books.

Schmid, P. (2005). Facilitative responsiveness: Non-directiveness from anthropological, epistemological and ethical perspectives. In B.E. Levitt (Ed.), *Embracing nondirectivity: Reassessing person-centered theory and practice in the 21st century* (pp. 75–95). Ross-on-Wye: PCCS Books.

Seligman, M.E.P. & Csikszentmihalyi, M. (2000). Positive psychology: An introduction. *American Psychologist, 55*: 5–14.

Shlien, J.M. (2003). Creativity and psychological health. In P. Sanders (Ed.), *To lead an honourable life: Invitations to think about client-centered therapy and the person-centered approach* (pp. 19–29). Ross-on-Wye: PCCS Books.

Stober, D.R. & Grant, A.M. (2006). Toward a contextual approach to coaching models. In D. R. Stober & A. M. Grant (Eds), *Evidence based coaching handbook: Putting best practices to work for your clients.* Hoboken, NJ: Wiley.

Vansteenkiste, M. & Sheldon, K.M. (2006). There's nothing more practical than a good theory: Integrating motivational interviewing and self-determination theory. *British Journal of Clinical Psychology, 45*: 63–82.

Wampold, B.E. (2001). *The great psychotherapy debate: Models, methods, and findings*. Mahwah, NJ: Lawrence Erlbaum.

Whybrow, A. (2008). Coaching psychology: Coming of age. *International Coaching Psychology Review, 3*, 227–240.

Wilkins, P. (2005). Person-centred theory and 'mental illness'. In S. Joseph & R. Worsley (Eds), *Person-centred psychopatholgy: A positive psychology of mental health* (pp. 43–59). Ross-on-Wye: PCCS Books.

Worsley, R. (2001). *Process work in person-centred therapy*. Basingstoke: Palgrave.

Worsley, R. (2004). Integrating with integrity. In P. Sanders (Ed.), *The tribes of the person-centred nation: An introduction to the schools of therapy related to the person-centred approach* (pp. 125–48). Ross-on-Wye: PCCS Books.

Worsley, R., & Joseph, S. (2007). *Person-centred practice: Case studies in positive psychology*. Ross-on-Wye: PCCS books.

5

The Gestalt Approach to Coaching

Peter Bluckert

Practitioners from a clinical background will be familiar with Gestalt from Gestalt therapy; what may be less well known is the coherent body of theory and practice relating to applications of Gestalt at the organizational level. This chapter describes the key aspects of the Gestalt theoretical tradition and sets out a conceptual and methodological framework for a Gestalt coaching approach.

THE THEORETICAL TRADITION

Gestalt coaching derives its theory and practice from Gestalt psychology; Gestalt therapy where the primary focus has been on individuals and, more recently, the application of Gestalt to wider systems such as couples, families, teams and organizations. However, Gestalt therapy is not simply a direct extension of Gestalt psychology. The pioneers of Gestalt therapy absorbed several philosophical and psychological traditions. The period from the 1950s to the 1980s, and particularly the earlier years when much of the influential work was done, was for many a time of deep questioning and dissatisfaction with the status quo. There was a desire for change and a belief that it could happen. Those early founders, Fritz and Laura Perls and Paul Goodman, confronted the Freudian-based psychoanalytical establishment and embraced the radicalism of the time.

They found their influences from psychoanalysis and Gestalt psychology, from field theory, existential philosophy and the humanistic therapy movement of the time. In 1951, Perls, in collaboration with Goodman and Hefferline, published the seminal Gestalt text: *Gestalt therapy: Excitement and growth in the human personality*, 'the cornerstone of the Gestalt approach' (Latner, 1992: 15).

Gestalt psychology was developed in Germany in the early 20th century by Max Wertheimer, Wolfgang Köhler and Kurt Koffka who were interested in the nature of perceptual experience. They challenged the belief that there is an 'objective reality' and sought instead to understand how we make sense of our experience, moment by moment, against the background of the field which includes our current mental models and historical experience. They believed that people strive to impose order and meaningful wholes on what they see and experience. The German word Gestalt, which does not easily translate into English, most approximates to words like pattern, shape, configuration, or meaningful organized whole.

From field theorists such as Kurt Lewin the concept of interconnectedness was adopted – that people exist as part of an environmental field and behaviour can only be understood in relation to that field. An important implication here for organizational consultants, facilitators and coaches is that *you* cannot be outside of the field. The notion of the neutral practitioner exerting no influence on the system you are working with is rejected in the field perspective. The intervener may not be a member of the group or system but as Perls, Hefferline and Goodman (1951: xi) said, 'the whole determines the parts'; if you are part of the field it impacts you and you impact it.

The existential philosophy roots come from Kierkegaard, Sartre and Heidegger with their themes of personal responsibility, freedom and authenticity. In relational terms Buber's philosophy of dialogue based on I–Thou connection, taken later into the therapeutic relationship as the dialogical method, was also influential. Phenomenology, which grew out of existentialism, advocates the value of staying as closely as possible to here-and-now data, rather than interpreting or judging it. In fact, Perls called Gestalt the 'psychology of the obvious'.

Description, says Clarkson (2004: 4), is more important than interpretation. What this means in practice is an emphasis on descriptive rather than evaluative feedback and an honouring of the coachees' own words, meanings and subjective experience. It calls on the coach to be observant of the body language and energetic presence of their client, fully attend to emotional needs as they arise and be aware of the contact (connection) issues within the relationship. Intrinsic to this approach is that the coach needs to focus on his/her own subjective experience and share this appropriately as part of an authentic dialogue. This sharing of the coach's interior and exterior world in the service of the client is known as *the use of self*.

THE GESTALT PERSPECTIVE OF HUMAN FUNCTIONING

Gestalt is a needs-based approach to understanding human functioning and behaviour. Through effective self-regulation people gratify needs and eliminate tensions. At the physical level this is self-evident. As a need such as hunger emerges it becomes an increasingly dominant *figure* against the background (*ground*) of that person's experience. This produces a state of temporary imbalance until that need is met, when it then dissipates with a consequent withdrawal of interest and energy. This process was first described in Goldstein's (Hall & Lindzey, 1957) research where he offered the concept of *organismic self-regulation.* According to Goldstein there is a biological law of balance inherent in human nature and we are programmed to move towards the best form possible to find that balance.

Melnick and Nevis (2005) acknowledge the contribution that Goldstein's work made to our understanding of self-regulation as primarily a physiological process focusing on survival and self-preservation, and differentiate it from another important Gestalt concept, *creative adjustment.* This is the notion that we are always seeking to do the best we can in any given circumstances to meet our needs, find solutions to our problems, achieve our goals and derive satisfaction from our lives. Through creative adjustment Melnick and Nevis (2005: 22) suggest that 'change can happen quickly and permanently'.

MAIN ASSUMPTIONS AND BELIEFS

Underpinning all Gestalt-based work is the following set of core assumptions and beliefs:

- Gestalt practitioners believe that *people are always doing the best they can* (Melnick & Nevis, 2005: 13). This belief emanates from the Gestalt perspective of resistance as a meaningful and healthy act when understood from the position of the so-called resistor. Indeed, the Gestalt concept of *creative adjustment* is founded in the belief that people make the best decisions and alter behaviour towards the best outcomes available *within* the external constraints and their own perceptions of what is possible at that time. With this in mind Gestalt can be seen as a positive psychology.
- The Gestalt theory of change, the *paradoxical theory of change* (Beisser, 1970), states that change occurs when one is fully in contact with 'what is', the truth of our experience, rather than trying to be different or disowning parts of ourselves. We must become our truth first before we can move from it. In translating this for the coach, Siminovitch and Van Eron (2006: 52) say, 'A fundamental intervention in Gestalt coaching is to sharply focus attention on what already exists for the client in the present, with the paradoxical result of initiating a profound experiential shift towards something new'. As a consequence of this theoretical perspective the skills and methods are used to support the client to get in contact and stay in contact with 'what is'. *Contact,* a core construct in Gestalt, is defined by Stevenson (2004: 5) as 'the psychological process whereby I allow myself to meet my self (as in memories and imagination); to meet a person, group, or organization; or to meet the environment: a sunset … and I can most effectively make such contact by staying present-centred'.
- A fundamental premise of all Gestalt-based work is that through heightened *awareness* people can more readily organize themselves into new ways of seeing, choosing and acting. Out of this awareness we energize ourselves and take actions that lead to the achievement of important goals. In completing these cycles we assimilate learning as well as gain closure around issues. Implicit in this assumption is that we may not attain our goals if they are based on impoverished awareness.
- In rejecting the notion of 'objective reality' Gestaltists consider the idea of 'multiple realities' to be more useful. By valuing multiple perspectives and realities people can be taught how to minimize conflict by welcoming differences and using them creatively.
- Behaviour can be strategic, meant to achieve a goal, or intimate, intended to enhance connection among people. These ways of relating need to be balanced differently in accord with the nature and function of each relationship.

- Individual behaviour cannot be fully understood without reference to its context. Each situation contains its own dynamic, requiring the coach to appreciate systems and levels beyond the individual. This is known as the *field perspective*.
- The power of *unfinished business* drains energy, focus and motivation and holds us back from fulfilling our potential and seeking out new possibilities existing in our current situation. Our unfinished situations may block us from opening ourselves to the awareness of those possibilities.
- The exploration of here and now, immediate experience, provides opportunities for learning and growth. This accounts for the classic Gestalt question, 'What are you aware of now?'

DISTINCTIVE FEATURES

As Saner (1999: 6) puts it, 'one of the distinguishing features of Gestalt is its emphasis on the role that awareness plays in achieving effective behaviour and a healthy way of life'. Gestalt focuses on the individual's (or system's) experience in the present moment, the environmental context or 'field' in which this takes place and the self-regulating adjustments people make as a result of the overall situation. The Gestalt coach is interested in how their client meets or fails to meet their needs and assists them to better understand their own process, especially their styles of relating and their habitual thinking and behavioural patterns. This emphasis on awareness as the change agent means that the Gestalt coach needs to facilitate heightened awareness.

Carter (2004) identifies practitioner identity and the effective use of self as the key determinants of the master practitioner. To this I would add the capacity to use the Cycle of Experience (Figure 5.1) as the orienting framework for appreciation of process issues and as the basis for intervention decisions. For the coachee to experience the support they require for deeper, reflective work, the coach also needs the capacity to build trust, respect and connection. It is generally acknowledged that the quality of the coaching relationship is a critical factor in successful coaching outcomes. With these notions in mind I now offer a framework for Gestalt coaching practice, whether or not this is practised in the organizational context (Table 5.1).

Table 5.1 A framework for Gestalt coaching practice

Defining features	Guiding theoretical perspectives
A focus on *the need-fulfilment process* – how we satisfy (or not) needs, achieve closure around issues, assimilate learning, and achieve desired goals	The Cycle of Experience
	Interruptions to contact
A focus on how to use self	Presence and the intentional use of self as instrument of change
A focus on the coaching relationship	Authentic dialogue

A. THE NEED-FULFILMENT PROCESS

The Cycle of Experience as the orienting framework

The Cycle of Experience is the Gestalt model for understanding how we satisfy (or not) our needs and achieve closure around issues. It is the primary orienting framework for a

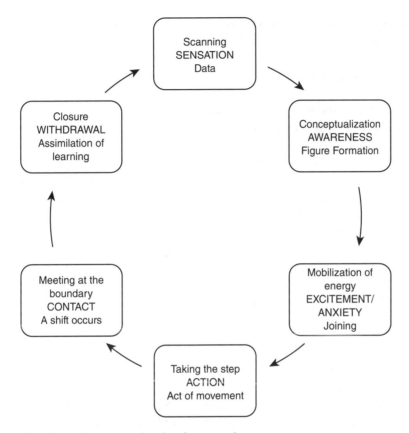

Figure 5.1   Cycle of experience as orienting framework

Source: Adapted from Siminovitch and Van Eron (2006)

Gestalt-oriented coach providing a reference point for tracking what Siminovitch and Van Eron (2006: 53) call 'the natural and ongoing experiential processes of need-fulfilment at any level of system'. It equally helps the coach identify where people and systems may be stuck, providing clues as to how to intervene. The Cycle of Experience is typically represented as a staged process (Figure 5.1), beginning with sensation, moving through awareness and energy mobilization to action and contact, producing resolution, closure and withdrawal of interest.

For the most part people complete Cycles of Experience in an uncomplicated way, especially when it comes to meeting their physical needs. I qualify this with the words 'for the most part', because even at the physical level we do not always engage in a healthy flow. Sometimes, for very good reasons, we cut corners with ourselves and go without sufficient food, sleep, exercise or relaxation.

The process can be far more complex at the social, emotional and spiritual levels. A very common emotional 'figure' in the workplace is the issue of inclusion, yet many people go through prolonged periods feeling devalued, ignored or sidelined by a boss or the organization. When this happens their energy can be stuck in a negative focus leading to self-defeating activity. This is known as an unfinished situation or 'unfinished business'.

Interruptions to contact. So, what gets in the way of completing cycles? The following *interruptions to contact* are sometimes presented as forms of unconscious resistance but may be more usefully understood as aspects of creative adjustment. From this perspective there is a positive dimension although they can also limit our capacity to make strong, lasting and authentic contact.

Gestalt theory identifies four major interruptions to contact – *introjection, retroflection, projection and confluence.* They connect and interrelate in complex and important ways, particularly introjection and retroflection, which have marked relevance for the coach.

Introjection refers to the process of 'swallowing' whole the beliefs, attitudes, values and edicts of significant others. This especially happens in early life and many of these introjections are useful, even necessary if an individual is to become adequately socialized into the norms of their culture. When parents tell their children not to put their fingers into an electrical power socket they want this to be introjected. At the societal level, there are countless norms which nations need their citizens to introject – driving on the correct side of the road being a simple example. Companies seek to instil values and behaviours in their staff – customer service and continuous improvement, for example, and working with the leadership agenda and corporate values.

The negative consequences of introjection occur when internalized 'shoulds' and 'should-nots', 'oughts' and 'ought-nots' prevent people from being able to seek and achieve satisfaction of personal needs. The young girl who grows up with the message 'put others first', may struggle to assert her own needs in adult life. She may hardly allow herself to recognize her own needs. When asked by her coach, 'What is it you want from your life?' or 'Where do you want your career to go?' this woman is likely to look perplexed and reply 'I really don't know. I don't often think about those kinds of things'.

A far-reaching implication of introjection is that we never fully know how much, or little, of what we think and believe about the world is undigested material from our pasts – a recycling of other people's views, opinions and mental frameworks. From this perspective the developmental aspect of coaching is about the coachee's sense of purpose and helping them to discover what they really think and believe, what they want from their work and wider life, and who they really are and want to be. As they proceed on their journey they will probably decide to hold on to much of what they introjected, but from the knowledge that they have examined it and made it their own. They may equally cast off or re-evaluate some previously held truths.

Retroflection means to turn inward upon oneself. We retroflect when we believe it would be unwise, even dangerous, to speak or act out what we inwardly wish to say or do. We perceive that there is simply too little support and safety to do otherwise. In the workplace people retroflect to protect their careers or for political reasons on such a regular basis that it can become a behavioural norm.

Working in the organizational context coaches are regularly confronted with retroflection. Whether their work is with individuals, training groups, teams or the entire system they cannot avoid retroflection. Bottling up of unexpressed views and feelings can be understood as an example of creative adjustment. We may wish to avoid hurting the other person, it may be a bad time, or the individual is simply unavailable to deal with directly. Retroflection of different or challenging views may be the wisest course of action when there is a real question of what is safe to share in a given context.

However, there are consequences of habitual retroflection. Turning inward what needs to be expressed outwardly can have serious effects on our health and well-being and diminishes the quality of relationships. Instead of being comfortable in the other person's company we either minimize contact, because it's too difficult, or stay in superficial connection.

While retroflection clearly impacts at the individual and relationship level it can also have a critical impact on organizational performance. Individual team members are often caught up in a culture of retroflection where people go through the motions of teamwork and collaboration but at a deeper, more significant level keep their real thoughts and feelings to themselves. This leads to a withholding of energy and full commitment to the enterprise of which they are part. Their behaviour is often interpreted as resistance but from their perspective it is the best course of action. Given these dynamics it's vital that coaches operating in corporate environments understand the nature of organizational power dynamics if they are to intervene effectively.

B. HOW TO USE SELF

Presence and the intentional use of self as instrument of change

From a Gestalt perspective coaches inevitably bring their presence into the coaching situation. The more relevant questions are about how well they understand their presence and what it evokes in others, to what extent it is grounded and integrated, and whether the coach can bring flexibility and intentionality to it.

Presence is not the same as charisma or style which can certainly be aspects of presence but only go part of the way towards capturing it. Our presence emanates from our ways of being and acting in the world. It contributes to whether we attract and interest others; it can also be a critical factor in distancing them or putting them off. It is the source of the coach's capacity to influence and equally it can explain lack of impact. For example, the coach may not be filling their space in a room, perhaps coming through too timidly. This may be due to shutting parts of themselves off from a belief that they do not belong in that arena. The result can be a severe loss of power and the coach may look back with disappointment and regret that they did not establish their presence sufficiently strongly to have impact. Siminovitch and Van Eron (2006: 51) unpack the notion of presence and practitioner identity in the following way: life experiences; an intellectual repertoire; particular skills or strengths as well as weaknesses or vulnerabilities; spiritual values and beliefs; and physical presence itself. Presented in this way it is clear that everyone brings their presence whether or not others see them as charismatic.

From a practitioner perspective the coach needs to appreciate the impact of their signature presence and may need to learn how to use different aspects of self – soft and hard, loud and quiet, strong and mild – to become a more finely tuned instrument of change. One of the best ways coaches gain a deeper appreciation of their presence is through actively seeking feedback from the widest range of sources.

As the coach begins to understand their presence they can develop more assurance and creativity in their interventions. The nature of those interventions will depend on what the coach believes most valuable at the time. The Cycle of Experience, the key orienting model of the Gestalt coach, indicates that much of the early work that establishes the safe foundations for developmental work lies at the awareness-raising stage. Raising awareness is therefore a core competency.

In setting out his main activities of a Gestalt practitioner, Nevis (1987: 57) offers two important pointers to working at the awareness stage of the Cycle:

- Attend, observe and selectively share observations of what you see, hear and feel.
- Attend to your own experience (feelings, sensations, thoughts, etc.) and selectively share these, thereby establishing your presence in doing so.

These direct the coach to what they are noticing in their coachee or client system, in themselves, and the relationship between. The term 'selectively share' is important here and is where the finer art of coaching applies. Well-timed, skilful articulation of observations is the hallmark of the highly accomplished coach. Clumsy, ill-timed interventions can risk the safety, trust and confidence so vital to the working alliance.

Bringing intentionality to coaching interventions also has a tactical dimension. In the early stages of a coaching relationship the presence which most lends itself to awareness-raising can be evocative in nature – one which is softer and leaning towards support. On some occasions with some coachees and corporate cultures this approach may not always be enough or sufficiently valued. A stronger, more provocative presence may be necessary to gain attention. It can be important in these circumstances to alter one's energetic presence in order to match the different energy of the coachee.

C. THE COACHING RELATIONSHIP

Authentic dialogue

We should not underestimate the importance of the coach–coachee relationship in determining coaching outcomes. The relationship is the vehicle through which the coachee stretches and challenges him or herself, goes to their learning edge and, with support, stays there long enough to deepen awareness and learn something. The importance of establishing and maintaining a contactful, trusting connection makes it one of the primary challenges for any coach. From a Gestalt perspective the responsibility for building this lies with both parties and the nature of the connection has certain defining features. Gestalt coaches put themselves into the relationship to be fully present with all that this means – in terms of their strengths and skills, their flaws and vulnerabilities. The Gestalt coaching presence requires what Yontef (2002: 18) describes as '*authenticity, transparency, and humility*'.

Starting from this position the Gestalt coach strives to develop a quality of interaction grounded in inclusion, collaborative partnership, strong contact and a commitment to dialogue. The coach is encouraged to learn the messages from relational Gestalt therapy of the importance of compassion, kindness, empathy and humility. The Gestalt coach works as much from their heart as from their head and gut.

However, this emphasis on supportive, empathic behaviours does not simply mean 'being nice'. There is a time when the most supportive thing a coach can do is bring a tough, challenging presence. Coachees can be complex, confusing, frustrating, irritating and downright disingenuous. There will be occasions when it seems impossible to reach and make connection with the coachee. These are the times when the coach's commitment to 'unconditional positive regard' will be most severely tested. The clue here is in the word authenticity; to be authentic requires honesty. When the coach steps too far back from that he/she will not be fully present or available to engage in genuine dialogue.

Implicit in the Gestalt relational approach is the notion that the coach as well as the coachee will be changed by the work undertaken together. The coach should expect to be moved and impacted by the process. The coachees' story, their struggles, their joys and their pain will touch you and remind you of your own. The very nature of the dialogue requires this openness to meeting at the boundary, where the coachee may never have been before, especially in a professional environment.

Dialogue moves beyond discussion when what Buber referred to as the I–It relationship is transformed into I–Thou connecting. When we are related to as an 'It' we feel like an object. When we are related to as 'Thou' we experience our personhood. The contact becomes more real, immediate and interesting. The challenge then for the Gestalt coach is to get into contact with their coachee, work with the emerging process, and let go of the need for certainty and control. This involves what Yontef (2002: 18) calls 'surrendering to the between', that which is co-created by both coach and coachee. Allan and Whybrow (2007: 136) describe how the attention to the relationship and the spirit of enquiry means that something new can emerge that was not in the minds of either party when the dialogue started. It is in this potentially very creative way that something completely appropriate for the current situation is generated.

It is here that we capture the essence of Gestalt: that the *whole can be greater than the sum of the parts*. If the coach is genuinely engaged in the experience there will be learning and growth available for them also. If the coach stays firmly in control and is unable to surrender to the 'in between' then opportunities for learning will be missed and the message to the coachee is that coaching is a one-way learning process. The implications of the Gestalt relational approach may present as intriguing and exciting with the possibility of a high level of practitioner satisfaction. That is undoubtedly true but the approach can also be daunting. To be appropriately transparent to others and present oneself in a genuine manner requires a good deal of personal courage as well as comfort in one's own skin. It may seem far easier and safer to hide behind the protection of the expert role.

All this probably points to the best-fit coaching clients for a Gestalt approach. They are likely to be relational and reflective by nature with a healthy interest in their interior as well as exterior worlds and not overly needy of structure and certainty.

METHODS AND TECHNIQUES

Creative experimentation

Known as 'experiments', these Gestalt exercises are designed to explore the coachee's experience through active, behavioural or imaginative expression, in addition to thinking aloud and conversational discourse. The aim of an experiment is to increase and expand awareness and insight. They can also provide a channel for release of emotion.

Many people are aware of the Gestalt two-chair exercise though the formulaic nature of this process runs counter to the spirit of the experiment. Gestalt experiments always begin with an idea and an invitation. They are invented in the moment through a creative process of dialogue between the coach and the coachee and with their contracting-in and acceptance. This co-creation of the experiment frees up the client to take the initiative. Experiments stimulate experiential learning and the best experiments are a product of imagination and intuition and can utilize metaphor, fantasy, visualization and symbolism.

Experiments can be used in one-to-one coaching and are frequently used in group situations such as workshops and team development processes.

The focus on the here and now

Gestalt is a present-centred approach. If we are interested in helping people become more conscious of themselves and others, then this requires a focus on the here and now. Figure formation, awareness and contact all occur in the present. Making new choices, taking significant decisions and creating new solutions happen in the Now. Discovering what we want and need happens in the Now.

This is not to deny the importance of past events. Indeed one of Gestalt's contributions is the understanding of unfinished business from the past and how we can work with it. From a Gestalt perspective, however, what is important is not the past event per se; rather what effect it is having in the present situation. If, for example, I have had a negative experience with a previous boss which I was unable to gain closure around, then I may treat my current boss with distrust and keep my distance. By increasing my awareness in the present moment I may discover and learn more about how my current behaviour has echoes of my past. My behaviour becomes more meaningful to me and I recognize that actually my boss is quite a different individual, the circumstances are now significantly different, and I do not need or want to replay an old pattern. Awareness in the Now produces the possibility of behaviour change going forwards. In Gestalt practice the focus is on whatever is going on right now, either with an individual client, between the members of a group or team, within the coach and between the coach and the client. We can describe this as current reality.

The coach encourages the client (individual or group) to become curious, interested in and aware of, their own process. This is most obviously achieved by asking questions which raise awareness. Examples would be: 'What are you aware of right now?'; 'What do you notice in yourself and others?'; 'What do you want to know or ask here and now?'; 'What do you want?'; 'How will you go about getting what you want?'; 'What is happening for you right now?' All these questions have some common factors. The first is that they are 'how' and 'what' questions. 'Why' questions tend to take people into explaining and justifying themselves which may not lead to heightened awareness and contact. The second is that they are present tense. They are located in the Now and are likely to produce more direct contact with immediate thoughts, feelings and needs.

In addition to asking questions it is helpful to prefix statements by the pronouns 'I' and 'you'. In groups, group members may refer to someone else in the room as he, she, him or her rather than speaking directly to the person and using the pronoun 'you'. This can leave the person feeling as if they do not exist. Another outcome is that it keeps things more psychologically distant. The other person is at arms length – outside the range at which meaningful contact can happen. When this type of communication occurs it rarely engages people. It can produce an uneasy feeling that someone is being made invisible, an Object, an 'It'.

Groups and individuals who are rarely asked the sorts of questions listed above such as 'What are you aware of now?' will sometimes experience some initial confusion. They feel that they have been put on the spot – asked for an answer that they do not seem to have. Part of the reason for this is that they go looking for a deep and meaningful motivation which must lie behind the question. They over-complicate it, instead of noticing the obvious, which is right there in front of them. They embark on a futile mission of trying to discover what lies under the stone rather than what is sitting on the stone. Awareness training then becomes part of the process – helping people use their full range of senses in the here and now. The Gestalt practitioner acts as an educator and guide in awareness-raising.

If we view Gestalt from the perspective of 'method' then the capacity to work in the here and now is an essential aspect. For many coaches-in-training and more experienced practitioners, this may be a critical area of development.

APPLICATION

In a very real sense Gestalt principles and methods underpin all coaching and mentoring practice because *all good coaching and mentoring is based on raising awareness as the starting point for learning and change*. In that sense every coach can benefit from a certain amount of Gestalt training and Gestalt-based coaching can be used in all coaching contexts.

That said, there are reasons why some contexts will be more appropriate than others. *The manager as coach* asked by his/her company to adopt more of a coaching style of management, will at best receive a short training in coaching skills, usually two to five days in duration. It will probably focus around a coaching model such as GROW and involve a limited amount of practice. The internalizing of a Gestalt informed conceptual and methodological framework in such a short developmental timeframe is unrealistic and is therefore rarely used in this context.

We should notice however that the R in GROW stands for Reality and is the equivalent to the 'What is' in Gestalt. The Gestalt contribution to coaches using the GROW model would be to raise awareness more fully before rushing to Options and Wrap-up. Furthermore, the growing appreciation that line management coaching is less to do with coaching 'sessions' and more with in-the-moment coaching 'conversations' indicates that the here and now' awareness-raising focus of Gestalt has a great deal of applicability in everyday, anytime coaching encounters.

The best-fit contexts for a Gestalt coaching approach may be *executive/leadership coaching, developmental coaching and team coaching*. Coaches operating in these contexts often bring previous relevant training and development, which prepares them for working in this way. A significant proportion of executive coaches come from psychological, psychotherapeutic or counselling backgrounds where they may have already undertaken a primary or secondary level of Gestalt education.

These coaching contexts also tend to give the coach longer to work with their coachee or client system (team). This is important to the Gestalt coach because it provides the opportunity to more deeply understand the coachees' process, gain a better sense of their habitual behavioural and ideational patterns, and explore how these serve them well and how they interfere with the achievement of their goals. This is equally true in the team context where suboptimal group dynamics, team norms and behaviours may be blocking high performance.

EVALUATION

The key strengths lie in the optimism, directness and power inherent in the Gestalt approach. Organizational life, indeed life in general, forces people to address an increasing level of complexity and chaos. Leaders and managers often experience prolonged periods of anxiety and stress from living life in the executive fast lane. They have to dig deep into their capacity to self-support. This can challenge their capacity to stay optimistic, positive and healthy. They can get stuck in negative spirals for prolonged periods yet hardly appreciate the effect on their own well-being, let alone on their colleagues and close ones. The freeing up of that energy, releasing the person from being trapped in unfinished business or redundant ways of seeing and acting can be nothing short of liberating and life-enhancing.

To work in a Gestalt way the coach needs to adopt a positive, optimistic, supportive stance and offer what Siminovitch and Van Eron (2006: 51) call 'a safe arena where vulnerability, strong emotions and failure can play themselves out in the service of learning and growth'. Finding such a place for deeper reflection and self-disclosure is rare for business leaders who typically believe that they must remain self-contained and on guard.

Nonetheless, the Gestalt method will be counter-cultural for some clients. The deceptively simple yet profound notion that awareness itself leads to change, and that change happens just by paying attention to 'what is', rarely forms part of a coachees' mental model. Executives may be sceptical of it and impatient to see proof. If they do not see it quickly they can lose interest and commitment. Some managers and leaders operating in fast-paced, numbers-driven business environments may not be the natural client group for Gestalt coaching. Awareness-focused work may seem just too slow for them. This type of client also tends to see results only in terms of tangible outcomes and benefits. If the session hasn't produced a concrete action plan then it may be dismissed as esoteric or subtle.

There are occasions in coaching when the coachees' presenting issues could suggest a therapeutic response. Well-trained and supervised coaches understand that in these moments, despite any glaring therapeutic issues facing them, they need to resist the clinical invitation. Though the Gestalt coach may sometimes chose to step back from more intensive personal growth work, the Gestalt approach nevertheless offers great scope for satisfaction in the role. The emphasis on Presence and the Use of Self as Instrument invites the coach to bring himself or herself more fully to what they do. This is not a method that asks the coach to learn a set of tools and techniques to use on someone else. From a Gestalt perspective, awareness is the most powerful instrument of change.

With this comes the hard and disciplined part. If coaches are going to intentionally use presence to intervene more effectively, then they have to understand more about who they are and what they bring to the coaching encounter. The critical issue here is the self-development work that this requires. While many coaches recognize this and proactively search out the kinds of places that provide a vehicle for their own learning and growth there are those who back off from the journey. The Gestalt approach may not appeal to them because they can see that it takes a long time, and perhaps some pain along the way, to gain mastery.

Gestalt theory is an eclectic mix of old and new concepts and beliefs. It draws on philosophy, psychology and humanistic psychotherapy to create a broad canvas onto which the practitioner can bring their own unique style and creativity. Because Gestalt is not formulaic or prescriptive the approach is always in a state of emergence as new generations make their own mark in response to the ever-changing field and the contexts in which they work.

What has been important to me about Gestalt is that its philosophical principles draw on deep wisdom that speaks to a set of truths I recognize for myself. In translating those into my own practice as a consultant and coach I find their simplicity and sophistication speak to others also.

FURTHER READING

Bluckert, P. (2006). *Psychological dimensions of executive coaching*. London: Open University Press. (The only coaching book which focuses on the application of Gestalt principles and methods to the executive coaching context.)

Nevis, E.C. (1987). *Organizational consulting: A Gestalt approach*. New York: Gestalt Institute of Cleveland and Gardner Press. (The definitive book on how Gestalt can be applied to organizational consulting.)

Perls, F.S., Hefferline, R.F., & Goodman, P. (1951). *Gestalt therapy*. New York: Julian Press. (The 'bible' of Gestalt therapy and an essential read for all those wanting to gain a fuller appreciation of Gestalt.)

DISCUSSION QUESTIONS

- How do you relate to the Gestalt core assumptions and values?
- What are the best ways to facilitate heightened awareness in self and others?
- How can we skilfully enhance contact in one–one and group situations?
- When we use our self in the coaching relationship what is appropriate/inappropriate to share and disclose?

REFERENCES

Allan, J. & Whybrow, A. (2007). Gestalt coaching. In S. Palmer & A. Whybrow (Eds), *Handbook of coaching psychology.* London and New York: Routledge.

Beisser, A.R. (1970). The paradoxical theory of change. In J. Fagan & I.L Shepherd (Eds), *Gestalt therapy now* (pp. 77–80). New York: Harper and Row.

Bluckert, P. (2006). *Psychological dimensions of executive coaching.* London: Open University Press.

Carter, J. (2004). Carter's cube and a Gestalt/OSD toolbox: A square, a circle, a triangle, and a line. *OD Practitioner,* Special Issue *36*: 4.

Clarkson, P. (2004). *Gestalt counselling in action.* London: Sage.

Farrands, B. (2012). A Gestalt approach to strategic team change. *OD Practitioner, 44*(4).

Hall, C.S. & Lindzey, G. (1957). *Theories of personality.* New York: John Wiley and Sons.

Latner, J. (1992). The theory of Gestalt therapy. In E.C. Nevis (Ed.), *Gestalt therapy: Perspectives and applications.* New York: Gestalt Institute of Cleveland and Gardner Press.

Melnick, J. & Nevis, S.M. (2005). The willing suspension of disbelief: Optimism. *Gestalt Review, 9*: 10–26.

Nevis, E.C. (1987). *Organizational consulting: A Gestalt approach.* New York: Gestalt Institute of Cleveland and Gardner Press.

Nevis, E.C. Melnick, J., & Nevis, S.M. (2008). Organizational change through powerful micro-level interventions. New York: *OD Practitioner, 40*(3).

Perls, F.S., Hefferline, R.F., & Goodman, P. (1951). *Gestalt therapy.* New York: Julian Press.

Saner, R. (1999). Organisational consulting: What a Gestalt approach can learn from Off-Off Broadway Theater. *Gestalt Review, 3*: 6–21.

Siminovitch, D.E. & Van Eron, A.M. (2006). The pragmatics of magic: The work of Gestalt coaching. *OD Practitioner, 38*(1).

Simon, S. (2009). *Applying Gestalt theory to coaching.* Gestalt International Study Center.

Stevenson, H. (2004). *Paradox: The Gestalt theory of change* (unpublished paper). Retrieved from www.clevelandconsulting group.com.

Stevenson, H. (2008). *Emergence: The Gestalt approach to change* (unpublished paper). Retrieved from www.cleveland consultinggroup.com.

Yontef, G. (2002). The relational attitude in Gestalt therapy. *International Gestalt Journal, 25*(1): 15–35.

6

Existential Coaching

Ernesto Spinelli

Existential theory in general concerns itself with the exploration and clarification of what it is to be a human being and how human beings experience their particular way of being.

Existential coaching explores these same issues from within the focused perspective of those matters related to professional, managerial and leadership development and performance as expressed and lived by individual clients, be they persons or organizations. Most typically, existential coaching seeks to assist clients to clarify the dilemmas that arise when an individual or an organization experience challenges to their continuity, beliefs, values and aspirations and identity as a consequence of personal, professional and interpersonal challenges to their way of being.

Existential coaching, in common with existential theory in general, has no single founder or authoritative source (Yalom, 1980; Spinelli, 2005). It is, more correctly, made up of a confederation of perspectives and practices that have been influenced by, and derived from, a 20th century philosophical approach known as phenomenology. Nonetheless, its multitude of manifestations agree upon a number of key foundational principles (Cooper, 2003). As has been argued elsewhere (Spinelli, 2007), three of these principles are pivotal in delineating existential theory's stance toward the human condition and, as well, are particularly pertinent to existential coaching practice.

A. RELATEDNESS

At its simplest, the principle of relatedness argues that all human beings are always *beings-in-relation* in that we express ourselves through, and are shaped by, an inter-relational grounding or context. Existential theory proposes a view of being that is founded upon a process-like 'flow' of being. It also proposes that human beings' reflective experiences of this 'flow' impose an inevitable act of interpretation which substantiates, structures or 'thing-ifies' this flow such that what is process-like is experienced by us as being predominantly substance-like. In doing so, human beings construct and engage in an interpreted world that appears to be made up of separate and distinct structures. Among these structures, perhaps most notably, is that structure that we label 'the self' (Spinelli, 2005).

Through the principle of relatedness, existential theory challenges a persistent assumption held by Western culture in general: that the self is a self-contained unit, understandable within his or her or its own set of subjectively-derived meanings and behaviours. From the standpoint of relatedness, the problems and concerns presented by coaching clients can no longer be seen as being solely their own, in any exclusively individualistic sense. In like manner, existentially-attuned executive coaching challenges the idea of an organization as being exclusively under-standable within his or her or its own set of subjectively-derived meanings and behaviours.

In sum, relatedness reveals 'the total, indissoluble unity or interrelationship of the individual and his or her world ... in the truest sense, the person is viewed as having no existence apart from the world and the world as having no existence apart from persons' (Valle & King, 1978: 7).

B. UNCERTAINTY

All human beings share various existential qualities or 'givens' of existence: we experience our existence through our bodies and within conditions of time and space; we struggle with and are sustained by the possibilities and limitations of the meanings we construe about any and every facet of our lives; and we maintain hopes and plans and expectations with the awareness that our lives as human beings are temporal and reveal an inevitable movement towards death. At the same time, *how* each of us lives with and gives expression to these universal 'givens' remains unique to each being (Cohn, 1997; Jacobsen, 2007). In many ways, these 'givens' can be considered as certainties of being.

The 'givens' of existence may set the boundaries to who and how and what and when we can be; but within those boundaries there exists an openness of possibilities – and, hence, uncertainty rules. The second principle espoused by existential theory argues that, within the parameters of these 'givens', there exists is an inevitable and inescapable *uncertainty* or incompleteness in any and all of our interpretative reflections on or about self, others and the world in general.

This uncertainty is not just about the realization that the unexpected can and does occur in our lives. Rather, existential uncertainty is a constant feature of living that also permeates what appears as the predictable or habitual in our lives. This uncertainty acts as a continual reminder that no one of us can ever fully know with complete and final certainty what and how the world will be, or others will be, or even 'I' will be, in any given set of circumstances. Common statements such as 'I never thought I would act like that'; or 'She just can't make sense of what's going on in the world any longer'; or 'This organization has made all the right changes but still doesn't seem to be able to achieve its goals' point us to positions that at least temporarily acknowledge the inevitable uncertainties of being.

C. EXISTENTIAL ANXIETY

Anxiety, from an existential perspective is the ongoing and unavoidable felt experience that arises as a consequence of relational uncertainty. Existential anxiety refers first to the uneasy experience accompanying the awareness of the ultimate incompleteness or openness of all our reflective interpretations – including, of course, all of those interpretations that serve to define and maintain 'the self'. Second, existential anxiety also refers to the inevitable unease and insecurity that arises when we attempt either to deny, or claim to have resolved or set aside, the dilemma of this openness – not least, for example, when we attempt to 'capture' self (and other) into fixed categories, typologies, characteristics and behaviours.

Existential theory argues that anxiety permeates *all* reflective experience. However, rather than being only or necessarily a debilitating, disruptive or problematic presence that must be reduced or removed, this anxiety can also be stimulating, can put us in touch with our sense of being alive, and is the source to all creative and original insight and decision making. The dilemma raised by existential anxiety is not so much *that* it is, but rather *how* each of us 'lives with' it.

Taken together, these three basic principles of relatedness, uncertainty and existential anxiety give shape to a view of human development that, unlike many others adopted by coaches, rejects any straightforward uni-directional perspective or 'growth-model'. Instead, it places human beings within a far more relationally open-ended – and hence uncertain and anxiously-experienced – trajectory whose focus and direction cannot be set or maintained by the individual alone.

DISTINCTIVE FEATURES

Existential coaching adopts a stance that in many profound ways provides the means for a structured critique regarding how contemporary coaching and its aims are predominantly understood and practised. This alternative perspective does not sit easily with a number of current approaches to coaching theory and practice. This challenging view of coaching was recently summarized by Mandic who argued that existential coaching:

> firmly and explicitly challenges the Modernist picture of the individual, which claims that we are composite of a body and mind, or in similar terms, of the material and the mental. This corresponds to an 'inner' and 'outer' way of describing ourselves and to the idea that we are rational subjects striving for autonomy from and control over objects or our environment. In contrast, existential coaching rejects any mechanistic, causally-determined, 'push/pull' picture of the individual. (Mandic, 2012: 21–22)

One consequence of this view is that existential coaching rejects the assumption that coaching can attend to and alter or amend 'parts' of an individual or an organization without such interventions affecting the *whole* of the being in ways which remain currently unpredictable. Instead, existential coaching's primary focus is on the client's *worldview* – which is to say, the whole range of beliefs, values, attitudes, assumptions, affects, feelings and behaviours that make up, maintain and identify a person's or organization's 'way of being'. Through this focus, existential coaching proposes that the concerns presented by clients are not to be seen as alien obstacles to the maintenance of the current worldview, but rather as consequential expressions of it.

Further, existential coaching rejects the view that a perceived issue, concern, block, or disorder should be seen as being *solely* problematic and instead proposes that expressions of dissonance, limitation and disorder may well also be crucial to the continued – and desired – maintenance of the client's current worldview. While by no means dismissive of problem- or solution-focused interventions, existential coaching urges patience and caution in providing such without first considering the impact upon the worldview arising from the removal or reduction of such concerns and issues. Not to do so might well generate unhelpful solutions that do not sufficiently address the primary concerns being raised for that particular client. Equally, although the solutions provided may well minimize or remove presenting problems, their very removal or reduction may bring to light far more disquieting concerns.

In taking such stances, existential coaching shifts the focus of coaching in various ways. For one, it is much more concerned with the descriptive investigation of *how it is to be in a given set of relational circumstances* and *conditions* than it is with any interventions centred upon directive change. In this sense, existential coaching is more akin to research enquiry focused on understanding than it is with the coach's directive attempts to provide novel ways for the client to be and to do. As Mandic states:

> [for many approaches, their coaching attitude] prioritizes the *epistemological* (knowing how to, or knowing what to do) over the *ontological* (how we are being); the existential position takes the ontological as fundamentally prior and therefore necessary to the coaching framework. (Mandic, 2012: 22)

Unlike a good number of coaching perspectives that emphasize broadly positive, self-actualizing possibilities for clients, existential coaching recognizes and gives equal emphasis to the divided stances, aims and aspirations that may well exist as competing values and beliefs which express the client's worldview. In general, existential theory argues that the client's experience of 'what and how it is for me to exist' is rarely entirely complete, coherent or consistent. Instead it reveals 'a complex combination of opposites, some reconcilable, others incapable of being resolved or harmonised' (Cherniss, 2006, as cited in Gray, 2006: 21). This foundational stance is well summarized as a warning of sorts to coaches by Bluckert: 'Many ... coaches begin with a strong tendency to look for the solution to the client's problem in the external reality – the outer game. They eagerly race towards a practical set of actions before fully understanding the complexities of the issue in the first place' (Bluckert, 2006: 48).

Perhaps most centrally, the expertise most associated with existential coaching is that of *un-knowing* (Spinelli, 1997, 2007). Un-knowing refers to that attempt on the part of the coach to remain as open as possible to what presents itself in the coaching relationship and to treat the seemingly familiar, assumed to be understood or understandable, as novel, unfixed in meaning and, hence, accessible to previously unexamined possibilities. The attempt to 'un-know' directs both the coach's and the client's primary focus to 'what is there' as opposed to 'what once might have been there' or 'what may one day be there'. Further, it challenges the technical authority of the coach as well as the client's own demands to be the recipient of that authority. Although the stance of un-knowing may, for some coaches, seem unusual or even antithetical to the coaching enterprise, various views expressed by coaches from differing traditions are in close agreement. For example, Lee (2003) has written on leadership coaching that 'the creation of a learning space depends on a particular quality of the coach that we might describe as "not knowing" ... the coach's capacity for openness, reflection, questioning, wondering and entertaining possibilities ... a willingness to stay with the uncertainties without reaching prematurely for fact or reason' (Lee, 2003: 63).

In adopting this stance of un-knowing, the whole focus of existential coaching centres upon what is taking place *directly* between coach and client. This focus serves to expose and clarify *in the immediacy of the current coaching relationship* the self-same interrelational issues that clients experience within their wider world relations. In other words, from the standpoint of existential theory, the coaching relationship is seen to be the 'microcosm' which both explores and expresses the 'macrocosm' of the client's currently lived experience (Cohn, 1997; Spinelli, 1997, 2001; Strasser & Strasser, 1997). This view is only just beginning to be addressed by coaching in general. Coaches have tended to be somewhat reluctant, if not unwilling, to bring explicitly this key assumption within existential coaching into their discourse and interventions with their clients. Nonetheless, this reluctance has recently been challenged by the Bluckert, who has written: 'the very dynamics occurring in the coaching relationship may be a mirror image of clients' experiences in their workplace relationships and they may be completely unaware of it' (Bluckert, 2006: 48). In other words, in avoiding or minimizing the significance of their own presence in the coaching relationship, those coaches who remain naive to its impact and usefulness inadvertently bestow considerable weaknesses and limitations upon their enterprise.

METHODS AND TECHNIQUES

Existential coaching offers a particular way of addressing and working with the inescapable tensions and paradoxes that make up the human experience of being. Specifically, it assists clients in looking again at the presenting concerns or aspirations they have brought to coaching from the standpoint of *conflictual worldview polarities.*

The worldview reveals a system of dynamic, intersecting polarities. Typical among these are polarities such as: good/bad; acceptance/rejection; trust/suspicion; control/letting go; risk/security; action/stasis; reason/intuition; intellect/emotion; and attachment/separation (Spinelli, 2007).

A worldview stance locates itself either at each extreme of any polarity or, more commonly, somewhere between these (such as at the mid-point of the continuum or closer toward one extreme or the other). Following the pioneering work of the American existential therapist, Rollo May, existential coaching explores the dilemmas presented by coaching clients as *challenges that have provoked polarity disturbance within the currently maintained worldview* (May, 1994). The shift in worldview polarity location provokes a (usually temporary) sense of dislocation that can be experienced as either stimulating or disquieting. In either case, what is being experienced is conflict within the worldview. Those conflicts that we experience as stimulating suggest our willingness to restructure or reconstitute one or more aspects of our current worldview. Alternatively, events or circumstances that are experienced as undesirable or threatening challenges to the currently maintained worldview provoke attempts to avoid, minimize or deny the challenges that arouse the felt experience of conflict and thereby protect the current worldview.

The exploration and clarification of conflictual worldview polarities highlights the existential contention that to associate issues of conflict *solely* with experiences of debilitation and disorder is far too limiting a perspective for coaches to take. The felt experience of unease, disturbance and tension which is so characteristic of conflict can be as much the source point for creativity, possibility, novelty and engagement as it might be about distress and suffering. As such, conflict is neither 'good' nor 'bad', 'positive' nor 'negative' in and of itself. Like so much else expressive of human experience, it is the particular stance adopted toward the focus point of the conflict which determines the degree to which the conflict is experienced as being constructive or destructive (Spinelli, 2007).

Considering all of the above from a coaching standpoint, what on the surface may appear to be the *same* source of challenge, will be experienced in uniquely differing ways ranging from debilitating disturbance to creative and liberating possibility. It is only by considering the relationship between that challenge and any *particular* worldview that the specific impact of that challenge can be discerned. While it is the case that all polarity challenges provoke the worldview, existential coaching argues that in order for the coach to assist clients as adequately as possible, it is critical to clarify the *specific and unique* meaning and felt experience of that challenge.

In addition, existential thought highlights two significantly different conditions that can generate conflict, namely conditions of dissonance (dissonant conflict) and conditions of consonance (consonant conflict).

Dissonant conflict arises from challenges that provoke the experience of a lack of fit, or tension, or contradiction in the currently maintained worldview. The following are two examples of dissonant conflict:

(a) David insists that he is an inspirational leader in his management team, but he constantly has to find new members for his team to replace those who resign on grounds that highlight various limitations in his leadership skills and qualities.
(b) Organization X presents itself as a leader in change but is deeply resistant to novel possibilities in management.

In each example, a dissonance between the maintained worldview and actual lived experience provokes the conflict. Dissonant conflict can only be resolved through the re-constitution of the worldview. For example,

(a) David comes to accept that his view of himself as an inspirational leader is inadequate. Instead, it is more accurate for him to state that he might be so some of the time but that equally there are times when he is anything but inspirational to others.
(b) Organization X acknowledges that its view of itself as a leader in change is currently inadequate and sets about re-organizing its management structure so that it is more in keeping with its philosophy.

Consonant conflict arises from challenges that reveal previously unforeseen or insufficiently considered aspects of a currently maintained worldview. Unlike *dissonant conflict*, which reflects a lack of fit with lived experience, *consonant conflict* originates from the unexpected or undesired implications that come with the continuing maintenance of a particular worldview. Consonant conflict may be disorienting and undesirable, but it emerges as a consequence of its consistency and compatibility with the currently maintained worldview. The following are two examples of consonant conflict:

(a) Margaret considers it essential that she, as team leader, demands what she refers to as 'brutal honesty' from all members of her team, as well as herself, so that, together, they will produce the very best results for her company. At the same time, her maintenance of this demand makes Margaret feel alone, or isolated or unappreciated or diminished by others.
(b) Organization Y proudly presents itself as a leader in change and sets specific requirements for its management leaders that reflect its change-focused ethos. It emerges that very few desirable managers work well within this ethos and that fewer still are willing to remain associated with the organization.

Consonant conflict, unlike dissonant conflict, cannot be resolved by reconfiguring the worldview – not least because the client will resist all such attempts to do so. Instead, its possible resolution lies in the client's new-found willingness to accept and embrace of the previously unconsidered, unexpected and uneasy consequences that arise from the continued maintenance of the desired worldview. For example:

(a) Margaret realizes that she stands by her view regarding honesty, and while this does not alter her experience of aloneness, isolation and lack of appreciation by others, she discovers a resoluteness that she did not previously appreciate.
(b) Organization Y explores its own attitude to change by investigating what it is about its identity, ethos or structure that may be placing undesirable limits upon its managers. In doing so, possible changes to its overall change-focused ethos are highlighted for consideration.

Many coaches all too often have a tendency to consider and seek the resolution of conflict only from the perspective of dissonant conflict; rarely is consonant conflict given adequate consideration. In taking this position, coaches may, in some instances, inadvertently exacerbate the risk that the attempted 'resolution' of a client's conflict will, instead, generate unexpected and unwanted shifts in anxiety far more debilitating than any being provoked by the presented experience of conflict.

Overall, the existential coach's primary role lies in the attempt to *be with* and *be for* the client. In *being with* the client, existential coaches seek to give expression to their respect for, and acceptance of, their client's worldview as it presents itself in their current encounter. In *being for* their clients, existential coaches express their willingness to attempt a challenging, non-judgemental descriptively-focused exploration of that worldview.

In this dual aim, they seek first to disclose, together with their client, the underlying, often implicit and inadequately acknowledged conflictual worldview polarities which threaten the maintenance of the client's worldview as it is currently construed and expressed. At the heart of this enterprise lies the attempt to ensure their clients' experience of 'being heard' accurately so that in turn clients may begin to hear their own statements more accurately and honestly. This predominantly receptive stance requires on the part of the coach the abdication of such security that comes with assumptions such as directing change or of 'the expert's' superiority of knowledge and status. Further, the adoption of this stance and attitude removes from coaches much of their professional mystique as well as a good deal of the power that may come with it.

Existential coaching neither embraces nor dismisses any particular method or technique available to coaches so long as the technique serves the primary enterprise of a descriptively-focused exploration of the client's worldview from the contextual focus of the client's presenting concerns. Nonetheless, this focus on descriptive exploration requires coaches to develop specific attitudes and skills designed to assist descriptively-focused enquiry. Two such attitudinal approaches can be briefly summarized:

A. THE PHENOMENOLOGICAL METHOD

One particularly useful and powerful way to assist the coach in becoming attuned to the client's worldview as it expresses itself is to apply what has become known as *the phenomenological method* of investigation. This method can be most easily summarized by highlighting three pivotal 'steps' (Ihde, 1986; Spinelli, 2005, 2007).

Step one: Bracketing

This first step urges coaches to set aside their initial biases and prejudices, to suspend expectations and assumptions – in short, to *bracket* all presuppositions regarding the client as far as possible. Instead, coaches are encouraged to attune their focus to 'what presents itself as it presents itself' so that the client's currently lived worldview can be more adequately disclosed and, in turn, so that any subsequent reconstructions of it will fit its meanings and values.

Step two: Description

The second step enjoins coaches to: 'describe, don't explain'. Rather than attempt to immediately analyse or transform the client's concerns on the basis of the coaches' preferred theories or hypotheses, the step of description urges them to remain initially focused on that information which arises from a concretely-based descriptive exploration of the client's worldview. The focus of this step centres more on the elaboration of the 'what and how' of a client's experience than it does on the explanation of its 'why'.

Step three: Horizontalization

The third step further advises coaches to avoid placing any unsubstantiated hierarchies of significance or importance upon the client's statements of experience, and instead to treat each as initially having equal value. It proposes that coaches avoid jumping to conclusions as to what really matters to the client or, indeed, what it may be that the client is seeking to address and resolve. In essence, horizontalization reminds coaches to treat the import and significance of all statements made by clients as being initially unknown to them.

Even from this very brief summary, it should be apparent that each 'step' in the phenomenological method is, more accurately, a particular point of focus rather than an entirely independent activity that can be wholly distinguished from the remaining two. Equally, any attempt to be successful or proficient in the phenomenological method will reveal the impossibility of its fulfilment. Even so, while coaches may be unable to achieve complete bracketing, pure description or total horizontalization, they are certainly capable of attempting each with increasing adequacy and, by so doing, are likely to become more aware of any number of unintended and undesirable biases that dominate their investigations. What is more, this self-same act of bias recognition can invoke for the coach a greater degree of caution in adhering too closely or uncritically to the immediate prejudices that he or she may have imposed upon the investigation from its earliest stages.

B. DESCRIPTIVE QUESTIONING

An extension of the phenomenological method that has been proposed by the present author emphasizes a form of enquiry designed to clarify a client's experience from the standpoints of its *embodiment*, *metaphorical equivalence* and *narrational scene setting* (Spinelli, 2007).

Viewed existentially, many statements made by clients regarding their experiences of someone or of some event (such as 'I'm stuck', 'I'm so angry', 'I'm not sure how to go about fulfilling my potential' and so forth) *suggest* a clear and understandable meaning but are descriptively far too abstract and detached from the client's lived experience of them. Descriptive questioning provokes a more descriptively adequate set of statements regarding the experience and, by so doing, re-awakens their felt experience in the immediacy of the coaching relationship.

In general, descriptive questioning concerns itself with the attempt to clarify clients' relations to their felt experience so that these are more adequately 'owned' by or accessible to them. A brief example should clarify each of these descriptive focus points.

Alice, a senior manager in an international organization, has come to coaching because she wants to explore future directions for her career. She states that she 'feels blocked' and can see nothing in her future that excites or stimulates her.

From the standpoint of *embodiment*, descriptive questioning assists Alice in locating her experience of 'feeling blocked', either in parts or the whole of her body. For instance: 'Where, if anywhere, in her body does she experience "feeling blocked"? What, more precisely, is that feeling? What effect does it have upon the whole or parts of her body? Does it provoke particular statements and emotions?'

From the standpoint of *metaphorical equivalence*, descriptive questioning urges Alice to explore what the experience of 'feeling blocked' is *like* for her. For instance: 'If it were like a shape, an object, a sound, a colour, a song, a statement and so forth, what would it be?'

From the standpoint of *narrational scene setting,* descriptive questioning encourages Alice to focus on specific narrative instances that have provoked her experiences and to recapture their details as though constructing a scene setting. For instance, Alice's most recent experience of being blocked occurred at a meeting with her team. Narrational scene setting encourages Alice to rebuild that scene through the description of such questions as: 'Who was there?' 'Where did they sit or stand?' 'How (in what position) did everyone present sit or stand?' 'What was the room like?' 'What clothes were she and other people wearing?' 'What objects were in the room?' Any specific scene setting can then be compared and contrasted to other scenes in Alice's experience that also provoked feelings of being blocked. Rather than encourage any changes or re-constitutions of such scenes, narrational scene setting, like embodiment and metaphorical equivalence, serves to enhance a descriptive focus that re-connects clients to their experiences in their immediacy and in the presence of their coach.

APPLICATION

It can be argued that the existential approach is amenable to every form of coaching, since all of the concerns relevant to coaching are most usefully explored when considered in relation to the specific context of a person's or organization's worldview. Nonetheless, the approach is particularly useful when working with issues of transition or progression and advancement in work, where dilemmas are often about risks to security and continuity, challenges to beliefs, values and aspirations and re-constituting identity.

In addition, existential coaching may be especially valuable when working with clients who find themselves at a crisis point in their lives, who have come up against a loss of meaning or direction, or who are attempting to cope with sudden and dramatic changes in a variety of professional or personal circumstances. Similarly, those clients who enter a foreign culture (or shift from one organizational culture to another) or who are members of a minority group within a dominant organizational or cultural setting may find existential coaching to be of particular worth.

Recent papers on existential coaching have highlighted its applications in the areas of major life and work decisions (LeBon and Arnaud, 2012), career development (Pullinger, 2012) and leadership development (Jopling, 2012).

In general, those clients who value the reflective, exploratory and challenging qualities of existential coaching are likely to most benefit from it. It is equally likely, however, that some clients will struggle with its emphasis on descriptive exploration rather than prescriptive change or goal setting.

EVALUATION

Overall, existential coaching's emphasis on ontological 'being qualities' and worldview exploration, as opposed to the development and refinement of the coach's 'doing' skills and repertoire, runs counter to both explicit and often implicit assumptions and emphases within coaching as understood by a significant number of its approaches. Whether this divergence will eventually prove to be its greatest strength or weakness remains to be seen. Even so, while existential coaching is undoubtedly less focused upon providing the means for immediate shifts in specific behaviours and performance, its concern to extend clients' understanding of their stance to life and how this stance impacts upon their affects and behaviour is as likely to provoke performance-focused change as is any other model of coaching.

What direct research evidence currently exists for the effectiveness of existential coaching is extremely limited. In part, this is likely due to the currently small number of coaches who have trained sufficiently to practise this approach. Equally, its philosophical assumptions reveal a decidedly different set of principles regarding what constitutes evidence and how such may be examined (Spinelli, 2005). Whether these principles can be 'translated' in order that they may be examined and tested within more commonly assumed criteria also remains, as yet, uncertain. Even so, a recent research paper by Krum has provided some initial data on the effectiveness of existential coaching in reducing work-related stress (Krum, 2012). Utilizing an action research approach, the results indicate 'that existential coaching can be a way of reducing stress by helping clients understand that openness to experience is a way of gaining insight into their need for control' (Krum, 2012: 57).

In addition, clients' self reports related to the outcomes associated with existential coaching are generally highly positive and emphasize the felt sense of a greater congruence with lived experience and through this, a greater clarity regarding aims, values and identity. Within the context of executive and transformational coaching, clients have reported improvements in managing complexity, ambiguity and anxiety as well as a greater degree of personal and interpersonal responsibility.

While it can stand as a model of coaching in its own right, the descriptive focus that is so central to existential enquiry can assist coaches from whatever orientation or model to consider more adequately and more clearly their own stance, and to recognize how they may be confused or uncertain about various basic principles or practices that their model espouses. In short, existential enquiry can assist both coaches and their clients in 'owning' their experiences, approach, values and beliefs so that their concerns can be more adequately explored.

At the same time, existential coaching's emphasis on descriptive inquiry is not for those who prefer 'performance-attuned' input and solutions. As this chapter has attempted to summarize, an existential approach, while initially attractive to many, also demands of coaches a high degree of commitment to a broadly philosophically-attuned mode of thought and practice. While undoubtedly rewarding for some, not all coaches will be drawn to what it offers.

Nonetheless, it is the view of the present author that in locating itself primarily within a predominantly organizational context, coaching (however unwillingly or inadvertently) is also adopting a relationally-attuned or inter-relational perspective akin to that which lies at the heart of existential thought and practice. An increasing number of coaches and coaching trainers have sought to demonstrate that it is this very same inter-relational assumption that provides a baseline grounding in the clarification, challenge and attempted resolution of the issues being brought by coaching clients (Sieler, 2003). Nonetheless, the revolutionary impact of this perspective has not yet been sufficiently addressed nor considered. Existential coaching is currently at the forefront of such explorations and, in the long term, this may well turn out to be its most significant contribution to the advancement of the coaching profession as a whole.

FURTHER READING

There exists, at present, very little literature specifically focused on existential coaching. However, many of the central ideas and practices that would inform existential coaching have been elaborated in writings dealing with existential psychology and therapy. Among these, I would recommend the following to interested readers:

Deurzen, E. van (2001). *Existential counselling and psychotherapy in practice.* London: Sage.
Jacobsen, B. (2007). *Invitation to existential psychology.* Chichester: Wiley.
Spinelli, E. (1997). *Tales of un-knowing: Therapeutic encounters from an existential perspective.* Hay-On-Wye: PCCS Books.
Spinelli, E. (2007). *Practising existential psychotherapy: The relational world.* London: Sage.
These texts have been noted by reviewers as particularly clear and accessible accounts of existential theory. In addition, all provide examples from general life and professional practice to which many coaches can connect both personally and professionally.
Recently, an edited text specifically focused on existential coaching has been published. Some of the papers therein are highly relevant; others seem to me to be somewhat tangential to the approach. As such, I can only offer a cautious recommendation:
Deurzen, E. van & Hanaway, M. (Eds) (2012). *Existential perspectives on coaching.* London: Palgrave Macmillan.

DISCUSSION QUESTIONS

- How do the theoretical underpinnings of existential coaching act as challenges to your own perspective? How would you respond to these challenges?
- Existential coaching argues that the coaching relationship can be best employed when the issues brought by the client are considered within the immediacy of the relationship itself. How would this view impact on your coaching style?
- Existential coaching distinguishes between dissonant and consonant forms of conflict. What examples of each have been noted from your own practice?
- Existential coaching argues that its emphasis on relatedness is of particular relevance to coaching that would take place within organizations. What view do you take? What sort of impact do you think it would have?

REFERENCES

Bluckert, P. (2006). *Psychological dimensions of executive coaching.* Berkshire: Open University Press.
Cherniss, J. (2006). Introduction to *Political ideas in the romantic age: Their rise and influence on modern thought* by I. Berlin. Princeton, NJ: Princeton University Press.
Cohn, H.W. (1997). *Existential thought and therapeutic practice.* London: Sage.
Cooper, M. (2003). *Existential therapies.* London: Sage.
Gray, J. (2006). The case for decency. *New York Review of Books,* LIII (12): 20–2.
Ihde, D. (1986). *Experimental phenomenology: An introduction.* Albany, NY: State University of New York.
Jacobson, B. (2007). *Invitation to existential psychology.* Chichester: Wiley.

Jopling, A. (2012). Coaching leaders from an existential perspective, in E. van Deurzen and M. Hanaway (Eds), *Existential perspectives on coaching*. London: Palgrave Macmillan, pp. 72–83.

Krum, A. N. (2012). How can ideas from the existential approach enhance coaching for people with work-related stress? *International Journal of Evidence Based Coaching and Mentoring*, Special Issue No.6, pp. 57–71.

LeBon, T. & Arnaud, D. (2012). Existential coaching and major life decisions, in E. van Deurzen and M. Hanaway (Eds), *Existential perspectives on coaching*. London: Palgrave Macmillan, pp. 47–59.

Lee, G. (2003). *Leadership coaching*. London: CIPD.

Mandic, M. (2012). Authenticity in existential coaching, in E. van Deurzen and M. Hanaway (Eds), *Existential perspectives on coaching*. London: Palgrave Macmillan, pp. 21–31.

May, R. (1994). *The discovery of being*. New York: Norton.

Pullinger, D. (2012). Career development as a life changing event, in E. van Deurzen and M. Hanaway (Eds) *Existential perspectives on coaching*. London: Palgrave Macmillan, pp. 60–71.

Spinelli, E. (1997). *Tales of un-knowing: Therapeutic encounters from an existential perspective*. London: Duckworth.

Spinelli, E. (2001). *The mirror and the hammer: Existential challenges to therapeutic orthodoxy*. London: Sage.

Spinelli, E. (2005). *The interpreted world: An introduction to phenomenological psychology* (2nd ed.). London: Sage.

Spinelli, E. (2007). *Practising existential psychotherapy: The relational world*. London: Sage.

Strasser, F. & Strasser, A. (1997). *Existential time-limited therapy: The wheel of existence*. Chichester: Wiley.

Valle, R.S. & King, M. (1978). *Existential-phenomenological alternatives for psychology*. Oxford: Oxford University Press.

Yalom, I. (1980). *Existential psychotherapy*. New York: Basic Books.

7

Ontological Coaching

Alan Sieler

Ontology is the study of being, in particular the investigation of the nature of human existence (Honderich, 1995). Ontological coaching focuses on the way of being of clients. Way of being is regarded as central to how people learn, function and change and is considered to be the underlying driver of behaviour and communication, for it is where an individual's perceptual patterns and attitudes exist, many of which can be deep-seated and out-of-awareness. Ontological coaching seeks to respectfully facilitate the transformation of being, which can include deep change, resulting in the client: (i) becoming a very different observer of themself and the world, (ii) making significant behavioural change, including relating more constructively with others and (iii) expanding what is possible in how they can create their future.

Ontological coaching has a robust theoretical basis consisting of four inter-related components. Heidegger's phenomenological analysis of being (Heidegger, 1962, 1971, 1999), supported by Gadamer's approach to hermeneutics (Gadamer, 1994), forms a major philosophical cornerstone of ontological coaching. Maturana's biology of cognition (Maturana and Varela, 1980, 1987) comprises the second part of ontological coaching's theoretical basis, with the work of Wittgenstein (1958), Searle (1969, 1979) and Austin (1973) in the philosophy of language being the third component. The fourth component is provided by philosophical investigations of the body, in particular the writings of Merleau-Ponty (1962) and Dewey (1929).

Flores integrated of the ideas of Heidegger, Gadamer, Maturana and Searle (Winograd & Flores, 1986) to form an initial body of knowledge that has been further developed and is now known as Ontology of the Human Observer (Sieler, 2003).

Within the theory that underpins ontological coaching at least seven premises can be identified:

1. All learning and change happens in the nervous system and coaching seeks to constructively influence change in the structure of the nervous system.
2. Humans exist in three inter-related existential domains of language, emotions and body, which constitute their way of being; what takes place in people's lives occurs in these domains.
3. The dynamic interplay between the three existential domains of language, emotions and body shapes perception and behaviour, and can be equated to the dynamic structure of the nervous system.
4. Humans are self-referencing beings: how the world is viewed and engaged with is always relative to what is important or deeply matters in the world of the individual, i.e. his or her concerns.
5. Humans are relational and conversational beings interacting with the world from their existential domains to take care of concerns.
6. Change occurs through perturbance of the client's habitual ways of thinking and perceiving, which may trigger changes in the domains of language, emotions and body to generate new perceptions and behaviours.
7. Humans are biological-cultural beings with ways of being that always exist in a cultural context, which can be important to consider in the facilitation of change.

DISTINCTIVE FEATURES

The dynamic interplay between language, emotions and body is referred to as the *way of being*. The essential goal of the coach is to be a catalyst for change by respectfully and constructively perturbing the coachee to enable him or her to self-generate constructive new perceptions and behaviours that are consistent with what they want to gain from coaching.

The coaching engagement proceeds through five main phases: (i) the coach being in his or her most resourceful way of being for the client, which includes ensuring deep respect for the client at all times, (ii) conversation for clarity, (iii) conversation for exploration and possibility, (iv) conversation for action and (v) long-term follow-up.

Being in the most resourceful way of being for the client

A primary responsibility of an ontological coach is to manage his or her own way of being in the coaching conversation. The only place he or she can coach from is their own way of being, which will affect how (i) acutely they observe the specifics of the coachee's way of being and (ii) they facilitate potential shifts in the coachee's way of being. For example, prior to a coaching appointment with a senior executive in a major finance corporation, a coach recognized feeling intimidated by the coachee, being anxious and having negative thoughts about being equal to the task of coaching someone so senior in the organization. He could not shift feeling intimidated merely by changing his thoughts, so focused on his body and breathing, adopting a posture and breathing pattern from which he felt competent and confident, practising this as he walked to the appointment and maintaining it during the conversation.

A critical task for the coach is to create a safe environment for inquiry, learning and discovery through a deeply respectful professional relationship with the coachee. This means regarding the coachee as a legitimate other. Two challenges in maintaining a safe environment are:

(i) respectfully initiating a different and potentially sensitive direction in the conversation; and

(ii) the coach not being too attached to his or her ideas of where the conversation 'should go'.

For example, a coachee identified improving self-confidence as the key coaching issue. The coach assessed that the coachee had a negative view of herself (referred to as a core negative self-assessment) that she was not aware of. The coach said, 'Sometimes we get in our own way by having one or more negative opinions about ourselves without knowing this. I'm wondering if you would like to explore whether you do have a negative view of yourself which is holding you back.'

Conversation for clarity

Developing a shared understanding with the client of the issue(s) to be covered and desired coaching outcomes is essential and is central to the contracting arrangement between coach and coachee. In organizational coaching the coachee's manager may also be part of the contracting and evaluation process, as illustrated in the following example. After a conversation with Stella and her line manager, the following coaching outcomes were identified:

1. first and foremost, greater self-confidence and an enhanced sense of self-worth
2. to be more able to deal with, and express, how she is feeling, rather than keep it inside and get to a breaking point
3. to not to take things personally, which is associated with becoming more resilient
4. to have a more strategic mind-set and not be as operationally oriented – to be able to stand back and observe the bigger picture
5. to express her point of view clearly and firmly in meetings, including having another perspective on senior people present at the meeting
6. to delegate and not be caught up in completing the details of various tasks – to know the deliverables required, where they fit in the larger scheme of things and to delegate to others in the team
7. through delegation to gain more from the variety of specialized expertise within her team.

The coach also ensured there was a shared understanding with Stella's manager about observable changes in Stella's behaviour that would be evidence of the fulfilment of the coaching outcomes. These were:

- 'doing less doing', with her team doing much of the detailed work
- asking the appropriate questions – ones that indicated a strategic focus, such as 'How does this relate to the business objectives?'
- being prepared to express well-thought-out 'push-back' or alternative opinions in meetings, especially where more senior personnel were present
- by coping effectively with setbacks, rather than getting down or despondent and dwelling on what 'went wrong', she would move forward to different issues.

After three 90-minute conversations, Stella declared she had gained what she wanted from the coaching, rating her self as 8–9 out of 10 on the issues she presented for coaching, compared with 2–3 at the commencement of coaching. Her manager agreed with Stella's assessments stating, 'The coaching has been a very worthwhile investment'. The significant shift that occurred in Stella's way of being was a combination of (i) eradicating a core negative self-assessment (self-belief), (ii) freeing herself from the debilitating effects of an ever-present mood of anxiety and (iii) developing a postural configuration in which she felt fully worthy and legitimate, and therefore confident, in herself as a person.

Conversation for exploration and possibility

Most of the coaching engagement occurs in this phase as the coach explores the client's way of being. In doing so the coach seeks to respectfully and constructively perturb the client's habitual ways of perceiving themselves and their circumstances to enable different and more helpful perceptions to become available as the basis for more effective behaviour. Important specifics of this phase are provided in the next section on methods and techniques.

Conversation for action

The main benefit of ontological coaching is enabling the coachee to observe and shift aspects of their own way of being beyond the coaching engagement and therefore enhance their behavioural flexibility for future challenges. Conversation for action is about orienting the client to application of what has been learned. For example, in supporting the coachee to confidently and constructively express her thoughts in business meetings, the coach asked three questions about future action:

> How will you cue yourself to notice what is happening in your thinking, emotions and posture during the meeting? How exactly will you make the necessary adjustments that will allow you to say what you want to – will it commence with your breathing and posture or with different thoughts? How will you take the posture, breathing, moods and thoughts to other areas of your life?

Long-term follow-up

This final phase of the coaching engagement involves contacting the client 2–3 months after the formal end of the coaching to inquire about the sustainability of the coaching, specifically if the coachee has successfully applied different perceptions and behaviours, as well offering further support if appropriate.

ESSENTIAL PROCESSES AND DYNAMICS OF ONTOLOGICAL COACHING

An important part of the process of ontological coaching is how the coach uses his or her interpretations of the coachee's way of being. Decisions are continually being made about what interpretations are likely to be most relevant and beneficial for the coachee. Part of working respectfully with the coachee consists of a combination of:

- asking questions to affirm if the interpretations are relevant; for example, 'What would you say is your mood about this situation? Would it be fair to say that this is a negative mood?'
- offering distinctions for the coachee to consider; for example, 'My guess is that you are experiencing a mood of resentment about this situation. Can I explain what I mean and see if you agree?'

An indispensable part of this process is the coach being open and flexible. Sometimes the conversation may move in a certain direction but not proceed far because it does not 'connect' with the coachee, or he or she does not give permission to proceed further. This is why it is essential that the coach is not attached to his or her interpretations and provides the emotional context for the coachee to decline to respond to the coach's initiative. Ontological distinctions are only useful if they 'hit the mark' and speak to something significant for the coachee, providing a new insight or perspective.

The main features of the methodology of ontological coaching will now be outlined, with coaching examples in each of the three domains of language, emotions and body provided to illustrate a range of methods and techniques.

METHODS AND TECHNIQUES

Ontological coaching goes beyond Descartes' conception of being human as 'I think, therefore I am'. From an ontological perspective, human cognition is more than thinking. To consider humans only as thinking beings runs the risk of focusing on the domain of language and not explicitly attending to the equally important domains of emotions and body in the facilitation of learning and change. Although other approaches to coaching are attentive to the importance of emotions (for example, psychodynamic and cognitive behavioural approaches, Gestalt, NLP, positive psychology) and the body (Gestalt, NLP), ontological coaching's methodology is unique in the explicit integration of language, emotions and body.

Language

While all other coaching traditions work in the domain of language, ontological coaching is differentiated from other traditions by (i) the explicit premise that language generates reality and (ii) the unique techniques that operationalise this premise. The main linguistic techniques of ontological coaching are the:

- application of a unique approach to listening as a critical part of language and its central role in generating reality
- utilization of the model basic linguistic acts to facilitate shifts in speaking and listening
- application of a typology of conversations
- moving beyond the subtle, yet powerful, negative affects of cultural–historical narratives.

One of the premises of ontological coaching is that language generates reality. The coach listens for how the coachee is explicitly and implicitly using language, as well as how he or she is not using language. An ontological coach is specifically listening for the following aspects of language: underlying concerns; basic linguistic acts (renaming of speech acts), including core assessments; types of conversations; and cultural–historical narratives.

Underlying concerns and core assessments are the hidden sides of coachees' language, that is, what exists in their listening that is not being articulated. Every issue for coachees is underpinned by something that matters to them – a concern. Heidegger emphasized that although we are always taking care of concerns, we rarely articulate what our concerns are. It can be especially revealing for coachees to understand what is behind their issue. Some specific questions can be helpful to assist them:

- What is at stake for you here?
- What is missing that is important for you?
- What is not being taken care of that matters to you?

The effect of such questions could be illustrated with an example of working with Helen. Her speciality in a pharmaceutical company is sales management; however, eight months prior she was transferred to an unfamiliar marketing management role, and provided with little support to learn the skills and knowledge for her new role. She seemed good-natured about the experience, saying that was part of corporate life, yet the coach assessed she had been putting on a 'happy face' to herself and the company. Asking how she felt about the way she had been treated by the company revealed that she was upset, as tears welled up. Exploration of underlying concerns through the question 'What wasn't taken care of that deeply mattered to you?' resulted in Helen recognizing that her dignity as a person had not been respected. The theme of taking care of her dignity was primarily explored through the domain of moods and emotions and is outlined in the next section.

The utilization of basic linguistic acts, derived from Searle's set of speech acts (Searle, 1969) is a major feature of the coaching methodology, these being: assertions, declarations, assessments (a subset of declarations), requests, offers and promises. An example illustrates the utilization of some of these acts in coaching conversations.

Jake's work team in the oil industry was consistently well short of meeting its weekly targets for the production of different lubricant products, resulting in delays in customer deliveries. Coaching with Jake and the planner who issued the weekly schedule enabled them to see that the weekly schedule was a request and that by not discussing the schedule Jake implicitly accepted it and was making a promise or commitment to deliver the weekly target. As a result of the coaching Jake and the planner met every week to discuss the forthcoming schedule to ensure explicit agreement about the weekly target, which is a particular type of conversation called 'conversation for the coordination of action'.

Core assessments are the fundamental beliefs and values people have about themselves, others, their situations in life and the world in general. They are central to how humans function as linguistic beings, providing an 'internal reality' from which the world is observed. A negative core assessment acts like a prison, closing off possibilities and restricting participation in different aspects of life. While these assessments do not 'announce themselves' the coach can discern their likely presence. The coach can offer an interpretation of their existence in the coachee's life and, if there is agreement, through a process called grounding assessments assist the coachee to see if the beliefs have been lived as if they are factual (a very common occurrence) and if there is any substance to them beliefs (which typically there is not).

Moods

Moods are subtle, enduring and pervasive emotions, continually influencing perception and behaviour. Ontological coaching utilizes a framework entitled 'Some Basic Moods of Life' (Sieler, 2007), which provides interpretive structures of eight moods. These interpretative structures consist of four components:

(i)   how the mood can be created
(ii)   the typical linguistic or narrative structure
(iii)   the behavioural predispositions
(iv)   the likely postural configuration that reflects the embodiment of the mood.

The coach listens for the language of moods as well as observing their somatic manifestation in the coachee's postural configuration.

Returning to the coaching example with Helen in the pharmaceutical company, the coach noted that in the realization that her dignity had not been taken care of, Helen had mentioned that the situation was not fair, given her hard work and success in the sales role. An assessment of not being treated fairly is part of the language of the mood of resentment, which is often subtle yet persistent and pervasive anger. Helen was not comfortable with saying she was angry but she could see how she continually had this feeling of being 'put upon' that had not gone away, that she was resentful and her enthusiasm and energy for her work had been dampened.

In the previous example of coaching Stella on the key issue of lack of confidence, she agreed that she lived with a mood of anxiety, which is persistent background fear of things going badly and of not being able to deal with them. The behavioural manifestation of anxiety is consistently being alert for threats and engaging in protective behaviour to avoid the harm that accompanies perceived threats. For Stella, a consistent fear and threat was that others were making negative judgements about her work; consequently she worked long hours at the office and at home to 'cover all bases' in order to ensure she had anticipated and prepared a response to potential criticism.

The domain of the body

Nineteenth century German philosopher Friedrich Nietzsche captured the pivotal role of the body when he wrote, 'Our most sacred convictions are … judgements of our muscles' (Nietzsche, 1968: 173). The importance of the somatic domain is that it is where the embodiment of change takes place. One procedure that can be highly effective in taking care of concerns and in diminishing the restrictive effects of core negative assessments is the use of the linguistic act of declaring, in which specific words are spoken from a body posture and with a voice tonality (indicative of emotional state) that are congruent with the words.

This can be illustrated with an example of coaching Stephen, a highly regarded manager who had been offered the role of Chief Operating Officer in a fast-growing telecommunications company. Despite his excellent record as a manager, Stephen lived from the core negative self-assessments of 'I'm not good enough' and 'I'm not worthy'. After he realized there was no substance to these assessments he was invited to stand and make a declaration.

An important part of this procedure is for the coach to: (i) suggest and negotiate an appropriate brief statement that will be spoken, (ii) invite the coachee to notice how they speak, inviting them to assess and self-adjust whether there is congruence between their words, voice tonality and how they are holding their body and (iii) seek permission to make suggestions.

Stephen and the coach worked with the declaration 'I am a legitimate, worthy and competent person, and I am a learner'. Stephen spoke his declaration nine times and despite his strong scepticism about the value of this process was surprised about the noticeably positive difference he felt about himself, which he described as being more solid and assured. He subsequently accepted the role of Chief Operating Officer.

Key considerations in the coach's way of being

There are three important issues for ontological coaches to continually keep in mind if they are to maintain a constructive relationship with the coachee:

1. An emotional orientation of humility and not arrogance. The coach becomes arrogant by being too attached to his or her own ideas, forgetting that these ideas are interpretations and falls into the trap of 'knowing' the best direction for the conversation. The coach is always a learner, privileged by the coachee's willingness to be coached and has the responsibility to be at his or her resourceful best, being flexible in how to use his or her expertise for the benefit of the coachee.
2. Recognizing that the coach does not directly cause change but is a catalyst for change. As was presented at the beginning of the chapter, a basic principle of the biology of cognition is that change primarily occurs from within the nervous system, as a result of the system being perturbed by an external agent. All a coach can do is perturb the coachee's overall biological structure, which may trigger a shift in the nervous system and the development of a more resourceful way of being. The artistry of ontological coaching is to know how and when to constructively perturb the coachee's way of being.
3. The courage to be 'respectfully firm'. There may be occasions when coachees appear to avoid an aspect of their way of being that the coach considers important. In extreme cases, coachees may take over the conversation. It is essential that the coach respectfully maintains his/her authority and is not put 'off balance' by the coachees' behaviour. The ontological coach needs to respectfully share his/her observation/interpretation of the coachees' behaviour, seek his/her response and inquire if there is permission to explore the issue not being addressed.

APPLICATION

Ontological coaching is applicable to the entire range of coaching contexts and genres covered in Section II. In reflecting on the coaching engagements with Stella, Helen, Jake and Stephen it can be seen that the genres of skills and performance coaching, leadership coaching and developmental coaching were covered. The relevance of ontological coaching to the manager as coach, executive coaching and cross-cultural coaching is evident in the following examples.

Executive coaching

Working relationships between senior executives and members of the board are critical for the company's future. Sometimes decisions can leave a residue of negativity that persists and compromises relationships, with important business conversations not happening.

As Managing Director of a medium-sized, family-owned bus building company employing 200 people, Giovanni had experienced a significant breakdown with a decision by the Board of Management. They had overruled Giovanni and brought in consultants to look at the company's manufacturing process. Although the consultants had completed their work and the board's decision had been made more than eight months prior to the coaching conversation, Giovanni said that the decision 'still sticks in my gut'. Giovanni agreed with the coach's interpretation that he was still in a mood of resentment with the board. He did not want to leave the company, yet continually felt negative towards board members, which was 'not helping me or the company'.

Part of the structure of resentment is continuing to fight against, and not accept, what has happened and cannot be changed. Giovanni agreed this was exactly what he had been doing. He said, 'I was professionally slighted by that decision – it was as if I didn't know and all my experience counted for nothing. My thinking has been continually preoccupied with what was done and how I disagreed with it'. Through the conversation he began to more fully appreciate the damaging consequences of his mood and stated, 'It really is time I put this behind me'. The coach worked with Giovanni to facilitate small yet important shifts in his posture to ensure that he no longer held remnants of resentment. This allowed him, through requests, to initiate conversations with members of the board, including the future chairperson, that had not been happening. In a follow-up coaching session, Giovanni reported on a marked improvement in the quality of his conversations with the future chair, and how much more relaxed and better he felt within himself.

Cross-cultural coaching

The increasingly globalized world of business presents new challenges to ensure effective communication between personnel with diverse cultural backgrounds across different locations. Different cultures reflect different ways of being. Each culture provides a frame of meaning and associated assumptions about how to understand and behave in different situations. Business performance and productivity is built on people working together effectively (coordinating action) to reach objectives, which is underpinned by shared meaning. Ensuring there is shared meaning in business communication can make a significant difference to the operation of a team.

Susan leads a risk team in a major bank, with the members of her team being in Australia and India. Her communication with the members of the team in India is via email and telephone, the latter including phone conferences. Susan was frustrated that her colleagues in India seemed to agree about tasks to be done but did not complete them; i.e. they had made promises (commitments) that they did not keep, engendering lack of trust.

Working from the ontological perspective that listening is meaning and is the crucial factor in communication, the coach explored the general hypothesis that Susan had assumed a shared understanding that did not exist between herself and team members in India. Cultures can be viewed as forms of deep listening, consisting of core assessments, social norms and practices, and cultural narratives that subtly inform members of a culture how to perceive and respond to situations. Within the general hypothesis the coach tested the relevance of two specific hypotheses to the communication breakdown Susan was dealing with. The first hypothesis was that 'saving face' is a significant part of Asian cultures that can result in the cultural practice of saying 'yes' when the listener does not understand. The second hypothesis was related to the influence of gender relationships, specifically males regarding themselves as being superior to females, which in Susan's situation may be the male members of her team in India not accepting her authority as manager and therefore not accepting her ideas, suggestions and requests.

Susan's acceptance of the possible relevance of the above two cultural influences, which included not being resentful of their existence, was the basis for the inclusion of a communication strategy in phone conversations with her colleagues in India. The strategy was to ensure explicit shared understanding of tasks to be completed and the availability of relevant resources in a manner that was not offensive. Conversationally, the implementation of the strategy was as follows:

> Thank you for our discussion. I'd like you to help me out here if you could – I'm not sure if I have done a very good job making clear what I'd like done. Could you please tell me your understanding of what you will be doing from our discussion and don't worry if it is not accurate because it was probably me not being clear enough in the first place?

This was followed by ensuring there was explicit shared understanding of the availability of relevant resources for the tasks to be completed. The coach emphasized the importance of being genuine in her requests, reflected in her voice tonality, which was indicative of her emotions and body posture being congruent with her words.

Health coaching

Juliette had been treated by a number of physiotherapists and chiropractors for significant pain and restriction in the movement of her neck and head. Recently she had been told that there was a problem with a disc in her neck. Intrigued that she didn't have pain and restriction all the time, Juliette was interested in exploring another avenue to complement the work of somatic practitioners. She was drawn to ontological coaching because of the inclusion of the domain of the body in the coaching methodology.

The coach ensured that Juliette understood he was not a somatic practitioner and was willing to do his best to see how an ontological approach could contribute to lessening the pain associated with the movement of her neck. After exploring when Juliette most noticed the restriction and discomfort in her neck, the coach asked what turned out to be the most significant question in the conversation (based on the notion of 'concerns'), which was, 'How does the discomfort and restriction in your neck take care of you?'

Juliette's initial response was a lengthy silence, after which she said, 'My first thought was that it doesn't but then I think there is some purpose there. I think it protects me from being responsible.' The coach and Juliette then explored the areas of her life where she considered she avoided responsibility, along with her moods, overall story and key assessments that accompanied this mode of being. Juliette was then invited to stand up and adopt the full body configuration that went with avoiding responsibility. Not surprisingly, she noticed the pressure she was putting on her neck. Juliette and the coach further explored the language and moods that accompanied the posture of not being responsible.

The coach ask Juliette to 'shake off' the unhelpful posture by gently moving her hips and shoulders, swinging her arms, taking some easy deep breaths and then to sit down again. She and the coach discussed the areas of her life in which she assessed she was responsible and she was asked to consider the difference in her language and moods from when she was avoiding responsibility. The coach invited Juliette to stand up again, move to a different spatial position from where she stood in the posture of avoiding responsibility and to adopt a full body configuration of being responsible. She was asked what specific differences she noticed in her posture compared with being 'in a body of avoiding responsibility'.

The main self-observation for Juliette was that she felt so much freer in her neck, which was amazing to her. The coach asked her to move back and forth between the postures of avoiding and accepting responsibility in order for her to gain a clear somatic feel of the difference between each dynamic body disposition. Once this was complete Juliette was asked, 'Which way of being in the body is preferable for you?' She replied enthusiastically, 'This one', referring to the body of accepting responsibility. As a closing comment the coach reinforced that the coaching conversation complemented the work of Juliette's somatic practitioners by saying, 'Please continue to use the services of the physiotherapist and chiropractor to ensure that your neck does fully recover'.

EVALUATION

While ontological coaching has the capacity to provide significant value across all genres and contexts for coaching, it is important to be mindful of some key considerations that, if not attended to, can act as constraints and limitations of this coaching methodology:

- Some coachees may be reluctant to explore the domains of emotions and body. The essential task of the ontological coach is to respect the boundaries of the coachee and to work skilfully in the area of language to generate shifts in perspectives and behaviour, which may spontaneously produce emotional and somatic shifts.
- Ontological coaches are not psychotherapists or somatic therapists. The coach has a fundamental responsibility to know his/her own coaching boundaries and not go beyond these. This is a critical aspect of the coach managing his/her own way of being in the coaching conversation. Boundaries are defined by the coach recognizing his/her levels of comfort and knowing his/her competence.
- Technical proficiency in the coaching methodology is not sufficient. The coach always coaches from life experiences, which can provide an invaluable experiential 'feel' for the challenges the coachee is dealing with. For example, coaching in the business world requires a sound general understanding of the nature of organizations, the nature of leadership and managerial responsibility, and daily life in the workplace.

- The coaching methodology is based on substantive and coherent theory of human perception and behaviour that provides a viable alternative approach to psychology for facilitating sustainable behavioural change.
- Working in the three domains of language, emotions and body provides the coach with the flexibility of multiple areas of engagement. The coach can recognize when the opportunities for learning and change have become exhausted in one domain and seek permission to focus on another domain. For example, new insights and behavioural shifts can open up for the coachee in the domains of moods and the body that are not possible while the conversation remains in the language domain.
- The role of the body in coaching ensures learning is embodied and consolidated.
- Ontological coaching offers a uniquely powerful way of intervening in organizational dynamics and culture. It provides an in-depth framework for positioning human interaction as a core business discipline and practice.

The general benefit of ontological coaching is that coachees experience shifts in their way of being, enabling them to become a different and more powerful observer of themselves, others and how they can constructively engage in the world. The coaching not only supports the coachee to deal with the problematic issues that were presented for coaching, but also positions them to be more resilient and adaptable for dealing with future problematic circumstances.

Ontological coaching is beneficial across a wide range of coaching contexts and genres because it deals with the fundamental ways people understand themselves, the world and what is possible for them in life. The coaching methodology facilitates the emergence of new perspectives as the basis for the development of expanded ways of thinking and increased behavioural flexibility, all of which have become so essential in increasingly unpredictable and uncertain times.

FURTHER READING

Sieler, Alan (2003). *Coaching to the human soul: Ontological coaching and deep change*, Vol. I. Melbourne: Newfield-Australia.

Sieler, Alan (2007). *Coaching to the human soul: Ontological coaching and deep change*, Vol. II. Melbourne: Newfield-Australia.

Sieler, Alan (2012). *Coaching to the human soul: Ontological coaching and deep change*, Vol. III. Melbourne: Newfield Institute.

(Volumes I, II and III of *Coaching to the human soul* are the detailed exposition of the methodology and theoretical underpinnings of ontological coaching. Volume I covers the specifics of the linguistic basis of the coaching methodology. The focus of Volume II is the emotional domain, which includes an extensive coverage of the model Some Basic Moods of Life. Volume III examines the biological thinking that underpins ontological coaching as well as providing a philosophical basis for the domain of the body and an in-depth conceptual and practical framework for coaching to the body. All volumes provide a wide range of coaching examples and practical activities.)

Winograd, T. & Flores, F. (1986). *Understanding computers and cognition.* Reading, MA: Addison-Wesley. (While the orientation of this book is the design of computer-based systems that facilitate human work and interaction, it provides a worthwhile introduction to the ideas of Heidegger, Maturana and Searle that comprise the theory behind ontological coaching. Winograd and Flores position ontology as a contribution to the emergence of a new intellectual paradigm that is new ground for rationality, which combines traditional rational thinking with intuitive–interpretive thinking.)

DISCUSSION QUESTIONS

- When you consider current issues you are dealing with in your personal and professional life, what aspects of your way of being (language, emotions and moods and body) are helpful and not helpful?
- As a coach, how could you apply a way of being approach in your coaching that will be beneficial for your clients?
- As a coach, how could you benefit by paying attention to your mood and body posture when coaching?

REFERENCES

Austin, J.L. (1973). *How to do things with words* (2nd ed.). Cambridge, MA: Harvard University Press.

Dewey, J. (1929). *Experience and nature.* La Salle, IL: Open Court.

Gadamer, H-G. (1994). *Truth and method* (2nd ed., Rev.). New York: Continuum.

Heidegger, M. (1962). *Being and time.* Trans. J. Macquarie & E. Robinson. San Francisco, CA: Harper.

Heidegger, M. (1971). *On the way to language.* Trans. P. D. Hertz. San Francisco, CA: Harper.

Heidegger, M. (1999). *Ontology – the hermeneutics of facticity.* Trans. J. van Buren. Bloomington, IN: Indiana University Press.

Honderich, T. (Ed.). (1995). *The Oxford companion to philosophy.* Oxford: Oxford University Press.

Maturana, H.R. & Varela, F. (1980). *Autopoeisis and cognition: The realization of the living.* Dordrecht: Reidel Publishing.

Maturana, H.R. & Varela, F. (1987). *The tree of knowledge: The biological roots of human understanding* (Rev. ed.). Boston, MA: Shambala.

Merleau-Ponty, M. (1962). *Phenomenology of perception.* Trans. C. Smith. London: Routledge and Kegan Paul.

Nietzsche, F. (1968). *The will to power.* Trans W. Kaufman & R.J. Hollingdale. New York: Vintage.

Searle, J.R. (1969). *Speech acts: An essay in the philosophy of language.* Cambridge: Cambridge University Press.

Searle, J.R. (1979). *Expression and meaning.* Cambridge: Cambridge University Press.

Sieler, A. (2003). *Coaching to the human soul: Ontological coaching and deep change*, Vol. I. Melbourne: Newfield-Australia.

Sieler, A. (2007). *Coaching to the human soul: Ontological coaching and deep change*, Vol. II. Melbourne: Newfield-Australia.

Sieler, A. (2012). *Coaching to the human soul: Ontological coaching and deep change*, Vol. III. Melbourne: Newfield Institute.

Winograd, T. & Flores, F. (1986). *Understanding computers and cognition.* Reading, MA: Addison-Wesley.

Wittgenstein, L. (1958). *Philosophical investigations* (3rd ed.). Englewood Cliffs, NJ: Basil Blackwell and Mott.

8

Narrative Coaching

David Drake

Narrative coaching is a mindful, experiential and holistic approach to helping people to shift their stories in order to generate new options and new results. It is unique in that it takes a whole person and whole system approach to coaching. It works with people at three primary levels: (1) it draws on *narrative psychology* to understand clients as *narrators* in support of their development and performance; (2) it draws on *narrative structure* to understand the material that is *narrated* and enable the reconfiguration of their stories; and (3) it draws on *narrative practices* to understand the dynamics in the *narrative field* and guide them across developmental thresholds. The core narrative coaching model integrates these three levels into a unified process of change. As it enters its second decade, narrative coaching is increasingly informed by narrative design as a pioneering theory of adult development connecting mindsets, behaviors and environments (see Drake 2012). It offers practitioners a way to do deep work simply yet is agile enough to address the complex issues of our time.

A BRIEF BACKSTORY

In her marvellous history of the narrative turn in the social sciences, Czarniawska (2004) provides an overview of the three main fields that fed into what became narrative studies and are, therefore, key to understanding narrative coaching as noted above: literary theory, humanities and psychology. The literary study of narratives focused on an analysis of texts. For example,

Burke (1969) described the central elements of a narrative as a Pentad: 'what was done (*act*), when and where it was done (*scene*), who did it (*agent*), how he did it (*agency*), and why (*purpose*)'. Bruner (2002) later added the 'coda' as a sixth element to refer to the meaning and implications of stories. With the rise of literary hermeneutics came a growing interest in the analysis of interactions of the text *and* the reader.

The resulting interest in issues such as power and discourse paved the way for the narrative frame to move into the humanities (e.g. political science, sociology and anthropology). In developing a broader understanding of stories as central to the fabric of social life and a contextual understanding of action, scholars such as phenomenologists Berger and Luckmann (1966) and the anthropologist Geertz (1978) provided important insights into the processes by which we narrate our socially constructed experience. As part of this process, individual stories came to be seen as shaped by the frames and forces of collective and cultural narratives. Of particular importance for narrative coaching in this regard is Campbell's (1973) work on the heroic journey, van Gennep's (1960) work on rites of passage and Turner's (1969) work to extend this model into broader cultural life. Together, they provide a theoretical and practical frame for working with people's stories in support of change.

William James was a seminal figure in bringing a narrative frame to the third field, psychology. For example, he (1927) wrote about the distinction between the *I* (the subject) and the *Me* (the object) – a distinction carried forward as the *self-as-knower* and the *self-as-known* (Hermans, 2004) and the *author* and the *actor* (Mancuso & Sarbin, 1983). This dialectic reflects the ongoing tensions for people in negotiating their narrative identity over time – moving between presenting identities that are socially acceptable and functional (Me) and embodying identities that are personally authentic and flourishing (I). The roots of a narrative approach to coaching can be seen through these three fields as a movement from *text* (literary theory and narrative structure) to *context* (humanities and narrative practices) to *subtext* (psychology and narrative psychology in particular) – a progression that was accelerated by the rise of postmodernism and the shift from 'stories-as-objects' to 'stories-in-context' (Boje, 1998). While psychology has emerged as the dominant discourse in coaching, coaches would do well to also engage literary theories and the humanities if they want to truly understand how best to work with clients and their stories.

Narrative therapy pioneers such as Michael White and David Epston (White, 1988; White & Epston, 1990) helped lead the way in this regard, e.g., by advocating for the deconstruction of dominant narratives, the externalization of problems, and the identification of 'unique outcomes' or 'exceptions' (Hewson, 1991) in a person's life as contradictions to internalized dominant narratives. Coaches can use this work to help people explore alternative territories and new possibilities by renegotiating the relationships between their sense of self and their stories, their internal experiences and their external narratives, and their narrative patterns and their narrative desires.

Narrative coaching is, however, more than just narrative therapy adapted for a coaching context. For example, narrative coaching:

- makes more overt use of the rites of passage frame as a systemic theory of change
- draws on Jungian psychology to address the personal and collective unconscious

- draws on attachment theory to address pre-verbal narratives
- incorporates somatic practices to engage and adapt embodied narratives
- incorporates mindfulness practices and field theory as keys for listening
- attends to issues of power in terms of development more than justice
- moves between decentered and centered positions in service of outcomes.

MAIN CONCEPTS AND ASSUMPTIONS OF A NARRATIVE APPROACH

The stories people tell about their lives are of considerable importance in coaching because there is an intimate connection between the ways in which people narrate their identities and enact their lives. Stories provide powerful openings to explore these connections because they bring to the surface how people construct and navigate their world and can be used to guide them in making any shifts. Narrative coaches use the narrative material and patterns in clients' stories to help them identify and cross developmental thresholds and as a structure for making internal or external changes in doing so. To do so, they tend to take a spiralling approach to client stories to get to the crux of the matter rather than a linear path to get to goals or plans, focus astutely on one thing at a time like a bird circling a tree, and help clients identify simple pivots they can use to sustain the changes back in their life. They are regularly asking themselves as they listen to clients, 'What does this person need most from me right now?'

Often what people are looking for is an opportunity to reconfigure the literal and representational elements in their stories to liberate new possibilities. This is important because people are continually attempting to clarify, claim and convince others of their identity through *positioning* (Davies & Harré, 1990) themselves in both their internal constructions and their external interactions. Narrative coaches help people notice the ways in which they currently position themselves and other characters in their stories and to explore how they might enhance or reconfigure their positional repertoire (Hermans, 2004) in order to increase their options. This fits with the overall aim in narrative coaching to help people express themselves with more authenticity and agency through the embodiment and enactment of new stories. The integration of the research on attachment theory into narrative coaching (Drake, 2009) provides a frame for working with preverbal, somatic patterns in order to enable these deeper shifts. For example, in coaching an academic who struggled to emotionally engage with others I used real-time feedback, modelling and improvisation to work with his body posture and voice.

DISTINCTIVE FEATURES

Listening as a method for change

A core feature of narrative coaching is the search for elements in people's stories that are 'amenable to challenge, redefinition, or alternative interpretation so that a new definition of the problem can emerge' (Coulehan, Friedlander, & Heatherington, 1998: 18). One of the core skills narrative coaches use in doing so is what Reik (1998) called the 'third ear – what I think of as including the 'third eye' – based in a non-judgemental presence, an engaged mindfulness and a multilayered attention to what emerges in the conversation. Listening to people's stories in this way enables narrative coaches to pay close attention to the nuances of what is said and not said verbally and non-verbally in sessions, and also to be more aware of the ways in which their own conscious and unconscious formulations are shaping the conversation (Drake, 2010). This is important because stories are not objects that exist intact with a client, but are co-created in the course of a coaching session. As a result, listening precedes talking in narrative coaching rather than the usual frame in which listening is what we do after we stop talking.

Listening in this way enables coaches to connect to the whole person and thereby open up a wider range of material for coaching in service of the client's objectives. In this sense, listening can be seen as a 360° experience and not a dyadic transaction. A key role for coaches then is to 'invite people to see their stories from different perspectives, to notice how they are constructed (or even that they are constructed), to note their limits and influences, and to discover other possibilities' (Freedman & Combs, 1996). It is about helping people to notice the differences between the stories they are telling and the stories they are living as well as to identify narrative 'data' from their lives that would support an alternate view of who they are and/or how they want to be in the world. For example, I invited a client who looked longingly off into space after stating her issue to follow her gaze (and used my hand to point in the same direction to pace her and focus her attention) and to verbalize the untold story that was playing in her mind. In doing so, she was able to access feelings of grief that had yet to find a place in her story or in the decision she brought to coaching.

Working with peoples' stories and the characters in them is powerful because it gives them access to aspects of themselves that are often hidden yet in motion in their psyche. This is important because development generally occurs for people outside their habitual plot lines and their psyche's defenses. Narrative coaches support this process through listening in a way that is active yet non-directive, engaged yet non-attached, deeply present yet keenly observant. The process often feels quite slow, for the participants (and for any observers such as when I demonstrate the work), yet often yields significant breakthroughs in a brief period of time. In this way, narrative coaching is both gentle and robust – a valuable combination at a time when people yearn for more meaningful connections *and* faster, more adaptive results.

Essential processes and dynamics

Narrative coaching presumes that: (1) identity is situated; (2) discourse is powerful; (3) growth is spiral; and (4) re-storying is possible. Each process is particularly linked to one of the four phases in the core narrative coaching model (Figure 8.1): (1) How is the person Situated (with the coach and within the story)? (2) What is the person Searching for? (3) What needs to Shift in order to fulfil that desire? (4) How will the person Sustain the change? This human-centered approach to coaching moves beyond modernist assumptions, linear development models, extroverted goal orientation and lingering biases toward behaviorism to create a truly post-professional and integrative approach to developing people. It shifts the emphasis from the coach and coaching methodologies to the coaching relationship and the stories that emerge there.

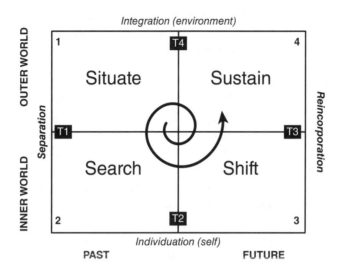

Figure 8.1 Narrative coaching model

Identity is situated

Who we are is an ongoing dynamic process that provides us with both a sense of continuity as seen in our narrative patterns and adaptability as seen in our narrative choices. Our identity and the schemas we rely on to narrate our experience are heavily influenced by our personal and collective sense of time and space, hence their situated nature. Narrative coaching overtly addresses the environmental and situational forces that shape clients' identities, stories and behaviors. In doing so, it shares Boscolo and Betrando's (1992) belief that 'the present is the only time frame for action, which means that all problems are problems of the present' (p. 121). Narrative coaches work in the moment with what IS as revealed through the unfolding narration, more so than most other approaches where there is a tendency to prematurely move to what COULD BE. This requires coaches to non-judgmentally witness the client and gracefully hold the stories as they are presented before any invitations are extended to try to change them (see Gallwey, 2009/1981). Doing so offers clients the opportunity to stand more fully in the truth of their experience as the precursor to meaningful development and change.

Coaches can therefore use the stories that are shared as valuable resources because they make visible clients' otherwise invisible identity processes – their 'theory of events' (Foucault, 1965) – and thereby shed light on the dynamic interplay between their identity, narrative and performance (Eakin, 1999; Mishler, 1999). This can be seen in a client who gained new insights into the stress he often experienced through exploring his stories about helping others: unpacking his familial identity as the hyper-responsible oldest son (identity), uncovering his fears of what happens when you don't help (narrative) and addressing his tendencies to micromanage others at work (performance). In working his stories, I helped the client see himself as someone who could choose what role he wanted to play in responding to others (identity), learn how to de-escalate his anxieties to create more space for a new story to form (narrative) and increase his delegation skills to allow others to do more for themselves (performance).

Discourse is powerful

Narrative coaches help people examine their assumptions about reality through a deep engagement with their stories. In doing so, they track not only the person's choices of language and narration, but also the broader discourses their stories reflect. The aim is to bring to light the client's unique schemas and internalized narratives that have shaped how they tell their stories and live their lives. However, it is important to remember that, if people are to adopt new behaviors or attain new results, they must embody an identity and discourse from which to do so and from which the desired behaviors naturally arise. If they are to sustain this new identity, they need to regularly enact these new behaviors – and the stories that go with them. This is because in order for new stories or new relations between stories to take hold in a people's life, they must build on elements of familiar stories in order to 'scaffold' their ascendance (Drake, 2008; Gergen & Gergen, 2006).

Therefore, a key task in narrative coaching is to introduce clients to the distinction between their traditionally *available narratives* and their latent *potential stories* (Drake, 2007). Available narratives are drawn from the vocabulary and grammar, the plot lines and historical conventions, and the beliefs and norms of their cultural systems (Freedman & Combs, 1996). As people begin to recognize the limitations inherent in their available narratives, they can create more distance from these narratives, see them more clearly and surface other 'selves' they could draw on to achieve what they are looking for in their lives or work. As potential stories become more available, other 'sympathetic' and previously neglected aspects of the person's experience (and the related discourse) can be expressed (White & Epston, 1990) and embodied. For example, I worked with a client who wanted to make a career transition into coaching with a new firm, but who was concerned that most of her skills would be relegated to the back office as they had in previous roles. I introduced the idea of working in the 'front office'; however, she felt apprehensive and not ready. I helped her to develop a transition plan based on using her existing skills in new ways in the front office as scaffolding for the role she truly wanted.

Growth is spiral

Peoples use *emplotment strategies* (Hermans & Kempen, 1993; Mattingly, 1994) to make sense of and choices about their experience as a means to define their identity, community, values, etc. These strategies operate largely at non-conscious and somatic levels, but they can be made conscious and malleable through coaching. Therefore, narrative coaches track the ways in which peoples organize their stories, e.g. which events are included, which themes they organize around, which characters are portrayed as significant and which voices are privileged in the telling (Botella & Herrero, 2000). It is particularly useful to listen for what is missing – the gaps (Drake, 2007) – where people's typical emplotment strategies have broken down and are no longer working. It is in these discrepancies between what we expected and what actually happened – what Bruner (1990) called 'breaches of the commonplace' – where growth most often occurs because they provide an opening for a pivot, a change in the trajectory of the story and the teller. These gaps can be marked by laughter, looking away, gaps in narration, changes in energy, etc. and often signal the proximity to a threshold in the client's development (as seen in Figure 8.1)

These spaces are often reached through spiralling upward (like a bird circling up above a tree) to help the client gain a new perspective or insight or spiralling downward to help a client reach a make a new decision or take a new action (like a bird circling to find a new branch upon which to rest). The outcome of the coaching process is often the release of the old story and the start of a new one rather than just restoring a sense of 'normal' to the disrupted plot. For example, a workshop participant started with a story about how his firm poorly handled the departure of a close colleague. 'It was not supposed to be this way' in his view. Drawing on this phrase, I asked him if this situation was ultimately about a challenge to his values. It took him a number of spirals through the topic to come to the realization that it had raised doubts about his own decision to seek partnership. Once he got to the crux of the matter, he was able to identify a more fulfilling course of action – and he eventually became a partner but on more solid ground.

Re-storying is possible

Narrative coaches help people to discern what they are ultimately trying to accomplish with the stories they currently tell (and for whom) as the foundation for exploring new options. 'Re-storying' is the process of creating a new, more powerful, alignment between the three pillars of development in narrative design theory – mindset, behavior and environment – to bring them to life. In order for these kinds of shifts to occur, people first need to loosen their *narrative grip* on the past, present and/or future (Boscolo & Bertrando, 1992) to create the space for new stories about themselves and others. Narrative coaches can draw on a repertoire of experiential, imaginal and somatic activities that have been developed to help people release stories that no longer serve them and step into new ones. For example, narrative coaches can invite clients to enact their metaphors as openings between the known and the unknown that are often the birthplace of new insights and new possibilities.

For example, I was asked to coach a key contributor in a manufacturing company to help her address some difficult relational and performance issues. Her initial stories were of anger at her employer and her colleagues. However, through exploring her story more fully she was able to reframe the issue as one in which she felt her professional passions had been compromised as the company had grown significantly. Her willingness to engage in these deeper truths emerged from a conversation about a pet and, with that, what 'home' meant for her. In the end, what she wanted was the chance to leave with dignity and the courage to return to the work she loved. To do so, she needed to shift from what she came to call her 'they don't appreciate or respect me' story to her 'I want to do what I love' story. In the end, she left the organization, moved to a new city and found a new job where she could thrive again. I helped the Vice President of Human Resources reflect on how much the culture had changed over the years and what they needed to adjust in order to retain their legacy talent.

THE ROLE OF THE NARRATIVE COACH AND THE RELATIONSHIP

[Our] role is correspondingly delicate. It may still not be, though, 'to change [their] story, for this is to deny it; it is, rather, to expand and deepen the story, thus releasing the energy bound within it.' (Houston, 1987: 99)

Given the co-creative nature of stories, it is no surprise that the nature of the coaching relationship and the roles a coach adopts are critical. The flexibility of narrative coaches to move in and out of client stories as needed is important and requires real-time attention to points of leverage in people's experience and narration to support their development. For example, I have supported breakthroughs for people through conversations that focused on (1) eating dinner, (2) unpacked moving boxes, (3) a childhood mentor and (4) a dream of riding a boat down the river. Each of these stories served as a portal to a larger theme and a developmental threshold to cross: (1) the need to make a major lifestyle and career change; (2) the anticipatory grief for an ill spouse; (3) the platform to celebrate and extend a new business direction; and (4) the end of a dysfunctional pattern in work relationships and a move to a new job.

A narrative coach creates a holding container in which people can courageously and creatively bring their narrative material into the world; helps them experience and explore new ways of relating to it; and invites the client into the possibility of a new story in the moment. In order to do this, narrative coaches provide both an interpersonal structure, e.g. a safe space, and a narrative structure, e.g. Bruner's (1990) notions of *landscapes of action* and *landscapes of consciousness,* to help people fully engage with their stories. Otherwise, their stories can easily devolve into non-productive habitual tales or detached chronicles, and the process degrades into an abstract analysis. These two structures are best seen as sources for potential questions rather than as expectations to which people and their stories must conform. Taken together, they have been described by clients and workshop participants as 'sacred spaces' and 'narrative ceremonies'.

In coaching this way, I often literally and figuratively move between centered and decentered positions relative to my clients – often facing the client at the start to build sufficient rapport and trust, then decentering myself by shifting my position to be more at an angle to explore the narrative material with the client, and recentering myself when stronger relational connection is needed (e.g. due to increased vulnerability) or a new experience seems called for in the moment. In moving back and forth, the coach continues to triangulate between the client, the stories and themselves as each interacts with the other in the field between them. It allows the coach to move between first, second and third positions in NLP terms yet always keep the stories present and owned by the client. This freedom to center oneself as a powerful, yet humble practitioner is one of the critical differences between narrative therapy and narrative coaching, and reflects the greater focus on shorter interventions and outcomes in coaching. A light, yet disciplined touch is required by coaches to remain full present and fully trust the process as they move in and out of people's stories.

To support themselves to do so, narrative coaches stay as much as possible in the moment, in *storytime* and *storyspace*, as the narration unfolds in the course of a session. The focus here is on the story as it is being told in the here and now. In doing so, coaches continually bring people back into their present experience in order to connect the proverbial 'dots' and provide a more solid basis for change. Gallwey's (2009/1981) work on the inner game and Kramer's (2007) work on relational meditation are both helpful here. For example, stories about the past and future are explored through questions such as, 'When have you been here before?' and 'When might you be here again?'; but the answers are brought back into the moment by asking questions such as, 'What are you thinking or feeling about X right now?' This stance is based on the belief that people need experiences not explanations if they are to create and sustain meaningfully change. A coaching session is like a lab in which clients work with the elements in their stories to try out new combinations and new options right then and there.

METHODS AND TECHNIQUES

An early source for this approach was the notion of *dialogical space*, wherein 'new relationships are established between existing story parts or new elements are introduced' (Hermans, 2004: 175) and the work from narrative researchers on how people 'locate characters in their stories in relation to one another and in relation to themselves' (Riessman, 2002) and how they position and 'reposition these characters … within a constantly moving interpersonal field' (Anderson, 2004: 317). In my doctoral work I drew on Jung's (1970) work with dreams and asked myself, 'What if we extended this theory of dreams to the study of narratives? What if the characters in the stories we choose to tell are all parts of ourselves, projected onto familiar forms as a means to work through developmental issues or needs in our identity?' (Drake, 2003: 245). As a result, I suggested that narrative work is a trialogic process between the narrator, the listener and the story itself. It offers a view that the characters, objects and events that appear in our stories are systematically related to the other figures in ways that are important to explore.

I used this research to develop *the narrative diamond* (Drake, 2007) as a framework that narrative coaches can use to listen to their clients' stories in new ways. It is unique in that the coach moves his or her attention between the client (the narrator), the stories (the narration) and the openings for change (the narrative elements) like a master chef would in the kitchen. Narrative coaches help clients step into their stories in the session through witnessing what *is being said*, recognizing what *is not being said* by advocating for the whole story, inviting them to step into what *wants to be said* by working with the narrative elements seen in a character(s) (e.g. person, place, metaphor, phrase, object) and building on what *is being said differently* through focusing attention on the shifts that are already emerging in the field.

APPLICATIONS

Narrative coaching is based in a unique philosophical stance and a distinct set of methodologies. One of its greatest strengths is that it draws from narrative design theory – and the set of literatures upon which it is based – and therefore provides a more holistic approach to understanding and facilitating development and change. As a result, narrative coaches can bridge the psychological and the systemic, the conscious and the non-conscious, the behavioral and the cultural in working at a number of levels with clients' stories. The following are three of the ways in which it has been applied.

Developmental coaching

A narrative approach can be particularly useful in working with people at turning points in their life or work. For example, in working with a client who had been promoted to Vice President of Engineering, he traced his career trajectory in an attempt to understand the difficulties he was experiencing in his new role. In doing so, he identified the three stages of his career as 'expert, manager and leader' and we explored his stories about himself at each stage and the stories others had of him as he advanced. In comparing these stories, he recognized that in large part he still identified with his old role (particularly as the 'expert') and acted accordingly. I helped him craft an identity story in which he could truly see himself as a leader and recognize what he would need to let go of and become comfortable with in order to more fully embody and successfully deliver on his new role We also addressed issues related to how the promotions had affected his identity and role at home.

Internal coaching skills programmes

A narrative approach works quite well in supporting organizational culture/change projects through aligning personal/career stories and organizational/strategic stories and developing a shared coaching mindset and coaching capabilities. For example, as part of my work with a global professional services firm, over 200 coaching champions were invited to share stories of how their coaching conversations had changed through the work we had done and how this was helping them to meet the increased demands on their teams. They shared stories about what had changed for them personally as well as what changes were happening for their teams and clients. As these stories spread, there were noticeable shifts in their openness to learning, engagement with coaching, versatility in talking with clients and the overall vibe in many of their teams. Coaching was no longer seen as formal, obligatory and generally unidirectional sessions dutifully done a few times a year, but rather as a natural, invitational and mutual way that conversations could be framed and business could be done.

Cross-cultural coaching

Stories have seven primary functions relative to culture. They help us to: (1) claim and navigate our formal and informal memberships; (2) establish and sustain social identities; (3) discern influential cultural/contextual norms; (4) observe ourselves from other vantage points; (5) negotiate our identity performances in key environments; (6) test and rehearse new selves; and (7) situate ourselves in a meaningful larger narrative (Drake, 2008). Each of these functions came into play in a leadership development programme I did for a federal government client. I realized on the first day that my design was not working as well as I had hoped. The primary disconnect was between the classic leadership theories upon which the program was based (mainly drawn from white men of privilege in academia) and the lived experience of this group (mainly women who were non-privileged and in low-status roles). After recognising my own unconscious bias, I jettisoned most of the curriculum, invited them into story circles to share what leadership looked like and meant in their cultures, and designed an approach with them to address their needs as leaders in their organizations.

EVALUATION

Much of the research that has informed narrative coaching to date has been drawn from efforts in related fields such as narrative psychology and narrative medicine. As a result, a key focus over the past ten years has been the theory building and process development that have been essential for establishing the critical philosophical foundations for and core applications of this approach. In building on these traditions and developing its own, narrative coaching seems to work best with people who have (1) a comfort with mindfulness and self-reflection; (2) a willingness to work at emotional, metaphorical and non-rational levels and a patience with non-linear processes; (3) an awareness of and ability to articulate their experience; and (4) the necessary ego strength to be able to self-disclose through their stories and work with their shadows. Obviously, this approach is more challenging and less effective if any of these four conditions are not present in the coach and/or the client.

Narrative coaching is a process that focuses on situated narrative identity, growth as a spiralling process, the power of discourse and the possibilities for new stories. It is based in a commitment by narrative coaches to (1) be mindful and compassionate; (2) listen deeply and respectfully; (3) engage courageously and fluidly with stories in the field; and (4) help people pivot in the direction of new ways of being and acting in the world. In thinking narratively, coaches place more emphasis on generating experiences and less on rushing to interpretation, meaning, or action. It does not matter which stories peoples choose to share first; narrative coaches trust that peoples will begin at the level at which they are ready and the critical themes will be forthcoming regardless.

Therefore, the aim is to create a rich narrative field, notice what appears, remain connected even in silence, actively engage with the narrative material as it emerges and trust that any story or set of stories is a portal into the larger issues at play. At the same time, narrative coaches know that the stories told in coaching sessions, even if they have served as a transformational vehicle in that setting, must survive the 'retellings' if peoples are to sustain the changes they have begun. As a result, there is a greater than usual attention paid to the fourth phase (Sustain) in the narrative coaching model so they can with increasing consistency apply what they have experienced and learned.

Ultimately, people can only see as far as their stories will take them and they can only act as far as their stories will back them. As such, the narrative coach helps people to connect their personal stories with the social contexts from which they came and to which they will return in new ways. There is a strong focus on helping clients prepare themselves to return to their world so that the seeds of their new stories will grow and flourish (Hewson, 1991). They often report leaving a session or workshop with an embodied sense of 'coming home to themselves' and a greater ability to literally return home with success. As narrative coaching has evolved over the past ten years, it has become a powerful method for helping people to (1) become more aware of their stories, (2) recognize how these stories shape their identity and behavior at both conscious and unconscious levels, (3) understand that these stories are personally and socially constructed and (4) be more authorial in aligning their stories with identities and actions that would enable them to live more fully and authentically.

FURTHER READING

Freedman, J. & Combs, G. (1996). *Narrative therapy: The social construction of preferred realities.* New York: Norton and Co. (This excellent introduction to narrative therapy features a good blend of theoretical and practice considerations.)

McKee, R. (1997). *Story: Substance, structure, style and the principles of screenwriting.* New York: HarperCollins. (The master when it comes to understanding screenwriting; he brings together a classic literary knowledge with a sound knowledge of contemporary culture in providing a deep resource on narrative structure.)

Schank, R.A. (1990). *Tell me a story: A new look at real and artificial memory.* New York: Charles Scribner's Sons. (Reading this book on how to create better transfer of learning and sustainable change in managers and leaders was influential in my development. An educator, he writes with a sound grasp of the research on schemas and other concepts from cognitive science, but does so from a starting point of the mind as a storyteller.)

DISCUSSION QUESTIONS

- Based on your background, what are your primary frames for listening to your client's stories?
- What does that help you hear? What might you be missing based on the frameworks offered in this chapter?
- What do you do when you feel resonance with a client's story? A clash with the client's story?
- Based on what an observer would see if they were watching you coach, what implicit stories seem to inform your sense of your role as a coach?

REFERENCES

Anderson, T. (2004). 'To tell my story': Configuring interpersonal relations within narrative process. In L.E. Angus & J. McLeod (Eds), *Handbook of narrative and psychotherapy: Practice, theory, and research* (pp. 315–329). Thousand Oaks, CA: Sage Publications.

Berger, P.L. & Luckmann, T. (1966). *The social construction of reality.* New York: Doubleday.

Boje, D.M. (1998). The postmodern turn from stories-as-objects to stories-in-context methods. *Research Methods Forum*. Retrieved January 7, 2006, from www.aom.pace.edu/rmd/1998_forum_postmodern_stories.html.

Boscolo, L. & Bertrando, P. (1992). The reflexive loop of past, present and future in systemic therapy and consultation. *Family Process*, 31, 119–130.

Botella, L. & Herrero, L. (2000). A relational constructivist approach to narrative therapy. *European Journal of Psychotherapy, Counselling & Health*, 3(3), 407–418.

Bruner, J. (1990). *Acts of meaning*. Cambridge, MA: Harvard University Press.

Bruner, J. (2002). *Making stories: Law, literature, life*. Cambridge, MA: Harvard University Press.

Burke, K. (1969). *A grammar of motives*. Berkeley, CA: University of California Press.

Campbell, J. (1973). *The hero with a thousand faces*. Princeton, NJ: Princeton University Press.

Coulehan, R., Friedlander, M.L., & Heatherington, L. (1998). Transforming narratives: A change event in constructivist family therapy. *Family Process*, 37, 17–33.

Czarniawska, B. (2004). *Narratives in social science research*. London: Sage.

Davies, B. & Harré, R. (1990). Positioning: The discursive production of selves. *Journal for the Theory of Social Behavior*, 20(1), 43–63.

Drake, D.B. (2003). *How stories change: A narrative analysis of liminal experiences and transitions in identity*. (Dissertation), Fielding Graduate Institute, Santa Barbara.

Drake, D.B. (2007). The art of thinking narratively: Implications for coaching psychology and practice. *Australian Psychologist*, 42(4), 283–294.

Drake, D.B. (2008). Thrice upon a time: Narrative structure and psychology as a platform for coaching. In D.B. Drake, D. Brennan & K. Gørtz (Eds), *The philosophy and practice of coaching: Issues and insights for a new era* (pp. 51–71). San Francisco: Jossey–Bass.

Drake, D.B. (2009). Using attachment theory in coaching leaders: The search for a coherent narrative. *International Coaching Psychology Review*, 4(1), 49–58.

Drake, D.B. (2010). What story are you in? Four elements of a narrative approach to formulation in coaching. In S. Corrie & D. Lane (Eds), *Constructing stories, telling tales: A guide to formulation in applied psychology* (pp. 239–258). London: Karnac.

Drake, D. B. (2012). An introduction to narrative design. Narrative Design Labs. San Francisco: Center for Narrative Coaching & Leadership.

Eakin, P.J. (1999). *How our lives become stories*. Ithica, NY: Cornell University Press.

Foucault, M. (1965). *Madness and civilization: A history of insanity in the age of reason*. New York: Random House.

Freedman, J. & Combs, G. (1996). *Narrative therapy: The social construction of preferred realities*. New York: W.W. Norton and Company.

Gallwey, T. (2009/1981). *The inner game of golf*. New York: Random House.

Geertz, C. (1978). *The interpretation of cultures*. New York: Basic Books.

Gergen, M.M. & Gergen, K.J. (2006). Narratives in action. *Narrative Inquiry*, 16(1), 112–121.

Hermans, H.J.M. (2004). The innovation of self-narratives: A dialogical approach. In L.E. Angus & J. McLeod (Eds), *Handbook of narrative and psychotherapy: Practice, theory and research* (pp. 175–191). Thousand Oaks, CA: Sage Publications.

Hermans, H.J.M. & Kempen, H.J.G. (1993). *The dialogical self: Meaning as movement*. San Diego, CA: Academic Press.

Hewson, D. (1991). From laboratory to therapy room: Prediction questions for reconstructing the 'new-old' story. *Dulwich Centre Newsletter*, 3, 5–12.

Houston, J. (1987). *The search for the beloved: Journeys in sacred psychology*. Los Angeles, CA: Jeremy P. Tarcher.

James, W. (1927). *Psychology: Briefer course*. New York: Henry Holt & Company.

Jung, C.G. (1970). *Psychological reflections*. Princeton, NJ: Princeton University Press.

Kramer, G. (2007). *Insight dialogue: The interpersonal path to freedom*. Boston, MA: Shambhala.

Mancuso, J.C. & Sarbin, T.R. (1983). The self-narrative in the enactment of roles. In T.R. Sarbin & K.E. Scheibe (Eds), *Studies in social identity* (pp. 233–253). Westport, CT: Praeger.

Mattingly, C. (1994). The concept of therapeutic 'emplotment'. *Social Science Medicine*, 38(6), 811–822.

McKee, R. (1997). *Story: Substance, structure, style and the principles of screenwriting*. New York: HarperCollins.

Mishler, E.G. (1986). The analysis of interview-narratives. In T.R. Sarbin (Ed.), *Narrative psychology: The storied nature of human conduct* (pp. 233–255). Westport: Praeger.

Reik, T. (1998). *Listening with the third ear: The inner experience of a psychoanalyst* (12th ed.). New York: Farrar, Strauss and Giroux.

Schank, R. (1990). *Tell me a story: A new look at real and artificial memory*. New York: Charles Scribner's Sons.

Turner, V. (1969). *The ritual process: Structure and anti-structure*. New York: Aldine Publishing Co.

van Gennep, A. (1960). *The rites of passage*. London: Routledge and Kegan Paul.

White, M. (1988). The process of questioning: A therapy of literary merit? In M. White (Ed.), *Collected papers* (pp. 37–46). Adelaide, South Australia: Dulwich Centre Publications.

White, M. (2000). *Reflections on narrative practice: Essays and interviews*. Adelaide, South Australia: Dulwich Centre Publications.

White, M. & Epston, D. (1990). *Narrative means to therapeutic ends*. New York: W.W. Norton & Company.

9

Psychological Development in Adulthood and Coaching

Tatiana Bachkirova

This chapter discusses a range of theories and research about developmental changes in the psychological make up of adults which influence coaching practice. Being part of the wider area of knowledge about adult development these theories suggest that people differ in ways that could not be explained by personality types, learning styles or personal preferences, all of which are usually seen as relatively stable for each individual. They advocate that people undergo significant changes during their adult life, for example in the way they make meaning of their experiences, reason about their values and act. The changes of these capacities occur in a logical sequence of stages and influence the way people feel, make meaning and engage with their environment. This development can be further stimulated and facilitated by appropriate support and challenge within the coaching process. Understanding developmental trajectories may help coaches to be better equipped to address the diverse needs of their clients.

Adult development theories are based on the three major areas of research or strands:

- The first strand began with the important work of Jean Piaget (1976). It emphasizes developmental changes in reasoning and meaning-making which extend, for example, to moral reasoning (Kohlberg, 1969); intellectual development (Perry, 1970); reflective judgement (King & Kitchener, 1994); and 'orders of mind' (Kegan, 1982, 1994).
- The second strand is ego development, with its origins in the research of Jane Loevinger (1976, 1987). It focuses on the development of self-identity and the maturity of interpersonal relationships and has been further extended to include post-autonomous ego development by Cook-Greuter (1999, 2004) and action logics by Torbert (1991) and Torbert & Associates (2004).
- The foundation of the third strand is the research of Clare Graves (1970) into levels of existence, which was later extended into 'worldviews' and 'values' by Beck and Cowan (1996) and is known as 'Spiral Dynamics'.

Further theories and research findings suggest that other aspects of personal development also occur in sequential stages, for example, emotions (Goleman, 1995), needs (Maslow, 1954) and spiritual awareness (Fowler, 1981). In this chapter, these aspects will be called 'developmental lines' as suggested by Wilber (1999). The continuing contribution of Ken Wilber (1999, 2000, 2006) to this approach is difficult to overestimate. He pulls together many theories and research findings relevant to this approach, creating a compelling picture of integral individual development that incorporates a range of developmental lines. It becomes apparent that all these studies are conducted in the tradition of developmental structuralism, which looks for patterns that connect specific psychological phenomena.

It is important to mention that all these theories were not developed for coaching. Their main purpose was the understanding of human nature and more specifically – individual differences. However, some practical applications of the above theories were gradually developed, such as Kegan and Lahey (2009), Berger and Fitzgerald (2002) and Berger (2006, 2012). In this chapter these theories and their practical applications will be discussed together with another theory-based approach to developmental coaching (Bachkirova, 2011). This approach consists of a theory specifically developed for coaching practice which is based on a new conceptualization of the self leading to a range of specific mechanisms for facilitating change in coaching.

DISTINCTIVE FEATURES

One of the most important principles of the theories of the psychological development in adulthood is '*holarchy*' (Wilber, 2006). There is a holarchical relationship between atoms, molecules, cells and whole organisms; therefore it is not possible to go from atoms to cells by 'skipping' molecules. Applied to the stages in adult development it is claimed that adults take a considerable time to develop through each stage and stages cannot be 'skipped', because each is built upon the previous one.

Another principle is the independent development of various developmental aspects (cognitive, emotional, moral, etc.). This means that for each individual, development of a number of aspects could be far from synchronic. Figure 9.1 represents a snapshot in time of how an individual's development might look if we were able to measure development of each developmental line. This representation, however abstract, could be useful in dispelling the myths of the simplicity of categorizing people and the validity of quick conclusions about their overall development. This may also indicate the futility of attempts to use one line for describing development of another in spite of the disagreement between some authors. For example, Loevinger believed that 'If the stages really reflect a common "deep structure", the stages of those variables should all proceed in tandem' (1987, p. 242). Similarly, other authors (Beck & Cowan, 1996; Wade, 1996, Laske, 2006) argued that it is their theories that describe such a structure. However, Wilber (2000) disputes such claims and the whole idea of overall development:

> Although substantial empirical evidence demonstrates that each line develops through these holarchical stages in an invariant sequence, nonetheless, because all two dozen of them develop relatively independently, overall growth and development is a massively complex, overlapping, nonlinear affair, following no set sequence whatsoever. (Wilber, 1999, pp. 291–292)

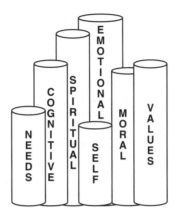

Figure 9.1   Example of a combination of the developmental lines in an individual

It can be noted that different theories of psychological development argue for a different number of stages in the developmental lines they study. This is not problematic: according to Wilber (2006) as in map making, the way to divide and represent the territory is somewhat arbitrary – it is not important 'how you slice and dice development'. At the same time, some common patterns can be identified suggesting similarities in 'slicing the developmental pie'. According to one of the patterns, development proceeds from the 'pre-conventional level to the 'conventional' and then to the 'post-conventional level' (Kohlberg, 1969). Similarly to this general pattern, Table 9.1 also describes only three stages of development under the names of Unformed, Formed and Reformed Ego, which will be further discussed later in this section (Bachkirova, 2011).

My choice to reduce the number of stages is made for simplicity and because various statistical data suggest that these are the most characteristic for the majority of adults (Beck & Cowan, 1998; Wilber, 2000; Torbert, 1991). It could be argued therefore that these stages will be typical in the clientele of coaches. These stages are described in four major aspects of the individual: cognitive style, interpersonal style, conscious preoccupations and character development as most descriptive according to Loevinger (1976). The main input for each of these aspects is drawn from the theories of Kegan (1982), Graves (1970), Wade (1996), Torbert (1991), Cook-Greuter (1999) and Wilber (2000) with the use of another simplifying meta-perspective on these theories offered by McCauley et al. (2006).

Table 9.1 indicates individual differences in people that cannot be explained by personality theories, but allow instead further understanding of the way that clients may change in the process of development. Acknowledgement of these differences can help to see why some coaching approaches might be better suited than others when working with people at different developmental stages. Appreciation of these differences is important for coaches themselves and the changes they undergo. Bachkirova and Cox (2007) argue that coaches who are aware of their own stages of development might be in a better position to understand their own role

Table 9.1 A cumulative description of the three stages in adult psychological development (Bachkirova, 2011, p.49)

Stages	Unformed ego	Formed ego	Reformed ego
Cognitive style	Socialized mind	Self-authoring mind	Self-transforming mind
(based mostly on Kegan)	Ability for abstract thinking and self-reflection	Can see multiplicity and patterns; critical and analytical	Systems view; tolerance of ambiguity; change from linear logic to holistic understanding
Interpersonal style	Dependent	Independent	Inter-independent
(Loevinger and Cook-Greuter)	Conformist/self-conscious	Conscientious/individualist	Autonomous/Integrated
	Need for belonging; socially expected behaviour in relationships; peacemakers/keepers	Separate but responsible for their own choices; communication and individual differences are valued	Take responsibility for relationship; respect autonomy of others; tolerance of conflicts; non-hostile humour
Conscious preoccupations	Multiplistic	Relativistic/Individualistic	Systemic/integrated
(Graves)	Social acceptance, reputation, moral 'shoulds and oughts'	Achievement of personal goals according to inner standards.	Individuality; self-fulfilment; immediate present; understanding conflicting needs
Character development	Rule-bound	Conscientious	Self-regulated
(Loevinger, Cook-Greuter and Kolhberg)	'Inappropriate' feelings are denied or repressed. Rules of important others are internalized and obeyed	Self-reliant, conscientious; follow self-evaluated rules; judge themselves and critical of others	Behaviour is an expression of own moral principles. Concerned with conflicting roles, duties, value systems

in the coaching process and the dynamics of the coaching relationship and thus be able to articulate, influence and change more critical situations in the coaching process. Also, the practical applications of some theories described, for example, by Berger and Fitzgerald (2002), Kegan and Lahey (2009) and Berger (2012), show how useful these theories can be for coaching practice.

However, it has to be said that the theories of psychological development in adulthood are also known for their complexity and particularly for their labour-intensive instruments used to identify developmental stages. Lahey and associates (1988) developed the subject–object interview (SOI), which is used for the assessment of 21 gradations within Kegan's orders of mind. It requires 60–90 minutes of recorded interview and a highly skilful scoring of the transcript. Although Berger's recent work (2012) makes the process of identifying developmental stages much clearer and appealing to try, it is still a significant challenge for coaches. There is also the Washington University Sentence Completion Test used to measure Loevinger's (1976) stages, which has been updated by Cook-Greuter (2004) as the Leadership Development Profile (LDP). Individual assessment with these tools can only be done through relevant organizations and there are many aspects of the measurement process that can potentially interfere with the quality of it such as verbal fluency and educational and social background (McCauley et al., 2006; Manners & Durkin, 2001). Although the commitment of these organizations to improving the quality of these instruments and inter-rater reliability amongst their trained scorers is reassuring, the actual fact that the assessment is done through the third party can deter coaches from using them.

With an intention to avoid the issue of measurement I have suggested a different theory that involves concentrating on the themes that clients are concerned with in different periods of their lives (Bachkirova, 2011). I argued that clients' concerns and their goals themselves show a pattern that is developmental. Therefore, I proposed that for the purpose of coaching there is no need to assess where each client is according to any scale – instead coaches can and should work with *developmental themes* that are brought by clients themselves. These themes are not only about goals – they are about the challenges that people face in life, what they find difficult, what their life circumstances demand from them. The pattern in the themes (Table 9.2) indicates the stage of ego development in each client which would help to shape an individual approach to coaching, i.e. offering coaching towards a healthy ego, coaching the ego or coaching beyond the ego (Bachkirova, 2011).

Table 9.2   Three groups of developmental themes with the corresponding approach to coaching

Themes of Unformed ego	Themes of Formed ego	Themes of Reformed ego
Decision-making in difficult situations with a number of stake-holders	Coping with high amount of self-created work	Dissatisfaction with life, in spite of achievements
		Internal conflict
Taking higher level of responsibility than they feel they can cope with	Achievement of recognition, promotion, etc.	Not 'fitting in'
	Interpersonal conflicts	Search for meaning in life
Work–life balance connected to inability to say 'no'	Drive for success and underlying fear of failure	Overcoming life crisis
		Initiating a significant change
Performance anxiety	Problem solving	Dealing with personal illusions
Issues of self-esteem	Learning to delegate	Staying true to themselves in a complex situation
	Stress management	
Coaching towards a healthy ego	**Coaching the ego**	**Coaching beyond the ego**

Ego in this theory is a neurological network of mini-selves according to the explanation of the mind as modular (e.g. Gazzaniga, 1985; Kurzban, 2012). Each mini-self is a combination of brain/mind states and processes that are involved in the organism's engagement with a certain task or more precisely, it is a particular pattern of links between different areas of the brain that become activated or inhibited when the organism is involved in an act. Both the consciousness (*rider*) and the unconscious automatic processes of the whole organism (*elephant)* are involved in the functioning of the ego (Haidt, 2006; Bachkirova, 2011).

The ego could be developed to various degrees and described as unformed, formed or fully formed. When the ego is fully developed the mind/brain can act or refrain from action if necessary in a way that reasonably satisfies the organism as a whole with all the multiplicity of its needs and tasks. With the *unformed ego* there are needs that remain unsatisfied and tasks unfulfilled. The sign of a fully *formed ego* is the capacity of the whole organism to take ownership of the past, withstand anxiety about what the future holds and build relationships with others without losing the sense of who they are. Their choices may be constructive or destructive, but they are made according to their own criteria. At the same time this stage of ego development is associated with other developmental challenges. The sense of control and self-ownership may lead to an overestimation of what is possible and realistic for the organism, which may result in a lack of attention to and even abuse of the body when working to achieve some specific targets. The third category, a *reformed ego*, represents capacities of the ego that go beyond those of the formed ego. There is a much more harmonious relationship between the elephant and the rider, manifested in the ability of the organism to tolerate the ambiguity of some needs and tasks, thus minimizing energy wasted on conflicts between the various mini-selves (Bachkirova, 2011, 2012).

Influencing development in coaching

Although coaching may seem to be a perfect way to influence development as described, the idea of actively influencing development is contentious among different authors. Some strongly advocate the need for development (Laske, 2006) others are more tentative (Kegan, 1982; Berger, 2006; Bachkirova, 2011). For example, Kegan suggests that the quality of psychological support for an individual who is facing transition or a new developmental task will be higher if the coach is 'developmentally-minded'. The main value is for the client to be in the presence of someone 'who can see, recognize and understand who the person is and who he or she is *becoming*' (Kegan, 1982: 260) (emphasis added). However, Kegan also expressed an important concern about overzealous attempts to change someone developmentally: 'amongst the many things from which a practitioner's clients need protection is the practitioner's hopes for the client's future, however benign and sympathetic these hopes may be' (1982: 295).

It is important to emphasize that the nature of development as discussed in this chapter is a complex process that involves a combination of known and unknown, internal and environmental factors. The shift from one stage to another may even take years to be noticed and recognized. However, once understood, these theories may be so attractive that some coaches are seduced into using them inappropriately, designing and suggesting interventions to 'move' clients from one stage to another. The main danger of this approach is that it may create the illusion that significant developmental shifts can be induced by sufficient motivation and effort. It may also distract coaches from attending to the client's other concerns which may actually be more relevant to them and have greater urgency. Berger also warned about hasty judgements of developmental stages, particularly in organizational contexts (2006) and about simplistic interpretations of this theoretical perspective.

At the same time, we do see again and again that the coaching process, even if it aims at specific and pragmatic goals, provides important conditions for potential developmental shifts in individuals. By engaging with the presenting task, coaches inevitably evaluate a fit between the existing capabilities of the client and the complexity of a task. This prompts them to create appropriate conditions for a developmental shift if necessary and that shift may well happen. It is interesting to notice at the same time how some traditional coaching approaches could be more suited for coaching clients at specific stages of development. For example, Person-centred coaching and Transactional Analysis (TA) have good methods suitable for coaching towards a healthy ego. Cognitive-behavioural and Solution-focused would resonate well with a Formed Ego. The Existential approach or Gestalt approach, on the other hand, would be sufficiently challenging for coaching beyond the ego (Bachkirova, 2011).

This means that coaches working in different traditions can work developmentally and be successful in promoting development without focusing on moving the client to the next stage of development. At the same time their knowledge of the theories of development can help them to recognize where the main challenges for the client are and to understand why their traditional approach may not work. In terms of the process, according to my theory of client development in coaching (Bachkirova, 2011) the developmentally-minded coach would approach a new assignment initially in the same way as any other coach: identifying the clients' needs, exploring their situation fully and clarifying their goals. This task should not be minimized by the focus on the clients' stage of development. However, the developmental coach would gradually gain a sense of the state of the client's ego from taking into account the issues they both identified, the challenges the client faces and the difficulties he/she experiences. The task of the coach is to engage with whatever issue/goal is presented, but noticing at the same time a pattern in these: a developmental theme. His/her job between the sessions is to explore these patterns and consider relevant coaching strategies through reflection on the previous sessions, preparation for the coming sessions and discussion of these cases in supervision.

METHODS AND TECHNIQUES

In Kegan's (1982) approach to development, an important mechanism of change is a shift from subject to object which coaching can usefully influence. Things that are Subject in Kegan's theory can prompt us to action but cannot be observed or reflected on. We cannot stand back and take a look at them because we are embedded in them. On the other hand, things that are Object for us are 'those elements of our knowing or organizing that we can reflect on, handle, look at, be responsible for, relate to each other, take control of, internalize, assimilate, or otherwise operate upon' (Kegan, 1994: 32). It has been said that to be Subject is to 'see with' rather than to 'see through' (Drath, 1990). A good example is 'cultural blindness' as described by Drath (1990: 486), who suggests that

we see with our culture-bound norms and expectations, accept them as given, and cannot examine them for what they are – that is, we cannot see through them. Our cultural heritage is something we are, not something we have. The culture holds us; we are embedded in it and cannot rise above it.

It is natural, therefore, that the more individuals can take as Object, the more complex their worldview becomes, because they can examine and act upon more things. The mechanism of the shift from Subject to Object could be considered as an essential element of coaching. It is one of the functions of coaches to watch for the re-absorption of insight in the client and to help build *psychological muscle* in order to hold something out from a person as an Object. As Berger and Fitzgerald (2002: 31) say: 'one of the most powerful interventions coaches can provide is simply help to keep critical insights alive for their clients'.

Here is an example from the coaching process: in his new role of head of department, a client received feedback suggesting that his way of one-to-one communication with people made some of his staff uncomfortable. He asked his coach to help him to respond to this feedback, which he found puzzling. They explored this feedback together with the coach's own observations of his interactions with her and others. It appeared that the client's style involved unusually long pauses that people perceived as withdrawals. These apparently made those colleagues, who were more self-conscious than others, feel insecure. The client was not aware of this. His style was so much a part of who he was that he could not reflect on the effect of it on other people. As the result of coaching, his style has gradually changed from being Subject into Object, leading to the client's increased ability to notice it and modify it when necessary.

Kegan and Lahey (2009) also proposed the idea of *immunity to change* suggesting that many people who sincerely want to change may not be able to do so because they are directing a lot of productive energy towards a hidden competing commitment. For example, the client may genuinely want to empower others and to delegate, but finds himself regularly sorting the problems by himself. His competing commitment may be to be personally useful with a 'big assumption' behind it that he might not be deeply satisfied when he is in a second line of action. Kegan and Lahey (2009) also developed an exercise of four columns to identify a big assumption, to make it 'object' for a person, which may lead to a new, more 'spacious' mental structure, able to accommodate a wider range of links. In this example, the definition of individual hero could expand into someone who is a hero by virtue of empowering others.

In Berger (2012) we can find many overall strategies of working with clients if their stages of development are identified. She suggests various ways of identifying key strengths, blind spots and central areas of growth for the clients at each stage, and comments on pitfalls that coaches may face with these client groups. For example, coaching the self-authored type of clients (formed ego as an equivalent) Berger recommends *exploring dichotomies, uncovering assumptions, questioning certainty and seeking wise mentors and thinking partners*. What is particularly important in Berger's position to the developmental perspective on coaching is the emphasis not only on techniques and methods of working with clients but also the attitude and intention of the coach (2012: 93). For example, she argues that simply learning about theories of development is developmental. Engaging with these theories coaches begin to ask themselves the developmental questions the theory asks and begin to listen in a different way to their own answers.

In my approach to developmental coaching three further mechanisms for development are proposed: improving quality of perception, working with the multiplicity of self-models and working with the elephant (unconscious, automatic parts of mind/brain and body). It is postulated that attention to these aspects in developmental coaching will enhance the client's engagement with the change they are aiming at.

Improving the quality of perception

In order to improve the quality of perception both internally and externally, coaches traditionally aim at development of active listening skills, observation skills, attention to body language, etc. However, it is important to know what we are up against when we try to improve it – what prevents us from seeing things as they are. According to Krishnamurti (1996: 54), it is only through understanding the nature of the trap that one can be free of it. Therefore, in coaching, *conditioning and self-deception* could be addressed as two main issues which interfere with the quality of perception.

Conditioning indicates issues of 'second-hand knowledge' absorbed from the culture of organizations, circles of friends, society as a whole, in ways that prevent change and development. Exposing and counteracting these influences is useful in developmental coaching. Another obstacle to perception is *self-deception*. Whilst during conditioning the filters impacting perception of reality are polished by influential others, in self-deception this job is done internally. There is a significant body of literature (Ames & Dissanayake, 1996; Fingarette, 2000; Goleman, 1997; Gur & Sackheim, 1979; Lewis, 1996) that offers useful insights into the psychology of self-deception in individuals, explaining cases based on cognitive incompetence, faulty thinking, irrational beliefs and unconscious psychological mechanisms. Working with the holes in clients' perceptions created by self-deception is another task of developmental coaches.

Working the multiplicity of self-models

Self-models or various stories of the self are put together by the linguistic function in the rider which have evolved with our ability to use language. They are not the same as mini-selves that constitute the ego. Although these stories help to create a coherent and reasonably consistent image of ourselves, some of them may be less than helpful in the process of change. Coaches can help clients in *accepting the fact of multiplicity.* Seeing the multitude of self-stories is helpful for many reasons (Rowan, 2009; Carter, 2008). Research by Linville (1987), for example, found that the more distinct self-descriptions of themselves participants were able to produce, the less they were likely to become depressed and even suffer somatically when under stress. Accepting multiplicity of self-models leads to conscious openness to experimenting with new roles that are often useful in coaching. It would also help if these conscious representations of our engagements with the world corresponded to how we actually act, to our actual mini-selves and this could also be a topic in developmental coaching (Bachkirova, 2011).

Working with the elephant

The third mechanism of change, *working with the elephant* (the emotional unconscious mind and the body), is about better interaction between the rider and the elephant in the process of change. This is possible through promotion of *soft thinking* (Claxton, 1999: 146) in addition to traditional hard reasoning which tend to involve the inhibition of other parts of the mind. Soft thinking instead implies a soft focus, 'looking at' rather than 'looking for' (Claxton, 1999; Claxton & Lucas, 2007) without forcing out new, unstable and fragile ideas that come from the unconscious. Gentle, rather than 'incisive' questioning and simply slowing down also promote soft thinking.

Another way of working with the elephant is better *communication with the emotional body*, improving two-way traffic between the rider and elephant. The language of the elephant is non-verbal, so the developmental coach promotes attention to emotions and other signs that may not be easy to articulate: physical feelings, images and dreams, guesses, fleeting thoughts, hunches. Gendlin (1962, 2003) for example, suggests a method of 'focusing': inviting the messages from the elephant, looking not only for unarticulated, but pre-logical, pre-conceptual, just felt dimensions of experiencing. In communicating messages to the elephant the use of imagery and metaphors is recommended and awareness of a particular sensitivity of the elephant to both the relationship with the coach and the coach's attitude towards the client (Bachkirova, 2011).

Although these mechanisms indicate the potential for development in any coaching process, each of these would need to be approached differently when applied to different stages of ego development. For example, in terms of improving the quality of perception, working with the unformed ego needs more attention to conditioning: giving priority to experience and own voice, while the formed ego is more susceptible to self-deception, so the priority should be given to external input, feedback and discrepancies (Bachkirova, 2011).

APPLICATION

There is an obvious connection between the approaches to coaching based on theories of psychological development in adulthood and *developmental coaching,* which is concerned with holistic changes in the person. If clients are dealing with important dilemmas or transitions in their lives (a theme that often occurs in developmental coaching) this perspective may help coaches and clients to understand that transitions may be not just an adjustment to environmental changes but also an internal process that has specific features. This can be helpful for clients as it will help them to understand what they are going through and to see the specific landmarks of this process.

In relation to *team coaching*, this approach makes clear why group work is sometimes difficult. For example, when individuals, at different stages of development, are intensely involved in the same process, the chances of serious misunderstandings are numerous. However, opportunities for expected and unexpected growth may also be present. Theories of psychological development may help to explain the reasons for disagreements and conflicts. They may also help coaches to find an overall perspective which allows for the integration of the different needs of individuals into the value system of the team.

The coach's own stage of development is also important. To be of most help to the client the coach should be able to recognize where the client is on the developmental line. As has been said already, people find difficulty in recognizing stages of development that come later than their own and consequently may not be optimally helpful as coaches in such cases. At the same time it could be argued that within certain coaching genres, for example skills coaching, such a discrepancy is less important.

EVALUATION

The approach to coaching based on psychological development theories can be highly valuable for coaching practice providing knowledge about an important dimension of clients' individual differences. However, this approach is not without controversies. Sometimes it causes unease in some coaches and sometimes it leads to overzealous and uncritical acceptance of its tenets. We also need to acknowledge considerable restrictions to the competent use of the diagnostic instruments which prevent wider applications of these theories in coaching practice.

First of all it is important to address the concern about this approach expressed by some coaches who believe that theories of psychological development imply a judgement about the level of development. This is seen as going against an implicit characteristic of coaching as non-judgemental. Without minimizing the significance of this concern it is important to notice that similar judgements are made on an everyday basis for all sorts of reasons including those which are fairly justified. Coaches reflect on such judgements individually and in supervision to evaluate their effect on the coaching process. What usually matters is the purpose of the judgement (or a better term – assessment) and the validity of it. The purpose of such an assessment in coaching is to facilitate a better fit between the environment and the client's capacity for dealing with it. In this case assessment is done in the best service of the client. The validity of the assessment depends on the quality of the theory that advocates it and the quality of the actual assessment.

This leads us again to issues related to the instruments for assessment of the individual development. As already discussed, in order to know the stage of development of the client, coaches seem to have various options. One option is to use independent assessments of the client's stage through specific instruments such as LDP, which are available, but quite expensive additions to the coaching itself. Another option is to invest into training and to learn to score SOI which is complex, time-consuming, but can be developmental in itself. Yet another option is to learn about developmental themes (Bachkirova, 2011), which is less precise than the above instruments but more precise than an 'educated guess' – an option that is available to anyone interested in these theories.

The last two options may sound imperfect but they have certain advantages. First of all, the coaches' assessment of the client's stage will be a tentative one and they will remain open to other interpretations of their judgement. (With the use of two previous instruments the temptation to see their results as 'truth' is much higher.) Second, in my view, coaching is valuable when coaches give respectful attention to the voices of *all* the client's states and stages and not only to 'the centre of developmental gravity'. Having a healthy doubt about the client's stage would help to keep the coach's attention fresh and open to these voices.

I also would like to express my concern about the over-enthusiastic voices in the coaching field: not only advocating such theories as potentially useful, but claiming a precision of assessment that is impossible to justify and putting pressure on coaches to be assessed and to assess clients as if it were an 'ethical obligation'. Learning about these theories should be an opportunity rather than a demand. It is better for coaches to learn about adult development not in order to avoid some potential harm that is difficult to justify. A better motive is to see more dimensions in themselves, their clients and the process of coaching. Realization of this complexity can enrich coaches' capacities for reflection and effective interaction with others providing more openings to their growth as a person, and it is the coach as a person, rather than the application of particular techniques or methods, that makes a difference in coaching practice.

FURTHER READING

Bachkirova, T. (2011). *Developmental coaching: Working with the self*. Maidenhead: Open University Press. (Describes a theory of adult development that is specifically created for coaching and the practical approach based on this theory.)
Berger, J.G. (2012). *Changing on the job: Developing leaders for a complex world*. Stanford, CA: Stanford University Press. (A practical and thoughtful adaptation of the original Kegan's theory, particularly valuable in the organizational context.)
Kegan, R. (2001). *The evolving self: Problem and process in human development*. London: Harvard University Press. (An original work of Kegan and an excellent introduction to his theory in spite of being conceptually challenging.)

DISCUSSION QUESTIONS

- What do you see as particularly developmental aspects of your approach to coaching?
- What other themes of coaching can be added to Table 9.2 that describe the typical developmental themes of the unformed, formed and reformed ego?
- What is your view on potential discrepancies between the levels of development of the coach and client? How could they affect the coaching process?

REFERENCES

Adams, G. & Fitch, S. (1982). Ego stage and identity status development: A cross sequential analysis. *Journal of Personality and Social Psychology, 43*, 574–583.
Ames, A. & Dissanayake, W. (Eds) (1996). *Self and deception: A cross-cultural philosophical enquiry*. Albany, NY: State University of New York Press.
Bachkirova, T. (2011). *Developmental coaching: Working with the self*. Maidenhead: Open University Press.
Bachkirova, T. (2013). Developmental coaching: Developing the self. In J. Passmore, D. Peterson, & T. Freire (Eds) *The Wiley-Blackwell handbook of the psychology of coaching and mentoring* (pp.135–154). Chichester: John Wiley and Sons Ltd.
Bachkirova, T. & Cox, E. (2007). A cognitive developmental approach for coach development. In S. Palmer & A. Whybrow (Eds), *Handbook of coaching psychology: A guide for practitioners* (pp. 325–350). London: Routledge.
Beck, D. & Cowan, C. (1996). *Spiral dynamics*. Oxford: Blackwell.
Berger, J. (2006). Adult development theory and executive coaching practice. In D. Stober & A. Grant (Eds), *Evidence based coaching handbook: Putting best practices to work for your clients*. Chichester: John Wiley.

Berger, J. (2012) Changing on the job: Developing leaders for a complex world. Stanford, CA: Stanford University Press.

Berger, J. & Atkins, P. (2009). Mapping complexity of mind: Using the subject-object interview in coaching. *Coaching: An International Journal of Theory, Research and Practice,* 2(1), 23–36.

Berger, J. & Fitzgerald, C. (2002). Leadership and complexity of mind: The role of executive coaching. In C. Fitzgerald & J. Berger (Eds), *Executive coaching: Practices & perspectives* (pp. 27–58). Palo Alto, CA: Davies-Black.

Carter, R. (2008). *Multiplicity: The new science of personality.* London: Little, Brown.

Claxton, G. (1999). *Wise-up: The challenge of lifelong learning.* London: Bloomsbury.

Claxton, G. & Lucas, B. (2007). *The creative thinking plan: How to generate ideas and solve problems in your work and life.* London: BBC Books.

Cook-Greuter, S. (1999). *Postatonomous ego development: Its nature and measurement.* (Doctoral dissertation). Harvard Graduate School of Education at Cambridge, MA.

Cook-Greuter, S. (2004). Making the case for developmental perspective. *Industrial and Commercial Training,* 36(7), 275–281.

Drath, W. (1990). Managerial strengths and weaknesses as functions of the development of personal meaning. *Journal of Applied Behavioural Science,* 26(4), 483–99.

Fingarette, H. (2000). *Self-deception.* London: University of California Press.

Fowler, J.W. (1981). *Stages of faith.* New York: Harper & Row.

Gazzaniga, M. (1985). *The social brain.* New York: Basic Books.

Gendlin, E. (1962). *Experiencing and the creation of meaning: A philosophical and psychological approach to the subjective.* Evanston, IL: Northwestern University Press.

Gendlin, E. (2003). *Focusing.* London: Rider.

Goleman, D. (1995). *Emotional intelligence.* New York: Bantam Books.

Graves, C. (1970). Levels of existence: An open system theory of values. *Journal of Humanistic Psychology,* 10(2), 131–154.

Gur, R. & Sackheim, H. (1979). Self-deception: A concept in search of a phenomenon. *Journal of Personality and Social Psychology,* 37, 147–169.

Haidt, J. (2006). *The happiness hypothesis.* London: Arrow Books.

Hawkins, P. and Smith, N. (2006). *Coaching, mentoring and organizational consultancy: Supervision and development.* Maidenhead: Open University Press.

Kegan, R. (1982). *The evolving self: Problem and process in human development.* London: Harvard University Press.

Kegan, R. (1994). *In over our heads.* London: Harvard University Press.

Kegan, R. & Lahey, L. (2009). *Immunity to change: How to overcome it and unlock the potential in yourself and your organisation.* Boston, MA: Harvard Business Press.

King, P.M. & Kitchener, K.S. (1994). *Developing reflective judgment: Understanding and promoting intellectual growth and critical thinking in adolescents and adults.* San Francisco, CA: Jossey-Bass.

Krishnamurti, J. (1996). *Questioning Krishnamurti.* London: Thorsons.

Kohlberg, L. (1969). *Stages in the development of moral thought and action.* New York: Holt, Reinhart and Winston.

Kurzban, R. (2012). *Why everyone else is a hypocrite: Evolution and the Modular Mind.* Princeton, NJ: Princeton University Press.

Lahey, L., Souvaine, E., Kegan, R., Goodman, R., & Felix, S. (1988). *A guide to the subject-object interview: Its administration and interpretation.* Cambridge, MA: Harvard University, Graduate School of Education, Laboratory of Human Development.

Laske, O. (2006). From coach training to coach education. *International Journal of Evidence Based Coaching and Mentoring,* 4(1, Spring), 45–57.

Lewis, B. (1996). Self-deception: A post modern reflection. *Journal of Theoretical and Philosophical Psychology,* 16(1), 49–66.

Linville, P. (1987). Self complexity as a cognitive buffer against stress-related illness and depression. *Journal of Personality and Social Psychology,* 52, 663–676.

Loevinger, J. (1976). *Ego development: Conceptions and theories.* San Francisco, CA: Jossey-Bass.

Loevinger, J. (1987). *Paradigms of personality.* New York: M. H. Freeman.

Manners, J. & Durkin, K. (2001). A critical review of the validity of ego development theory and its measurement. *Journal of Personality Assessment,* 77(3), 541–567.

McCauley, C., Drath, W. Palus, P., & Baker, B. (2006). The use of constructive-developmental theory to advance the understanding of leadership. *The Leadership Quarterly*, 17, pp. 634–653.

Maslow, A. (1954). *Motivation and personality*. New York: Harper.

Perry, W.G. (1970). *Forms of intellectual and ethical development in the college years*. New York: Holt, Rinehart and Winston.

Piaget, J. (1976). *The psychology of intelligence*. Totowa: NJ: Littlefield, Adams & Co.

Rowan J. (2009). *Subpersonalities – the people inside us*. London: Brunner-Routledge.

Torbert, W. (1991). *The power of balance*. Newbury Park, CA: Sage.

Torbert, W. & Associates. (2004). *Action inquiry: The secret of timely and transforming leadership*. San Francisco, CA: Berret-Koehler.

Wilber, K. (1979). *No boundary.* Boston, MA: Shambhala.

Wilber, K. (1999). *One taste: The journals of Ken Wilber.* Boston, MA: Shambhala.

Wilber, K. (2000). *Integral psychology.* London: Shambhala.

Wilber, K. (2006). *Integral spirituality*. Boston & London: Integral Books.

10

The Transpersonal Approach to Coaching

John Rowan

The transpersonal is the land of creativity, of playfulness, of no boundaries, of no restrictions, of endless joy. It is full of imagery, guided fantasies, unguided fantasies, sudden leaps, unpredictable discoveries. It is the most fun of any approach to coaching. That is why I love it.

The transpersonal is a level of consciousness where we admit that we are spiritual beings with a soul and a spirit. As we know from the work of Ken Wilber (2000), it is usual to distinguish between the pre-personal, the personal and the transpersonal, and this seems clear enough. The personal is the ordinary everyday consciousness with which we are all familiar; the pre-personal is all that comes before that in the process of development, and is well described in developmental psychology generally; and the transpersonal is that which genuinely goes beyond the personal into the realm of the sacred, the numinous, the holy, the divine. That is all well-trodden ground. It has often been pointed out that society helps us to develop out of the pre-personal into the personal, and even helps us through the early development of the personal into the mature ego that is favoured in our society generally. Society does not, however, help us on into the transpersonal. That is something for each person to initiate and take responsibility for. And just because society is not interested in the transpersonal, it is a realm which is disputed and subject to warring factions.

However, since the founding of the *Journal of Transpersonal Psychology* in 1969 and the formation of the Association for Transpersonal Psychology in 1972, the transpersonal has been studied scientifically, and in 1996 the British Psychological Society founded the Transpersonal Psychology Section, which publishes the peer-reviewed *Transpersonal Psychology Review.*

This and the publication of a variety of books (e.g. Cortright, 1997; West, 2000; Wilber, 2000; Ferrer, 2002; Rowan, 2005), have made the subject respectable and well based.

Let us look at some of the boundaries which should help to clarify the matter.

The transpersonal is not the extrapersonal

A distinction has been drawn by Alyce and Elmer Green (1986) between the extrapersonal and the transpersonal. The point is that the extrapersonal can sometimes be simply a gift that the person has. It can simply be a wild talent, perhaps present from an early age. The whole range of the paranormal comes in here, as representing the extrapersonal.

The transpersonal is not the same as the right brain

There is a lot of interest these days in the two halves of the brain, and it is often said that our civilization neglects the right brain and overstresses the left brain. There may be something in this, and there is no wish here to pour cold water on the whole idea, particularly in view of the recent work of Ian McGilchrist (2009), but it is important to make the point that to locate the transpersonal in the right brain is a mistake. It is a mistake because it necessarily lumps the transpersonal with the pre-personal.

The transpersonal is not the New Age

There is a good deal of interest these days in the New Age and in my travels I have seen whole sections of bookshops and even whole bookshops, devoted to it. But the general attitude of the New Age seems to be undiscriminating and even to be against the whole idea of discrimination. The New Age people love the transpersonal, but the transpersonal people do not love the New Age.

The transpersonal is not religion

The most general use of the word 'religion' is to mean an organization of some kind. But the transpersonal is to do with personal experience, which may or may not be expressed in religious terminology. And if it is expressed in some religious way, it is just as likely to be some little-known religion such as paganism, animism, polytheism or pantheism, as one of the better-known and better-organized religions. In other words, the transpersonal is a realm of personal discovery, not something which one joins.

The transpersonal is not the spiritual

Even more importantly, the word spirituality is used so vaguely and generally that we have to question its value. There can be pre-personal spirituality (which includes fundamentalism and is often fear-based), personal spirituality (which produces all kinds of good works such as schools and hospitals) and transpersonal spirituality. In the early 1970s Roberto Assagioli described the transpersonal as:

> a term introduced above all by Maslow and by those of his school to refer to what is commonly called spiritual. Scientifically speaking, it is a better word; it is more precise and, in a certain sense, neutral in that it points to that which is beyond or above ordinary personality. Furthermore it avoids confusion with many things which are now called spiritual but which are actually pseudo-spiritual or parapsychological. (Assagioli, 1991: 16)

I think this is a very important point, because the word 'spiritual' is beginning to be used much more these days, not least by people who want to obscure the kinds of distinctions we have tried to make here.

Within the transpersonal

Now within the transpersonal, there is an important distinction to be made, which I think is most clearly put by Ken Wilber (2000). Transpersonal 1 is variously called the Subtle, the realm of the soul, the superconscious, the heart centre, the intuitive mind, the psychic centre, the *antaratman* and so forth. Its distinguishing feature is that it shows forth the divine in the form of symbols and images, which are accessible and reasonably familiar to all. So it is the realm of archetypes (Shadow, Anima, Puer, etc.), deities, nature spirits, standing stones, wells, trees, rivers and so forth – all things which are accessible to all of us and which point to the divine if approached in the right way. In yoga it is called the *bhakti* approach and it is the realm of compassion of a deeply emotional kind. And in coaching it is the realm of linking – a psychological connection with another person where the usual boundaries seem to fall away (Rowan, 2005).

Transpersonal 2 is the further stage of transpersonal development, where we are able to give up all the symbols and images, all the comfortable distinctions and divisions, and move into the deep ocean of spirituality, where there are no signposts and no landmarks. This is variously called the Causal, the overmind, the bliss mind, the pure self, formless mysticism, *jnana* yoga, the witness, cessation, the Void, Big Mind and so forth. This is less often used in coaching and I shall explain why this is a mistake.

However, Transpersonal 1 can be used quite readily, because it is more accessible and more coaches have had some experience of it, particularly if they have been through a psychosynthesis training, where a good deal of attention is paid to it. Sir John Whitmore, for example, has used ideas from psychosynthesis a good deal, such as subpersonalities, guided imagery and the superconscious (Whitmore & Einzig, 2007). In what follows, we will give many examples of how it can be used in coaching.

DISTINCTIVE FEATURES

The transpersonal tradition is devoted to the idea of development and holds that we are all on a path of psychospiritual development whether we know it or not and whether we like it or not (Wilber, 2000). At the same time it recognizes that at the extreme point of development the whole idea disappears because it holds that the central part of a person was never born and will never die. This is part of the mystical tradition that we have named as Transpersonal 2 in the Introduction. This tradition recognizes that people go through stages in their lives when predictable issues have to be faced and dealt with. What we do not do is to ascribe a great deal of importance to them except as illusions to be seen through. In fact, from a transpersonal point of view, the whole object of therapy is to get rid of illusions and false assumptions. Similarly with coaching, what holds people back is not the facts of their situations, but the false assumptions they make about them. As Mark Twain once said, 'It is not the things we don't know that hold us back, it is the things we do know for sure that just ain't so!' And this rather comedic dictum alerts us to the fact that the transpersonal is a field full of fun, a district full of delight, an arena full of artistry, of affability, of the amazing and the adventurous.

One of the main illusions which has to be faced and dealt with is the false belief that we are determined by our previous experiences. The word that is unfortunately too often used for this is 'conditioning' and this is believed in as a real entity with its own fixed laws. From a transpersonal point of view, conditioning may well apply to rats and other organisms, but not to the human soul, which is unconditioned. This is certainly so at the level we have called Transpersonal 1, where we are more inclined to say that 'Wounds are for healing'.

However, there is an interesting contribution which has been made by Whitmore (2002). He suggests that people in business and elsewhere have two forms of development which can get separated, with unfortunate results. One is the everyday development, which is objective, quantitative, psychological, out there – mainly concerned with what we have named as the personal: material things and socially approved achievements. He says that many people act as if this were all there is. The other is transpersonal development, which is more qualitative, aspirational, spiritual and mainly concerned with the inner world. He suggests that we look at these as two dimensions at right angles to each other. The horizontal dimension he calls the psychological/quantitative and the vertical dimension the spiritual/qualitative. This gives us a graphic space where we can plot the position of a given person at a given time.

He goes on to say that if a person were balanced between these two, we would get a neat diagonal line on such a graph, showing equal progress along both dimensions. But what so often happens is that a person, let us say a businessman, crawls along the bottom of the graph, paying much attention to the psychological and the quantitative – or in other words, his work – but none or a minimal amount to the spiritual or the qualitative. (Of course it would also be possible, if less common in our society, to pay attention only to the spiritual/qualitative dimension, and be equally unbalanced in that way.) But what may happen then is that the person hits a crisis of meaning. This very often takes the form of a break of some kind, forcing the person to rethink their whole life. It can then be a wake-up call, leading the person to take up coaching, for example, as a way out. 'When we hit the crisis wall, we tend to bounce back in shock and into temporary confusion and performance regression for a while, but we are at the same time pulled upwards toward the ideal eventually to discover a more balanced path' (Whitmore, 2002: 123). This can then lead to an increased wisdom in leading our life in a less one-sided and unbalanced way.

This means that people who come in to transpersonal coaching as clients have often hit this wall: 'This crisis was typically associated with mid-life, but we are now seeing it among many younger people too' (Whitmore & Einzig, 2007: 126). In transpersonal coaching we are able to recognize such moments and help the clients to use better maps of their world. Such development is not the gradual increase in ability which we found earlier on the path, but rather a step-function change, involving the rejection of much that we took for granted at earlier ages. It is here that the transpersonal can become important, as giving us the guideposts needed for the next phase of our development.

There is a very important theoretical point to be made here. Quite recently was launched the idea of the Wilber-Combs Matrix (Wilber, 2006: Ch. 4). This says that although fully reaching a mystical *stage* takes appropriate work in psychospiritual development, having an experience of such a *state*, in a temporary way, is open to all. We have always known that a peak experience can come to anyone: what we are now saying is that we can turn this on at will, without the use of meditation or drugs; all we have to do is ask. Then, along came Genpo Roshi (Merzel, 2007) to tell us how. We do not have the space here to spell this out in detail, but it informs the rest of this chapter.

Essential processes/dynamics

From a transpersonal point of view, there are no fixed processes or dynamics, because everything is fluid and open to change all the time. It is a truly experimental point of view, which simply says – 'Let's try it and see'. Taking nothing for granted is easy at the level of Transpersonal 1, because we can now see that nothing is absolutely true. However, there is one theory which turns out to be particularly helpful at this stage. It is called 'Theory U' and it comes from the book *Presence* written by Senge, Scharmer, Jaworski and Flowers (2005). However, full details will not be given here, because although it is excellent, it is also quite time-consuming, because it involves taking the coachee through seven stages in the work.

The idea is that in transpersonal work we are continually trying to engage with the creativity of the client. Our job is very often to help the client to bring out his or her latent creative spirit. In transpersonal work we are not only 'listening for the large life' (Williams and Menendez, 2007), we are also listening for the deep life. It is certainly possible to say, with Dave Ellis, that 'coaching gives the opportunity to think what they've not thought, say what they've not said, dream what they've not dreamt and create what they've not created' (Ellis, 1995).

Creativity and imagery

However, the main tools of the transpersonal coach are intuition (Charles, 2004) and imagery. At the level of Transpersonal 1, intuition has become our main way of thinking, our main platform for interacting with the client. And imagery is our main tool. Instead of saying 'What happened in that meeting with your boss?' we might say – 'When you imagine that meeting with your boss, what is the image which comes to mind?' And we then allow that answer to sink in to our consciousness and evoke a response in us. We enter into the imaginal world using our intuition.

Again, if a client has a problem with something or somebody, we can ask – 'If that …. turned into an animal, what would that animal be?' And if the person answers – 'A rat' – the next question is – 'How do you feel about rats?' This often leads into more insight into the nature of the problem. Or if the client produces an image spontaneously, we might become interested in what archetype it represented: at this level archetypes become very real. The anima and the animus, for example, can be very much worthwhile exploring, as strongly affecting perception of a person or event (Woolger, 1990). What I love about the transpersonal approach is that it releases a huge supply of creativity, both in the coach and in the coachee, at every point along the way.

Psychosynthesis (Brown, 2004) explains this by saying that we all have a superconscious or higher unconscious, at the other end, so to speak, from the more familiar lower unconscious. There is some rich material available now, such as, for example, the recent book by the late Ian Gordon-Brown and Barbara Somers (2008), which offers a panoply of guided fantasies and other materials which can be adapted for coaching. Another useful book comes from Charles (2007) about visualizations.

Dreams are not often mentioned in relation to coaching, but at this level dreams can be very useful in throwing light on everyday issues. The point of this is to undermine the client's taken-for-granted way of seeing the world and question radically the assumptions which are holding the client back. This questioning also affects the issue of goals. Sometimes the client's goals are just as dubious as any of the other assumptions which may be holding the client back.

Role of the coach and relationship with a client

From a transpersonal point of view, the role of the coach is that of a companion along the way. There is no assumption of expertise, or leadership, or superiority in any way. It is more like a wise companion on a journey, who does not argue about the way, does not criticize any mistakes, encourages the weary, witnesses the struggles, offers a presence that is nourishing and warm. But also a companion who is creative and arouses creativity in the coachee. Both can see, sometimes quite suddenly, some new aspect of the problem or of the solution that had not appeared before. And in this respect the coach can become a trickster, using insights that the coachee may never have come across, both wise and stimulating.

The relationship is undemanding, supportive, realistic, truthful, observant and continually offering to go into different dimensions with the client. Williams and Menendez (2007) say that 'The power of a strong collaborative relationship cannot be underestimated' (p.152), but the transpersonal relationship goes further than that – it opens up a space in which both client and coach can co-create together, in a deeply spiritual way. As Whitmore and Einzig (2007) say, the client may be seen by the coach in the light of 'Here is a soul who has challenges and obstacles to overcome on her journey through the university of life. This is another such learning opportunity' (p.122).

It is these other dimensions that make the difference between a transpersonal coach and some other kind. The coach might say: 'What does your soul say about this?' This would be an invitation to enter the Subtle realm (Transpersonal 1), as might be the simple question: 'What image does that bring to mind?' Even a basic question like: 'Who would know the answer to that? Fact or fiction, past or present?' would be likely to take the client into the Subtle realm. The Subtle realm allows for the possibility that the answer to a problem might lie outside a person, rather than inside them. It allows for the possibility of inspiration. Thanks to the inspiring work of Genpo Merzel (2007) we now know how to access parts of the coachee that he or she may never have considered possible – the creative self, the self who knows the answer, the unlimited self. And thanks to the work of Hermans, as adapted recently (Rowan, 2010), we now have a complete theory of how this may be possible, using the new concept of I-positions rather than the older idea of subpersonalities.

And when we come to Transpersonal 2 all the symbols and images and archetypes disappear, and we are left with no signposts and no handrails and no landmarks. This can sometimes be accessed by such a simple question as: 'What would an impersonal Witness say about this?' More commonly, the invitation would be to go to a place where there are no problems and look at the issues from there. Suppose we dropped all the labels such as: 'This is a problem'. 'This not the way it should be', 'This is hurtful'. What if the situation just *Is*? From the phrase 'This is wrong' we simply drop the word 'Wrong'. This is a different dimension and not every client is ready for this, by any means. But with the right person, at the right moment, it can hit a unique button not accessible by other means. This is quite different from the Subtle, though both are within the transpersonal. It is in this area that we find mindfulness to be of use (Passmore & Marianetti, 2007). Mindfulness is a practice that has been known for many years to be proven as a way to increase well-being among clients and coachees (Shapiro et al., 1998; Kabat-Zinn, 1990) and research has shown it to be valuable in many different spheres of work (Segal et al., 2002). Those of us who work in the transpersonal area see it as much more than just a useful technique, but rather as a way of deepening the whole coaching experience.

At a more prosaic level, the coach can simply call on the value of imagery. In the DVD of Einzig and Whitmore (2008), where the latter is coaching a client from the local government field, the coach deliberately encourages the client to bring up an image of a safe place, a place of peace and nourishment, for example. This is used later to help solve a problem for the client. And it is also clear from this example that the coach is really in there with the client, joining with the client in a common endeavour. The transpersonal coach is not an impartial observer, but a real participant in the action, risking his or her own presence in the act.

Tasks and goals of the traditions

The main goal of the transpersonal coach is to enable the client to disengage from whatever beliefs are holding him or her back from his or her higher or deeper possibilities. The human mind is infinite and the human soul is divine, and most clients do not realize this. Nor do they recognize, very often, the creativity within them that they can call upon at any time.

The task for the coach is to enable the client to work at the level most appropriate for him or her. It is said in therapy that some clients need glue, while others need solvent. This is also true in coaching. Some coachees need help in consolidating their previous gains and finding more applications for what they know already. Others need help in getting rid of false assumptions and false trails, and finding new directions. Some coachees need a combination of both – discovering, for example, the best ideas on negotiation, so as to yield the optimal result for all the parties involved. A useful new book from this point of view is Sarah Rozenthuler (2012). From a transpersonal perspective, everyone is right and the trick is to enable the client to discover that and use such insights productively. Unlike New Age approaches, transpersonal coaching has a place for the negative and recognizes that destruction has a value alongside creation, and is indeed part of the same process.

In fact, the kind of thinking found at the transpersonal level of functioning is very interesting in itself. It operates according to the laws of what Wilber calls vision-logic and what others have called dialectical logic. It has also been called second-tier thinking (Beck & Cowan, 1996). First-tier thinking is limited by the either-or: if I am right the other guy is wrong. In second-tier thinking I can be right and the guy who disagrees with me can be right too. Another way of putting this is to say that in second-tier thinking we start to see the value of paradox. The screen saver on my computer says: 'Of course it matters. Of course it doesn't matter. Of course it matters. Of course it doesn't matter…' and so forth endlessly. If I hold only 'of course it matters' I can get weighed down by responsibilities. If I hold only 'of course it doesn't matter' I can be irresponsible and unreliable. But if I hold both, in suspension, so to speak, then I am properly responsible but not weighed down by that.

The transpersonal approach adopts a sceptical attitude to the concepts of goals and tasks. At lower levels such ideas are very useful and indeed inevitable, but at the transpersonal levels there is a radical questioning of such notions. People often come into transpersonal coaching at moments of crisis: 'It is the individual's ability to live through and be transformed by the crisis (from base metal to gold as in the alchemist's crucible) that differentiates the leader from the rest' (Whitmore & Einzig, 2007: 129). This is not the language of goals and tasks – it is the language of transformation and the language of the transpersonal. 'Having clear outcomes at the outset is one thing, but this type of work is much more organic and can often meander, diverge and reconnect as the client gains understanding of the next step on their change journey' (Coldman, 2007: 10). In transpersonal coaching, in other words, we are more concerned with opening out possibilities than with finding fixed answers to problems.

METHODS AND TECHNIQUES

The transpersonal tradition is rich in techniques, because it is so open to creativity. Techniques are invented or modified in virtually every session. There is a particularly strong emphasis on imagery, as the imagination is seen as the best entry point for transpersonal insights. Very often there is much more trust in images than in words. Whitmore and Einzig (2007) have made the point that all the techniques of psychosynthesis are useful in transpersonal coaching. Psychosynthesis is of course a well-established discipline in psychotherapy and has made an impact wherever it has been used (Parfitt, 2003). If the coachee has a superconscious as well as a lower unconscious, that can be called upon in case of need: it is the source of creativity and fresh thinking and being.

One of the most important techniques pioneered by psychosynthesis, and mentioned a number of times by Whitmore for example, is based on the idea that people are multiple rather than just always single. He uses the word subpersonalities to introduce this idea, but more recently the term I-positions has been found to carry fewer possibilities for misunderstandings and reification (Hermans, 2004).

Some coaches have told me that they cannot use the idea of I-positions in their work because they work on the phone and cannot see the client move about. But this is a false belief. I myself have certainly said to a phone client – 'See if you can imagine that woman sitting in a chair near you. Move the chair if it makes it easier. As you see her sitting there, how would you describe her?' That went all right and I then went on to ask her to talk to the other person, and say all the things she really wanted to say. From there it was only a step to say – 'Now switch over and sit in the other chair and be her.' And this dialogue then carried on until a useful terminus was reached.

More important than any of these techniques, however, is the recognition that we are dealing here with a very specific level of consciousness, and that no one will be able to use such methods convincingly if they have not had at least a glimpse of this level of consciousness, which Wilber (2000) calls the Subtle, Hillman (2006) calls the soul and which Cortright (2007) calls the psychic centre. Transpersonal work is not just about using certain methods, but also of adopting this central outlook. And one way of attaining this state of consciousness is mindfulness (Passmore & Marianetti, 2007).

Some people are very reluctant to admit that they have a soul. There are many ways to get round this. One is simply to rename it: such terms as 'higher self', 'inner teacher', 'wise being', 'psychic centre' or even just 'heart' may be enough to make this acceptable. Another way is to use the concept from Transactional Analysis (TA) of the 'Nurturing Parent': it is not often realized that this concept contains most of the elements necessary to the soul. Like the soul, it is often neglected and only needs to be brought into action by paying attention to it. Another way is to ask the client to think of someone they would really trust to have the answer or give understanding: I have had Sir Alex Ferguson, Sherlock Holmes, Aldous Huxley and many others standing in for this role. Simpler still is to ask the client to think of a stranger from another land who has been everywhere and seen everything, and has become very wise. What would this character say about the question? Even simpler is to ask to speak to the Big Mind of the coachee. At the level of Big Mind (Merzel, 2007) there are no problems.

Another technique is to ask the client to imagine something ideal and removed from the current scene. Williams and Menendez (2007) call this 'stepping into the future' and Whitmore and Einzig (2007) call it 'what makes your heart sing?' The client is asked to bring this to life as if it is happening now. When this has been done, the client is asked – 'What year, what month is it now?' When this has been answered convincingly, the next question is – 'What happened in the previous year to make that possible?' And so we go backwards until the present is reached, whereupon the client is asked to take the first step forward and see what that feels like.

APPLICATION

There seems little to be said about application of this approach to various genres and contexts of coaching. There are a few pioneers such as Whitmore who experiment in introducing the elements of transpersonal work in leadership coaching and in team coaching, but no research-supported publications are available that can give a reasonable review of such attempts. It could be argued that any genre of coaching (performance coaching, career coaching, life coaching, developmental coaching) may have a transpersonal dimension in it if the mind-set of the coach includes this dimension. This is strongly suggested by the work of Law et al. (2010), which contains many valuable findings in this area. That the transpersonal is also historically important for coaching is emphasized by Williams (2012).

EVALUATION

The transpersonal tradition is so undeveloped in comparison with most of the other approach to coaching that it is relatively hard to conduct a systematic or evidence-based evaluation of it. However, there is now a well-developed tradition of transpersonal research and it is only a matter of time before it is applied to coaching (Braud & Anderson, 1998; Bentz & Shapiro, 1998; Heron, 1996).

One piece of research that was done confirmed that intuition was highly cultivated in transpersonal therapists. The transpersonal coach relies heavily on intuition, because this is part of the deal at the Subtle level: instead of intuition being a chancy and momentary thing, it is the main way in which we think. This is quite a new way of experiencing intuition, but of course it does depend upon the relationship between coach and client; as always, it takes time to build up the kind of trust which enables such things to emerge.

Similarly with the kind of deep empathy we have called linking, where there is a kind of union with the client, and some say that an energy flow can be detected (Rowan & Jacobs, 2002; Cameron, 2004). Tobin Hart (1997) talks about transcendental empathy quite convincingly. I have recently been arguing that 'working at relational depth' is essentially a transpersonal approach (in Knox et al., 2013).

Who for?

It is obvious that the transpersonal approach is not for everyone. It suits best people who are creative and open to new ideas. It also suits people who have taken some steps in their own psychospiritual development, sufficient to have opened their eyes to the power of the imagination. Such people are more common nowadays, because we have gone beyond the old Jungian statement that such interests are only for the second half of life. Younger people are now waking up to the potential of the transpersonal in their lives.

FURTHER READING

Gordon-Brown, I. & Somers, B. (2008). *The raincloud of knowable things: A practical guide to transpersonal psychology.* Dorset: Archive Publishing. (A beautiful book, which gives a real feel of working in a transpersonal way.)

Rowan, J. (2005). *The transpersonal: Spirituality in psychotherapy and counselling* (2nd ed.). London: Routledge. (Gives the basic structure of the transpersonal and warns against many of the most common errors in this area. Extensive material on actual practice.)

Whitmore, J. & Einzig, H. (2007). 'Transpersonal coaching', in Passmore, J. (Ed.), *Excellence in coaching.* London: Kogan Page. (Useful statement of the original ideas behind transpersonal coaching.), London.

Wilber, K. (2006). *Integral spirituality.* Boston, MA: Integral. (Gives the full story about the Wilber-Combs Lattice and much else besides.)

DISCUSSION QUESTIONS

- What is the best word to use for the part of us which belongs to the spiritual realm? Soul, Higher Self, Inner Teacher, Anima, Daimon, Antaratman, Bliss Self, Guardian Angel? All these and many others have been used.
- Sir John Whitmore has suggested that rather than talk about Spirituality, it might be better to talk about Values. Such a word is more acceptable to more people, yet it points in the right direction. In what way they are different?
- People sometimes say that they can't do imagery. Jean Houston gets them to start by looking for a few seconds at a candle flame, then closing the eyes and looking at the after-image. Then see this ball of light turn into a sunflower with bright yellow petals, a brown seeded centre and a long green stalk. Why not try it?
- If a coachee says they cannot use intuition, suggest that they pick a problem with no solution and then go into a place of not knowing and wait. This is an easy experiment to make. Because it is an experiment, no answer is guaranteed.

REFERENCES

Anthony, R. Ecker, B., & Wilber, K. (Eds) (1987). *Spiritual choices.* New York: Paragon House.

Assagioli, R. (1991). *Transpersonal development.* London: Crucible.

Beck, D. & Cowan, C. (1996). *Spiral dynamics.* Oxford: Blackwell.

Bentz, V.M. & Shapiro, J.J. (1998). *Mindful inquiry in social research.* Thousand Oaks, CA: Sage.

Braud, W. & Anderson, R. (Eds) (1998). *Transpersonal research methods for the social sciences: Honoring human experience.* Thousand Oaks, CA: Sage.

Brown, M.Y. (2004). *Unfolding self: The practice of psychosynthesis.* New York: Helios Press.

Cameron, R. (2004). 'Shaking the spirit: Subtle energy awareness in supervision', in Tudor, K. & Worrall, M. (Eds), *Freedom to practise: Person-centred approaches to supervision.* Ross-on-Wye: PCCS.

Charles, R. (2004). *Intuition in psychotherapy and counselling.* London: Whurr.

Charles, R. (2007). *Your mind's eye.* Woodbridge: Selfheal Books.

Coldman, D. (2007). 'Beyond results: When clients seek deeper understanding'. *The Bulletin of the Association for Coaching* 10 9–11

Cortright, B. (1997). *Psychotherapy and spirit: Theory and practice in transpersonal psychotherapy.* Albany, NY: SUNY Press.

Cortright, B. (2007). *Integral psychology: Yoga, growth and opening the heart.* Albany, NY: SUNY Press.

Einzig, H. & Whitmore, J. (2008). Transpersonal coaching DVD. London: Association for Coaching.

Ferrer, J. (2002). *Revisioning transpersonal theory: A participatory vision of human spirituality.* Albany, NY: SUNY Press.

Gordon-Brown, I. & Somers, B. (2008). *The raincloud of knowable things: A practical guide to transpersonal psychology.* Dorset: Archive Publishing.

Green, E.E. & Green, A.M. (1986). 'Biofeedback and states of consciousness', in Wolman, B.B. & Ullman, M. (Eds), *Handbook of states of consciousness.* New York: Van Nostrand Reinhold.

Grof, S. (1988). *The adventure of self-discovery.* Albany, NY: SUNY Press.

Hart, T. (1997). 'Transcendental empathy in the therapeutic encounter'. *The Humanistic Psychologist* 25/3 245–270.

Heron J. (1988). *Cosmic psychology.* London: Endymion Press.

Heron, J. (2004). *Co-operative inquiry: Research into the human condition.* London: Sage.

Hillman J. (1975). *Re-visioning psychology.* New York: Harper Colophon.

Hillman J. (1997). *The soul's code.* New York: Bantam.

Houston, J. (1996). *A mythic life.* New York: Harper Collins.

Kabat-Zinn, J. (1994). *Wherever you go, there you are: Mindfulness meditation in everyday life.* New York: Hyperion.

Knox, R., Murphy, D., Wiggins, S., & Cooper, M. (Eds) (2013). *Relational depth: New perspectives and developments.* Basingstoke: Palgrave Macmillan.

Law, H., Lancaster, L., & DiGiovanni, N. (2010). 'A wider role for coaching psychology – applying transpersonal coaching psychology'. *The Coaching Psychologist* 6/1 22–30.

Liss, J. (1996). 'The identification approach'. *Energy & Character* 27 45–60.

Maslow, A.H. (1970). *Religion, values and peak experiences*. New York: Viking.

McGilchrist, I. (2009). *The master and his emissary*. New Haven, CT: Yale University Press.

Merzel, D.G. (2007). *Big mind, big heart*. Salt Lake City, UT: Big Mind Publishing.

Parfitt, W. (2003). *Psychosynthesis: The elements and beyond*. Glastonbury: PS Avalon.

Passmore, J. & Marianetti, O. (2007). 'The role of mindfulness in coaching'. *The coaching psychologist* 3/3 131–137.

Rozenthuler, S. (2012). *Life changing conversations*. London: Watkins.

Rowan, J. (2005). *The transpersonal: Spirituality in psychotherapy and counselling* (2nd ed.). London: Routledge.

Rowan, J. (2010). *Personification*. Hove: Routledge.

Segal, Z.V., Williams, J.M.G., & Teasdale, J.D. (2002). *Mindfulness-based cognitive therapy for depression*. London: Guildford Press.

Senge, P., Scharmer, C.O., Jaworski, J., & Flowers, B.S. (2005). *Presence: Exploring profound change in people, organizations and society*. London: Nicholas Brealey.

Shapiro, S.L., Schwartz, G.E., & Bonner, G. (1998). 'Effects of mindfulness-based stress reduction on medical and premedical students'. *Journal of Behavioral Medicine* 21/6 581–599.

Sperry, L. (2007). *The ethical and professional practice of counselling and psychotherapy*. Boston, MA: Allyn & Bacon.

Starhawk (1989). *The spiral dance* (2nd ed.). San Francisco, CA: Harper & Row.

Thich Nhat Hanh (1995). *The heart of understanding: Commentaries on the Prajnaparamita Heart Sutra*. Berkeley, CA: Parallax Press.

Wade, J. (1996). *Changes of mind: A holonomic theory of the evolution of consciousness*. Albany, NY: SUNY Press.

West, W. (2000). *Psychotherapy and spirituality*. London: Sage.

Whitmont, E. (1969). *The symbolic quest*. Princeton, NJ: Princeton University Press.

Whitmore, D. (2004). *Psychosynthesis counselling in action* (3rd ed.). London: Sage.

Whitmore, J. (2002). *Counselling for performance* (3rd ed.). London: Nicholas Brealey.

Whitmore, J. & Einzig, H. (2007). 'Transpersonal coaching', in Passmore, J. (Ed.) *Excellence in coaching*. London: Kogan Page.

Wilber, K. (2000). *Integral psychology*. Boston, MA: Shambhala.

Wilber, K. (2006). *Integral Spirituality*. Boston, MA: Integral.

Williams, P. (2012). 'Looking back to see the future: The influence of humanistic and transpersonal psychology in coaching psychology today'. *International Coaching Psychology Review* 7/2 223–236.

Williams, P. & Menendez, D.S. (2007). *Becoming a professional life coach: Lessons from the Institute for Life Coach Training*. New York: W. W. Norton.

Woolger, R.J. (1990). *Other lives, other selves: A Jungian psychotherapist discovers past lives*. Wellingborough: Crucible.

11

The Positive Psychology Approach to Coaching

Ilona Boniwell, Carol Kauffman and
Jordan Silberman

Positive psychology coaching (PPC) is a scientifically-rooted approach to helping clients increase well-being, enhance and apply strengths, improve performance and achieve valued goals. At the core of PPC is a belief in the power of science to elucidate the best approaches for positively transforming clients' lives. The PPC orientation suggests that the coach view the client as 'whole' and that the coach focus on strengths, positive behaviours and purpose. These, in turn, are used as building blocks and leverage points for coachee development and performance improvement. The positive psychology movement has developed the theoretical and research foundations for PPC and provided an arsenal of models and interventions that are invaluable for coaching practice. The present chapter is designed to provide an applicable overview of PPC and to help coaches find specific ways in which PPC can be utilized to optimize the effectiveness of their coaching practices.

Positive psychology arose largely from a shift in the interests of many academic psychologists. Before the recent shift within the field of psychology, most psychologists focused on ridding the world of mental illness, while paying little attention to the enhancement of positive mental health. Although some psychologists researched well-being before the official launch of positive psychology in 1998, these early investigations pale in comparison to the 2000 articles, chapters and books that are now published annually on positive psychology (Diener, 2007).

Both positive psychology and coaching philosophy are inconsistent with interventions that are disproportionally or inappropriately driven by pathology-focused medical models. Linley and Harrington (2005) note that coaching involves a focus on the positive aspects of human nature, and on inspiring growth and change. Gable and Haidt (2005) suggest that 'positive psychology is the study of the conditions and processes that contribute to the flourishing or optimal functioning of people, groups, and institutions'. This definition encompasses much of what one would hope to observe in any coaching engagement. Indeed, coaching has been described as a 'natural home' for positive psychology, suggesting that coaching is an ideal vehicle through which the science of positive psychology can be applied.

With its origins in academia, it is not surprising that the scholar–practitioner model has been implicitly integrated into PPC (Grant, 2006). A recent definition of coaching psychology suggests that it is 'grounded in established adult learning or psychological approaches' (Palmer & Whybrow, 2005), alluding to the scientific underpinnings that are becoming an increasingly integral part of coaching practice. Positive psychology coaches attempt to weave the 'straw' of research into the 'gold' of artful coaching.

PPC is deeply influenced by a number of psychological paradigms. For example, it has a great deal in common with humanistic psychology. Both orientations focus on developing talents, building self-efficacy and moving individuals toward self-actualizing goals.

The cognitive-behavioural model currently influences PPC far more than psychoanalytic perspectives. This may reflect the academic origins of positive psychology and the shift from psychoanalytic to cognitive-behavioural approaches that has occurred in academia during the past few decades.

This chapter explores the processes and tools of PPC. It describes positive psychology theories, and explores how they can impact the approach taken toward the client, the issues focused upon and the co-construction of coaching relationships. Specific interventions are discussed, with an eye toward the kinds of goals that clients bring to their sessions. In this way, we explore how positive psychology can inform the process as well as the content of coaching.

DISTINCTIVE FEATURES

Coaching for change, positive emotions and strengths

Before describing the goals and tasks of PPC, it is helpful to explore the importance of interventions designed to increase well-being. We now know that we can reliably increase life satisfaction and other measures of psychological well-being (Boniwell, 2008; Kauffman, 2006; Seligman, Rashid, & Parks, 2006; Seligman, Steen, Park, & Peterson, 2005), and that interventions designed to do so may provide measurable benefits that extend far beyond simply 'feeling good'. A recent meta-analysis of more than 350 studies indicates that, although 'feeling good' is a temporary experience, positive emotion can help build enduring personal resources. Positive emotions enhance cognitive, affective and physical resilience, and broaden our repertoire of thoughts and behaviours (Fredrickson, 2001). Hundreds of studies have reported associations between positive emotion and tangible outcomes such as higher wages, customer satisfaction, creativity, big-picture thinking, physical health, quicker cardiovascular recovery and work engagement (Lyubomirsky, King, & Diener, 2005).

These benefits may give rise to a frequently-observed positive upward spiral. The increased positive affect that clients tend to experience often leads to a broadening and building of their thought–action repertoires. This fosters big-picture thinking and creativity, and gives clients access to a wider range of choices. These benefits may then help clients achieve goals, overcome challenges and perform more effectively, which may in turn boost positive affect, inciting the next iteration of the upward spiral toward improved performance and life satisfaction.

In addition to promoting positive affect, another significant goal of PPC is *directed purposeful change*. This is facilitated in part by employing successful transition models. All significant models of change in human behaviour distinguish between several stages, including pre-contemplation, contemplation, preparation, action and maintenance (Prochaska, Velicier, Rossi, & Goldstein, 1994). The coach assists the coachee through the change process, providing challenges and support that are appropriate for the coachee's current stage of change. As we will see below, interventions based on hope psychology provide important insights for facilitating change. Here we emphasize that focusing on what is 'right' with a person reduces resistance throughout the change process. Applying positive psychology interventions to promote well-being, helping clients achieve the tangible benefits of well-being and facilitating lasting change, are some of the many goals of PPC.

Perhaps the most ambitious positive psychology initiative has been the development of the *Values in Action Institute Inventory of Strengths* (VIA-IS) (Peterson & Seligman, 2004), a carefully developed classification of character strengths. After consulting with numerous experts, Peterson and colleagues identified 24 strengths of character that are valued by most of the world's cultures. These qualities include critical thinking, humour, spirituality, hope and many others. The VIA-IS is a 240-item self-report questionnaire that assesses these character strengths, each categorized within six virtues (Dahlsgaard, Peterson, & Seligman, 2005). Virtues are defined as 'the core characteristics valued by moral philosophers and religious thinkers', while character strengths are 'the psychological ingredients' – i.e., processes or mechanisms – that define the virtues (Peterson & Seligman, 2004). The five highest strengths are often referred to as 'signature strengths', which are celebrated and exercised frequently. The VIA survey is available free of charge online (www.AuthenticHappiness.org) and provides a list of top strengths.

The following exemplifies how positive psychology tools like the VIA can be integrated into coaching models in common use. Many coaches use the 'GROW' model as a way to structure the coaching session. This model incorporates the coachee's *goals*; the *reality* of the coachee's current circumstances, resources and obstacles; the *options* available for moving toward a goal; and the *will/way forward*, that is, the personal importance of a goal that ignites the coachee's motivation and the specific action steps needed for goal achievement (Whitmore, 2002).

The VIA has facilitated a new approach to this process. One frequently used PPC exercise involves finding ways in which coachees can apply their strengths to achieve desired outcomes. The coach might describe the process to the client using an image similar to the following: 'Visualize yourself on one side of a gap, with the goal on the other side. Now, let's construct bridges over that gap. Let's consider your top five strengths and see how each one can be used to connect you to what you truly want to be.' If the client's top strength is curiosity, we would begin there. For example, we might encourage a CEO to use his or her creativity to improve products that have been profitable in the past. The coach and coachee then develop an action plan, a road map for traversing the aforementioned bridge. The coachee is then asked to create another bridge based on his or her second-highest strength and to repeat the process until five bridges have been developed. This step-by-step process integrates the VIA with established coaching approaches for translating brainstorming into action. This approach can easily be translated into an unstructured, emergent process. When coaching in the 'options' phase, for example, the coach might use knowledge of strengths to ask powerful and inspirational questions that reveal a broader range of choices. Such questions can be as simple as: 'how can you use your strengths in this situation?'

Essential processes and the coaching relationship

The following section explores how a positive psychological orientation influences assessment, coach expectations and the coaching relationship.

Assessment. PPC offers a clear and articulate assessment of the coachee's strengths, orientation toward well-being, life satisfaction and potential routes to peak performance. There is a wide array of empirically supported assessments available, some of which have been tested on nearly 2,000,000 participants. These include the VIA inventory, the 'satisfaction with life scale', the 'meaning in life questionnaire' and many others. Additional measures are available for the assessment of optimism, hope, career self-efficacy, positive emotion and many other positive constructs (Lopez & Snyder, 2003). They are helpful with a wide range of clients, from those whose performance is merely adequate to those who have achieved the highest levels of performance.

Expectations and coaching orientation. It is known that an instructor's expectations of a student powerfully affect student performance. Teachers who genuinely believe that their students have great potential are more likely to have students who perform well on objective measures of academic success (Rosenthal & Jacobson, 1968). Similarly, a body of research on 'affective priming', suggests that expectation has a tremendous impact on client functioning. When people are informed that they or their group generally do poorly on a task, their performance declines. In contrast, groups or individuals who are told that they perform well tend to do better than those who expect themselves to do poorly (Cooperrider, Whitney, Stavros, & Fry, 2003). Positive psychology coaches seek to harness this 'Positive Pygmalion' effect; it is crucial that coaches identify reasons to genuinely believe in the potential of their clients.

The coaching relationship. There are several studies now conducted within the coaching context (De Haan, 2008; Gyllensten & Palmer, 2007; O'Broin & Palmer, 2010). that confirm the psychotherapy research (e.g. Horvath & Bedi, 2002) clearly suggesting that the relationship is a key ingredient in successful outcomes A positive psychological approach is highly congruent with the Co-active Coaching model proposed by Whitworth, Kimsey-House and Sandahl (1998). They emphasize an egalitarian approach in which coaches engage in active listening, powerful questioning, designing actions, goal setting and managing accountability.

Another important role of the coaching relationship is achieving an optimal balance between positive and negative. It is important to note that, contrary to misperceptions, positive psychologists do not endorse unbridled positivism. The field advocates a shift to a greater focus on the positive, but does not ignore negative issues or emotions that warrant attention. This approach is based in part on a solid foundation of research. Fredrickson and Losada (2005) have demonstrated that high performing teams are characterized by a ratio of positive to negative emotions of approximately three (positives) to one (negative). Negative emotions encountered in such teams include criticism, anger and anxiety. PPC involves a coaching relationship in which there is a productive ratio of positive to negative emotions and interactions; coaching relationships should not, by any means, be relentlessly positive. The evidence suggests, in fact, that ratios of positive to negative exceeding 11:1 give rise to performance that is just as poor as the functioning associated with excess negativity (Fredrickson & Losada, 2005). When investigating this phenomenon, performance of businesses was operationalized to include parameters such as customer satisfaction, profitability and team members' performance reviews. PPC puts this research into practice by structuring the coaching encounter as an active synthesis of support and challenge, addressing both positive and negative emotion and experience.

METHODS AND TECHNIQUES

The following section provides a brief description of several evidence-based interventions that are often used in PPC. Originally validated as stand-alone exercises to be completed without the help of a coach, in practice, however, these tools are often offered as part of the ongoing coaching process, integrated into powerful combinations of interventions (Kauffman, 2006).

Three good things. One of the most powerful and well-studied of all positive psychology interventions, it is also one of the simplest. The instructions are straightforward. Every night, just before going to sleep, write down three things that went well during the day. This deceptively simple exercise has been shown to increase happiness and decrease depressive symptoms for at least six months (Seligman et al., 2005). The exercise may feel too simple-minded to be useful, but it is important to remember that studies have clearly demonstrated the remarkable effectiveness of this simple intervention.

Variants of this exercise have also been scientifically investigated, always with promising results. If the coachee feels that a meeting has been disastrous, for example, the coach might simply ask the coachee to name three things that went well with their project today. The coach might then ask what the client did to make those positive things happen. By no means would the coach minimize negative aspects of the meeting; he or she would simply try to cultivate a ratio of positivity to negativity that is likely to promote success. Another variant is useful when unfinished business causes people to lose sleep. Rather than ruminating about problems that have arisen or may arise, it is useful to ask, 'When was I at my best today?' Clients often remember positive events that they would otherwise have overlooked (Sheldon & Lyubomirsky, 2004).

Three question process. This exercise is a modification of the Meaning, Pleasure, Strengths (MPS) Process, proposed by Tal Ben-Shahar (2007) in his book *Happier.* In a nutshell, it involves asking a coachee three questions:

- What gives you meaning?
- What gives you pleasure?
- What engages you?

These are straightforward questions, that, however, one does not pose oneself often. It is important to encourage your client to take some time reflecting on these questions and avoid jumping to conclusions too fast. The next step involves discovering where and how the answers your coachee comes up with overlap. What activities would bring them meaning, engagement and pleasure? How can they further use the three question process to make important decisions in their lives?

Gratitude visit. For many people, the gratitude visit exercise can be genuinely 'life changing'. Instructions for this exercise are as follows. Think of a person to whom you feel gratitude for something he or she has done in the past. Draft a concrete and well-written letter to this person, describing what the person did and how it affected your life. Next, call this 'gratitude recipient' and arrange to meet with him/her. When you meet, read your letter aloud. Both individuals generally find this experience to be extremely meaningful (Seligman, 2002). This exercise can also be adapted for the work setting. If a manager is angry at an employee and feels an impulse to counterproductively chastise the employee, then it may be helpful for the manager to identify things the employee has done that inspire feelings of gratitude. Doing so may reveal a more balanced picture of the individual in question, defuse anger and set the stage for faster resolution of the problem. Both the preparation and feedback on this exercise should be addressed within the coaching session.

Savouring. Noticing and savouring life's pleasures, both those that are subtle and those that are spectacular, can powerfully enhance well-being. According to Bryant and Veroff (2007), 'people have capacities to attend, appreciate, and enhance the positive experiences in their lives'. Coaches can encourage clients to find specific positive experiences in their daily lives, and focus intentionally on these experiences. This technique might be considered a specific type of mindfulness skill and is an excellent way to help busy executives slow down and manage stress. Research has shown that positive emotions arising from this technique can buffer one from stress and lead to quicker cardiovascular recovery after difficult experiences (Fredrickson, 2006; Tugade & Fredrickson, 2004).

Best possible future self. This exercise is similar to the coaching technique of 'futuring' and is similar in spirit to the 'miracle question'. Coachees are asked to imagine that everything has gone the way they wanted and that all goals have been realized. They are asked to vividly imagine this future. Coachees can also do this as homework, typically during a period of approximately four weeks, bringing the results back to the session. This exercise enhances optimism and helps elucidate priorities and goals. It is hardly surprising that an increase in happiness usually follows from this exercise.

Using your strengths in a new way. This exercise involves choosing a top strength and applying it in a new way, every day, for one week. On the first day, the client simply identifies situations in which signature strengths are already in action. Clients then brainstorm new ideas, identifying novel approaches to applying their strengths (see case example of Antonia, described below). Clients may also find it helpful to identify ways in which they can apply their strengths to improve or make the most of a trying situation. To ameliorate public speaking anxiety, for example, clients might apply their gratitude, love of learning, or capacity to love. This may help them focus on their core strengths or values, and find the energy and resolve necessary to move forward effectively.

Applying strengths proved invaluable for Antonia, an executive coach, who referred frequently to other coaches. Unfortunately, these referrals were not reciprocated and Antonia could not afford to lose business. Her top strengths were teamwork and authenticity. When being coached herself, Antonia was challenged with the following questions: 'You use your teamwork to serve others, but why not also apply your teamwork strength to help those who count on you for support?'; 'What about "Team Antonia?"'; 'How can you use this strength on behalf of the people to whom you are most responsible, including yourself?'

As a reflexive giver, Antonia demonstrated a novel application of her teamwork strength. She needed a few strong reflections and repeated exploration of this positive challenge, as she defaulted to helping others at her own expense. However, because we were harnessing an established strength, this orientation soon led to a cascade of new possibilities that she could contemplate. She realized that she was largely the author of her own dilemma. As a result, Antonia was better able to find ways in which she could apply her strength of authenticity to attract more clients. This process could then be integrated into the GROW model for translating insight into action and accountability (Kauffman, 2006).

APPLICATION

The following describes how positive psychology theories and tools may be particularly useful when applied within specific coaching genres such as life coaching, performance coaching, executive coaching and team coaching.

Life coaching

Empirically-validated positive psychology interventions can be invaluable in the context of life coaching. The approaches and research of self-determination theory (SDT) and self-concordance theories (SCTs) are particularly informative. SDT (Ryan & Deci, 2000) postulates the existence of three inherent universal needs, or basic psychological nutrients:

Autonomy: the need to choose what one is doing, being an agent of one's own life.

Competence: the need to feel confident in doing what one is doing.

Relatedness: the need to have human connections that are close and secure, while still respecting autonomy and facilitating competence.

SDT asserts that satisfaction of these needs enhances motivation and well-being, and that deficiencies of these needs undermine effective functioning and well-being. These needs, moreover, may inspire progression from extrinsic to intrinsic motivation, thus enabling individuals to feel more self-determined. Self-determination, in turn, is associated with higher self-esteem, improved weight loss management, success in alcohol treatment programmes, work enjoyment and other positive outcomes (Ryan & Deci, 2000).

PPC applies SDT in many ways. The coach supports the client's autonomy by enabling clients to make their own decisions. Coaches may also help clients achieve or enhance competencies by guiding them through the applications of strengths, and by identifying evidence supporting the use of these strengths. Finally, relatedness is encouraged when the coach expresses empathy, demonstrates understanding and finds ways to help clients enhance their existing relationships. Interventions such as the 'random acts of kindness' technique (Lyubomirsky, 2008) are also frequently used, in part to help satisfy the client's relatedness needs.

SCT, like SDT, is applied frequently in the context of life coaching. The coach helps the client ensure that his/her goals are self-concordant (i.e., based on fundamental human needs), inspired by lifelong passions and consistent with core values. Both working toward and achieving these goals is likely to enhance well-being.

Skills and performance coaching

Many PPC theories and tools can be useful in the context of skill and performance coaching. These include theories of flow and peak performance states, theories of explanatory style, interventions such as the 'best possible future self' exercise and many others. For the present discussion, we focus on an area of positive psychology that is particularly important for skill and performance coaching: cognitive hope theory.

Contrary to common misconceptions, hope is more than 'wishful thinking'. Rick Snyder and Shane Lopez, the leading researchers on hope theory, have carefully elucidated and defined the construct of hope. According to this cognitive theory of hope, the construct is comprised of two aspects: 'waypower' and 'willpower'. Waypower is a process that involves identifying goals and finding ways to achieve goals despite obstacles. Willpower involves a general belief in one's own ability to achieve goals (i.e., 'agency beliefs') (Snyder et al., 1991). Pathways thinking (i.e., generating several feasible routes toward a goal) is crucial; the first pathway toward a goal that is considered or attempted may not be the best path available. If the primary pathway is unavailable, a hopeful person will find an alternate route (Snyder, 2003).

Research suggests that a hopeful disposition yields many benefits. Hope inhibits handicapping and self-deprecatory thoughts, as well as negative emotions. Hopeful people focus more on disease prevention and hopeful athletes exhibit better athletic performance. In fact, up to 56% of the variance in females' athletic success can be attributed to hope (Curry, Snyder, Cook, Ruby, & Rehm, 1997). Hope may also promote academic achievement and is one of the strongest predictors of overcoming adversity (Snyder, Rand, & Sigmon, 2002).

PPC builds on both aspects of hope, in order to help clients improve their performance. During coaching sessions, agency and pathways thinking are often described as WILL power and WAY power. Both are essential for successful performance. Self-efficacy, which is very similar to agency thinking, is crucial for behaviour change; self-efficacious individuals are more likely to make an initial decision to change, generally devote greater effort to achieving change and persevere longer in the face of adversity (Bandura, 1994). While many coaches address agency beliefs in a way that is consistent with research literature, few take full advantage of this rich body of scientific findings. We know, for example, that an individual's prior successes are the most powerful source of self-efficacy, followed by vicarious experiences (e.g., observing the success of another person whom you believe has similar skills). Maddux (2002) suggests that 'imaginal' experiences (e.g., imagining ourselves or others behaving effectively in hypothetical situations) can also boost self-efficacy. Verbally persuading individuals of their efficacy, in contrast, is only occasionally successful (Bandura, 1994).

Executive coaching

According to positive psychology research, top performers have very specific goal setting habits. It is often assumed that these individuals set high goals, while low achievers set low goals. However, evidence suggests that top achievers know their capabilities and set goals that are only slightly above their current performance levels (Latham, 2000). Conversely, low achievers are unaware of their ability levels and often set goals that are unrealistically ambitious. Top achievers also set goals based on their strengths, building their personal and professional lives on these personal assets. They learn to recognize and develop their talents, find roles that suit them best and creatively invent ways to apply their talents and strengths when necessary.

Assessing and applying strengths can serve many purposes beyond enhancing well-being. Knowledge of strengths can be used to re-craft jobs, negotiate development challenges, construct teams on the basis of complementary strengths profiles and build better relationships with colleagues and superiors. These types of applications often play a central role in executive coaching.

Importantly, some of the concepts in PPC may need re-branding when applied to the executive context so to speak the language of the client. For example, when introducing the notion of strengths, it might be more helpful to talk about engagement. The impact of positive emotions can be introduced in terms of increased productivity, whilst development of happiness may be positioned as work-life balance.

Team coaching

PPC also lends itself well to team coaching for businesses and organizations. One development in positive psychology is the study of organizational dynamics that produce exceptional outcomes. Cameron, Dutton and Quinn (2003) have proposed that this process depends largely on positive emotions that are contagious and that broaden our repertoires of thoughts and behaviours (Fredrickson, 2003). They assert that positive emotions give rise to a wide range of desirable organizational behaviours, such as creativity, tolerance of failure and transformational leadership. These outcomes, in turn, promote further positive emotions. PPC can be used to help teams capitalize on this knowledge of positive group dynamics. Positive psychology coaches help teams identify and build on positive emotions through investment in high-quality connections and relationships (Dutton & Heaphy, 2003), random acts of kindness (Lyubomirsky, 2008) and other strategies.

EVALUATION

Positive psychology and PPC, in contrast to traditional approaches, explicitly focus on character strengths, well-being and the things that make life worth living. Coaching and positive psychology are natural allies in their explicit concern with enhancement of optimal functioning and well-being, their challenge of traditional assumptions about human nature and their use of a strengths-based approach to performance improvement. As an applied tradition, PPC serves a dual function. On the one hand, it provides a context in which the scholarly ideas of positive psychology can be applied and evaluated. On the other hand, it enables practitioners to understand how the sound base of theory and research provided by positive psychology can give rise to successful intervention and change.

Some may wonder if the benefits of PPC arise simply from being reassuring, caring and kind to clients. These are certainly important aspects of any therapeutic relationship, including PPC, but PPC cannot be reduced to these relatively 'non-specific' factors. PPC is a complex confluence of science and art. Coaches utilize a variety of highly developed and evidence-based coaching tools to help clients achieve optimal performance.

When focusing on the positive, the potential exists for lack of balance; insufficient attention may be devoted to negativity, or to deeper, underlying issues (Popovic & Boniwell, 2007). One of the greatest emotions scholars, Richard Lazarus (2003: 94), challenges the implicit message of separation between positive and negative, arguing that they are two sides of the same coin: 'God needs Satan and vice versa. One would not exist without the other. We need the bad, which is part of life, to fully appreciate the good. Any time you narrow the focus of attention too much to one side or another, you are in danger of losing perspective'. The realities of life and coaching most often fall between positive and negative extremes. If the psychology of the past made the major mistake of focusing on the negative – often at the expense of the positive – is positive psychology not making the same mistake by allowing the pendulum to swing in the opposite direction? An informed PPC practitioner can draw on work in post-traumatic growth and resilience (Tedeschi & Calhoun, 2004) as well as meaning and benefit-finding (Baumeister & Vohs, 2002), but this may not be enough to equilibrate the aforementioned pendulum to a position along the positive–negative spectrum that is optimal for a given client.

Finally, positive psychology has been criticized for adopting an exclusive focus on the individual and thereby placing responsibility for happiness squarely at the individual level (Held, 1999). This may sound noble, but it may also give rise to an unintended conclusion: victims of unfortunate circumstances can be blamed for their own misery. Instead of acknowledging the socioeconomic forces that may have contributed to an individual's psychological struggles, we may implicitly and unintentionally highlight an individual's failures to exhibit the necessary optimism, strength, virtue and willpower to be happy despite challenges. Held (1999: 980) writes:

> In my own experiences as … a clinical psychologist, I have repeatedly noticed that some people seem to feel guilty, defective, or both when they can't feel good. They sometimes apologize for not being able to smile in the face of adversity, as if they were committing an act of treason by feeling and acting unhappy.

This appears to reflect an unspoken cultural mandate, which holds that unhappiness is intolerable and should therefore be abolished. The mandate may paradoxically decrease subjective well-being, the very condition it is designed to enhance. For some people who face trying circumstances, it may be possible to apply the tools of positive psychology in order to improve psychological well-being. For others, doing so is simply infeasible. It is crucial that coaches do not imply, even unintentionally, any culpability in those whose circumstances have made it difficult to achieve lasting happiness.

In conclusion, we have argued that PPC is a constructive coaching tradition that combines the very essence of coaching with a robust theoretical and empirical base. As coaches begin to apply the approach they may find that the dichotomy between positive and negative is somewhat misleading; it is rare for coaches to focus exclusively on either positive or negative issues. We call for a balanced approach to PPC that moves away from ideological biases on either side, an approach that combines positive psychological science with coaching intuition to positively transform the lives of coaching clients.

FURTHER READING

Biswas-Diener, R. (2006). *Practicing positive psychology coaching*. New Jersey: John Wiley & Sons. (The only useful manual of PPC offers insightful exercises to help practitioners develop an experiential understanding of positive psychology principles.)

Boniwell, I. (2012). *Positive psychology in a nutshell*. Maidenhead: The Open University Press. (Currently in its third edition, this balanced introduction to positive psychology provides a thorough and engaging overview of the field.)

David, S., Boniwell, I., & Ayers, A. (2013). *Oxford handbook of happiness*. Oxford: Oxford University Press. (A major up-to-date academic volume on positive psychology benefiting from an excellent 'applications' section, where coaches would find many useful tools and suggestions for practice.)

Haidt, J. (2005). *The happiness hypothesis: Finding modern truth in ancient wisdom*. New York: Basic Books. (An enjoyable and extremely well-written introduction to the positive psychology field that interweaves positive psychology theory with ancient wisdom.)

DISCUSSION QUESTIONS

- In what way can coaches usefully incorporate positive psychology into their practice?
- How can a business coach frame the validated positive psychology interventions in a context that is appropriate for a corporate client?
- What is new in positive psychology for the experienced coach?
- What are the main limitations of a paradigm focusing exclusively on the 'positive'?

REFERENCES

Bandura, A. (1994). Self-efficacy. In V.S. Ramachaudran (Ed.), *Encyclopedia of human behavior* (vol. 4, pp. 71–81). New York: Academic Press.

Baumeister, R.F. & Vohs, K.D. (2002). The pursuit of meaningfulness in life. In C.R. Snyder & S.J. Lopez (Eds), *Handbook of positive psychology* (pp. 608–18). New York: Oxford University Press.

Ben-Shahar, T. (2007). *Happier.* New York: McGraw-Hill.

Boniwell, I. (2008). *Positive psychology in a nutshell.* London: PWBC.

Bryant, F.B. & Veroff, J. (2007). *Savoring: A new model of positive experiences.* Mahwah, NJ: Lawrence Erlbaum Associates.

Cameron, K.S., Dutton, J.E., & Quinn, R.E. (2003). *Positive organizational scholarship.* San Francisco, CA: Berrett-Koehler.

Cooperrider, D., Whitney, D., Stavros, J., & Fry, R. (2003). *Appreciative inquiry handbook.* San Francisco, CA: Berrett-Koehler.

Curry, L.A., Snyder, C.R., Cook, D.L., Ruby, B.C., & Rehm, M. (1997). The role of hope in academic and sport achievement. *Journal of Personality and Social Psychology, 73*(6): 1257–67.

Dahlsgaard, K., Peterson, C., & Seligman, M.E.P. (2005). Shared virtue: The convergence of valued human strengths across culture and history. *Review of General Psychology, 9*(3): 203–13.

De Haan E (2008). *Relational coaching: Journeys towards mastering one-to-one learning.* Chichester: John Wiley & Sons.

Diener, E. (2007). Myths in the science of happiness, and directions for future research. In M. Eid & R. Larsen (Eds), *The science of subjective well-being* (pp. 493–514). New York: Guilford.

Dutton, J.E. & Heaphy, E.D. (2003). The power of high-quality connections. In K.S. Cameron, J.E. Dutton, & R.E. Quinn (Eds), *Positive organizational scholarship: Foundations of a new discipline.* San Francisco, CA: Berrett-Koehler.

Fredrickson, B. (2006). The broaden and build theory of positive emotions. In M. Csikszentmihalyi & I. Csikszentmihalyi (Eds), *A life worth living: Contributions to positive psychology.* New York: Oxford University Press.

Fredrickson, B.L. (2001). The role of positive emotions in positive psychology: The broaden-and-build theory of positive emotions. *American Psychologist, 56*(3): 218–26.

Fredrickson, B.L. (2003). Positive emotions and upward spirals in organizations. In K.S. Cameron, J.E. Dutton, & R.E. Quinn (Eds), *Positive organizational scholarship: Foundations of a new discipline.* San Francisco, CA: Berrett-Koehler.

Fredrickson, B.L. & Losada, M.F. (2005). Positive affect and the complex dynamics of human flourishing. *American Psychologist, 60*(7): 678–86.

Gable, S. & Haidt, J. (2005). What (and why) is positive psychology? *Review of General Psychology, 9*(2): 103–10.

Gyllensten, K. and Palmer, S. (2007). The coaching relationship: an interpretative phenomenological analysis. *International Coaching Psychology Review, 2*(2): 168–177.

Grant, A. (2006). A personal perspective on professional coaching and the development of coaching psychology. *International Coaching Psychology Review, 1*(1): 12–22.

Held, B. (1999). The tyranny of the positive attitude in America: Observation and speculation. *Journal of Clinical Psychology, 58*(9): 956–91.

Horvath, A.O. & Bedi, R.P. (2002). The alliance. In J.C. Norcross (Ed.), *Psychotherapy relationships that work: Therapist contributions and responsiveness to patients.* New York: Oxford University Press.

Kauffman, C. (2006). Positive psychology: The science at the heart of coaching. In D. Stober & A. M. Grant (Eds), *Evidence based coaching handbook: Putting best practices to work for your clients* (pp. 219–54). Hoboken, NJ: John Wiley & Sons.

Latham, G. (2000). Motivating employee performance through goal setting. In E.A. Locke (Ed.), *Handbook of principles of organizational behavior* (pp. 107–19). San Francisco, CA: Blackwell.

Lazarus, R.S. (2003). Does the positive psychology movement have legs? *Psychological Inquiry, 14*: 93–109.

Linley, A. & Harrington, S. (2005). Positive psychology and coaching psychology: Perspectives on integration. *The Coaching Psychologist, 1*(1): 13–17.

Lopez, S. & Snyder C.R. (2003). *Positive psychological assessment: A handbook of models and measures.* Washington, DC: American Psychological Association.

Lyubomirsky, S. (2008). *The HOW of happiness.* New York: Penguin Press.

Lyubomirsky, S., King, L., & Diener, E. (2005). The benefits of frequent positive affect: Does happiness lead to success? *Psychological Bulletin, 131*(6): 803–55.

Maddux, J.R. (2002). Self-efficacy: The power of believing you can. In C.R. Snyder & S.J. Lopez (Eds), *Handbook of positive psychology* (pp. 277–87). New York: Oxford University Press.

O'Broin, A. and Palmer, S. (2010). Exploring key aspects in the formation of coaching relationships: Initial indicators from the perspectives of the coachee and the coach. *Coaching: An International Journal of Theory, Research and Practice, 3*(2): 124–143.

Palmer, S. & Whybrow, A. (2005). The proposal to establish a special group in coaching psychology. *The Coaching Psychologist, 1*(1): 5–12.

Peterson, C. & Seligman, M.E.P. (2004). *Character strengths and virtues: A handbook and classification.* Washington, DC: American Psychological Association.

Popovic, N. & Boniwell, I. (2007). Personal consultancy: An integrative approach to one-to-one talking practices. *International Journal of Evidence Based Coaching and Mentoring, 5*: 24–9.

Prochaska, J.O., Velicier, W.F., Rossi, J.S., & Goldstein, M.G. (1994). Stages of change and decisional balance for 12 problem behaviours. *Health Psychology, 13*(1): 39–46.

Rosenthal, R. & Jacobson, L. (1968). *Pygmalion in the classroom: Teacher expectation and pupils' intellectual development.* New York: Holt, Rinehart, & Winston.

Ryan, R.M. & Deci, E.L. (2000). Self-determination theory and the facilitation of intrinsic motivation and well-being. *American Psychologist, 55*: 68–78.

Seligman, M.E.P. (2002). *Authentic happiness.* New York: Free Press.

Seligman, M.E.P., Rashid, T., & Parks, A. (2006). Positive psychotherapy. *American Psychologist, 61*(8): 774–88.

Seligman, M.E.P., Steen, T., Park, N., & Peterson, C. (2005). Positive psychology progress: Empirical validation of interventions. *American Psychologist, 60*(5): 410–21.

Sheldon, K.M. & Lyubomirsky, S. (2004). Achieving sustainable new happiness: Prospects, practices and prescriptions. In P. A. Linley & S. Joseph (Eds), *Positive psychology in practice.* Hoboken, NJ: John Wiley & Sons.

Snyder, C.R. (2003). *On the trail of the elusive 'false' hope phenomenon.* Paper presented at the 2nd Annual Positive Psychology Summit, Washington, DC, October, 2003.

Snyder, C.R., Rand, K.L., & Sigmon, D.R. (2002). Hope theory: A member of the positive psychology family. In C.R. Snyder & S.J. Lopez (Eds), *Handbook of positive psychology.* New York: Oxford University Press.

Snyder, C.R., Harris, C. Anderson, J.R., Holleran, S.A., Irving, L.M., Sigmon, S.T., et al. (1991). The will and the ways: Development and validation of an individual differences measure of hope. *Journal of Personality and Social Psychology, 60*(4): 570–85.

Tedeschi, R.G. & Calhoun, L.G. (2004). Post-traumatic growth: Conceptual foundations and empirical evidence. *Psychological Inquiry, 15*(1): 1–18.

Tugade, M.M. & Fredrickson, B.L. (2004). Resilient individuals use positive emotions to bounce back from negative emotional arousal. *Journal of Personality and Social Psychology, 86*(2): 320–33.

Whitmore, J. (2002). *Coaching for performance.* Boston, MA: Nicholas Brealey.

Whitworth, L., Kimsey-House, H. & Sandahl, P. (1998). *Co-active coaching.* Mountain View, CA: Davies-Black.

12

Transactional Analysis and Coaching

Rosemary Napper and Trudi Newton

Transactional Analysis (TA) developed as a theory in social psychology from the late 1950s, as a way to identify how behavioural patterns of communicating reveal something of the psycho-dynamics of the internal world of individuals. This connection between the interpersonal and the intra-psychic was a radical departure from the psychological frameworks predominant at the time, as were the humanistic values underlying TA which inspire optimism about human nature and development:

- People are OK
- Everyone can think
- Therefore people can decide to change if they wish

This concept of 'OK-ness' is central and applied to both the attitude towards self and towards others and is the core of practice in all fields of application of TA. It is both easy to grasp and difficult to define: to respect and value both self and others is one way to express this aspiration. In coaching, an aim is that the client resolves their situation with this frame of mind.

Eric Berne, the originator of TA, was concerned to create a psychology which could be easily understood by the client, to emphasize the mutuality between practitioner and client. Diagrams are commonly used to express concepts, which are identified in colloquial, everyday language.

The number of concepts defined within TA is in the hundreds (*Clarke's Dictionary of TA has over 300 diagrammed concepts*). All TA concepts interlink as a set of maps – some are 'topographical', featuring observable behaviours, some are 'geological' depicting the underlying inner world and some are 'global' providing connections with wider contexts of systems.

The illustration (Figure 12.1) shows the contribution TA can make to inform the coach about their practice. 'I' (the coach) can monitor my internal structural ego states in order to: (a) be fully present and engaged; (b) identify some of the ulterior messages and transferences being communicated unconsciously by 'YOU' (the client) as you tell your stories; and (c) consider my rationale in selecting my interventions.

TA provides the practitioner with many concepts to consider the personality of the client. Contemporary TA, rather than 'labelling', focuses on strengthening each person's capacity to feel, think and behave in the present (the structural Adult ego state) and to take into account 'IT' – the systems or organization. TA has several ways to identify the culture created by the structures and dynamics of systems, and how culture can significantly influence the thoughts, feelings and behaviours of its participants. The coach working with a contract within an organization needs an understanding of when a consultancy intervention to the system itself might be valuable, and the opportunity to communicate this information. Often the client's stories will involve 'THEY' and the TA coach has a range of frameworks to assess the power that others have in the system and their impact on the client. 'WE' is the communication between coach and client.

This psychological framework is called 'transactional' analysis rather than interactional analysis, in order to emphasize the notion of exchange. With every verbal or non-verbal interaction recognition is exchanged which may be either positive or negative, about the individual's being or actions. Traditionally termed 'strokes', this concept is central to considering how individuals develop and maintain their internal patterns of feeling and thinking, their sense of 'OK-ness' and their patterns of behaviour. The success of coaching is often due to the consistent

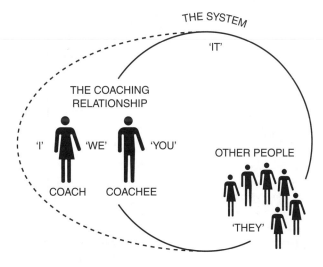

Figure 12.1 Three–cornered contract

one-to-one attention of a coach, who regards their client with respect and value and provides sustained positive recognition both unconditionally and conditionally, often resulting in a sense of well-being that provides a positive base for coaching.

DISTINCTIVE FEATURES

The core TA concept of structural ego states describes personality and is the source of either autonomous or archaic behavioural modes. There is often confusion between ego states and behaviour; in this chapter we differentiate between observable behavioural modes and the internal world of structural ego states.

TA offers the coach a framework of behavioural modes to choose from in their responses in the coaching conversation (Temple, 2004; Figure 12.2). The five positive modes invite the client to be fully present and to assess the reality of the situations presented in the session. The mode the client responds with is an indicator of whether s/he is engaged in the here and now, or has contaminated feelings and thoughts rooted in past experiences.

The Adult structural ego state is the major asset of a coach; the capacity for most of their energy to be focused into the current experience with the client. The client can also consider their own capacity for presence rather than being stuck in repeating the thoughts, feelings and behaviours of past experiences (the structural Child ego state) or regurgitating the thoughts feelings and behaviours of powerful others from their past; bosses, teachers, parental figures

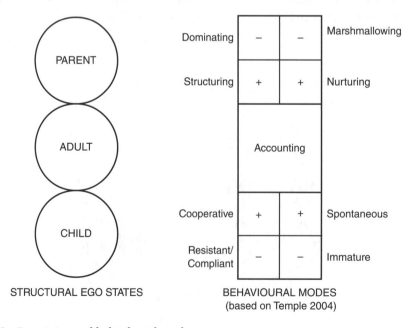

Figure 12.2   Ego states and behavioural modes

(the structural Parent ego state). The coach may pick these up by sensing inauthenticity in the client. The client's Adult will be evident as he becomes aware of a sense of autonomy, fresh perspectives and of respect and valuing of self and others.

Three further major concepts are discussed here that are invaluable in TA coaching:

1. *Contracting.* The processes used by the coach to clarify tasks and goals in the coaching, the psychological aspects of the relationship between coach and client and any others involved, and the boundaries of these relationships.
2. *Role theory.* A map for the coach's thinking in order to understand the realities of the client's situation; to provide prompts for asking powerful questions about the clients perspective on their context; and to check the fit of client feelings and behaviours, the expectations of those whom they need to relate to and the prevailing culture.
3. *Psycho-education.* Developing the clients' psychological perspectives on how humans communicate and relate to one another.

Contracting as a principle is central to TA practice. The overall purpose of the contract is to co-create boundaries to the work and to the roles of all concerned in order to provide sufficient protection for client, practitioner and organizations, and to delineate what can be included and what is outside the boundaries of the contract. Contracting clarifies the key issues, how to monitor progress and identify when other interventions are needed and how to evaluate the return on investment. In this way the potential of the coach, the client and any systems involved can be maximized.

Often in coaching the contract is multi-party as in Figure 12.3a (English, 1975). The diagrams show three stakeholders, but there can be more. In an organizational setting there will often be some representative of IT (the system such as Human Resources, or a line manager, or the director), and a contract made between the coach (or a coaching consultancy) and the system. This will include the purpose of the coaching, the information to be exchanged in each direction including the limits of confidentiality and the business aspects such as fees and time. In life coaching the system may be the family – without a direct contract with the coach – so in the initial contracting the coach will enquire of the client what impact the coaching might have on the family and vice versa in terms of money, time, goals and other pressures. Ideally the agreements made between the I and YOU (the client) and I and IT (the system), alongside the agreements YOU have made with IT will be in the TA spirit of open communication and thus in harmony, as in the equilateral triangle diagram above. However, this is not always the case, or equilibrium may not be maintained over time; contracting is often an ongoing process (Micholt, 1992; Napper & Newton, 2003).

There are three aspects to contracting:

(i) *The practical or business aspects:* How long, when, where, how much,?
(ii) *The professional aspects:* Who will be involved? For what purpose/s? What processes will be used? How will this be monitored and evaluated?
(iii) *The psychological aspect of the contract:* What each party holds in mind. These thoughts and feelings may be expressed and heard in subtle ways. If not openly communicated they are likely to distort the contract, and cause rupture to the practical, professional or affective aspects, as in these examples:

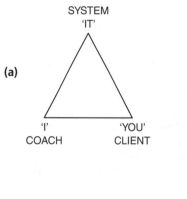
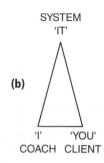

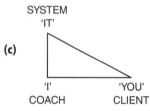
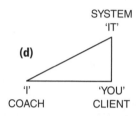

Figure 12.3

Figure 12.3b: a sense that the coaching is going nowhere, e.g. the manager as coach and her subordinate spend their sessions complaining about the leadership team in the organization

Figure 12.3c: a client who is going through a divorce and has not mentioned this underlying stress to his leadership coach out of fear that the company will find out and demote him, and who therefore does not show up to a session

Figure 12.3d: a situation where the company has sent someone for career development and withheld the information that they want rid of the staff member, so the sought promotion cannot be realized within the organization, regardless of how the client develops.

The psychological aspect of the contract is the most powerful influence with regard to protection, permission and maximizing potential, and so a key aspect throughout the coaching.

Role theory in TA (Schmid, 2006) is invaluable in coaching – any difficulties the client is experiencing can be considered in terms of role. The model can be helpful for the coach to consider how they inhabit the role of coach and what it means to be a client.

A role is defined as a consistent pattern of feeling, thinking, perspective on reality, behaviours and relationships. This is an extension of the definition of ego states through the addition of 'perspective on reality'. This implies involving the Adult ego state to assess a situation from the viewpoint of the system, other people, the required tasks and protocols, the appropriate behaviours, thinking frameworks and emotions. A role is a psychological concept and the descriptor of 'inhabiting' each role expresses the notion of how living a role *is*, from the inside out.

The role concept suggests that there are various 'worlds' which we inhabit (illustrated in Figure 12.4):

- the private world where we live our different roles such as parent, daughter, friend, and which may also involve the world of a community where we may live – roles such as neighbour, citizen and so on;
- the professional world where we may have a variety of roles each requiring particular expertise (not to be confused with a job title) such as budget-holder, designer, seller, complaints-taker, problem-solver and so on;
- roles in the organizational world such as leader or public-relations advisor, or, in the family, head of household. Roles in the organizational world involve representing the system or organization.

Some of the difficulties that people encounter are due to confusion between their 'role worlds'. A father of lively teenage children may contaminate his manager role with the same feelings and behaviours towards subordinates as he expresses at home and get negative reactions. The

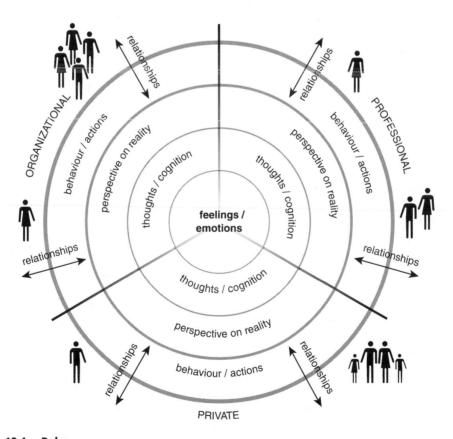

Figure 12.4   Roles

woman who takes her role of negotiator home when parenting small children may find she is creating many problems for her whole family through her way of thinking about competing needs and wants. In both cases the coach will encourage articulation of feelings and thoughts and question how these fit the reality of the roles in context.

Some confuse roles within the same 'world' and this can create difficulties in terms of inappropriate behaviours and relationships. A project manager will have a number of roles – managing the flow of tasks; budgeting; informing different people about their roles in relation to the project and so on. A skills-development coach using TA may be a sounding board to help delineate these different roles and identify the different behaviours required; managing task flow between project members requires different behaviours from informing those outside the project of what is required of them.

Role confusion can be particularly difficult for the manager as coach, both for subordinates and for the manager/coach themselves. Coaching supervision helps clarify the different roles and how best to signal to those being managed when the manager is in a directive manager role, and when they are using a coaching approach to management.

Frequently the client finds solutions when the TA coach asks the client to identify the perspectives on reality held by the system and those he or she relates to. Sometimes these are clouded by archaic perceptions from past experiences. Two examples:

- Someone feeling trapped by their family and marriage might realize that it is in their 'breadwinner' role that these feelings are engendered and that this role has become confused with the roles of lover, playful parent and home-maker. Discovering this means that the client can identify alternative conversations and family agreements which could be made, and can generate options where the breadwinner role is less overpowering.
- Promotion from team member to team leader frequently generates role confusion and conflicts. Coaching will include sharing information in order to increase understandings about rivalry and transferences to leaders, as well as supporting the client in exploring the different perspectives and behaviours that are required by the new organizational role, alongside managing different sets of relationships and their own transference of past feelings and responses.

Psycho-education has been a predominant thread throughout the development of TA, providing concepts to inform thinking. The emphasis on mutuality and transparency of thinking was part of the TA revolt against the mysticism of traditional psychoanalysis and has led to the sharing of ideas and concepts for use in everyday life. An understanding of general patterns of 'what makes human beings tick' can expand and enhance the structural Adult ego state perspectives on reality, and normalize what might seem frightening for those who have not previously considered a psychological 'take' on relationships with individuals and groups.

TA, with its emphasis on everyday language for many psychological concepts, can readily be understood. For example, when coaching someone in a new role it can be helpful to ask how old they feel in this role. If the reported age is of a small child, it can open up further enquiry about who the powerful parent-like figures seem to be, how they behave and how the client feels they ought to behave, and whether these responses come from a 'here and now' reality or are an echo of past experiences – perhaps long past actual experiences of, for example, starting a new school. Such transferences of past relationships are common – and unhelpful as they are not rooted in the current reality, and may invoke and establish patterns of inappropriate behaviour.

METHODS AND TECHNIQUES

TA has developed some key methods for practice which are valuable for coaches and also borrows techniques from many other approaches adding to them a viewpoint of TA theory. Two chair techniques from Gestalt are used in TA with three chairs (or mats to stand on) to investigate the resources from the past available in the Child ego state experience and from significant others in the Parent ego state, with an evaluation of the options generated by the Adult ego state in regard to the current situation. Scaling, adopted from solutions-focused approaches, is a common practice, to help clarify significance in the Adult ego state. Metaphor and associations, common in psychodynamic ways of working, are also used to uncover some of the feelings and thoughts deep in the inner world, whilst symbols often used in transpersonal approaches are used to highlight particular aspects of the self.

Two methods and one technique are elaborated in this section: (i) contracting and the TA use of confrontation within the process; (ii) the technique of using objects to uncover the imago, concerning the relationship between an individual and others; and (iii) story-telling is a significant thread through all TA practice which can be used as a systemic method in coaching

Contracting is both a central concept in TA and a way of working. Several techniques facilitate contracting (Napper & Newton, 2003; Sills, 1997). Consideration of the practical, professional and psychological aspects of the contract as discussed earlier, provide a focus for questioning by the coach who is listening (with their full focus on the reality of the relationships between all parties), for what is emerging in terms of sufficient protection for each party, sufficient permission for what is/is not included in the conversation, in order to maximize the potential of client, coach and system.

The nature of the contract agreed may vary:

1. A 'soft' contract involves agreeing boundaries for exploration, in order to see what emerges as significant, e.g. a career development coach might make an exploratory contract with a client in their mid-forties to investigate together what emerge as life priorities in the broadest sense, in order to determine how the career fits their life overall. This may determine techniques – for example, a symbolic large-scale drawing of a river of life and all the contributories so far, with space to imaginatively continue.
2. A 'hard' contract is where goals are specified in measurable terms, usually involving particular behaviours and time-scales. This often comes after a period of exploration, or as a mini-contract within a wider soft contract for growth and development, or as specific to a type of coaching. For example, in parent coaching, a contract might be made for a parent to go out with their partner once a week, and not talk about their kids, having put aside sufficient money to pay for the child-care needed.

A type of questioning described in TA as confrontation – that is, putting the reality in front of all involved, using whichever of the five effective behavioural modes invite the client to access their Adult ego state energy and thus fully take into consideration their reality – is shown here as an example of re-formulating a contract with the director-owner of a small company:

Coach: So, what do you want to focus on today? (orienting/structuring mode)

Client: I'm not sure. I've made some notes – there's lots going on with the new staff taken on, and I'd like to talk through how I'm finding them; there's the new sales which we have nearly landed, and the office move …

Coach: Sounds a lot! How are you feeling with all this going on? (nurturing mode)

Client: To be frank – relieved! The taking on new staff hasn't been the problem I thought it would be, and although I miss those who've left and their skills, I'm not missing the level of support they required!

Coach: What do you highlight as the most significant in the long list you gave just now? (accounting mode)

Client: Well, I'm concerned with who is going to be in charge when I take a couple of days off next week – I probably need to put that high on today's list.

Coach: That sounds important for you (co-operative mode) … and I am wondering about your tone of voice when you mention time off (accounting mode) … (with a laugh). What are you NOT telling me?! (spontaneous mode)

Client: (laughs) Ah! Long term I want to get this job down to four days a week and be able to take a three-month sabbatical!

Coach: Oh, so that's our real contract for these coaching sessions! (co-operative mode) not just dealing with the issues arising (accounting mode). It seems that we've taken a few sessions to get here (structuring mode); and maybe we've now got sufficient trust between us to work with what is most vital for you (nurturing mode).

Client: Yes … I've only just now realized as I said it, that's my real agenda!

The shifting energy in the client indicated that he moved into his Adult ego state and out of his Child ego state transference to the coach where he considered that he had to bring 'proper problems' to the 'expert' rather than his real desires. This was bought about eventually by the Coach using the spontaneous mode to confront the here and now of the client; her felt sense at first was that the client did not sound fully engaged, whatever behavioural mode she used to invite him.

Imago is the TA term for describing the psychological relationship between an individual and others. It can be usefully employed when a client wants to explore his or her relationships with others in the workplace, or the family, or amongst friendship networks. A toy-box of objects, a bag of pick and mix sweets, a button box, or some other collection of different symbols are used to represent the client and others. The client uses their intuition to place these different people in relation to self and each other. This is a visible expression of the psychological distance experienced in by the client. The creation of this imago on the table or floor becomes a 'third' which can be viewed from various angles and distances and discussed. These different perspectives on the imago, plus the coach's curiosity, often bring to the surface factors in the 'unthought' known of the client about individuals and about the systemic culture. This powerful technique invariably releases a range of new information for Adult consideration by both client and coach.

Story-telling, whether about present circumstances, past events, or the organizational context, is a valuable strand of the coaching conversation. *Script* is the TA concept used to describe repeating or stuck patterns of behaviour, feelings, thoughts and perspectives of individuals; repeating patterns of ulterior messages within the system or organization can show the character of its culture. Script and culture can both be helpful resources and can also be sources of 'stuckness'. Both the content and the processes of the stories told represent fractals of the individual's life-script and the 'cultural script' of the system.

The coach's task is to listen out for when the script or culture is stuck or unhelpful to the individual and/or organization and to confront the client in such a way that their Adult can assess the reality of what they are saying. The multi-cornered contract can support the coach to give feedback about unsupportive organizational culture which may require consultancy; and for the coach to reflect back to the individual when patterns from the past may be getting in the way of the present, or when the culture might be blocking the individual's potential and creating an impossible task. Whilst the coach holds an unconditional positive regard for the individual and system (summed up as OK-ness), the coach also raises questions when they hear of blockages. These may be evident in the story itself, or can show up at the micro-level of vocabulary – words such as 'everyone', 'no one', 'always' 'never', or in blocking or tangential responses, or in the client's despair at a seeming lack of options. Re-storying, in partnership with the coach, can then evolve new options.

APPLICATION

The process and purpose of TA coaching is autonomy and change. This could be described as strengthening the Adult ego state of the person in the client role through a contracted and confronting dialogue with the Adult ego state of the person in the coach role. Three case studies are described below – the first two interlink and were part of a larger cultural change project within a public sector organization, where external consultants determined that training for a coach approach to management, plus team coaching were two elements invigorating the culture change.

A long-standing manager, Dave had been referred for coaching as he showed signs of stress. He agreed with the new approach yet found it difficult to engage in with his team and was uncertain about his authority. The Human Resources Director joined for a three-way meeting once Dave and the coach had explored the professional and psychological contract for working together. As a result there was agreement to provide coaching for Dave's team to enable them to get to grips with the impact of organizational changes on their roles, and to consider the role of the team in the new structures. The following illustrates how two coaches shared similar TA models with manager and team.

Management coaching

The coach working with Dave used the template of behavioural modes; he found having a map in his mind helpful. Dave was concerned with how to be in charge and recognized he needed to provide both structure/orientation and nurture, neither of which he had experiences in his structural ego states to draw on. Clarke and Dawson (1998: 103) suggest that this can be thought of as a highway with two clear 'lanes', the negotiable and the non-negotiable. This helped, for instance, to differentiate a manager using the (negotiable) coach approach, e.g. to provide the boundaries around a team member goal setting for themselves and providing (non-negotiable) direction, e.g. with health and safety compliance.

In addition to being in charge the coach manager needs to take account of what is happening (accounting), co-operate when staff take charge of a piece of work and be spontaneous and think outside the box. This model proved extremely valuable to Dave who shared it at a team coaching to explain his role and range of styles. Three months later at the next three-way meeting he reported feeling much less stressed; the stand-off style of conflict within the team lessened, communication increased and attitudes to the senior leadership function within the organization became much more positive. Eventually he reflected to his coach how she had modelled for him, without comment, these different ways of being in charge in their relationship.

Team coaching

The second coach spent time exploring with the team the psychological level of the contract, by telling and inviting stories about how things held in mind and not expressed can cause ongoing rumblings or even explosive conflicts – how organizational change often triggered thoughts and feelings that can lead to tricky interactions. She followed this with interactive psycho-education on 'OK-ness' linked to the fight, flight, freeze instinctive responses (Figure 12.5), giving and inviting examples from the team.

The value of the positive OK-OK (flow) position was evident to the team. Also evident was the difficulty of holding this when someone else invited you from their negative position – 'I'm Not OK and You're Not OK' tries to get others to join in moaning, the 'I'm Not OK You Are' person goes looking for an 'I'm OK and You're Not' person to prove them right (and vice versa!). Ideas emerged among the team for how to work together better, which one member turned into posters for their offices.

The other part of the team coaching explored Schmid's (2006) roles theory. Each person made a personal chart for each 'world' of roles; sharing these facilitated new appreciation of each other and helped everyone clarify their own and each other's current roles in the workplace. The organizational arena proved fascinating for the team who had never before differentiated times when they and their manager represented the organization, regardless of professional expertise and opinion. What also became apparent for everyone was how miscommunication can happen and how one role area can contaminate or exclude another – when

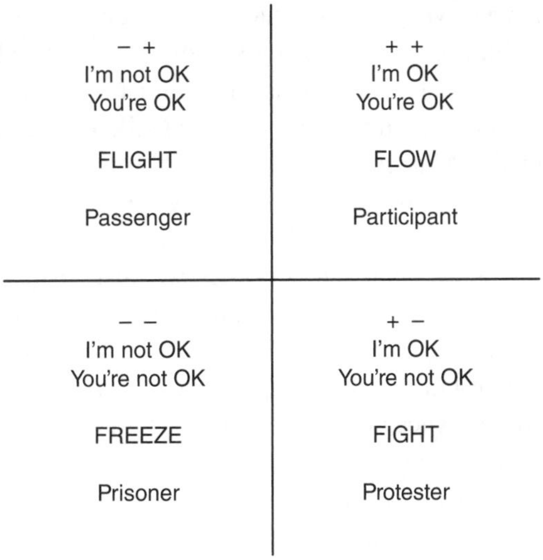

− + I'm not OK You're OK FLIGHT Passenger	+ + I'm OK You're OK FLOW Participant
− − I'm not OK You're not OK FREEZE Prisoner	+ − I'm OK You're not OK FIGHT Protester

Figure 12.5

being a parent interferes with working arrangements and others' workloads, or taking work home impacts on family life. The team identified the need for 'contracting' so as to clarify boundaries and give everyone concerned a chance to say what is on their mind, prior to making decisions about what to do.

This work with the team was useful for Dave in clarifying that his role is primarily organizational, and his job is to carry and inspire his team with the organization's' purpose and values, explore the relationship between his team and other teams it works with, and enable members to maximize their own potential and contribute to the organization's whole.

Cross-cultural career coaching

The following case study illustrates both an approach to career change and overtly cross-cultural work. Using the concept of stuck script as an internal reference point the coach was able to work sensitively with difference while acknowledging the recognition and shared values between coach and client that formed a sound basis for working together.

Marsha, a black woman, made a private approach to a coach, a white woman, about her career. She felt in a rut in a private sector managerial post but did not know what she wanted to do instead. Surfacing the psychological level of the contract proved important – why had she chosen this person as a coach? What impact might their different cultures and ethnicities make? It turned out that she admired her entrepreneurship in setting up a coaching business and that she wasn't sure whether race and cultural differences would help or hinder: however, there was agreement that these could be raised by either. Without explaining TA ideas of script the coach asked Marsha to tell her what was her favourite story around the ages of five to seven. The intention was multiple: to find if there were any kernels of unrealized dreams that might contribute to career decisions, to check on levels of optimism and idealism, and to invite the resources of creativity, intuition and imagination of the Child ego state via positive memories.

The traditional folk story that Marsha told involved a little girl going on a long journey that was very hard work, meeting up with a wicked witch and a wise woman along the way. Marsha had forgotten the purpose of the girl's journey and found it hard to imagine the ending. Rather than asking 'powerful questions' a TA approach considers whether to make the intention behind a query evident by expressing the thought behind the question. The coach wondered aloud about the parallels between the story and what Marsha had already shared about her current situation. Marsha's response was a 'light-bulb' moment of realization, which illuminated the possibility of stepping out of this frame of reference into 'a different story' – one that she made up in the present.

As the story-making frame seemed useful, Marsha agreed to make up lots of stories and look for others that appealed in films, books and the media. The themes that emerged were: to use her hands in making things, being independent and providing a service to black women– combining a positive psychology framework of 'the pleasurable, engaged and meaningful life' with TA ideas about life-script. Marsha decided that a portfolio career beginning with one day a week whilst reducing her well-paid employment time might be a fulfilling experiment. She set up a small business making greetings cards for the Afro-Caribbean community, volunteered as a mentor for women setting up their own businesses and gradually shifted to a three-day week, employing others to help make the cards. A critical moment occurred when the coach was able to say: 'being black is one of your unique strengths – it's OK to build on it!'

EVALUATION

The use of colloquial language for TA terminology is problematic. Different cultures interpret the terms differently, the terms can seem loosely defined or simplistic and over time terminology can seem outdated. Despite the original intent to use everyday language, some TA terms use unusual vocabulary, e.g. imago.

The diagrams used in TA can be critiqued as reification, reducing the complexity of the human experience and taking away from the uniqueness of the individual. However, the diagrams are merely metaphors, visually depicting what can take many words of description.

There are four fields of TA qualification: psychotherapy, counselling, organizations and education. The psychotherapy field has dominated in the English-speaking world in terms of numbers of trainees, qualified practitioners and articles written (the other fields are more numerous, for instance, in the German-speaking world). This bias has meant a focus on psychopathology in the literature and training, whereas the other three fields have a positive psychology focus on strengthening health more appropriate to coaching.

As coaching has developed strongly since the beginning of the 1990s it has been adopted as one way of practising in the organizational field (executive coaches, leadership coaches, team coaches) and mentoring and skills coaching are some of the professional roles in the Educational field. Within TA the field of Counselling is defined in relation to European practice and includes coaching, personal consultancy, team facilitation, non-managerial supervision, life-skills learning, mentoring, advising and guidance, as well as therapeutic counselling. Thus coaching is a recognized professional practice, but does not have a field of its own, as the different types of coaching are seen as context specific, each with their own frame of reference and with a specific contracted role. One implication is that coaches need to know when to refer on to other types of practitioners – an advantage for a TA coach who is being able to do so to others with a TA framework for thinking.

FURTHER READING

TA is primarily an oral tradition, passed on through teaching and learning workshops and conferences around the world. *The Transactional Analysis Journal* (published by Sage) provides a place for theoretical development and *IJTAR* (*The International Journal of Transactional Analysis Research*) is a free online international journal of TA research. However, there is a comparative lack of books, and few references to examples or theory, on TA coaching. The books mentioned here are, in our view, the most useful for coaches wanting to develop their TA practice.

Napper, R. & Newton, T. (2000). *Tactics: Transactional analysis concepts for all trainers, teachers and tutors & insight into collaborative learning strategies.* Ipswich: TA Resources. (This book focuses on how TA can be used to inform the process of adult learning and describes learning as making changes to attitudes and feelings, understanding and knowledge, and behaviours and skills. This correlates with the perspective on coaching as a space for individualized learning. A key theme is a developmental model that can be applied to development within a programme of coaching, a coaching session, or the process of starting a new job.)

Erskine, R. (Ed.) (2010) *Life scripts: A transactional analysis of unconscious relational patterns.* London: Karnac. (This book has a chapter on coaching which focuses on the individual in their context. This analyses the interlocking aspects of the cultural script of the organization and that of the individual client, and how this manifests in the coaching process. This book contains many other chapters focusing on contemporary use of the life-script concept in psychotherapy.)

Cochrane, H. & Newton, T. (2011). *Supervision for coaches: A guide to thoughtful work.* Ipswich: Supervision for Coaches Publishing. (Coaches looking for supervision on their work usually find a choice between business consultancy or psychotherapy-based models; this TA-based book aims to create something specific to coaching, combining practical guidance for supervisors with reflection on the underpinning 'roots' of supervision, including recent theories of adult learning. Included are sections on working with groups and working as external supervisor for internal coaches.)

Lapworth, P. & Sills, C. (2011). *An introduction to transactional analysis.* London: Sage. (This book is an introduction to TA, which focuses on a relational approach to practice. It is illustrated throughout with an example of TA used in executive coaching, although without any systemic context and a frame of reference which tends to the psychotherapeutic. This book has developed an idiosyncratic take on ego states and provides three different models.)

DISCUSSION QUESTIONS

- To what extent can TA provide a meta-language for a variety of different approaches in coaching?
- To what extent does the inner world of the coach impact the client and the coaching relationship? And how can this be contracted for and form a valuable aspect of TA coaching?
- What do you think are the benefits of using TA as a framework for thinking about systems in terms of structures, dynamics and culture?

REFERENCES

Berne, E. (1964) . *Games people play.* New York: Grove Press.

Clarke, J.I. & Dawson, C. (1998). *Growing up again* (2nd ed.). Center City, MN: Hazelden. (Original work published 1989.)

Cochrane, H. & Newton, T. (2011). *Supervision for Coaches: A guide to thoughtful work.* Ipswich: Supervision for Coaches Publishing.

English, F. (1975). The three-cornered contract. *Transactional Analysis Journal* 5:4, 384–5.

Erskine, R. (Ed.) (2010). *Life scripts: A transactional analysis of unconscious relational patterns.* London: Karnac.

Lapworth, P. & Sills, C. (2011). *An introduction to transactional analysis.* London: Sage.

Micholt, N. (1992). Psychological distance & group interventions. *Transactional Analysis Journal* 22:4, 228–233.

Napper, R. & Newton T. (2000). *Tactics: Transactional analysis concepts for all trainers, teachers and tutors & insight into collaborative learning strategies.* Ipswich: TA Resources.

Schmid, B. (2006 [1994]). Role concept, transactional analysis and social roles. In G. Mohr & T. Steinert (Eds.), *Growth and change for organizations: Transactional analysis new developments 1995–2006* (pp. 32–61). Pleasanton, CA: International Transactional Analysis Association.

Sills C. (Ed.) (1997). *Contracts in counselling.* London: Sage.

Temple, S. (2004). Update on the functional fluency model in education. *Transactional Analysis Journal* 34:3, 197–204.

13

The NLP Approach to Coaching

Bruce Grimley

Dilts, Grinder, Bandler and DeLozier (1980: 13) argued that Neuro-linguistic Programming (NLP) is a 'model for transforming environmental variables into the class of decision variables, it is a model to give people choice where previously they had no choice'. A popular working definition of NLP suggests it is an attitude with a methodology that leaves behind a trail of techniques. In this chapter I discuss how this attitude is formalized within the presuppositions of NLP; how the methodology is that of modelling and how the trail of techniques are the models which are created through modelling projects. The first two models published were the Meta Model and the Milton Model (Bandler & Grinder, 1975a, 1975b; Grinder & Bandler, 1976; Grinder, DeLozier, & Bandler, 1977).

In Grimley (2013: 27) I suggested that NLP coaching is an amalgam of two definitions: it is an approach to coaching which has modelling at its heart and makes use of the patterns developed from modelling projects, yet it follows the definition introduced in the introduction to this Handbook, namely that it is 'a human development process that involves structured, focused interaction and the use of appropriate strategies, tools and techniques to promote desirable and sustainable change for the benefit of the coachee and potentially for other stakeholders'.

Despite the technical overtones and the sense of a human as the modern biocomputer (Lilly, 1967), which appears to characterize NLP, the first exemplars for NLP models were very human: Fritz Perls, Virginia Satir and Milton Erickson. From modelling these therapists came the idea that each human is different and an appreciation that there are powerful systemic relationships between the conscious mind and unconscious mind based upon personal histories and internal representations of those histories.

The starting point for NLP coaching is necessarily the presuppositions that underpin NLP. Any system of knowledge has to have a point when it has to accept something at face value because it cannot prove what it accepts. NLP presuppositions are described as 'a pedagogical device to assist people new to NLP in making the required transitions in their thinking to the new forms of perception and thought implicit in the technology' (Bostic St. Clair & Grinder, 2001: 202). The best known NLP presupposition comes from Korzybski (1994: 58): 'A map is not the territory it represents, but if correct, it has a similar structure to the territory, which accounts for its usefulness'. For example, a deeply held belief such as 'I am hopeless' is never a 'reality' but a way in which we choose to represent ourselves within a particular context. The understanding for the NLP coach is that humans act not upon the world, but upon their representation of the world, and it is this representation that the NLP coach works with.

DISTINCTIVE FEATURES

Building on the notion of representation, NLP coaching does not focus so much on the content of the coachee's reality (details of the story), but rather on the process (how the details are consistently related and coded) or the pattern. Grinder explained how 'the single most pervasive influence in NLP is the paradigm that was current in linguistics at the time of the creation of NLP' (Bostic St. Clair & Grinder, 2001: 66), namely Transformational Grammar. Before his NLP publications Grinder, in writing about Transformational Grammar claims that 'linguistics will be the single most important activity in liberating one's head from the structure imposed by one's native language' (Grinder and Elgin, 1973: 8).

Within Transformational Grammar, the deep structure represents the basic grammatical relationships from which a sentence is derived. In NLP this is termed 'First Access' (F^1 or FA). It is the term given to preverbal sensory uptake of information and represents *sensory maps of reality* based upon neurological transforms. Linguistic transforms, acting as a sub-system, are then applied to these preverbal maps of reality (F^2) and at both of these levels the modelling processes of Deletion, Distortion and Generalization occur according to the processing rules of each level. Empirical research has found support for the weak version of the Sapir Whorf hypothesis (Hoijer, 1954), suggesting that even though language does not prevent sensing in the sensory apparatus it does have a strong affect on how that sensory information is coded and stored. Once applied to the sensory environment according to cultural rules, language then begins to determine what is experienced and what is not (Brown & Lenneberg, 1954; Carmichael, Hogan, & Walter, 1932).

The reason people often struggle to make changes is that they regard their internal brain architecture as immovable. They mistake their map of reality, for reality; like eating the menu at a restaurant mistaking it for the real food. This is because people take experiences in their personal history and embody the meanings created at that time. The sub-system of language then embeds this embodiment further in our neurology within multiple frames and at different levels (e.g. identity, meaning, ability, others, time, purpose) – so all experience is deleted and distorted through sensory and linguistic filters to accord with the generalizations created within personal history. If as a result of our personal history we come to the conclusion within a particular context that we are hopeless, then the cognitive dissonance theory predicts that if any experience provides evidence contrary to this belief a negative drive state will develop (Festinger & Carlsmith, 1959). To reduce dissonance, ideally the coachee will change. However, rather than change and believe they are 'capable' the coachee will often distort and delete incoming information to accord with the neurologically and linguistically embodied generalization. Thus the belief 'I cannot change' or 'I am hopeless' becomes a self-fulfilling prophesy. Bateson suggests that to be infinitely intelligent implies we have to be infinitely flexible. He argued that we have an emotional commitment to the solutions we discover and it is this psychological commitment that makes us rigid in operation and blind to alternative patterns of operating (Bateson, 1972).

The reason NLP coaching is believed to be so effective is because in its model of human functioning it makes explicit the dual information-processing systems of sensory transforms (F^1) and Linguistic transforms (F^2) and their systemic interaction. In the NLP model, because primary information-processing is via F^1 transforms this is where the leverage in coaching is.

Brookes and Coue (1922: 18–19) similarly point to the poverty of the simple cognitive model of human functioning. Their main conclusions were:

1. Every idea which exclusively occupies the mind is transformed into an actual physical or mental state.
2. The efforts we make to conquer an idea by exerting the will only serve to make that idea more powerful.

From the above, it can be seen that the main concept underlying the NLP approach to coaching is that humans construct their reality and do so through multiple information systems which are systemically inter-related. Much of this 'reality' is unconscious, thus much of the coaching needs to communicate at this unconscious level. How the coachee represents his/her world phenomenologically is always the topic of coaching and changing these representations so as to support well-formed outcomes generated at the beginning of coaching is the purpose of NLP coaching. NLP generally adopts the position of Mischel (1968) concerning personality and regards personality and the associated cognitive and affective strategies as situational rather than biological.

Coaching process

Using the main pillars of NLP coaching: Outcome, Acuity and Flexibility (O'Connor & Seymour, 1995), the coaching process focuses on three main questions:

1. Do coachees know specifically what they want?
2. Can they keep their senses open so they know what they are presently getting?
3. Do they have the flexibility to keep changing till they get what they want?

Change during coaching is enabled through the five core NLP processes (Bostic St. Clair & Grinder, 2001: 198–9):

1. The Meta Model, designed to verbally challenge the mapping between first access to the outside world through our senses and our linguistically mediated mental maps.
2. Operations that define over-representational systems and their sub-modalities.
3. Reframing patterns, so that representations are placed in a different cognitive structure.
4. Anchoring, so that undifferentiated groupings of representations are brought together for purposes of integration.
5. The Milton Model, where representations are shifted using linguistically mediated maps without the need to map those representations into the client's conscious understanding.

Changes, however, are irrelevant if the coachee does not know what they wish to achieve and the context within which they wish to achieve that outcome. The role of the NLP coach is then to assist the coachee in understanding what they want. This is more complex than it may seem, because just as within psychology we have the concept of a false self (Winnicott, 1960), so too within coaching we can imagine the concept of a false outcome. This is an outcome which lacks authenticity. Such an outcome will also lack ecology and 'parts' within the mind–body system will object to aspects of such an outcome. It has been described as 'shoulding' ourselves (Tagg, 1996), or 'musterbating' (Ellis, 1980). Very often within NLP coaching, the process of clarifying the outcome is sufficient to bring into play underused internal resources which may lead to the desired outcome without further coaching. During the clarification part of NLP coaching 11 variables need to be addressed effectively (Grimley, 2013: 195). The coachees are asked if the outcome is:

1. *Specific.* In NLP terms, 'Can you put it in a wheelbarrow?' For example, success cannot be put in a wheelbarrow. However, a coaching certificate, a business contract, or £10,000 are more tangible.
2. *Measurable.* What is the scale whereby you will measure your outcome? How will you calibrate your successful outcome compared to your own previous performance or the performance of other people?
3. *Achievable.* This question does not imply only the strength of the coachees' beliefs in their ability to achieve this result. It also addresses the question if this can be done by another human being.
4. *An appropriate chunk size.* Needed in order for the coachee to congruently take immediate action. For example, completing a doctorate needs to be chunked down.
5. *Within an appropriate time frame.* Over what time will you achieve your outcome?
6. *Ecological.* Is there any part of the coachee that objects to the well-formed outcome? If there is such a 'part' it needs to be satisfied before the outcome can be called 'well-formed'.
7. *Stated in the positive.* In NLP the representation of the outcome needs to be sensory based. This cannot be done in negative terms.
8. *Preserving the positive.* All change involves transformation from the old to the new. It is essential that what is valued in the old is preserved effectively in the new outcome.
9. *Owned.* Coachees cannot own the outcome of getting a promotion. However, they can own the outcome of engaging in behaviours and language which will increase the probability of obtaining a promotion.
10. *Motivating.* Motivation is the fuel enabling coachees to travel from where they are to where they want to be. It is inevitably related to what is important at the level of values. The outcome needs to be compelling at every level in order to maintain the change process when rewards do not appear to be forthcoming and obstacles emerge. For example, the key to individual change may be anchoring pleasure to outcomes and pain to

non-achievement. Once done automatic decision making inevitably leads to self-directed change (Robbins, 1986; Grant, 2001).

11. *Future paceable.* Every 'well-formed' outcome in NLP can be imagined as being achieved at a later date. If the coachee cannot imagine themselves achieving their outcome in the future and being very excited about that achievement there is a lack of 'ecology'.

Very often in NLP coaching the five core NLP processes will be utilized to facilitate the point at which coachees can access their Well-Formed Outcome phenomenologically. It is at this stage, if needed, that the coach works with the coachee to understand what he/she is presently getting (developing self-awareness) and working at what needs to change (flexibility). The role of the coach throughout this process is to support and facilitate an exploration of what coachees value, how this is related to their identity and what beliefs, strategies, behaviour and language are needed to relate to others in such a way that their outcome becomes manifest and their environment systemically supports them.

Because NLP believes everybody is different, this means everyone's outcome is going to be different in certain ways. The NLP coach needs to spot these differences and always work with the map of the coachee. It may be tempting to look at the psychological literature and make certain generalizations when we put our professional robe on. We may 'know' that leaders tend to be proactive, move towards well defined goals, are stable, extraverted and internally referenced when making decisions. However, to impose these generalizations upon a coachee who wishes to develop leadership qualities, without taking considerable time to appreciate their current map of the world through congruent matching and pacing, would be incongruent to NLP coaching.

Even though NLP coaching already had a significant array of tools useful for operating technically as an NLP coach, during the late 1980s and after parting with Bandler, Grinder developed New Code NLP, initially with DeLozier (DeLozier & Grinder, 1987). This was because within the NLP fraternity there was a 'hardening of the categories' so to speak. Grinder found that NLP students were using the NLP patterns in a way that was not ecological, there was a lack of grace and elegance and a part of the evidence for this was that NLP coaches could not apply NLP patterns to their own lives effectively. New Code NLP sought to take NLP back to the systemic principles which Bateson espoused and an appreciation of the unconscious mind which had been left behind. An appreciation for such a coaching perspective comes also from Bandler, the other co-founder of NLP: 'there is one thing that delineates when someone knows what NLP is. It is not a set of techniques – it is an attitude' (Bandler, 1985: 155). Likewise Linder-Pelz states that she aims to reduce NLP coaching 'to basics and principles rather than tools' (2010: 53). Michael Hall makes a similar point arguing that the NLP presuppositions are devices to 'suggest the kind of attitude or a meta-state frame that transforms us so that our practice of NLP moves to a higher level of mastery' (Hall & Bodenhamer, 2003: 40). This means that even though an NLP coach needs to be able to spot a Meta Model violation and ask the appropriate question, if he or she does not do this in the appropriate way and at the appropriate time the question will be counterproductive.

The ability to use the NLP patterns in this ecological way is something that comes with experience. Coding this ecology in such a way that trained NLP coaches can consistently provide empirically validated results is a challenge that NLP has yet to master.

METHODS AND TECHNIQUES

Taking into consideration the importance of the systemic perspective rather than the mechanical use of tools as discussed above, let us now look at some of the techniques that an NLP coach might adopt.

The Meta Model

The Meta Model is the first model of NLP. It consists of 13 syntactic patterns in human speech along with the appropriate challenges. Questions assist a coachee to elaborate a hitherto impoverished map of the world, resulting in much greater choice. These patterns are grouped into the three modelling processes of Deletions, Distortions and Generalizations, for example if the coachee complains: 'They never listen to me', the NLP coach could respond:

1. Who never listens to you? (recovering *deleted* information)
2. How do you know they never listen to you? (checking for behavioural evidence and accurate calibration of that behaviour to an internal state, Listening to ensure the coachee's meaning-making is not *distorted*)
3. NEVER listens to you? (accentuating the *Generalization* so as to trigger an internal search for exceptions to the rule)

In NLP coaching the Meta Model is essentially a linguistic model to clarify what the coachee is saying, primarily for the sake of the coachee. Often it transpires that the coachee does not really know what they are talking about and this in itself is a useful coaching challenge, as the language we use is an intrinsic part of the systemic loop which creates our phenomenological experience and therefore our behaviour. The key to using the Meta Model effectively is ensuring good rapport is generated and then maintained.

When coachees use language they can be encouraged to use it to express what they are experiencing at a deeper level, ensuring the surface structure of their words are connected to the deeper structure of the reference experience, or to influence what they are experiencing at a deeper level. In both ways words and syntax are effective representations whereby we literally 'inform' our phenomenological experience. We use our language to either consolidate or change our unconscious maps of the world. Coachees who are aware of the powerful effect of their words are in a better position to use language in either of the above ways.

The Meta Model can appear quite complex when read as a linguistic treatise (Grinder & Bandler, 1976). However, if we think of the basic clarifications questions: How? What? When? Who? and Where? it becomes easier to incorporate them into a coaching strategy. Grimley (2010: 250–251) suggests a strategy for using Meta Model type questions consisting of five basic steps:

1. Establish rapport.
2. Listen intently.
3. As you listen run an internal video in your head.
4. When the verbal does not translate into visual format ask a Who? How? When? Where? or What? question until it does.
5. Ensure you consistently match and pace your coachee's map of the world and retain rapport at all times.

Milton Model

Just as the Meta Model uses language in order to challenge sentences which are not well-formed and thus help represent the deep structure of reference experience, so conversely the Milton Model uses language in an ill-formed way with the purpose of overloading the conscious mind, so as to access the unconscious processes: 'You are sitting down in that chair and can begin to relax now'. The coachee cannot deny they are sitting in a chair; however, the conjunction 'and' is used to link this irrefutable truth to a suggestion. The Milton Model uses the principles of acceptance and utilization whereby the coachee's model of the world is maximally used, by accepting it, matching it and pacing it. Because the nature of Milton Model language patterns is such that they are ill-formed, the conscious mind becomes overloaded and access to the unconscious mind becomes possible. If an idea is then accepted by the unconscious mind it becomes a part of 'reality'.

However, to accept something consciously is to accept it only analytically and for consideration. For Brooks and Coue a thought is a force: 'every idea which enters the conscious mind, if it is accepted by the unconscious, is transformed by it into a reality and forms henceforth a permanent element in our life' (Brooks and Coue, 1922: 54–5). Erickson was a master of matching, pacing and then communicating with the unconscious mind of his patients so as to lead them into a new reality. For Gilligan, who also modelled Erickson, Hypnosis, is nothing unnatural. Trance is simply a special learning state that occurs whenever identity is threatened, disrupted, or needs to reorganize. Hypnosis is the social tradition that can provide a ritual space and process to receive and positively guide the trance process in helpful ways (Gilligan, 2013). In NLP coaching it is said there is no such thing as a resistant coachee, only an inflexible coach. If there is resistance in the coaching intervention it is because the coach is not matching, pacing and ensuring they are in rapport with their coachee. As we can see below, these are all aspects of the Milton Model which are important for a successful coaching intervention.

Matching, pacing and leading

Matching is a rapport-building technique of feeding back the behavioural patterns of the person being coached. It is recognized that people who are really 'getting on' are almost in a dance. If one person touches their ear, often within a few minutes the other person will match with a 'hand to face' gesture of some kind. Similarly, pacing is feeding back the cognitive patterns of the person being coached. If, for example, the coachee talks exclusively about the future and does so using abstract language, the coach repeats these patterns back to the coachee.

Critics of NLP sometimes suggest that matching and pacing is being false or incongruent. However, NLP practitioners see these as building bridges so that the map of the coachee can be more fully appreciated. Matching and pacing is the precursor for leading. It is possible to identify whether or not the coach is matching and pacing effectively. When they do something differently from how the coachee usually behaves, after a time lag the coachee follows them.

The purpose of leading is to widen coachees' repertoires and to provide them with greater choice in their life. In order to know what set of skills or state they require, coaches must have established what their coachees' well-formed outcome is. For example, if they wish to network more effectively with the aim of building their business, and during the establishment of rapport the coach has noticed that the coachee displays a pattern of moving away from undesirable situations rather than moving towards desirable ones, the following challenge might be useful:

> Coach: You have told me how you would rather stay in and have other people contact you, and you have also let me know about the anxiety you feel in talking to others about what you do. So I would like you now to see yourself and your business, which is important to you, in five years' time. As you stay in waiting for others to make the move, imagine what that does for your bank balance. Looking at yourself now in this situation from that place in five years' time, what could be the first thing you do to make a difference and build your business?

The coachee then may be supported by the coach in a process whereby they search for the most appropriate action in the immediate present to change their situation. This leading process, however, would not be effective if the matching and pacing were not present, and during the rapport-building process the appropriate cognitive filters had not been picked up and made use of by the coach to lead the coachee to a new reality supporting their well-formed outcome using the coachee's own cognitive preference.

Using metaphor

Just as humans replace objects with words, so too, by using metaphor the coach can replace the coachee's problem with another problem, within which lies a solution. A well-created metaphor will bypass the analytical mind and will be accepted by the holistic mind of the unconscious, becoming a 'reality' for coachees. As their conscious mind focuses on the content which is different from the coachee's situation, the unconscious mind resonates with the structure of the metaphor leading to a solution.

Anchoring

Anchoring formats in NLP were developed by Bandler and Grinder as a result of modelling Erickson's style. They found that Erickson would use particular cues as post-hypnotic triggers to help a person change their internal state at some time in the future. Anchoring is a natural phenomenon and is similar to classical conditioning (Dilts & DeLozier, 2000). Whereas in classical conditioning the conditional stimulus and conditional response were always external, anchoring formats have been generalized in NLP to be used for internal events, too. In coaching therefore, the thought of giving a presentation can be anchored to a feeling of relaxation within the whole body. After successfully making use of anchoring in coaching the coachee can forget about the procedure and will find that the context of giving a presentation in the future automatically triggers the feeling of relaxation. As with metaphor as a coaching tool, the unconscious mind is utilized in setting up the new reality and when this occurs no effort is required by the conscious mind. Anchoring of course happens every day naturally and often in a negative way. If someone is consistently irritated by another's behaviour they are naturally anchored. Whenever this behaviour occurs they move into this predictable negative state. This can be changed in NLP coaching by setting up another more productive emotional state to be associated with the other person's behaviour.

Framing and reframing

Framing and reframing is essentially taking what a person says and putting it into a cognitive frame which is useful. 'I am hopeless' can produce a sense of achievement when the coach points out that it is an excellent strategy for getting out of doing the dishes. In NLP coaching this would be an example of a 'context reframe', building upon the NLP presupposition that all our behaviour is useful in some context. A content reframe, by contrast, will build upon the NLP presupposition that all behaviour has a positive intention. In response to 'I am hopeless' the coach could say 'that means you really care about your performance which is the first step in making wonderful improvement'.

Framing is of course more important than reframing: DeLozier is said to have argued that an ounce of framing is worth a pound of reframing. The more the NLP coach can from the outset act in a congruent and professional way, the more the initial frames will be set for a good coaching intervention and reframing will not be needed to such an extent in these cases.

Logical levels

The relevance of the logical levels model is that it overtly introduces the concept of systems thinking. The idea of logical levels was developed by Dilts (1990) and based upon the concept of logical types formulated by Whitehead and Russell (1910) and used by Bateson (1972). According to the model there are six levels (spirit; identity; beliefs and values; capability; behaviour; and the environment). Each level synthesizes, organizes and directs the class of activity at the level below it. So changing something at a higher level will necessarily change something at a lower level; however, change at a lower level would not necessarily change the element above (see Figure 13.1).

At an individual level there is a recognition that no behaviour stands alone. In order to understand a behaviour effectively we need to understand where this behaviour occurs, when it occurs, how it occurs, what are the beliefs which underpin such behaviour, what values drive such behaviour, who would engage in such behaviour and of what, such behaviour is a part, in the wider sense of shared outcomes and common visions. The logical levels model is thus a very

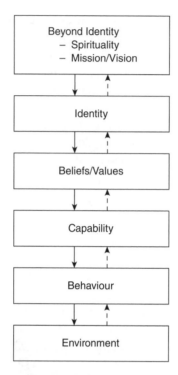

Figure 13.1   Logical levels model (adapted from Dilts, 1990)

useful framework for exploring and modelling a coachee's current map of the world in a particular context at different levels of information-processing. Often coaches can direct coachees
to step away from the spaces on the floor and observe themselves behaving in an environment,
or observe their physiology as they process a belief. This provides an extra description for coachees to assist them become more self-aware and thus closer to that situation in which they can
make the necessary adjustment to their current map of reality. The logical level model is also
very useful within organizations. By modelling different departments at different levels, business coaches can assist coachees in understanding where there is a mismatch and work to generate greater rapport at that level.

Eye-accessing cues

In the film *The Negotiator* actor Samuel Jackson tells fellow hostages that he knows a group
member is lying, because his eye movements went up and to the right when he spoke rather than
up and to the left. To suggest the NLP paradigm supports such a contention as Wiseman et al.
(2012) do is to misrepresent NLP. The empirical evidence for the NLP recognition of eye-
accessing cues seems very mixed. Eye movements may be related to several undefined sources

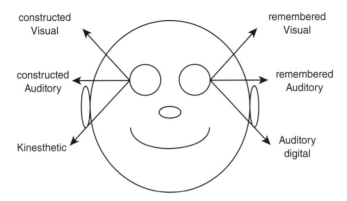

Figure 13.2   Eye Accessing cues (adapted from Dilts et al., 1980)

of variance and as a general rule the eye-accessing cues posited by Dilts et al. (1980) need to be calibrated to each individual coachee. If every time the coachee talks about a particular problem they look down and to the right, and they do this consistently, according to the NLP model they are accessing a kinaesthetic internal representation. Theoretically, they would respond much more quickly and accurately to the question 'and how do you feel about that?' compared with the questions 'how do you see that?' or 'how does that sound to you?' The key for an NLP coach in using eye-accessing cues is to calibrate effectively and understand that the purpose of this observation is simply to engage more effectively with the coachee's unconscious map of the world in the problem context. Figure 13.2 illustrates the hypothesized relationship between eye position and representational system.

APPLICATION

NLP coaching puts an emphasis on rapport and many coaches find its personable paradigm well buttressed with a richness of philosophy and techniques. This allows them to develop their coaching style effectively and without constraints on their own personality. If coaches have a preference for detail, they will enjoy coaching using the Meta Model. Alternatively, coaches who prefer to look at the bigger picture will enjoy making use of the Milton Model and logical levels in their coaching approach. Coaches who deal with cross-cultural issues find NLP coaching very useful because the Meta Model assists coachees in developing an awareness of their own cultural values, beliefs and attitudes. With the rich repertoire of coaching techniques NLP coaching can then be effectively used to help the coachee express such beliefs and attitudes in an elegant manner within a different culture. The Meta Model is especially useful for assisting such coachees to examine their own unexplored assumptions and stereotypes about the behaviours of those in other cultures.

When coaching in a specific competency is called for, either in an executive or managerial role, NLP is well-suited because of the emphasis on integration of the skills into an unconsciously competent format. For instance, anchoring is something that consistently and naturally occurs; one cannot avoid anchoring. The NLP coach is simply a professional person who is aware of the ubiquitous nature of such a process and will use it in an ethical way. This means that integration of NLP coaching skills into an executive or managerial role is seamless and does not create resistance in those being coached. Often, issues of fit come to the fore in both team and career coaching. NLP places great emphasis on goal setting and creating frames that work for individuals and teams; however, it also places an equal emphasis on the mind–body system and the need for ecology and congruence in the lives of those who seek to work as part of a team or to develop their career.

EVALUATION

One of the particular strengths of NLP as a coaching paradigm is its accessibility. Any would be coach looking to start coaching practice will have no difficulty in sourcing an NLP trainer. The down side of this accessibility is a lack of standardization. A new coach can obtain an NLP practitioner certificate after only five days training packed into a hall with 600 other delegates. At the other end of the spectrum one can find NLP practitioner trainings which have at least four trainers, 36 days training, course work, examinations and supervised practice. NLP and coaching can also now be studied at postgraduate level at universities in the UK and abroad. It is therefore a case of *caveat emptor* as an NLP practitioner certificate is not necessarily evidence of NLP coaching competency. There is also mis-information about NLP which is easily accessible and can lead people astray. Another difficulty with NLP coaching is that although there is plenty of anecdotal evidence for its effectiveness in print and on the web, there is little empirical evidence in academic literature for its efficacy in the context of coaching. This is beginning to be addressed by the NLP community, but it is a long and winding road that needs to be travelled.

NLP as a coaching paradigm may still need to find a validated empirical evidence base. However, it is a dynamic coaching paradigm which has tremendous potential simply because of its appreciation of the consistent operation and influence of the unconscious mind and the need to communicate at that level within the coaching intervention.

FURTHER READING

Grimley, B (2013). *Theory and practice of NLP coaching.* London: Sage. (A handbook on the psychological theory and practice supporting NLP coaching.)

Hall, M. & Duval, M. (2004). *Meta coaching, Volume 1 and Volume 2.* Clion, CO: Neuro Semantics Publications. (An NLP coaching handbook.)

Tosey, P. & Mathison, J. (2009). *Neuro-linguistic programming: A critical appreciation.* London: Palgrave Macmillan. (A critical exploration of NLP.)

DISCUSSION QUESTIONS

- Milton Erickson used to create a different model of working for each client as he believed each client was different. How is it possible to evaluate a paradigm which changes at each session?
- Many people seek to characterize NLP coaching in terms of basic principles and attitudes rather than prescriptive steps. Why do you think this is?
- If you were a successful coach who was using NLP coaching with good results would you be concerned with the lack of empirical evidence for NLP coaching in the academic literature?

REFERENCES

Bandler, R. (1985). *Use your brain for a CHANGE*. Moab, UT: Real People Press.

Bandler, R. and Grinder, J. (1975a). *Patterns of the hypnotic techniques of Milton H. Erickson MD, Volume 1*. Capitola, CA: Meta Publications.

Bandler, R. & Grinder, J. (1975b). *The structure of magic: A book about language and therapy*. Palo Alto, CA: Science and Behaviour Books.

Bateson, G. (1972). *Steps to an ecology of mind*: Chicago, IL: University of Chicago Press.

Bostic St. Clair, C. & Grinder, J. (2001). *Whispering in the wind*. Scotts Valley, CA: J&C Enterprises.

Brooks, C.H. and Coue, E. (1922). *Practice of autosuggestion*. New York: Dodd, Mead and Company.

Brown, R. & Lenneberg, E. (1954). A study in language and cognition. *Journal of Abnormal and Social Psychology, 49*, 454–462.

Carmichael, L., Hogan, P., & Walter, A. (1932). An experimental study on the effect of language on the reproduction of visually perceived forms. *The Journal of Experimental Psychology, 15*, 73–86.

Cox, E., Bachkirova, T., & Clutterbuck, D. (2010). *The complete handbook of coaching*. London: Sage.

Grinder, J. & DeLozier, J. (1987). *Turtles all the way down: Prerequisites to personal genius*. California: Grinder & Associates.

Dilts, R. (1990). *Changing belief systems with NLP*. Capitola, CA: Meta Publications.

Dilts, R., Grinder, J., Bandler, R., & DeLozier, J. (1980). *Neuro-linguistic programming, Volume 1: The study of the structure of subjective experience*. Capitola, CA: Meta Publications.

Dilts, R. & DeLozier, J. (2000). *Encyclopedia of systemic neuro-linguistic programming and NLP new coding*. Scotts Valley, CA: NLP University Press.

Ellis, A. (1980). The general theory of RET. In W. Dryden (Ed.) *The essential Albert Ellis: Seminal writings on psychotherapy*. New York: Springer Publication Company.

Festinger, L. & Carlsmith, J.M. (1959). Cognitive consequences of forced compliance, *Journal of Abnormal and Social Psychology, 58*, 203–210.

Gilligan, S. (2013). *An Interview with Dr Stephen Gilligan*. By Chris & Jules Collingwood, Sydney, Australia. www.stephengilligan.com/interviewA.html, retrieved 4th January 2013.

Grant, A.M. (2001). Neuro-associative conditioning. *Australian Psychologist, 36*(3), 232–238.

Grimley, B. (2010). The Meta Model in McMahon,G &Archer,A (Eds) (2010)*101 Coaching Strategies and Techniques*. London & New York: Routledge.

Grimley, B. (2013). *Theory and practice of NLP coaching: A psychological approach*. London, Sage.

Grinder, J. (2005). *Coaching for coaches: Two interviews with John Grinder – Uncensored*. 2005 Interview. www.empowered tolearn.com/GrinderInterview2005.htm, retrieved 28th December 2012.

Grinder, J. & Bandler, R. (1976). *The structure of magic 2: A book about communication and change*. Palo Alto, CA: Science and Behaviour Books.

Grinder, J., DeLozier, J., & Bandler, R. (1977). *Patterns of the hypnotic techniques of Milton H. Erickson MD, Volume 2*. Capitola, CA: Meta Publications.

Grinder, J.T. & Elgin, S.H. (1973). *Guide to transformational grammar: History, theory, practice*. New York: Holt, Rinehart and Winston Inc.

Hall, M. & Bodenhamer, B. (2003). *The user's manual for the brain, Volume 2*. Carmarthen: Crown House Publishing.

Hoijer, H. (Ed.) (1954). *Language in culture: Conference on the interrelations of language and other aspects of culture*. Chicago, IL: University of Chicago Press.

Korzybski, A. (1994). *Science and sanity: an introduction to non-Aristotelian systems and general semantics* (5th ed.). New York: Institute of General Semantics.

Lilly, J.C. (1967). *Programming the human biocomputer*. Berkeley, CA: Ronin.

Linder-Pelz, S. (2010). *NLP coaching: An evidence-based approach for coaches, leaders and individuals*. London: Kogan Page.

Mischel, W. (1968). *Personality and assessment*. New York: Wiley.

O'Connor, J. & Seymour, J. (1995). *Introducing NLP Neuro-Linguistic Programming*. London: Thorsons.

Robbins, A. (1986) *Unlimited Power*. New York: Free Press.

Tagg. J. (1996). *Shoulding Yourself, shoulding others*. http://daphne.palomar.edu/jtagg/should.htm, retrieved 5th January 2013.

Whitehead, A.N. & Russell, B. (1910). *Principia mathematica*. Cambridge: Cambridge University Press.

Winnicott, D. W. (1960). Ego distortion in terms of true and false self. In *The Maturational process and the facilitating environment: Studies in the theory of emotional development* (pp. 140–152). New York: International UP Inc, 1965.

Wiseman, R., Watt, C., ten Brinke, L., Porter,S., Couper, S-L., & Rankin,C. (2012). *The eyes don't have it: Lie detection and neuro-linguistic programming*. www.plosone.org/article/info%3Adoi%2F10.1371%2Fjournal.pone.0040259, retrieved 5th January 2013.

Contexts and Genres

14

Skills and Performance Coaching

Bob Tschannen-Moran

Skills and performance coaching (SPC) is, perhaps, the original and most common genre of coaching: assisting someone to learn how to do something better.

As children, from the time of learning how to walk and talk, we were taught by others using a combination of two processes: instruction and incentives. These significant others told us what to do and how to do it correctly. They may have also offered incentives, such as rewards, compliments, or punishments to get us to do the work and master the domain. The assumptions here include that there is a right way to do something, that the instructor knows that way and that the instructor must teach and motivate the learner to learn that way.

Although it is not uncommon for these same processes to be used with adults, especially when it comes to training and knowledge transfer, research by educators and psychologists (e.g. Knowles, Holton, & Swanson, 2011) has documented the limitations of this approach. There are many ways to do things and adults, deep down, are no different than toddlers learning to walk: we like to figure things out for ourselves, for our own reasons, in our own way, on our own schedule and with our own resources. For SPC to be effective, therefore, it needs to take these and other autonomy-related factors into consideration.

DISTINCTIVE FEATURES

One distinctive feature of SPC stems from the fact that it relates to particular domains of human functioning with clear performance standards. Unlike other forms of coaching, the scope and success of which may be entirely defined and determined by the coachee, SPC often involves meeting external requirements established by others. Even when the desire to improve skills and performance is motivated intrinsically, the standards themselves are typically defined by others. An athlete does not improve performance, for example, without knowing the rules of the game; neither does an actor improve performance without the response of the audience. So, too, with engineers, teachers and surgeons: there is no way for them to improve their skills apart from the context of physical laws, organizational requirements and the standards of their professions. When it comes to SPC, then, coaches are assisting people to improve their ability to function in relationship to not only their own but also to externally-defined dynamics. To accomplish this, coaches must assist coachees to:

1. *Find positive motivation.* SPC invites coachees to find positive, intrinsic motivation to meet those externally-defined requirements. This requires coaches to shift coachees from aversive motivators, such as fear and disgust, to attractive motivators, such as hope and competence. Assisting coachees to develop a clear and compelling vision of performance mastery, what is wanted rather than what is not wanted, is critical to continuing skills and performance improvements.
2. *Expand mindful awareness.* What is happening right now? What really matters? When things work well, what do they look, sound and feel like? Assisting coachees to attend to these things, in-the-moment and without judgement, facilitates what Gallwey (2008) calls 'natural learning'. A clear and accurate appreciation of what is happening in the present moment underlies skills and performance improvements in every arena.
3. *Build self-efficacy.* Beyond ideas of right and wrong doing there is a field wherein people can find the confidence to initiate and sustain performance improvements. SPC enables coachees to play in that field through verbal persuasion, somatic awareness, vicarious learning and mastery experiences (Bandura, 1994, 1997). It seeks to build the self-efficacy of coachees in specific areas of responsibility and interest.
4. *Recognize learning opportunities.* Skills and performance improvements require understandings and environments that support movement, innovation and resilience for learning and growth. Coaching assists coachees to recognize and develop such opportunities.
5. *Design learning experiments.* 'Nothing is as dangerous as an idea,' wrote Émile Chartier, 'when it is the only one you have' (cited in O'Hanlon & Beadle, 1997: 31). The operational task of SPC is to generate and test out multiple ideas for skills and performance improvements instead of getting wedded to a single course of action.
6. *Support perseverant efforts.* Practice may not make perfect, but it does lead to improved skills and performance when engaged in over extended periods of time. SPC therefore assists coachees to persevere while implementing new behaviours, especially in the wake of setbacks. Finding fulfilment in the ups and downs of the learning process itself is a key aspect of SPC.
7. *Savour every success.* SPC strives to assist coachees to experience and celebrate mastery in their desired areas of performance improvement. Quick wins, whether large or small, build self-efficacy and long-term success.

Artfully handling these seven tasks requires coaches to engage in eight critical functions:

1. *Identifying a learning need with intrinsic value.* The first challenge of SPC is to connect external performance requirements with internal desires and ambitions. Until coachees want to learn something for their own good reasons, the process of coaching will revert to instructions and incentives. Interviewing coachees as to what and how they want to learn is the start of SPC.
2. *Listening to understand and support.* Because SPC works with external performance requirements, extending empathy is another one of its essential processes. The route to performance mastery is filled with thrills and agonies, each of which requires supportive, emotionally-intelligent understanding.

3. *Discovering capacities, strengths and resources.* Another challenge of SPC is to shift coachees from a problem-solving to a strengths-building focus. Expanding on what people already know and do well is a more effective and enjoyable way to learn than identifying and fixing problems. To facilitate transformational change, therefore, SPC investigates assets more than deficits.

4. *Observing examples of successful accomplishment.* More than other forms of coaching, SPC requires a clear picture of successful accomplishment. What does it look like to do something well? Instead of describing this to coachees, SPC gets coachees to discover it for themselves through the observation of role models and the exploration of their methods and techniques.

5. *Formulating a vision of personal mastery.* SPC also invites coachees to envision themselves performing at higher levels of mastery. It is one thing to observe others; it is another thing to imagine following in their footsteps. Through visualization exercises and other creative activities, SPC assists coachees to move from mimicking to personal anticipation, appropriation, adoption and assimilation.

6. *Brainstorming innovative designs and strategies.* The process of generating multiple possibilities for self-directed skills and performance improvements, without regard to their value, feasibility or desirability, is an essential process of SPC. Since there is no way to predict which designs and strategies will prove most effective for any given person to actually realize his or her vision, SPC encourages coachees to experiment with different approaches and contexts that fit with their interests, abilities and experiences.

7. *Practising and refining new behaviours.* The biggest challenge of SPC is often to keep people moving forward over time. Both advances and setbacks can stall the process of behaviour change, as people become either satisfied or discouraged. The role of SPC is to align internal understandings and external environments so that coachees persistently make adaptive choices and sustain new behaviours.

8. *Celebrating improvement.* The old adage 'Nothing breeds success like success' speaks to a key source of self-efficacy in generating performance improvement. SPC assists coachees to experience quick wins and to appreciate their accomplishments before moving on to new goals and possibilities.

Once coachees experience the thrill of successfully improving their skills and performance through the adept handling of these critical functions, it leads naturally to continued interest in additional observations and conversations. Rather than being dreaded, they are welcomed. Coachees become fully engaged in the coaching process and the spiral dynamic of continuous performance improvement, with coaches becoming partners on the journey to success rather than instructors (Corcoran, 2005). This dynamic, described fully in Tschannen-Moran and Tschannen-Moran (2010), is well illustrated by a Möbius-strip model of the coaching process that revolves around four conversations: Story, Empathy, Inquiry and Design (SEID) (Figure 14.1). Each will be considered in turn.

Story

Coaching begins when coachees share their stories. These stories reflect the sense coachees make of their experiences. They are never the experiences themselves; they are rather an attempt to understand, value and shape their experiences in ways that make sense and guide future actions.

Since coaching works with the stories coachees tell, both to themselves and to others, it is possible to change everything. Tell a new story, in a new way and we get a new experience (Bandler & Grinder, 1975). That is especially true when we begin to work with the attributions of cause and effect that are explicit and/or implicit in most stories (Loehr, 2007: 4). Coaches listen for those attributions, since they illuminate a coachee's path of development. For example:

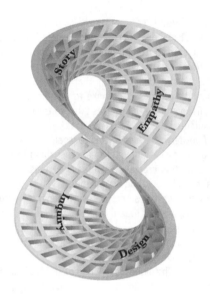

Figure 14.1   A Möbius-strip model of SPC

- What is the overarching theme? Does it lie more with danger or opportunity?
- Where is the locus of control? Does it lie more with the coachee or with others?
- What is the language of capacity? Does it lie more with skills or resources?
- How is the objective defined? Does it lie more with metrics or morale?
- What is happening with energy? Is it emptying out or filling up?
- What is happening with values? Are they being honoured or compromised?
- What is happening with needs? Are they being met, denied, or sacrificed?

There is no end to the attributions we can listen for and find, since there is no end to the stories coachees can tell. The secret is to listen mindfully, without judgement or haste. It is tempting to rush coachees through the telling of their stories in order to get to new approaches and designs. People want things fixed and they want them fixed fast. But visions, goals and designs based on unappreciated stories often generate unhappy results. Instead of skills and performance improvements, we get more of the same. Instead of learning and growth, we get stuck in the muck. Story listening is the first step and a key element to SPC.

Empathy

Although empathy has long been recognized as a critical part of therapy it is not often talked or written about in the context of SPC. Yet empathy has much to do with skills and performance improvements.

When listening to coachee stories, it is important to distinguish between pity, sympathy and empathy. Pity is feeling sorry for someone, which does not foster change. Sympathy is emotional contagion or sharing someone's feelings, which can lead to advising, rescuing and defending behaviours. Empathy, the respectful, no-fault understanding and appreciation of someone's experience, is an orientation and practice that fosters radically new change possibilities.

Empathy does this by shifting the focus from particular strategies to universal needs. Most of the stories people tell are about the strategic designs and efforts that either did or did not work. That is, in fact, why they tell their stories: because they feel good or bad about something that has happened. Often, however, they misattribute their feelings to the designs themselves rather than to the underlying needs. As a result, they get caught up in a self-defeating cycle of interpretations, judgements, criticisms and diagnoses (Rosenberg, 2005: 52 ff.).

To express empathy, coaches can use the Nonviolent Communication model developed originally by Marshall Rosenberg (2005). Upon hearing a story, coaches can notice and reflect back the coachee's feelings and needs in ways that release tension, facilitate calm and expand awareness. To do this effectively requires fluency in the language of authentic feelings and universal human needs (d'Ansembourg, 2007). Noticing and mirroring such feelings and needs are two more key features of SPC.

Inquiry

Inquiry without empathy is interrogation. That is why SPC moves from Story to Design through Empathy and Inquiry. Once coachees feel safe and heard at the level of their feelings and needs, they become open to exploring new ways of looking at themselves and what they are doing. Such openness generates alternative stories and, in turn, alternative designs.

When it comes to improving skills and performance, adult learning theories and growth-fostering psychologies suggest that appreciative, strengths-based inquiries are more effective and empowering than analytic, deficits-based inquiries. Given that many if not most stories are told from a deficits-based framework, it is immediately reorienting to ask open-ended, strengths-based questions, such as:

- What would success look like? What else would it look like?
- What's working with your approach? What else is working? What else?
- What talents and abilities are serving you well? What else?
- What's the best thing that's happening now? What else?
- What fills you with energy and hope? What else?
- What enables you to do as well as you are doing? What else?
- What is the positive intent of your actions? What else?
- What resources do you have available? What else?

The point of such inquiries is to elevate the focus, self-efficacy, resourcefulness and wherewithal of coachees. The more focused coachees are on their problems, deficits and limitations, the less likely they are to imagine and pursue new possibilities. Appreciative, strengths-based inquiries turn that around. They remind coachees that they have what it takes to learn what they want to learn.

They also remind coachees that stories of hardship, difficulty, frustration and failure do not represent the whole story. The point of asking 'What else?' on multiple occasions is to raise the awareness of coachees as to other ways of telling the story. Knowing that in every situation something is always working, no matter how bleak or discouraging things may appear, coaches can be courageous in their inquiries to find high points worth celebrating.

In addition to discovering the best of what is, coaches can also inquire into the best of what might be. This can be done either directly ('If you could wave a magic wand and make any three wishes come true, wishes that would infuse you and this situation with energy and life, what would they be?') or indirectly ('If a miracle happened tonight to make these problems disappear, what would be the first thing you would notice when you woke up in the morning?'). Either way, the point is to prime the pump with a compelling vision before moving into design. Such inquiry and imagination are two more key aspects of SPC.

Design

When coachee stories are listened to and reframed properly, through empathy and inquiry, strategic designs for skills and performance improvements often emerge organically from the coachees themselves. Little or no instructions or incentives are required and are, in fact, often counterproductive (Knight, 2011). Coaches should therefore aim to assist coachees to become detached from both the fear of failure and their own illusions as to what is or should be happening; it is then, and only then, that they become fearless in the pursuit of those things which will enable them to learn and grow.

The key in SPC, then, is for coaches to avoid reintroducing judgemental frames as to how things are to be done 'correctly' or even 'better'. The best strategic designs evolve from experiments with no preconceived ideas as to outcomes. What works for one person may not work for another. Strategic designs can well be thought of, therefore, as games to be played and learned from rather as blueprints, plans and prescriptions to be followed.

Brainstorming is an essential part of playing that game and a useful tool for developing smart designs, especially when coachees and coaches take turns coming up with possible ideas. Basic protocols for brainstorming include:

- setting a minimum number of possibilities to generate
- setting a time limit to keep things moving rapidly
- withholding judgement or evaluation of possibilities
- encouraging wild and exaggerated possibilities
- letting no possibility go unsaid
- building on the possibilities put forth by others
- combining and expanding possibilities.

A central question around which to brainstorm is 'What could I pay attention to that would improve my skills and performance in this situation?' This makes learning both self-directed and enjoyable. By getting coachees to identify what is important, without telling them what to do, they are nudged to make new choices and to try new behaviours with a minimum of resistance. The non-judgemental focus enables the voice in the head to get out of the way.

Whatever gets generated through brainstorming, SPC assists coachees to winnow through the options and to implement strategic designs in incremental timeframes. Small, manageable designs that rapidly give people an experience of improvement and success do much to bolster the self-confidence and learning of coachees over time. These successes can then be celebrated, while setbacks can be appreciated as new grist for the coaching mill. Brainstorming, experimenting and appreciating are key works of SPC that keep the process moving forward (Alexander & Renshaw, 2005; Cox, 2006).

Case study

Jack was frustrated, confused and anxious. As a 63-year-old probation officer, he wanted nothing more than to do his job well and to retire with full benefits in a few years' time. Yet day after day, week after week, Jack found himself procrastinating on some of the most important aspects of his work: writing and filing reports on a timely basis. His desk was filled with piles of paper, he was missing deadlines and his boss had given him an ultimatum: get on top of things, or else. 'You better not lose this job,' his wife implored at one of their increasingly tense moments. Perhaps coaching could help.

During Jack's initial session he shared with me the story of how far behind he was with his paperwork, how overwhelmed he was by the work and how ashamed he felt to be a procrastinator. 'This is all my fault,' he said ruefully, 'and I'm not getting any younger. Whether I retire here or get fired, it will probably be my last best job.' I reflected back his concern, but not his attribution of blame. I reflected back his anxiety, but not his fatalism. Instead, I guessed that his concern and anxiety might be surfacing because of his very real needs for contribution and security. I could hear the air slowly release over the telephone. 'It's important for me to do a good job,' he said, 'you heard that right. I just wish it wasn't such a struggle.' 'So you also need ease and assistance,' I said. At that, the tension let up even further.

I asked him to tell me a story about the best contribution he ever made as a probation officer. He choked up as he told me about his relationship with Kevin, a teenager who was on the edge of throwing his life away. He visited Kevin after hours and saw him through the process of getting off probation. 'That's the best,' Jack said, 'when someone like Kevin actually makes it clean rather than ending up with a long prison sentence, or worse.' 'That's quite a contribution,' I observed, 'it's almost like you saved somebody's life. I can hear what it means to you in your voice.'

From that simple, values-oriented, strengths-based inquiry, Jack started to shift from a storyline of failure and being overwhelmed to one of meaningfulness and purpose. He also began to connect the dots, all on his own, between paperwork and contribution. In an instant, he no longer saw paperwork as busywork; he suddenly saw it as an integral part of his contribution. 'I'm going to figure this out,' he said, 'I'm going to learn how to do this. For the first time in my life, I'm going to stop procrastinating.'

Week after week we brainstormed ideas and ran experiments: throwing all the clutter off his desk into a box for immediate gratification; noticing and logging what his office looked like at the start and end of each day; inviting his wife over for an office clean-up party; finishing all paperwork on Wednesdays; or reviewing his notes in the car before leaving a client location. He would start every coaching conversation with new stories as to what was happening and how he was feeling. As the stories came out, we would go through the same process of empathy and inquiry on the way to new designs.

This process also quickened an increased awareness of his needs. He noticed how tired he felt, for example, because his needs for rest and play were not being met. 'How can I take any time off,' he exclaimed, 'when my office is such a wreck! I have to work all the time just in case someone wants something and I'm the only one who can find it – which sometimes takes me several hours.' He also felt frustrated because his need for interdependence was not being met. 'I'm not the only one who is falling behind,' he said, 'and I'm really not sure how to streamline my reporting.' 'Where could you go with those concerns?' I asked. 'I could talk with my boss about both,' he replied, 'perhaps I could show him a report to get his feedback on the essential elements.' 'Would you be willing to summarize that feedback in the form of a check-list that you could share with me?' I asked. Jack agreed happily.

Two weeks later Jack was beaming at the start of our call. 'You'll never guess what happened,' he bragged. 'You got the clean-office award!' I laughed. 'Not yet,' he said, 'but people are talking. I had those conversations with my boss and with his boss. We talked about the need for a succession plan and they agreed to hire two more probation officers. In addition, my boss circled the information he wanted on my reports. I've been writing way too much! No wonder I was falling behind. Now my reports are getting easier and soon we'll be able to distribute the work better in the office. I feel like a new man.'

'You sound like a new man,' I reflected back with sincere enthusiasm. 'I *am* a new man,' he said, 'I took a half day off work last week to go to the dentist. And I've started walking in the morning with my son's dog. I'm just more relaxed and even my boss has noticed the difference. He complimented me recently and asked me to handle something when he was going to be out of the office. It wasn't six weeks ago that he was avoiding me and not giving me work. Even other people have noticed the difference. Things have really turned around.'

The breakthroughs this coachee achieved and the progress he made were due to the raised awareness he had as to the connection between his feelings, needs and strategies for meeting those needs. Instead of dealing directly with 'his problems' of procrastination and organization, we used his awareness and stories of contribution to step above the fray and to design new possibilities for getting help and streamlining his reporting. That shift made all the difference and his competence and self-efficacy grew and enabled him to learn how to meet the tasks at hand and to take better care of himself in the process.

RELATIONSHIP WITH THEORETICAL TRADITIONS

As presented here, SPC is related most closely to the following theoretical approaches to coaching: solution-focused, person-centred, narrative, cognitive developmental, positive psychology and Neuro-linguistic Programming. Each approach will be considered in turn as it relates to skills and performance coaching, but the following recognitions are held in common between them all, either explicitly or implicitly:

- People are inherently creative and capable.
- Learning takes place when people take active responsibility for constructing meaning from their experience (either confirming or changing what they already know).
- The meanings people construct determine the actions they take.
- Every person is unique and yet all people have the same universal needs.
- Empathy, mutuality and connection make people more co-operative and open to change.
- People don't resist change; they resist being changed.
- The more people know about their values, strengths, resources and abilities the stronger their motivation and the better their changes will be.

These recognitions challenge the presuppositions of behaviourism and provide yet another framework for calling into question the use of instructions and incentives in SPC. Although it is tempting to tell people how to do things better, to make them practice and to reward their progress, such approaches fail to inspire and leverage the best of human learning and functioning. Indeed, they can just as easily undermine motivation, provoke resistance, usurp responsibility, rupture relationships, ignore reality, discourage risk-taking, limit imagination and restrict results (Kohn, 1999). They may 'work' in the short run (if 'work' is understood as compliance) but they seldom work in the long run (if 'work' is understood as mastery) and they rarely generate significant improvements, at least not until they are abandoned in favour of self-directed learning. In skills and performance coaching, using the SEID model can turn things around by drawing upon these different theoretical approaches.

With its focus on the desired solution state, rather than the problem(s) coachees want to solve, solution-focused coaching is perhaps the theoretical tradition most closely aligned with SPC as presented here. Assisting coachees to focus on what they want, rather than on what they don't want, is a fundamental task of effective SPC. Like solution-focused coaching, SPC also understands that the more we talk about our problems, the more entrenched our problems become. So SPC keeps the coaching conversation focused on what it looks and feels like to perform and be at one's best. It is important for that vision of personal mastery to have a somatic component. As jazz saxophonist Charlie Parker famously said about music, 'If you don't live it, it won't come out of your horn.' This fits in with Parker's legendary notion that the way to mastery is to 'practice, practice, practice – and then, when you finally get up there on the bandstand, you forget about all that and just wail.' Trying to fix what's wrong often makes the problem(s) more entrenched. Instead, language that describes and epitomizes what's right makes the solution(s) more likely. Solution-focused language is itself a solution and effective SPC consistently brings coachees back to solution-focused language during coaching conversations.

This is quite similar to the Rogerian components of client-centred therapy (Rogers, 1951/1988). If one starts from the stance that people are their own best experts, then it naturally follows that coaching is more about strengthening functionality than repairing dysfunctionality.

Carl Rogers' stance that people are intrinsically motivated to grow into optimal functionality is both an obvious and guiding principle of SPC. People do not seek SPC unless they want to improve and that happens most fully when their best attributes are recognized and called forth by the coaching process itself. The coach does not need to tell a coachee what's wrong; people become coachees because they know something is wrong in a specific area of endeavour. The surprise of SPC using the SEID model is the discovery that coachees also know best how to fix what's wrong with their skills and performance. They do not need to be taught by others as though they were elementary-school students; they can seek and find their own solutions with minimal direction and instruction from their coaches. The coaches' roles are to motivate, encourage, inquire and guide people in designing their own best solutions. No two solutions work equally well for any two coachees. Solutions must be tailor-made and the best tailors are the coachees themselves.

For that to happen, as narrative coaching recognizes, coachees must learn to sing a new song and tell a new story. The grip of the old story, that 'I see a problem,' has to be loosened in order for the new story, that 'I see a possibility,'' to take hold. With the vision of a possibility clearly in mind, coachees often surprise both themselves and their coaches with the approaches and solutions they devise. That is what cognitive developmental coaching identifies when it suggests that the process of making changes works best when it is chosen by the coachee rather than the coach. Only coachees know fully who they are and who they are becoming. Excellent SPC leverages that truth to facilitate a more rapid development into skills and performance mastery. There is, indeed, always a 'grain of mystery' to the developmental process and that is as true for SPC as for any other developmental process. Skills and performance coaches would do well to take that into account, to not take themselves too seriously and to not give themselves too much credit. When SPC works it is because it has unlocked the inherent potential of the coachee rather than because the coach has done such a great job.

Although a relatively recent addition to the field, positive psychology coaching (PPC) fits right into this conversation of theoretical traditions that relate to SPC. All of the traditions discussed so far focus more on the positive than on the negative aspects of human nature and on ways to inspire rather than to push coachees into performing at their very best (Fredrickson, 2009). The old adage, 'When I insist, you resist,' is especially true in SPC. The more coaches seek to get coachees to do it the coach's way, the more likely it is that coachees will push back – whether obviously or in more subtle ways. The more coaches facilitate coachees to find their own way into greatness, on the other hand, so as to build on their own, unique positive qualities and strengths, the more ready, willing and able coachees become to do just that.

The NLP approach to coaching represents one more, important tradition that reflects the SEID model of SPC presented here. The notion that reality is self-generated by the stories that we tell ourselves and others represents an enormous leap of faith that coachees consistently discover to be true when they make the leap. Giving empathy to coachees for their painful stories and inquiring into their best possible stories enables them to stop being stuck and to design new ways forward that are often surprising to their coaches in both kind and degree. NLP starts from that stance when it assumes that coachees' come to coaching with all the resources they need to change, even if they are unaware of them or if these resources are unavailable to them at the time. The process of coaching, then, is comparable to a treasure hunt: coachees and coaches go hunting together to discover the designs that will bring out a coachee's greatness. When NLP asserts that reality is self-generated, it recognizes a coachee's ability to improve by appreciating their best qualities, maximizing their resources and developing their ability to use those resources in new and creative ways. By joining up with coachees through rapport-building exercises and focusing consistently on what coachees want, rather than on what they do not want, coaches engage the unconscious mind of coachees in the change process until it becomes a conscious part of who they are and who they are becoming. Once coachees become aware of and embrace their potential, all manner of change becomes possible, even in the face of great adversity and obstacles.

Many of these different theoretical traditions were brought into play by Gallwey with his approach to 'Inner-Game' coaching, first applied to tennis in 1974 and later to other fields of human endeavour. He, too, recognized the debilitating impact of reparative coaching models, as well of instructions and incentives, on the internal dynamics that make for optimum skill development and performance improvement. Ironically, he noted, the more important the stakes, in terms of the external requirements and reinforcements, and the more coaches work to point out problems and instruct people in the 'right' way to do things, the more people distracted become from their own 'natural learning' style (Gallwey, 2008: 22).

Although Gallwey's first book marked a turning point for athletic coaching and is frequently hailed as a milestone in the modern coaching movement (particularly after publication of *The inner game of work*, in 2000), his Inner-Game principles are inextricably tied to the theoretical traditions discussed here as well as to the research and practice in adult education and learning theories dating back more than a century. Lindeman (1926) and Knowles (1950) were two of the early pioneers in this field and the characteristics of adult learners, highlighted by Knowles in particular, frame a strong theoretical base for why reparative, instructional and compensatory models so often interfere with high performance.

Instructions come with an implicit 'should' as to what is to be done and how it is to be done, undermining autonomy and self-direction. Adding compensatory incentives only makes this worse. Instructions also build more on the experience base of the coach than of the coachee, which may or may not be viewed as relevant and workable in the eyes of the coachee. They imply that there is a 'right' way to do something, while extrinsic incentives feel more like enforcement than support. In short, the use of instructions and incentives violates much of what has been learned when it comes to adult education and learning theory. Gallwey (2000, 2008) was right when he asserted there must be a better way to learn. The SEID model of SPC takes those considerations into account.

These recognitions also explain why SEID represents such a promising model for SPC. When the coaching process assists coachees to explore their stories with empathy and inquiry, rather than with evaluation and interrogation, it produces freedom, stimulates curiosity, elevates self-efficacy and leverages latent competencies in the service of desired outcomes. Such coaching sets aside the notion of there being one 'right' way to do something; it rather invites coachees to become fully engaged in the process of discovering their own unique designs for skill and performance improvements without suffering the stress of having to do things 'correctly'.

EVALUATION

Human learning and growth is a natural process that can be facilitated as well as impeded by the intervention of others, including coaches. The more coaches tell their coachees what to do, how to do it and why to do it, the more resistance gets triggered and the less learning takes place. It may be usual and customary to give instructions and provide incentives, but these approaches can be counterproductive to skills and performance improvements.

Taking this into account, effective SPC assists coachees to find their own path and get out of their own way in the service of desired outcomes. That is recognized, albeit in their unique ways and from different vantage points, in the different theoretical traditions highlighted earlier. Through cultivating motivation, expanding awareness, building self-efficacy, framing opportunities, designing experiments, structuring repetition and savouring success, coaches enable coachees to progress more easily and effectively than when they are left to their own devices. That is because people tend to be their own worst enemies when they are not performing as they would like. They pressure themselves into doing things 'right' and 'get down' on themselves when they do things 'wrong', as if their very identities depended upon the outcome. These dynamics tend to immobilize people and make things worse.

SPC can break that juggernaut through empathy and inquiry, effectively freeing coachees to play with alternative designs and strategies rather than to push for perfect performance. This requires fluency on the part of coaches in the languages of empathy and inquiry, as well as attentiveness to the stories being told. Through listening, noticing, exploring, experimenting and enjoying the process of discovery, coachees can learn to take their skills and performance to ever higher levels of mastery.

Although SPC as described here cannot make everyone the first among many in their areas of interest, it can bring out their very best and can make them very happy with their skills and performance. That, in the end, is the goal of all SPC: to evoke greatness from coachees within the capacities of their mental, emotional and physical abilities. SEID then, can be understood as a dance, where Story and Design flow from and are set to the music of Empathy and Inquiry.

FURTHER READING

Alexander, G. & Renshaw, B. (2005). *SuperCoaching: The missing ingredient for high performance*. London: Random House. (Focused on improving the quality of coaching in business settings, this book identifies 12 Core Competencies for SPC to effective).

Gallwey, W.T. (2008). *The inner game of tennis: The classic guide to the mental side of peak performance*. New York: Random House. (Originally published in 1974, this book makes the case for 'natural learning' with a minimum of instructions and incentives. To encourage 'natural learning', Gallwey discusses the value of non-judgemental awareness, creating images, letting things happen and relaxed concentration. His 2000 book, *The inner game of work*, is also useful in relation to coaching.)

Senge, P.M. (2006). *The fifth discipline: The art & practice of the learning organization*. New York: Doubleday. (With a nod to Gallwey, Senge further describes how to optimize the learning process. This book has helpful chapters on personal mastery, mental models, shared vision and team learning.)

Hall, L.M. & Duval, M. (2004a, 2004b); and Hall, L.M. (2007). *Meta-coaching*: Vols I–III. Clifton, CO: Neuro-Semantics Publications. (With frequent references to Gallwey's *Inner Game*, these books on coaching for change, structuring coaching conversations and facilitating self-actualization present a detailed discussion of how to unleash people's creativity and natural ability to learn.)

Tschannen-Moran, B. & Tschannen-Moran, M. (2010). *Evocative coaching: Transforming schools one conversation at a time*, San Francisco, CA: Jossey-Bass. (Written by my wife, a professor of educational leadership at the College of William & Mary in Williamsburg, VA and me, this book describes the dynamics and application of the SEID coaching model so as to improve the quality of instruction and leadership in schools.)

DISCUSSION QUESTIONS

- In what areas of human endeavour do you excel? How did that mastery come about?
- What has been your best experience of learning a new skill? How would you relate your learning process to the SEID model?
- What has been your best experience of facilitating someone else to learn a new skill? What approach did you take and how would you relate that approach to the SEID model?

REFERENCES

Alexander, G. & Renshaw, B. (2005). *SuperCoaching: The missing ingredient for high performance*. London: Random House.

Bandler, R. & Grinder, J. (1975). *The structure of magic I: A book about language on therapy*. Palo Alto, CA: Science and Behavior Books, Inc.

Bandura, A. (1994). Self-efficacy. In V.S. Ramachaudran (Ed.), *Encyclopedia of human behavior* (Vol. 4, pp. 71–81). New York: Academic Press. (Reprinted in H. Friedman [Ed.]. [1998]. *Encyclopedia of mental health*. San Diego, CA: Academic Press.)

Bandura, A. (1997). *Self-efficacy: The exercise of control*. New York: W.H. Freeman.

Corcoran, J. (2005). *Building strengths and skills: A collaborative approach to working with coachees*. New York: Oxford University Press.

Cox, E. (2006). An adult learning approach to coaching. In D.R. Stober & A.M. Grant (Eds), *Evidence based coaching handbook: Putting best practices to work for your coachees* (pp. 193–217). Hoboken, NJ: John Wiley & Sons.

d'Ansembourg, T. (2007). *Being genuine: Stop being nice, start being real*. Encinitas, CA: PuddleDancer Press.

Fredrickson, B. (2009). *Positivity*. New York: Crown Publishers.

Gallwey, W.T. (2000). *The inner game of work: Focus*. New York: Random House.

Gallwey, W.T. (2008 [1974]). *The inner game of tennis: The classic guide to the mental side of peak performance*. New York: Random House.

Hall, L.M. (2007). *Meta-coaching: Vol. III Unleashed! A guide to your ultimate self-actualization*. Clifton, CO: Neuro-Semantic Publications.

Hall, L.M. & Duval, M. (2004a). *Meta-coaching: Vol. I For higher levels of success and transformation*. Clifton, CO: Neuro-Semantic Publications.

Hall, L.M. & Duval, M. (2004b). *Meta-coaching: Vol. II Coaching conversations for transformational change*. Clifton, CO: Neuro-Semantic Publications.

Knight, J. (2011). *Unmistakable impact: A partnership approach for dramatically improving instruction*. Thousand Oaks, CA: Corwin.

Knowles, M.S. (1950). *Informal adult education*. New York: Association Press.

Knowles, M.S., Holton, E.F., & Swanson, R.A. (2011). *The adult learner* (7th ed.). Burlington, MA: Butterworth-Heinemann.

Kohn, A. (1999). *Punished by rewards: The trouble with gold stars, incentive plans, A's, praise, and other bribes*. New York: Houghton Mifflin.

Lindeman, E. (1926). *The meaning of adult education*. New York: New Republic.

Loehr, J. (2007). *The power of story: Rewrite your destiny in business and in life*. New York: Free Press.

O'Hanlon, B. & Beadle, S. (1997). *A guide to possibility land: Fifty-one methods for doing brief, respectful therapy*. New York: Norton.

Rogers, C.R. (1951/1988). *Client-centered therapy: Its current practice, implications, and theory*. London: Constable & Robinson Ltd.

Rosenberg, M.B. (2005). *Nonviolent communication: A language of life*. Encinitas, CA: PuddleDancer Press.

Senge, P. (2006). *The fifth discipline: The art & practice of the learning* organization. New York and London: Doubleday Business.

Tschannen-Moran, B. & Tschannen-Moran, M. (2010). *Evocative coaching: Transforming schools one conversation at a time*. San Francisco, CA: Jossey-Bass.

15

Developmental Coaching

Elaine Cox and Peter Jackson

Development is widely understood to mean growth of intellectual, emotional or some other capacity over time and so coaching that is described as developmental would aim to support the coachee to make the changes necessary to grow and mature. In this chapter we consider that development must involve progress and expansion of some kind. As Sugarman (2001) confirms, development is a concept that centres on a value-based notion of improvement. So, inherent in developmental coaching is an assumption of movement from where the client is now to where he or she wants to be, whether that is in relation to making practical changes in the work environment, making changes in response to emotional pressure or making changes in levels of understanding and responses to the world around them. To be developmental the coaching has not merely to focus on problem-solving but also on ensuring that client capacity is built through that problem-solving.

Definitions of developmental coaching

In much of the coaching literature developmental coaching is described in human capability and potential terms. For example, Sperry (2002: 142) sees developmental coaching as recognition by the coach or manager of an employee's skills and potential, and the provision of opportunities to develop or use those skills in the course of their work. Hunt and Weintraub (2002: 5) similarly define developmental coaching as an interaction between two people, often a manager and an employee, aimed at helping the employee learn from the job in order to promote his or her development. The process they describe involves the coachee being encouraged to reflect on current work challenges and to self-assess his/her performance. The ultimate aim is for the employee to recognize and address the gap between perceived achievement and expected achievement. Such developmental coaching, they argue, is always driven by the individual's agenda, rather than the organization's agenda. So it would appear that even in the organizational setting the value judgement under-girding the desired improvement can be that of the coachee.

Thus one definition of developmental coaching, especially as conceived in organizational settings, is concerned with professional and career development: providing opportunities for people to progress within the organization. However, in this chapter we present an extension of this view of developmental coaching – we are concerned with helping clients to expand in outlook and attitude as individuals as they work through their life experiences. We agree with Taylor, Marienau and Fiddler (2000: 10) who define adult development as 'a process of qualitative changes in attitudes, values and understanding that adults experience as a result of ongoing transactions with their social environment.' Development occurs when new learning, however achieved, becomes absorbed into who we are and how we work – into our 'pre-reflective experience' (Cox, 2013).

Developmental coaching in this second definition can therefore be viewed as a natural progression from the skills and performance focused coaching suggested by Sperry and Hunt and Weintraub. Coaches working across a whole spectrum of contexts have realized that as people enhance their skills and performance they also develop as people. As their functioning improves so their confidence and self-efficacy improves; they learn more about themselves and expand their perspectives. Accordingly, developmental coaching could be seen as a progressive step in the provision of coaching; from skills coaching (developing the technical mastery of aspects of a particular activity) through performance coaching (developing the effective deployment of skills in complex contexts), to developmental coaching (helping the person change in order to engage in a different way with current and future challenges). This progression is depicted in Figure 15.1, where we illustrate the movement from what might be seen as the fundamentally behavioural coaching offered by the skills coach, through performance coaching, to a more constructivist, developmental approach, which, as well as addressing immediate needs, takes a longer-term, more evolutionary perspective on the client's growth. To sum up, skills are contained in the presenting challenge; performance calls on creative judgement to recruit appropriate skills;

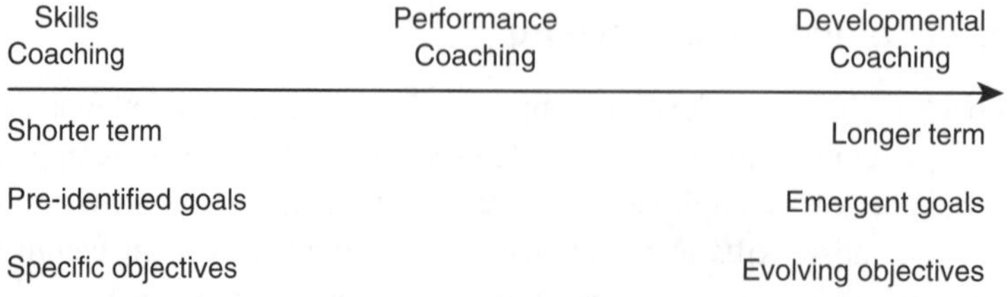

Skills Coaching	Performance Coaching	Developmental Coaching
Shorter term		Longer term
Pre-identified goals		Emergent goals
Specific objectives		Evolving objectives

Figure 15.1   Skills, performance and developmental coaching – an evolution

development calls on some kind of re-evaluation of the system of judgement. Unsurprisingly, such an intervention may be 'relatively long-term (usually more than six months), and emphasizes personal rather than technical or business issues' (Berman and Bradt, 2006: 245).

Background to developmental coaching

Knowles, Swanson and Holton (2011) confirm that adults do not become adults in an instant and that a developmental process is involved. However, they claim that adult development theory, which might be expected to shed light on the developmental process, is currently little more than an array of untested theories and models. The theories fall into three main categories:

1. physical changes – e.g. theories of maturation and ageing, such as those discussed by Schaie and Zanjani (2006)
2. cognitive or intellectual development – theories such as Perry's (1970) or Kegan's (1994), discussed by Bachkirova in Section I of this volume and in Bachkirova (2011)
3. life-span development (theories such as Erikson's (1974), or Levinson's (1978), which are based on social role perspectives).

Sugarman too, has described the imprecision surrounding the term 'development', suggesting that no matter how much data could be collected about an individual life it would still not enable us to define what is meant by the term unless we were to say that 'whatever happens across the life span is what constitutes development' (2001: 3). However, as Sugarman suggests, this negates the idea of development enhancing interventions (such as coaching) since there could be no judgement as to what would be better or preferable: from this viewpoint, she argues, 'any life course is as good (or as developed) as any other, there are no grounds for attempting to influence it'.

Sugarman (2001) goes on to describe how attempts have been made to define development empirically by reference to norms that suggest that certain aspects or stages of development may be expected to happen to the majority of people during their life. In Erikson's (1974) theory, for example, there are eight stages of development which unfold as we go through the life-span. Each involves the resolution of a crisis. According to Erikson, this crisis is a turning point involving increased vulnerability and enhanced potential. The more a crisis is successfully resolved, the healthier our development will be. For other researchers development is an adaptive response to new priorities and opportunities through the life-span. Levinson's studies suggest that the (male) life cycle is composed of a series of age-related developmental periods: childhood and adolescence; early adulthood; middle adulthood and late adulthood. Between each of the periods are transitions, such as the mid-life transition, which provide developmental opportunities. Levinson also believed that there are transitional periods in late adulthood and argued that 'as long as life continues, no period marks the end of the opportunities and the burdens of further development' (Levinson, 1978: 244).

These models, however accurate and useful they seem, have been criticized for discouraging individuality and exceptionality: any concentration on life as a series of stages implies a form of mechanical predictability that seems curiously at odds with the dynamics of change and individual variability. It could be argued that it is impossible to fully capture the considerable complexity of the tasks and processes involved in adult development. As Kolb (1984: 138) notes, 'The paths of development can be as varied as the many systems of social knowledge'. By extension, we would argue that any particular model of development is a partial perspective and cannot reflect the range of developmental opportunities evident in coaching practice. This range is highlighted by Bachkirova (2011: 125), who argues that clients' themes are inherently developmental: 'formulated from their own perspectives of their overarching needs and challenges'.

In the next section we look at the distinctive features of developmental coaching. This is followed by a discussion of its relationship with the theoretical traditions or approaches outlined in Section I of this book. We conclude with an evaluation that identifies some of the limitations and benefits of this genre.

DISTINCTIVE FEATURES

The developmental coaching perspective is built on a complex worldview that assumes that the world is unitary and interactional. At the heart of this lies the belief that man is adaptive: people are seen as active organisms that have free will, rather than as merely reactive creatures. Knowles et al. (2011: 24) suggest that individuals who accept this perspective tend to 'emphasize the significance of processes over products and qualitative change over quantitative change'. They also tend to emphasize the importance of the role of experience in constructing, facilitating or inhibiting the course of development.

This constructivist worldview is also evident in much coaching literature. For example, following Kolb (1984), Hunt and Weintraub (2004: 42) claim that the underlying assumption of developmental coaching is that employees will learn more when pursuing goals that they have defined, rather than goals defined by others. There is a substantial body of evidence to support the view that self-directed learning results in better outcomes than learning based on demands for compliance to the goals of others (see Knowles et al., 2011). From this it can be deduced that responsibility is also an important issue. Coaching is founded on an understanding of individuals as responsible for their own development (i.e. they are self-directed) and that their learning derives from tackling their own problems and solutions.

As intimated above, it could be argued that all coaching approaches are in some way developmental. Coaches make the assumption that when they work with the whole person (i.e. with emotions as well as cognitions) it is developmental coaching, but few use that term in order to describe their work. Most choose to use a term that describes either the target audience for their coaching: executives, leaders, teams, peers; or the context in which they are coaching: life coaching, career coaching or cross-cultural coaching. A quick look at the other chapters in this Handbook confirms this. The focus for coaching is on how to help clients deal with or remove the obstacles to growth and to facilitate the conditions that are conducive to their fulfilment. It therefore follows that development, whether overtly stated or not, is an integral part of all coaching contexts and genres.

We would argue, for example, that transformational coaching is in fact a type of developmental coaching, since it too is concerned with helping the client to think and act differently in response to a dilemma. However, it proposes that developmental change can be achieved quite quickly or even that it can be manufactured. Consequently, developmental coaching differs in one significant regard from the model of transformational coaching in that it holds that development is a gradual, organic, even a lifelong process. Development is not instantaneous or even discernable – it has been argued that development sometimes takes years or even decades (Berger & Fitzgerald, 2002; O'Connor & Lages, 2007) – so a short-term coaching relationship may only be a small part or a small phase in the client's developmental journey: just one ingredient in the client's developmental 'stew'.

In another example, O'Connor and Lages (2007: 230) have argued that developmental coaching is important for supporting leaders, since at higher levels of development 'people construct their world and understand differently; they are able to think more systemically, make finer distinctions and see the world as a bigger place, because they are not so identified with parts of their own ego'. However, developmental coaching in an executive and leadership context can also be quite different from some other forms of coaching in that it does not necessarily prioritise the organizational agenda. A systemic perspective is always important in order to work with the alignment of the individual and organizational needs: yet in some approaches the priority is to align the client's capabilities to the client's role in the organization – i.e. the organizational agenda is privileged; while in developmental coaching it may be a more open agenda of the fit between the two. The possibility that the coachee may seek a better fit elsewhere is always a possibility with developmental coaching and should probably be contracted for at the outset with sponsors.

Goals and tasks of the developmental approach

Merriam and Clark (2008: 29) suggest that the goal of development is unclear. They ask:

> Is it to achieve an end point, such as self-actualisation (Maslow, 1970), or a fully integrated ego (Loevinger, 1976) or a more permeable and inclusive perspective (Mezirow, & Associates 2000)? Or as Riegel (1973) and others see it, is development dialectic in nature, a function of the 'constant interaction of the person and the environment' (Tennant & Pogson, 1995: 199) with no end point?

In developmental coaching, however, we suggest, the goal is much clearer: the client agenda is paramount and it is clients' goals that prevail. This suggestion builds on the premise that we all construct our own perspectives of the world based on individual experiences and perceptions; taken with the questions posed by Merriam and Clark above, it would imply that any developmental coaching intervention needs to be holistic and client-centred. It tends to involve not merely helping clients to achieve their full potential at work or improving their performance in specific areas, but also enabling them to make conscientious decisions, understand their values and beliefs, take appropriate risks or discover their purpose. This experience may well lead them to considerations outside the immediate concern of skills, performance or advancement within the prevailing organizational frame.

In an attempt to explain the goals of the developmental approach, we asked ourselves why we refer to it as 'developmental'. We found two answers. Firstly, the term 'developmental coaching' is intended to reflect something of the experience that is being created for the client. Whether the trigger for coaching is presented as a performance issue, a project issue or a career issue, the aspiration is to facilitate some *progressive* and *permanent* change. By *progressive* we mean a change that takes the client, over a period of time, to some kind of enrichment of their engagement with their personal, social and career context. By *permanent* we mean that the solution should extend beyond the presenting trigger and create some greater, sustainable capacity in the client. The second answer reflects the core belief that the capacity of the system in which the client sits (organization, family, society) is itself enhanced by the individual's capacity and so the changes initiated have a secondary developmental capacity beyond the client's immediate situation. In summary, we see the goal of development as being a widening of the client's perspective and enhanced ability to engage with the world.

These arguments for using the term 'developmental' have implications for the way in which the coach works. For example, it seems an inevitable consequence that learning sits at the centre of the relationship and that it is a concept of learning specifically related to the experience of the individual, hence it is constructivist and experiential (see also Cox, 2013). There is a close parallel here with the concept of Process Consultation (Schein, 1987, 1998). Schein (1987: 30) argues that a Process Consultation approach will 'increase the likelihood that the immediate problem will be solved, but, even more important, the client learns the skills of problem-solving so that he or she can continue to solve problems after the consultant leaves'. So, one of the main tasks is to ensure some ongoing improvement in the coachee's ability to respond to future events.

The role of the coach and relationship with clients

In the absence of a single theoretical framework, the concept of development (and particularly the progressive outcome) may be problematic. Although we can argue that it is only the client's perspective that matters, the evaluation of such a situation is both subjective and contextual, in that the client may perceive an improvement differently at different times. Similarly, the possibility of the coach taking a longer-term perspective than the client at a particular point in time could be considered a heavy responsibility and a luxury that does not sit well with the other principles of this approach to coaching. Put simply, it is not for the coach to decide that something will be good for the client 'in the end' just as it is not for the coach to decide where 'the end' is, or if there is such a thing at all. This dynamic creates a greater role for the ongoing process of contracting and re-contracting, of asking permission, of challenging by consent. A coach should not necessarily see this as a constant topic of conversation, but it should be a constant concern.

The ambiguity of the concept of 'progress' (Prescott, 2010) means that contracting, especially the triangular contract with organizational sponsors, should be approached as far as possible on the level of process and shared understandings, rather than specific outcomes and measures. Acknowledging current debates about return on investment, we realize this is an unfashionable formulation that may appear impracticably purist. In practice, however, it need not be. Taking a developmental approach does not mean taking the individual's side at the expense of the organization. It does imply that attention is given to the individual and the sponsor (possibly facilitated by the coach) sharing an understanding of their respective needs and aspirations. There will be times where there is insufficient overlap between these aspirations; in such cases the facilitation of progress for the individual may mean their leaving the organization. If this possibility is unacceptable to the organization then a developmental approach may not be the most suitable. The contracting process can therefore, in some cases, be a significant help in moving an unsatisfactory situation forward. It also sets up a level of communication that is likely to support the ongoing development of the individual within the management processes of the organization. Most managers appreciate the benefits that a three-way contracting process can bring and tend to have a more open attitude towards outcomes as a result.

The attitude that expresses itself in contracting – essentially the negotiation of the purpose of the coaching intervention – is also reflected in the progress and the relationship. There are many characteristics of the developmental coaching relationship that are common to most if not all non-directive approaches, including the emphasis on the client's agenda, their ability to seek and implement solutions and the avoidance of advice giving. From a developmental perspective, however, any experience of problem-solving is equally a learning opportunity for the client. Hence the developmental coach is perhaps less concerned with the immediacy of the presenting problem and may be even more wary of the urge to 'help out'. The coach is more likely to rely on his or her 'presence' to support their clients and may have to help them to hold an uncomfortable level of uncertainty. This can be difficult and coaches must constantly question their own motivation to intervene and the extent to which they may be becoming enrolled in the dynamics of the client's system. In earlier work, Jackson (2005) identified a typology of coaching genres. Developmental follows what he calls a 'flexible personal methodology' evidenced by an interest in the use of the relationship with the coach as the developmental influence. In this genre there is an emphasis on mutual exploration rather than on targets or performance measures.

It follows that developmental coaching is humanist and person-centred in outlook. It has much in common with the Rogerian belief in the human orientation towards self-development. Yet it must be acknowledged that there are likely to be more procedural elements than in person-centred counselling. In parallel to the way that the stakeholding is shared between coachee and sponsor through the triangular contract with the coach, the agenda in development coaching is balanced between the behavioural/performance outcome and the human potential outcome. That is to say that unconditional positive regard does not have centre stage as it does with person-centred counselling by virtue of the fact that this is coaching. Systemic demands on the individual are the occasion and the objective (however the individual eventually decides to deal with them), and development is the solution. It may well be the case that developmental coaching is practised by those whose preference in the field of therapy would be for the humanistic approaches. Developmental coaching may also be organizationally sponsored, not simply as an employee support or benefit, but as a means to organizational ends: there is recognition of the individual's development occurring within the organizational context with which it interacts.

In terms of activities there may be a wide variation in the choice of techniques and tools, and indeed a wide variation in the range of attitudes to their use among coaches. There is a tendency to focus more on the relationship as developmental rather than the use of procedural techniques (Jackson, 2005; Bachkirova, 2011). Hence the developmental coach will tend to reflect on process, limit questions of content and embrace ambiguity as ways of enriching the developmental relationship. Procedural tools where used may focus on the learning process, for example reflective and observational logs, experimenting with problem-solving or communication patterns that are less preferred by the client (e.g. in terms of Myers-Briggs, Kolb or other typologies). Direct challenge is used with caution and is likely to be focused on process as there is otherwise a risk that it may mask an unacknowledged desire in the coach to lead the client's agenda or solutions. With an emphasis on presence and on the client's own processes, sessions may be marked at times by a quiet, contemplative atmosphere.

In keeping with the outlook described in the discussion of contracting above, clients tend to describe outcomes in terms of what has been learnt *beyond* the presenting topic. For example, 'I feel more able to deal with things' (presenting topic: project management); 'I'm communicating more effectively with people inside and outside work' (presenting topic: career). As a consequence of the emphasis on process, clients also report a sense of feeling understood, or that the coach has unusual insight.

From the above it could be inferred that any opportunity the coach takes to widen the coachee's perspective and transform the way he or she thinks will lead to development. Indeed, there are a number of widely used models of developmental coaching that can support the process amply. The differences in a developmental approach are not necessarily in the tools and behaviours deployed by the coach, but in how these might be subtly different as they emerge from a different ethical and philosophical position. In what follows we seek to illustrate this by comparing Goodman's developmental coaching process with the more familiar GROW model (West & Milan, 2001).

Goodman's (2002: 138) developmental coaching process involves four steps that have their basis in research in the adult learning and development field:

1. asking for meaning
2. building a new perspective
3. creating a bridge
4. developing action.

The first step, asking for meaning, involves asking questions that enable both the coach and the client to arrive at a deep understanding of the issue or dilemma that the client is facing. For the developmental coach, what Mezirow and Associates (2000: 22) would call 'disorienting dilemmas' are an important sign that the client is ready to make some significant and possibly developmental shift. The dilemma could suggest that the current way of making meaning is inadequate. A full understanding of the issue therefore not only helps the coach to understand the problem, but it also provides possibly a first chance for the client to tell their story and undertake some reframing of the issue (Cox, 2013). Once understanding is achieved; the client's perspective of the dilemma is laid out for examination and the way is open for alternative perspectives or read-ings of the story to be proposed. Goodman describes how the coach must first validate the client's current construction of the situation, but once the client feels safe and 'held' then new angles can be explored.

Step 2 involves the overt introduction of new perspectives and new options which open up choices for the client. It is here that we begin to see how the GROW model has parallels with this developmental coaching process. 'Asking for meaning' serves the same function as the reality check that is the 'R' part of GROW and 'Building a new perspective' corresponds to the exploration of Options (the 'O' in GROW). The exploration of options helps the client's under-standing of the different forces that influence the dilemma.

Step 3, 'Creating a bridge', is a vital process that is not explicitly addressed in GROW, but according to Goodman helps to 'minimize the client's sense of loss by identifying and retaining some aspects of the old behaviour' (Goodman, 2002: 145–6). By reflecting on past fears and relating these to the nature of the challenge ahead, clients are enabled to move forward with a sense that their new options or perspectives have connection and relevance to their (previously articulated) reality. A similar strategy was advocated by William Perry and is well described by Kegan (1994: 277–8).

In step 4, which involves developing action, there is a direct correspondence with the 'W' in the GROW model (Will). At this point in the process a plan is developed that details what the client will do to implement change and, vitally, the coach helps the client to rehearse that change. Once more the holding environment is important: Goodman emphasizes that 'asking the client to envision the change before implementing it can increase his or her sense of control' (Goodman, 2002: 150).

RELATIONSHIP WITH THEORETICAL TRADITIONS

Developmental coaching, as we have seen, turns out to be more theoretically grounded than other genres; or to be more accurate it is multi-theoretically grounded. Indeed, it could be argued that each coaching approach involves the development of the client from its own perspective and so every theory is a theory of developmental coaching. However, for the purposes of this chapter we have chosen just four linking theoretical approaches: person-centred; cognitive-behavioural; narrative; and cognitive developmental.

The person-centred approach

The person-centred approach is the most obvious candidate for alignment with developmental coaching. Rogers's construct of the actualizing tendency is grounded in the belief that human beings have an inherent tendency or motivation towards growth and development, with the fundamental qualities in human nature being viewed as those of growth, process and change. In Rogers's theory, 'man is an actualizing process' (Van Belle, 1980: 70). Horney (1950) also highlights 'the struggle toward self-realization', suggesting that if obstacles to growth were removed, we would naturally develop into all that we were capable of becoming. This theory underpins the way person-centred coaching works – to examine obstacles in the client's agenda. Similarly, the developmental coach may work with these concerns through identifying values, encouraging reflexivity and challenging inconsistencies and limiting assumptions.

The cognitive-behavioural approach

The cognitive-behavioural approach also shares many of the aims of developmental coaching: to facilitate self-awareness through an exploration of internal dialogue and automatic thoughts; the development of sustainable thinking skills; and the imperative to look at different perspectives. The focus is also on sustaining results over time: neither approach expects a 'quick fix' for the client. Developmental coaches may also draw on specific cognitive-behavioural techniques such as the exploration of the client's beliefs and the consequences of holding those beliefs if they have been unproductive in the past. However, and without claiming that the outcomes are necessarily different in some cases, the cognitive behavioural approach's tendency towards working with the *process* or *mechanism* of sense making is different from developmental coaching's concern with working with the *person*.

The narrative approach

Developmental coaching involves the in-depth exploration of client issues and so cannot help but draw on a narrative approach. The development of stories and accounts are important, particularly at the beginning of the developmental relationship. However, although clients are experts in their own lives, they do tend to focus on particular aspects of the account and downplay others. In addition, recounted sets of events are just one explanation, and developmental coaching, like narrative, recognizes that these are just one story created to help clients 'understand and give meaning to aspects of their lives' (Cox, 2013: 41).

The cognitive-developmental approach

The cognitive-developmental approach to developmental coaching involves unequivocal engagement with adult development theory, such as that propounded by Kegan (1982, 1994), and claims that that there are patterns of maturation in adulthood that involve the achievement of increasingly higher (and measurable) levels of self-awareness and cognitive capacity. The theory posits that behaviour can be understood, explained and even predicted, as adults make progressive developmental changes through the life-span (Lucius & Kuhnert, 1999; O'Connor & Lages, 2007).

In forms of coaching where this theory is made explicit, coach and client both need to be familiar with the theories that might guide an overt movement towards a higher level of development. Coaching with such an explicit focus on movement towards higher levels or stages of cognitive, emotional and ego maturity differs significantly from the developmental coaching approach described in this chapter, since it overtly uses a developmental framework to guide the coaching endeavour (for an example, see Bachkirova and Cox, 2007).

Laske's (2008) work, which he describes as 'evidence-based developmental coaching', is another example of an overtly theoretically guided approach. His emphasis is on facilitating an understanding of current levels of development as identified by a number of measures derived from developmental theories. Laske draws heavily on the work of Kegan (1982, 1994), Basseches (1984) and Jaques (1994) to create a constructive-developmental framework for guiding adult development. He argues that 'not only the coachee (client), but the coach as well, is naturally engaged in a journey across the life span that determines his or her Frame of Reference' (Laske, 2008: 78).

Some developmental coaches may find that Laske's synthesis of developmental models and its explicit use as a framework transgresses the content/process boundary that particularly defines developmental coaching as described above. It takes some of the content agenda away from the client. It may also be seen to imply that some levels of maturity are intrinsically better than others, with the danger then, as Brookfield (2000: 124) recognizes, that we make 'the explicit judgement that some states of being are better than others'. There is nonetheless something to be gained from it. As is the case with many such systematic models it may provide a framework which helps the client express and describe their own developmental aims; if it is helpful for the client to be able to say that they would like to demonstrate, in Kegan's (1994) terms, a more characteristically 'Level 4' way of making sense of their world, then it may not matter whether the coach feels that 'Level 4' is a valid theoretical construct or not. Similarly, it may provide a way of opening useful enquiries ('what would it look like if you were looking at this in a Level 4 way?') And finally, it may provide the coach with a framework for helping the client's investigation. The important thing here is that the model need not be held to be right for it to be useful.

Interestingly, Laske (2008) has argued that all behavioural coaching, of whatever persuasion, has developmental foundations and that all adults have what he calls 'developmental intuitions'. What they lack, he claims, is only a methodology and notation for using them professionally. Laske is emphasizing here the inherent human tendency towards growth and development, and reinforces Sugarman's (2000) claim that the values underpinning the concept of development precede all empirical observation.

EVALUATION

As we have seen, developmental coaching is a genre of coaching where the primary purpose is not to address one specific area of a client's work or life, but to help them to achieve personal growth which will assist in a variety of different areas of their life and in the development of flexibility in their responses to their environment. Developmental coaching therefore has a much broader remit than some other forms of coaching. Developmental coaching is concerned with helping people to perform in response to an altered way of conceptualizing the world. However, it does also focus on the presenting problem as the driver for change. In developmental coaching, therefore, there is a fine balance between seeing the problem as need and seeing it as opportunity – the presenting problem provides the immediate driver for finding a solution, but also, inherently, the opportunity to develop beyond that solution.

The strengths of developmental coaching lie in the support provided for the client to grow and change. Clients are encouraged to explore work and life issues from a perspective of future efficacy and efficiency, not merely in relation to short-term solutions. Developmental coaching therefore is aimed towards permanent change.

The limitation of developmental coaching is, as discussed earlier, the lack of an overarching theory to guide its practice. We have shown how many theories have some relevance for this genre, but that no one theory can be invoked. This has three significant consequences: first, it makes it difficult and complex for the coach when looking for the evidence base to guide their practice. Second, it places a high degree of responsibility on the coach to ensure that the client understands and is a willing participant in the developmental approach, over and above other options available. Finally, because of its less procedural, more personal approach, it places a greater responsibility on the coach to examine and explore their own responses to the coaching experience through supervision and reflective practice (Bachkirova, Jackson, & Clutterbuck, 2011).

FURTHER READING

Bachkirova, T. (2011). *Developmental coaching: Working with the self.* Maidenhead: Open University Press. (Provides a theory and framework for developmental coaching.)

Flaherty, J. (2005). *Coaching: Evoking excellence in others.* Oxford: Elsevier Butterworth-Heinemann. (Describes a coaching process that is inherently developmental.)

Sugarman, L. (2001). *Life-span development.* Hove: Psychology Press. (A wide range of developmental concepts and theories are described.)

DISCUSSION QUESTIONS

- As a developmental coach, what would it look like to be a 'good-enough' coach?
- When you work with a client, do you hold a picture of where your client needs to get to? What determines this picture? Should you invite your client to challenge this picture?
- At what level of learning do you feel you need to work with this client? At what level of learning would you like to work in your own supervision?

REFERENCES

Bachkirova, T. (2011). *Developmental coaching: Working with the self.* Maidenhead: Open University Press.

Bachkirova, T. & Cox, E. (2007). A cognitive-developmental approach for coach development. In S. Palmer & A. Whybrow, *Handbook of coaching psychology.* London: Routledge.

Bachkirova, T., Jackson, P., & Clutterbuck, D. (Eds) (2011). *Coaching supervision: Theory and practice.* Maidenhead: McGraw-Hill.

Basseches, M. (1984). *Dialectical thinking and adult development.* Norwood, NJ: Ablex.

Berger, J. & Fitzgerald, C. (2002). Leadership and complexity of mind: The role of executive coaching. In C. Fitzgerald & J. Berger (Eds), *Executive coaching: Practices & perspectives* (pp. 27–58). Palo Alto, CA: Davies-Black Publishing.

Berman, W. & Bradt, G. (2006). Executive coaching and consulting: Different strokes for different folks. *Professional Psychology: Research and Practice, 37*(3): 244–53.

Brookfield, S. (2000). Transformative learning as ideology critique. In J. Mezirow & Associates (Eds), *Learning as transformation.* San Francisco, CA: Jossey-Bass.

Cox, E. (2013). *Coaching understood: A pragmatic inquiry into the coaching process.* London: Sage.

Erikson, E.H. (1974). *Dimensions of a new identity.* New York: Norton.

Goodman, R. (2002). Coaching senior executives for effective business leadership: The use of adult developmental theory as a basis for transformative change. In C. Fitzgerald & J. Berger (Eds), *Executive coaching: Practices & perspectives* (pp. 135–53). Palo Alto, CA: Davies-Black Publishing.

Horney, K. (1950). *Neurosis and human growth.* New York: Norton.

Hunt, J. & Weintraub, J. (2002). *The coaching manager.* London: Sage.

Hunt, J. & Weintraub, J. (2004). Learning developmental coaching. *Journal of Management Education, 28*(1), 39–61.

Jackson, P. (2005). The development of a five-dimensional typology of approaches used by independent UK coaching practitioners. *International Journal of Evidence Based Coaching and Mentoring, 3*(2), 45–60.

Jaques, E. (1994). *Human capability.* Falls Church, VA: Cason Hall.

Kegan, R. (1982). *The evolving self: Problem and process in human development.* London: Harvard University Press.

Kegan, R. (1994). *In over our heads.* London: Harvard University Press.

Knowles, M.S., Swanson, R.A. & Holton, E.F. III. (2011). *The adult learner: The definitive classic in adult education and human resource development* (7th ed.). Oxford: Elsevier.

Kolb, D. (1984). *Experiential learning.* Englewood Cliffs, NJ: Prentice Hall.

Laske, O. (2008). Mentoring a behavioural coach in thinking developmentally: A dialogue. *International Journal of Evidence Based Coaching and Mentoring, 6*(2): 78–99.

Levinson, D. (1978). *The seasons of a man's life.* New York: Knopf.

Loevinger, J. (1976). *Ego development: Conceptions and theories.* San Francisco, CA: Jossey-Bass.

Lucius, R. & Kuhnert, K. (1999). Adult development and the transformational leader. *Journal of Leadership Studies, 6*(1/2): 73–85.

Maslow, A.H. (1970). *Motivation and personality* (2nd ed.). New York: Harper & Row.

Merriam, S.B. & Clark, M.C. (2008). Learning and development: The connection in adulthood. In C. Hoare (Ed.), *Handbook of adult development and learning.* New York: Oxford University Press.

Mezirow, J. & Associates (2000). *Learning as transformation.* San Francisco, CA: Jossey-Bass.

O'Connor, J. & Lages, A. (2007). *How coaching works.* London: A. & C. Black.

Perry, W.G. (1970). *Forms of intellectual and ethical development in the college years.* New York: Holt, Rinehart and Winston.

Prescott, T. (2010). Why is progress a controversial issue in coaching? *International Journal of Evidence Based Coaching and Mentoring,* Special Issue No 4: 21–36.

Riegel, K. (1973). Dialectic operations: The final period of cognitive development. *Human Development, 16*: 346–70.

Schaie, K.W. & Zanjani, F. (2006). Intellectual development across adulthood. In C. Hoare (Ed.), *Handbook of adult development and learning.* New York: Oxford University Press.

Schein, E. (1987). *Process consultation (Vol II): Lessons for managers and consultants.* Reading, MA: Addison-Wesley.

Schein, E. (1998). *Process consultation revisited: Building the helping relationship.* Reading, MA: Addison-Wesley.

Sperry, L. (2002). *Effective leadership.* New York: Brunner-Routledge.

Sugarman, L. (2001). *Life-span development* (2nd ed.). Hove: Psychology Press.

Taylor, K., Marienau, C., & Fiddler, M. (2000) *Developing adult learners: Strategies for teachers and trainers.* San Francisco, CA: Jossey-Bass.

Tennant, M. & Pogson, P. (1995). *Learning and change in the adult years.* San Francisco, CA: Jossey-Bass.

Van Belle, H. (1980). *Basic intent and therapeutic approach of Carl R. Rogers.* Toronto: Wedge.

West, L. & Milan, M. (2001). *The reflecting glass.* London: Palgrave MacMillan.

16

Transformational Coaching

Peter Hawkins and Nick Smith

Transformational coaching enables coachees to create fundamental shifts in their capacity to change their habitual ways of doing things in their work and their lives. This is achieved through transforming their ways of thinking, feeling and behaving in relation to specific situations that they find problematic. It is our contention that this transformation is delivered through focusing on the shift that needs to happen live in the coaching space so that a sustained change takes place beyond the coaching session.

Transformational coaching sits at one end of a spectrum of coaching (Hawkins & Smith, 2013) and has one key outcome: shifting the meaning scheme or action logic of the coachee. This outcome derives from the work of Mezirow (1991) who laid out the psychological processes by which adults learn and, most importantly, change their behaviour. Mezirow explained that a 'meaning scheme' is made up of specific beliefs, attitudes and assumptions that are responsible 'behind the scenes' for generating our reflexive, emotional reactions to life events. Shifting these patterns of thinking is an example of what Bateson (Bateson, 1985: 283–306) termed 'Level II learning'. Later in this chapter we link this with the work of neuroscientists who have understood the mechanisms by which adults can learn new habits, a process that involves recreating 'brain plasticity' in the adult. Neuroscience helps us understand why this outcome is possible and shows us the processes that facilitate such changes. It tells us that by making implicit beliefs and memories explicit, neuroplastic changes in the brain are triggered that first generate unlearning and so dissolve specific existing neuronal networks (Doidge, 2010: 233). This offers the possibility of creating a new set of connections with different meanings attached and therefore different behaviours, feelings and outcomes.

DISTINCTIVE FEATURES

The key outcome is facilitated by three transformational practices that are applied during coaching:

1. Working on multiple levels at the same time

To effect change with the client, the coach needs to be able to work on multiple 'levels' at the same time (that is, to attend to the physical, psychological, emotional and purposive elements of what is going on and how they combine in the present situation). The change in perspective has to be 'embodied' (i.e. the coachee needs to be able to think, feel *and* do differently) for it to be truly transformational.

2. Shift in the room

Transformational coaching therefore focuses strongly on freeing the coachee's 'stuck' perspective within the session, live in the room. The process, by which the coach helps the client to experience an integrated transformation of perspective, is termed 'creating shift in the room'. A method of first matching and then mismatching the coachee is used to create such a transformational shift and use is made of the CLEAR model to achieve this.

3. Four levels of engagement

As Mezirow reminds us, a change in perspective comes through a change in the coachee's assumptions, values and beliefs about the presenting issue. Transformational coaches use the 'four levels of engagement' model to map the connection of these assumptions to the reflex feelings that drive the behaviours, that then generate the specific responses which an executive is trying to modify. The importance of this 'four levels' model is that it helps us track when we are working with assumptions and when we are working with the phenomena generated by assumptions.

In this chapter after exploring the background to transformational coaching, we illustrate how transformational coaching focuses on creating a shift in the thinking, feelings and behaviour of the coachee at each stage of the CLEAR process (**C**ontracting, **L**istening, **E**xploring, **A**ction, **R**eview). We end by showing how it differs from other coaching approaches and evaluate its use.

History and roots of transformational coaching

As coaches, we have worked with senior executives exploring how they could be more effective at work. Most coaching sessions created new awareness and insight for the coachee. They would leave with good intentions to use this insight to create a better reality back at work.

Often, however, they would return to the next session having 'failed' to follow through. They would use phrases such as: 'I was too busy'; 'other issues came up'; 'it was more difficult than I thought'. In supervision, we would share our frustration and blame the coachee or their organization for the lack of change.

After becoming aware of this pattern, we started to ask the more searching question: 'what could we change in our coaching practice that would increase the amount of follow through in the good intentions of our coachees?' We were reminded of executive teams we worked with that had met regularly and agreed to do something, only to return several weeks later, collectively frustrated by the fact that nothing had happened (see Hawkins, 2011). We realized that there was a fundamental difference between 'agreeing to act' and 'acting'. Intellectual agreement to an action is worlds away from an embodied commitment to make something happen. In the initial discussion, however, they can easily look the same.

RELATIONSHIP WITH THEORETICAL TRADITIONS

We then explored what we could do as coaches that would encourage 'embodied commitment' in the coachee, not just intellectual insight and good intention. We drew on a number of key theories and methodologies:

Psychodrama (Moreno, 1972) showed the importance of the 'cathartic moment' of emotional expression and embodying and trying out new ways of being.

Gestalt psychology (Polster & Polster, 1973; Clarkson & Mackewn, 1993, Bluckert, this volume) underlined the focus on shifting how the client is aware of themselves and their relationship with the coach.

Gendlin's 'focusing' (Gendlin, 1978) explained the notion of the 'felt shift'. Gendlin discovered that success in psychotherapy is linked to how clients talk about the issue being addressed and how they focus on physical sensations in relation to the issue. Creating a 'felt shift' in the internal response to the issue creates a more sustained change than mere insight (what NLP might call 'creating a new emotional anchor').

Systemic family therapy clarified the process of creating a systemic shift in interlinked relationships (Minuchin & Fishman, 1981).

Levels of learning (Argyris & Schön, 1978; Bateson, 1985). Bateson distinguished four types of 'learning':

Zero Learning: describes many processes that in everyday speech are termed 'learning', but which are only about the acquisition of data; these may lead on to 'learning' but are not learning events in themselves.

Learning Level I: concerns skills learning, making choices within a simple set of alternatives, called single-loop learning by Argyris and Schön (1978). It involves re-arranging the current information into new connections.

Learning Level II: happens when the assumptions within which Level I learning takes place are challenged, called double-loop learning by Argyris and Schön (1978). Here we are challenging the frame in which we had previously understood the problem.

Learning Level III: According to Bateson (1985) learning at Level III is likely to be rare. It involves seeing the world as it is, rather than how someone wants it to be. It is the realm which can be talked of only in symbolic and paradoxical language because it is stripped of personal colour and concern. According to Bateson (1985), to the degree that a person achieves Learning III, 'the 'self' will take on a sort of irrelevance'.

Recent developments in neuroscience

Recently, there has been tremendous progress in discovering more about the brain and its relationship to coaching (for example, Rock & Page, 2009; Brown & Brown, 2012; Rogers, 2012). This material is useful in helping us understand why techniques do or do not work. Some scientific insights from the 1960s have also been foundational in developing our theory. One important piece of research showed that human beings function from three different centres of the brain: the neocortex, the limbic and the reptilian (MacLean, 1990). Each centre has an entirely different 'approach' to the way it reacts to the world around us. Lewis, Amini and Lannon (2001: 63) argue that those enabling change need to focus on 'limbic resonance, regulation and revisioning'. Whereas coaching has often focused upon the cognitive aspects of the neocortex, neuroscience is indicating that fundamental change also requires a shift in the patterns of relating that are embedded in the limbic brain. In order to understand the way in which our coachees respond to situations, it is important for us to see which 'brain' is driving the responses they are making. Being aware of the coachee's current 'action logic' allows us as coaches, first to match for rapport, then to mismatch for change.

Outcomes of transformational coaching

By integrating these different approaches, we have been experimenting with a form of coaching that focuses on two further outcomes that support 'shifting the coachee's meaning scheme':

1. *Enabling 'Level II' learning* (Argyris & Schön, 1978; Bateson, 1985), by creating a shift in the coachee's mind-set and emotional framing of his/her reality, rather than simply focusing on other choices within the current set of perceived possibilities. This helps the coachee create a new meaning scheme.
2. Moving beyond new awareness and insight, to *create a 'felt shift' live in the room*, where the coachee's whole way of engaging with the issue has changed, including: language and metaphors; body language (posture, breathing, tone, tempo, pitch and rhythm of voice); way of relating to the coach (such as engagement and eye contact); an increase in embodied, energetic commitment to action; and newly rehearsed ways of moving the presenting issue forward.

As we utilized this more in our practice, we discovered that the approach created a more lasting impact than other approaches. In supervision, where we started to use a similar transformational approach, coaches were returning to sessions excited about the changes they had produced. Furthermore, some coaches were returning saying they did not even have to follow through with their plan for change, as it was almost as if the other parties had heard the supervision session and had anticipated the changes. At first this seemed rather magical, but then we realized, from a systemic perspective, that if one part of the system fundamentally changes, the rest of the system adapts to align to it.

The conclusion from our explorations, and from those of our supervisees, was that if the change does not start in the coaching room, it is unlikely to happen back at work.

Key elements of transformational coaching

1 The CLEAR model

CLEAR is a process model indicating a way of constructing a coaching dialogue and has become a core practice in transformational coaching. It has five stages, each requiring different relational skills. In CLEAR, the coach starts by *Contracting* with the coachee both on the focus of the work and any boundaries they wish to place around it. This contracting is an iterative process during a session and across sessions. Then the coach *Listens* to the issues the coachee brings, listening not only to the content, but also to the feelings accompanying the content and ways of framing the story used by the coachee. The coach needs to let the coachee know that they have not only heard the story, but have 'got' what it feels like to be in that situation. This process helps to create 'match' between the two and develop necessary rapport and limbic resonance (Lewis et al., 2001) to enable the coach, at a later time, to 'mismatch' for change. Only then is it useful to move on to *Explore* with the coachee what options for change they have. This is done by understanding what is happening in the dynamics, both in the work relationships and also what may be paralleled in the coaching relationship playing out in the room, before facilitating the coachee to explore new *Actions* live in the session. Finally, the coach *Reviews* the process with the coachee and agrees next steps.

The use of CLEAR is necessary but not sufficient for practising transformational coaching. In order to get to the nub of the problem, coaches also need to have a 'compass' that steers them towards the critical area for change. New coaches often have a natural tendency to focus either on facilitating problem-solving or exploring feelings. This can influence how they react when they start listening to the client. Those coaches who are practical, logical and data focused feel comfortable in encouraging their client to go deeper into the detail and then move swiftly to facilitating a solution. Others may immediately seek out the feelings in the situation and try to bring those out more clearly, holding off from offering practical solutions. Neither is wrong, as an initial starting point, but context requires an ability to use both of these perspectives.

Initial preferences therefore are not always a useful guide for coaches in a coaching session. To be able to help coachees navigate from the initial data and explanations they brought, to a new perspective that allows them to be and act differently, coaches need some sort of 'map' showing how the issue has been constructed over time and a notion of where they need to concentrate, in order to create this substantial shift in perspective.

2 Exploring the four levels

The 'four levels of engagement' model (Figure 16.1) explains how the coach can avoid 'problem-solving' or ventilation of feelings as a default coaching outcome and helps create a

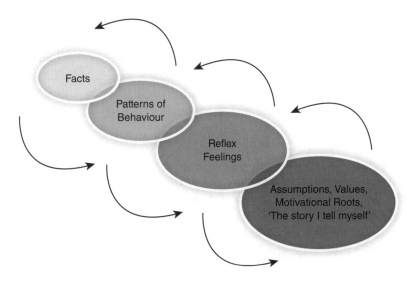

Figure 16.1   Four levels of engagement

developmental/transformational intervention for coachees. Awareness of the model allows the coach to see whether he/she is dealing with facts, patterns of behaviour, reflex feelings or assumptions. If the entire content of the conversation has focused upon facts and behaviours, then the coach knows that, in order to help the coachee move on, it will be necessary to help them look at the reactive feelings driving the habitual behaviours these events evoke. It also shows that to create sustainable change, coachees need to understand their internal dialogue, which generates any dysfunctional feelings or emotional responses in the situation in which they find themselves (i.e. their assumptions).

   This simple but profound model offers a map of where coach and coachee need to get to in their coaching conversations and how to decide which questions to ask next. It is a helpful map for all who wish to develop transformational coaching skills. In a world in which people seek out 'quick fixes' and formulae for success, this could be seen as another 'golden bullet', a recipe for transformation every time. It isn't. However, although it is not prescriptive in shaping a coaching conversation, it is indicative of the ground that needs to be covered. It is both art and science. We explore below how this model fits with the CLEAR process for trans-formational coaching. To start, we explore the four levels to see how they might be understood and used.

Level 1 Data   When starting a new coaching conversation, most coaches want to gather data, asking, for example: 'What does the issue look like? How often does it happen? What are the consequences? Who is involved?' As experience and confidence are gained, coaches probably need a lot less detail before moving things forward for the coachee. Level 1 therefore focuses on the details of the events that are being discussed. It generates a list of facts (this issue happened with this person, on this date and yielded these results).

The detail, though, can be confusing. If coaches are being told about random events with no apparent connection, they have no means of helping coachees understand what is happening. If events are truly random, the coach and coachee cannot easily learn from them. To understand whether these facts are random or a habitual response, they need to go to Level 2 and see if the behaviours recur.

Level 2 Patterns of behaviour

A unique response to a situation is simply a random behaviour, in the sense that we cannot predict it. However, if we find there is a habitual response to the same type of event, it shows a pattern of behaviour. If the behaviours, that relate to the specific event the coachee brought, turn out to show a repeating and often long-standing habitual pattern, the coach knows that it is highly likely that they can help the coachee. First to help them understand and then, if they wish, to transform these reactions so that they are not locked into repeating the same outcomes. Being clear what the repetitive behaviour looks like brings some awareness as to what might be happening but, of itself, will not help to shift 'stuck' behaviours, for insight alone does not create transformation. It needs something more.

If we look at the reason such behaviour patterns are created, we find that most are formed as a strategic and practical response to a difficult situation we found ourselves in. A lot of the more fixed patterns we have go back to our childhood. When working with successful business executives, we find the reason that they bring the 'strategy' now is that 'what got them here won't get them there' (Goldsmith, 2008): the specific behaviour response that worked well for them for many years won't work now. The benefits of the strategy start to run out and they find that unless they can change their responses they may not be able to continue any higher on their career path. Such ingrained behaviours are difficult to let go of. Therefore in working to change these behaviour patterns first we need to be highly appreciative of their previous value and then encourage them to be 'parked' with due respect and gratitude.

Level 3 Reflex feelings

Repetitive behaviours are driven by emotions that appear as a reflex reaction to a situation we find challenging. When we have experienced a difficult, upsetting or traumatic situation, we put in place a strategy that will protect us from this sort of shock happening to us again in the future. As a child, if I experience my teacher making fun of me in a class, I might decide that I will never volunteer to do anything in public, when large groups of people are involved. I will keep my head down. This strategy then successfully minimizes my likelihood of being ridiculed in public over the next 25 years. However, when I start climbing the promotional ladder, I am expected by my bosses to be more proactive in public and stand up and challenge what is being said around me. What I experience though when I am in a public situation and I know I will be asked to be proactive in discussions, is an immediate reflex emotional response in the pit of my stomach. I feel sick and anxious. These feelings drive me to 'keep my head down'. Such reflex emotional responses are at the root of protecting ourselves from things that could be 'dangerous' to us. It is a 'homeostatic' trigger for keeping things safe. Homeostasis is the human body's response for protecting it against random and potentially dangerous change. Our bodies are 'physically wired' to keep body temperature and heart rate within specific bounds and if our body goes outside those ranges, it employs a wide variety of 'physical' and 'emotional' means to get things back 'in the groove'. A homeostatic principle operates in our limbic brains to keep us safe and in familiar territory too.

Feelings can trap coach and coachee by their intensity and their engaging qualities, but we cannot change the emotions by solely focusing on these emotions. We can only change a recurring emotional pattern by exploring the assumptions and beliefs they are rooted in.

Level 4 Core assumptions

To change feelings, we need to look at core assumptions, because these generate the reflex feelings that drive the behaviours that create the type of event we are trying to change. At Level 4 it is possible to uncover and articulate the story being told by the coachee when faced with specific events. For example, if I have not had a very distinguished academic history, when faced with 'clever people', I might tell myself 'I need to constantly prove that I am as good as they are'. I might then come across as competitive and bombastic with colleagues and clients. When I reach a certain level in my organization, these dysfunctional responses could hurt my credibility and that of my company.

Level 4 is populated by core assumptions about:

personal reality ('I am hopeless at confronting powerful people')

strongly held values ('I am only here to serve others')

guiding principles ('being competitive with others is the worst kind of pride').

By uncovering the narrative at this level, coachees can check whether it is simply a fossilized remain from a previous era in their life (e.g. a now dysfunctional response to the trauma of being humiliated publicly in adolescence) or whether it has current validity. To shine a light on this aspect of the coachee's beliefs, the coach can simply start by asking 'What is the assumption you are making about this sort of situation?' If this question draws a blank, the coach can proceed more creatively. For instance, if our coachee is finding it hard to be proactive in large groups, we would instead look to the future and suggest to the coachee that he/she thinks about what it would look like to be able to act in the way they would most like to in these public situations. 'First tell me what I would see if you were doing this really well?' They might describe 'I would be standing confidently!' ('What would that look like specifically?') 'I would be standing in a relaxed way, shoulders down, looking from side to side, making eye contact with people, slowing down my speech etc ...'. Once we have a picture of what this changed behaviour would look like, we can move to the third level and ask 'For you to behave like that, how would you need to feel in that situation?' 'Well I would need to feel confident, happy, engaged with everyone and wanting to contribute!' At this point when we are clear what the feelings would need to be to generate the behaviours, we would then move to the fourth level. 'So in order to feel like that, what would you need to believe about yourself, other people or the situation itself?' 'To feel like that I would need to believe that I have something that others want to hear; that I am as good as everyone else; and that people want to hear what I have to say!' 'Right so what do you think your assumptions are at the moment?' Often they are the reverse of the positive assumptions they have just constructed. To construct a more positive set of core assumptions we have to create a new, short, positive assumption 'mantra' and also find a strong positive experience of feeling confident, happy, engaged and wanting to contribute wherever they have felt that reflex in their life before (not necessarily in a business context). This emotional anchor is then joined with the new assumption to allow a new pattern of behaviour. This needs to be practised regularly in order to increase the new neural pathway of new behaviour in this type of situation.

Mapping the CLEAR process onto the four levels

Taking a typical transformational coaching session, the CLEAR process can be mapped onto the four levels of engagement (Figure 16.2). This is not prescriptive, but shows a general intent and flow in the coaching session. If coaches are going to create a process map for a session, in order to create a shift in the room, they must contract clearly as to the best outcome for the coachee. In transformational coaching the coach would look at how long the session is going to last and, rather than focusing on broader goals, encourage the coachee to think carefully about what specifically they want to have been changed by the end of the session.

'What would good look like, for this session to be a real success for you?' 'In the 40 minutes we have together, what is the real stretch that you need to make to move things forward?'

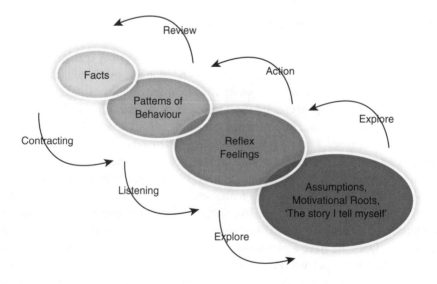

Figure 16.2 CLEAR and four levels of engagement

By working with the coachee to look at what a successful next step would require, the coach helps the coachee to visualize and/or rehearse the goal and therefore be more likely to achieve it.

Contracting (Levels 1 and 2)

Effective executive coaching requires at least a three-way contract between the coach, the coachee and the organizational client. The coachee's sponsor is the representative of the organization and is responsible for the organization learning and benefiting from this coaching relationship. The sponsor is not just there to support the coachee's learning, but has an important role in locking the relevant bits of the coachee's learning back into the wider system's learning. Three-way contracting is a way of getting traction between individual coachees, their organizations and the work of the coach. Contracting, in our view, should also include connection to the needs of the stakeholder community in which the organization exists as well as connection to the needs of the coaching profession. With each client we need to reflect on the appropriate stakeholders we need to bear in mind.

The Contracting phase in CLEAR is importantly different from, say, the GROW model (Whitmore, 1992) because it focuses upon the shift needed now in the room, as well as acknowledging the broader goals of the coaching process. This phase is not just relevant at the very beginning of each session, but whenever during a session the coach feels some shift has occurred that may have refocused what might be important to work on. Contracting is expected to be an iterative process within each session, as well as between sessions.

Listening (Levels 2 and 3)

The Listening phase is used to uncover details of the situation to be worked upon. If coachees report issues in their usual way, it will not help them to see things differently and will not generate new possibilities for the coach or coachee to play with. It is important therefore to interrupt habitual responses in the coachee at this early stage. While listening, the coach can also test the coachee's flexibility to think and behave differently, by interrupting the pattern of delivery. For example, if the coachee appears to be going into 'automatic pilot' in their description of the problem, the coach might interject and either register an alternative view of the assumptions being made or ask a catalytic question (e.g. 'If that wasn't the reason, what else might have been going on?').

The coach needs to listen with their ears to what is happening in the situation (what has been tried, what has worked or not worked) and listen with their body to what is not being voiced, what this situation has 'cost' the coachee and others involved, and what is the degree of urgency in coming to a resolution.

By mapping the listening phase of CLEAR onto the four levels, it can be seen to use the facts (Level 1), the behaviours (Level 2) and the feelings generated (Level 3), in order to understand what has been done already and what the activity has cost the coachee emotionally.

Explore (Levels 3 and 4)

The Explore phase starts to build on what has already been discussed and searches for new possibilities for change. This stage of the coaching relationship is nurtured through a process of skilful dialogue. Powerful questions are core, as they enable the coachee to explore the situation from different standpoints, generating new perspectives and possibilities. Useful types of coaching questions here include:

Closed questions – seeking data ('How many apples do you have?')

Open questions – seeking information ('Can you tell me about your apple trees?')

Leading questions – seeking information and indirectly shaping the answer ('Why do you like apples best?')

Inquiry questions – inviting active inquiry ('What are the criteria for judging the best apple?')

Transformational or mutative questions – inviting active inquiry that not only assists the coachee in thinking outside their current frames and mind-sets, but also creates an emotional shift in the person being asked ('What would it take for you to begin to like apples?')

At this point we often use Heron's Confronting, Catalytic and Cathartic interventions (Heron, 2001) to move coachees towards seeing the story they are telling themselves. The objective is to create a wider range of choices from which coachees can choose a better way forward. It also starts the process of making their assumptions more explicit or indicates the sort of story they are telling themselves about the situation.

Action (Levels 4, 3 and 2)

Having created some different options and then decided on a course of action, it is vitally important that the transformational coach creates time and space for coachees to rehearse what they will say and do to address the issue they have discussed.

If coachees do not rehearse the way in which they want to behave differently and do not practise it, and in the process receive clear feedback on how they are coming over, they are less likely to do things differently outside the coaching session. So the action stage requires the relational skills of inviting the coachee to embody that change, live in the room. 'So you will confront this issue with your colleague when you meet with them next Tuesday. Show me how you will do that. Try out your first few sentences. Talk to me as if I am the colleague.' This would be followed by direct feedback from the coach and an encouragement to do a second and third rehearsal. The coach focuses on the coachee creating an authentic, embodied shift in how they relate to the other person. This will manifest in new ways of breathing, posture, eye contact and different energy, as well as new language and metaphor.

Review (Levels 1–4)

In the final part of the session, the objective is to help the coachee review what has worked and what would be more effective next time. It helps them to see the web of connections between different parts of the process and how different questions sharpened and focused the inquiry. This feedback is of huge benefit for the learning of both coach and coachee, and allows both to 'bank' new ways of doing things and take confidence from the session, so that they have the opportunity to behave differently in new circumstances in the future.

The transformational coaching process

The craft of the coach is multilayered, requiring high levels of attention and awareness and openness to using oneself in the service of what needs to change in the system. The coach begins by listening intensely and responding with 'fearless compassion' to the client in the room and their wider system outside. The coach is silently holding the questions:

'What is the shift that needs to happen in this wider system?'

'What needs to shift in the relationship between this individual and the issue they are describing?'

'For those shifts to occur, what needs to shift right now in this individual?'

The coach then turns the focus back to the 'system that is live in the room' – themselves and the coachee and the relationship between them – all the while holding the following questions in mind:

'To be in service of those changes, what needs to shift in my relationship to this coachee right now?'

'What do I need to alter in my being to help bring that about?'

The coach holds these questions internally, not trying to work out an answer intellectually, but waiting for a felt sense of what is necessary for the intended transformative purposes.

Understanding of the coachee's situation starts with the larger view of the system of which they are a part. From here it moves to the specifics at play in the present relationship. However, the change *process* moves differently. It goes the other way round. It starts with the individual in the present moment, then reverberates through the relationship between coach and coachee and later instigates a change in the coachee's relationship with the wider system.

What do the 'shifts' look like?

'Shift in the room' will, to differing degrees, impact all four levels of the coachee's engagement with the coach. If coachees have a moment where they realize that the way they had been thinking about things is not the only way, this triggers a set of reactions at all levels.

Physical appearance changes. Coachees might look brighter, more open and engaged, have livelier energy. Posture, breathing, voice tone, etc. model a change in the way they relate physically in the situation.

In the room, coachees adopt new behaviours in relation to the coach and the issue they brought. Their behaviour is less predictable and more experimental, and less reflective or 'in their head'.

The feeling tone changes for the person – from locked and stuck to energized and hopeful. There is often a 'Derrrr!' response – the person laughs, hits palm of hand on forehead in disbelief that they have really believed this story for so long. That lightening of tone and laughter is a strong clue to the shift having taken place.

The story being told is now clear to coachees and, because of that, it holds far less power. The mind-set shifts and there appear to be possibilities that were not there before of doing things differently.

Transformational coaching is not the only useful form of coaching, but it is the most effective for trying to enable embodied, level two learning that creates a shift in consciousness and a sustained shift in how the coachee is engaging at work. Below we present a continuum of coaching that showed the relationship of transformational coaching to skills, performance and developmental coaching (Figure 16.3).

When looking at the continuum of coaching we see that transformational coaching is not just situated at some point along a continuum of coaching practice. Our experience is that it is a way of coaching any coachee need, whether skills, performance or developmental.

If, for example, we look at skills coaching we can simply focus on getting the necessary details about the activity over to the coachee so that they can adequately perform the skill in the future. If we are teaching someone how to, for example, use the latest Microsoft operating system we can just give the details and sequences they need to know to utilize it. In transformational mode, however, we would look at what is holding the person back from learning this. There may be a broader pattern of response to new technology: ('Yes, I am a bit phobic about new technology generally!') or when faced with new learning: ('I feel physically sick, and quickly panic and find it hard to remember what is being told to me.') or there is an habitual story being told: ('I keep thinking I am hopeless at this sort of thing and that I am going to annoy people because I am so stupid!'). From there the coach could help the coachee set up a new 'story' and a new emotional anchor, so that learning technical things generally will be easier.

This is not to say we should use transformational coaching the whole time, but rather when the issue is less technical and more to do with the way a person approaches their learning. The same principle would be true for performance and developmental coaching. If, for example, the reason for performance coaching is simply a lack of understanding as to how someone can work with time management, prioritization, development of staff, engagement with stakeholders, or

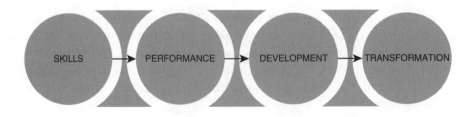

Figure 16.3   The coaching continuum

become strategic about the direction of the business unit, then performance coaching is necessary and sufficient. If, however, these issues highlight that the individual finds it difficult to take authority and is constantly drawn to doing things rather than leading them, transformational coaching may be more relevant.

Developmental coaching is less focused on the coachee's current role and more on longer-term career and personal development. Besides helping the coachee develop competencies and capabilities, it will include more focus on the development of the whole person and their broader human capacities, showing how they can use their current role to develop capacity for future roles and challenges. Thus there is more focus on second order or double-loop learning (Argyris & Schön, 1978: Hawkins, 1991). Developmental coaching tends to focus on increasing capacity within one life stage and in what Torbert (2004) describes as a particular 'action logic', by which he means 'the way the coachee frames the world both cognitively and emotionally'. In contrast, transformational coaching will be more involved with enabling the coachee to shift levels or 'action logics' and thereby make a transition from one level of functioning to a higher one.

EVALUATION

From what has been discussed so far, we can see that transformational coaching is not an answer to every coaching need. It is focused at one end of the coaching spectrum. Using a transformational approach in skills and performance coaching could, for instance, be experienced as intrusive and threatening, unless there was a contract with the coach and the coachee to take a much broader and deeper view of the issues at hand. Transformational coaching requires the coachee to have an active agenda of transformation and the coachee an active need to change. The agenda for transformational coaching is second order change. First order change is simply the sort of change that requires addition or subtraction of what is already there. Therefore it works within the current bounds of existing assumptions. Second order change is achieved when there are radical changes in assumptions about significant elements of life. They are what Mezirow (1991) called perspective transformations. It is this type of change that transformational coaching addresses; if someone does not want or need to shift core assumptions in order to change, then this type of coaching could be experienced as intrusive.

Transformational coaching comes into its own when coachees want or need to create a radical shift in the way they operate. Transformational coaching looks at supporting a step change in someone's approach to a situation. It could be used where the person does not have the luxury of gradual personal development. This suggests that in the fast pace of today's corporate life, this type of coaching has strong relevance, particularly for those in senior positions, where the consequence of slow personal change is the coachee's inability to step up to meeting the demands of the work and potentially their quick dismissal.

When new or experienced coaches are trained in transformational coaching, the first stage is to help them learn the various models, both theoretically and practically. After they have created a strong practical foundation we remind them that ultimately transformational coaching is an attitude, based on a core belief that change starts with oneself as coach and in the here and now.

Although the underlying models can at first seem quite complex, transformational coaching focuses on three simple questions:

What is disconnected that needs to be connected?

What is the truth that needs to be spoken?

What is the shift that needs to be enabled?

In asking these questions the coach applies them to all parts of the system: 'What is disconnected within the client organization?'; 'What is the shift that needs to be enabled right here in the room?'; 'What is the truth that needs to be spoken by me, by the coachee, in the organization and between the organization and its stakeholders?'

The world is changing faster than most humans are able to adapt. Learning ways of accelerating depth transformation is an urgent and important calling. Our hope is that Transformational Coaching will make a contribution to this challenge.

FURTHER READING

Bateson, G. (1985). *Steps to an ecology of mind*. New York: Ballantine Books. (This ground-breaking book explores how ideas interact and how systems of thought sustain themselves and evolve. It is not an easy read, but is a seminal work for this type of change.)

O'Neill, M.B. (2000). *Coaching with backbone and heart: A systems approach to engaging leaders with their challenges.* San Francisco, CA: Jossey-Bass. (Mary Beth O'Neill communicates the practicalities of the task of coaching leaders, the importance of a systemic understanding and the necessity of business understanding, and provides particular insight into what we have called 'fearless compassion'.)

Hawkins, P. & Smith, N. (2013). *Coaching, mentoring and organizational consultancy: Its supervision and development* (2nd ed.). London: Open University Press. (This significantly expanded text sets systemic transformational coaching in a broader context and also looks at the way in which transformational coaching skills apply to the practice of executive coaching supervision.)

DISCUSSION QUESTIONS

- What range of client coaching needs do you think require transformational coaching?
- How would you contract differently for transformational coaching as opposed to performance coaching?
- What techniques would you use to ensure that the change begins to happen live in the coaching session?

REFERENCES

Argyris, C. & Schön, D. (1978). *Organizational learning*. Reading, MA: Addison-Wesley.

Bateson, G. (1985). *Steps to an ecology of mind*. New York: Ballantine Books.

Brown, P. & Brown, V. (2012). *Neuropsychology for coaches: Understanding the basics*. Maidenhead: McGraw-Hill, Open University Press.

Clarkson, P. & Mackewn, J. (1993). *Fritz Perls*. London: Sage.

Doidge, N. (2010). *The brain that changes itself.* Victoria: Scribe.

Gendlin, E.T. (1978). *Focusing* (1st ed.). New York: Everest House.

Goldsmith, M. (2008). *What got you here won't get you there: How successful people become even more successful.* London: Profile.

Hawkins, P. (1991). The spiritual dimension of the learning organisation. *Management Education and Development, 22*(3).

Hawkins, P. (1994). The changing view of learning. In J. Burgoyne (Ed.), *Towards the learning company.* London: McGraw-Hill.

Hawkins, P. (2005). *The wise fool's guide to leadership.* Winchester: O Books.

Hawkins, P. (2011). *Leadership team coaching: Developing collective transformational leadership.* London: Kogan Page.

Hawkins, P. & Smith, N. (2013). *Coaching, mentoring and organizational consultancy: Supervision and development* (2nd ed.) Maidenhead: Open University Press.

Heron, J. (2001). *Helping the client.* London: Sage.

Lewis, T., Amini, F., & Lannon, R. (2001). *A general theory of love.* New York: Vintage Books.

MacLean, P.D. (1990). *The triune brain: Role in paleocerebral functions.* New York: Springer.

Mezirow, J. (1991). *Transformative dimensions of adult learning.* Oxford: Jossey-Bass.

Minuchin, S. & Fishman, H.C. (1981). *Family therapy techniques.* Cambridge, MA: Harvard University Press.

Moreno, J.L. (1972). *Psychodrama* (Vols. 1–3). Boston, MA: Beacon Press.

Polster, E. & Polster, M. (1973). *Gestalt therapy integrated.* New York: Random House.

Rock, D. & Page, L (2009). *Coaching with the brain in mind: Foundations for practice.* Hoboken, NJ: John Wiley

Rogers, J. (2012). *Coaching skills: A handbook* (3rd Ed.). Maidenhead: Open University Press.

Torbert, W. (2004). *Action inquiry: The secret of timely and transforming leadership.* San Francisco, CA: Berrett-Koehler.

Whitmore, J. (1992). *Coaching for performance.* London: Nicholas Brealey.

17

Executive and Leadership Coaching

Jon Stokes and Richard Jolly

Executive Coaching is a term used broadly to cover work with executives from middle management upwards or sometimes even to those in junior roles deemed to have high potential. It is used most effectively with those individuals who have significant responsibility for the current and future success of an organization and who have the potential to develop and change. While sometimes used for individuals who are performing poorly or having a negative effect on those they lead, remedial work is not its primary focus.

The needs of such a diverse group vary considerably and thus so does the extent to which the coaching relationship needs to be one of teacher or trainer versus facilitator or consultant, or how much it should focus on management skills (getting things done through others) versus the leadership role (creating an environment where others feel inspired and want to follow).

Too broad a definition renders the term Executive Coaching virtually meaningless since it can and sometimes is used to cover any form of training or development activity carried out on a one-to-one basis by a coach with an executive. Consequently we reserve the term for work with senior level executives that focuses on the executive becoming more self-aware in order to carry out their leadership role more effectively (Levinson, 1996; Peterson, 1996; Kilburg, 2000; Fitzgerald & Berger, 2002).

Executive coaching could therefore be defined as a form of personal learning and development consultation provided by someone external to the organization who focuses on improving an individual's performance in the quintessentially executive role of balancing the forces of co-operation and competition in an organization (Barnard, 1938). It can be distinguished from mentoring, which is typically a more informal relationship with a more experienced colleague (Clutterbuck & Megginson, 2005) and from coaching received from an individual within the same organization, typically the individual's manager (Landsberg, 1997).

While a senior executive's role will include elements of both management and leadership, executive coaching focuses primarily on the latter. Management is essentially the skill of working with 'the known' within defined and existing parameters and constraints, and focuses on achieving controlled and quantifiable task objectives. Leadership focuses primarily on what is 'not known', the future and on what changes will be required. It is often about emotions rather than facts; it is about people and relationships rather than tasks. Whereas management aspires to be a science, leadership will always remain an art. What is required of those in senior roles in organizations is usually far more about leadership than management. Indeed, making the shift from manager to leader, from relying on an operational perspective to employing a strategic one, from a mind-set of controlling events to a mind-set of enabling others, and achieving a better understanding of the organization as a whole, are just some of the reasons individuals seek executive coaching.

In this chapter we recognize that leadership, as an activity rather than a role, is not something confined to the top of an organization. Leadership exists at all levels in an organization, and thus much of what we say will also have more general application.

DISTINCTIVE FEATURES

Briefly summarized, executive coaching is a professional and confidential partnership relationship between a senior executive and coach involving:

- ongoing confidential meetings (lasting between one hour and a full day) organized on a regular basis for a period of six months or longer
- the primary goal of improving the executive's leadership skills
- some assessment of the individual's current effectiveness in the leadership role
- very often the use of data from psychometric and other assessment and feedback tools
- a relationship of challenge and support
- building on strengths as well as how to manage or change weaknesses
- an objective of both behavioural change and increased personal maturity and wisdom.

Opinions vary as to the extent to which the coach should be held responsible for ensuring that organizational goals are achieved. Arguably, the tension between personal self-interests and organizational group interests lies at the very heart of what a senior leader in a firm has to manage. Having the coach take sides on these questions could defeat the executive's challenge of taking up their authority effectively, and runs the risk of becoming a sophisticated form of staff supervision.

Certainly, clarity about accountability for how the coaching will contribute to organizational effectiveness must form a central part of the setting up of any executive coaching assignment. But it must remain the executive's task to interpret how best to achieve organizational goals as opposed to someone external to the organization. Having a coach who simply directs the coachee about the right and wrong course of action, though often a relief to both parties, may discourage executives from exploring the issues for themselves and from fully taking up their authority and accountability.

A coaching assignment should ideally be a partnership between the executive, the coach and the organization working together. However, in the real world of organizations, and especially large bureaucratic organizations in difficulty, such ideal goals are not always easily achieved. Given the increasingly complexity of organizational structures in firms around the world (in particular the rise of matrix structures – Bartlett & Ghoshal, 1990), the executive may have multiple lines of accountability to persons with conflicting views and interests. The aims and strategies of an organization rarely remain uncontested for long among its senior executives. Nevertheless, the aim must be that the executive, the coach and other key stakeholders work to create a partnership that ensures that the executive's development advances the organization's overall business objectives.

For example, the CEO of a particularly entrepreneurial conglomerate sought coaching to help him take up his role. Being new to the role of CEO and having to navigate not just a wide range of stakeholders within the portfolio of companies within the group, but also the often radically-changing perspective of the founder/chairman, this individual needed help with operating in a situation of considerable ambiguity and change. This involved discussions with the various stakeholders to develop a clearer understanding of what success meant for the CEO in his role, as well as helping him develop his capacity to stay with the uncertainty of not being able to clarify key elements of success.

Background and context

Up until the mid-1980s, the coaching of executives (though that term was rarely used) was provided informally either by internal Human Resource professionals, usually with a remedial emphasis, or by an external professional whose primary role was that of trusted advisor from a legal, accounting or marketing background. It had no established theoretical framework and practitioners generally had little or no formal training. A rare exception was the method of Organizational Role Analysis developed by a group connected with the Tavistock Institute in London during the 1960s whose theoretical framework derived from anthropology, sociology and psychoanalysis. This used a systems thinking perspective to understand the relationship between individual personality, the role, the work and the organization in the way that an individual operates as a leader (Newton, 2006).

During the late 1970s and beyond, a combination of factors served to open up a demand for the specialist professional executive coach. Changing attitudes to authority and the desire for more diversity at the top of organizations posed a challenge to accustomed ways of leading and managing (Drucker, 1993; Handy, 2002). This led to a demand for professionally trained coaches with expertise in human psychology and relationships in the workplace beyond simply being experienced Human Resources professionals or trusted professional advisors (Kilburg, 2000). Four major factors drove these changes:

1. Less stress on formal hierarchy and more emphasis on the right to express individual views meant that leaders needed to learn a broader repertoire of skills for influencing and motivating, especially with groups within society that had not previously had a place at the top (Hirschhorn, 1997). Although traditionally considered bastions of confidence and power, in which position in the hierarchy guaranteed a degree of respect and influence, the impact of social and economic changes made organizations increasingly unstable, fractured arrangements. Senior executives no longer felt they could trust the corporation to look after them and increasingly could not rely on alliances with their peers in a rapidly changing, highly competitive environment (Miller, 1993; Krantz, 1998). These demands combined to drive many senior executives to seek individual confidential relationships of counsel in which they could develop new skills and have the space and time to reflect on the increasing pressures of organizational leadership (Orenstein, 2007).
2. At the same time, and partly in response to the same factors, Human Resources departments were enlarged and began placing a greater emphasis on development activities for staff. Development was not just for staff requiring remedial attention, but began to be seen as a right, as well as a way of retaining the best staff. It was also seen as a strategy for changing the culture of a whole firm via personal performance coaching across groups of leaders (Tichy, 2004).
3. The breakdown of traditional, hierarchical institutions in the west meant that individuals seeking success needed to do so by better managing themselves personally and professionally, and by improving their own performance through their own efforts and will. Because of this, the self-help book and self-development programme industries burgeoned at an astonishing rate. The expansion of executive coaching could be seen in the context of a more general expansion of a cultural norm of individualized personal development. This put the stress on personal effectiveness as the new, more meritocratic route to success, wealth and happiness (Wuthnow, 1996; Frey & Stitzer, 2002).
4. The rise of a more explicitly merit-based approach to the promotion of executives, rather than simply age or longevity in the organization, or whether they knew the right people, created new opportunities for achievement-oriented managers from different social and educational backgrounds. This also increased the pressures on individuals to perform. Such pressures have led to managers working increasingly long hours, thus changing the traditional culture where seniority meant fewer hours. Today, the more senior is an executive, the harder he or she has to work, and the more permeable the traditional work versus personal life boundaries have become (Reeves, 2001). Helping leaders to manage the continual challenges of finding some sort of balance between the various roles in their lives has become a recent additional important role for coaches.

Among the main proponents of executive coaching have been Marshall Goldsmith, Warren Bennis, Jim Kouzes and Tim Gallwey (Goldsmith, Lyons, & Freas, 2000). Gallwey (2000), in particular, revolutionized the field by suggesting, based on his experience as a tennis coach, that expertise as a manager was often a handicap to being an effective coach, since it encouraged the coach to 'tell' the 'trainee' how to do it, as opposed to using a facilitative approach to provide the conditions that enable the coachee to learn from their experiences of success and failure and to reach their own conclusions and devise their own responses. This is now the stated aim of most executive coaches.

The evolution of executive coaching has led to the field rapidly becoming professionalized, with specialist organizations being formed to promote the interests of executive coaches, such as in the Association for Professional Executive Coaching and Supervision (APECS), in the United Kingdom (www.apecs.org) and the Worldwide Association of Business Coaches (WABC) in the United States (www.wabccoaches.com).

Several factors distinguish executive coaching from other forms of coaching:

- The primary client is the organization and its various stakeholders rather than simply the individual, who is seen as located and therefore to be understood within a wider system of roles and accountabilities.
- Executive Coaching always involves an intent to align the capabilities of the individual with the ambitions of the organization, and to work to support and achieve the organization's overall purpose and objectives.
- The aim of coaching will usually be informed by, and often agreed with, the individual's line manager, to whom some form of feedback before, sometimes during and generally at the end of a period of coaching is appropriate.
- Matters of purely private concern and interest, with no implications for the sponsoring organization, are not the primary focus of executive coaching, although they will often be a necessary component to address in order to help the executive improve his or her performance.
- The coach's fees are therefore generally paid by the organization and not personally by the executive.

These rules are not hard and fast, however, and require a degree of flexible interpretation. People are generally motivated at work by personal needs, not all of which are the concern of the organization. For example, in the real world even the most committed and hard-working executive will go through periods of doubt and frustration with his organization and will inevitably at times consider a career elsewhere. Indeed, such reactions may be a normal response. On other occasions, significant events in the personal life of an executive may cause that person to be distracted from their work role. It would be naïve to prohibit such conversations, as they are part of the process of helping executives develop greater self-awareness.

Why do leaders seek executive coaching?

Executives typically seek coaching during times of transition, when they are taking up a new position or joining a new organization, or when they are facing new personal challenges either from colleagues or subordinates within the organization, or when addressing difficult issues in their private lives.

Life at the top can be lonely and the higher the executive rises the less frequent and less reliable the feedback from colleagues becomes. Individual agendas multiply and conflict. Leaders need on occasion an independent sounding board; someone who can assist them in working through problems and potential solutions and to create a space for thinking in the executive's otherwise action-packed working life (Bruch & Ghoshal, 2002). The everyday challenge to doing this is well captured in the phrase 'when you are fighting off the alligators, it's hard to remember you were trying to drain the swamp'. Some leaders, given their achievement orientation, get so preoccupied with 'fighting alligators' that they can fail to focus on the actions critical to achieving their own and the organization's ambitions. Leaders need to take responsibility for draining the swamp and this involves the ability to set and follow through on their key priorities.

Those new to leadership roles, or who have recently moved into a new position, need to actively integrate themselves into the role and the organization. Senior leaders of the order of 30–50% fail or have left within 18 months of a new appointment (Watkins, 2003). Similarly, those facing new challenges in their role, such as how to exert influence on a broader stage as a consequence of organizational expansion, will need new capabilities in motivating and persuading. What has led to their success so far is unlikely to be sufficient going forward. Managers are not promoted to leaders because they were good at their previous role, but rather because there is a hope that they will be able to develop, learn and adapt their behaviour to be successful in the new role. Many managers derail because of their inability to change their behaviours as they become more senior (Van Velsor & Leslie, 1995). Executive coaching can help them adapt to the new role demanded of them by their organization.

Those who aspire to leadership generally have a strong drive towards power, achievement and success. Consequently, some common problems are:

- a need to dominate and control
- a focus on action, rather than thinking
- a need to be right
- impatience
- a need to be associated with success and to avoid failure
- a high need for self-determination
- a need to feel powerful
- a need to know
- an exaggerated sense of responsibility
- over-commitment
- a struggle to balance work demands with other areas of their life.

Topics such as these will be among the key agenda items for any leadership coaching assignment.

Goals and tasks of executive and leadership coaching

Undoubtedly, executive coaching has at times been in danger of becoming an over-used management fad, particularly when it is being prescribed without a great deal of thought being given to its objectives (Berglas, 2002).

As mentioned earlier, executive coaching has a broad remit and will vary at one extreme from relatively superficial external goals to perhaps more profound internal change. Building on Argyris and Schön (1978) in relation to levels of learning, we identify three levels of activity:

Level 1 Behaviour change – normally achievable in the relatively short term. It requires focused feedback, a commitment to change, the development of alternative behaviours and practice as well as reinforcement.

Level 2 Self-image – the stories we tell ourselves about ourselves and how we view ourselves both consciously and unconsciously, impact our self-confidence and our sense of ourselves as either victim or agent in the world. For example, if a client is not able to imagine him or herself as a partner in a professional practice firm then it is highly unlikely that he or she will be promoted to such a position. Such questions go beyond mere professional identity. They generally touch on deep-rooted conflicts that all human beings face. Issues of self-confidence and self-doubt may need to be tackled.

Level 3 Purpose and meaning – questions of personal purpose, as well as how to contribute to a greater organizational purpose, lie at the heart of a leader's motivations. The greatest leaders in history have acquired their commitment through the crucible of difficult experiences, turning these from potential trauma into sources of inspiration and courage. While executive and leadership coaching can benefit from studying such great leaders, it has been suggested that many leaders are in fact 'twice born' (Zaleznik, 1992), in the sense of having experienced events which have made them feel different from their peer group, leading them to step outside of focusing on their everyday living and to observe life audaciously, resulting in a new beginning in their attitude to life.

For example, a recently elected leader of a large international professional services firm requested help with being able to be 'tougher' in his leadership style. At the level of behaviour change we worked on his tendency to a conciliatory, conflict avoiding style of interpersonal interaction. He needed to balance his personal preference for friendly relations and compromise over asserting what he truly felt was in the best interests of the firm. This preference touched on his image of himself as a thoughtful person concerned with the welfare of others. However, this was at the cost sometimes of the welfare of the whole organization where tough decisions about individuals were required to improve profitability. Beyond this he was able to see that the way in which he sought purpose and meaning was focused too narrowly on leading the executive team as opposed to leading the firm, and beyond that, influencing the quality of service provided to clients by the profession as a whole. In this example we can see that problems that were first described in purely behavioural terms reflected concerns at both the levels of self-image and purpose and meaning. Remaining at the purely behavioural level would not have touched on these deeper levels making sustained behavioural change less likely.

Four central dilemmas can be said to lie at the heart of effective leadership:

- the strategic longer-term perspective versus the operational day-to-day perspective
- being directive versus enabling others
- getting ahead versus getting along with others
- being empathic versus being ruthless.

Successful leaders are rare because balancing and optimizing these conflicting tendencies requires great skill; human beings generally have a preference towards one or the other polarity. The executive coach's task is to help the leader to hold and bear the tension between the forces pulling in one direction or another, to provide a sounding-board and a container (Stokes, 1994), as well as a space in which the leader can reflect on personal preferences and ethical dilemmas. Thus the executive coach's task should be to strive to add value in the job of balancing and optimizing these dilemmas in order to improve leadership effectiveness, more than any particular quantitative business or management outcome.

Berglas (2002) suggests that the executive coach requires a degree of psychological training and sophistication and both Berglas (2002) and Peltier (2009) have identified areas where technical competence might reasonably be expected from an executive coach. These include:

- an understanding of personal, organizational and group psychology and dynamics, and their impact on individuals and teams
- appropriate business knowledge
- methods of leadership, team and organizational development
- leadership and team assessment methodologies
- certification with a range of psychometric instruments
- an understanding of how to promote the adult learning process.

With these dilemmas and competencies in mind, we have identified how coaching senior executives to lead effectively benefits from a sequence of four essential steps:

1. Know yourself

Self-awareness is the first step. Typically, the coaching will ask: What motivates you? How do others perceive you? Why would anyone want to follow you?

2. Own yourself

Being prepared to be accountable for the effect we have on others comes next. Coaching questions might include: What is the impact you have on others, both positive and negative? Who might find your style, attitudes or values motivating or difficult?

3. Be yourself

A lack of authenticity is often one of the first criticisms that will be made of a new leader. If there is a gap between 'talking the talk' and 'walking the walk' there is little chance of sustained support. Executives need to be clear about their own values and sticking to them also requires courage.

4. Help others to do the same

A key aspect of good leadership is bringing on and supporting other voices of leadership. The coach will ask such questions as: Does your leadership style enable others to take up leadership roles? Effective leaders empower others, not simply themselves.

These are matters and questions to which responses and decisions are not easy, or even possible to find without support. They require sustained effort, credible feedback and, on occasion a willingness to face painful emotional truths. Having the benefit of a period of reflection, with an executive coach who is independent of the organization and who has no personal or political agenda of his or her own, can enable a more balanced, objective and effective approach to these questions.

RELATIONSHIP WITH THE THEORETICAL TRADITIONS

The intentions of senior executive and leadership coaching are broad and ambitious hence the theoretical, psychological and philosophical traditions upon which it draws – from eastern philosophies to neurophysiology through to psychoanalysis to systems thinking – are similarly wide in sweep. This type of coaching may draw on any of the theoretical traditions outlined in Section I of this Handbook, all of which may provide complementary insight into three of the essential functions of leadership.

- Personal leadership – what do I as a leader stand for in terms of my purpose and values in this organization?
- Team leadership – how do I influence and persuade others to follow me and to work together collaboratively?
- Organizational leadership – how are the external and internal structural and systemic factors best managed in a strategy that will achieve the organization's objectives?

However, the theoretical approaches that executive coaches most commonly draw on include the following.

The psychodynamic approach

Those working within this tradition combine insights from psychoanalysis about the nature of emotional conflict and psychological defences in individuals and groups with the 'systems' perspective on organizations. An early example of applying systems thinking to coaching is the Organizational Role Consultancy methodology (Krantz & Malts, 1997; Newton, Long, & Sievers, 2006) developed at the Tavistock Institute. This is a relatively formal methodology and a precursor of executive coaching that emphasizes that executives are part of a system, rather than simply being individuals with specific personalities. The nature of the psychosocial system needs to be understood during coaching if that individual is to take up his or her role effectively in the organization. To what extent the executive's personality influences the behaviour of the organization or alternatively how much the dynamics of the organization are determining the executive's feelings and behaviour are two questions central to this approach. Nowadays, most executive coaches would recognize that attention to the dynamics of the organizational system is as much part of executive coaching as is a focus on personal psychology.

The cognitive-behavioural approach

This approach focuses almost entirely on the individual rather than the group or the system and on the way in which certain cognitive assumptions are interfering with the executive's capacity to take a leadership role. It is particularly relevant where an individual leader is emotionally inhibited or overwhelmed by anxieties, for instance in situations of conflict, in large meetings or in informal social settings. Helping the executive replace dysfunctional thought patterns with more adaptive versions is central to this approach.

The transactional analysis approach

The Parent-Adult-Child perspective of transactional analysis sheds light on the way in which scripts and games are played out in organizations between managers and staff; how a leader may be experienced as 'parental' and thereby provoke manipulative 'child' behavioural response in the behaviour of followers. The concept of 'life-script' or repetitive patterns in relationships of dependency is key.

The existential approach

This approach stresses how each individual is the ultimate source of accountability and how members of organizations can easily lose sight of their capacity to make choices and become trapped in a victim mentality where they come to believe they are unable to change themselves or their circumstances. It focuses on the value of authenticity and the significance of trust and truth telling in organizational leadership.

EVALUATION

Measuring the effectiveness of a leader is complex. Are external effectiveness criteria, such as the profitability, share price or longevity of the business, most telling? Or is the judgement of followers, as measured by the responses of those who choose to follow – their 'approval rating' – most important? Studies of leadership often confuse these two very different questions. In fact, as a broad generalization, no substantial, generally accepted objective evidence has yet been put forward demonstrating that better leadership in and of itself yields better results, higher profits, or indeed any other objectively measurable organizational outcome. Indeed, it is highly unlikely that this could ever be demonstrated convincingly, since the number of variables determining profitability that would need to be controlled for any degree of scientific precision is effectively infinite. Such things as chance events, the history of the firm before the leader took office, its network of commercial relationships, the efforts of others, the failure of significant competitors, the recruitment of new personnel and the ownership of previously undervalued technologies to name just a few. Whilst influenced by the leader they are not uniquely the leader's responsibility. Leadership can only really be quantitatively measured by just one criterion – how many others wish to follow?

The nature of what constitutes 'good leadership', like beauty, can more be said to lie as much in the eye of the beholder as in any objective criterion. Furthermore societies differ in the ideals they expect of a leader. If this is accepted, then qualitative rather than quantitative analysis and evaluation will be more fruitful and revealing. Two fundamental reasons for this are:

Leadership is at root a relationship between followers and the leader; the power of a leader comes from the followers. This is a fact that both leaders and followers often forget. The leader is dependent entirely on his or her followers who decide whether or not to follow. The leader is thus also a product of the group – it is the group that gives sanction and power to the leader. When, as is often the case with leaders who have been in power too long, these facts are forgotten the leader quickly loses power and often becomes accusatory towards his followers.

Leadership is about values and qualities of courage, self-sacrifice, judgement and character are significant. These are not qualities which can be measured objectively or learned in management training. Whilst an element of these qualities may be genetically determined, generally they arise out of tough personal experiences turned to personal benefit, often through the mentorship of others more experienced than the novice leader. An entirely normal and untroubled life to date is generally a poor preparation for a leadership role. Such individuals are less likely to have the strong inner drive to change things, or to have developed a robust personal conviction that they are right when the going gets tough. As a consequence the executive coach will at times need to work with some powerful psychological dynamics in the coaching relationship.

Research on the outcome evaluation and efficacy of executive coaching is in its infancy (Kilburg, 2000; Orenstein, 2006). This is in part due to the limited quality of the studies (Kampa-Kokesch & Anderson, 2001) and partly the difficulty of measuring efficacy in an evolving field (Lowman, 2001). To ask 'does executive coaching work?' is too broad a question, better to ask 'what works, with whom, to achieve what aim, by what criterion?' Certainly many studies show that executives receiving coaching value it highly and do change (e.g. Jones, Rafferty, & Griffin, 2006) and this evidence is building (Passmore, 2006). Effective research in the future will need to focus on the more specific variables of aim, method, client and coach variables, amongst others.

The executive coach's primary purpose then, is to enable the senior executive to take up his or her leadership role more effectively, to manage the conflicting force of co-operation and competition within the organization, and to balance the competing interests of the long list of stakeholders who must be satisfied if the organization is to prosper. The executive coach's client relationship is inevitably twofold, comprising both the individual in the coaching session and the organization that provides that individual with their executive authority. Methods and theories of executive coaching may vary but all share a common aim of enabling the executive to grow, learn and develop and to use their authority more effectively. Few organizations that have the ability to sustain success are simple systems that can achieve complete alignment amongst all of their stakeholders. Rather, they are complex political, social and emotional systems that need to mirror the complexity of their environment (Ashby, 1956). Whilst this remains the case the purposes, methods and measures of Executive Coaching will remain equally and entirely properly debated and contested.

FURTHER READING

Goldsmith, M., Lyons, L., & Freas, A. (2000). *Coaching for leadership*. San Francisco, CA: Jossey-Bass. (A broad-brush introduction with contributions for many of the foremost figures in the field, though with a strong US bias.)

Fitzgerald, C. & Berger, J.G. (2002). *Executive coaching*. Mountain View, CA. Davies-Black. (Provides an introduction to the various practices and perspectives of practitioners in the field.)

Heifetz, R.A. (1994). *Leadership without easy answers*. Cambridge, MA: Harvard University Press. (An original and penetrating analysis of leadership from the Kennedy School of Government at Harvard University that is relevant to anyone coaching someone in a leadership role.)

Scoular, A. (2011). *Business coaching*. London: Financial Times Prentice Hall. (An excellent practical introduction for anyone interested in training as an executive coach.)

DISCUSSION QUESTIONS

- What are some of the potential pitfalls that an executive or leadership coach should beware of?
- What are valid reasons for an organization to request coaching for an executive?
- Under what circumstances is it not appropriate to provide executive coaching?

REFERENCES

Argyris, C. and Schön, D. (1978). *Organizational learning*. Reading, MA: Addison-Wesley.

Ashby, W.R. (1956). *An introduction to cybernetics*. London: Chapman & Hall.

Barnard, C.I. (1938). *The functions of the executive*. Cambridge, MA: Harvard University Press.

Bartlett, C. A. & Ghoshal, S. (1990). Matrix management: Not a structure, a frame of mind. *Harvard Business Review*, 68(4), July–August: 138–45.

Berglas, S. (2002). The very real dangers of executive coaching. *Harvard Business Review*, 80(6), June: 86–92.

Bruch, H. & Ghoshal, S. (2002). Beware the busy manager. *Harvard Business Review*, 80(2), February: 62–9.

Clutterbuck, D. & Megginson, D. (2005). *Mentoring in action: A practical guide for managers*. London: Kogan Page.

Drucker, P. (1993). *Post-capitalist society*. Oxford: Butterworth-Heinemann.

Fitzgerald, C. & Berger, J. (Eds) (2002). *Executive coaching: Practices & perspectives*. Palo Alto, CA: Davies-Black Publishing.

Frey, B. & Stitzer, A. (2002). *Happiness and economics*. Princeton, NJ: Princeton University Press.

Gallwey, T. (2000). *The inner game of work: Overcoming mental obstacles for maximum performance*. London: Orion Business Books.

Goldsmith, M., Lyons, L., & Freas, A. (2000). *Coaching for leadership*. San Francisco, CA: Jossey-Bass.

Handy, C. (2002). *The age of unreason: New thinking for a new world*. London: Random House.

Hirschhorn, L. (1997). *Reworking authority*. Cambridge, MA: MIT Press.

Jones, R.A., Rafferty, A.E., & Griffin, M.A. (2006). The executive coaching trend: Towards more flexible executives. *Leadership & Organizational Development Journal*, 27(7): 584–96.

Kampa-Kokesch, S. & Anderson, M. (2001). Executive coaching: A comprehensive review of the literature. *Consulting Psychology Journal: Practice and Research*, 53: 205–28.

Kilburg, R.R. (2000). *Executive coaching*. Washington, DC: American Psychological Association.

Krantz, J. (1998). Anxiety and the new order. In E. Klein, F. Gabelnick & P. Herr (Eds), *Leadership in the 21st century*. Madison, CT: International Universities Press.

Krantz, J. & Maltz, M. (1997). A framework for consulting to organizational role. *Consulting Psychology Journal*, 49(2): 137–51.

Landsberg, M. (1997). *The Tao of coaching*. London: Harper Collins.

Levinson, H. (1996). Executive coaching. *Consulting Psychology Review*, 48(2): 115–23.

Lowman, R. (2001). Constructing a literature from case studies: Promises and limitations of the method. *Consulting Psychology Journal*, 53: 119–23.

Miller, E.J. (1993). *From dependency to autonomy: Studies in organization and change*. London: Karnac Books.

Newton, J., Long, S., & Sievers, B. (2006). *Coaching in depth – the organizational role analysis approach*. London: Karnac Books.

Orenstein, R. (2006). Measuring executive coaching efficacy? The answer was right here all along. *Consulting Psychology Journal,* 58: 106–16.

Orenstein, R. (2007). *Multidimensional executive coaching*. New York: Springer.

Passmore, J. (2006). Coaching psychology: Applying an integrated approach in education. *Journal of Leadership in Public Services*, 2(2): 27–33.

Peltier, B. (2009). *The psychology of executive coaching: Theory and application*. London: Routledge.

Peterson, D. (1996). *Executive coaching at work: The art of one-on-one change*. Consulting Psychology Journal, 48: 78–86.

Reeves, R. (2001). *Happy Mondays – putting the pleasure back into work*. London: Momentum.

Stokes, J. (1994). Institutional chaos and personal crisis. In A. Obholzer & V. Roberts (Eds), *The unconscious at work*. London: Routledge.

Tichy, N. (2004). *The leadership engine: How winning companies build leaders at every level*. London: Collins Business.

Van Velsor, E. & Leslie, J. (1995). Why executives derail: Perspectives across time and cultures. *Academy of Management Executive*, 9(4): 62–72.

Watkins, M. (2003). *The first 90 days*. Boston, MA: Harvard Business School Press.

Wuthnow, R. (1996). *Poor Richard's principle*. Princeton, NJ: Princeton University Press.

Zaleznik, A. (1992). Managers and leaders: Are they different? *Harvard Business Review,* March–April: 129–35.

18

The Manager as Coach

Andrea Ellinger, Rona Beattie and
Robert Hamlin

The purpose of this chapter is to explore the concept of the 'manager as coach' and to integrate recent empirical research that has explored aspects of this form of coaching. In this chapter we examine distinctive features associated with the concept of the 'manager as coach' which include: the beliefs that exemplary managers serving as coaches have; the catalysts for managerial coaching, managerial coaching skills; the requisite effective and ineffective behaviours of managerial coaches; and the contextual factors that may be influential in promoting a 'manager as coach' approach in organizations. The chapter also draws upon other theoretical perspectives associated with coaching and examines their applicability to the 'manager as coach' approach. Furthermore, it examines the empirical research that has explored the impact of coaching in workplace contexts and concludes with suggested readings and discussion questions.

'Instructing subordinates' (Kraut, Pedigo, McKenna, & Dunnette, 1989), 'training-coaching' (Yukl, 1994 [1981]) and 'providing growth and development' (Morse & Wagner, 1978; Yukl, 1989, 1994 [1981]) have been previously identified in past managerial behaviour research and resulting taxonomies as components of managerial roles, or as a subset of the leader role (Mintzberg, 1990, 1994). The importance of coaching and developing employees as a core managerial activity established by Evered and Selman (1989) has been further supported with research which has suggested that coaching is at the heart of managerial effectiveness (Hamlin, Ellinger, & Beattie, 2006). Since Human Resource practices have increasingly devolved to line managers, employee expectations have grown with respect to their development and the importance of talent management has required that managers assume more predominant roles as coaches and developers of their employees. Coaching by managers has progressively gained currency, as evidenced by CIPD Learning and Development Surveys (2006, 2007) which revealed 47% of line managers were using coaching in their work and significant activity was being undertaken to develop internal coaching capability by managers. The respondents of the EFMD/European Mentoring Coaching Council (EMCC) survey (2009) on the state of coaching and mentoring also acknowledged that line managers are effective at enhancing performance and skills through coaching. Therefore, the concept of the 'manager as coach' is not a new phenomenon and is one that continues to gain purchase in the practitioner and scholarly literatures. Reviews of the literature on managerial coaching have become more prevalent within the management and Human Resource development literature along with other fields like nursing (Batson & Yoder, 2011; Ellinger et al., 2006; Hagen, 2012).

Yet, despite the growing interest in the manager as coach concept and the apparent benefits associated with managerial coaching for employees, managers and for the organization, there has been a 'relative paucity of resources aimed specifically at helping managers to coach people better' (Peterson & Little, 2005: 179). Further, Gilley, Gilley and Kouider (2010: 53) have suggested that 'few empirical studies of managerial coaching skills, optimal conditions, or its benefits to individuals and organizations'appear in the academic literature. Therefore, to address the criticisms that managerial coaching is somewhat prescriptive, atheoretical and still considered to be in its infancy, this chapter synthesizes the empirical research on managerial coaching to inform academics, researchers, practitioners and clients about this prevalent form of coaching.

DISTINCTIVE FEATURES

Coaching has often been perceived as a remedy for poor performance (Fournies, 1987). However, more recent conceptions of coaching have moved beyond a deficit orientation to one of a developmental orientation, in which coaching is considered to be a day-to-day, hands-on process of helping employees recognize opportunities to improve their performance and capabilities (Orth, Wilkinson, & Benfari, 1987; Popper & Lipshitz, 1992), of empowering employees to exceed prior levels of performance (Burdett, 1998; Evered & Selman, 1989; Hargrove, 1995) and as a process of learning designed to provide guidance, encouragement and support to the learner (coachee) (Redshaw, 2000). Mink, Owen and Mink (1993) have conceived coaching as a process in which the coach creates an enabling relationship with others to help them learn, so that improved performance is a by-product of learning. More contemporary perspectives have considered coaching as being synonymous with facilitating learning (Beattie, 2002; Ellinger, 1997; Ellinger & Bostrom, 1999).

While coaching is often provided by a coach external to the organization who provides contracted coaching services to the client, in contrast, the 'manager as coach' concept refers to a manager or supervisor serving as a coach or facilitator of learning in the workplace setting, in which he or she enacts specific behaviours that enable his/her employee (coachee) to learn and develop (Beattie, 2002; Ellinger & Bostrom, 1999; Talarico, 2002). The goals associated with managerial coaching are often to improve an employee's performance through learning, but may also be multifaceted. For example, promoting an understanding of the employee's strengths and weaknesses through the provision of extensive feedback and encouraging self-awareness that may influence personal relationships and work behaviours may be additional goals associated with this form of coaching. In essence, managerial coaching refers to managers being coaching resources to their employees within their organizations.

Heslin, Vandewalle and Latham (2006: 872) acknowledge that 'managers vary in their willingness to coach their employees', despite the importance of coaching as a managerial activity. Further, others contend that the 'managerial coach' is a rare species and that 'managers infrequently engage in coaching' (Gilley et al., 2010: 62). Managers may lack the time or requisite skills and capabilities to coach, are not encouraged or rewarded for coaching, or may perceive it to be an unimportant managerial role (Goleman, 2000; Hunt & Weintraub, 2002a). Yet for those managers who do perceive themselves as managerial coaches, a 'coaching mind-set' (Hunt & Weintraub, 2011) or a set of beliefs about being a managerial coach (Ellinger & Bostrom, 2002) are considered to be necessary prerequisites, along with specific skills and capabilities that enable the manager to coach effectively. More recently, Heslin et al. (2006: 896) have suggested that implicit person theories 'appear to affect the extent to which they coach their employees'.

The manager as coach mind-set

Managers who have become effective coaches have the following characteristics in common: an attitude of helpfulness; less need for control; empathy in dealing with others; openness to personal learning and receiving feedback; high standards; a desire to help others to develop; a theory of employee development that is not predicated on a 'sink or swim' approach; and a belief that most people do want to learn (Hunt & Weintraub, 2002b, 2011). Based upon their work with managers who have become coaching managers, Hunt and Weintraub consider these attitudes and beliefs to constitute the coaching mind-set. Although empirical research on this aspect of coaching is limited, Ellinger and Bostrom (2002) identified three major categories of beliefs held by exemplary managerial coaches, namely beliefs about their managerial roles and capabilities, beliefs about learning and the learning process and beliefs about learners. First and foremost, these managers believed that coaching employees and facilitating their development is their role and what they are expected to do. Furthermore, they drew distinctions between coaching, which is 'all about people – helping them grow and develop' and management, which is 'telling people what to do' (Ellinger & Bostrom, 2002: 156). For these managers, managing was often about telling, judging, controlling and directing, whereas being in a 'coaching mind-set' was about empowering, helping, developing, supporting and removing obstacles. It was recognized that managers often had to move between these roles because certain circumstances might require role switching.

In terms of their capabilities, these exemplary managers believed that they had skills, process capabilities and experiences to coach their employees effectively. Their self-efficacy was evident, as was their ability to establish trust, rapport and to build relationships with their employees, because they cared enough to want to help them. In terms of the beliefs about learning and the learning process, these managers considered learning to be important, ongoing and shared. Furthermore, learning was most effective when it was integrated with work, when feedback was provided and when learners (coachees) were encouraged to learn for themselves. The final category of beliefs identified in Ellinger and Bostrom's empirical study of exemplary managers reflected beliefs about learners. Such managers considered their coachees to be capable and willing to learn and recognized the need for learners to possess a solid foundation of information and a need to understand the whys. More recently, Anderson (2013) examined the factors that affect managers' propensities to assume coaching roles and found that leader-team relationships and occupational self-efficacy were predictive of managerial coaching behaviours, thus underscoring the importance of relationships and self-efficacy.

The catalysts for coaching opportunities

Since coaching is often an informal learning strategy that is used by managers, understanding the catalysts for initiating a coaching dialogue with employees is also important. Mumford (1993) has acknowledged that any managerial activity contains the potential for learning and may include some of the following: a new assignment; a new challenge; a new project; a shock or crisis; problem-solving within a group; differing standards of performance; an unsuccessful piece of work. Similarly, research by Ellinger (2003) on the catalysts for coaching by managers revealed the following triggers: gaps and deficiencies of existing employee skills; political and high consequence issues; assignments; projects; employee transitions; and developmental opportunities.

The skills and behaviours required for coaching

The skills associated with managerial coaching have been described in the practitioner-oriented literature and include: listening skills, analytical skills, interviewing skills, effective questioning techniques and observation skills. Gilley et al. (2010) found that a manager's ability to motivate, encourage growth and development, communicate appropriately and possess skills necessary for the job, were predictors of coaching. The actual behaviours identified have typically included giving and receiving performance feedback, communicating and setting clear expectations, and creating a supportive environment conducive to coaching (Graham, Wedman, & Garvin-Kester, 1993, 1994; King & Eaton, 1999; Marsh, 1992; Mobley, 1999; Orth et al., 1987; Phillips, 1994, 1995; Zemke, 1996).

In terms of coaching skills, McLean, Yang, Kuo, Tolbert and Larkin (2005) developed a self-assessment based upon a four-dimension coaching model. This model suggests that the 'manager as coach' reflects four aspects of managerial behaviour. The 'manager as coach' should: communicate openly with others; take a team approach instead of an individual approach with tasks;

value people over tasks; and should accept the ambiguous nature of the working environment. Their findings suggest that managerial coaching is a multidimensional construct that supports their four-dimension coaching model. In responding to this work, Peterson and Little (2005) questioned whether the team approach is a primary component of effective coaching, since coaching is often considered a one-on-one managerial intervention. Further, they noted that other factors associated with coaching skills should be considered, such as: developing a partnership, effective listening skills and providing feedback, as well as capabilities for facilitating development. In response to Peterson and Little's criticism, Park, Mclean and Yang (2008) added a component related to facilitating development and have subsequently tested this revised instrument which has evidence of validity.

In light of the Park et al. (2008) instrument, interest in managerial coaching skills and expertise as a direction for research has emerged in the literature: Park et al. (2008) found a positive influence of managerial coaching skills on employees' personal learning, organizational learning and turnover intentions, while Hagan (2010) examined managerial coaching expertise within a Six Sigma context. Ahmadi et al. (2011) examined managerial coaching expertise in relation to quality of work-life and found it was an important factor in quality of work-life. In a more recent study that explored managerial coaching expertise and learning outcomes within a high-performance work team context, Hagan (2012) found a significant positive relationship between the level of coaching expertise and team learning outcomes.

However, while it is important to possess coaching skills and expertise, translating such skills into practice must be accompanied by behaviours that enable managers to perform in a 'manager as coach' capacity. Therefore, previous research focused managerial coaching behaviours. For example, incorporating Schelling's eight behaviours associated with successful sales managers, Graham et al. (1994) interviewed account representatives and obtained ratings of their respective manager's coaching skills prior to the implementation of a coaching skills training programme. The findings supported the existing literature on coaching concerning the importance of providing feedback, setting clear expectations and creating a climate for coaching that involves a positive trusting relationship. Ellinger's (1997) and Ellinger and Bostrom's (1999) research identified a taxonomy of thirteen managerial coaching behaviours that included both facilitating and empowering behaviours (see Table 18.1). Similarly, Beattie's (2002) research on managerial coaching in the context of a social service organization revealed twenty-two discrete effective facilitative behaviours that were classified and allocated into one of nine identified behavioural categories.

Subsequent comparative analyses between the Ellinger and Beattie taxonomies have revealed a high degree of congruency in managerial coaching behaviours (Hamlin, Ellinger, & Beattie, 2006). More recent research by Longenecker and Neubert (2005), Powell and Doran (2003), Shaw and Knights (2005) and Amy (2005) have offered additional support for these behavioural findings. Additionally, Noer (2005) and Noer, Leupold and Valle (2007) have suggested that managerial coaching is a dynamic interaction between three sets of behaviour: *assessing*, *challenging* and *supporting*.

Table 18.1   Behavioural taxonomies

Ellinger's (1997) and Ellinger and Bostrom's (2002) Behavioral Taxonomy	Beattie's (2002) Behavioural Taxonomy
The empowering cluster consisted of the following behaviors: • question framing to encourage employees to think through issues; • being a resource – removing obstacles; • transferring ownership to employees; • holding back – not providing the answers. The facilitating cluster consisted of the following behaviors: • providing feedback to employees; • soliciting feedback from employees; • working it out together – talking it through; • creating and promoting a learning environment; • setting and communicating expectations; • stepping into other to shift perspectives; • broadening employees' perspectives – getting them to see things differently; • using analogies, scenarios, and examples; • engaging others to facilitate learning.	Beattie's behavioural categories consisted of: • thinking – reflective or prospective thinking; • informing – sharing knowledge; • empowering – delegation, trust; • assessing – feedback and recognition, identifying developmental needs; • advising – instruction, coaching, guidance, counselling; • being professional – role model, standard setting, planning and preparation; • caring – support, encouragement, approachable, reassurance, commitment/involvement, empathy; • developing others; • challenging employees to stretch themselves.

Contextual factors influencing managerial coaching

Scholars have acknowledged that creating a culture of coaching is important in promoting managerial coaching behaviours (Evered & Selman, 1989; Hunt & Weintraub, 2002b, 2007). However, empirical research exploring such contextual influences on managerial coaching has been very limited. Beattie (2006) found that environmental factors such as political, economic, societal and technological trends influenced the management framework and learning needs within the two organizations she studied. In terms of the organizational influences, she identified history, mission and strategy, structure, and culture as impacting the context for managerial coaching. Specifically, in these organizations, the aspirations to become learning organizations contributed to line managers' roles as coaches and developers. In terms of Human Resource development strategy, the provision of training for managers to assume developmental roles by supporting their learning needs was also a critical influence.

However, organizations that do not have the same employee development aspirations or infrastructures to adequately prepare managers to assume coaching roles, often do not effectively leverage managers as coaches. Furthermore, there is a paradox when managers become coaching managers because they 'must both coach and evaluate direct reports' (Hunt & Weintraub, 2002b: 16). It is possible that the evaluative component of their position may detract from employees being open about their 'concerns, problems, and mistakes' (p. 17). As alluded to in Ellinger's (1997) research, the importance of managers being able to role switch and to recognize when they need to focus on developmental coaching, or when they need to wear a more directive managerial hat, is critical and requires 'significant emotional maturity' (Hunt & Weintraub, 2002b: 17).

THE RELATIONSHIP WITH THE COACHEE

In the absence of their wanting to be coached, it is often difficult if not virtually impossible for the manager to coach his or her employees. The coaching relationship established between the manager and employee (coachee) must be one that is based on mutual trust and openness. The manager must believe that he or she is capable of serving as a coach, can leverage coaching opportunities and can effectively engage behaviours that facilitate coachees' learning. Coachees, according to Hunt and Weintraub (2002b), should possess an ability to reflect on their actions from an objective point of view; curiosity about their actions and those of others; acceptance that others may possess more knowledge; the ability to share their self-observations with the manager without shame; a willingness and capacity to listen and be receptive to feedback; and motivation to improve and learn through the process of coaching.

Although managerial coaching can be provided as a structured intervention, often, as Hunt and Weintraub (2002b) advocate, coaching should be 'slipped into' (p. 18) the manager's daily routine. Managers are in the unique position of interacting with their employees on a regular basis, are responsible for their employees' performance and often can leverage on-the-job learning. Therefore, managerial coaching often becomes an informal activity that is initiated through a dialogue with the coachee. In many cases, the coaching dialogue may begin as a result of a performance gap or performance deficiency, but a coaching dialogue may also be initiated as a result of a developmental opportunity that the manager has identified and which will promote the coachee's learning. It may also be a result of several of the other aforementioned catalysts for coaching. When the catalyst occurs, either as a result of the manager or coachee's initiative, it is then important for the manager to determine the most appropriate behaviours to engage. In many situations, the manager may engage in a conversation with the coachee that integrates question framing techniques to encourage the coachee to think for him/herself. It might also be that the manager provides feedback to the coachee, or engages in a role-play activity. The manager may engage several behaviours or may determine that a select few are more relevant from those sets of behaviours identified in the empirical research.

RELATIONSHIP WITH THEORETICAL TRADITIONS

The managerial coaching literature has been criticized for being atheoretical. However, there are many philosophical underpinnings associated with coaching and a review of these theoretical traditions offers some potential grounding for the 'manager as coach' concept. Specifically, these include the solution-focused approach to coaching (Cavanagh & Grant, 2010), the behavioural approach to coaching (Peterson, 2006) and the cognitive approach/cognitive behavioural coaching (Williams, Edgerton, & Palmer, 2010).

The solution-focused approach to coaching

Grant (2006) has acknowledged that 'solution-focused' coaching has its roots in Erikson's approach to strategic therapy. Therapists had become disenchanted with the diagnostic medical approach and began to 'simply ask questions that focused their clients' attention on building solutions' (Grant, 2006: 74). The application of this to workplace coaching and particularly to the 'manager as coach' form of coaching, is predicated upon a number of key principles as follows:

problems stem from a limited repertoire of behaviour

the focus is on constructing solutions

the notion that the coachee, rather than the coach, is the expert in his/her own life

the coach helps the coachee to recognize resources

there is an action orientation, specific goal setting

change can occur in a short period of time, designed for each coachee, future oriented

coaching engages the coachee

the coach actively challenges the coachee to think in a new way.

Cavanagh and Grant (2010) suggest that the solution-focused approach to coaching is constructionist in orientation and they assert that the client is capable of solving his/her own problem. Further, principles of self-directed learning influence the 'solution-focused' approach.

The following example illustrates the applicability of the 'solution-focused' coaching approach to the manager as coach form of coaching:

'Planning the Party' – Hank and his Two Young Employees

Hank, a mid-level manufacturing manager in a consumer goods company, described working with two younger employees who assumed responsibility for planning a holiday party for the division. Since they lacked experience with event planning, Hank indicated that they collectively met and talked about some ideas. Hank said, 'I prodded them to tell me where they were at, what thought processes they were using, how they came to their conclusions … just asking those kind of probing questions … and by questioning, they began to fold the brainwork in which to guide [their] direction'. This approach was in alignment with Hank's value of 'people owning the work … that the people doing the work know best how to do it'.

Behavioural coaching

Coaching is about behaviour change, although not from a mechanistic, stimulus-response perspective, but rather from a whole-person approach (Peterson, 2006). Classic behavioural change techniques often include modelling, feedback, shaping and successive approximation, self-management, rewards and reinforcers and behavioural practice (Peterson, 2006). Peterson suggests that a behaviour-based approach to coaching 'starts with clarity around what really matters to people and then helps them get there' (Peterson, 2006: 74).

The following example illustrates the applicability of the behaviour-based coaching approach to the 'manager as coach' form of coaching:

'You're Not Perfect Either' – Glen and Bob

Glen, a mid-level employee development manager in a manufacturing context, described Bob's behavior as very disrespectful to other employees during a meeting. Glen said, 'I sat down with that Bob and held the mirror and we went over the impact of what had taken place … .' Bob agreed that he should not have done what he did and that he could see 'the negative situation that occurred and where I shut everybody up'.

Cognitive coaching and cognitive behavioural coaching

Cognitive coaching theory draws upon cognitive therapy which suggests that one's moods are strongly related to and triggered by one's cognitions or thoughts (Auerbach, 2006). Therefore, the cognitive approach often assists clients 'in identifying errors in their thinking and aiding them in adopting more accurate, useful cognitions' (Auerbach, 2006: 104) and helps them to 'learn more realistic ways to approach the world' (p. 105). Drawing upon work done by Costa and Garmston (cited in Auerbach, 2006); 'cognitive coaching enhances the ability of the person being coached to examine their patterns of thinking and behaviour, and to reconsider the underlying assumptions that precede actions' (Auerbach, 2006: 109). Similarly, according to Williams, Edgerton and Palmer (2010), cognitive behavioural coaching is 'an integrative approach which combines the use of cognitive, behavioural, imaginal and problem solving techniques and strategies within a cognitive behavioural framework to enable coaches to achieve their realistic goals' (Palmer & Szymanska, 2007: 86 in Williams et al., 2010: 37).

The following example illustrates the usefulness of the cognitive coaching approach for managers:

'Making a Change' – Howard and John

Howard, a senior-level financial manager in a consumer goods company, was aware of a change that John wanted to make in his department, but suspected it would have negative organizational consequences and alienate an employee. John had difficulty in understanding the potential consequences so Howard encouraged him present the idea at a staff meeting. The other staff members agreed that the change was necessary but the way in which the change was proposed would indeed alienate the employee. Howard said, 'we did a lot of role playing during the process [of many meetings with John] … really trying to get John to try and understand the emotional feelings that the employee would be feeling.' By helping John to 'step into this person's shoes', Howard was trying to enable him to see the situation differently.

The 'manager as coach' form of coaching can be informed by many perspectives and a variety of approaches can be adopted to enable managers to become optimally effective in coaching their employees. Many managers do not have counselling, psychology, or therapy backgrounds. Therefore, they need to be exposed to such approaches and appropriately trained so that they can use tools and techniques that are theoretically grounded but practical.

EVALUATION

Scholars suggest that the benefits of coaching are enormous and associated with: producing long-lasting learning; contributing to high levels of motivation; and improving and enhancing employee performance, working relationships, job satisfaction, and organizational commitment (Anon, 2001; Redshaw, 2000). More specifically, as a performance improvement strategy, the literature suggests that coaching positively impacts individual, team and organizational performance (Ellinger et al., 2010; Gilley et al., 2010; Hagen, 2012). Previous research by Good (1993) found that sales managers' investment of time for coaching impacted salespeople's skills. Specific coaching behaviours have also been directly correlated with net increases in sales (Graham et al., 1994). Further, improvements in systems, cost savings and knowledge sharing may be directly attributed to coaching interventions when managers serve as coaches for individuals or teams of employees (Ellinger, 2003). Yet, overall, the empirical research on the efficacy of managerial coaching is still underdeveloped (Agarwal, Angst, & Magni, 2009; Gilley et al., 2010; Hagen, 2012; Yukl, 1994 [1981]).

To address these shortcomings, in recent years a few studies have been conducted that report on the impact of managerial coaching. Ellinger, Ellinger and Keller (2003) found that warehouse employees' perceptions of the extent of their respective supervisors' coaching behaviours were significant predictors of job satisfaction and job performance. Hannah's (2004) case study on supervisory coaching within the British Rail context revealed that, with supervisory coaching, employee competence improved and the resulting service consistency increased passenger satisfaction with customer service received. Shaw and Knights (2005) also found that introducing a coaching style as a preferred leadership style within a small to medium-sized enterprise (SME) resulted in enhanced knowledge and potential growth, along with improved communications and interpersonal relationships. Further evidence of the benefits of managerial coaching have been provided by Elmadag, Ellinger and Franke (2008), whose study found that managerial coaching had a stronger influence on frontline employee commitment to service quality than formal training or rewarding; Agarwal et al. (2009) conducted a multi-level exploration of the effects of managers' coaching intensity on the performance of their direct reports. Their findings 'add to the small but growing body of evidence in support of the value creation potential of a developmental style, as opposed to a command-and-control style' (p. 2125). Ellinger et al. (2011) examined the influence of managerial coaching behaviour on relationships between organizational investments in social capital and employee work-related performance. Findings suggested that 'the influence of managerial coaching was considerably stronger under conditions of low coaching than high coaching' (p. 79), which was unexpected. In more recent research, Ellinger et al. (2012) explored the influence of managerial coaching and formal training on job and organizational engagement. Findings suggested that managerial coaching is positively related to both types of engagement. Wang's (2012) survey-based research examined the influence of incentive pay and training and managerial coaching on the relationships between research and development employees' characteristics and innovative behaviour in the Taiwanese context. She found that such Human Resource management approaches and managerial coaching positively moderated these relationships. Lastly, Gomez and Gunn (2012) sought to determine if managers who coach become better leaders. Using a mixed methods design, they developed a new taxonomy that describes the components of managerial coaching and leader development activities. Their findings suggest 'a clear, strong and positive correlation between managerial coaching and leader development' (p. 77).

Although recent research has found that managerial coaching has been linked to many positive employee and organizational outcomes, it is important to acknowledge that not all managerial coaching is effective. Attention to ineffective managerial coaching behaviour has been equally underdeveloped; however, recent comparative analysis has revealed considerable consistency among ineffective managerial behaviour. Ellinger, Hamlin and Beattie (2008) have found that the predominant ineffective behaviour held in common among all three studies was an autocratic, directive, controlling, dictatorial managerial style, which is often associated with a 'traditional bureaucratic management paradigm'. This paradigm has been characterized by command, control, compliance and coercive styles of management, which is not considered appropriate for promoting a 'coaching management paradigm' that encourages empowerment, inclusion and participation. Another commonality revealed in the research was the use of ineffective communication and poor dissemination of information, along with the use of inappropriate behaviours and approaches which included, among others, not spending enough time with employees.

Overall, this growing base of empirical research continues to offer support for the efficacy of managerial coaching in workplace contexts. However, scholars are advocating more comprehensive research that examines the antecedents or factors that influence managerial coaching, the skills and behaviours that managers possess and enact, factors that might influence the managerial coaching process and the outcomes that emanate from such coaching (Batson & Yoder, 2012; Ellinger et al, 2006; Hagen, 2012). The apparent benefits of managerial coaching have been established primarily for those recipients of coaching. However, future research should continue to examine the benefits that managers receive from serving as coaches and being engaged in coaching relationships relative to their own learning and development (Gomez & Gunn, 2012). And, because there are likely drawbacks to managerial coaching, more research is needed to better understand its limitations within workplace contexts.

FURTHER READING

Cox, E. (2013). *Coaching understood: A pragmatic inquiry into the coaching process.* London: Sage Publishers, Ltd. (This book introduces a cyclical coaching model that articulates how coaching works as a 'facilitated, dialogic, reflective learning process' (p. 1). Specific chapters focus on listening, clarifying, reflecting, questioning which are critical behaviors enacted by managers who assume coaching roles.)

Hunt, J.M. & Weintraub, J.R. (2011). *The coaching manager: Developing top talent in business* (2nd ed.). Thousand Oaks, CA: Sage. (This revised edition, similar to but expanded beyond the first edition, is intended to help managers become more effective developmental coaches as well as create organizational contexts conducive to coaching.)

Hunt, J.M. & Weintraub, J.R. (2007). *The coaching organization: A strategy for developing leaders*. Thousand Oaks, CA: Sage. (This book provides an overview of how leaders and Human Resource professionals can build organizational coaching capability by using developmental coaching and other forms of coaching to enhance organizational results.)

DISCUSSION QUESTIONS

- When considering the manager as coach, what compelling personality traits and other features and characteristics distinguish exemplary managerial coaches?
- We can see from the growing base of empirical research that managerial coaching can be very effective and linked to many important outcomes. Yet, the manager-coach is a relatively rare species. How do we encourage more managers to adopt the coaching role? What must organizational leaders and managers do differently to create the context and culture for coaching?
- What research can be done in exemplary coaching organizations to provide more contextual understanding of the factors that can facilitate the adoption of this role and minimize hindrances?

REFERENCES

Ahmadi, S.A.A., Jalalilan, N., Salamzadeh, Y., Daraei, M., & Tadayon, A. (2011). To the promotion of work life quality using the paradigm of managerial coaching: The role of managerial coaching on the quality of work life. *African Journal of Business Management, 5*(17), 7440–48.

Agarwal, R., Angst, C.M., & Magni, M. (2009). The performance effects of coaching: A multilevel analysis using hierarchical linear modelling. *The International Journal of Human Resource Management, 20*(10), 2110–34.

Amy, A.H. (2005). Leaders as facilitators of organizational learning. (Unpublished Doctoral dissertation. Regent University at Virginia Beach, VA.)

Anderson, V. (2013). A Trojan horse? Managerial coaching and theories of leadership. *Human Resource Development International, 16*(3), 1–28.

Anonymous (2001). Mentoring and coaching help employees grow. *HR Focus, 78*(9), 1–6.

Auerbach, J.E. (2006). Cognitive coaching. In D.R. Stober & A.M. Grant (Eds), *Evidence based coaching handbook* (pp. 103–27). Hoboken, NJ: John Wiley & Sons.

Batson, V.D. & Yoder, L.H. (2012). Managerial coaching: A concept analysis. *Journal of Advanced Nursing, 68*(7), 1658–1669.

Beattie, R.S. (2002). Line managers as facilitators of learning: Empirical evidence from voluntary sector. *Proceedings of 2002 Human Resource Development Research and Practice across Europe Conference*. Edinburgh: Napier University, January.

Beattie, R.S. (2006). HRD in the public sector: The case of health and social care. In S. Sambrook & J. Stewart (Eds), *Human resource development in the health and social care context*. London: Routledge.

Burdett, J.O. (1998). Forty things every manager should know about coaching. *Journal of Management Development, 17*(2), 142–52.

Cavanagh, M.J. & Grant, A.M. (2010). The solution-focused approach to coaching. In In E. Cox, T. Bachkirova, & D. Clutterbuck (Eds), *The complete handbook of coaching* (pp. 54–67). London: Sage Publishers, Ltd.

Chartered Institute of Personnel and Development (CIPD). (2006). *Learning and development survey*. London: CIPD.

Chartered Institute of Personnel and Development (CIPD). (2007). *Learning and development survey*. London: CIPD.

The EFMD/EMCC Survey on the state of coaching and mentoring (2009). Belgium: Brussels. Available at www.efmd.org.

Ellinger, A.D. (2003). Antecedents and consequences of coaching behavior. *Performance Improvement Quarterly, 16*(1), 5–28.

Ellinger, A.D., Beattie, R.S., Hamlin, R.G., Wang, Y., & Trolan, O. (2006). The manager as coach: A review of the empirical literature and the development of a tentative model of managerial coaching. In *Proceedings of the Seventh International Conference on HRD Research and Practice Across Europe* (CD-Rom). Tilburg, The Netherlands.

Ellinger, A.D. & Bostrom, R.P. (1999). Managerial coaching behaviors in learning organizations. *Journal of Management Development, 18*(9), 752–71.

Ellinger, A.D. & Bostrom, R.P. (2002). An examination of managers' belief about their roles as facilitators of learning. *Management Learning, 33*(2), 147–79.

Ellinger, A.D., Ellinger, A.E., & Keller, S.B. (2003). Supervisory coaching behavior, employee satisfaction, and warehouse employee performance: A dyadic perspective in the distribution industry. *Human Resource Development Quarterly, 14*(4), 435–58.

Ellinger, A.D., Ellinger, A. E., Bachrach, D.G., Wang, Y., & Bas Elmadag, A.B. (2011). Organizational investments in social capital, managerial coaching and employee work-related performance. *Management Learning, 42*(1), 67–85.

Ellinger, A.D., Hamlin, R.G., & Beattie, R.S. (2008). Behavioural indicators of ineffective managerial coaching: A cross-national study. *Journal of European Industrial Training, 32*(4), 240–57.

Ellinger, A.D., Musgrove, C.F. & Ellinger, A.E. (2012). Examining the relationships between employee development, engagement, and service climate. Refereed Working Paper. In *Proceedings of the UFHRD Europe 2012 Conference* (CD-ROM). Portugal.

Ellinger, A.M. (1997). Managers as facilitators of learning in learning organizations (Unpublished Doctoral dissertation, University of Georgia at Athens, GA.)

Elmadag, A.B., Ellinger, A.E., & Franke, G.R. (2008). Antecedents and consequences of frontline service employee commitment to service quality. *Journal of Marketing Theory and Practice, 16*(2), 95–110.

Evered, R.D. & Selman, J.C. (1989). Coaching and the art of management. *Organizational Dynamics, 18*, 16–32.

Fournies, F.F. (1987). *Coaching for improved work performance*. Kansas, MO: Liberty Hall Press.

Gilley, A., Gilley, J.W. & Kouider, E. (2010). Characteristics of managerial coaching. *Performance Improvement Quarterly, 23*(1), 53–70.

Goleman, D. (2000). Leadership that gets results. *Harvard Business Review*, March-April: 78–90.

Gomez, E. & Gunn, R. (2012). Do managers that coach become better leaders? An exploration into the relationship between managerial coaching and leader development. (Unpublished Master's Thesis, School of Management, Blekinge Institute of Technology: Sweden.)

Good, D.J. (1993). Managerial coaching as a sales performance moderator. *Journal of Marketing – Theory and Practice, 1*(3), 74–83.

Graham, S., Wedman, J.F., & Garvin-Kester, B. (1993). Manager coaching skills: Development and application. *Performance Improvement Quarterly, 6*(1), 2–13.

Graham, S., Wedman, J.F., & Garvin-Kester, B. (1994). Manager coaching skills: What makes a good coach? *Performance Improvement Quarterly, 7*(2), 81–94.

Grant, A.M. (2006). Solution-focused coaching. In J. Passmore (Ed.), *Excellence in coaching: The industry guide* (pp. 73–90). London: Kogan Press.

Hagen, M. (2010). Black Belt coaching and project outcomes: An empirical investigation. *Quality Management Journal, 17*, 54–67.

Hagen, M. (2012). Managerial coaching: A review of the literature. *Performance Improvement Quarterly, 24*(4), 17–39.

Hagen, M. & Aguilar, M.G. (2012). The impact of managerial coaching on learning outcomes within a team context: An analysis. *Human Resource Development Quarterly, 23*(3), 363–88.

Hamlin, R.G., Ellinger, A.D., & Beattie, R.S. (2006). Coaching at the heart of managerial effectiveness: A cross-cultural study of managerial behaviours. *Human Resource Development International, 9*(3), 305–31.

Hannah, C. (2004). Improving intermediate skills through workplace coaching: A case study within the UK rail industry. *International Journal of Evidence Based Coaching and Mentoring, 2*(1), 17–45.

Hargrove, R. (1995). *Masterful coaching*. San Diego, CA: Pfeiffer & Company.

Heslin, P.A., Vandewalle, D., & Latham, G.P. (2006). Keen to help? Managers' implicit person theories and their subsequent employee coaching. *Personnel Psychology, 59*, 871–902.

Hunt, J.M. & Weintraub, J.R. (2002a). How coaching can enhance your brand as a manager. *Journal of Organizational Excellence, 21*(2), 39–44.

Hunt, J.M. & Weintraub, J.R. (2002b). *The coaching manager: Developing top talent in business*. Thousand Oaks, CA: Sage.

Hunt, J.M. & Weintraub, J.R. (2007). *The coaching organization: A strategy for developing leaders*. Thousand Oaks, CA: Sage.

Hunt, J.M. & Weintraub, J.R. (2011). *The coaching manager: Developing top talent in business* (2nd ed.). Thousand Oaks, CA: Sage.

King, P. & Eaton, J. (1999). Coaching for results. *Industrial and Commercial Training, 31*(4), 145–8.

Kraut, A.I., Pedigo, P.R., McKenna, D.D., & Dunnette, M.D. (1989). The role of the manager: What's really important in different management jobs. *The Academy of Management Executive, 3*(4), 286–93.

Longenecker, C.O. & Neubert, M.J. (2005). The practices of effective managerial coaches. *Business Horizons, 48*, 493–500.

Marsh, L. (1992). Good manager: Good coach? What is needed for effective coaching? *Industrial and Commercial Training, 24*(9), 3–8.

McLean, G.N., Yang, B., Kuo, M.C., Tolbert, A.S., & Larkin, C. (2005). Development and initial validation of an instrument measuring managerial coaching skill. *Human Resource Development Quarterly, 16*(2), 157–78.

Mink, O.G., Owen, K.Q., & Mink, B.P. (1993). *Developing high-performance people: The art of coaching*. Reading, MA: Addison-Wesley.

Mintzberg, H. (1990). The manager's job: Folklore and fact. *Harvard Business Review,* March–April: 163–73.

Mintzberg, H. (1994). Rounding out the manager's job. *Sloan Management Review, 36*(1), 11–26.

Mobley, S.A. (1999). Judge not: How coaches create healthy organizations. *The Journal for Quality and Participation, 22*(4), 57–60.

Morse, J.J. & Wagner, F.R. (1978). Measuring the process of managerial effectiveness. *Academy of Management Journal, 21*(1), 23–35.

Mumford, A. (1993). *How managers can develop managers* (2nd ed.). Aldershot: Gower.

Noer, D. (2005). Behaviorally based coaching: A cross-cultural case study. *International Journal of Coaching in Organizations, 3*, 14–23.

Noer, D.M., Leupold, C.R. & Valle, M. (2007). An analysis of Saudi Arabian and US managerial coaching behaviors. *Journal of Managerial Issues, 19*(2), 271–87.

Orth, C.D., Wilkinson, H.E. & Benfari, R.C. (1987). The manager's role as coach and mentor. *Organizational Dynamics, 15*(4), 66–74.

Park, S., McLean, G.N. & Yang, B. (2008). Revision and validation of an instrument measuring managerial coaching skills in organizations. In T.J. Chermack, J. Storberg-Walker, & C.M. Graham (Eds), *Proceedings of 2008 Academy of Human Resource Development Conference* (CD-ROM). Panama City Beach, FL, February.

Peterson, D.B. (2006). People are complex and the world is messy: A behavior-based approach to executive coaching. In D.R. Stober & A.M. Grant (Eds), *Evidence based coaching handbook* (pp. 103–27). Hoboken, NJ: John Wiley & Sons.

Peterson, D.B. & Little, B. (2005). Invited reaction: Development and initial validation of an instrument measuring managerial coaching skill. *Human Resource Development Quarterly, 16*(2), 179–83.

Phillips, R. (1994). Coaching for higher performance. *Management Development Review, 7*(5), 19–22.

Phillips, R. (1995). Coaching for higher performance. *Executive Development, 8*(7), 5.

Popper, M. & Lipshitz, R. (1992). Coaching on leadership. *Leadership & Organization Development Journal, 13*(7), 15–18.

Powell, T. & Doran, M. (2003). Managers' perceptions of their role in facilitating employee learning. *Proceedings of 2003 International Academy of Human Resource Development conference,* University of Minnesota, Minneapolis, MN, June.

Redshaw, B. (2000). Do we really understand coaching? How can we make it work better? *Industrial and Commercial Training, 32*(3), 106–8.

Shaw, S. & Knights, J. (2005). Coaching in an SME: An investigation into the impact of a managerial coaching style on employees within a small firm. *Proceedings of the Sixth international conference on HRD research and practice across Europe,* Queens Hotel, Leeds, May.

Talarico, M. (2002). Manager as coach in a pharmacy benefit management organization: A critical incidents analysis. (Unpublished Doctoral dissertation, University of Minnesota at Minneapolis, MN.)

Wang, Y. (2012). R & D employees' innovative behaviors in Taiwan: HRM and managerial coaching as moderators. *Asia Pacific Journal of Human Resources*. DOI: 10.2222/j.1744–7941.2012.00049.x

Williams, H., Edgerton, N., & Palmer, S. (2010). Cognitive behavioural coaching. In E. Cox, T. Bachkirova, & D. Clutterbuck (Eds), *The complete handbook of coaching* (pp.37–53). London: Sage.

Yukl, G. (1989). Managerial leadership: A review of theory and research. *Journal of Management, 15*(2), 251–89.

Yukl, G. (1994 [1981]). *Leadership in organizations* (3rd ed.). Upper Saddle River, NJ: Prentice Hall.

Zemke, R. (1996). The corporate coach. *Training, 33*(12), 24–8.

19

Team Coaching

David Clutterbuck

The instinct to work in teams can be observed widely in social species, from apes to wolves. Through such collaborations, tasks can be accomplished more effectively (although there are significant exceptions) and individual learning rapidly shared with the rest of the team members.

Team coaching in the workplace is a relatively recent concept, although it is well-established within the world of sport. However, as discussed later, the structure, aims, processes and inter-dependencies of sports teams are significantly different from those in the workplace – to the extent that the validity and safety of transfer between the two worlds is low (Keidel, 1987).

Although a Google search indicates that Team Coaching is offered as a service by many training and consultancy organizations, there seems to be little consistency of definition or practice. The situation is not helped by the fact that the evidence-based literature on team coaching is woefully thin. The first substantive attempt to define team coaching was by Hackman and Wageman (2005), who describe it as a direct intervention with a team intended to help members make coordinated and task-appropriate use of their collective resources in accomplishing the team's work. My own definition, based on listening to how team coaches describe their role, is: 'a learning intervention designed to increase collective capability and performance of a group or team, through application of the coaching principles of assisted reflection, analysis and motivation for change'. The contrast in theoretical approach here is between short-term performance orientation and the concept of the team as a learning organism (Marsick, 1994; Clutterbuck, 1996, 2000).

Skiffington and Zeus (2000) present the team coach as someone who facilitates problem-solving and conflict management, monitors team performance and coordinates between the team and a more senior management sponsor. This construct presupposes a very hands-on role for the team coach and a high level of responsibility for team performance, which is absent in both the Hackman/Wageman and Clutterbuck definitions. Similarly, Thornton (2010) defines it as 'coaching a team to achieve a common goal, paying attention to both individual performance and to group collaboration and performance' – placing the emphasis on achieving a solution to a specific problem, rather than on building the team's overall capacity to sustain performance. Hawkins (2011) proposes a systemic perspective, defining systemic team coaching as: 'a process, by which a team coach works with a whole team, both when they are together and when they are apart, in order to help them improve their collective performance and how they work together and also how they develop their collective leadership to more effectively engage with all their key stakeholder groups to jointly transform the wider business'. This definition assumes the context is a leadership team or executive board. However, the systemic perspective has value at all levels of team. Techniques, such as socio-mapping (Bahbouh & Warrenfeltz, 2004; Willis, 2012) help illuminate the mechanics of human interaction within the team. Relationships with other teams and stakeholders above, below and at the same organizational level are also significant issues in team performance and hence valid areas for exploration within team coaching.

There are, therefore, as with coaching itself, several alternative perspectives about the role and function of team coaching. The common factors, however, include:

- an acceptance by the team and the team coach that a coaching approach is appropriate and beneficial
- a focus on performance (though whether this is a cause or effect of learning differs)
- an emphasis on conversations between team members, aimed at making more effective use of collective skills, knowledge and interests.

Proponents of team coaching argue that coaching an individual without attempting to influence the immediate human systems in which they operate reduces the impact of the coaching intervention. Teams develop habitual behaviours and norms, which exert considerable entropic energy to undermine individual and collective change (Valley & Thompson, 1998). An important component of this dynamic is the team's mental model, which becomes rigid and less likely to be challenged as circumstances change.

Like individuals, team effectiveness can also be undermined by quality of thinking. Addressing and improving the quality of thinking, for both individual issues and more broadly, is the core of coaching and this applies equally to individuals and the collective work group (Rogers & Blenko, 2006). In addition, teams have many of the characteristics of organisms. Team personality, which has been widely studied (Van Vianen & de Dreu, 2001; Gustavsson & Baccman, 2005), appears to be a valid but under-explored concept and teams also develop collective norms about issues such as time orientation.

The context of team coaching is significantly different from that of one-to-one coaching. Among the principal differences are:

Confidentiality: even with a high degree of psychological safety, team members may be reluctant to disclose to a group of colleagues, or to admit weaknesses to their boss.

Pace of thinking and deciding: some members of the team may reach a conclusion faster than others. Where the coach in a one-to-one relationship can adjust pace to the speed of the coachee's mental processing, the team coach needs to be able to hold the attention and interest of the vanguard, while ensuring the rearguard are able to catch up at their own pace.

Scope of topic: team coaching can only deal effectively with issues in which all the team members have a stake. Sometimes this involves helping team members recognize the mutual benefits and value of supporting a colleague.

Building trust within the coaching relationship: while team members will vary in the level of trust they place in the coach, progress can normally only be made when the team as a whole is ready to trust both the coach and the process.

Team coaching also differs significantly from team building, team facilitation, process consultancy and other related interventions. Clutterbuck and Hawkins each present different, but broadly consistent rationales for these distinctions in terms of purpose, style, duration of intervention, nature of learning and other characteristics.

DISTINCTIVE FEATURES

Features of team coaching, such as the setting of goals, are dependent on the stage of team development and on the specific characteristics of the team. Although it is common to refer, for example to *the leadership team*, the collective leadership may not be a team at all (Katzenbach, 1998). A group is distinguished from a team in various ways, but some of the most common (Hackman, 1990; Thompson, 2000) are:

- shared goals and purposes
- structured communications
- allocated responsibilities and accountabilities
- a level of interdependence
- willingness of members to place the collective goal above their own priorities
- clear boundaries (who is and is not included)
- operation within a social systems context (i.e. it is part of a larger organization, to whose goals it contributes).

Team coaching is also commonly used at the time of team formation, particularly when a project team is strategically or economically important for the organization. The process of transition through forming, storming, norming, performing and transforming (Tuckman and Jensen, 1977) benefits from some process management and team coaching is claimed to speed up the time it takes to reach the performing stage (Hackman & Wageman, 2005; Jackson & Taylor, 2008). Hackman and Wageman build on the work of Gersick (1988, 1989) to suggest that team coaching interventions should be structured to fit the stages of psychological and process development of the team. What this means in practice is that at the early stages of team formation, team coaching should be focused on clarifying the team task, setting norms of how to work together, defining boundaries and roles and gaining motivational momentum. At the mid-point of the team's development (or of a project assignment), it is ready to reflect on the task and the processes for achieving it. Towards the end of the project's assigned time, team members become open to a review of learning, both individual and collective.

Team coaching may also be remedial, in the sense that a team may need practical assistance in addressing specific issues of performance (e.g. achieving rapid improvements in productivity or customer service) or collective behaviour (e.g. managing conflict). The majority of case studies in Clutterbuck (2007) relate to these two categories, with building a team from a group as a common sub-theme. Wageman, Nine, Burruss and Hackman (2008) maintain strongly that focusing team coaching on interpersonal relations (the core of team building) does not reliably improve team performance, but that team coaching is most effective when focused on motivation (the effort people put in), strategies for performance and increasing the level of skills and knowledge within the team. However, case study evidence tends to suggest that increasing mutual trust and respect does have an impact on performance. A pragmatic perspective, suggested by Clutterbuck (2007), is that behavioural interventions are more likely to improve performance when aimed at specific team processes or objectives.

Where the group already exhibits most or all of the characteristics of a team, the coaching goals tend to relate to specific areas of performance. One way of categorizing these is as:

interpersonal dynamics – issues such as recognizing and managing conflict, increasing collective emotional intelligence and building and sustaining an appropriate coaching climate

temporal issues – for example, how the team balances its emphasis on past, present and future; and time management

managing key processes – goal setting and management, functional analysis, innovation, decision making and communication.

In all of these areas, the core task of the coach goes beyond making the team aware of problems and helping it develop solutions for the present – that is more typically a task for facilitation. Team coaching goes several steps further, helping the team to develop the capacity (skills, knowledge and capability) to manage these issues more effectively on its own.

Role of coach and relationship with clients

Team coaches can operate from four perspectives or relationships with the team. At the simplest level, the team coach is also the team leader – by analogy, the team captain, who is both leading the team and engaging in the collective task. This is a role that involves multiple conflicts. Ferrar (2006) lists a number of barriers to effective line manager coaching, some of which apply equally to individual and collective coaching. These include difficulties in achieving full openness, pressure on the line manager to work to short-term agendas, groupthink and the tendency of managers to adopt parent–child behaviours towards direct reports. Wageman, Nine, Burruss and Hackman (2008), in a recent study of 120 top teams, concluded that the role of line manager as coach is typically less effective than using a coach who is not engaged in the team task.

A second role for the team coach is the equivalent of the touchline manager, who is not part of the play, but can observe, give feedback and bring the team together for reflection. Ferrar's barriers to effectiveness still apply, but the coach is potentially able to apply a wider perspective from not being engaged in the task. Whether this actually happens may depend on how much of their attention is devoted to managing other stakeholders.

A third perspective is equivalent to being in the stands, unable to influence the play in real-time, but able to help the team think strategically about what is its task and the processes it uses to achieve it. Here, Ferrar's barriers become less significant.

Finally, there is an external perspective – the coach, who does not observe the team at all, but who relies on evidence the team itself gathers, either intrinsically or from third parties (for example, through customer surveys). This is qualitatively a very different role, as it involves helping the team to develop and pursue its own learning agenda.

An issue for the team coach in all these perspectives is how to balance collective coaching with additional, individual coaching. The team leader and team manager as coach will need to be careful not to alienate some individuals by being perceived as offering other team members proportionately more coaching (or by offering them too much!) A useful process in this context is the *team development plan* – an amalgam of personal development plans and the business plan. Clarity around individual coaching needs and opportunities for peer coaching are important elements of this working document.

Also important contextually is the nature of the team itself. There are several ways in which teams can be classified. For example, the degree of task interdependence has a significant impact on the type and frequency of communication needed, the nature of relationships within the team and the potential for role conflict. The flow of work within the team provides another method of classification (Ratliff, Beckstead, & Hanke, 1999), from simple teams where everyone does the same task, to relay teams where tasks are different and sequential, through integrative teams where everyone does a different task at the same time (e.g. an operating theatre) and finally problem-solving teams where the process and procedures may be defined as the task progresses.

In a study of how teams learn (Clutterbuck, 2000), I identified six major team types, each of which had different issues in terms of their learning dynamics. These are basically:

Stable teams – where membership and tasks are constant over a long period. Stable teams have advantages in terms of learning (strong learning partnerships can develop) but over time group norms tend to narrow creative thinking and reduce experimentation.

Cabin crew teams – where the task remains the same but membership is constantly changing. Examples include film crews and some aspects of police work. The benefit of having lots of people to learn from may be outweighed by the lack of opportunity to form strong, long-term learning partnerships.

Standing project teams – relatively stable new teams drawn from a variety of other teams and working on usually short-term projects. By the time the team has gone from storming to performing, it has often reached the end of its lifetime, so the learning can easily be lost.

Evolutionary teams – longer-term projects, where the tasks and the membership change over time, with new people taking over as the project moves into new phases. A major problem for learning in this context is failure to educate newcomers in the history of the project.

Developmental alliances – teams set up specifically for learning (for example, action learning sets). An issue here is the relative priority given to membership of this team compared with other, task-focused teams, to which members may belong.

Virtual teams – teams with fuzzy boundaries, or geographically dispersed. Here the learning problem may be creating opportunities for collective reflection.

Whatever method of team classification is chosen (and there are several more), team coaches need to be aware of the functional dynamics of the teams with which they work and adapt their approach accordingly. In many cases, the team itself may not be consciously aware of its functional dynamics, nor of the implications these may have in terms of performance management.

Similarly, the team coach needs to be aware of the extensive spectrum of influences on team performance and team learning. Some of the most significant include:

Diversity – Homogenous teams tend to provide higher levels of customer service, but lower levels of creativity. Heterogeneous (diverse) teams vice versa. According to Early and Mosakowski (2000), mildly diverse teams perform least well, because they tend to fractionate into sub-teams; but highly diverse teams can perform exceptionally well when they spend time developing rules for personal and task communication, shared expectations about roles and performance, norms for conflict management and a sense of common identity. Although they do not specifically make a link with team coaching as a means of achieving these characteristics, it is likely to be much harder without external intervention.

Conflict management – Not all forms of conflict are damaging. While conflict based on emotion and personality tends to undermine team performance, conflict of ideas and approaches can be highly efficacious. The key is for the team to develop language and protocols that recognize conflict at an early stage, steer it towards dialogue around ideas and approaches, and allow for collaborative, no-fault solution-finding (Jehn & Mannix, 2001).

Communication – Communication within the team is critical in maintaining workflow, sharing learning and maintaining social identity. Teams may also adopt any or all of three strategies in communicating to key external audiences: ambassadorial (managing team reputation with top management); task-coordinating (liaising with other teams and stakeholders); and environmental scanning (Ancona & Caldwell, 1992). The effectiveness of these strategies in managing team reputation varies over time.

Based on responses from a survey of team coaching practitioners, Hawkins (2011: 156–166) offers a perspective on the qualities required for an effective team coach. He divides these into general competencies and capabilities, including contracting, rapport-building, use of questioning and facilitation methods and reviewing; systemic capabilities, including understanding systems levels and organizational politics, and linking team coaching with other aspects of organizational change; and capacities, ranging from self-awareness and self-ease, through ethical maturity. At a basic level, most of the competences and capacities would also be expected of a competent one-to-one coach – it is the adaptation to team dynamics and interconnecting systems that differentiates the team coach's role. The range of tools and processes the team coach requires is therefore wide and arguably much wider than for one-to-one coaching.

A central issue in team coaching and essential in contracting is clarity of responsibility. There are typically four major stakeholders in externally resourced team coaching: the team; the team leader/manager; other team members (i.e. apart from the manager); and the sponsor. Many teams are in fact composed of sub-teams, with considerable variation in their willingness and ability to collaborate.

Issues that need to be foreseen and managed include:

- The team leader's behaviour or competence may be one of the primary reasons for poor team performance – hence there is a potential for conflict of loyalty.
- The team and the leader may have different agendas, as may the sponsor.

How team coaching is different

We have already explored how team coaching differs from individual coaching. However, it is often confused with team leading, team building and team facilitation. In each case, there are some overlaps in role, but also considerable distinguishing features. Tables 19.1 and 19.2 illustrate some of these overlaps.

Table 19.1   Differences between team leading and team coaching

Issue	Leader-as-manager	Leader-as-coach
Task Goals	Set goals for and with the team	Help establish processes for setting and reviewing goals
	Develop commitment to the goals	
	Review progress against the goals	Explore alignment between personal, sub-group and team goals
		Help explore the causes of setbacks/progress failures
Learning goals	Establish development needs of each team member Agree PDPs	Help establish processes for integrating individual and team development plans
Visioning	Articulating the team's ambitions internally and to external stakeholders (e.g. higher management)	Testing the quality and viability of the vision and how it influences day-to-day activity
	Contextualizing the vision within the corporate vision	Helping the team articulate the *values* behind its vision
Coordination	Ensuring that everyone understands their roles and responsibilities	Giving feedback on processes and procedures; and on how the human factor affects these
	Reviewing and improving work processes, in consultation with the team	Helping the team question its processes and approaches
	Planning and strategizing	Developing strategy skills
Problem-solving and decision-making	Demonstrating effective decision-making and problem-solving behaviours, by involving team members and achieving consensus	Helping the team improve its problem-solving and decision-making processes

(Continued)

Table 19.1 (Continued)

Issue	Leader-as-manager	Leader-as-coach
Conflict management	Pre-emptive action to identify, discuss and prevent potential conflict	Giving feedback to ensure that conflict is recognized
	Mediating and agreeing rules that will reduce conflict	Improving the team's ability to manage conflict
Communication	Demonstrating effective communication Being available when needed	Helping the team understand the theory and practice of communication
	Creating opportunities for communication to occur	Helping investigate and learn from communication failures
Learning processes	Ensuring the team takes time to reflect and review	Helping the team build the skills and processes of reflective dialogue
Boundary management	Protecting the team from external threats and interference	Helping the team review and improve its boundary management
	Resource acquisition	
Performance management	Clarifying expectations of performance Appraisal	Exploring the influences on performance at both individual and team levels
	Recognizing and rewarding performance	

Reproduced with permission of the publisher and author (Clutterbuck, 2007)

Table 19.2 Team coaching vs. team facilitation

Attribute	Team Coach	Team Facilitator
Use/generation of feedback	Gives or helps team use and also receive feedback	Helps team generate mutual feedback
Engagement	Within the team or engaged with the team	Detached from the team
Learning process	Shares the learning process	Directs/manages the learning process
Action/ monitoring	Intellectual, emotional and practical support through the changes	Process support for the changes
Relationship	Reagent	Catalyst
	Coach acquires learning or change through the process	Facilitator remains largely unchanged
Learning conversation	'Open' dialogue – structure generated from within	'Directed dialogue' – structure emerges from the facilitator's observations
Enablers	Working within team dynamics	Understanding team dynamics
Outcomes	Team and individual achievement	Agreement on team direction and method

Source: reproduced with permission of the publisher and author (Clutterbuck, 2007)

Team coaching is also different from group therapy, although some of the same techniques may be used on occasion. Corey (2004: 4) describes some of the values of group therapy as 'practising new skills … feedback and insights of other members as well as the practitioner … opportunities for modelling'. However, the members of a therapy group have few of the characteristics of a team; the aim of group counselling is to achieve individual improvements, rather than a common goal. A clue to the difference lies in Corey's explanation: 'The role of the group counsellor is to facilitate interaction among the members, help them learn from each other, assist them in establishing *personal* goals, and encourage them to translate their insights into personal plans that involve taking action *outside* of the group' (Corey, 2004, emphasis added). Team coaching, by contrast, emphasizes *collective* goals and action *within* the team.

RELATIONSHIP WITH THEORETICAL TRADITIONS

While team coaching in sport is closely associated with *sports psychology* as a source of evidential and philosophical grounding (Weinberg & Gould, 2007), these do not necessarily provide a basis for understanding team coaching in the workplace. The extent to which sports coaching approaches can be transferred to the workplace is hotly disputed. Katz (2001) points to a number of fundamental differences in context between the two roles:

> Sports coaching is about winning/beating the competition; work teams place greater emphasis on co-operation and collaboration.
>
> Sports coaching involves a great deal of practice for periodic short bursts of exceptional performance; coaching in the workplace is typically about achieving consistent, long-term performance improvements. (Exceptions, where the analogy may work better, include emergency services and the military.)
>
> Coaching is only one of many influences on team performance in the workplace – resource availability, team structure and task design all play an equal or greater role.

According to Keidel (1987), there are three layers of interdependence in sports teams:

1. pooled, where team performance is the sum of individual performances (for example, baseball or cricket)
2. sequential, where team performance relies on a mixture of individual and orchestrated performance (for example, football)
3. reciprocal, where team performance is more than the sum of individuals (for example, basketball).

The equivalent work teams might be: sales, where everyone works independently; assembly manufacture, where work is passed from one to the next; cross-functional task force, where there is continuous involvement by all team members. Using the wrong analogy, or an analogy that fits only partially, can be disruptive to team performance.

Team coaching relates to *performance coaching* in that teams have goals, which must be achieved. Goal clarity is typically seen as at the heart of performance coaching, although Megginson (2007) and Clutterbuck (2008) argue strongly that too narrow a focus of goals is dysfunctional. Like individuals, teams have a variety of potential or real barriers that prevent them achieving their performance potential. These include:

- the tendency towards social loafing (Ringelmann, 1913)
- poor prioritization of goals
- failings in leadership
- collective self-limiting beliefs.

The task of the team coach includes helping the team identify barriers to performance, designing appropriate strategies to overcome those barriers and creating the time and motivation to implement those strategies. It also involves stimulating open dialogue around individual and collective behaviours, which contribute to good and poor performance.

All teams that have been in existence for more than a short period have a history. The members may also import into the team their own history (or baggage) from other teams, either within the organization or outside. Awareness of one's own and others' histories and their impact on collaborative behaviours may be low. Psychodynamic conversations can help the team recognize, accept or challenge, and manage these histories.

Cognitive behavioural approaches are sometimes associated in team coaching with motivational processes by identifying and eliminating behaviours, which are not conducive to achieving collective goals or collaboration, or by embedding new behaviours, which are. A specific application here is the development of coaching and co-coaching behaviours within the team. Because effective coaching is a consensual activity, it requires an attitudinal and behavioural shift on the part of the line manager as coach and on the part of other team members as coachees. (In practice, much of the coaching may also take place between peers within the team.) Agreeing and implementing appropriate feedback systems is integral to this behavioural change process.

However, cognitive behavioural approaches also have a role to play in helping the team develop more rigorous decision-making processes. 'Groupthink' is a constant danger in the team context (Janis, 1972). For teams at the top, the frequency of substantive decisions is also associated with team (and organizational) performance (Mankins & Steele, 2006). Effective decision making requires processes that challenge rationalizations and raise awareness of psychological traps in thinking – for example, our tendency to attach higher significance to events that have strong emotional impact (Hammond, 2006).

Solutions-focused coaching and positive psychology approaches provide an alternative perspective for team coaching methodology. The solutions-focused team coach helps the team extract from its experience the strengths and characteristics of its behaviours and processes when things are going well. S/he uses questions such as:

- What positive moments were there in this gloomy period?
- What happened to make them different?
- What can we learn from these highlights that would help us tackle the issue differently?
- How could you create more of those moments – make them the dominant theme?
- If you had already resolved the problem, what would you and others have done?

The discipline of *family therapy* (Nichols & Schwartz, 1991) may also inform team coaching processes, by focusing attention on the systems within the team and in the team's interactions with the external world. Like the family therapist, the team coach helps the team recognize interaction patterns that might otherwise not have been apparent and helps the team establish new behavioural norms, which may have a positive impact on the entire team system. One of the most obvious applications here is overcoming a problem that team leaders, who have attended behavioural training programmes (for example, in coaching skills), often encounter – the team members may be resistant to the new behaviours, with the result that the leader is rapidly rehabituated to behave as before. Viewing the change as a team change, rather than one of leadership style, and addressing the team from a systemic perspective, can provide a powerful means of ensuring that the intended new leader behaviours stick.

Team coaching can also apply much of the learning relating to *group therapy*. Therapy and coaching generally differ in that the former emphasizes cognitive and behavioural dysfunction and the latter emphasizes building on existing competencies; this broad differential can be observed between group therapy and team coaching. However, many teams do exhibit dysfunctional behaviours, especially in terms of conflict, groupthink, collective avoidance or delusion, resistance to change, defensive behaviour and so on (Corey, Covey, Callanan, & Russell, 1992). Group therapy has well-established processes for managing all of these issues.

In *developmental coaching*, the objective is self-awareness. Collective self-awareness is a more complex concept, which requires an integration of self-knowledge and knowledge about the fears, motivations, ambitions and emotions of other team members. By raising collective awareness – through dialogue and use of mutual feedback – the team coach equips the team to engage in systematic, sustainable change. Team coaching also shares with developmental coaching a focus on assisting transitions between developmental levels or stages. Where developmental coaching incorporates models of individual maturation (e.g. Erikson, 1974; Kegan, 1982), team coaching helps groups achieve transitions in collective maturation. The most common model for this is Tuckman and Jensen's (1965, 1977) forming, storming, norming, performing and adjourning. However, this model appears to relate only to project teams with a finite life, or to the early stages of new teams of other types. There does not seem to be a substantive model relevant to stable teams in their maturity (and possibly, decline).

EVALUATION

The paucity of evidence-based literature on team coaching makes it difficult to conduct a substantive evaluation.

Some observers contest the validity of team coaching as a genre, on the basis that it is no more than facilitation or team development, and that part of the essence of coaching is that it is an individual process. Taking these arguments in turn, we have already discussed a number of salient differences between team coaching and facilitation. The validity of these distinctions is still open to debate. An argument could be made, for example, that there is enough similarity between the two roles to depict a sub-genre of a coaching style of facilitation, or alternatively, a facilitative style of coaching. As to whether coaching can only be an individual process, interesting forms of peer coaching in groups have been described by, among others, McNicoll (2008). Group supervision can also be seen as a well-established analogy of coaching (Hawkins & Smith, 2006).

Team coaching can be highly demanding of the coach since there is the need to manage simultaneously the coaching process and the interactions of team members. It requires considerable skill to avoid common pitfalls, such as:

assuming the team leader's role or responsibilities. An ineffectual leader may abdicate difficult tasks or decisions to the coach

becoming subverted into existing group norms or thinking patterns

creating dependency – the degree of intimacy and frequency of interaction can gradually create conditions where the team looks to the coach to solve its problems. Instead, the team coach should be focusing from the beginning on helping the team learn how to coach itself.

While one-to-one coaching now has broadly accepted codes of ethical practice, the ethics of team coaching, as a relatively new workplace discipline, are much less distinct. Some of the ethical issues that have emerged in workshops include:

- In individual coaching, the well-being of the client normally comes before that of the organization. But how does the coach balance the welfare of an individual versus that of the team as a whole?
- The team has been set very challenging goals, which demand long hours. The coach can see that this is having a negative affect on the home lives and health of some team members. The team say they are prepared to live with these conditions for a period, because the project is high-profile and will be beneficial in terms of their careers. However, the coach suspects that some people are going along with this view because they do not want to let down their colleagues.
- When is it appropriate to advise breaking up a dysfunctional team; and when should we try to fix it through coaching?
- When is it *not* appropriate to take on a team coaching assignment?
- The team leader is manipulative and dishonest towards the team. The coach knows his real intentions, but the team does not.
- It is clear to the coach that there is a serious issue, which the team is avoiding; (for example, dysfunctional behaviour of a key member who has unique knowledge or special client relationships). The team leader has warned the coach against addressing this issue, but s/he knows the team cannot make real progress without dealing with it.

The answers to these dilemmas are not always straightforward, especially given that there are multiple stakeholders involved in a team coaching assignment.

The nature, context, content and skills base for team coaching are still evolving and it is difficult to predict what standards will eventually emerge. There is an urgent need for empirical research to determine the roles and boundaries of team coaching, the minimal competencies and experience required to be effective in the role and good practice in such areas as contracting, process management and evaluation. Team coaching may be the newest kid on the coaching block, but it is growing up fast!

FURTHER READING

The most comprehensive and approachable analysis of team dynamics is Leigh Thompson's *Making the team* (Prentice Hall, 2000). Wageman et al. (Harvard Business School, 2008) built on Gersick's (*Academy of Management Journal*, 1988) evidential analysis to draw conclusions about the timing of coaching interventions. There are now three books covering the specific topic area of team coaching: Clutterbuck (2007), Thornton (2010) and Hawkins (2011), all referenced below.

DISCUSSION QUESTIONS

- Currently, team coaching as described in this chapter is focused mainly on senior leadership teams or high-risk project teams. What would be the value of offering team coaching to a much wider spectrum of teams at different levels? What would need to happen to bring this about?
- Different definitions of team coaching emphasize either achieving specific and immediate performance goals, or building longer-term sustainable capacity. Are these definitions compatible, or do they describe two discrete approaches?
- Hawkins (2011: 169–182) discusses briefly the requirement for supervision for team coaches. In what ways might supervision for team coaches differ from supervision for coaches working in a one-to-one context?

REFERENCES

Ancona, D.G. & Caldwell, D.F. (1992). Bridging the boundary: External activity and performance in organizational teams. *Administrative Science Quarterly, 37*: 634–65.

Bahbouh, R. & Warrenfeltz, R. (2004). *The Application of Sociomapping to Executive Team Development,* www.hoga nassessment.com/hoganweb/documents/ApplicationOfSociomapping.pdf.

Clutterbuck, D. (1996). Developing learning teams. *Training Officer*, July/August.

Clutterbuck, D. (2000). *Learning teams report.* St Albans: Exemplas.

Clutterbuck, D. (2007). *Coaching the team at work.* London: Nicholas Brealey.

Clutterbuck, D. (2008). Are you a goal junkie? *Training Journal*, May: 43–6.

Corey, G. (2004). *Theory and practice of group counselling* (pp. 4–5). Florence, KY: Thomson Brooks/Cole.

Corey, G., Corey, M.S., Callanan, P., & Russell, J.M. (1992). *Group techniques.* Pacific Grove, CA: Brooks/Cole.

Early, P.C. & Mosakowski, E. (2000). Creating hybrid team cultures: An empirical test of transnational team functioning. *Academy of Management Journal, 11*: 231–41.

Erikson, E.H. (1974). *Dimensions of a new identity.* New York: Norton.

Ferrar, P. (2006). The paradox of manager as coach: Does being a manager inhibit effective coaching? (Unpublished Masters dissertation, Oxford Brookes University, Oxford.)

Gersick, C. (1988). Time and transition in work teams: Toward a new model of group development. *Academy of Management Journal, 31*: 9–41.

Gersick, C. (1989). Marking time: Predictable transitions in task groups. *Academy of Management Journal, 32*(2): 274–309.

Gustavsson, B. & Baccman, C. (2005). Team-personality: How to use relevant instruments to predict team performance. *Paper presented at the 47th annual conference of the International Military Testing Association*, Singapore, November.

Hackman, J.R. (1990). *Groups that work (and those that don't): Creating the high performance organization.* London, HarperBusiness.

Hackman, J.R. & Wageman, R. (2005). A theory of team coaching. *Academy of Management Review, 30*(2): 269–87.

Hammond, J. (2006). The hidden traps in decision-making. *Harvard Business Review*, January: 118–26.

Hawkins, P. (2011) *Leadership team coaching.* Kogan Page, London

Hawkins, P. & Smith, N. (2006). *Coaching, mentoring and organizational consultancy.* Maidenhead: McGraw-Hill.

Jackson, K. & Taylor, I. (2008). *The power of difference: Exploring the value and brilliance of diversity in teams.* London: Management Books 2000.

Janis, I.L. (1972). *Victims of groupthink.* Boston, MA: Houghton Miffin.

Jehn, K.A. & Mannix, E.A. (2001). The dynamic nature of conflict: A longitudinal study of intragroup conflict and group performance. *Academy of Management Journal, 44*(2): 238–51.

Katz, N. (2001). Sports teams as a model for workplace teams: Lessons and liabilities. *Academy of Management Executive, 15*(3): 56–7.

Katzenbach, J.R. (1998). *Teams at the top.* Boston, MA: Harvard Business School Press.

Kegan, R. (1982). *The evolving self: Problem and process in human development.* London: Harvard University Press.

Keidel, R. (1987). Team sports as a generic organizational framework. *Human Relations, 40*: 591–612.

McNicoll, A. (2008). Learning at the leading edge. *Paper presented at the bi-annual conference of the New Zealand Association of Training and Development*, Auckland, May.

Mankins, M. & Steele, R. (2006). Stop making plans: Start making decisions. *Harvard Business Review, June:* 76–84.

Marsick, V. (1994). Trends in managerial reinvention: creating a learning map. *Management Learning*, 25(1): 11–33.

Megginson, D. (2007). An own-goal for coaches. *Paper presented to the European Mentoring and Coaching Council UK annual conference*, Ashridge Business School, April.

Nichols, M.P. & Schwartz, R.C. (1991). *Family therapy: Concepts and methods.* Upper Saddle River, NJ: Allyn and Bacon.

Ratliff, R., Beckstead, S.M., & Hanke, S.H. (1999). The use and management of teams: A how-to guide. *Quality Progress, June,* 31–38.

Ringelmann, M. (1913). *Aménagement des fumeurs et des purins.* Paris: Librarie Agricole de la Maison Rusique.

Rogers, P. & Blenko, M. (2006). Who has the D? How clear decision roles enhance organizational performance. *Harvard Business Review, January*: 53–61.

Skiffington, S. & Zeus, P. (2000). *The complete guide to coaching at work.* New York: McGraw-Hill.

Thompson, L. (2000). *Making the team: A guide for managers.* Upper Saddle River, NJ: Prentice Hall.

Thornton, C (2010). *Group and Team Coaching.* London: Routledge.

Tuckman, B.W. (1965). Developmental sequence in small groups. *Psychological Bulletin, 63*: 384–99.

Tuckman, B.W. & Jensen, M. (1977). Stages of small group development revisited. *Group and Organizational Studies*, 2: 419–27.

Valley, K. & Thompson, T.A. (1998). Sticky ties and bad attitudes: Relational and individual bases of resistance to changes in organizational structure. In M.A. Neale & R. Kramer (Eds), *Power and influence in organizations.* Thousand Oaks, CA: Sage Publications.

Van Vianen, A.E. and de Dreu, C.K. (2001). Personality in teams: Its relationship to social cohesion, cohesion and team performance. *European Journal of Work & Organizational Psychology, 10*(2): 97–120.

Wageman, R., Nine, D., Burruss, J., & Hackman, R. (2008). *Senior leadership teams: What it takes to make them great.* Boston, MA: Harvard Business School Press.

Weinberg, R.S. & Gould, D. (2007). *Foundations of sport and exercise psychology.* Champaign, IL: Human Kinetics.

Willis, P (2012) Sociomapping in Mars 500. *Paper to British Psychological Society, Department of Occupational Psychology. Annual conference*, January 11–13.

20

Peer Coaching

Richard Ladyshewsky

Peer coaching is a process involving a coach and a coachee, with relatively equal status, focusing on expanding, refining and building new skills and competencies in training and workplace situations. The peers normally have similar training or background preparation which enhances mutual support.

Peer coaching was developed extensively in the early 1980s as part of teacher development, where much of the earlier literature can be found (Ackland, 1991; Joyce & Showers, 1982; Showers, 1984; Skinner & Welch, 1996). It was seen as an effective strategy for classroom teachers to get non-evaluative feedback from a peer teacher regarding curriculum implementation and teaching effectiveness. Both teachers and health professionals have used this approach as a support strategy to improve professional practice (Ladyshewsky, 2004; Sekerka & Chao, 2003; Skinner & Welch, 1996; Waddell & Dunn, 2005; Wynn & Kromrey, 1999). In the business or organizational context, the approach has been used to build skills, to support people in leadership and management development programmes and to promote transfer of training (Ladyshewsky, 2007, 2012; Ladyshewsky & Ryan, 2006; Peters, 1996).

This chapter provides an overview of peer coaching starting off with an introduction to the context of peer coaching. This is followed by a discussion of the distinctive features of peer coaching along with a conceptual model for this developmental strategy. Lastly, theoretical perspectives that underpin peer coaching are described. Examples are offered throughout to illustrate this genre in practice. Peer coaching can be applied to a wide range of peer groups, of any age and in many sectors, but for the purposes of this chapter, the focus is on its use in the training environment and workplace.

THE CONTEXT OF PEER COACHING

A key goal of a peer coaching relationship is to provide the coachee with a development experience that is built around trust and confidentiality. This experience is typically driven by the coachee, who recognizes a development need and seeks the support of a peer coach. The coaching is most often used to help the coachee achieve a specific set of skills that lead to competency, although the potential to assist in other areas, such as accelerated academic achievement, is also a possibility, depending on the skill of the coach.

The efficiency and effectiveness of this coaching genre is enhanced when participants are given initial training in coaching skills, contracting and reflective journaling. Ongoing support to participants in the form of a peer coaching orientation also promotes ongoing success.

While peer coaching can occur naturally, failure to formalize the process and train participants may impact on rapport-building, development of trust, confidentiality, status and power and final learning outcomes. Training ensures that the important features of equality and mutuality in the relationship are maintained (Damon, 1984; Damon & Phelps, 1989). Equality in the relationship is critical if self-disclosure is to be encouraged. This self-disclosure leads to a sense of mutuality or connectedness in the relationship. This in turn promotes deeper conversations about development, practice and learning which are necessary for gaining the insights needed for escalating skill development and knowledge acquisition.

Ideally, the coachee, in consultation with the coach, works collaboratively to create a development plan (Knowles, Holton, & Swanson, 1998) that specifies the goal to be achieved along with the resources and strategies that will be employed. Strategies for evaluating progress are also included in the plan along with key performance indicators that measure success. The collaborative creation of a development plan, driven largely by the coachee's needs, ensures that the plan is owned by the coachee. It maps out the accountability of the parties involved and assists the coach and coachee to maintain focus during their sessions. Often, the arrangement is reciprocal, with each party alternating between the role of coach and coachee. This is often referred to as 'reciprocal peer coaching' and each coachee would have a specific development plan (Ladyshewsky, 2002).

The task of the coach is to create a trust-filled open space for self-disclosure whereby the coachee can explore development needs in an experiential manner (Kolb, 1984). This goal is accomplished through regular meetings with the coachee whereby the coach uses open-ended and probing questions that encourage the coachee to explore his or her thinking and action, generate new conclusions and apply the learning to future experiences. The goal of the coaching is to remain objective and non-evaluative in order for the coachee to make self-discoveries that progress development, learning and skill.

Peer coaching is a laterally directed learning strategy in which individuals seek support from those whom they see as equals. This is different from a vertically directed learning strategy whereby a supervisor, for example, coaches the subordinate. This vertical strategy can be referred to as the 'manager as coach' and is fraught with status–solidarity issues and evaluation, which impact on equality and mutuality (Ladyshewsky, 2010a). This is absent or minimal when peers coach each other because of the equality in status and power.

Tasks that enhance peer coaching are the use of reflective journals (Kerka, 1996; Ladyshewsky, 2007). Reflective journaling requires the coachee to review their practice as part of their skill development. The coachee reviews these reflections so that they can bring them to the coaching session. The coach, through the use of open-ended and probing questions, assists the coachee to see patterns in their reflections and reviews. The coachee then gains greater insights into the knowledge, skills and attitudes that influence their progress.

DISTINCTIVE FEATURES

D'Abate, Eddy and Tannenbaum (2003) conducted a comprehensive review of developmental interactions such as coaching, mentoring and tutoring, and were able to map specific features of these interventions. They classified these interactions into five areas: participant demographics; interaction characteristics; organizational distance/direction; purpose of the interaction; and degree of structure. Their research reveals a significant amount of inconsistency and overlap between peer coaching and other developmental interactions.

The defining features of peer coaching which manifest consistently in the literature are: a lateral organizational direction to the relationship; a focus on specific objectives; feedback as a central part of the development experience; and observation of practice (D'Abate et al., 2003). This observation can be direct or indirect. Other dimensions of the relationship which appear throughout the literature, but to a lesser extent, are interaction characteristics which have bi-directional benefit and a focus on short-term performance. Behaviours in peer coaching are directed towards achieving learning goals. Behaviours are highly collaborative, with mutual problem-solving focused on achieving developmental outcomes. Further, aiding and befriending are also consistent behaviours which are designed to provide emotional support in the process (D'Abate et al., 2003).

As noted earlier, the peer coaching relationship develops in response to an identified learning need in the coachee. Hence, engagement in the relationship is often a voluntary one; although more structured programmes can be implemented into the workplace or training environment. The coachee sees value in a strategic learning partnership and the process of building a supportive relationship begins.

One model of peer coaching, although very clinically focused, is described as having five stages: forecasting; training with demonstration of new practice behaviours; opportunities for practice; non-evaluative feedback; questioning and self-assessment (Waddell & Dunn, 2005). Jewett and Macphee (2012) describe a peer coaching programme embedded into a graduate literary course for teachers. This programme followed a structured model, with participants selecting coaches and undergoing three cycles of coaching. The programme used observation, videotape and reflective journaling to promote skill development.

An eight stage model that outlines the features, processes and roles in a peer coaching relationship has also been described (Ladyshewsky & Varey, 2005). These eight stages were conceptualized by comparing and contrasting different types of coaching relationships. They were then modified specifically to create and sustain the dynamics needed for a successful relationship by trialing them in practice. Each step in this eight stage model is directed towards achieving the specific and necessary outcomes essential to the overall success of the development interaction. Failure to fulfil each stage of the process is likely to lead to negative consequences in the relationship. These factors are explained more fully in Table 20.1.

Table 20.1 Eight stage peer coaching model

Step	Description	Objective of each stage (desired outcome)	Impact of stage if not executed properly
1	Assessment & Trust Building	Peers assess each other for personal compatibility and suitability of partnership.	Trust and understanding are not built into the relationship, mutuality and equality suffers and relationship fails.
2	Planning	Timing and place for peer coaching sessions are established. Commitment is made to a structured process.	If sessions are cancelled, inconvenient, inappropriately timed or consistently interrupted – sessions may be seen as unproductive and motivation to participate declines.
3	Formalizing Process & Scope	The coachee's particular needs and the scope of the sessions are determined, based on priority of interests and available time.	If the coachee's needs do not drive the process and scope – actions will not be relevant. Commitment wanes.
4	Defining Purpose & Goals	Coach explores with the coachee potential learning objective(s). Goals and objectives are further defined.	Unless both parties gain this understanding only symptomatic surface level solutions are discovered and main goals will not be achieved.
5	Clarifying Facts & Assumptions	Coach asks the coachee to separate assumptions from facts and offers non-evaluative feedback and perspectives to assist in gaining objective clarity.	If the coachee is not challenged, they may not develop self-awareness and insights into how to progress development.
6	Exploring Possibilities	Conversations move from correctly identifying the issue, event or dilemma to developing possibilities for solutions. The coachee finds their own path out of the learning development plan assisted by the coach who creates space for exploration of different scenarios. This creates commitment to the action.	If the range of solutions are not constructed by the coachee, they are disempowered and become dependent on the coach. Lack of exploration creates the risk of partial solutions being implemented due to lack of meta-cognitive reflection. Risk of constraints emerging, which block progress, due to lack of exploration.
7	Gaining Commitment to Actions	Conversation moves to creating verbal commitment to identified actions with clear outcomes.	If actions are vague they are difficult to act on with confidence and the assessment of directly attributable outcomes is difficult – reducing further reflection and learning.
8	Offering Support and Accountability	Coach offers follow-up support with genuine interest in coachee's results. Follow up is structured by the coach to assist in motivation, learning support and ongoing trust building.	Without authentic support in the relationship, follow up is seen purely as accountability. Relationship becomes strained and trust declines and is likely to stop with only one or two cycles.

There are other specific features and processes of the peer coaching relationship which get less attention in the literature (D'Abate et al., 2003). The duration of the interaction can vary, depending on the needs of the coachee. For the most part, however, the literature suggests that the relationship is generally of a shorter term, as it is focused typically on developing a skill, after which the relationship ends. The schedule of meetings is typically regular, as this keeps the coachee engaged, motivated and supported during the change process.

Trust, confidentiality and matching

Trust and confidentiality are important cornerstones of a successful peer coaching interaction. Given that the relationship is housed within a training or workplace environment, the coach is often, but not exclusively, selected from within that sector. Hence, issues of trust and confidentiality are magnified. Coachees may approach coaches because of previous experiences of working together, or through recognition of skill sets useful for their development. Coaches should be external to any line management or direct report relationship to ensure relationships are status and power neutral and therefore equal and open to mutual discourse. Otherwise, the relationship is no longer 'peer' based. These matching issues are important considerations for a successful engagement.

Formality

An element of formality to the peer coaching process is also helpful as it facilitates the achievement of outcomes by ensuring the coach and coachee stay focused on previously agreed goals. Formality involves having a regular meeting schedule, ensuring dialogue is focused on learning goals and the development plan, incorporating information from the learning journal and keeping discussions non-evaluative through the use of open-ended and probing questions. It is critical that time is provided within the work and training environment for the coaching to take place.

This formality keeps the ownership and direction of the process conceptually in the hands of the coachee, even if the interaction has been suggested by the coachee's manager as a development strategy through the performance management process. The formality maps out an agreed upon process, the accountability of coach and coachee as well as others in the plan, such as the manager, the Human Resources professional or other experts. Issues of confidentiality, disclosure and trust become more central to the contracting process along with the scope and nature of the development plan. Having these mapped out in advance ensures the experience is focused on learning and development.

Non-evaluative feedback

Given that coaching is typically established to work on a development need or skill deficiency, some assessment of performance growth is needed. This assessment or feedback can be formal or informal, and is aligned to the goals and key performance indicators in the development plan. The coachee needs this information to pace their learning and to map their progress. The role of the coach is to encourage the coachee, through the provision of 'non-evaluative' feedback on progress, to assist in confidence building, motivation and self-efficacy.

The coach must also be very sensitive to the feedback that is offered to the coachee, especially in the early part of the relationship. In order to preserve the equality and mutuality of the relationship, feedback should be non-evaluative (Showers, 1984). If feedback starts to become evaluative, then the status–solidarity dimension (Baker, Jensen, & Kolb, 2005) between the coach and coachee changes and equality disappears. This is because the coach has shifted role from peer coach to peer reviewer. This change in role, which often occurs insidiously without the coach realizing it, may strain the relationship. When evaluation enters the relationship, the coachee is less likely to self-disclose and the mutuality of the relationship suffers because underlying expectations of how the relationship is supposed to work become violated. Luft and Ingham (1955) describe changes in interpersonal interactions when these are influenced by issues such as evaluation or power.

The coach can ensure that feedback is non-evaluative by using open-ended and probing questions. This type of questioning helps the coachee to reflect deeply on their experiences and skills – a critical component of experiential learning (Kolb, 1984) and deep learning (Boud, 1993; Marton & Saljo, 1976). Who, what, where and how questions are particularly useful as they help the coachee explore and self-evaluate their skills and performance (Zeus & Skiffington, 2002). For example, in helping a coachee to develop conflict management experience following a negative experience where they lost their temper in a group, a peer coach may ask, 'who do you think you could call upon in the group to help diffuse tension?'; 'what evidence do you have to support your claim that they don't like you?'; 'where could you implement changes in the meeting structure to manage conflict?' 'Why' questions, in contrast, push the coachee towards having to justify action, which may strain the relationship. Using the same example, if the coach asks, 'why did you lose your temper in that meeting?' the coachee may become defensive.

Other important communication skills needed by the coach include active listening skills, the ability to use verbal and non-verbal communication strategically and also employ emotional intelligence (Goleman, 1995; Merlevede, Bridoux, & Vandamme, 2001).

Termination of the relationship occurs when the objectives of the development plan have been achieved or learning has reached a plateau and the parties agree to disband. This does not preclude the peers from coming together once again if a new development need arises, or the old plan needs revisiting.

Peer coaching is distinct, yet symbiotic, with other forms of coaching such as: skills and performance coaching (SPC); executive and leadership coaching; and the 'manager as coach' models. It is often used synonymously with mentoring but is, in fact, quite distinct.

Skills and performance coaching

Peer coaching is focused largely on developing skills and performance as a result of the insights gained from collaboration with one another. It is a short-term initiative driven by specific goals and development plans. On this level, it is very similar to skills and performance coaching (SPC), where improving ability is the focus. However, the coach, in SPC, usually has greater expertise and competence and is commissioned to help the coachee. This greater expertise is important in some forms of SPC (Sue-Chan & Latham, 2004), as the coach is seen to be more credible. The loss of the 'peer' element, however, increases the likelihood of coachee movement into the 'hidden or private' window (Luft & Ingham, 1955) and the concomitant reduction in self-disclosure.

Executive and leadership coaching

Executive and leadership coaching can also be peer based, with the coach being internal or external to the training environment or workplace. This coaching engagement may be commissioned by the executive/leader as part of their development, be aligned to a leadership development programme, or assigned by superiors as a strategy to 'smooth out rusty edges' in an otherwise promising leader. When one gets to executive ranks, however, the availability of peer coaches within the organization is limited. Those that are available are often competing for the same position(s) one level above and are therefore not appropriate for peer coaching. The co-operative element that peers are able to use to build the learning partnership is difficult to achieve in this instance. Instead, the relationships are often competitive. Peer coaches for these executives need to be sought externally.

Mentoring

Mentoring and coaching are often used interchangeably in the literature. Some authors do not see a difference at all (Sperry, 1996) whereas others see definitive distinctions (Chao, 1999; Waddell & Dunn, 2005). Structured mentoring programmes in organizations are more often downward in orientation and often internal to the organization. Further, the object of development is often general or holistic and long term. The matching process is also quite formal and guided by the formality of the programme (D'Abate et al., 2003). The mentor is also in a higher status position, given their experience, age and seniority. This influences the solidarity between the parties (Baker et al., 2005) by the understanding that the mentor has a large role to play in driving the direction of the relationship. This same structure can also be seen in informal mentoring relationships that emerge serendipitously. These informal mentoring relationships are still downward in orientation, long term, and focused on holistic or general issues. Peer coaching is clearly based on equality, which has a differential impact on the status–solidarity relationship. As noted earlier, peer coaching is also more aligned to specific skill development, is of short-term duration and driven by specific goals, which from the description above, is distinct from mentoring.

RELATIONSHIP WITH THEORETICAL TRADITIONS

Peer coaching can be linked to the following theoretical traditions: solution-focused coaching; person-centred coaching; and cognitive behavioural approaches to coaching. The extent to which the coach is able to apply these theoretical approaches to the developmental interaction depends on the coach's knowledge and ability to practise within these theoretical frameworks.

Solution-focused approach

Given that peer coaching is directed towards achieving a specific skill or improving performance, guided by a goal and development plan, its forward development nature parallels the solution-focused approach to coaching (Greene & Grant, 2003). Solution-focused coaches encourage the coachee to focus on desired future states and then help them to discover how they might achieve these using skills they already possess (de Shazer, 2005).

The peer coach within the solution-focused approach would support the coachee in defining goals and exploring strengths that they already possess which might be used to reach these goals. By focusing on solutions and goals, rather than on problems, energy can be directed towards achieving targets, rather than trying to fix problems. This creates attention density (Rock & Schwartz, 2006) and strengthens learning pathways in the brain that facilitate learning. Goal setting theory (Locke, 1996), like solution-focused coaching, is geared towards helping the coachee focus on the outcomes they are seeking. Within this genre, the coach must help the coachee to frame the goals and tasks in a way that they can embrace and take ownership of them. For example, in solution-focused coaching, a coachee who is frustrated with conflict in the workplace would be assisted by a peer coach to explore their strengths in managing conflict. These strengths would be harnessed to assist the coachee in developing a preferred conflict-free workplace; rather than focusing on the problems causing the conflict, solutions that remedy the situation receive energy.

Person-centred approach

The person-centred approach to coaching, sometimes referred to the humanistic approach, flows from the work of Carl Rogers and focuses on helping the individual to develop their potential as a human being (Carlopio, Andrewartha, & Armstrong, 2005). Abraham Maslow, another proponent of the humanistic approach, referred to this as self-actualization (Carlopio et al., 2005).

A peer coach who embraces this humanistic philosophy would assist the coachee by using a development interaction to first understand the human experience of the coachee. Through this understanding, the coach could then support the coachee to examine their unique context, to develop further self-awareness in the coachee and to help the coachee seek choices that have meaning and value. For example, a peer coach may assist a coachee to discover how work events relate to life experience. Through this understanding, the coachee may gain insights into their behaviour and how this might link to workplace behaviour.

Cognitive behavioural approach

The cognitive behavioural approach to coaching is focused on helping the coachee become aware of thought processes, often contradictory or sabotaging, which have a negative impact on behaviour and skills achievement. Most behaviours have cognitive underpinnings (Urdan & Midgley, 2001) and in order to regulate behaviour more effectively, individuals need to consider the combination of the environment, thoughts, feelings and behaviours (Grant, 2001). Being able to self-regulate emotion and cognition in combination with training programmes that include coaching has demonstrated significant long-term gains in performance (Grant, 2001).

The peer coach's role in this theoretical approach is to assist the coachee to examine thoughts, feelings and behaviours in a range of situations. Hopefully, the coachee gains new insights into how these factors link into their thinking and how this drives behaviour. Through these insights, the coachee can begin to manage the change process towards skill acquisition by managing the thought processes that block growth and development. Using a conflict management example, a peer coach may help a coachee to see how their thoughts about situations are lacking real evidence. This may free the coachee to move forward, realizing that fears or beliefs that they have held about conflict are inaccurate.

Learning theory approach

Peer coaching is particularly aligned to theories of learning that see co-operation among peers as an essential prerequisite for cognitive growth. The intellectual disagreements that occur during these discussions create conceptual conflicts that motivate individuals to seek out new information (Johnson & Johnson, 1978; Johnson, Johnson, & Smith, 1998; Johnson, Maruyama, Johnson, Nelson, & Skon, 1981). Most of the literature supporting peer assisted learning appears to fall within this theoretical dimension. Peers are a compelling source of conflict because they speak on levels which can be easily understood by one another (Damon, 1984; Foot & Howe, 1998). Further, the informal communication between peers is less threatening; hence, there is potential for deeper engagement in the learning experience.

Transfer of learning is also facilitated by a socio-cognitive learning approach and is paralleled by the discussions about training and application to work that take place during peer coaching. Vygotsky (1978, 1986) reports that peers benefit from one another by internalizing the cognitive processes implicit in their interactions and communications. The peer dialogue that results emulates several critical features of rational thinking, in particular: the verification of ideas; the planning of strategies; the symbolic representation of intellectual acts; and the generation of new solutions. Vygotsky argues that social and cognitive interaction with a more capable peer allows a slightly less capable peer to enter new areas of potential. For example, the coach and coachee could be engaged in a debate about the roles and responsibilities of a manager to mediate conflict. The engagement of the two parties in this discussion, directed by the coachee's desire to improve their conflict management skills, may shift the coachee's perspective towards a more positive perspective.

These theoretical perspectives can all be applied within peer coaching (Jewett & MacPhee, 2012). The application depends in part on the goals and objectives of the coachee, and the ability of the peer coach to work within the theoretical paradigm. In leadership development, the application of all of these theoretical perspectives would be important. First, a solution-focused approach would challenge the coachee to visualize themselves as an effective leader and work towards that vision. In order to move towards this goal, a person-centred approach would be important to consider the human experience of the leader and how this is influencing their development. A cognitive behavioural approach would assist the leader in understanding thought processes that may have developed from their experience, which are limiting performance. Lastly, a learning theory approach would be applied to challenge the leader's thinking in order for them to consider other perspectives defining their actions.

EVALUATION

Through an evaluation of the tradition of peer coaching, it becomes apparent that this model is an excellent learning strategy for the development of skills and to enhance performance. This stems from the fact that individuals at comparable points in their professional development often make similar information-processing errors. Hence, partnerships where individuals are at the same level can be of great assistance because both individuals see and experience their learning challenges in similar ways. For individuals at a novice level (Oldmeadow, 1996), problem-solving typically involves the use of a backward or deductive reasoning process to sort through hypotheses (Patel & Kaufman, 1995). For example, a novice physical therapist may have to explore six different hypotheses to arrive eventually at a decision about a client's physical diagnosis. This problem-solving process is quite different from ones used by those who are more advanced in their skills base (Oldmeadow, 1996). Individuals at this expert level use a forward or inductive reasoning process by applying previous knowledge frameworks (Patel & Kaufman, 1995). For example, a senior physical therapist may recognize very early in the interaction that a client has a specific shoulder problem they have seen many times before. The strategies to manage this client are very clear because they fit the clinician's pattern of experience. Hence, the value of peer coaching for individuals who are at similar developmental levels (Ladyshewsky, 2010b) is supported by information-processing theory.

Limitations related to peer coaching largely relate to the skills base of the coach in building the relationship, maintaining confidentiality, building trust, keeping the dialogue non-evaluative and applying the correct practice within a theoretical framework (e.g. solution focus). The ability to embed experiential learning principles into the coaching experience is also an important aspect that ensures a successful learning experience. Reflective questioning, theory building and re-application of experience must be modelled in the coaching framework. The ability to build development plans around goals also influences success. Hence, the strength of this intervention rests on how well prepared are participants and how well the organization supports this learning strategy within the training or developmental process.

Strengths of the peer coaching model are its ability to promote deep reflection (Jewett & MacPhee, 2012), to build understanding and application of knowledge, theory and skills in a non-threatening and non-evaluative manner. Peer support is a strong psychological factor in promoting and maintaining goal activity. A further strength of the approach is that it can be implemented at relatively low-cost for an organization. As a result, it can be an effective organizational learning strategy that can be used to build learning within an organization, increase transfer of training (Baldwin & Ford, 1988) following training and development initiatives, and facilitate positive returns on training investments.

Peer coaching, while sharing many features of other forms of coaching, achieves its unique outcomes through the nature of the partnership which is based on equality and mutuality. This fosters self-disclosure and engagement in the learning process. The importance of keeping the relationship equal, by having clear developmental plans in place and keeping feedback non-evaluative, preserves the relationship and the benefits that ensue. Peer coaching can operate within several of the theoretical traditions provided the coach has the skill and understanding to practise within these frameworks. It is an excellent organizational learning tool.

FURTHER READING

Ladyshewsky, R. (2012). Chapter 9: The role of peers in feedback processes. In Boud, D. and Molly, E. (Eds), *Effective feedback in higher education: Understanding it and doing it well.* Milton Park: Informa UK Ltd. (This chapter explains theoretical and practical principles of establishing peer feedback systems in academic and work integrated learning settings. A range of examples are provided, for example, a hospital-based work integrated learning placement and a business leadership course. Paired and group peer feedback systems are described.)

Jewett, P. & MacPhee, D. (2012). A dialogic conception of learning: A collaborative peer coaching model. *International Journal of Mentoring and Coaching in Education, 1*(1): 12–23. (This paper describes the theoretical principles behind a peer coaching programme designed for teachers in a postgraduate literacy course. The paper offers a robust description of an embedded peer coaching programme within a university course and would be helpful to those considering building peer coaching programmes in to their academic courses.)

Ladyshewsky, R. (2010b). Building competency in the novice allied health professional through peer coaching. *Journal of Allied Health, (39)*2: e75–e80. (This paper looks at novice practitioners and outlines how they can use peer coaching to build their competency. Whilst using health care as the background, the principles are extendable to any profession. Theoretical principles behind problem-solving and reasoning are outlined and linked to a description of a peer coaching programme. The challenges that peers may face in this structured learning process are detailed along with information on the role of the supervisor.)

DISCUSSION QUESTIONS

- What cultural practices would you need to address in your work and training environment in order to implement a peer coaching strategy. For example, are participants willing to expose learning needs? Would the time spent in learning concern those whose focus is productivity?
- To what extent does the need to appear competent and capable in the eyes of peers interfere with the ability to engage in a peer coaching relationship? How does vulnerability factor into the coaching relationship?
- Where could you make a first step in establishing a peer coaching relationship or programme in your work or training environment? Consider what you might need to do in order to make it successful.

REFERENCES

Ackland, R. (1991). A review of the peer coaching literature. *Journal of Staff Development, 12*(1): 22–6.

Baker, A., Jensen, P., & Kolb, D. (2005). Conversation as experiential learning. *Management Learning, 36*(4): 411–27.

Baldwin, T. & Ford, J. (1988). Transfer of training: A review and directions for future research. *Personnel Psychology, 41*(1): 63–105.

Boud, D. (1993). Experience as the base for learning. *Higher Education Research and Development, 12*(1): 33–44.

Carlopio, J. Andrewartha, G., & Armstrong, H. (2005). *Developing management skills* (3rd ed.). French's Forest, NSW: Pearson Australia Group.

Chao, R. (1999). Invited reaction: Challenging research in mentoring. *Human Resource Development Quarterly, 9*(4): 334–8.

D'Abate, C., Eddy, E., & Tannenbaum, S. (2003). What's in a name? A literature-based approach to understanding mentoring, coaching, and other constructs that describe developmental interactions. *Human Resource Development Review, 2*(4): 360–84.

Damon, W. (1984). Peer education: The untapped potential. *Journal of Applied Developmental Psychology, 5:* 331–43.

Damon, W. & Phelps, E. (1989). Critical distinctions among three approaches to peer education. *International Journal of Educational Research, 13*: 9–19.

de Shazer, S. (2005). *More than miracles: The state of the art of solution-focused therapy*. Binghamton, NY: Hawthorn Press.

Foot, H. & Howe, C. (1998). The psychoeducational basis of peer assisted learning. In K. Topping & S. Ehly (Eds), *Peer assisted learning* (pp. 27–43). London: Lawrence Erlbaum and Associates.

Goleman, D. (1995). *Emotional intelligence*. New York: Bantam Books.

Grant, A.M. (2001). Coaching for enhanced performance: Comparing cognitive and behavioural approaches to coaching. *Paper presented at the 3rd International Spearman Seminar -Extending intelligence: Enhancement and new constructs*, Sydney. Retrieved 10 November 2008 from www.psych.usyd.edu.au/coach/CBT_BT_CT_Spearman_Conf_Paper.pdf.

Greene, J. & Grant, A. (2003). *Solution-focused coaching: A manager's guide to getting the best from people*. London: Pearson. education.

Jewett, P., & MacPhee, D. (2012). A dialogic conception of learning: A collaborative peer coaching model. *International Journal of Mentoring and Coaching in Education, 1*(1):12–23.

Johnson, D. & Johnson, R. (1978). Cooperative, competitive, and individualistic learning. *Journal of Research and Development in Education, 12*(1): 3–15.

Johnson, D., Johnson, R., & Smith, K. (1998). Cooperative learning returns to college: What evidence is there that it works? *Change, 30*(4): 27–35.

Johnson, D., Maruyama, G., Johnson, R., Nelson, D., & Skon, L. (1981). Effects of cooperative, competitive, and individualistic goal structures on achievement: A meta-analysis. *Psychological Bulletin, 89*(1): 47–62.

Joyce, B. & Showers, B. (1982). The coaching of teaching. *Educational Leadership, 40*(1): 4–8.

Kerka, S. (1996). *Journal writing and adult learning* (Report No. EDO-CE- 96–174). (ERIC Document Reproduction Service No. ED399413). Washington, DC: Office of Educational Research and Improvement.

Knowles, M., Holton, E., & Swanson, R. (1998). *The adult learner* (5th ed.). Woburn, MA: Butterworth-Heinemann.

Kolb, D. (1984). *Experiential learning*. Englewood Cliffs, NJ: Prentice Hall.

Ladyshewsky, R. (2002). A Quasi-experimental study of the differences in performance and clinical reasoning using individual learning versus reciprocal peer coaching. *Physiotherapy Theory and Practice, 18*(1):17–31.

Ladyshewsky, R. (2004). The impact of peer coaching on the clinical reasoning of the novice practitioner. *Physiotherapy Canada, 56*(1): 15–25.

Ladyshewsky, R. & Varey, W. (2005). Peer coaching: A practical model to support constructivist learning methods in the development of managerial competency. In M. Cavanagh, A. Grant & T. Kemp (Eds), *Evidence-based coaching:* Vol. 1: *Theory, research and practice in the behavioural sciences* (pp. 171–82). Bowen Hills, QLD: Australian Academic Press.

Ladyshewsky, R. & Ryan, J. (2006). Peer coaching and reflective practice in authentic business contexts: A strategy to enhance competency in post-graduate business students. In A. Herrington & J. Herrington (Eds), *Authentic learning environments in higher education* (pp. 61–75). Hershey, PA: Idea Group Publishing.

Ladyshewsky, R. (2007). A strategic approach for integrating theory to practice in leadership development. *Leadership & Organization Development Journal, 28*(5): 426–43.

Ladyshewsky, R. (2010a). The manager as coach as a driver of organizational development. *Leadership and Organizational Development Journal, 31*(4): 292–306.

Ladyshewsky R. (2010b). Building competency in the novice allied health professional through peer coaching. *Journal of Allied Health, (39)*:2;e-75–e-80.

Ladyshewsky, R. & Flavell, H. (2012). Transfer of training in an academic leadership development program for program coordinators. *Educational Management Administration and Leadership, 40*(1): 127–147.

Locke, E. (1996). Motivation through conscious goal setting. *Applied and Preventive Psychology, 5*: 117–24.

Luft, J. & Ingham, H. (1955). *The Johari window: A graphic model for interpersonal relations*. Los Angeles, CA: University of California Western Training Laboratory.

Marton, F. & Saljo, R. (1976). On qualitative differences in learning. I. Outcome and process. *British Journal of Educational Psychology, 46*: 4–11.

Merlevede, P., Bridoux, D., & Vandamme, R. (2001). *Seven steps to emotional intelligence*. Carmarthen: Crown House.

Oldmeadow, L. (1996). Developing clinical competence: A mastery pathway. *Australian Physiotherapy Journal, 42*(1): 37–44.

Patel, V. & Kaufman, D. (1995). Clinical reasoning and biomedical knowledge: Implications for teaching. In J. Higgs & M. Jones (Eds), *Clinical reasoning and the health professions* (pp. 117–28). Oxford: Butterworth-Heinemann.

Peters, H. (1996). Peer coaching for executives. *Training and Development Journal, 50*(3): 39.

Rock, D. & Schwartz, J. (2006). *The neuroscience of leadership*. Retrieved May 2006 from www.strategy-business.com/article/06207.

Sekerka, L. & Chao, J. (2003). Peer coaching as a technique to foster professional development in clinical ambulatory settings. *Journal of Continuing Education in the Health Professions, 23*(1): 30–7.

Showers, B. (1984). *Peer coaching: A strategy for facilitating transfer of training*. Eugene, OR: Oregon University Center for Educational Policy and Management.

Skinner, M. & Welch, T. (1996). Peer coaching for better teaching. *College Teaching, 44*(4): 153–6.

Sperry, L. (1996). Executive consulting, psychotherapy, and coaching. In L. Sperry (Ed.), *Corporate therapy and consulting*. Philadelphia, PA: Brunner/Mazel.

Sue-Chan, C. & Latham, G. (2004). The relative effectiveness of external, peer and self-coaches. *Applied Psychology: An International Review, 53*(2): 260–78.

Topping, K. & Ehly, S. (Eds) (1998). *Peer assisted learning*. London: Lawrence Erlbaum and Associates.

Urdan, T. & Midgley, C. (2001). Academic self-handicapping: What we know, what more there is to learn. *Educational Psychology Review, 13*(2): 115–38.

Vygotsky, L. (1978). *Mind in society*. Cambridge, MA: MIT Press.

Vygotsky, L. (1986). *Thought and language*. Cambridge, MA: MIT Press.

Waddell, D. & Dunn, N. (2005). Peer coaching: The next step in staff development. *Journal of Continuing Education in Nursing, 36*(2): 84–9.

Wynn, M. & Kromrey, J. (1999). Paired peer placement with peer coaching: In early field experiences: Results of a four-year study. *Teacher Education Quarterly, 26*(1): 21–38.

Zeus, P. & Skiffington, S. (2002). *The coaching at work tool kit*. Roseville, NSW: McGraw-Hill.

21

Life Coaching

Anthony Grant and Michael Cavanagh

One way to develop an understanding of life coaching is to contrast it with counselling and mentoring, and executive and workplace coaching. Counselling tends to focus on helping people regain functionality in their lives, whereas mentoring involves one person with expertise in a specific area helping another in making significant transitions in knowledge, work or thinking (Megginson & Clutterbuck, 1995). Executive coaching focuses on helping clients who have managerial responsibility in organizations to achieve goals that improve their professional performance, and consequently the effectiveness of the client's organization (Kilburg, 2000). Executive coaching is typically (but not always) paid for by the organization. Workplace coaching takes place in work settings with non-executive employees. It may include on-the-job coaching by line managers and supervisors, aimed at improving productivity and developing an individual worker's skill.

In contrast to the above, life coaching typically tends to focus on goals that fall within the personal sphere rather than the work or employment sphere. In brief, the overarching aim of life coaching is sustained cognitive, emotional and behavioural changes that facilitate goal attainment and the enhancement of well-being in one's life (Douglas & McCauley, 1999).

Life coaching takes a personal values-based, holistic approach to personal change and development: the coachee spends time examining and evaluating his or her life, and then systematically makes life-enhancing changes with the support of a coach. Key issues often focus on work–life balance, dealing with stress, managing finances, enhancing relationships and generally developing a more fulfilling and purposeful life. Some life coaches have specialities, such as a focus on helping people work through major life transitions or developing new career directions; others focus on helping people develop a clear sense of purpose and life direction; others may work with specific at-risk clients groups helping those clients develop life-skills or overcoming certain challenges. Life coaches tend to provide a service to individual clients, rather than to commercial business organizations.

THE HUMAN POTENTIAL MOVEMENT AND LIFE COACHING

Life coaching appears to have its roots in humanistic traditions of psychology (e.g. Maslow, 1954) and the practices of the Human Potential Movement (HPM) (for a detailed discussion, see Spence, 2007). One of the key influences was the Erhard Seminars Training (EST programmes) developed by Werner Erhard (Kirsch & Glass, 1977). These were marketed as personal transformation and could be considered as drawing on the same social impetus that later gave rise to life coaching. Indeed, one of the early pioneers of commercial life-coach training, Thomas Leonard, drew heavily on these approaches in the life-coach training offered by his company, Coach U.

Parallel with the growth of HPM and the life-coaching genre, psychologists were also drawing on validated clinical and counselling psychology and offering life-coaching services. As far back as Filippi (1968) and Ponzo (1977) there have been discussions in the psychology literature about the need for counsellors to act as life-skills coaches. Albert Ellis (e.g. Ellis & Harper, 1961), one of the founders of the cognitive behavioural approach, frequently prefigures, although he did not use the term in his work. Similarly, commentators such as Thompson (1980) predicted that by the year 2000 psychologists would have increased their emphasis on life quality enhancement as opposed to remedial therapy.

Despite these early trends, psychology as an academic discipline and a helping profession tended to be associated, at least in the public's mind, with mental illness and the treatment of distress, rather than the promotion of well-being. Psychology did not truly engage with until the early pioneers of commercial life coaching in the US, such as Thomas Leonard, had raised the profile of life coaching and life-coach training during the late 1980s and early 1990s. However, at this time life coaching was still viewed by many as being faddish, theoretically incoherent, New Age and more of a network marketing opportunity than a solid theoretically-grounded helping modality.

However, as public interest in life coaching has developed there has been a significant shift towards a theoretically-grounded and empirically-validated approach to life coaching. Some of the drivers of this include interest from researchers and academics in the use of life coaching as a methodology for developing understanding of the processes underpinning human change and development (Grant, 2003); greater sophistication in the consumers of coaching services (both clients and trainee coaches) (Jarvis, 2003); and the increasing involvement of psychologists who offer life-coach training courses. In addition, a number of universities worldwide now offer postgraduate degrees in coaching.

The literature on life coaching also reflects this shift, with increasing numbers of life-coaching books being published that are explicitly grounded in evidence-based methodologies (e.g. Grant & Greene, 2001; Neenan & Dryden, 2002; Dunbar, 2010; Dryden, 2011). This trend toward a more professional approach is also reflected in the fact that professional bodies such as the Psychological Societies of Australia, Britain, Denmark, Ireland, South Africa and others have established groups focused on coaching.

Emergence of evidence-based approaches

An evidence-based approach to life coaching can be distinguished from approaches to coaching that are based on ad hoc adaptations of 'pop-psychology' or personal development programmes. Adapted from its use in medical settings, the term 'evidence-based coaching' refers to the intelligent and conscientious use of best current knowledge in making decisions about how to deliver coaching to coaching clients, and in designing and teaching coach training programmes (Sackett, Haynes, Guyatt, & Tugwell, 1996). Best current knowledge is up-to-date, empirically valid and conceptually coherent, from relevant areas such as behavioural science, adult education, business and philosophy.

Evidence-based approaches to life coaching came to the fore with the establishment of peer-reviewed coaching-specific journals such as the *International Journal of Evidence-based Coaching and Mentoring* (2003), the *International Coaching Psychology Review* (2006) and *Coaching: An International Journal of Theory, Research and Practice* (2008). Indeed, the total number of peer-reviewed coaching-specific publications has increased dramatically. However, despite these recent developments and the increased flow of coaching-related research, research specifically into life coaching is surprisingly scarce. A literature search of the peer-reviewed literature, as presented in the data base PsycINFO in August 2008, using the key words 'life coaching', found a total of 59 citations. The majority of these were reviews of books on life coaching, or editorials or details of book chapters which were about life coaching. There was a total of only 23 peer-reviewed papers on life coaching.

However, this is not a completely stagnant field. The same literature search conducted in January 2013 found a total of 128 citations. An important development in the literature on life coaching, and one that has implications for the broader coaching industry, is the fact that there are an increasing number of citations documenting the use of life coaching in with a wide range of health, medical or social problems. For example, life coaching has been used to help individuals make lifestyle adjustments in order to help them deal better with issues such as aphasia (Worrall et al., 2010), and diabetes (Newnham-Kanas, Morrow, & Irwin, 2011; Schneider et al., 2011), and with middle aged and older men in service club settings in remote areas such as Western Australia, in order to help them reduce body mass index, increase physical activity and change their dietary habits (Aoun, Osseiran-Moisson, Shahid, Howat, & O'Connor, 2012). Exploratory studies have also looked at the effectiveness of using holistic life coaching for breast cancer survivors (Shearsmith, 2011), and life coaching has even been used with individuals with severe mental illness in Japan to help improve their quality of life (Yoshida, Ito, & Ogawa, 2011).

This emerging body of research suggests that life coaching may be moving out of the personal development genre and starting to become integrated into broader health enhancement programmes. This is a most welcome development, as the empirical literature, such as it is, suggests that life coaching has the potential to be a useful adjunct to established medical and health delivery services,

Although the literature on life coaching is developing, there is still not yet a coherent body of work in this area. The fact that there is relatively little research means that there is little solid empirical data to guide the conscientious professional life coach. Consequently, in order to design and deliver solid life-coaching services, the professional life coach needs to be well-versed in identifying relevant knowledge from related areas such as counselling psychology, positive psychology, theories of adult learning and human development. Thus the scholar practitioner model may be a useful professional framework for life coaching. The scholar practitioner knows how to access, evaluate and adapt information in order to best meet the needs of their client. Such a stance towards professional practice requires constructive self-reflection (McGonagill, 2002) and an explicit articulation and examination of the assumptions, methods and techniques used in life-coaching practice.

DISTINCTIVE FEATURES

Understandings of life coaching vary in the extent to which they focus on personal development compared to the achievement of performance targets. Approaches fall on a continuum between facilitation of self-directed learning at one end and the sort of direct instruction found in sport coaching or educational tutoring at the other. Most approaches to life coaching fall in between these two ends of the continuum. The role of the life coach is seen as to conduct coaching conversations in which the coach asks direct, personal and often challenging questions that help the coachee focus on clarifying and exploring ways to achieve their goals. In the life-coaching relationship, the coach primarily plays the role of a facilitator of change; it is the client's responsibility to enact change (Whitworth, Kimsey-House, & Sandahl, 1998).

Underlying the practice of life coaching are the assumptions that:

People have considerable latent potential.

Significant human change is possible.

The client is resourceful (although they may not be aware of such resources).

There is an absence of serious mental health problems in the life-coaching client.

Life coaching is not focused on repairing psychopathologies.

Life coaching is an inherently goal-focused process.

Change can happen in a short period of time.

The client is willing to do the work of change.

Much life coaching takes place over the telephone. Indeed, some life coaches never meet their clients face-to-face. There has been some controversy over whether face-to-face or phone coaching is more effective, although some of this debate appears to have been fuelled by a need to promote specific proprietary coach training systems that use face-to-face coaching methodologies (see Corbett, 2006). In fact there is a growing body of evidence from the mental health area that phone coaching can be effective (Evans, Morgan, Hayward, & Gunnel, 1999) and it has been shown that peer coaching by phone can be very effective in enhancing professional skills in the workplace (Gattellari, Donnelly, Taylor, Meerkin, Hirst, & Ward, 2005). Recent research in the area of executive coaching suggests that there may be little difference in outcomes realted to the quality of the working alliance or in problem resolution, thus offering tentative evidence that distance coaching may be as effective as face-to-face coaching (Berry, Ashby, Gnilka, & Matheny, 2011). Indeed its exponents argue that phone coaching, when conducted properly, is very time efficient and facilitates a direct, honest and intimate relationship in which the absence of physical cues actually enhances rapport through the need for in-depth listening (Hymer, 1984). However, clearly further research is needed here.

The internal structuring of life-coaching sessions, whether by phone or face-to-face, is another key area in need of further research. There is evidence that highly structured interventions may be very effective. For example, Howard, Kopta, Krause and Orlinsky (1986) found that the frequency of counselling sessions was not related to client improvements, rather the structure and intensity of sessions were the key important factors. Furthermore, there is good evidence that effective change requires scaffolding. Scaffolding is a strategy that involves supporting novice learners by making the initial learning context quite simple and this is done by initially limiting the complexities of the context and gradually removing those as learners gain the knowledge, skills and confidence to cope with the full complexity of learning target (Young, 1993). At the same time, an over-structured approach to life coaching may be alienating for some clients, particularly where the coach's relationship building skills are not sophisticated or where the coach is not able to tailor his/her approach to suit the needs of the individual client.

Individual approaches to life coaching will vary depending on factors such as the coach's training, theoretical approach, personal preferences and personality, and client needs and expectations. However, the degree to which life coaches adopt a systematic structured approach to coaching is unclear. What is clear is that many of the proprietary commercial life-coach training programmes place great emphasis on structure. This is because highly structured, systemized life-coaching programmes that emphasize technique and methodology are easier to teach to potential life coaches than programmes that require broad understanding of theoretical principles and empirical evidence. The 'seven steps to your ideal life' approach is easier to understand than programmes that teach from theory into practice. Thus a highly structured, systemized approach is well-suited to the teleclass teaching and the highly heterogonous student populations that are frequently found in commercial life-coach training programmes (Grant & O'Hara, 2006).

Contracting and payment issues

The great majority of problems that might emerge in life coaching can be circumvented by having clear, detailed and explicit up-front contracting. Contracting is a core process in life coaching and is used to make explicit the nature of the coaching relationship, the expectations and responsibilities of all parties, including costs, confidentiality issues, legal disclaimers and payment procedures and cancellation fees. A life-coaching contracting agreement typically also includes a mental health/illness disclosure clause along the lines of 'coaching is not therapy and does not aim to treat psychological problems. The client agrees to disclose full details of past or present psychological or psychiatric treatment. If such issues become salient during the coaching relationship the coach may recommend referral to an appropriate and qualified specialist.' Written contracting can also be an effective way of enhancing commitment to the change process (see, for example, Leung, 1974; Neale, Singleton, Dupuis, & Hess, 1990).

Life-coaching clients are often asked to pay for their coaching service in advance and this requirement may also be part of the written coaching agreement (Leshinsky, 2007). However, the issue of advance payment for coaching services is somewhat controversial. It is often justified to clients by claiming that it enhances commitment to the coaching process. But emphasis on advance payment may be distasteful for some life-coaching clients, giving the impression that the life coach is more interested in running a smooth, coach focused business operation than focusing on client needs. Interestingly, executive coaching services, which are perceived as being more professional than life-coaching services, are typically paid for following delivery.

A key difference between life coaching and executive or workplace coaching is that the life-coaching client is typically paying for the coaching service themselves, and this can impact on the dynamics of the coach–client relationship. Where in executive coaching the coaching engagement is frequently overseen by an internal sponsor such as a Human Resources or learning and development professional, in life-coaching the coachee is the paying client and there is no third party involved. This means that life coaching may be at greater risk of derailment, and life-coaching clients should always check to see if their life coach has a supervisor or mentor coach who oversees their life-coaching practice.

Goal setting in life coaching

Little research has focused on the process of goal setting in life coaching, but anecdotal evidence suggests that the completion of some type of structured life inventory is often used as a precursor to goal setting in this context. These inventories can range from idiosyncratic 'ideal life' checklists to the use of scientifically validated inventories such as the Quality of Life Inventory (QOLI) (Frisch, 1994). Inventories such as the QOLI are well-suited for goal setting in life coaching because of their clear non-pathological orientation and their emphasis on strengths as well as problems. The QOLI assesses life satisfaction in 16 domains of life including health, home, money, work, relationships and play and can be used as an outcome measure to assess the effectiveness of the coaching intervention.

The number of goals set in life coaching will vary. Some life coaches suggest that clients focus on only one or two goals, others encourage clients to set more and address whole of life issues (Williams & Davis, 2002). Often, life coaching clients will be encouraged to complete a written pre-prepared form detailing their goals, and possibly writing down the costs and benefits of goal attainment.

On the other hand, some life-coaching programmes pay little attention to the quality of the goal identification process itself. Rather, the main focus of attention is placed on developing motivation to change, designing action plans, overcoming barriers to change and supporting the client in making these changes. While these are important facets of coaching, they are dependent on the quality of the goal. Motivation will pall and the best action plan will ultimately fail to deliver what the coachee is looking for if the goal is inappropriate.

Many life-coach training organizations teach relatively simplistic approaches to goal setting; for example, goal setting approaches that stop at the notion of 'SMART' goals (specific and stretching, measurable, achievable, realistic and time-framed). While there is good evidence that goals that meet these criteria can be effective (Locke, 1996), other dimensions of goals are also important. For example, goals should be self-concordant. That is, they should align with the client's personal values (see Sheldon, 2001). Similarly, locus of control and whether goals are approach goals or avoidance goals have a major impact on satisfaction and well-being. Some life-coaching programmes do indeed place great emphasis on the explicit articulation of the client's values in the goal setting process. However, it is equally important that sufficient time be given to discussing the goals under consideration, rather than rushing to set a goal and quickly moving on to action: the 'rush to closure' can lead to derailment later in the coaching process.

Monitoring and evaluation between sessions

Good-quality life-coaching interventions place significant emphasis on pre-session preparation and the monitoring and evaluation of between-session action steps (sometimes called fieldwork or homework). Life-coaching clients are often asked to complete a pre-session form in which they detail their progress to date, how they have been feeling since the last session and what they want to get out of the upcoming session. Although such forms may appear simplistic, such pre-session work may help the client move from a contemplative to deliberative or action-focused mind-set (Gollwitzer, 1999) and such mind-set shifts can significantly impact on client engagement and goal attainment.

Following the life-coaching session, many coaches ask their clients to complete a post-session self-evaluation form detailing the specific action steps to be completed before the next session, and asking the client to reflect on any insights or learnings that may have arisen in the coaching session. Such reflective practices are fundamental to creating purposeful change (Argyris, 2002) and are part of the self-regulation cycle of goal setting, action planning, acting, monitoring, evaluating and change that essentially underpins all forms of purposeful human change (Carver & Scheier, 1998).

A significant part of the life coach's role involves keeping the client on track for success. This is not always easy. Many people come to life coaching with the desire to create change. Fewer stay self-motivated as the work of change becomes real and difficult. For most people purposeful change is not easy. If it were easy then there would be no need for coaches or other professional change agents. Some life coaches request an email from the client each time the client completes one of the between-session action tasks. It can be helpful in maintaining motivation for the client to have to report their progress to the coach between coaching sessions. However, in their quest to help the client achieve their goals, novice or unskilled life coaches may seek too much between-session contact with the client and this may result in fostering dependency on the coach, a reduction in the client's sense of control and autonomy, or simply creating too much for the client to do, leading to feelings of overwhelm. In these cases goals set in coaching can begin to feel like gaols.

Ending the coaching relationship

Even with clear up-front contracting about the coaching relationship, the termination phase of the life-coaching relationship, as in therapy and mentoring, can be a difficult process for both coach and client (for a detailed empirical analysis of relationship endings, see Clutterbuck & Lane, 2004). Where the coaching relationship has not been great, both parties may avoid discussing issues related to the termination of the coaching. In this situation at best there may be a brief 'thanks for your help, I'll be in touch' comment. Even worse, the client, feeling resentful and somewhat aggrieved, may simply keep cancelling meetings and let the coaching relationship drift away.

Where the coaching relationship has been good, both parties may avoid the question of whether the coaching engagement has reached a natural end-point and may seek to continue coaching beyond its usefulness. It is natural to feel sadness when an important relationship is coming to an end – such close relationships have typically been formed based on discussion of personal and often emotionally-laden material (Cavanagh & Grant, 2004). However, it is important for both coach and client to recognize that coaching is ultimately a professional relationship, not a personal one. The coach's role is to prepare the client for the termination phase from the beginning of the coaching engagement. After all, one key aim of coaching is that the client becomes their own coach!

Ideally the initial life-coaching contract should detail how the coaching relationship will be reviewed and terminated. Many coaching contracts state a set period of time, or a fixed number of sessions following which the coaching will be reviewed and a decision made to continue or not. The temptation for the inexperienced life coach may be to press for continuation in the pursuit of building their coaching business. The temptation for the client in this situation may be to avoid a discussion about the termination process and carry on with the coaching in order not to upset the coach. The danger in this is that the client may come to feel that coaching (and the coach) is not serving their needs and at worst, come to resent the time and costs coaching places on them. Clearly this is an unsatisfactory outcome for both coach and coachee.

Given that coaching relationships per se can arouse significant emotions for both the coach and the client (Cox & Bachkirova, 2007), the professional coach has a responsibility to proactively manage the termination process. It is important to recognize that the coaching relationship is a multifaceted one with at least three sub-themes: (i) a valued relationship, (ii) trust and (iii) transparency (Gyllensten & Palmer, 2007). Termination should therefore be dealt with in a way that is transparent, builds trust and recognizes the value of the past relationship.

Termination of a life-coaching engagement may be brought about not only by a pre-agreed timeframe. It may happen quite organically. It should be recognized by the coach that the dynamics of the relationship will change significantly over time. When the client first starts coaching, and intimacy between the coach and client is relatively low, the coach's energy and enthusiasm may be high and delivering tangible benefits may be at the forefront of the coach's mind in each session. As the relationship develops, greater intimacy between coach and client may lead to less focus on tangible benefits. In short, the coaching sessions become less about goal attainment and more like supportive counselling, or even friends having a nice chat. When this starts to happen, it may be a sign that the coaching relationship has run a natural course, irrespective of any predetermined timeframe. The coach needs to address this issue by holding an open and frank review session in which the client has the opportunity to talk about the coaching and then set new goals, make purposeful and specific changes in how the coaching is conducted, or take a break from coaching for a while.

Controversial points in life coaching: coach or couch?

Although the relationship between life coaching and counselling is complex, one key difference between life coaching and therapeutic counselling or psychotherapy is that therapeutic counselling and psychotherapy mainly focus on helping people recover from psychological distresses, and life coaching is not focused on addressing this. Rather, life coaching is about fine-tuning one's life.

The reason for emphasizing the distinction between the therapeutic foci of counselling and the aim of life coaching is because most lifecoaches are not trained, registered or licenced as mental health professionals (Bachkirova, 2007; Grant & Zackon, 2004). Clearly, the public is at risk when life coaches who are untrained in mental health interventions attempt to treat psychological problems such as depression, acute anxiety, substance abuse or major relationship difficulties, or because they do not recognize or take into account the nature of the vulnerabilities of people with mental health problems (Cavanagh, 2005).

This is not to say that life coaches cannot coach people who are suffering from such problems. There is emerging research suggesting that coaching in conjunction with medical interventions can be very successful. Indeed, a well-trained life coach who works in conjunction with a trained (mental) health professional may be able to significantly speed the client's recovery. Edelman et al. (2006) describe how a whole-person approach to treating and minimizing cardiovascular risk factors which used health coaches alongside medical practitioners was successful in terms of increased exercise, weight loss and decreased risk of coronary heart disease.

The key issue here is that coaches should know the limits of their expertise and they should work with appropriately trained professionals in designing interventions with the client.

However, the boundaries between a life-coaching relationship and a counselling or psycho-therapeutic relationship are not clearly defined. The conversation can easily turn from coaching to counselling. Given that it has been found that between 25% and 50% of people seeking life coaching have clinically significant levels of psychopathology (Green et al., 2006; Spence & Grant, 2007), it may well be that some clients are using life coaching as de facto forms of therapy. Thus, life coaches have an unequivocal duty of care to ensure that they can recognize the limits of their competencies and make appropriate referrals (Cavanagh and Buckley, Chapter 28, this volume; Spence, Cavanagh, & Grant, 2006). As there is increasing interest in using life-coaching methodologies with at-risk or vulnerable populations, a more ethically-grounded approach to the use of life coaching with at-risk populations or with individuals with major physical or mental health problems is for health professionals themselves to become trained in life-coaching methodologies (Anderson, Williams, & Kramer, 2012; Passmore, 2009), and this may be the main way in which the life-coaching genre will develop over the coming years.

RELATIONSHIP WITH THEORETICAL TRADITIONS

Such assumptions suggest that professional life coaching has very clear links to at least four established theoretical traditions. First, life coaching tends to make explicit the relationships between thinking, feelings, behavioural and the external situation or environment, echoing the central aspects of cognitive behavioural approaches. Second, life coaching is solution-focused, focusing on goals rather than the past, and assumes that the client has resources, strengths and abilities hereto unrecognized. Third, life coaching draws very heavily on humanistic values central to the person-centred tradition. Finally, life coaching is increasingly aligned with positive psychology, with its emphasis on understanding the nature of the life well-lived and the use of a grounded systematic approach to achieving that life.

The notion that most people have latent potential dates back to Aristotle and can be followed through to Maslow (1968) and more recently into the Positive Psychology movement (Ryff & Singer, 2008). Indeed, there is substantial empirical evidence that people have considerable latent potential which can be brought to the fore in many areas of life, including sports, human performance broadly defined, education, business and mental health (for in-depth analysis, see Druckman & Bjork, 1991). Further, solution-focused approaches to human change, which explicitly operationalize the assumption that people have unacknowledged resources, have been found to be effective ways of helping people in a wide range of settings (Kim, 2008; Stams, Dekovic, Buist, & de Vries, 2006).

However, the a priori assumption that clients who present for life coaching do not have clinically significant levels of mental health problems may not be justified. Green, Oades and Grant (2006) surveyed a total of 107 potential life-coaching clients from a community sample and found that 52% had clinically elevated scores (a score of two standard deviations above the mean) on the Brief Symptom Inventory (BSI) (Derogatis & Melisaratos, 1983). The BSI is a frequently used and well-validated screening tool that is designed to be used with both clinical and non-clinical populations. Spence and Grant (2007) found that 25% of 84 participants in life coaching had clinically elevated BSI scores. These findings suggest that some individuals who seek life coaching may have higher than average levels of psychopathology, and these findings clearly do not support the assumption that there is an absence of serious mental health problems in life-coaching clients. These findings have important implications and challenges for the ethical practice of life coaching and more research is needed in this area.

EVALUATION

However, from the perspective of practice, the lack of clear training guidelines, industry regulation and rigorous accreditation still represent real risks to the emerging profession of life coaching. At present there are no barriers to entry in life coaching. Anyone, with or without training, can offer life-coaching services. It is this lack of standards that has led to the variability in quality of service offered by life coaches and in turn led to its poor reputation even within the wider coaching industry.

There is a further challenge that faces life coaching that is perhaps more worrying than the quality of service issues that arise with under-trained coaches. A basic tenet of all professional codes of ethics is the requirement that professionals know the limits of their expertise and operate within those limits. There are within the wider life-coaching industry individuals who are offering coaching services aimed at addressing serious difficulties for which they have no training or qualification beyond their own assertion of expertise. For example, untrained individuals are offering coaching for such conditions as ADHD (Attention Deficit Hyperactivity Disorder), anorexia or relationship difficulties, and so the previously-noted shift towards trained professionals using life-coaching methodologies with such populations is a welcome emerging trend.

In the area of practice development, the grounding of practice in theoretically coherent and evidenced-based models is the major challenge facing life coaching. For the industry to develop into a recognized area of professional practice, the development of a research-based body of knowledge is essential. This raises a further challenge for life coaching – namely moving from an individual proprietary approach to practice towards a community of practice approach. To date the coaching industry has tended strongly toward basing practice on commercially owned proprietary models of coaching – many claiming to be the most or even only effective coaching model available. For coaching to progress beyond a proprietary product model of service to a genuine profession, there needs to be greater openness to having one's models of practice held up to rigorous peer-reviewed evaluation. More importantly, the widespread sharing of this research for the information and development of industry-wide practice is a key element in the creation of a profession of life coaching. This is a significant challenge to the way the life-coaching industry appears to be organized at the moment.

Evidence-based life coaching conducted by properly trained coaches who work within a scholar–practitioner model has terrific potential to contribute to the well-being of individual clients and communities. In effect, evidence-based life coaching conducted by well-trained practitioners has the potential to offer a much needed service in our society, where people can take time to review their life directions, take stock, explore new life options, develop new directions and get support in creating purposeful change and enhancing their well-being.

An evidence-based approach to life coaching has great potential as a means of facilitating positive change. Yet life coaching is frequently undervalued as a human change methodology. Greater status appears to go to executive, business or workplace coaching. There is something of false distinction in this. Drawing strong boundaries between life coaching and other forms of coaching neglects the commonalities of practice among them. At present, there are few encouragements for practising life coaches to develop a stronger research and knowledge base. However, this is a challenge to the industry – to step into the power of its own change methodology – both in terms of practice development, and demonstration of the efficacy and value of that practice. Perhaps the last word on the relative value of life coaching compared to other applications of coaching should go to Dr Patrick Williams (Williams & Davis, 2002): 'No matter what's on your business card, if you're coaching a breathing client, you're life coaching because they have a life.'

FURTHER READING

Grant, A.M. & Greene, J. (2004). *Coach yourself: Make real change in your life* (2nd ed.). London: Momentum Press.
Neenan, M. & Dryden, W. (2002). *Life coaching: A cognitive-behavioural approach*. New York: Brunner-Routledge.
Whitworth, L., Kimsey-House, H., & Sandahl, P. (1998). *Co-active coaching: New skills for coaching people towards success in work and life*. Palo Alto, CA: Davies-Black.
Williams, P. & Menendez, D.S. (2007). *Becoming a professional life coach: Lessons from the institute for life coach training*. New York: Norton & Co.

DISCUSSION QUESTIONS

- What are differences (if any) between life coaching and counselling?
- Should life coaches receive training in mental health issues, and if so, what are the implications of that training?
- What role (if any) can life coaching play in physical and mental health rehabilitation?

REFERENCES

Anderson, S.K., Williams, P., & Kramer, A.L. (2012). Life and executive coaching: Some ethical issues for consideration. *APA handbook of ethics in psychology, Vol 2: Practice, teaching, and research* (pp. 169–181). Washington, DC: American Psychological Association; US.
Aoun, S., Osseiran-Moisson, R., Shahid, S., Howat, P., & O'Connor, M. (2012). Telephone lifestyle coaching: Is it feasible as a behavioural change intervention for men? *Journal of Health Psychology, 17*(2): 227–36.
Argyris, C. (2002). Double-loop learning, teaching and research. *Academy of Management Learning and Education, 1*(2): 206–18.
Bachkirova, T. (2007). Role of coaching psychology in defining boundaries between counselling and coaching. In S. Palmer & A. Whybrow (Eds), *Handbook of coaching psychology* (pp. 325–50). London: Routledge.

Berry, R.M., Ashby, J.S., Gnilka, P.B., & Matheny, K.B. (2011). A comparison of face-to-face and distance coaching practices: Coaches' perceptions of the role of the working alliance in problem resolution. *Consulting Psychology Journal: Practice and Research, 63*(4): 243–53.

Carver, C.S. & Scheier, M.F. (1998). *On the self-regulation of behavior*. Cambridge: Cambridge University Press.

Cavanagh, M. (2005). Mental-health issues and challenging clients in executive coaching. In M. Cavanagh, A.M. Grant, & T. Kemp (Eds), *Evidence-based coaching* (vol 1): *Contributions from the behavioural sciences* (pp. 21–36). Bowen Hills, QLD: Australian Academic Press.

Cavanagh, M. & Grant, A.M. (2004). Executive coaching in organisations: The personal is the professional. *International Journal of Coaching in Organisations, 6*: 6–15.

Clutterbuck, D. & Lane, G. (Eds) (2004). *The situational mentor: An international review of competences and capabilities in mentoring*. Aldershot: Gower.

Corbett, K. (2006). *The Sherpa report*. Cincinnati, OH: Sasha Corp.

Cox, E. & Bachkirova, T. (2007). Coaching with emotion: How coaches deal with difficult emotional situations. *International Coaching Psychology Review, 2*(2): 178–90.

Derogatis, L.R. & Melisaratos, N. (1983). The brief symptom inventory: An introductory report. *Psychological Medicine, 13*: 595–605.

Douglas, C.A. & McCauley, C.D. (1999). Formal developmental relationships: A survey of organizational practices. *Human Resource Development Quarterly, 10*(3): 203–20.

Druckman, D. & Bjork, R.A. (1991). *In the mind's eye: Enhancing human performance*. Washington, DC: National Academy Press.

Dryden, W. (2011). *Dealing with clients' emotional problems in life coaching: A rational-emotive and cognitive behaviour therapy (RECBT) approach*. New York, NY: Routledge/Taylor & Francis Group.

Dunbar, A. (2010). *Essential life coaching skills*. New York, NY: Routledge/Taylor & Francis Group.

Edelman, D., Oddone, E.Z., Liebowitz, R.S., Yancy, W.S., Jr., Olsen, M.K., Jeffreys, A.S., et al. (2006). A multidimensional integrative medicine intervention to improve cardiovascular risk. *Journal of General Internal Medicine, 21*(7): 728–34.

Ellis, A. & Harper, R.A. (1961). *A new guide to rational living*. Englewood Cliffs, NJ: Prentice Hall.

Evans, M.O., Morgan, H.G., Hayward, A., & Gunnel, D.J. (1999). Crisis telephone coaching for deliberate self-harm patients: Effects on repetition. *British Journal of Psychiatry, 175*: 23–7.

Filippi, R. (1968). Coaching: A therapy for people who do not seek help. *Zeitschrift Fuer Psychotherapie und Medizinische Psychologie, 18*(6): 225–9.

Frisch, M.B. (1994). *Quality of life inventory*. Minneapolis, MN: National Computer Systems.

Gattellari, M., Donnelly, N., Taylor, N., Meerkin, M., Hirst, G., & Ward, J. (2005). Does 'peer coaching' increase GP capacity to promote informed decision making about PSA screening? A cluster randomised trial. *Family Practice, 22*(3): 253–65.

Gollwitzer, P.M. (1999). Implementation intentions: Simple effects of simple plans. *American Psychologist, 54*(7): 493–503.

Grant, A.M. (2003). The impact of life coaching on goal attainment, metacognition and mental health. *Social Behavior and Personality, 31*(3): 253–64.

Grant, A.M. & Greene, J. (2001). *Coach yourself*. Cambridge, MA: Perseus Publishing.

Grant, A.M. & O'Hara, B. (2006). The self-presentation of commercial Australian life coaching schools: Cause for concern? *International Coaching Psychology Review, 1*(2): 20–32.

Grant, A.M. & Zackon, R. (2004). Executive, workplace and life coaching: Findings from a large-scale survey of International Coach Federation members. *International Journal of Evidence-based Coaching and Mentoring, 2*(2): 1–15.

Green, L., Oades, L., & Grant, A. (2006). Cognitive-behavioral, solution-focused life coaching: Enhancing goal striving, well-being, and hope. *The Journal of Positive Psychology, 1*(3): 142–9.

Gyllensten, K. & Palmer, S. (2007). The coaching relationship: An interpretative phenomenological analysis. *International Coaching Psychology Review, 2*(2): 168–77.

Howard, K.I., Kopta, S., Krause, M.S., & Orlinsky, D.E. (1986). The dose-effect relationship in psychotherapy. *American Psychologist, 41*(2): 159–64.

Hymer, S.M. (1984). The telephone session and the telephone between sessions. *Psychotherapy in Private Practice, 2*(3): 51–65.

Jarvis, J. (2003). *Coaching and buying coaching services*. London: Chartered Institute of Personnel and Development.

Kilburg, R.R. (2000). *Executive coaching: Developing managerial wisdom in a world of chaos* (pp. 53–67). Washington, DC: American Psychological Association.

Kim, J.S. (2008). Examining the effectiveness of solution-focused brief therapy: A meta-analysis. *Research on Social Work Practice*, *18*(2): 107–16.

Kirsch, M.A. & Glass, L.L. (1977). Psychiatric disturbances associated with Erhard Seminars Training: II. Additional cases and theoretical considerations. *American Journal of Psychiatry*, *134*(11): 1254–58.

Leshinsky, M. (2007). *Coaching millions: Help more people, make more money, live your ultimate lifestyle*. New York: Xeno Press.

Leung, P. (1974). The use of behavior contracts in employability development planning. *Journal of Employment Counseling*, *11*(4): 150–3.

Locke, E.A. (1996). Motivation through conscious goal setting. *Applied & Preventive Psychology*, *5*(2): 117–24.

McGonagill, G. (2002). The coach as reflective practitioner. In C. Fitzgerald & J.G. Berger (Eds), *Executive coaching: Practices and perspectives* (pp. 59–88). Palo Alto, CA: Davies-Black.

Maslow, A.H. (1954). *Motivation and personality*. Oxford: Harpers.

Maslow, A.H. (1968). *Towards a psychology of being*. New York: Wiley & Sons.

Megginson, D. & Clutterbuck, D. (1995). *Mentoring in action: A practical guide for managers*. London: Kogan Page.

Neale, A.V., Singleton, S.P., Dupuis, M.H., & Hess, J.W. (1990). The use of behavioral contracting to increase exercise activity. *American Journal of Health Promotion*, *4*(6), 441–7.

Neenan, M. & Dryden, W. (2002). *Life coaching: A cognitive-behavioural approach*. New York: Brunner-Routledge.

Newnham-Kanas, C., Morrow, D., & Irwin, J.D. (2011). Participants' perceived utility of motivational interviewing using co-active life coaching skills on their struggle with obesity. *Coaching: An International Journal of Theory, Research and Practice, 4*(2), 104–22.

Passmore, J. (2009). Coaching ethics: Making ethical decisions – novices and experts. *The Coaching Psychologist, 5*(1), 6–10.

Ponzo, Z. (1977). Back to basics: The counsellor-coach. *Canadian Counsellor, 12*(1): 55–8.

Ryff, C. & Singer, B. (2008). Know thyself and become what you are: A eudaimonic approach to psychological well-being. *Journal of Happiness Studies, 9*(1): 13–39.

Sackett, D.L., Haynes, R.B., Guyatt, G.H., & Tugwell, P. (1996). Evidenced based medicine: What it is and what is isn't. *British Medical Journal, 13:* 71–2.

Schneider, J.I., Hashizume, J., Heak, S., Maetani, L., Ozaki, R.R., & Watanabe, D.L. (2011). Identifying challenges, goals and strategies for success for people with diabetes through life coaching. *Journal of Vocational Rehabilitation, 34*(2), 129–39.

Shearsmith, A. (2011). An exploration of holistic life coaching for breast cancer survivors. *International Journal of Evidence Based Coaching and Mentoring, 5*, 120–38.

Sheldon, K.M. (2001). The self-concordance model of healthy goal striving: When personal goals correctly represent the person. In P. Schmuck & K.M. Sheldon (Eds), *Life goals and well-being: Towards a positive psychology of human striving* (pp. 18–36). Kirkland, WA: Hogrefe & Huber.

Spence, G.B. (2007). Further development of evidence-based coaching: Lessons from the rise and fall of the human potential movement. *Australian Psychologist, 42*(2): 255–65.

Spence, G.B. & Grant, A.M. (2007). Professional and peer life coaching and the enhancement of goal striving and wellbeing: An exploratory study. *Journal of Positive Psychology, 2*(3): 185–94.

Spence, G.B., Cavanagh, M.J. & Grant, A.M. (2006). Duty of care in an unregulated industry: Initial findings on the diversity and practices of Australian coaches. *International Coaching Psychology Review, 1*(1): 71–85.

Stams, G.J., Dekovic, M., Buist, K., & de Vries, L. (2006). Efficacy of solution-focused brief therapy: A meta-analysis. *Gedragstherapie, 39*(2): 81–94.

Thompson, A.S. (1980*)*. Counseling psychology in the year 2000. *Counseling Psychologist, 8*(4): 21–2.

Whitworth, L., Kimsey-House, H., & Sandahl, P. (1998). *Co-active coaching: New skills for coaching people towards success in work and life*. Palo Alto, CA: Davies-Black.

Williams, P. & Davis, D.C. (2002). *Therapist as life coach: Transforming your practice*. New York: Norton.

Worrall, L., Brown, K., Cruice, M., Davidson, B., Hersh, D., Howe, T., et al. (2010). The evidence for a life-coaching approach to aphasia. *Aphasiology, 24*(4): 497–514.

Young, M.F. (1993). Instructional design for situated learning. *Educational Technology Research & Development, 41*(1): 43–58.

Yoshida, K., Ito, J., & Ogawa, M. (2011). Model project of home-visit living-skills coaching for individuals with severe mental illness in Japan. *International Journal of Mental Health, 40*(4): 19–27.

22

Health and Wellness Coaching

Margaret Moore and Erika Jackson

The lifestyle-related chronic diseases heart disease, stroke and cancer account for 50% of deaths, while obesity, pre-diabetes and diabetes are reaching epidemic levels of prevalence in the US and spreading globally. US healthcare costs associated with lifestyle-related chronic diseases are estimated as 75% of total costs (Centre for Disease Control, 2013) and growing rapidly with an aging population engaged in unhealthy lifestyles. Former US Comptroller General, David Walker notes: 'Our current healthcare spending is unsustainable and could eventually bankrupt the country absent dramatic changes in our current healthcare programs and system' (Walker, 2012).

Health behaviours also include stress management interventions as evidence mounts for the role of chronic negative emotions in accelerating the onset of chronic diseases and early death (Cole, 2012), while mindfulness practices, which improve emotional regulation, have been shown to ameliorate a growing number of medical conditions (Marchand, 2012). Early research is showing that positive emotions and shared positive emotions in caring relationships improve mental and physical health (Fredrickson, 2010, 2013). A next research frontier is the role of meaning and purpose, and spirituality, in improving well-being; published research by Cole and Fredrickson has shown impairment of gene expression of the immune system in people with a low level of life purpose (Fredrickson et al., 2013).

The economic and clinical case for health-promoting behaviours as safe and effective interventions to help prevent and treat many chronic diseases is leading to a new medical domain, lifestyle medicine (American College of Preventive Medicine, 2009; Institute of Lifestyle

Medicine, 2013); the second edition of a lifestyle medicine textbook was published in early 2013 (Rippe, 2013).

Helping people take better care of their health is among society's most pressing priorities. In the US where employers assume a good deal of the responsibility for employee healthcare costs, organizational leaders are called upon to create workplaces that foster rather than damage health, to both reduce healthcare costs and improve productivity and engagement (Institute of Health & Productivity Management, 2013). Yet healthcare providers often do not have the skills, nor are they reimbursed to help people learn and sustain new health-giving habits and leave behind health-damaging ones. The healthcare system was designed to manage acute medical emergencies and conditions. It is not well-suited to helping people manage a lifelong journey of developing and sustaining health-promoting behaviours. To date, a focus on pre-scriptive and expert educational approaches to helping people adopt health-promoting lifestyles has shown limited success (Frates & Moore, 2013). To meet this compelling need over the past decade, thousands of health and allied health professionals have sought training as health and wellness coaches in many countries in order to apply a new skill set designed to facilitate autonomy and change.

What is a health and wellness coach?

Professional health and wellness coaches have emerged as experts who are competent in help-ing people become autonomous, self-motivated, confident, resilient and fully engaged in lead-ing a health-promoting lifestyle. Health and wellness coaching is a growth-promoting relationship designed to facilitate positive and sustainable changes that support optimal health including physical activity, nutrition, weight, stress management or emotional regulation, and life satisfaction. Health and wellness coaches typically help clients focus on their health goals, developing the behaviours, knowledge and skills needed to prevent or treat disease, tracking health outcomes along the way. Coaches may also provide expert guidance and advice where clients lack expert knowledge, and only in the areas where they have professional credentials, while facilitating referrals to other experts as needed.

In addition to professional coaches, credentialed health professionals (including physicians, nurses, nurse practitioners, physician assistants, exercise physiologists, dieticians, therapists, social workers, rehabilitation professionals) seek to combine coaching skills with their expert knowledge to help clients manage medical conditions such as heart disease, hypertension, dia-betes, obesity, arthritis, chronic pain, cancer and depression. Models of peer health and wellness coaching are also emerging (Thom & Bodenheimer, 2013).

Over the past few decades, social, behavioural, health and positive psychologists have devel-oped the scientific foundation on which health and wellness coaching competencies stand. Key research questions continue to be addressed:

- What behaviours lead to positive mental health or flourishing?
- Does mental flourishing improve physical health?

- Given the challenges many face in sustaining health behaviours, what enables consistent adoption of the behaviours shown to improve physical and mental health, such as exercise, healthful nutrition, weight management and mindfulness practices?
- Do coaching techniques improve mental and physical health outcomes?
- What neuroscience discoveries can be applied by coaches?

Researchers have shown that positive psychological states prevent and ameliorate major chronic diseases by improving the function of the nervous, immune and endocrine systems. In contrast, chronic emotional stress, loneliness, depression and low levels of life purpose impair these systems, making people vulnerable to chronic disease (Veenhoven, 2009; Cole, 2012). Positive psychology, the scientific study of what optimizes human functioning, provides a framework and many interventions for coaches to apply in helping clients improve psychological capacities related to well-being.

Psychologists have been recently joined by neuroscientists exploring the biological processes of neuroplasticity, the generation of new neural connections and integrated brain-wide networks (Hammerness & Moore, 2012). These networks are believed to under-gird the formation of new behaviours and the cognitive and emotional mind-sets needed to sustain them.

The coaching research literature while limited, with studies trailing the latest developments in coaching skills training, is beginning to show that coaching interventions, multiple in-person or telephone coaching sessions for three months or longer, are improving health outcomes for several chronic diseases including diabetes, heart disease, obesity and cancer survivors (Butterworth et al., 2006; Edelman et al., 2006; Spence et al., 2008; Galantino et al., 2009; Newnham-Kanas, Morrow, & Irwin, 2010; Wennberg et al., 2010; Wolever et al., 2010; Appel, 2011; Frates and Moore, 2013). In 2013, Wolever et al. published a systematic review of the health and wellness coaching literature to identify 284 articles that operationalized health and wellness coaching:

1. as a process that is fully or partially patient-centred
2. included patient-determined goals
3. incorporated self-discovery and active learning processes (versus more passive receipt of advice)
4. encouraged accountability for behavioural goals
5. provided some type of education along with using coaching processes
6. coaching occurs as an ongoing relationship with a coach who is trained in specific behaviour change, communication and motivational skills.

DISTINCTIVE FEATURES

Contrasting the medical expert approach and the coaching approach

The goal of a health and wellness coach is to elicit personal responsibility, focus and clarity, self-discovery, inspiration and self-efficacy, in order to help clients change for good. To the maximum extent possible, coaches facilitate a dynamic that allows clients to find their own answers, create their own possibilities and design their own experiments, rather than being directed to follow an expert-determined agenda. The coaching approach helps clients generate new insights, generating new brain connections and networks over time, which are not possible when a coach is directive or prescriptive. Although client-generated plans and behaviours have greater potential for lasting change (Deci & Flaste, 2006), it can be difficult for health professionals, who have been trained extensively as authoritative experts, to take off their expert hats and shift to a coaching approach.

Psychologists Deci and Ryan (2002) have identified a primal drive of human beings as autonomy. This drive is so strong that it triggers a deeply wired and rapid response to being told what to do – to resist or rebel, without a lot of thoughtful analysis. This resistance can lead one to do things that are not in one's best interest, especially in response to an expert who is judgemental or does not fully empathize with one's situation. Helping professionals can inadvertently create resistance, causing clients to pull away, rather than open up and collaborate. It is common for people to resist the counsel or prescription of a healthcare provider when they feel judged or do not feel appreciated or understood.

The best way to avoid or defuse resistance is to fully understand a person's need for self-determination, for autonomy, competence and connection. One methodology for eliciting autonomy taught to coaches and healthcare providers is Motivational Interviewing (Miller & Rollnick, 2012), which teaches useful tools for 'rolling with resistance'. Motivational Interviewing is a counselling methodology developed originally in the addiction field 25 years ago. It was designed to help people overcome ambivalence or resistance to changing behaviour. This methodology considers what is necessary to initiate and support change – summarized briefly as being ready, willing and able, and uses a decisional balance sheet to consider the pros and cons of the status quo and the change under consideration. Through a careful balance of open inquiry and reflective listening, interviewers elicit and selectively reinforce pro-change talk and minimize resistance. For example, a coach working with a client who smokes would genuinely acknowledge the benefits of smoking (e.g. smokers enjoy regular five-minute brain breaks to de-stress). When a client trusts that his coach is accepting and appreciative of his reasons to not change, he can become more open to collaboration and exploration of new possibilities.

In 2010, Pollak et al. explored the impact on weight loss counselling when physicians were trained in motivational interviewing techniques. After one visit, the patients whose physicians used motivational interviewing techniques (collaboration, empathy, open inquiry, reflections), lost an average of 1.6 kilos three months later. The patients whose physicians were not using motivational interviewing techniques gained or maintained weight. In a few moments coaches and healthcare providers can make a difference by using a collaborative and not prescriptive dynamic.

Table 22.1 lays out the distinctions between the expert approach, the main relational mode in healthcare, and the coach approach, what is needed to support personal responsibility and sustained engagement. While medical experts play an essential and life-saving role in diagnosing ailments, prescribing and delivering medicines and other interventions, the expert approach falls short when helping people figure out how to live their lives in a way that optimizes health.

Table 22.1 The expert vs. coach approach

Expert approach	Coach approach
Authority	Partner
Educator	Facilitator of change
Defines agenda	Elicits client's agenda
Feels responsible for client's health	Client is responsible for health
Solve problems	Foster possibilities
Focus on what's wrong	Focus on what's right
Has the answers	Co-discover the answers
Interrupt if off topic	Learn from the client's story
Working harder than the client	Client working as hard as the coach
Wrestle with client	Dance with client

Coaching is ideally not about following a formula or checklist. Each client is unique; coaching tools are applied uniquely. Coaches build and grow their toolboxes, ever learning over many years, to ensure that they have plenty of strategies to meet the seemingly infinite permutations and combinations of client's needs, resources, styles and challenges. The best coaching sessions are generative; a coaching conversation is often described by coaches as an 'intuitive dance' or as 'relational flow' (Moore et al, 2005). In moments of relational flow, both the coach and client are present, engaged, challenged and stretched to the outer edges of their abilities.

Coaching mechanisms and competencies

We propose four coaching mechanisms that are applied by health and wellness coaches to enable sustained change, a biological transformation of mind-set and behaviour. Then we explore the biological and scientific underpinnings of these mechanisms, followed by translating them into a set of coaching competencies. The first mechanism relates to designing a relationship that fosters brain learning, growth and change. The second and third mechanisms can be considered the twin engines of change, also central themes in motivational interviewing and self-determination theory. People need to want to change, so they need to be motivated and it has to come from within. The second twin engine is confidence. They need to believe they can do it, feeling both 'I want it', and 'I can'. Both need to be recharged frequently, even daily, to propel people forward. The last mechanism is the change process or journey itself, including assessments, visions, action plans, creative brainstorming, accountability and referrals.

Coaching mechanism #1: Growth-promoting relationships

Facilitate client-directed neuroplasticity
Coaches support clients in developing new behaviours and mind-sets by facilitating neuroplasticity over time, fostering the ideal conditions for a client's brain to change. Neuroplasticity

is the brain's ability to grow, adapt and change; rewiring the brain is the process that underlies biological self-determination. The physiological mechanism for change is generally understood as the process of neurons forging new connections, creating new pathways and networks in the brain (Hammerness & Moore, 2012). Robust neural networks that endure likely require months, or a year or more, of client-directed neuroplasticity.

Elicit mindfulness to generate self-awareness

Coaches in the health and wellness field typically complete mindfulness skills training and are able to bring a mindful, present state to coaching sessions to enhance a client's state of mindfulness. A coach's mindful presence is an important precondition to helping a client to become mindful during a coaching conversation, and encourages more mindful moments in a client's everyday life to improve self-reflection, self-awareness, self-regulation, self-compassion, positivity and creativity, all noted below as critical to the brain's change process. Enhanced mindfulness enables coaches to improve listening skills; for example, being more present and not distracted by thinking about what to say next. A mindful state helps coaches better sense a client's positive and negative emotions, important messengers for both client and coach.

Mindfulness, as described by Vago and Silbersweig (2012), is a temporary state of non-judgemental, non-reactive, present-centred attention and awareness. Mindfulness skills developed over time first bring self-awareness (one's ability to observe oneself impartially), followed by self-regulation (an ability to effectively manage or alter one's responses and impulses) and ultimately self-transcendance (the development of a positive and ever-evolving relationship between self and others that transcends self-focused needs and increases social connections).

Vago and Silbersweig propose that 'six neurocognitive component mechanisms, highly integrated and strengthened together through intentional mental strategies, underlie the practice and cultivation of mindfulness'. These mechanisms are valuable to coaching clients, and include intention and motivation, attention, emotion regulation, extinction and reconsolidation, non-attachment and de-centring. The first stage in the brain's creative process is described by Carson (2010), as the 'mindful absorb' brain state or 'brainset', where neural activity is largely at the back of the brain and the thinking, analysing and evaluating prefrontal cortex region is less active.

Facilitate full attention

Coaching conversations help clients to focus the brain's attentional resources on their personal ambitions and growth, enhancing the brain's ability to learn. A full focus of the brain's attentional resources is a first step in neuroplasticity. Undistracted attention, a state of full awareness, enhances neuronal activity by harnessing various regions of the brain, including the prefrontal cortex, sub-cortical limbic and brainstem areas, into an integrated coherent state. Attention enhances the responses of selected neurons under focus and reduces neural activity in other brain regions. An attentive brain can focus and learn without distractions, be productive and creative and make fewer errors (Hammerness & Moore, 2012).

Emotion regulation

Emotional states have an enormous impact on the brain's capacity for learning and coaches assist clients in developing optimal emotional states to support learning. The first step toward an 'organized mind' is to tame the negative emotional frenzy that many people deal with daily (Hammerness & Moore, 2012). Negative emotions reduce the brain's ability to learn, to take in new knowledge and skills, by impairing the function of the prefrontal cortex, impairing access to working memory which is the raw material for creativity, and hampering curiosity and cognitive agility.

A study of physician empathy (Hojat et al., 2011) concluded that patients whose physicians have high empathy scores were significantly more likely to have good control of blood sugar and cholesterol levels than physicians with low empathy scores. A coach's compassion makes an important contribution in helping clients handle their negative emotions. Most people, particularly those who have chronic diseases and feel badly about their personal contribution to a disease process, have a vocal inner critic, a voice that says 'I can't do this', 'I'm not good enough', 'I failed'. Self-criticism is a potent source of negativity that depletes brain resources, making it hard to move forward.

When coaches radiate warmth, patience and empathy, clients are better able to let go of the past, accept themselves and feel self-compassion. It can be difficult for healthcare providers to be patient and empathetic when people are not making progress, and yet acceptance and empathy are essential if coaches are to help clients loosen the grip of negative emotions and self-talk.

Neff (2011) has studied the value of self-compassion as a method of processing negative emotions, to suffer well. Self-compassion towards one's negative emotions leads to a softer, kinder motivation that improves the brain's ability to learn and change. Unfortunately, fear of failing, of being a failure, is not an optimal source of motivation. In contrast, Neff's formula for self-compassion is an excellent guide for coaches; it starts with a mindful acceptance of negative emotions, followed by a heartfelt connection to others who share similar negative emotions and last, self-kindness, perhaps crossing one's hands over the heart area for a moment.

Goleman (2006) suggests that there are two types of emotional reactions: low road and high road. Low road reactions occur automatically, such as when we hear a sudden noise in the night and our heart jumps. High road reactions occur when we reappraise the situation, halting the further release of stress hormones adrenaline and cortisol. Reappraisal dampens the overactive amygdala (the inner 'uh-oh' voice). When we reappraise events, we are more likely to remember the content of those events. When we can mindfully distinguish between an event and our interpretations of it, we are setting the stage for optimistic reappraisal. The reappraisal process is a matter of becoming aware of often-unconscious interpretations, bringing relevant filters (values, beliefs, culture) to consciousness and introducing positive changes in our perspectives.

A task of a coach then is to support clients in making reappraisal a conscious, ongoing process. Optimistic reappraisals are important in building a client's internal resources. Reappraisal is not about suppressing emotion, a function that the brain is not equipped to perform. In fact, suppression leads to higher levels of negative emotions and worsening disease symptoms. We are also vulnerable to errors and poor judgements when brain function is impaired by fear. The coaching conversation can bring this often-unconscious process to the conscious mind, where it can be named and normalized. Calming the amygdala by naming the threat enables more activity in the problem-solving portion of the brain.

Fredrickson (2009) has shown that positive emotions improve attention, open-mindedness, creativity and the ability to reach a strategic perspective. Further, when we are able to attain and sustain a positive emotion to negative emotion ratio above 3:1, resilience passes the tipping point needed to adapt and change. Positive emotions are vital for brain learning in-the-moment and for a client's change success over time.

In each coaching session, coaches create an oasis for clients, one that is calm, mindful, undistracted and positive. Coaches also help clients become more self-compassionate toward their negative emotions and inner critics and develop a level of positive emotions needed for curiosity and creativity, leading to new insights and possibilities. Coaches support clients in learning from their behavioural experiments, to substitute curiosity for negative self-talk that can come from perceived failure.

Foster creativity

Coaching at its essence is a creative process, helping clients create neuronal connections and networks, imagine new possibilities and develop new behaviours and mind-sets. In addition to the 'mindful absorb' brain state mentioned above, Carson (2010) has identified six other brain activation states or 'brainsets' that enable the creative process, starting with a mindful absorbing of new information, reasoning or thinking about a problem to solve, envisioning or imagining a possible outcome, brainstorming to generate new possibilities, a flow state that produces a creative outcome and an evaluation phase to enable sifting through options and implementing a creative design. Coaches and clients can learn to direct their attention to different brain regions for different creative stages. For example, the focused left prefrontal cortex is ideally suited to the reasoning and evaluation phases, but dampens inputs from other brain regions needed for more defocused imagining, brainstorming and flow states which activate the right prefrontal cortex and other brain regions.

Meaning-making to connect the dots

Coaches help clients tame their emotional frenzy and distractions, bring mindful attention to their motives and goals, then foster cognitive agility and creative brainstorming in order to arrive at a strategic big picture, 'connecting the dots' or generating new perspectives (Hammerness & Moore, 2012). The brain is a connection machine, constantly making connections to reflect conclusions about how everything fits together, to make meaning of 'it all' (Kegan, 1982). We are constantly trying to interpret the meaning of what happens to us, what others do and what the effects are. Most activity in the brain involves creating connections between existing neurons and pruning these connections. Every piece of data, each idea, habit and thought is made up of a set of connections among neurons. Making new connections is pleasurable. When we create a new connection, we experience a positive charge of energy – the *aha* of insight, temporarily opening our minds to new possibilities. A client's self-generated insights are important in supporting neuroplasticity.

The human brain makes patterns of connections in our ongoing quest for meaning – our mental maps. The maps that convey information that is most accessed and get the most repetitions get further hardwired and become more likely to be activated in the future.

Coaching sessions explore and make meaning of a client's values, vision, health, way of life and learning, challenges and experiences along the journey of change. Clients move an automatic pilot mode of living into the spotlight of awareness, thoughtful reflection and take their personal relationship with health to a higher level of evolution. Instead of sacrificing health to meet life's demands, health becomes essential to meeting those demands. The meaning of health and one's ability to change the course of health and life has changed for good.

Coaching competencies for the growth-promoting relationship

Attend to self-care. Become a master at self-coaching and self-care as a role model for clients and to bring mindfulness, compassion, positive emotions and creativity to coaching sessions.

Elicit mindfulness. Facilitate a calm, mindful and curious focus of attention on a client's state of health and well-being which expands self-awareness of deficits and awakens the desire for possible benefits of positive change. Mindfulness helps clients become more curious and objective, less reactive to the ups and downs of change, and more self-aware of what's working, or not, and why.

Radiate compassion. Empathize with a client's negative emotions, show acceptance and foster a non-judgemental and affirmative perspective ('Let's appreciate and learn from the past and move forward to build a better future'). Deploy inquiries that encourage the client's story to expand awareness of their feelings and underlying needs.

Encourage autonomy. Put clients in the driver's seat and yourself in the passenger seat, by undistracted listening, curious and open-minded inquiry, refraining from mindless advice giving and helping clients to make choices by brainstorming a few options to select from.

Generate positivity. Help clients consider, appreciate and unpack sources of positive emotions, past accomplishments, strengths, life circumstances, relationships and shift to a positive frame of negative experiences and events.

Practice creative inquiry and reflections. Alternate open questions with reflections to help clients generate new insights, perspectives and meanings that support experimenting with new behaviours. Acknowledge and unpack insights and perspectives to help them stick and provide energy for forward movement.

Coaching mechanism #2: Elicit self-motivation

There are two general categories of motivation – external and autonomous – as defined by Deci and Ryan (2002). Then, there are two kinds of external motivation. External motivation, or external regulation, occurs when an external human being, like a boss, spouse or mother, tells us what to do and we don't think much about it beyond 'I want to do what this person wants me to do to avoid conflict'. For example, a coaching client might say 'I'm exercising because my wife will get upset if I don't'. That is the extent of his exploration and reflection. A second form of external motivation is when we internalize the external desire, without a deeper alignment with personal values and desires, as an inner critic that says 'I should' or 'I ought' to exercise or eat better. While external motivation may work in the short term, it is not an effective form of motivation for the long term.

Autonomous motivation on the other hand does lead to sustainable motivation. Autonomous motivation often has a future orientation – for example, when we want to be fit and strong because we want to have the energy to make a difference every day, or don't want our children to have to take care of us if we have a heart attack or stroke. Connecting the behaviour to something in the future that we value, or the identity we want to project, is the type of motivation that has been shown to lead to sustainable weight loss. Then we have internalized our reason to do something, because it is good for our future or fits with the identity we aspire to. Future-oriented autonomous motivation is the kind of motivation that works best (Deci & Ryan, 2002).

The other type of autonomous motivation that is also valuable is the one that produces flow experiences in our lives. It happens when we love to do an activity in-the-moment – we just love our yoga class, or we are excited about cooking a new recipe, or can't wait to listen to music to relax. When we love to do something, we do it for its own sake. We do it because it taps into our strengths and it is fun and engaging. While that can be a powerful kind of motivation for health behaviours, it can take many years to find. We may never fall in love with exercising, cooking, or meditation. It is important to keep looking, but it may not come along quickly.

Coaching clients need support in developing a future-oriented autonomous motivation, digging deeper to get to the 'why behind the why'. A client who wants to lose weight may initially be focused on wearing smaller-sized clothes for a family celebration in a few months, and a coach may need to deepen the inquiry until a client has tapped into longer-lasting, more meaningful motivation, that will keep her on track while making dozens of health decisions each day. An example could be a heartfelt desire to be stronger and more energetic so as to not be physically dependent on her grown children as she ages as her mother has become.

Self-motivation is tapping into an energy source, or a life force, that is intrinsic and biological. It is often a heartfelt drive to help others, be a role model, make a difference in the world, to use our strengths competently and to make our lives meaningful. Authentic motivation improves cognitive function, attention, emotion regulation and creativity, bringing meaningful and dependable intentions to a challenging journey of change.

Coaching competencies for eliciting motivation

Ignite and sustain autonomous motivation. Help clients find health behaviours that are intrinsically motivating (enjoyed for their own sake) and/or discover internal motivation (articulating and valuing future personal benefit or desired future identity) for a health behaviour, for example, it will allow them to make a difference in the world or do more of things they treasure most, now and in the future. Help clients stay connected to their most heartfelt motivation so that the intention informs health choices in daily life.

Improve autonomous motivation. Help clients select behaviours that have the potential to enhance autonomous motivation quickly by delivering early noticeable benefits (more energy, better sleep, a calmer mind) within two weeks or so.

Coaching mechanism #3: Build confidence

While a high level of autonomous motivation is important to starting and sustaining a change journey, it is insufficient in the absence of self-efficacy or confidence in the face of one's obstacles. Capacity and confidence to change are typically built by diligent efforts over time. People have varying levels of self-motivation and confidence across a diverse set of eating, exercise, mindfulness, or emotional and self-regulation behaviours. If a client is reasonably confident and motivated to make even a small change, the success that follows will increase confidence and motivation further. Hence it's often important to help clients select a habit that, while a stretch, is within reach and will build confidence a little. A little success will improve motivation and confidence and get clients started on an upward spiral.

Most people who have struggled with weight loss or a chronic disease for some time, face many challenges that have led to failed change attempts and are stuck in a state called chronic contemplation. Self-efficacy is at a low level (Moore, 2006). Fredrickson (2009) has shown that not only do positive emotions allow us to be more open-minded and creative, but also they are a main variable in determining one's resilience to setbacks and adversity. Ideally each coaching session elicits and leverages a good dose of positive emotions. 'What's the best thing that happened to you in the past week? What are you enjoying most in your life right now? What's your favourite thing to do? What makes your thrive?' Coaches find ways to spark authentic positivity as a resource for creative brainstorming to bounce back from setbacks or circumvent challenges. Then when clients inevitably reach a roadblock, they can access more energy and creativity, improving the capacity to find new paths to rise above obstacles.

Another important approach to improving confidence is to help clients tap into another drive in Deci and Ryan's self-determination theory (Deci & Ryan, 2002): to be competent. People dislike being incompetent – we hate falling off our bikes, especially as adults. People are more competent and successful when they apply their values, strengths and talents, as learned from the research in the application of character strengths (Niemiec, 2013). When clients tap into their strengths in new and creative ways, their mental processing comes up with solutions more quickly.

The Transtheoretical Model of Change (Prochaska, 2005) gives tools to coaches that help clients determine client readiness for change of a given behaviour which is related to the level of self-efficacy. The model categorizes stage of readiness to engage in a behaviour and then measures the use of key variables that have been found to promote behaviour change. The four key variables are (1) stage of change, (2) decisional balance, (3) self-efficacy, i.e. examining challenging situations to create a personal relapse prevention plan and (4) processes of change. Most recently Norcross (2012) has translated the Transtheoretical Model of Change into a set of evidence-based emotional and behavioural processes that fit each of five stages of change:

psych (getting psyched), prep (getting prepared), perspire (take action), persevere (manage slips) and persist (maintain change).

Along the journey, coaches help clients deal with setbacks in order to fully harvest learning. Creative brainstorming or relational flow is common in most sessions in order to generate new insights and increase hope and optimism by coming up with creative possibilities to navigate around numerable challenges.

Coaching competencies for building confidence

Cultivate positive emotions. Begin sessions with positive topics–experiences, lessons, successes, strengths, which improve brain function including attention, memory and creativity, for more challenging topics later in sessions. Unpack and harvest positive topics and emotions at the close of sessions.

Leverage strengths. Help clients identify personal strengths and talents and brainstorm ways to deploy strengths in the pursuit of lifestyle change and better health.

Set stretch goals. Help clients set goals that stretch them a little so that they are engaging, but not too much so as to increase stress.

Identify systems of support. Help clients find people and informational resources to support gaining of knowledge and learning of skills just-in-time to enhance motivation, confidence, self-awareness and new insights, and support their goal attainment.

Enable hope. Help clients brainstorm on various paths to reach goals so that they appreciate that if one path doesn't work, one or more other paths are possible, which increases hope and confidence.

Coaching mechanism #4: Process of change

Just as organizations inch forward via projects that have strategies, goals, plans and timelines, coaching clients focused on health goals benefit from structured projects and processes. Coaching often starts with health and wellness assessments to support progress tracking. Then, just like an architect creates a picture of a new house, the brain needs a vision or picture of what the ideal future looks like, the 'envision brainset' in Carson's model of creativity (Carson, 2010). Next it is time to design experiments, goals and action plans that are set in motion to move clients toward their visions. Some clients prefer small steps while others want the challenge of bolder goals.

Behavioural or SMART goals, such as 'I will do three 30 minute yoga sessions per week', focus on engaging in new habits consistently and provide specific ways to measure the success of goals. Clients may decide to set skills-building goals such as learning how to lift weights safely, cook healthy meals, or meditate, or they may want to set 'performance' goals, such as reaching a certain weight or blood pressure level or completing a walking race.

Having clients determine how they want to be accountable is a critical step, as accountability to others is an important source of support. There are many mobile technology tools for tracking and accountability to self and others. Coaching organizations may provide online client files including assessments, tracking, goals records and journaling. The simplest approach is a regular progress report, perhaps weekly, monthly, or quarterly. Setting quarterly or annual milestones for review and celebration provide important validation of progress. Clients may also need the support of other health experts and therapists along the journey and coaches need to have a wide network of referrals and credible information sources at their fingertips.

Coaching competencies for the process of change

Complete baseline and outcomes assessments. Help clients increase self-awareness and get clear on how to measure success by completing baseline assessments and tracking improvements of health and wellness status, energy and vitality, mental health, life purpose and satisfaction. There is a plethora of mobile and computer tools to support assessment and tracking.

Clarify visions. Help clients define motivational vision statements or art forms (poems, photos, drawings) and specific behaviour, skills-building, or destination goals to provide a coherent structure for pursuing lifestyle change.

Design experiments. Help clients select goals and develop strategies, including environmental and social support, which enhance confidence, which in turn will improve autonomous motivation.

Design goal-tracking and accountability method. Help clients select types of goals and build in methods for commitment and accountability. Help clients decide on level of goal ambition (bold or baby steps) and goal time frames which will work best (3 months, 1 year, beyond).

Be prepared for referrals. refer and collaborate with other members of the healthcare team, including nurses, physicians, therapists and others, as well as evidence-based information sources.

RELATIONSHIP WITH THEORETICAL TRADITIONS

Along with positive psychology interventions, evidence-based theoretical models commonly translated into coaching competencies include the transtheoretical model (Prochaska et al., 1995) motivational interviewing (Miller & Rollnick, 2012), self-determination theory (Deci & Ryan, 2002), emotional intelligence (Goleman, 2006), mindfulness (Vago & Silbersweig, 2012), social cognitive theory (Moore & Tschannen-Moran, 2009) and empathy (Centre for Nonviolent Communication, 2013).

EVALUATION

As it gains recognition over coming years, health and wellness coaching and wide dissemination of coaching skills have the potential to be a transformational force in the healthcare system in many countries. Coaching competencies are widely applicable, in-person and telephone, individual and group, professional coaches, health professionals integrating coaching skills and tools into current protocols, and peer health and wellness coaches for community outreach.

Health and wellness coaches are not limited to helping clients improve diet and exercise. Health and wellness coaches address the whole person, what it means to thrive mentally and physically, and how to leverage the biology of change. The coaching relationship is designed to facilitate sustainable change, and optimize health and well-being. With self-determination as a driver, clients move from dependency to empowerment, thereby making longer-lasting, confidence building, internally motivated changes that are appropriate for their evolving lives. Given that chronic stress directly damages health, the positive emotions generated by coaching will potentially be shown to reduce the incidence of disease symptoms, preventable chronic diseases and early mortality.

When employers, clinical or health payor organizations require coaching for 'high-risk' employees, the coaching relationship is less likely to collaborative and client-centred. Such relationships may focus on external motivation and press clients to make behaviour changes in areas where they are not ready, undermining biological needs for autonomy and competence. Such models are evolving to a higher standard as professional coach standards improve, more evidence emerges and the pool of competent health and wellness coaches expands.

As is the case for any new professional domain, there is much progress to be made to enable health and wellness coaching to become integrated into mainstream healthcare and consumer wellness. A US volunteer organization, the National Consortium for Credentialing Health & Wellness Coaches (www.ncchwc.org) is developing standards, a national certification, as well as a collaborative research agenda to expand the evidence base. The Institute of Coaching, at McLean Hospital, a Harvard Medical School affiliate, is awarding coaching research grants and furthering the translation of science into best coaching practices in healthcare and beyond. The UK government's National Health Service held a health coaching summit in early 2013 to discuss how to study and expand health coaching initiatives.

Coaching competencies will continue to evolve as new discoveries are made by psychologists and neuroscientists. Coaching outcomes research addressing a wide spectrum of health and wellness needs from childhood to end of life is a vital endeavour to support the integration of coaching interventions into evidence-based medicine, healthcare and consumer wellness offerings.

FURTHER READING

Cooperider, D. and Whitney, D. (2005). *Appreciative inquiry: A positive revolution in change*. San Francisco, CA: Berrett-Koehler.

Kegan, R. & Lahey, L. (2009). *Immunity to change: How to overcome it and unlock the potential in yourself and your organization*. Boston, MA: Harvard Business Review Press.

National Health Service Health Coaching Summit (2013). www.pcc-cic.org.uk/article/presentations-health-coaching-summit-26-february-2013.

Video: www.youtube.com/watch?v=HqVy2Nwj8Xw&feature=youtu.be

DISCUSSION QUESTIONS

- What are the primary distinctions between health and wellness coaching and life coaching?
- What are the potential consequences of applying the expert approach with clients?
- What mindfulness practices would best support the coach in developing growth-promoting relationships with clients?

REFERENCES

American College of Preventive Medicine (2009). *Lifestyle medicine – Evidence review*. http://c.ymcdn.com/sites/www.acpm.org/resource/resmgr/lmi-files/lifestylemedicine-literature.pdf.

Appel, L.J. et al. (2011). Comparative effectiveness of weight loss interventions in Clinical practice. *New England Journal of Medicine, 365*(21): 1959–68.

Butterworth, S. (2006). Effect of motivational interviewing-based health coaching on employees' physical and mental health status. *Journal of Occupational Health Psychology, 11*(4): 358–65.

Carson, S. (2010). *Your creative brain*. New York: Wiley & Sons.

Centre for Disease Control and Prevention (2013), www.cdc.gov/chronicdisease/overview/index.cfm.

Centre for Nonviolent Communication (2013). www.cnvc.org.

Deci, E. and Flaste, R. (1996). *Why we do what we do: Understanding self-motivation*. New York: Penguin.

Deci, E. & Ryan, R. (2002). *Handbook of self-determination research*. Rochester, IL: University of Rochester Press.

Edelman, D. et al. (2006). A Multidimensional Integrative Medicine Intervention to Improve Cardiovascular Risk. *Journal of General Internal Medicine, 21*: 728–34.

Frates, B. and Moore, M. (2013) Health and wellness coaching: Skills for lasting change. Chapter 27. In J. Rippe (Ed.), *Lifestyle medicine* (2nd ed.). New York: CRC Press.

Fredrickson, B. (2009). *Positivity*. New York: Three Rivers Press.

Fredrickson, B. (2013). *Love 2.0*. New York: Hudson Street Press.

Fredrickson, B., Cole, S. et al. (2013). A functional genomic perspective on human well-being. *Proceedings of the National Academy of Sciences, 110*(22): 13684–89.

Galantino, M. L. et al. (2009). Longitudinal benefits of wellness coaching interventions in cancer survivors. *International Journal of Interdisciplinary Social Sciences, 4*: 42–58.

Goleman, D. (2006). *Emotional intelligence*. New York: Bantam Books.

Hammerness, P. & Moore, M. (2012). *Organize your mind, organize your life*. Harvard Health book. Ontario: Harlequin.

Hojat, M. et al. (2011). Physicians' empathy and clinical outcomes for diabetic patients. *Academic Medicine, 86*(3). 359–63

Institute of Health & Productivity Management (2013). www.ihpm.org/info/background.php.

Institute of Lifestyle Medicine (2013). www.instituteoflifestylemedicine.org.

Kegan, R. (1982). *The evolving self: Problem and process in human development*. Boston, MA: Harvard University Press.

Marchand, W. (2012). Mindfulness-based stress reduction, mindfulness-based cognitive therapy, and zen meditation for depression, anxiety, pain, and psychological stress. *Journal of Psychiatric Practice, 18*(4): 233–52.

Miller, W. & Rollnick, S. (2012). *Motivational interviewing: Helping people change*. New York: Guilford Press.

Moore, M. (2006). The obesity epidemic: A confidence crisis calling for professional coaches. White paper published by Wellcoaches Corporation, www.wellcoaches.com/images/whitepaper.pdf.

Moore, M. et al (2005) Relational Flow: A theoretical model for the intuitive dance. International Coach Federation Coaching Research Symposium Proceedings.

Moore, M. & Tschannen-Moran, B. (2009). *Coaching psychology manual*. Baltimore, MD: Lippincott, Williams & Wilkins.

Neff, K. (2011). *Self-compassion: Stop beating yourself up and leave insecurity behind*. New York: William Morrow.

Newnham-Kanas, C., Morrow, D., & Irwin, J.D. (2010). Motivational coaching: A functional juxtaposition of three methods for health behaviour change: motivational interviewing, coaching, and skilled helping. *International Journal of Evidence Based Coaching and Mentoring, 8*(2): 27–48.

Niemiec, R. (2013). Character strengths, a research update. *IPPA Newsletter,* 5(4). www.ippanetwork.org/newsletters/volume5/issue4/character_strengths_application/.

Norcross, J. (2012). *Changeology.* New York: Simon & Schuster.

Pollak, K.I., Alexander, S.C., Coffman, C.J., Tulsky J.A., Lyna, P., Dolor, R.J., & James, I.E. (2010). Physician communication techniques and weight loss in adults. *American Journal of Preventive Medicine, 39*(4): 321–8.

Prochaska, J, Norcross, J., & DiClemente, C. (1995). *Changing for good: A revolutionary six-stage program for overcoming bad habits and moving your life positively forward.* New York: William Morrow Paperbacks.

Rippe, J. (Ed.). (2013). *Lifestyle medicine,* (2nd ed.). New York: CRC Press.

Rosenberg, M.S. (2005). *Nonviolent communication: A language of life.* Encinitas, CA: Puddle Dancer Press.

Spence, G. et al. (2008). The integration of mindfulness training and health coaching: An exploratory study. *An International Journal of Theory, Research and Practice, 1*(2): 144–62.

Thom, D. & Bodenheimer, T. (2013). Impact of peer health coaching on glycemic control in low-income patients with diabetes: A randomized controlled trial. *The Annals of Family Medicine 11*(2): 137–44.

Vago, D. & Silbersweig, D. (2012). Self-awareness, self-regulation, and self-transcendence (S-ART): A framework for understanding the neurobiological mechanisms of mindfulness. *Frontiers in Human Neuroscience, 6*(296): 1–30.

Veenhoven, R. (2009). Enjoyment of life lengthens life: Findings and consequences. In T. Freire, (Ed.), *Understanding positive life: Research and practice on positive psychology.* (pp. 19–42). Lisboa, Portugal: Climpsi Editores.

Walker, D. (2012). Gambling with the future of healthcare. *Healthcare Finance News,* www.healthcarefinancenews.com/news/gambling-future-healthcare

Wennberg et al. (2010). A randomized trial of a telephone care-management strategy. *New England Journal of Medicine, 363*(13): 1245–55.

Wolever, R. et al. (2010). Integrative health coaching for patients with Type 2 Diabetes: A randomized clinical trial. *Diabetes Educator, 36*(4): 629–39.

Wolever, R. et al. (2013). A systematic review of the literature on health and wellness coaching: Defining a key behavioral intervention in healthcare. *Global Advances in Health & Medicine, 2*(4): 35–53.

23

Career Coaching

Bruce Hazen and Nicole Steckler

Career management is the conscious or unconscious process of managing our relationship to our work over a lifetime. Career coaches add value to this process by maximizing insights that are intrapersonal, interpersonal and market-based, and by turning those insights into action strategies. Career coaches bring the advantage of objectivity, information and planning to the pursuit of goals and can help with:

- choosing work (career decision making)
- moving up in a profession, job or organization (development strategy)
- moving out, by choice, of a form of work or an organization (career transition strategy to find work or create entrepreneurial work)
- finding work after job loss (job search strategy)
- planning for the end of paid work and the beginning of a period of generativity (focusing on the developmental issues of up-and-coming generations).

Insight is gained through a process of dialogue, appreciative inquiry, interpretation, reframing, assessment and other classic counselling techniques. In addition, information and education can also be a product of the career coaching process as the coach adds both wisdom and knowledge about various work cultures, processes and styles that clients may lack. Career coaching is therefore one of the most focused, result-oriented forms of coaching because of the clearly defined presence of work as an end goal. Achieving that goal also means a coach must prepare a client to enter the marketplace in a knowledgeable and astute way, exhibiting tactics and behaviours that are appropriate to that work culture.

The concept of vocational guidance was developing within North American schools in the early 1900s, and during that timeframe Frank Parsons was credited with founding career guidance and starting the Vocation Bureau of Boston. Subsequent research and models of career theory and guidance were developed throughout the 20th century by such thinkers as John Holland, Edgar Schein, Donald Super (Blustein, 2006) and, more recently, Charles Hakim (1994), Richard Bolles (2008) and Ken Dychtwald (2005). Career coaching, in particular, has been discussed by Feldman and Moore (2001), Colombo and Werther (2003) and, more recently, Bench (2008), although there remains little empirical research in this area.

DISTINCTIVE FEATURES

Goals and tasks of career coaching

Career coaching goals can range from the tactical and measurable (lost a job, need to find a new one) to the more intra-psychic and intangible. Coaches assist in the establishment of a satisfying marriage of work and current identity, where work fits the character, competencies, values and experiences of the coachee. At the same time, career coaching seeks to benignly disturb the current identity, then design and guide the experiments necessary to refine and develop that identity to its next stage of actualization.

Looking again at the five areas of career coaching work, there are key tasks that enable goals of coaching and career management to be realized (see Table 23.1). The goals in these areas are cognitive, emotional and behavioural.

Many of these career coaching goals and tasks are demonstrated by the case of a senior engineering manager in an international heavy manufacturing company who sought coaching as he anticipated the loss of his job when a product-line reached its projected end of life, and needed to define and choose among options, including:

- deciding to leave on his own by activating an early retirement
- considering unpaid work in retirement to fulfil sociopolitical values
- waiting to be laid off and receiving a severance package
- beginning a job search while currently working, so as to land a new job prior to job elimination.

The challenge for the coach was to utilize knowledge of work culture and client values to consider how age, gender, social class, language, family expectations, the larger culture and the economy all interact in career strategy design and execution. For example, entrepreneurial options might abound for an engineer in California. A French engineer might have a socially

Table 23.1 Goals, objectives and processes in career coaching

Goals of career coaching	Coachee objectives	Coaching processes
1. Choosing work	Gain self-insight and realistic knowledge of both self and the work culture coachee hopes to join. Learn the behavioural skills needed to study the market through networking. Feel confident enough to make a choice.	Conduct assessments. Gather family and personal history of work. Educate about skills, jobs and work organizations. Direct field research. Conduct behavioural skills practice (networking, interviewing).
2. Moving up in profession or organization	Advance in competency, complexity of work, authority and status.	Development planning. Assess and measure current and desired future state and help coachee measure and close the gaps that exist. Action learning design. Mentor or sponsor identification. New job launch plan.
3. Moving out, by choice	Leave a job, organization or profession in a timely and judicious way. Find or create a job or an entrepreneurial endeavour.	Define exit strategy and timing issues. Create a job search campaign. Assess entrepreneurial readiness and create a plan for starting a business. Create new job launch plan.
4. Finding work after job loss	Replace work lost due to poor performance, job elimination, retirement or other involuntary means.	Same as 'Moving Out' above with the addition of assessing and processing potential emotional, financial and skill deficit issues that temporarily lower client effectiveness. New job launch plan.
5. Ending current work	Retire (many definitions). Rehire into new or same roles/new or same organization. Volunteer. Mentor others.	Explore client values and framework for defining and living in retirement. Define roles, organizations and needs that contain work opportunities unfettered by the need for a full pay check or established 'job'.

sponsored financial system to lend predictability to retirement plans. A 28-year-old female engineer in Russia or Iran (or from similar cultures) might have cultural and family expectations that would weigh heavily in strategy design, even if the options under consideration were those listed above.

Career coaching contexts and roles

Career coaching takes place in a wide range of contexts and life stages. High schools, colleges and universities offer career services including assessment and advising. Individuals who lose their jobs as part of lay-offs are often offered outplacement services, usually from an outplacement firm on contract with the downsizing organization. Experiences in these two contexts, in particular, may colour the potential coachee's expectations of what career coaching has to offer. Other coachees may arrive at career coaching along a similar path to those seeking life coaching or leadership/job effectiveness coaching. Coachees may be motivated by dissatisfaction with their current work situation, by wanting to contribute more and seek advancement, by attraction to a different line of work, by an upcoming planned retirement and/or by experiencing transitions that could be described as 'mid-life crises'.

'Plan and implement' v. 'test and learn' approaches

Two guiding concepts of how career planning unfolds can be used to clarify the coaching process and the role of the career coach. The 'plan and implement' approach starts with analysis, followed by action, creating a linear path toward a clear goal; the 'test and learn' approach starts with action, followed by analysis, leading to other actions, creating a cycle of testing and learning (Ibarra, 2004).

Each of these approaches is based on different underlying assumptions about human personality. The 'plan and implement' philosophy builds on the notion that that each of us has a core 'true' self and that personality is consistent if not immutable. In this tradition career planning and/or transition builds on introspection and assessment in order to uncover an appropriate career fit for that individual. In contrast, the 'test and learn' approach takes as its starting place notions of human personality as a collection of 'possible' selves, including those that repel us as well as those that attract us. Within this philosophy career transition then becomes a process of what Ibarra (2004) calls 'crafting experiments': trying out new actions, professional relationships and stories that offer opportunities to explore 'possible selves' in a low-cost, low-risk way; then reflecting on the resulting experiences in terms of fit and crafting the next round of experiment, progressing, over time, from lower-risk exploratory experiments to more confirmatory experiments that would require greater investment.

These are useful to the coach as guiding frameworks and particularly useful at different career stages. For example, plan and implement may be particularly useful for job search after lay-off when the goal is immediate re-employment in a similar role; test and learn may be especially appropriate for a mid-career individual considering a significant change in profession.

Less obvious but equally important, is the internal preference the coachee (and the coach) may have for these styles of engagement with career planning. Some coachees may prefer a more mechanistic, linear, structured 'engineering' approach, while others may prefer a more organic, exploratory 'experiment' process. The successful career coaching outcome depends on fit between the coachee's career situation and goals/needs, the coachee's style preference and personality and the coach's strengths and preferences. The greater the breadth of skills and range of approaches offered by the coach, the greater the coach's flexibility and ability to meet the needs of a wide range of coachees.

The coach and coachee each come to the relationship with existing beliefs about career development and preferences for either a more organic or mechanistic process for coaching and for career exploration. Ideally, the coach is equipped to be able to work along the whole spectrum in order to match the coachee's needs, as well as expand the coachee's capacity to meet a real challenge that may not conform to their initial worldview. With a coachee whose natural preference is for a more linear, mechanistic process, the coach serves as a guide along the way in the more organic process of 'crafting experiments'. With a coachee whose natural preference is more evolutionary and organic, the coach provides guidance and structure as necessary for the coachee to reach his or her goals.

Life cycle of a career coaching relationship

Contracting

Contracting can be thought of as the coach and coachee coming together to decide what destination they are aiming for and what methods they want to use to get there. The coach must establish a connection and understanding of the coachee's current situation and partner with the coachee around change. The contracting stage clarifies roles and goals: What is the coachee seeking to accomplish and what role is he or she looking for the coach to play? In this phase the coach gauges the sophistication of the coachee to see if he or she has accurately differentiated between how the coach might act as a consultant, networking facilitator and/or introduction agent (likely roles) versus a talent agent, a publicist or recruiter (unlikely roles). Clarifying the role expectations of the coachee may lead to a referral for the type of service the coachee is seeking.

Sometimes contracting comes up again at a middle stage of a coaching engagement. For example, with a coachee who loses an engineering job as part of a corporate downsizing, the initial contract may be for job search. Through the initial coaching sessions an underlying awareness emerges that the coachee does not want to return to the same type of large corporate setting. ('So, you don't know what you want to do, but you know you don't want to go back to the cubicle farm?' 'Yes!') The coach expands the initial contracting to clarify whether there is an immediate necessity to find work, or whether the coachee has the financial and emotional capacity to explore career change at this time. If the latter, the contract switches out of the initial plan and implement job search agreement to more of a test and learn career change exploration.

Assessment

The assessment phase of coaching goes deeper into goals: what depth of career exploration is the coachee seeking? A primary value of assessment is the ability to get at skills and preferences in a more value-neutral way, away from the job/company context. Coachees identify what parts of previous jobs they have liked and disliked and what skills are personal strengths for them versus requirements of previous jobs. Multiple methods may be used: interviews (structured/ open-ended), psychometric instruments and/or self-reflection exercises are all options. Assessment can offer the coachee both objectivity and movement early in the coaching process.

At this point the focus also shifts into deeper assessment of the individual: how congruent are they with the goal being articulated? The process is different from psychological assessment, although occasionally coaching assessment uncovers a psychological dynamic that is interfering with career and relationships at work, in which case the coach would refer the coachee for psychological work prior to proceeding with career coaching.

Action planning

The heart of the action-planning stage is to agree upon the behaviours that will get the coachee to the goal agreed upon in the assessment stage. The degree of structure or spontaneity may differ depending on whether the pair use a more plan-and-implement or test-and-learn approach. With either approach the coachee and coach must define, at least roughly, a professional objective. In the 'test and learn' approach the objective may change as a result of the very method being used, but the process is never a random curiosity search. For that, there is no need to pay a coach.

Market inquiry

Next, the coachee collects data from the employment market and sifts though the evidence, analysing it as market feedback. One successful method for this process starts with designing a 'focus of inquiry' (Hazen, 2014) by identifying a set of problems, issues, needs and trends (PINT) for analysis, relevant to the markets of interest and about which the coachee would like to know more. This has the dual purpose of getting the coachee focused and knowledgeable about their job search or career change targets of interest in order to learn, and at the same time, position themselves as a somewhat knowledgeable peer in front of individuals who can start to get to know them as colleagues or 'tribe members'. This stage is the prelude to the employment stage, providing a chance to identify the areas in which coachees want to promote themselves. The career coach's role is both outward-focused and inward-focused in this stage; the coach is adding information and recommendations as to where to research (and with whom) and harnessing both their own knowledge and the knowledge and experience of previous clients to help in evaluating the results from the inquiry. The desired outcome is to narrow the inquiry down to the most fruitful areas of focus.

A critical point here is that the coach is chartered to hold awareness of the coachee's combined skills, values and interests and to be the constant reminder of their importance so the coachee is dissuaded from making an overly simplistic choice. For example, a coachee whose strengths are not in sales discovers an exciting new product which can only be accessed through an entrepreneurial track. Here the role of the coach is to feed back the data and his/ her own impressions that clearly pointed to a mismatch between the coachee's interests and skills, and the intense selling and marketing activity that would be required to start up this new business.

Respond and decide

A strong market inquiry stage leads naturally to responding to these discoveries or analyses with intensification of both focus and effort into a more select number of targets. While the market inquiry was more about outbound curiosity, the 'respond and decide' stage is more about responding to shared, mutual interest and intensifying efforts to promote yourself to the right audiences. If this stage is successful the ultimate result is an invitation or a contract to engage. An additional alternative at this stage is the entrepreneurial option, where coachees decide to become the owner–operator of their own business.

Entry plan

When the coachee is ready to accept a new position, the coach can act as corporate anthropologist to help the coachee anticipate the new roles, rules and expectations regarding entry into a new 'tribe'. This crucial stage is where the coachee learns the cultural customs of the newly chosen career and/or job in addition to acclimatizing to the new job responsibilities. A new job launch plan helps the coachee to harness the specific opportunities and resources available to them during the 'honeymoon' of the first few months in a new job.

When the coachee chooses the entrepreneurial option of starting a new business, the coach's role will differ, depending on the coach's background. One likely scenario may be that the coach guides or refers the coachee to someone who can guide the detailed construction of a business plan and or specialize in more quantitative analysis of financial aspects of their business idea (Horan, 1997, 2006).

Ending/disengagement

In the final phase of a career coaching engagement, the dual focus is both to help the coachee anticipate stages of future career development or distress, for which a career coach could be a resource. Disengagement can lay groundwork for prevention or early intervention if and when any bumps in the road present themselves.

In the phase immediately after a new job or artful career change, a not unexpected exhaustion often leaves coachees not very receptive to the notion of an 'always on' career management strategy. The coach can remind the coachee that if some unforeseen aspect of the new organization becomes problematic (and this is frequently the case), there is something they can do about it early on. The objective is to de-stigmatize and normalize the likely challenges that lie ahead, and to prepare the coachee to enter the next career phase with a greater sense of self-efficacy and empowerment.

RELATIONSHIP WITH THEORETICAL TRADITIONS

Career coaching uses a blend of different theoretical approaches. The following four are of particular relevance.

Cognitive–behavioural

Cognitive–behavioural approaches to coaching are particularly useful in working with two common career circumstances: coachees who have just been terminated or had their position eliminated, and coachees who are currently working through a conflict with their boss or have left an organization because of a conflict with their boss. This technique is particularly good for coachees who have anger or blame directed inward at themselves. For those individuals, the cognitive–behavioural model helps to clear the psychological obstacles before attempting to do career strategy work.

The coach's job is to listen for indicators of potentially irrational thinking such as the coachee's use of the phrases 'should', 'supposed to' and 'ought to'. For example, a coachee was having difficulty accepting and moving beyond job loss in a lay-off situation. While expressing the (irrational) belief that she was incompetent, she didn't believe that any of the other 30 people who were laid off were incompetent. The coach used a cognitive–behavioural approach to confront the discrepancy, observing, 'You said these other 30 were competent professionals doing good work, so according to your "should", they "should" still have their jobs. So, since they don't have their jobs, let's look for some other rational explanation for why you don't have your job.'

Narrative

Narrative approaches to coaching link well with some of the theories in the field of occupational psychology. Holland (1997) refers to the Personal Career Theory (PCT) that individuals develop as a way to explain their perception of how their career choices and results play out. When the personal narrative that accompanies their PCT seems to fail to provide an adequate context for the events or strivings that are emerging in an individual's work-life, help is often sought in the form of a coach.

We tend to screen out stories, facts and even observations that are not congruent with the selective perception that accompanies our current story or theory. The career coach's role is to:

- assist the coachee with insight into current identity
- differentiate what Drake (2007) refers to as the available stories offered by our context, history, culture, family and even vocabulary, and the potential stories that can be created or co-created for a more congruent or fulfilling future
- explain or normalize the shifts in identity that occur with development, trauma, new relationships and age
- expand the possibilities to create new identities through the creation or co-creation of new narratives about work that respect the shifts or changes that are taking place and reflect the co-defined realities of the coachee's emerging context.

The recrafting of one's story can be particularly challenging for the individual who is shifting their working identity to a new career, not just a new job. Ibarra (2004) describes the three stages that require an individual to create new stories about themselves as seeker, in between and 'ex'. The career coach can add value, speed and clarity to the creation of the new and various stories.

The coach can expedite the creation of new stories when working with coachees to interpret psychometric measures of their preferences and interests. Coaches can use the data as an opportunity to have coachees look at the other occupations that share the same interests and see these other occupations not as what they 'should become', but rather, as potential 'clients, customers or colleagues' in their future work. For example, consider a coachee who is a history teacher and 20-year veteran of the classroom, and whose Strong Interest Inventory (2004) indicates similar interest patterns with occupations such as marketing executive, graphic artist, teacher and technical writer. The coachee reacts negatively to the notion of becoming a marketing executive. The coach invites the coachee to transform that reaction by thinking of the marketing executive not as a career goal, but as a possible team-mate. The coachee re-narrates a story as: 'Maybe I work for a textbook publisher and I'm on a team with a marketing executive, a graphic artist, and a technical writer, working together to design a textbook cover that will get students interested in learning history'.

When coachees complete this exercise, they have created alternative stories about their working identities, starting with assessment-based data (as well as their coach's insights and observations) and projecting some of who they are or could be when inspired by some of that data.

Positive psychology

Career coaching draws many of its underlying assumptions from the theoretical perspective of positive psychology. A primary goal of career coaching is to assist the coachee in developing a nuanced understanding of his or her strengths and then translating or 'behaviouralizing' those strengths as they might be valued in the marketplace. A clear mutual understanding of the coachee's strengths is critical for constructing an answer to the question: 'What would success look like?'

Often, career coaches use approaches drawn from positive psychology to help coachees become aware of strengths that others perceive in them, as well as to revalue strengths of which they may already be aware. One approach used in leadership development contexts that may be adapted for use in career coaching is the 'reflected best self' exercise (Spreitzer, Stephens, & Sweetman, 2009), in which individuals solicit feedback from a cross-section of colleagues, customers, friends and family members who know them well, asking them to 'tell me about a time when you saw me at my best: what did I say or do, and what was the impact you observed?' This is especially useful with coachees who are struggling to translate their accomplishments into summarized form for their résumés and/or examples to share during employment interviews.

Person-centred

Coaches and coachees often strive to bring analysis and data to their process but the coaching experience is often used more as a thinking-out-loud laboratory, which makes the person-centred approach to listening and deeply acknowledging the coachee's experience one of the most useful career coaching approaches.

In some instances, career coaches are aware of their strengths but they value them as neutral or negative. The neutral quality is created by the mental 'tornado' that they are in as they mentally spin around various key questions without coming to closure. For example, a coachee may find he/she starts internal conversations about career change, maybe gathers a little information, gets distracted and moves on to other tasks, and then returns to the career question and starts the process all over again. The experience of many small whirlwinds throughout the day that never go anywhere is a depleting 'tornado' experience, creating zones of chaos and self-doubt as opposed to order or directionality.

Thinking of the career indecision 'tornado' as a set of run-on sentences, the person-centred coaching relationship inspires the coachee to better formulate the fragments and recursive thinking loops that have characterized their career change 'tornado' in order to present information to their coach. The process of creating and telling one's story often leads to insights – 'no, that's not quite how it happened' or 'I didn't realize I felt that way' – which create new awareness and understanding. Additional awareness and understanding often arise when the coach artfully acknowledges and/or reframes the patterns he or she is hearing in the coachee's story. The coach may at this juncture draw on narrative, cognitive–behavioural or other approaches for the next steps in the coaching process. All of them can be thought of as resting within the connectedness and trust created by the person-centred approach to listening and acknowledging the reality of the other person's experience.

EVALUATION

Career coaching is called for when coachees seek the benefit resulting from planned action, or when their personal career theories no longer seems to serve them in explaining the world of work and their place in it. Common constraints on the nature and success of career coaching include intra-psychic, interpersonal and socioeconomic constraints.

Intra-psychic and clinical issues may block client success. As coaches, we draw on psychological theories and traditions that are also the basis for therapy. When we assess the fabric of a coachee's life and start pulling a thread related to career, we can find ourselves unravelling marriage, family, alcoholism and/or depression issues that are not the purview of career coaches. Even with clinical background and training, the career coach has not entered into a therapeutic relationship and is not chartered to work in clinical areas and, therefore, runs the ethical risk of creating a 'dual relationship' with a coachee by engaging in psychotherapy in addition to career coaching. Psychological understanding is crucial so as to identify, but not treat, issues that are blocking progress. Referral knowledge is essential.

In other instances it is appropriate for the career coach to blend in other types of coaching. For example, career and leadership coaching may be called for by coachees who are struggling within a management role. Coachees may prematurely flee a job or organization (and seek career coaching) due to discomfort with the role of manager. They may seek new jobs rather than address style, skill or knowledge shortcomings that could be addressed through performance coaching to enable them to successfully sustain the leadership role.

Being patient with the initial goal assessment may be difficult. It is crucial to sort out the differences between a career change strategy and a job search strategy early in the engagement. The lack of clarity or ambivalence of many clients will require patience and careful assessment on the part of the coach to determine the mission of their work together. Impatience can result from a poor match between a goal-oriented coach who is working with an insight-oriented client wanting to experiment with defining a new working identity. Alternatively, career coaching may be offered as part of an outplacement service that is time-limited and driven by a sense of urgency or quality metrics that do not similarly compel the coachee.

The context of employer-paid career coaching can raise contextual issues. Coachees may question what is considered confidential and whether or not there is a real or perceived dual relationship when the coach is simultaneously operating as corporate 'HR professional' and an individual 'career coach' discussing personal development strategy with an employee.

Finally, there may be both cultural and economic constraints on career coaching. In more localized, tradition-driven, tribal or non-industrialized cultures, the few individuals who could use career coaching may find it lacking due to the fact that the majority of citizens have their career decisions defined and answered for them by the social context. Even in a more commercial or industrial culture, ability to pay for career coaching can be a constraint. There may also be a mismatch wherein the points in time when individuals are most in need of career coaching (job and income loss) coincide with times when they may be least able to pay for a coach's services.

Protracted economic recession has become both a regional as well as global economic constraint on the goals of career coaching. As recession takes its toll, it leaves a wake of unemployed workers at all levels that must struggle more than ever to find their occupational niche in a receding economy. In times like this, career and job search strategies are more essential than ever because competition in the market place is so intense. Career coaching then becomes most essential at a time when many clients might otherwise cut back on expenses for personal services in a way that may be 'penny wise and pound foolish'.

There are some realistic limitations on the career coach as well as the client in tough economic times. The coach must recalibrate options and timelines as well as client expectations. Not infrequently, the coach may be the bearer of harsh but realistic information about the constrained job market context or the reduced possibilities of making career changes. But it is essential to continue to offer encouragement on the basis of a very real fact; searching for work is a micro-economic strategy and clients may be ill-advised to conduct their micro-economic strategy on the basis of macro-economic statistics (i.e. national unemployment figures or general decline of sales in an industry sector).

It will also be increasingly important for career coaches to be cognizant of mental health and substance abuse issues that may arise with clients during periods of protracted unemployment (8–24+ months). Being sad or frustrated are normal human emotions to observe in clients during times of unemployment. When these emotional states progress to clinical depression, substance abuse, or frequent outbursts of anger or even violence, the career coaching will start to have diminishing effectiveness. It is then time to collaborate with a mental health counsellor to treat the emotional issues that are starting to eclipse the client's ability to execute on the career strategy.

A global issue is arising for government workers in industrialized open market countries. Tax revenues in many economies will drop and government employment will slow and experience significant lay-offs. In the past, these laid-off government workers would have simply switched their employment to a different local or national branch of government after a relatively short search for work. With government lay-offs happening at all levels simultaneously, re-employment in public sector work is less likely than ever. Former government workers will have to seek employment in the private sector and will have to learn a new work culture. Thus, career coaches must ideally have a 'bi-cultural' understanding of public and private sector values and styles to help clients make that cultural transition. As Clark (2012) suggests, these changes are beyond the control of individual institutions as well as the individuals that work in them. Because individuals can't change the economic environment they must adapt their personal business model to better match the circumstances they are in. Understanding personal business models and how to construct or modify them is the emerging skill set for both career coaches as well as their clients.

Work and the workplace are, for most of us, a compelling arena for our interest and investment. Career coaches are the 'investment advisors' for this part of our life portfolio. It is a form of coaching that is blessed with rich rewards for the coachee and the coach, due in no small part to the frequently measurable outcome of the coaching process: useful, observable work to which the talents of the coachee can be applied.

FURTHER READING

Butler, T. (2007). *Getting unstuck: How dead ends become new paths*. Boston, MA: Harvard Business School. (A nuanced approach to assessment of an individual's career development needs and change dynamics. Butler offers career coaching stories illuminating how his clients uncovered the underlying psychological dynamics behind their impasse and moved through a series of self-awareness exercises to clarity about next steps and action. Butler weaves the psychology of Carl Jung and David McClelland, among others, into a series of 'deep dive' exercises that culminate in a map of the individual's life interests, social motivators, themes and dynamic tensions.)

Clark, T., in collaboration with Osterwalder, A. and Pigneur, Y. (2012). *Business model you: A one-page method for reinventing your career*. Hoboken, NJ: Wiley. (Provides a practical methodology for clients to map key elements of their career onto a one-page summary of their own personal 'business model'.)

Ibarra, H. (2004). *Working identity: Unconventional strategies for reinventing your career*. Boston, MA: Harvard Business Review. (Ibarra offers a practical process for career reinvention based on inductive analysis of longitudinal observations of mid-life career changers. Ibarra honours the 'plan and implement' model of career development but expands beyond it to offer a rich and practical description of an alternative 'test and learn' approach. Many rich stories illustrate how a series of low-cost, low-risk experiments over time can enable profound career shifts.)

DISCUSSION QUESTIONS

- What boundary issues need to be negotiated early in a career coaching relationship? How can coaches and coachees become clear early on about mutual role and relationship expectations? Why is this important?
- How would you keep a client focused and motivated during a protracted job search in a down economy?
- What aspects of career coaching are most similar and different across cultural contexts?

REFERENCES

Bench. M. (2008). *Career coaching: An insiders guide*. London: High Flight Press.

Blustein, D. (2006). *The psychology of working: A new perspective for career development, counseling, and public policy*. Mahwah, NJ: Lawrence Erlbaum Associates.

Bolles, R.N. (2008). *What color is your parachute? A practical manual for job-hunters and career changers*. (Rev. and updated annually). Berkeley, CA: Ten Speed Press.

Butler, T. (2007). *Getting unstuck: How dead ends become new paths*. Boston, MA: Harvard Business School Press.

Clark, T., in collaboration with Alexander Osterwalder and Yves Pigneur. (2012). *Business model you: A one-page method for reinventing your career*. Hoboken, NJ: Wiley.

Colombo, J.J. & Werther, W.B. (2003). Strategic career coaching for an uncertain world. *Business Horizons*, 48(4): 33–38.

Drake, D.B. (2007). The art of thinking narratively: Implications for coaching psychology and practice. *Australian Psychologist*, 42(4): 289.

Dychtwald, K. (2005). *The power years: Pursue your dreams, deepen your relationships, achieve financial freedom*. Hoboken, NY: John Wiley & Sons.

Farren, C. (1997). *Who's running your career? Creating stable work in unstable times*. Austin, TX: Bard.

Feldman, D.C. and Moore, D. (2001). Career coaching: What HR professionals and managers need to know. *Human Resource Planning*, 24: 26–35.

Hakim, C. (1994). *We are all self-employed*. San Francisco, CA: Berrett-Koehler.

Hazen, B.B. (2014). *Answering the three career questions: Your lifetime career management system*. Portland, OR: Three Questions Consulting.

Holland, J.L. (1997). *Making vocational choices: A theory of vocational personalities and work environments* (3rd ed.). Odessa, FL: Psychological Assessment Resources.

Horan, J. (1997). *The one page business plan (for the creative entrepreneur).* Berkeley, CA: The One Page Business Plan Company.

Horan, J. (2006). *The one page business plan (for the professional consultant).* Berkeley, CA: The One Page Business Plan Company.

Ibarra, H. (2004). *Working identity: Unconventional strategies for reinventing your career.* Boston, MA: Harvard Business School Press.

Spreitzer, G., Stephens, J.P., & Sweetman, D. (2009). The best reflected self experiment with adolescent leaders: Exploring the psychological resources associated with feedback source and valence. *Journal of Positive Psychology*, 14(5): 331–48.

Strong Interest Inventory (2004). Mountain View, CA: CPP.

24

Cross-cultural Coaching: A Paradoxical Perspective

Geoffrey Abbott

Cross-cultural (or intercultural) coaching has emerged as a distinct practice in situations where cultural influences are identified as particularly relevant to the client's personal and professional development. A cultural issue that suggests a cross-cultural coaching intervention might be global in nature, such as in the expansion of a company across national boundaries into cultural environments that are 'foreign' on almost every indicator; or it might be as narrow as a shift of an employee from one department of a company to another. The practice of cross-cultural coaching can happen on an individual, group or organizational level. This chapter describes how cross-cultural coaching has emerged and examines the interrelationship with other forms of coaching – noting, paradoxically, that all coaching is cross-cultural – and none. Regarding the future, the main proposition is that high impact cross-cultural coaching requires engagement with uncertainty, change and complexity in community, organizational and group contexts. In particular, coaching can assist clients in embracing and managing core paradoxes that have the capacity to derail positive change and growth, and instead position them as positive creative sources of energy for development.

Cross-cultural coaching often occurs simply by way of the fact that the context is in some way 'cross-', 'multi-' or 'inter-' cultural. Some common examples include:

mergers and acquisitions (cross-border or in-country)

joint ventures and alliances (cross-border or in-country)

expatriate assignments (long-term sojourns and more fluid 'flexpat' arrangements) multicultural teams (geographically co-located and, increasingly, virtual)

international projects (commercial, aid, educational, etc.)

internal restructures

job shifts from one company to another, or one department to another

bi-cultural or mixed background coaching clients and so on.

An assumption of cross-cultural coaching is that there are multiple realities and that each situation within each of the above categories requires a unique approach. There is no 'Seven Steps – One Size Fits All' model. Coaching conversations become a means by which contextual forces can be given prominence – not discounted. Coaching is a medium by which the complexity of situations can be unpacked, moving clients from being overwhelmed and confused to situations where possibilities emerge.

The mobility of people and capital through globalization has seen an increase in the number of situations where cultural issues come to the fore. The most recent manifestation of this shift is the rapid economic expansion of the so-called 'BRIC' countries of Brazil, Russia, India and China (Goldman-Sachs, 2007) and other emerging economies. These countries are not only new players in the 21st century global economy (particularly in mergers and acquisitions), but they also have distinct cultures that are very different from those of the traditional economic powerhouses of the USA and Western Europe. In addition, the constant movement of peoples around the globe as refugees and migrants has added to the cultural diversity of workforces in many countries that were relatively monocultural through long periods of their history.

A related trend that has increased is the use of the internet for the normal conduct of international business activity. A decade ago, people wanting to conduct real-time interactions across borders were consigned to costly telephone calls, fixed point videoconferencing, or unreliable web-based technologies. Now, there is a plethora of possibilities. Skype is ubiquitous, allowing unlimited, acceptable-quality audio and video communication for little or no cost. A by-product of the technological advancement has been the growth of virtual teaming. For coaching, this has meant that coaches are increasingly being asked to engage with executives whose scope of influence ranges far outside their offices. Multicultural teams and geographically dispersed teams are common place, along with the challenges and possibilities that come from cultural and linguistic diversity. Even coaches (and the executives they coach) who don't travel outside their home town are now required to be culturally and internationally savvy.

The result is that coaching – particularly executive and business coaching – has become a necessarily cross-cultural practice. Nevertheless, many coaches have little or no specific knowledge, models, techniques or assessment tools that can assist them to deal with the reality of the intercultural practice of which they are part. This is not surprising, as few established models exist for coaching across cultures. In 2003, Rosinski published *Coaching across cultures* and invited coaches, organizations and individual clients to view culture as an advantage rather than as an obstacle. He provided tools and methodologies for coaches to use with clients to leverage cultural differences for individual, organizational, community and societal development. His contribution was to place culture as a key influence in coaching effectiveness. He drew together knowledge from disparate disciplines to give coaches a solid foundation for their practice.

Since then, other texts have given some attention to the cultural perspective in coaching, usually by way of a dedicated chapter (for example, Drake, Brennan, & Gørtz, 2008; Morgan, Harkins, & Goldsmith, 2005; Passmore, 2006; Stober & Grant, 2006). Another text that gives special attention to cultural issues in coaching is that of Law, Ireland and Hussain (2007). Most recently, Moral and Abbott (2011) have given an organizational context to the practice of international coaching, seeking to intertwine culture within traditional and new coaching themes. Gradually then, coaching texts and coach training programmes are recognizing the importance of cultural perspectives.

Predating coaching-specific literature, interculturalists such as Bennett (1993, 1998), Hofstede (1997), Trompenaars and Hampden-Turner (1998) and others have provided a wealth of information upon which coaches who work internationally can and do draw. Adler and Gundersen (2008) has also provided rich resource material and models from an organizational perspective for coaches in the international business field, giving particular attention to gender issues.

Cross-cultural psychology and management researchers have given prominence to the interplay of cognitive, behavioural and emotional factors in understanding and managing the pressures and complexities of cross-cultural situations. The concept of 'cultural intelligence' (Earley and Ang, 2003; Ang, Van Dyne and Tan, 2011) has emerged from the academic literature as a useful tool for those working interculturally. Cultural intelligence describes a person's (1) knowledge of cultural difference; (2) capacity to change behaviour to accommodate difference; (3) motivation to change behaviour in the light of knowledge of cultural differences and capacity to change; and (4) overall conceptual capacity to make sense of culturally diverse contexts. Similarly, the idea of a Global Mindset has been developed along with a measurement instrument to examine the factors that are involved in influencing people who are different from oneself. Again, the construct examines the interplay of cognitive, affective and behaviour elements in context. Ward, Bochner and Furnham (2001) explained how psychological impact of interacting with new cultures can be conceptualized through the interplay of cognitive, behavioural and emotional aspects. This is all useful knowledge for coaches who are assisting clients to deal with cultural complexity.

Many paradoxes have emerged in the expanding field of cross-cultural coaching. One is that the choice of a cross-cultural coaching intervention in itself reveals a level of awareness about culture that might render unnecessary such a culture-specific intervention. Another paradox is that to label the intervention as 'cross-cultural' may potentially undermine its effectiveness because this might detract from attention being given to other powerful factors that are impacting a change process.

Culture has been defined in so many ways that it is almost indefinable. Trompenaars and Hampden-Turner (1998: 6) suggest it is 'the way a group of people solve problems and reconcile dilemmas'. Schein (1999: 29) defines it as 'the sum total of all the shared, taken-for-granted assumptions that a group has learned through its history'. Hofstede (1997: 5) defines culture as 'the collective programming of the mind which distinguishes the members of one group or category of people from another'. Externally, it is manifested in symbols and artefacts. Internally, it resides in deeply embedded subconscious assumptions and patterns of thinking and feeling and acting. Culture is not static; cultural interaction inevitably results in some degree of change in the cultures of the interacting groups. Some changes are huge; others are imperceptible. The uncertain nature and practice of cross-cultural coaching reflects the muddiness and wooliness of the concept of culture itself.

Another paradox is that all coaching is cross-cultural; and yet no coaching is cross-cultural. That is, the individual identity of every person is always partly influenced by the cultures of the groups with which he or she interacts. Thus, any kind of coaching work will touch either implicitly or explicitly on the various cultural influences involved (team, family, community and so on). At the other extreme, it could be said that coaching can never be labelled 'cross-cultural' because so many influences impinge on the coaching engagement that to concentrate only on culture makes no sense.

A common implicit assumption in choosing 'cross-cultural coaching' in place of other genres of coaching is that somehow it is possible to isolate culture as a variable and treat it separately in developing strategies for development and change. While to some extent it is possible, from another perspective it is not. A holistic, integrationist, situational view of coaching would suggest that culture is inextricably linked with various cognitive, emotional, behavioural, structural and other influences. There is no resolution to these dilemmas or contradictory truths. It is a question of accepting a fundamental paradox in cross-cultural coaching that:

1. it is sometimes necessary and possible to deal explicitly and primarily with culture as a variable and influence in coaching (including measuring it and making generalizations on the basis of culture) – in other words to 'do' cross-cultural coaching and;
2. doing cross-cultural coaching is theoretically dubious and can be highly perilous.

Holding on to this paradox is essential for effective cross-cultural coaching. Difficulties arise when:

> The coach through his or her own expertise and interest in culture keeps the focus on culture when in fact there might be other issues and variables that need attention.

> A client or organization is blind to cultural factors and chooses a coaching intervention that is not culturally appropriate or is not able to take advantage of cultural perspectives and resources.

> The coach is not sufficiently skilled, experienced or knowledgeable around cultural issues to be able to identify, explore and leverage culture in the coaching engagement.

> Cultural stereotypes are mobilized and inadvertently reinforced in a form of sophisticated stereotyping (Osland, Bird, Delano, & Jacob, 2000). This point is critical and is covered below in the discussion of cultural measurement.

Coaching approaches that integrate culture into a holistic approach to individual and organizational change are finding favour. Wilber's Integral Model (Armstrong, 2009; Wilber, 2000) has been effectively utilized to position cross-cultural coaching. The Integral Model identifies four quadrants on a two-by-two matrix (see Figure 24.1). Culture is placed in the internal/collective quadrant. In integral coaching, the coach will work the coaching conversation around the four quadrants. The use of the model ensures that culture gets some attention in the coaching engagement. Similarly, Bolman and Deal's (2008) highly-practical four-frame model (from the organizational behaviour literature) includes a symbolic/cultural frame for analyzing any leadership challenge.

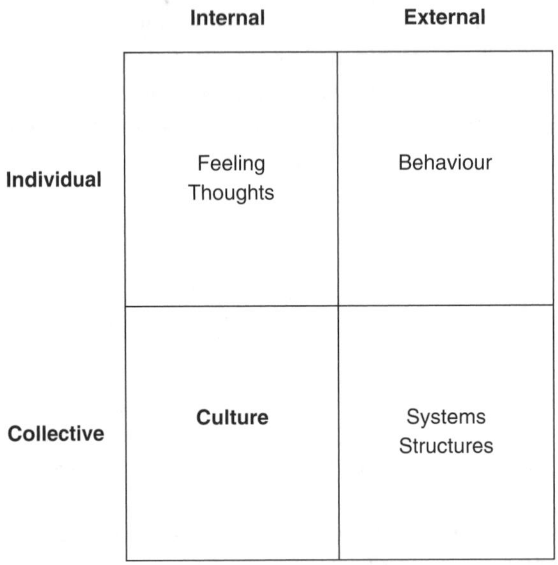

	Internal	**External**
Individual	Feeling Thoughts	Behaviour
Collective	**Culture**	Systems Structures

Figure 24.1   The integral model (adapted from Wilber, 2000)

Another theoretical framework that has significance for cross-cultural coaching is complexity theory. Climate change, resource shortages, technological developments, population movements and pressures, religious conflicts, political upheaval and so on have placed enormous pressures on organizations and individuals. In business, complexity theory is now being applied to assist executives to make sense of 'messy' or 'wicked' problems that on the surface appear insoluble. An example of the response of business to the growing complexity is the work of Snowdon and Boone (2007). The Cynefin framework they have developed proposes that problem situations need to classified as simple, complicated, complex or chaotic. Depending on the choice, the approach needs to be different. For complex problems – which are increasingly common – the first strategy is to 'probe', then to 'sense' and then to 'respond'. A coaching approach is based on open questioning which fits with the probing strategy. Cultural influences, which operate beneath the surface, are a natural sphere for probing and exploration in coaching, using some of the models described above.

Cavanagh and Lane (2012: 88) draw on the work of Stacey and others (e.g. Stacey, 2007) to examine how complexity theory can inform coaching. They pose several questions to the coaching community, including, 'Can we manage to organize as a profession in a way which honours the complex and chaotic contexts within which we work, rather than seek to codify the knowledge base so that it conforms to a traditional linear structure?' (Kolb: 1984)

The relevance of complex adaptive systems to cross-cultural coaching becomes apparent if we consider how complexity is embedded in cultural interactions. Cross-cultural coaching therefore, becomes a means of exploring possibilities and paradoxical thinking, in particular, is one method of generating nonlinear exploration Furthermore, practices developed in intercultural coaching may be of considerable relevance to other coaching approaches as complexity becomes the underlying context of our work.

DISTINCTIVE FEATURES

The defining feature of cross-cultural coaching is an assumption that culture has a major (and potentially positive) influence on individual and group performance, development and satisfaction. The influences operate interactively across the cognitive, behavioural and affective domains and the task of the coach is to work holistically with the client in ways that will assist them towards more satisfying and productive futures (Abbott, Stening, Atkins, & Grant, 2006). Beyond this assumption, the practice can vary as to how culture is mobilized. Cross-cultural coaching that is integrated with other approaches, is contextual and is grounded in action learning principles (Abbott & Grant, 2005), appears to provide opportunities for achieving personal and group development on many fronts. An action learning model is illustrated in Figure 24.2.

Though linear in stages one to five, in practice the model is much more fluid. In cross-cultural coaching, a fluid and dynamic action cycle is paramount because it provides a

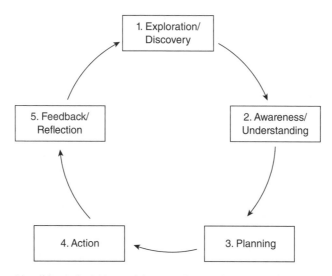

Figure 24.2   Action learning cycle (adapted from Kolb, 1984)

mechanism for clients (individual, team, organizational) to adjust and adapt to complex and changing circumstances. Regular periods of reflection in coaching sessions can give clients invaluable opportunities to step back and examine themselves – their feelings, thoughts and behaviours – in the evolving cultural context. Such reflection is valuable fuel for planning and action towards desired outcomes.

Unlike training, cross-cultural coaching provides ongoing opportunities to work through stages 3 and 4 of action learning – planned action based on enhanced awareness in context. Figuring out action strategies that foster the leveraging of difference through creative synergies takes time and in-depth discussion. Group training situations cannot always provide such opportunities. Following client action, coaching sessions provide further opportunities for clients to take action, then engage in creative dialogue about what happened (feedback and reflection – stage 5). Then, the ongoing process of coaching takes the client into further cycles of discovery, awareness-raising, action and feedback/reflection. Typically, a cross-cultural coaching intervention would run over eight to twelve sessions over six to twelve months, perhaps longer. The reason for a relatively long timeframe is that culture is often an underlying variable that is entwined in all aspects of the client's experiences. Working at this level is complex and requires a high degree of experimentation through the various stages of the action learning cycle.

Coaching across cultures requires a language to assist clients to make sense of their stories and to discuss cultural influences with a degree of depth and sophistication. Establishing such a vocabulary early can be helpful in tackling complex situations later on. One aim of cultural measurement frameworks is to give a terminology for discussing differences. Culture values, dimensions and orientations have been measured in various ways by many different interculturalists and values researchers (e.g. Hofstede, 1997, 2001; Kluckhohn, 1967; Schwartz & Bilsky, 1987; Trompenaars & Hampden-Turner, 1998). Hofstede's five dimensions (formerly four) were derived from a survey of IBM offices in the 1960s. They are commonly used in the cross-cultural area – including by coaches. The dimensions are:

1. power distance (high/low)
2. uncertainty avoidance (high/low)
3. individualism v. collectivism
4. masculinity v. femininity
5. long-term v. short-term orientations.

Similarly, Hampden-Turner and Trompenaars (2000) have identified seven common dimensions across which people tend to vary in response to common challenges faced by groups and communities. They promote the concept of cultural synergies – seeking to reconcile the dichotomies rather than to see them as incompatible. Looking for synergies is a common approach in cross-cultural training, yet in practice it is very difficult to achieve within limited timeframes and constructed training agendas.

Rosinski (2003) provided a Cultural Orientations Framework (COF) which distils various cultural measurement approaches into a 'coach-friendly' list of orientations. The questionnaire is straightforward and respondents simply rate what they believe their current orientation is against each item. For example, a respondent may express a high individualistic orientation, rather than a collectivist orientation. They also express their preferred orientation; that is, the questionnaire splits on 'current' orientations (which are determined to some extent by the context) and 'preferred' orientations. Although the COF has fixed categories and dimensions, Rosinski explains that there is scope for coaches to work with clients in context to develop new and more appropriate dimensions that suit the time, place, people and issues at hand.

In constructing the various measurement tools, the approach was to collect data from large samples across different cultures and then to use advanced multivariate statistical analysis to identify factors that represent cultural dimensions, orientations or values. In theory, some measurement of group culture is then possible, which can subsequently be used to compare with other groups and as a baseline for change processes (e.g. through coaching programmes, organizational change processes). Another paradox emerges. Quantifying culture in this way carries the assumption that as an influence it can be isolated. Once isolated, it can then in theory be 'dealt with'. With this assumption, we can potentially miss or underestimate the embedded nature of culture.

There have been vigorous debates about 'the best' cultural measurement system. While interesting from an academic perspective, they are not overly useful for those working with culture in situ. Values and culture are vague concepts at best and there will never be a perfect system. However, cultural orientations and dimensions can be useful road maps for coaches and clients who are working across cultures, always remembering that the map is not the territory. Coaches working across cultures need to make their own decisions and be prepared to engage clients in creative, messy, tentative and ongoing dialogue to help make sense of what is going on.

A real risk in using cultural measurement is to unknowingly enter the territory of 'sophisticated stereotyping' (Osland et al., 2000) and inaccurately or inappropriately label people, groups or societies. The dimensions and orientations are invaluable in conceptualizing the world of the client – for the coach and for the client – but they can lead to negative outcomes if not dealt with very carefully. Inexperienced coaches may use results from a cultural measurement test to make predictions or interpretations that are 'sold' to the client as fact. These can then take on a life of their own in the client's thinking, feeling and behaving, and in the way the coach designs and implements the coaching intervention. It all may sound highly scientific at the time but is likely at best to be of little real value to the client and at worst to be totally misleading.

An associated limitation of the measurement systems is that they are usually presented as dichotomies. Although it is common cross-cultural coaches to promote synergies between the opposites, the image of opposites remains – even in the use of Rosinski's COF with his emphasis on 'leveraging differences'. There remains a sense that by moving towards the other end of the scale from one's current orientations, there is a need to compromise or to somehow be 'less'. The outcome of a coaching conversation may result, for example, in a client believing that being 'more direct' in communication would be a wise strategy. Paradoxically, being diplomatic and indirect may be the client's major personal and professional strength. He/she may consciously or subconsciously pull back from using a core strength in a situation where even more rather than less of it may be required. In effect, the result, though not the coaching intention, could be that the client ends up as being somehow diminished.

Hampden-Turner and Trompenaars (2000) see different cultural approaches as mirror images of each other and as having very dynamic interaction. They plot their paired dimensions on 'x' and 'y' axes and suggest that the interaction of the variables is where the potential for growth and development resides. By further developing the idea of creative synergies it is possible to depict the orientations and dimensions in a way that promotes paradoxical thinking and leads clients towards more creative approaches. The use of the common two-by-two matrix assists in this process. An overarching two-by-two matrix by Berry (1997) illustrates the value of the matrix in supporting 'and' rather than 'either/or' approaches when dealing across cultures. Figure 24.3 illustrates the choices open to someone who is in contact with a different culture. Berry's context was acculturation across national borders; the model applies equally well in organizational mergers and other cross-cultural situations. The model suggests that there are four possible approaches:

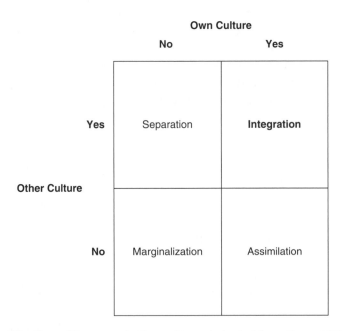

Figure 24.3   Identification with own and other cultures (adapted from Berry, 1997)

1. *Integration* occurs when there is an interest on behalf of the expatriate in both maintaining his or her original culture while being in daily interactions with other groups. Thus, some degree of cultural integrity is maintained, while at the same time the expatriate seeks to participate as an integral part of the larger social network.

2. *Assimilation* contrasts with integration and is where the individual does not wish to maintain his or her own cultural identity and seeks identification with and assimilation into the host culture. With expatriates, this is sometimes referred to as 'going native'.

3. *Separation* is when the individual places a value on holding on to his or her original culture and seeks to avoid interaction with the host culture. This stance is quite common with expatriate managers who may form enclaves (particularly in hardship posts). This was evident within a sample of expatriate managers in a recent coaching research study in Central America (Abbott, 2006).

4. *Marginalization* is the strategy adopted when there is little possibility or interest in cultural maintenance (often for reasons of enforced cultural loss) and little interest in having relations with others (often for reasons of exclusion or discrimination).

Integration has been found to be the most successful strategy in studies of acculturation; marginalization is the least; and assimilation and separation strategies are intermediate (Berry, 1997). This pattern has been found in almost every study and is present for all types of acculturating groups. The findings in organizational contexts are similar. A recent study of bicultural professionals (Tadmor, Galinsky, & Maddux, 2012) affirmed the advantages of integration as a strategy. They found that higher levels of 'integrative complexity' were associated with enhanced creativity and professional success. Counterintuitively, they found that marginalization was the second most effective strategy. Their reasoning was that marginalization avoids accepting one or other approaches as 'right', enabling a degree of flexibility.   Again, this kind of knowledge is useful for coaches working across cultures and assisting clients to raise awareness, make choices and design effective actions in their different contexts.

In a work context, the Harrison Assessment Paradox Graph (Harrison & Harrison, 2008) is a tool that attempts to promote a reconciliation of opposites through paradox theory. The tool is more designed for executive recruitment and job-fit purposes than for cross-cultural work per se, although the authors give weight to its cross-cultural application demonstrated through success in China. The tool also depicts apparently contradictory variables on two axes in a two-by-two matrix. The Harrison approach uses paradox theory, drawing on the work of Jung, Freud and others (Harrison & Harrison, 2008). According to paradox theory, our lives involve dealing with a series of paradoxes – twelve are listed. Each paradox is a relationship between two categories of traits, 'gentle' traits and 'dynamic' traits.

Being strong on both of the traits that make up the paradox is termed 'balanced versatility'. If the range of behaviour extends only to the 'dynamic' aspect of the paradox, it is called 'aggressive imbalance'. If the range extends only to the 'gentle' aspect of the paradox, it is called 'passive imbalance'. Imbalances have some counterproductive tendencies. A low range of behaviour on both aspects is called 'balanced deficiency' – with counterproductive tendencies (Figure 24.4).

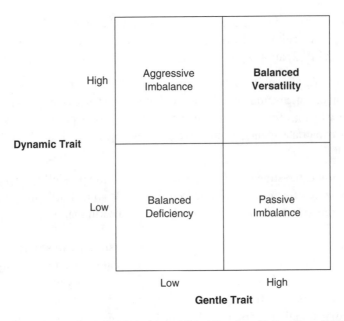

Figure 24.4   Trait interaction possibilities (adapted from Harrison & Harrison, 2008)

An example of balanced versatility in relation to the traits of 'certainty' and 'reflectiveness/openness' is given in Figure 24.5.

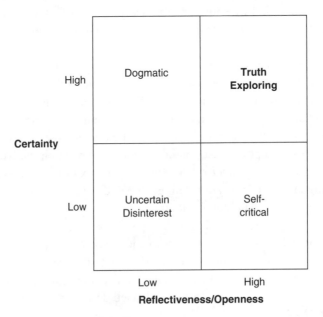

Figure 24.5   Certainty/reflectiveness paradox

The point of presenting this tool is not to argue for its scientific accuracy regarding the identification of universal paradoxes. In fact, the 'multiverse' (James, 1907) position proposed for cross-cultural coaching interventions would suggest that the concept of a fixed list of paradoxes makes little sense. Ideally, in each context the participants (clients and coaches) will construct relevant paradoxes through dialogue. The value is in suggesting to coaches that they use cultural dimensions measurements utilizing a paradoxical representational rather than a dichotomous depiction. For example, the individualism/collectivism dichotomy could be represented (see Figure 24.6). An illustration of how this might be applied to a coaching situation will be presented later in the chapter. With the assistance of paradox theory, the leveraging of differences through coaching can reframe cultural dimensions from dichotomies into orientations that can be held together and synthesized to develop approaches that are of most benefit to the client in specific contexts.

Even without measurement, a cross-cultural coaching intervention can be powerful in introducing a language for uncovering and naming issues which may be culturally underpinned. A point made often in the cross-cultural literature is that people are often blind to the nature and influence of culture in their lives and organizations. Coaches who are culturally savvy themselves can ask questions that can encourage clients to at least consider culture as a factor.

The role of coach

A key role of a coach working across cultures is to assist clients to notice the potential influence of culture in complex and changing environments. The action research framework positions the

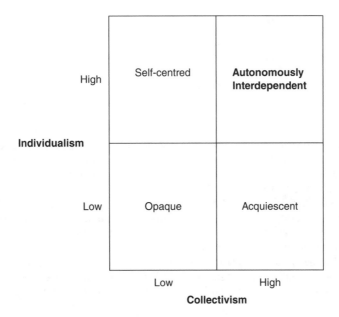

Figure 24.6   Individualism/collectivism paradox

coach as an active participant in the relationship – not a passive observer or simply someone who mirrors the world of the client. The questions asked by the coach and the choices about the process and direction of the coaching will have their own cultural biases. It is therefore paramount that coaches engage in their own processes of self-discovery and development. They then need to be appropriately explicit about their preferences and biases as they work with clients, and be very self-analytical about the way in which these forces may be operating. Abbott et al. (2006: 306) suggested that coaches working across cultures should have (in addition to generally accepted coaching competencies):

1. sound appreciation of the cultures of the client and the host country
2. self-awareness of the coach's own cultural background
3. personal experience in cultural adaptation and acculturation
4. familiarity with cross-disciplinary intercultural theory and research.

As noted earlier, a coach working across cultures is likely to use a cultural measurement tool of some kind. In training programmes, participants gain an understanding of cultural differences and hopefully a heightened awareness and understanding of who they are in relation to where they are and who they are with. The role of the coach beyond this is to explore reframing and managing of paradoxes to generate creative synthesis and inform action. The work of the coach is mainly in encouraging clients to develop narratives that include cultural sense making and shape futures that capture as many different dimensions and angles as possible. Put simply, the coach can help shape clarity in complexity.

Case study: Rafael Luz

The following case study provides an illustration of how cross-cultural coaching works in practice and also highlights how a paradox framework can assist in case conceptualization and development. The case study is of a Central American manager (Rafael Luz – not his real name) working in Central America with a European-based multinational company. The coaching programme with Rafael was one of 15 conducted as an action research doctoral study, examining how executive coaching could facilitate expatriate acculturation (Abbott, 2006).

Rafael Luz commenced his coaching programme while working in a middle management project role in finance and information technology. Rafael was formerly manager of operations and administration at the national airline. He had an engineering degree from an American University and an MBA from the top business school in Central America. The coaching programme comprised seven sessions of one to two hours over eleven months.

Rafael was dissatisfied with his limitations as an expert in finance and information technology. He was interested in developing his career and eventually being a general manager. The early coaching conversations gave Rafael an opportunity to give voice to a narrative that drew on his past successes as a manager in the local culture, and his academic and technical successes in a new culture (USA). The evolving narrative included reshaping his career back into the management stream within the multinational and perhaps extending beyond into management in local companies. Culture was deeply interwoven in each element of the coaching programme. No measurement tools were used.

Rafael clarified his goals, in particular his interest in improving his communication skills:

RL: One of the areas I don't really see as a weakness but one I would like to strengthen is communication. I don't see myself with problems on content. It is more externalizing those ideas to others.

GA (coach):   You had feedback that you had too much detail and you also said you liked detail?

RL: But I would be willing to trade it off if I could transfer it.

This was the entry point for a discussion about the company culture, which extended into a more general discussion about national culture and communication styles. The company culture at senior levels favoured direct communication with minimal up-front detail. In fact, detail was a major strength for Rafael. In cross-cultural terms, this could be presented as a dichotomy of direct and indirect communication (very commonly listed as a cultural orientation). The coaching could potentially have focused on pushing Rafael towards directness and away from his preferred style of giving large amounts of information.

From a paradox framework, this could be conceptualized slightly differently – as two related and conflicting variables of directness and detail (see Figure 24.7). The coaching conversation is a place where the contextual variables can be teased out and explored and so the task was to

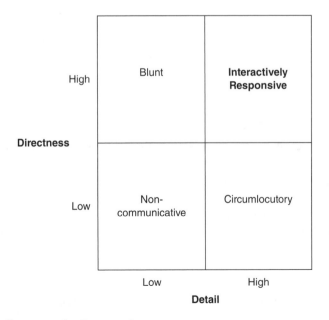

Figure 24.7   Rafael's communication paradox

unravel with Rafael what might be going on in the context and then to assist him to use his potential on each to maximize value from the other in a synergistic approach.

Rafael seemed high on detail but low on directness. When explored, it transpired that Rafael was actually quite comfortable with directness – but initially he saw it as a trade-off for his unique talents for managing enormous and complex detail across financial and technological fields. Although it was a trade-off he was prepared to enact, it was not attractive. In context, it emerged that Rafael was not asking enough direct questions to find out exactly how much detail was required at particular points in time. His challenge was to use directness at the front end of conversations to draw out the detail required in the context. The cultural issue was that in his previous management positions there had been an expectation that a presenter would provide considerable detail. The new assumption, organizationally and to some degree culturally-based, was that people expected a relatively short up-front delivery, followed by multiple exchanges to move through layers of detail that were behind the initial presentation.

The emphasis in the coaching was not to detract from Rafael's strength in the detail but to validate and manage that strength through utilizing a different kind of directness. The coaching sessions were dedicated to managing detail in a way that allowed it to be delivered rapidly and with focus at points when it was best needed. This approach fostered the 'leveraging of differences' in a dynamic way that went beyond the traditional cultural synergy approaches.

RELATIONSHIP WITH THEORETICAL TRADITIONS

Cross-cultural coaching cannot stand alone. Abbott and Rosinski (2007) have outlined how 'global coaching' incorporates the cross-cultural perspective and other perspectives, genres, or traditions of coaching. Following are four examples of how different genres were operating in the cross-cultural coaching with Rafael Luz.

Psychodynamic coaching

Cultural influences are often embedded deep in the subconscious. The coaching relationship carried high potential for transference and countertransference – with cultural undertones. The coach was an expatriate with a profile not dissimilar to the expatriate management group in-country and therefore could potentially be viewed by the client as representative of the multinational company norm. The coach's challenge was to be as aware as possible of any transference that might be occurring and to deal with it in the coaching dialogue.

Cognitive-behavioural coaching

Fundamentally, the coaching programme with Rafael was a behavioural change process. Part of the process was in-session training with Rafael on responding to direct questions with direct answers and in generating direct questions to be used to sharpen his interaction with senior expatriate executive. Cognitive reframing was required with Rafael to assist him in a shift from an assumption that 'direct communication managing complex detail are incompatible', to a new assumption that 'direct interactive communication can be highly effective in managing and communicating complex detail'.

Cognitive-developmental coaching

The coaching process had a strong developmental aspect. The conversations encouraged Rafael to see himself more objectively – that is, to step out of his role as a technical financial special-ist and to examine his potential and his future from a higher and wider perspective. The shift during the period of the coaching could be interpreted as typical of a manager expanding from Stage 3 to Stage 4 in Kegan's adult development model (Berger & Fitzgerald, 2002; Kegan, 1982, 1994). Berger and others have discussed how coaching programmes can be powerful in promoting experiential learning with associated cognitive developmental growth.

Positive psychology and solution-focused coaching

The coaching approach combined a focus on strengths with the opening up of new possibilities consistent with these coaching genres. Rafael's grasp of detail was portrayed as an asset to be managed rather than down-played. Similarly, coaching drew out strengths from Rafael's back-ground in being direct in his communication. Then, a very pragmatic contextual process followed to work those two strengths together for a solution that in the end paid enormous dividends.

The coaching sessions were devoted to validating Rafael's uniqueness and to allow him to design a future of his own making. Initially, the company seemed to be viewing Rafael as stereotypical of someone from the region who was buried in detail and unable to work at a high level with rapid-pace decision making. The coach's validation and valuing of Rafael's past, present and future assisted him to overcome the perceptions and to craft a role for himself that few would have envisaged possible.

The coaching dialogue gave attention to Rafael's past successes in Latin business contexts and grounded his future development on a successful integration with the organizational culture within which he was operating (consistent with Berry's integrationist strategy). This approach gave flesh to Rosinski's position of viewing culture as an opportunity rather than an obstacle to personal and professional development and is very much consistent with positive psychology principles.

EVALUATION

Cross-cultural coaching is difficult to evaluate as a context or a genre. When coaches integrate a cultural perspective, culture can be conceptualized and mobilized as a variable and be a pow-erful ally to coaches and their clients. However, culture can be unhelpful or even damaging when viewed as a separate or fixed variable that can be manipulated or altered. In this form, culture can be used to rationalize, excuse, dictate, glorify, or even dismiss aspects of client's development. The challenge is to be mindful of the potential for culture to be a major influence but to be very open-minded as to how it may be playing a part in the client's situation.

We are in an era when the challenges facing individuals and organizations are invariably complex. Culture is one variable that adds to the complexity. It also adds to the potential power of solutions because each different perspective holds a different way of tackling the challenge. Paradoxical thinking is one strategy that can assist coaching clients to draw across multiple perspectives and generate contextually effective solutions. Coaching can help them to find a degree of clarity in the complexity of their situations and equip them to make more effective decisions. At its worst, cross-cultural coaching could marginalize culture and give attention to the 'problem' of cultural differences. It could unknowingly become a vehicle for perpetuating stereotyping through the introduction and validation of rigid measurement systems that allow and even encourage simplistic interpretations of how people differ on the basis of culture. At its best, cross-cultural coaching is an inspired action-learning process that gives prominence to context where culture is explored and mobilized through conversations followed by client action. Appropriate terminologies are borrowed and constructed that give life to real issues that are playing out in the lives of clients. Clients are encouraged through narrative to take an expanding view of who they are and what they are doing on an individual, organizational, community and global scale.

As a final comment, the field of cross-cultural research and cross-cultural coaching has largely been driven by Western thinking and business practice. Different voices are emerging in intercultural research and in coaching and the future of cross-cultural coaching will be enhanced by this diversity. The application of paradoxical thinking to the world of coaching would dictate that diverse approaches be probed and synergized. Individual coaches require new ways of thinking – drawn from diverse traditions, practices and cultures – that can accommodate complex environments. They can then work with clients at a local level to assist them to create solutions that are likely to generate positive outcomes.

FURTHER READING

Adler, N.J. & Gundersen, A. (2008). *International dimensions of organizational behavior* (4th ed.). Cincinnati, OH: South-Western. (An excellent resource for coaches working with international companies.)

Moral, M. & Abbott, G. (Eds) (2011). *The Routledge companion to international business coaching*. London: Routledge. (Gives attention to coaching in an international business context. Each chapter contains theory, case studies, models and tools for coaches, executives and HR professionals. Issues covered include global virtual teams, international team coaching, collective intelligence, survival theory in international business, and global nomads.)

Rosinski, P. (2003). *Coaching across cultures: New tools for leveraging national, corporate and professional differences*. London: Nicholas Brealey. (Provides clear illustrations of how to leverage cultural differences. It also contains the Cultural Orientations Framework and a framework for Global Coaching. A 'must read' for any coaches working in intercultural environments.)

Snowden, D.J. & Boone, M.E. (2007). A leader's framework for decision making. *Harvard Business Review* (November): 69–76. (This article introduces some core elements of complexity theory and a way of conceptualizing problem situations that is 'gold' for coaches working in complex cross-cultural situations. Although it is mostly about leadership, the Cynefin Framework has much broader application.)

DISCUSSION QUESTIONS

- What is your experience of the culture–coaching relationship and how might you best leverage it to advantage in your context?
- On a scale of 1–10 (10 is high), how knowledgeable do you believe you are about cultural orientations and dimensions? When you reflect on your response, is they anything you think you need to do to best position yourself for success in your coaching-related work?
- The Cynefin Framework (Snowdon and Boone, 2007) suggests that complex problems first need to be 'probed'. What role do such frameworks have in coaching in complex intercultural environments?
- How might team, group and individual coaching approaches help people avoid falling into the trap of 'sophisticated stereotyping' on the basis of national culture?
- What kinds of tensions have you observed and experienced in cross-cultural situations. How might paradoxical thinking assist in creating energy and traction for coaching in such situations?
- How does your own cultural background influence the way that you interact with people in culturally diverse contexts? How might you make the most use of your cultural preferences and orientations?
- What is your favourite story about cross-cultural interaction? What meaning might this story have for the way you make sense of cross-cultural coaching?

REFERENCES

Abbott, G.N. (2006). Exploring evidence-based executive coaching as an intervention to facilitate expatriate acculturation: Fifteen case studies. (Unpublished Doctoral dissertation. Australian National University, Canberra.)

Abbott, G.N. & Grant, A.M. (2005). Evidence-based executive coaching and action research: A natural fit. In I.F. Stein, F. Campone, & L.J. Page (Eds), *Proceedings of the Second ICF Coaching Research Symposium*, 3 November 2004, Quebec City, Canada (pp. 22–9). Washington, DC: International Coach Federation.

Abbott, G.N. & Rosinski, P. (2007). Global coaching and evidence based coaching: Multiple perspectives operating in a process of pragmatic humanism. *International Journal of Evidence Based Coaching and Mentoring, 5*(1): 58–77.

Abbott, G.N., Stening, B.W., Atkins, P.W.B., & Grant, A.J. (2006). Coaching expatriate managers for success: Adding value beyond training and mentoring. *Asia Pacific Journal of Human Resources, 44*(3): 295–317.

Adler, N.J. & Gundersen, A. (2008). *International dimensions of organizational behavior* (5th ed.). Cincinnati, OH: South-Western.

Ang, S., Van Dyne, L., & Tan, M.L. Cultural intelligence. In R.J. Sternberg & B.F. Kaufman (Eds), *The Cambridge handbook of intelligence*. Cambridge: Cambridge University Press.

Armstrong, H.B. (2009). Integral coaching: Cultivating a cultural sensibility through executive coaching. In M. Moral & G. Abbott (Eds), *The Routledge companion to international business coaching*. London: Routledge.

Bennett, M.J. (1993). Towards ethnorelativism: A developmental model of intercultural sensitivity. In *Education for the intercultural experience* (pp. 21–71). Yarmouth, ME: Intercultural Press.

Bennett, M.J. (1998). Overcoming the golden rule: Sympathy and empathy. In M.J. Bennett (Ed.), *Basic concepts of intercultural communication: Selected readings* (pp. 191–214). Yarmouth, ME: Intercultural Press.

Berger, J.G. & Fitzgerald, C. (2002). Leadership and complexity of mind: The role of executive coaching. In C. Fitzgerald & J.G. Berger (Eds), *Executive coaching: Practices and perspectives* (pp. 27–57). Palo Alto, CA: Davies-Black Publishing.

Berry, J. (1997). Immigration, acculturation, and adaptation. *Applied Psychology, 46*(1): 5–34.

Bolman, L. G. & Deal, T.E. (2008). *Reframing organizations: Artistry, choice, and leadership*. San Francisco, CA: Jossey-Bass.

Cavanagh, M. & Lane, D. (2012). Coaching psychology coming of age: The challenges we face in the messy world of complexity. *International Coaching Psychology Review, 7*(1): 75–90.

Drake, D.B., Brennan, D., & Gørtz, K. (Eds) (2008). *The philosophy and practice of coaching: Insights and issues for a new era*. Chichester: Jossey-Bass.

Earley, P.C. & Ang, S. (2003). *Cultural intelligence: Individual interactions across cultures*. Stanford, CA: Stanford University Press.

Goldman-Sachs. (2007). *BRICs and beyond*. London: Goldman-Sachs Group.

Hampden-Turner, C. & Trompenaars, F. (2000). *Building cross-cultural competence: How to create wealth from conflicting values*. Chichester: John Wiley & Sons.

Harrison, A. & Harrison, D. (2008) *Assessment paradox graph*. Retrieved 26 July 2008 from www.harrisonassessments. com/

Hofstede, G. (1997). *Cultures and organizations: Software of the mind*. New York: McGraw-Hill.

Hofstede, G. (2001). *Culture's consequences: Comparing values, behaviors, institutions and organizations across nations.* (2nd ed.). Thousand Oaks, CA: Sage.

James, W. (1907). A pluralistic universe. In L. Menand (Ed), *Pragmatism: A reader* (pp. 132–8). New York: Random House.

Javidan, M., Teagarden, M., & Bowen, D. (2010). Making it overseas: Developing the skills you need to succeed as an international leader. *Harvard Business Review,* (April): 109–113.

Kegan, R. (1982). *The evolving self: Problem and process in human development*. Cambridge, MA: Harvard University Press.

Kegan, R. (1994). *In over our heads: The mental demands of modern Life*. Cambridge, MA: Harvard University Press.

Kluckhohn, C. (1967). Values and value-orientations in the theory of action: An exploration in definition and classification. In T.P.E.A. Shils (Ed.), *Towards a general theory of action*. Cambridge, MA: Harvard University Press.

Kolb, D. A. (1984). *Experiential Learning: Experience as the Source of Learning and Development*. New Jersey: Prentice Hall.

Law, H., Ireland, S., & Hussain, Z. (2007). *The psychology of coaching, mentoring and learning*. Chichester: John Wiley & Sons.

Moral, M. & Abbott, G. (Eds) (2011). *The Routledge companion to international business coaching*. London: Routledge.

Morgan, H., Harkins, P., & Goldsmith, M. (Eds) (2005). *The art and practice of leadership coaching*. Hoboken, NJ: John Wiley and Sons.

Osland, J.S., Bird, A., Delano, J., & Jacob, M. (2000). Beyond sophisticated stereotyping: Cultural sensemaking in context. *Academy of Management Executive, 14*(1): 65–79.

Passmore, J. (Ed.) (2006). *Excellence in coaching: The industry guide*. London: Kogan Page.

Rosinski, P. (2003). *Coaching across cultures: New tools for leveraging national, corporate and professional differences*. London: Nicholas Brealey.

Schein, E.H. (1999). *The corporate culture survival guide: Sense and nonsense about culture change*. San Francisco, CA: John Wiley and Sons.

Schwartz, S.H. & Bilsky, W. (1987). Towards a universal psychological structure of human values. *Journal of Personality and Social Psychology, 53*(3): 550–62.

Snowden, D.J. & Boone, M.E. (2007). A leader's framework for decision making. *Harvard Business Review* (November): 69–76.

Stacey, R.D. (2007). *Strategic management and organisational dynamics: The challenge of complexity* (5th ed.). London: Financial Times.

Stober, D.R. & Grant, A.M. (Eds) (2006). *Evidence based coaching handbook: Putting best practices to work for your clients*. Hoboken, NJ: John Wiley & Sons.

Tadmor, C.T., Galinsky, A.D., & Maddux, W.W. (2012). Getting the most out of living abroad: Biculturalism and integrative complexity as key drivers of creative and professional success. *Journal of Personality and Social Psychology, 3*: 520–542.

Trompenaars, F. & Hampden-Turner, C. (1998). *Riding the waves of culture: Understanding cultural diversity in global business* (2nd ed.). New York: McGraw-Hill.

Ward, C., Bochner, S., & Furnham, A. (2001). *The psychology of culture shock* (2nd ed.). Hove: Routledge.

Wilber, K. (2000). *Integral psychology: Consciousness, spirit, psychology, therapy*. Boston, MA: Shambhala.

25

Mentoring in a Coaching World

Bob Garvey

This chapter discusses the role, function and purpose of mentoring within a commercial world often dominated by talk of coaching. It draws on the literature of both mentoring and coaching and emphasizes the dynamics of dyadic developmental relationships. It also integrates mentoring and coaching practices into a broad category of one-to-one developmental dialogue.

The word 'mentor' comes directly from Ancient Greek and means 'of the mind'. The character, 'Mentor' was first introduced in Homer's epic poem, *The Odyssey*. According to The Oxford Dictionary, the term 'mentor' was first used in English to describe a developmental process in a letter from Lord Chesterfield to his son in 1750. It was later used by Lord Byron in his poems *The Curse of Minerva, Childe Harold's Pilgrimage* and *The Island* to describe characters of influence. However, probably the most significant volume on mentoring was Fénélon's (1651–1715) *Les aventures de Télémaque*.

Fénélon's (1808) work is a treatise on educational techniques. Based on Homer's *Odyssey*, it is a comprehensive description of the holistic learning and development of young Telemachus, King Odysseus' son. The work includes illustrative examples of learning from experience, reflective questioning and practical skills development, learning social awareness and self-awareness, role modelling and leadership development. Fénélon implied that leadership could be developed through guided experience. Louis XIV saw this as a challenge to his divine right, banished Fénélon to Cambrai and cancelled his pension. Nevertheless, Fénélon's work was very widely read throughout Europe and his influence is seen in the works of other writers on educational philosophy during the 18th century.

Caraccioli's book *Veritable le mentor ou l'education de la noblesse* published in 1759 was translated into English in 1760 and became *The true mentor, or, an essay on the education of young people in fashion*. This work describes mentoring from the perspective of the mentor. Caraccioli acknowledges the influence of Fénélon's work on his own and included a mentoring process model:

- observation leading to …
- toleration leading to …
- reprimands leading to …
- correction leading to …
- friendship leading to …
- awareness.

While the language in this model is archaic, it does contain some interesting parallels with both mentoring and coaching. For example, models of coaching for performance and mentoring in the education sector include 'Observation' as a key element of the process. 'Toleration' may be associated with patience and respect, perhaps even listening skills. 'Reprimands' and 'Correction' could be linked in modern thinking to feedback, demonstrations or searching for solutions to challenges. 'Friendship' is not normally an outcome of coaching but can be a natural consequence of mentoring. 'Awareness' is a key outcome for any coachee or mentee.

Another writer influenced by Fénélon was Rousseau. He was influenced by Fénélon's ideas on dialogue as an important vehicle for learning – we learn in conversation with others. It is no surprise then that Rousseau thought that the ideal model for learning effectively was one-to-one! Rousseau's '*Emile*' (1762) explores the learning and development of the central character, Emile, who is given a copy of '*Les aventures de Télémaque*' as a guide to his developmental journey. In '*Emile*', Telemachus becomes a model for learning, growth and social development.

Another writer from the 18th century produced three volumes called '*The Female Mentor*'. These were published in London in 1793 with the third volume in 1796. The author, Honoria (probably a *nom de plume*) identifies and describes the characteristics of the female mentor through a commentary and series of asides made throughout the volumes. These characteristics include patience, virtue, listening, challenge and support. The books are dedicated to Fénélon for sharing his approach to education and life.

The term 'coaching' first appears in English literature in Thackeray's '*Pendennis*' in 1849. Thackeray used the term 'coaching' as a pun, blending the idea of travelling in a horse drawn carriage from A to B (London to Oxford University) and helping someone to improve their academic attainment. During the 19th century, the term 'coaching' became associated with sport (rowing and cricket), life-skills development (e.g. parenting skills), craft skills and laboratory techniques. Coaching was for either performance improvement or for learning specific skills or tasks.

Mentoring and coaching share similar features in history. Both can be linked to education and learning and both are described as one-to-one processes. Recent European Mentoring Coaching Council (EMCC) research (Willis, 2005) indicates that coaching and mentoring are indeed similar activities and clearly demonstrates that coaches and mentors, in the main, share the same practices, skills and processes. However, what makes them distinctive is the context in which they happen, the purpose for which the conversation is conducted, mentoring tends to be voluntary and the move towards professionalizing coaching more so than mentoring.

In the last 40 years, mentoring activity has gained much momentum in private sector businesses, the public sector, small and large businesses and in education and social welfare. A recent survey in the UK Health Service (Healthcare Commission, 2005) estimated that 230,000 people participated in mentoring activity during 2004. The UK Health Service is the largest employer in Europe, with an estimated 1.3 million employees. If extrapolated out to other sectors, this would mean that 17% of the UK workforce would have experienced mentoring activity and this does not include educational and social mentoring activity. Therefore, in numerical terms mentoring reaches a huge number of people.

Coaching activity across Europe is also considerable. The recent Bresser Report (2008) suggests that approximately 17,000 businesses engage in coaching activity and practices are very diverse.

The rapid rise of both mentoring (Healthcare Commission, 2005) and coaching activity (Bresser, 2008) over a relatively short period has led to definitional confusion of both. There is much debate among academics and practitioners as to the true and distinctive nature of each. For example, Rosinski (2004) states:

> Although leaders can act as coaches, I have found that this role is often confused with mentoring. Coaches act as facilitators. Mentors give advice and expert recommendations. Coaches listen, ask questions and enable coachees to discover for themselves what is right for them. Mentors talk about their own personal experience, assuming this is relevant for the mentees. (Rosinski, 2004: 5)

I agree with Rosinski that mentoring is often associated with 'expert' knowledge sharing and advice giving, but it is also associated with listening, asking questions and enabling mentees to discover for themselves. A further point of confusion comes later in the same book where Rosinski goes on to say:

> In my view coaches are also responsible for transferring knowledge. Coaches don't simply help resolve coachees' issues. They actually share their knowledge so that coachees can become better coaches. For example the coach will briefly explain his frame of reference. (Rosinski, 2004: 245)

The above quote raises a problem because it is hard to distinguish between 'sharing knowledge' with the purpose of enabling someone to become a 'better coach' and talking, as a mentor, about one's 'own personal experience, assuming this is relevant to the mentee'. Rosinski's position raises the question of what the difference is between 'personal experience' and 'knowledge'. These points are discussed later in this chapter.

Gladstone (1988: 10) suggests that trying to define mentoring is difficult because

> ... it is as informal as pairing, as variable as the organizations in which mentors and protégés find themselves, and as idiosyncratic as the people involved.

Definition, by its very nature, seeks to simplify and reduce. It also, as can be seen above, attempts to polarize. In a world arguably dominated by cause and effect thinking, clear definition has a simplistic appeal. With social phenomena as complex as mentoring and coaching, definitional simplification is unhelpful. Lack of definition need not, however, be a problem. An alternative perspective explores the subtleties and complexities of the phenomena within their social contexts (see Bruner, 1985). Geertz (1971) suggests that this is called a rich or 'thick description'. The descriptions of mentoring offered below are not definitive but are a personal description of mentoring. There are four main elements:

First, mentoring is dependent on the human qualities of trust, commitment and emotional engagement. Often, in successful mentoring partnerships, the pair respect and like each other, and this may result in friendship.

Second, it includes the use of such skills as listening, questioning, challenging and supporting.

Third, central to mentoring is 'the mentee's dream' (Caruso, 1992). Mentoring is primarily for the mentee and the concept is therefore fundamentally associated with a desire to progress, to learn and understand and to achieve. People often engage in mentoring where the mentee is making a transition. For example, a new job, a promotion, a new stage of life, setting up a business, facing retirement, moving from unemployment to employment, reorganization or change.

Fourth, mentoring is a relationship between two individuals with learning and development as its core purpose. This relationship is a core part of the dynamic and it is here that mentoring activity starts to depart from coaching. Some of the relationship issues will be discussed later in this chapter but the following quote from Hunt and Weintraub (2002: 10) supports this view and emphasizes the 'emotional bond' as a key difference between mentoring and coaching: 'we believe that coaching doesn't necessarily require the type of emotional bond usually associated with mentoring'.

DISTINCTIVE FEATURES

This section briefly covers some of the main features of mentoring activity. These include:

- the relationship
- the social context
- the organizational context and mentoring
- the use of advice, knowledge or experience.

The relationship

As suggested above, central to mentoring is the idea that the 'relationship' plays an important part in facilitating learning. The affective side of mentoring plays a role, particularly in the light of the tendency for interpretations of mentoring and coaching to polarize; for example, to emphasize either the professional or the personal development of the mentee (Carruthers, 1993) or performance set against development or the long-term relationship versus short-term (Clutterbuck & Megginson, 2005).

De Haan (2008) also links coaching and mentoring activity and along with Sieler (2003) and Bluckert (2005) is one of the few authors to raise the importance of the relationship between coach and coachee. Hunt and Weintraub (2002: 9) stress the idea of a relationship over time as well as supporting the idea that coaching and mentoring are similar processes: 'Mentoring typically involves a more ongoing relationship. Effective mentors do use some of the same coaching practices'.

Ancient and modern mentoring literature has made the relationship point extensively (see, for example, Homer, 1184 [1250] BC; Caraccioli, 1760; Honoria, 1796; De la Mothe-Fénélon, 1808; Levinson, 1978; Torrance,1984; Bennetts, 1995, 1996; Hurley & Fagenson-Eland, 1996; Scandura, Tejeda, Werther, & Lankau, 1996; Hale, 2000; Samier, 2000; Friday, Shawnta, Friday, & Green, 2004). This literature either presents relationship building as key to achieving positive outcomes in mentoring or as problems associated with manipulation, favouritism or abuse.

Connor (1994) offers a rationale for integrating mentoring with the theory found in the kind of learning involved in counselling. Counselling practice highlights human qualities such as trust, openness, honesty and integrity. Additionally, notions crucial to workplace learning such as those of 'skills development', 'training for specific purposes', 'experiential learning' and 'situated learning' all relate to a model of learning which includes the concept of mentoring (Garvey, 1994c; Daloz, 1999).There are also connections here between those who view mentoring as a means to an end, such as learning for improved efficiency and effectiveness, and those who emphasize its wider psychosocial context (Kram, 1983) in which people are regarded as 'ends in themselves'.

Simmel (1950) explored issues of intimacy, secrecy, dependency, termination and triviality within dyads and observed that two is the maximum number of people needed for the security of a 'secret', suggesting that 'secrecy' places a mutual dependency on the relationship. In modern parlance, 'secrecy' could be replaced by the word 'confidentiality'. Confidentiality is fundamental to the success of both coaching and mentoring relationships (MacLennan, 1995; Clutterbuck & Megginson, 1999; Grodzki & Allen, 2005; Megginson, Clutterbuck, Garvey, Stokes, & Garrett-Harris, 2005). Modern writings on both mentoring and coaching regard dependency as a problem and also stress the allied notions of 'trust', 'commitment' and 'active involvement' as important elements of the relationship.

The certainty that any dyadic relationship may end can be a powerful influence on the partnership. Simmel suggests that the sense of the end can lead to either greater dependency or lack of trust. He also states that the sense of the end can bring the pair closer together. The coaching and mentoring literature discusses the issue of proper closures and endings of the relationship at some length (see Garvey, 1994b; Clutterbuck & Lane 2004; Grodzki & Allen, 2005).

'Triviality', Simmel suggests, is created by the initial expectations in the relationship failing to materialize in practice; and perhaps the frequency and sharing of experiences within the relationship contributes to a sense of 'triviality'. This can result in the dyad closing down as the pair or one of the pair runs out of things to say and gets bored! Consequently, there is a need for regular review and stimulation for it to deliver successful outcomes (see Neilson and Eisenbach, 2003).

Within any dyad there is potential for intimacy and the dyad provides the further potential for deep friendship with a tendency for intimacy and mutual dependence. Simmel makes it clear that this is not a consequence of the content of discussions but the uniqueness of the relationship. Intimacy exists 'if the 'internal' side of the relationship is felt to be essential; if its whole affective structure is based on what each of the two participants give or show only to the one other person and to nobody else' (Simmel, 1950: 126). In other words, the open nature and the confidentiality of the discussions provide the ingredients for intimacy.

In early research (Garvey, 1994a) a range of different people from different backgrounds described the 'quality' of their mentoring relationship in terms of:

- the wide ranging topics discussed in the partnership
- how many people within the organization knew that a mentoring relationship existed
- a 'tacitly understood' or 'explicitly understood' partnership at work
- the degree of activity within the partnership
- security and stability within the partnership.

These descriptions translated into a framework (Garvey, 1994c) that helps to describe the mentoring relationship and is referred to as the 'dimensions framework'. The participants in the research viewed these descriptions as important aspects of their natural and informal mentoring relationships. These dimensions offer the basis for a new approach to understanding both coaching and mentoring (Garvey, Stokes, & Megginson, 2009). This approach is not underpinned by simplifying definitions but, rather, by flexible description. The original descriptions were developed into the dimensions as follows.

Description 1, translated into the OPEN/CLOSED dimension. This dimension is about the content of the discussions. In an OPEN discussion, anything is on the agenda. If it is CLOSED, the discussion may focus on specific issues.

Description 2, translated into the PUBLIC/PRIVATE dimension. This is about who knows mentoring is going on in an organizational context and who ought to know.

Description 3, translated into the FORMAL/INFORMAL dimension. This is about the administration and management of the relationship. In a FORMAL arrangement, the mentoring pair may agree meetings in advance, take notes, time limit the discussion, agree to meet in a regular venue at regular intervals. If it is INFORMAL they will meet on an 'as required basis' and generally work on a 'go with the flow' basis.

Description 4, translated into the ACTIVE/PASSIVE dimension. This is about 'Who does what in the relationship?'

Description 5, translated into the STABLE/UNSTABLE dimension. This is about trust and consistency. It is about sticking to the ground rules while being prepared jointly to review them.

These dimensions represent points on a continuum. They are not fixed points but rather dynamic and subject to change over time as the relationship develops and matures. The research also identified that mentor and mentee often had a different perspective on their relationship and so, although these dimensions may be negotiated at the start of a mentoring relationship, they will require regular review over time. In this way, the rapport in the relationship is strengthened and this often leads to improved outcomes, as noted by Neilson and Eisenbach (2003).

The dimensions not only describe the dynamics of a mentoring relationship but also provide the basis of the ground rules and may help to develop mutual understanding between mentor and mentee. No one set of dimensions represent the ideal relationship.

The mentor's role therefore, is to listen, support and challenge and to do this in the context of:

- change and transition
- leadership development
- time management and work–life balance
- performance and behaviour
- motivation and confidence
- personal and people related issues
- thoughts and feelings on a range of issues.

The mentor will do this by:

- sensitively drawing on relevant experience and skills
- employing well-developed interpersonal skills
- relating well with people who want to learn
- having a desire to help and develop mentees
- being open-minded, flexible and recognizing his or her own need for support
- giving time and being willing to develop the relationship.

Given the similarities between coaching and mentoring practice discussed earlier in this chapter, this framework could be applied to either. I am convinced that many writers on coaching would agree with the above points but call the activity 'coaching' instead!

The social context

Mentoring is a dynamic activity and the form it takes within a social setting influences its potential for success or failure as a developmental intervention. Mentoring has both the potential to be genuinely supportive and helpful to people and abusive and manipulative (see Carden, 1990). Mentoring relationships can be about the exercise of power and control over others. In the UK, some associate mentoring with gratuitous advice giving, the 'old boys' networks, 'sitting with Nellie' or straightforward and old-fashioned nepotism. In part, this is because it is such an ordinary and natural human activity and difficulties in human relationships are a normal part of life. In addition, genuine practical and structural difficulties contribute to the success or failure of mentoring and on occasions, mentoring is subject to social and cultural pressures. Again, this is a departure from what is written about coaching, which is often positioned as 'clean' and 'objective'. Mentoring is potentially messy and therefore even less subject to strict definition than coaching as currently projected in the literature.

The organizational context and mentoring

Any honest investigation of mentoring will recognize its potential to become part of the 'shadow-side':

'The shadow-side activities have two distinct characteristics: they are outside ordinary management processes because they are covert, informal, or even unable to be discussed; and they are economically significant, in that they very often add direct or indirect costs, including lost opportunity costs, that escape ordinary accounting procedures (Egan, 1993: 33). This is not to say that their contribution is negative; on the contrary, as Egan puts it, 'Some shadow-side activities add value rather than cost' (1993: 33).

In a recent presentation about mentoring given by a Human Resources director, a fellow director remarked: 'All this mentoring stuff sounds a bit airy-fairy to me. I'm not having it in my department.' The Human Resources director replied, 'Well, you have it in your department whether you like it or not, you just can't stop it.'

Mentoring has the potential to offer value whether or not it is recognized as a formal process or system. This is because mentoring is a normal human activity and whether or not it is constructed as a formal scheme, it will exist because it links strongly to Erikson's (1995) 'generativity' concept. Erikson links generativity to the strong human desire to procreate but it is also about bringing on, influencing and supporting the next generation. As Garvey, Alred and Smith (1996: 13) point out: 'Mentoring is one way to satisfy the deep-seated desire to "leave an impression on the world", which is recognized as a characteristic of mature adulthood'.

Levinson (1978) also associates mentoring with the generativity concept and suggests that this contributes to the motivation to mentor. Generativity and the desire to influence is often observed when senior managers in organizations talk about 'giving something back to the organization'.

In sum, mentoring as a learning and supportive relationship has a vital part to play in developing learning in a whole variety of conditions.

The use of advice giving, knowledge or experience

The experienced mentor does not give gratuitous advice since, as Rosinski (2004) implies above, knowledge sharing or advice given with an assumption of relevance or without respect for the receiver is inevitably unhelpful. However, we are social beings who learn in a social context and according to Bruner (1985, 1990), we are shaped by the social contexts we inhabit.

In their notions of 'communities of practice' and 'legitimate peripheral participation', Lave and Wenger (1991) developed the idea of learning as a social activity within a social context. There seems little doubt that people learn by, through and with each other but there are various ways in which this can be done. Emler and Heather (1980) suggest that sharing knowledge is essential in human development: 'We are a successful species because we cheat; we tell each other the answers'. Knowledge or experience sharing and advice giving can be an essential part of learning: if we do not do this as a species, we commit the next generation to reinvent the wheel! As Sir Isaac Newton is deemed to have said 'If I have seen further, it is because I have stood on the shoulders of giants'. Knowledge is therefore a building process. If the mentor shares knowledge and experience with the intent of offering it up as options or choices for action or as a vehicle for further discussion, it establishes rapport, empathy, credibility and additionally, accelerates learning. Here the notion, so strongly promoted in the coaching literature, that the coach works with the coachee's agenda breaks down. If someone genuinely does not know or lacks experience or confidence in a new situation, then hearing of the others' experience, shared with the intent building a relationship, is reassuring, builds empathy and the relationship. If the coach or mentor is completely neutral, there is nothing to build a relationship upon. In my view, if conversational learning is relationship based, then there has to be something to build a relationship on and sharing experience offers one way to do this.

Knowledge economy

An important backdrop to mentoring and coaching activity is the concept of the knowledge economy. All economies are knowledge economies and they always have been, so the notion is not a new one. It is a fact that all forms of economic life depend on on some kind of specialized knowledge.

In recent times, this dependency has accelerated and with this comes new challenges. The intended consequences of the faster pace of economic life are one thing, but there are often unintended consequences as well and these not only bring about changes within organizations but also within societies. The pressures on people appear relentless and the dominant rhetoric in economic life is the accelerating pace of change, influenced by technological and political initiatives. If believed, the implications of this rhetoric for individuals are considerable. The need for people who are able to adapt to change rapidly, learn quickly and apply their knowledge to a range of situations has increased. In this climate, it is crucial for employees to have 'strong and stable personalities' (Kessels, 1996: 4) and mentoring has the potential to make a contribution. The expectation of change – conceived still by many as progress – is pervasive. The future is open; no one knows what it will be, but everywhere it is anticipated, planned for and predicted.

As a consequence, mentoring can help the individual to discover what sort of person he or she could be. Sometimes this involves learning and acquiring specific knowledge, specific skills and more often gaining inspiration, challenge, encouragement and support so that understanding develops and appropriate behaviour is acquired. Gladstone (1988: 21) suggests that 'successful mentors accept change willingly' and that 'mentorees are encouraged to devote their talents and energies to attainable goals and as a result they develop self-confidence'. Within the context of a knowledge economy, confident people are an important asset.

Although contexts and practices vary, the relational aspects between mentor and mentee help to create and support professional and academic development, personal development and learning. Mentoring makes a crucial contribution as the mentee integrates prior and current experience through meaningful and deep dialogue with the mentor. Mentoring is effective when learners are making transitions at key points in their educational or occupational careers. It helps, for example, in the following contexts:

- induction
- support to development
- social integration and cultural change
- diversity programmes
- talent management
- developing strategic capability
- career progression and job change
- support for learning on the job
- redundancy support
- leadership development.

RELATIONSHIP WITH THEORETICAL TRADITIONS

O'Brien (1995) describes a mentoring process embedded within change and development, and draws on psychodynamic principles for its ethical framework, while McAuley (2003) employs the psychoanalytic notion of transference and counter transference to develop and extend our understanding of the mentor/mentee relationship. Bennetts (1996) and Garvey (2004) link mentoring to Rogerian philosophy, and other writers (Gibb, 2004) consider ethical and boundary issues which relate to psychological frameworks. Baum (1992) applies Freudian psychology to mentoring relationships in the US, suggesting that within mentoring there is potential for narcissistic fantasy and Oedipal reality in mentoring relationships as the mentee pursues his or her 'dream'.

However, the coaching literature seems to be concerned with psychology far more than does the mentoring literature. An example is found in Lee (2003), where he refers to 'psychological mindedness' as an important element of a coach's practice and Bluckert (2006: 87) describes this as 'people's capacity to reflect on themselves, others, and the relationship in between'. He suggests that this is best done with an understanding and awareness of psychological processes. These ideas suggest that an understanding of psychology and therapeutic practice is a necessary requirement for mentors as well as coaches. Berglas (2002) in relation to coaching would agree. He considers that knowledge of psychology is necessary and asserts that only trained therapists should coach; but his position is not clear when he states:

> My misgivings about executive coaching are not a clarion call for psychotherapy and psychoanalysis [...] My goal, as somebody with a doctorate in psychology as well as serving as an executive coach, is to heighten awareness of the difference between a problem executive, who can be trained to function effectively, and an executive with a problem who can best be helped by psychotherapy. (Berglas, 2002: 89)

This quotation offers further insight into the complex and overlapping practices of mentoring, coaching and counselling. Alternative views suggest that mentoring is essentially two colleagues engaged in a purposeful conversation and therefore knowledge of psychology is not necessary for mentors.

Unlike coaching, where psychological methods often migrate to informing practice and brands of coaching (see, for example, Solution-Focused Coaching or Cognitive-Behavioural Coaching), mentoring draws on this literature to inform and challenge rather than create practice and here is another distinction between the two. Coaching is increasingly viewed as a profession with codes of practice and standards. This has the potential to exclude the practising manager who wants to use coaching as a way of managing. Mentoring is seen as a supportive activity available to anyone and requires some training and orientation to the task as well as some ongoing support.

EVALUATION

As with coaching, within mentoring there are opportunities for the organization, the mentor and the mentee to benefit from mentoring or purposeful conversations. In broad terms, this might be as follows:

For the mentee:

- improved performance and productivity
- career opportunity and advancement
- improved knowledge and skills
- greater confidence and well-being.

For the mentor:

- improved performance
- greater satisfaction, loyalty and self-awareness
- new knowledge and skills
- leadership development.

For the organization:

- staff retention and improved communication
- improved morale, motivation and relationships (less conflict)
- improved learning.

As human beings, we have the potential to be truly magnificent at relationships as well as to be exceptionally bad at them! Mentoring relationships are no different. Because mentoring is a natural activity, as a practice within an organization it will be present either by default or by design. If the best is to be achieved, mentoring activity does need some 'light touch' design and some core conditions need to be considered, such as:

- voluntarism and choice
- clear recruitment strategy
- training of mentors and mentees
- ongoing support for mentors and mentees if they require it
- a clear and transparent matching policy
- establishing reviewable ground rules
- ongoing review
- working with the mentee's agenda
- accepting mentoring as legitimate work (Alred & Garvey, 2010).

However, as I suggested in previous work, caution is necessary because:

> The real danger for mentoring is the tendency to adopt mentoring as a strategy for facilitating learning and change without due consideration for the social setting or the cultural context. All too often, mentoring is used as the 'fixer' of problems, a fast tracker to success, a 'cure-all' without due consideration for the wider social, political and economic context. An organisation can talk development as much as it likes but without real commitment to the notion then it is just another initiative to squeeze a little more out of people. (Garvey, 2004: 176)

Genuine and authentic intent is an essential ingredient for mentoring and coaching within an organization because holistic development is only achievable in a wholesome and honest environment.

Mentoring has a longer tradition than coaching but both activities share many of the same practices, applications and values. In the end, it comes down to a choice of terminology and the meaning associated with that terminology. Meanings, as Bruner (1985, 1990) tells us, are dependent on the social context so it is inevitable that the terms mentoring and coaching will mean different things to different people in different contexts. For me, the problem comes when either mentoring or coaching writers attempt to position one as fundamentally different from the other. Coaching has in recent times become the dominant term and the one with greater and more direct commercial interest. However, coaching as a concept is derived from mentoring and perhaps an argument is beginning to emerge for a multiple perspective approach to mentoring and coaching through description rather than definition. For the future, maybe a new term will emerge that will satisfy all interested parties but somehow, I doubt it!

FURTHER READING

Garvey, B., Stokes, P. & Megginson, D. (2009). *Coaching and mentoring theory and practice.* London: Sage. (A comprehensive and critical discussion of many aspects of mentoring and coaching.)

Garvey, B. & Alred, G. (2010). *The mentoring pocket book* (3rd ed.). Management Pocket Book Series – Mentoring. Hants: Arlesford Press Ltd. (A practical, no nonsense guide to mentoring.)

Riley, P. (1994). *Fenelon: Telemachus.* New York: Cambridge University Press. (Insights into historical perspectives on mentoring.)

DISCUSSION QUESTIONS

- Whose interests are served by trying to differentiate coaching and mentoring?
- What are the pros and cons of a descriptive approach to understanding coaching and mentoring?
- What is the role of advice giving within mentoring?

REFERENCES

Baum, H. (1992). Mentoring: Narcissistic fantasies and oedipal realities. *Human Relations*, 45(3): 223–45.

Bennetts, C. (1995). Interpersonal aspects of informal mentor/learner relationships: A research perspective. *Paper in Proceedings at the European Mentoring Centre Conference*, London, October.

Bennetts, C. (1996). *Mentor/learner relationships – A research perspective, making it happen,* South West Conference, Torquay, January.

Berglas, S. (2002). The very real dangers of executive coaching. *Harvard Business Review,* 80(6): 86–92.

Bluckert, P. (2005). Critical factors in executive coaching – the coaching relationship. *Industrial and Commercial Training,* 37(7): 336–40.

Bluckert, P. (2006). *Psychological dimensions of executive coaching.* Maidenhead: Open University Press.

Bresser, F. (2008). *Results of the European coaching survey.* Cologne: Bresser Consulting.

Bruner, J. (1985). Vygotsky: A historical and conceptual perspective. In J.V. Wertsch (Ed.), *Culture, communication and cognition: Vygotskian perspectives.* Cambridge: Cambridge University Press.

Bruner, J. (1990). *Acts of meaning.* Cambridge, MA: Harvard University Press.

Caraccioli, L.A. (1760). *The true mentor, or, an essay on the education of young people in fashion.* London: J. Coote.

Carden, A. (1990). Mentoring and adult career development. *Counselling Psychologist,* 18(2): 275–99.

Carruthers, J. (1993). The principles and practice of mentoring. In B. Caldwell & E. Carter (Eds), *The return of the mentor: Strategies for workplace learning.* Bristol: Falmer.

Caruso, R.E. (1992). *Mentoring and the business environment: Asset or liability?* Aldershot: Dartmouth.

Clutterbuck, D. & Lane, G. (2004). *The situational mentor.* Aldershot: Gower Publishing.

Clutterbuck, D. & Megginson, D. (1999). *Mentoring executives and directors.* Oxford: Butterworth-Heinemann.

Clutterbuck, D. & Megginson, D. (2005). *Making coaching work: Creating a coaching culture.* London: CIPD.

Connor, M. (1994). *Counsellor training: An integrated approach.* London: Kogan Page.

Daloz, L. (1999). *Mentor: Guiding the journey of adult learners.* San Francisco, CA: Jossey-Bass.

de Haan, E. (2008). *Relational coaching: Journeys towards mastering one-to-one learning.* Chichester: John Wiley.

De la Mothe-Fénélon, F.S. (1808). *The adventures of Telemachus* (Vols. 1 & 2) (trans. J. Hawkesworth). London: Union Printing Office.

Egan, G. (1993). The shadow side. *Management Today,* September: 33–8.

Emler, N. & Heather, N. (1980). Intelligence: An ideological bias of conventional psychology. In P. Salmon (Ed.), *Coming to know.* London: Routledge and Kegan Paul.

Erikson, E. (1995). *Childhood and society.* London: Vintage.

Friday, E., Shawnta, S., Friday, A., & Green, L. (2004). A reconceptualization of mentoring and sponsoring. *Management Decision,* 42(5): 628–44.

Garvey, B. (1994a). *Mentoring in the market place: Studies of learning at work.* (Unpublished Doctoral dissertation, University of Durham.)

Garvey, B. (1994b). Ancient Greece, MBAs, the Health Service and Georg. *Education and Training,* 36(2): 18–26.

Garvey, B. (1994c). A dose of mentoring. *Education and Training,* 36(4): 18–26.

Garvey, B. (2004). When mentoring goes wrong. In D. Clutterbuck & G. Lane (Eds), *Situational mentoring.* Aldershot: Gower Publishing.

Garvey, B. & Alred, G. (2010). *The mentoring pocket book* (3rd ed.). Management Pocket Book Series – Mentoring. Hants: Arlesford Press Ltd.

Garvey, B., Alred, G., & Smith, R. (1996). First person mentoring. *Career Development International,* 1(5): 10–14.

Garvey, B., Stokes, P., & Megginson, D. (2009). *Coaching and mentoring theory and practice.* London: Sage.

Geertz, C. (Ed.). (1971). *Myth, symbol and culture.* New York: Norton.

Gibb, S. (2004). The moral dimension of mentoring. In D. Clutterbuck & G. Lane (Eds), *Situational mentoring.* Aldershot: Gower Publishing.

Gladstone, M.S. (1988). *Mentoring: A strategy for learning in a rapidly changing society.* Research Document CEGEP. Quebec: John Abbott College.

Grodzki, L. & Allen, W. (2005). *The business and practice of coaching.* London: Norton.

Hale, R. (2000). To match or mis-match? The dynamics of mentoring as a route to personal and organizational learning. *Career Development International,* 5(4/5): 223–34.

Healthcare Commission (2005). *NHS national staff survey 2004 – Summary of key findings*. London: Healthcare Commission.

Homer (1184 [1250] BC). The Odyssey. In R. Lattimore (1965), *The Odyssey of Homer*. New York: Harper Perennial.

Honoria (1793). *The female mentor or select conversations* (Vols. 1 & 2). London: T. Cadell.

Honoria (1796). *The female mentor or select conversations* (Vol. 3). London: T. Cadell.

Hunt, J.M. & Weintraub, J.R. (2002). *The coaching manager: Developing top talent in business*. Thousand Oaks, CA: Sage.

Hurley, A.E. & Fagenson-Eland, E.A. (1996). Challenges in cross-gender mentoring relationships: Psychological intimacy, myths, rumours, innuendoes and sexual harassment. *Leadership and Organisation Development Journal*, 17(3): 42–9.

Kessels, J.W.M. (1996). Knowledge productivity and the corporate curriculum in knowledge management: Organization, competence and methodology. *Proceedings of the Fourth international ISMICK Symposium*, Rotterdam. October.

Kram, K.E. (1983). Phases of the mentor relationship. *Academy of Management Journal*, 26(4): 608–25.

Lave, J. & Wenger, E. (1991). *Situated learning: Legitimate peripheral participation*. Cambridge: Cambridge University Press.

Lee, G. (2003). *Leadership coaching: From personal insight to organisational performance*. London: CIPD.

Levinson, D. (1978). *The seasons of a man's life*. New York: Alfred Knopf.

McAuley, J. (2003). Transference, countertransference and mentoring: The ghost in the process. *British Journal of Guidance and Counselling*, 31(1): 11–23.

MacLennan, N. (1995). *Coaching and mentoring*. Aldershot: Gower Publishing.

Megginson, D., Clutterbuck, D., Garvey, B., Stokes, P., & Garrett-Harris, R. (Eds) (2005). *Mentoring in action*. London: Kogan Page.

Neilson, T. & Eisenbach, R. (2003). Not all relationships are created equal: Critical factors of high-quality mentoring relationships. *International Journal of Mentoring and Coaching*, 1(1). Retrieved from www.emccouncil.org.

O'Brien, J. (1995). Mentoring as change agency: A psychodynamic approach. *Counselling*, February: 51–4.

Rosinski, P. (2004). *Coaching across cultures*. London: Nicholas Brealey.

Rousseau, J. (1762). *Émile ou de l'éducation* [Emile: or, on education]. Geneva: A La Haye, Chez Jean Néaulme.

Samier, E. (2000). Public administration mentorship: Conceptual and pragmatic considerations. *Journal of Educational Administration*, 38(1): 83–101.

Scandura, T., Tejeda, M., Werther, B., & Lankau, M. (1996). Perspectives on mentoring. *Leadership & Organization Development Journal*, 17(3): 50–56.

Sieler, A. (2003). *Coaching to the human soul: Ontological coaching and deep change*. Newfield, VIC: Newfield-Australia.

Simmel, G. (1950). *The sociology of Georg Simmel* (trans. and ed. K. H. Wolff). Glencoe, IL: Free Press.

Thackeray, W.M. (1849). *The history of Pendennis*. Harmondsworth: Penguin.

Torrance, E.P. (1984). *Mentor relationships: How they aid creative achievement, endure, change and die*. Buffalo, NY: Bearly.

Willis, P. (2005). *EMCC competency research project: Phase 2*. Watford: European Mentoring and Coaching Council.

Professional Practice Issues

26

The Future of Coaching as a Profession

David Lane, Reinhard Stelter and
Sunny Stout-Rostron

The popularity of coaching is seen in an array of international coaching conferences, burgeoning coach training and education, and emergent professional bodies for coach practitioners. This escalating demand has motivated coach practitioners, consumers and educators of coaching to advocate the professionalization of the industry to ensure the quality of coaching services.

Coaching as a form of practice is now widely adopted, although recognition as a profession remains contentious and patchy, with different jurisdictions taking contrary views on its legitimacy. A growing awareness of the potential benefits to the industry of professional status has led to participation in international dialogues, such the Global Convention on Coaching (GCC) and the International Coaching Research Forum (ICRF). These dialogues have in turn helped to motivate initiatives on the definition of standards for coaching by various organizations including the Worldwide Association of Business Coaches (WABC), and a working group of Australian stakeholder organizations coordinated by Standards Australia. In 2012 an alliance of three organizations, the European Mentoring and Coaching Council (EMCC), the International Coaching Federation (ICF) and the Association of Coaching (AC), was formed and they opened an invitation for others to join.

This chapter outlines the criteria for a discipline to be accepted as a profession, briefly assessing the extent to which coaching complies. Potential lessons for coaching from the development of psychotherapy into a profession are then summarized, highlighting the fragility of the term 'profession' in contemporary society. The chapter goes on to outline key observations on professionalization, as distinct from 'professionalism'. Feasible options regarding the status of coaching as a true profession, or alternatively as an occupation maintaining professionalism are compared, and ongoing concerns and challenges are underlined.

Criteria for a profession

Generally accepted core features of a profession include the requirement for members to have formal academic qualifications; adherence to an enforceable code of ethics; practice licensed only to qualified members; compliance with applicable state-sanctioned regulation; and a common body of knowledge and skills (Spence, 2007: 261). This is a highly contentious area and there are many ways of viewing a profession.

From a legalistic perspective, a profession is established if some of the following criteria are embodied in a law or similar statues (DBVC, 2007):

- societal mandate (monopoly for professional practice)
- formalized curriculum/professional education
- plurality of theory and methods as the basis for the curriculum
- research foundation in relation to the professional practice
- governmental accreditation, professional licence
- quality assurance
- reflective professional competence
- standards of ethics
- specific career paths, professional trajectories and passages
- professional body – association with formalized rights and duties for their members
- financial independence of the single professional (employment, scale of fees).

Bennett (2006: 241–2) has reviewed the relevant literature and summarized the criteria to enable coaching to be determined a profession as follows:

1. Identifiable and distinct skills – i.e. skills that are widely accepted as required for the performance of skilled coaching.
2. Education and training required to acquire proficiency – for example, the minimum initial and ongoing training required to coach; generally accepted competences required for coaches; means of assessing competence.
3. Recognition outside the community as a profession – for example, recognition by established professions as a profession; government classification of coaching as a profession.
4. Code of ethics – a code of ethics for coaches defined, implemented, monitored and effectively enforced by a governing body, making coaching a self-disciplined industry.
5. Public service – public service by coaches that is motivated by altruism rather than financial gain.
6. Formalized organization – widely accepted and established professional association(s) representing the profession and those practising coaching.
7. Evaluation of merit (credentialling) and self-regulation of service – for example, definition of accepted requirements for coaches; systems for assessing competence; systems for monitoring and regulating service delivery by coaches; mechanisms for encouraging thought and discussion about the practice of coaching.
8. Established community of practitioners – for example, forums where coaches can network and exchange ideas on coaching; publications supporting the community of practitioners.
9. Status of membership in a profession – for example, recognition of coaches by their clients and the general public as members of a profession.

10. Public recognition – recognition by the general public that coaching is a distinct and established profession.
11. Knowledge base – coaching practice founded in theoretical and factual research and knowledge, with a defined body of knowledge, a defined theoretical foundation and ongoing evidence-based theoretical and practical research.

However, there is a long way to go before coaching can be defined as a profession in the narrowest sense. In the list of the criteria above none of these is fully realized in the professional field of coaching, either nationally or internationally. Bennett (2006: 242) highlighted the following critical gaps between the criteria listed above for a profession and the current practice of coaching:

- There are currently no generally accepted, identifiable and distinct skills for coaches.
- Training and/or education are not required before a person can practise as a coach, although various coach training programmes are available.
- The general public and related professions do not recognize coaching as a profession.
- There is not an established community of practitioners; for example, less than half the estimated coaches in the world belong to representative bodies such as the International Coach Federation (ICF).
- There is a lack of defined theory on which coaches base their practice.

Lessons from psychotherapy

In some ways the current position and disputes about status in the field of coaching mirror those around parallel fields such as psychotherapy. Indeed, the position of psychotherapy is illustrative of the type of problems coaching may face unless it adopts a strongly collaborative approach.

Various schools of psychotherapy have developed with their own philosophy, model of causation and intervention. Candidates were trained within one modality (i.e. speciality) and as standards developed each modality claimed its own standards body. Splits between members within single bodies led to even more forms of 'accreditation' and as new methods emerged additional accreditation bodies were formed. This is in contrast to physical medicine where the invention of a new treatment did not lead to multiple accrediting bodies with a single theory as the basis for registration and licence to practise. Practitioners are regulated as medics first and second by their specialism rather than their theories about human illness. In psychotherapy (and perhaps in coaching) any new theory, whether evidence-based or not, could gain adherents, thus creating new accrediting bodies.

As psychotherapy sought to gain 'respectability' in the form of statutory regulation, the problem was compounded by disputes between professional bodies as to which one represented the appropriate truth. Since the basis for practice was either theory and competences that had not been agreed, or an agreed knowledge base shared across all practitioners, it was difficult for statutory authorities to regulate. A 'Psychotherapy Regulation Act' could require 450 different models of practice to be listed, each with differing standards to cover the range of current practice. No jurisdiction would contemplate such complex legislation.

Eventually, attempts by the various groups to collaborate resulted in agreement to at least the hours of training and some common areas of knowledge (e.g. through the United Kingdom

Council for Psychotherapy (UKCP)). This has only been partly successful, with ongoing disputes between the members of these collaborative bodies and with members leaving, rejoining, leaving again and others forming their own new competitive collaboration. In Europe this confusion has lead to some countries restricting practice to medical practitioners and psychologists, as a sub-function within those professions, thereby denying psychotherapy as a separate profession. In others psychotherapy can be practised but only in a limited number of modalities. Forms of practice common (in the unregulated profession) in the UK would not be allowed in Germany or Spain. In the UK, the government is currently considering the regulation of psychotherapy and is also going down the restricted modality route with cognitive-behavioural, analytic, humanist and systems models being the preferred routes. The alternative favoured by the European Federation of Psychologists Associations (EFPA, www.efpa.eu) is to determine the guiding principles for practice (as for all other professions) rather than to treat psychotherapy as a practice of limited modalities.

In some countries where regulation has been attempted these issues have emerged and consequently some jurisdictions have restricted the rights to practise to a limited number of modalities or specific types of psychotherapy practice. Germany, for example, recognizes three modalities, whereas others have yet to regulate the psychotherapy profession at all. In the UK, there are multiple competing bodies which exist without a statutory framework although the authorities are currently considering regulation within four modalities. Thus a form of practice accepted in the UK (existential psychotherapy which has its own accrediting society) is not a permissible modality in Germany. In the USA, the position varies from state to state; what is included within the field also varies widely. This leads to considerable confusion about what is in and what is out, and has led to debates in some countries about how wide the field should be.

While psychotherapists worldwide fight among themselves about what is the best form of practice, others in the better established professions of psychiatry (which is state-regulated in most jurisdictions) and psychology (which is regulated in many) claim ownership of the field. Some influential voices in these fields fully deny that coaching is a separate profession and claim that it is an area of practice for their speciality rather than a separate field in its own right. As psychotherapists find themselves in territorial disputes with psychologists and psychiatrists they are also seeking to embrace the newer emerging fields, such as coaching, as their territory, arguing that coaching is a field that requires practice by a psychotherapist (Berglas, 2002).

The question is whether we wish to use this model for coaching. Even though it is acknowledged by the Global Coaching Community (GCC) that coaching is a unique synthesis of a range of disciplines (GCC, 2008: 5), attempts within coaching to seek professional standing have been hampered by its lack of conformity to the precedented basis for granting a right to be a profession. Given that each of the professional bodies within the coaching field take a different view of the criteria for professional status, gaining agreement as to what constitutes the 'profession' of coaching is difficult. Although different from psychotherapy, professional bodies in the coaching field are not accrediting bodies in themselves; they simply provide guidelines for 'professional' practice. Unless coaching can agree on the core principles (as, for example, in the EFPA model) then the negative effects of the regulation in psychotherapy may apply: either coaching is excluded from practice as in some European countries, or state regulators will determine which forms of practice are allowed or not, thereby excluding many practitioners.

Fragility of the term 'profession' in late modern society

During the last few decades, the concept of the profession has itself become fragile. The main reason for this process of disintegration is that professionals have been losing their monopoly of knowledge. This loss, in fact, is one of the fundamental reasons for the rapid development of the coaching industry: knowledge has become something that evolves in specific communities of practice. Knowledge is not a list of facts that is stable, but it is contextualized and relational – that is, it depends upon how and where it is being used and by whom. Furthermore, knowledge is democratized by being accessible through channels open to everybody, mainly through the internet. In that sense there is no profession that has exclusive ownership over the knowledge base in specific areas of expertise. Even within traditional fields such as medicine there is growing competition from alternative practitioners such as herbalists and homeopaths. The development in recent decades has shown that traditional professions, because of fast and diversified knowledge production and dissemination, no longer enjoy automatic respect from clients based on their superior access to information.

Consequently, it is crucial to think about an alternative understanding of the concept of profession. Drake (2007), for example, has argued that we have moved beyond the traditional profession towards a craftsperson's view of professional practice, blending science and art in what he terms the 'pursuit of conscious mastery'. This has clear implications for the professionalism of coaching. Drake (2009) has argued further that coaches need to move beyond their biases for their specialized, professional knowledge to make sufficient room for other forms of knowledge and toward an engagement in a mutual and co-creative process to formulate what is happening in the coaching conversation. Others have pointed to the client becoming their own 'self-coach'. Corrie (2009) provides a framework for the coach to share tools with the client.

It seems to be challenging and unhelpful to attempt a degree of conformance in the coaching field where coaching is established as a traditional profession, since:

- Coaching is not based on societal mandate or a monopoly for professional practice.
- Coaching is not subject to governmental accreditation or a professional license.
- Coaching has no quality assurance.
- Coaching has only voluntarily accepted standards of ethics.
- Coaching has no specific career paths, professional trajectories and passages.
- Coaching has no association with formalized rights and duties for their members.
- Coaching does not guarantee financial independence for the single professional (employment, scale of fees).

However, that does not prevent coaches working towards interdisciplinary co-operation, towards a multidisciplined professional or alternative perspective, towards agreeing key elements that might enhance the quality of the coaching offering to clients.

Traditional and alternative perspectives

Issues similar to those that have formed part of debates in other professions are emerging (Lane & Corrie, 2006). Some strongly support the view that coaching should conform to the traditional view of a profession. However, an alternative view states that professions should be recognized as institutionalized forms of power and that adopting the traditional approach could be detrimental to the future of coaching. In the literature on the sociology of the professions there are significant critiques of professions (see, for example, Larson, 1977; Johnson, 1995; Lo, 2004). These views are similar to those discussed by Lane and Corrie (2006), who argue that the knowledge to which professionals lay claim is arrived at and sustained through relationships with the state and the marketplace. Professions in general can also be seen as interest groups engaged in a collective mobility project to improve their economic and social standing. Power is gained through the attainment of professional autonomy by state licensing, which enables monopoly supply. This means that those who can most closely align themselves with power in the marketplace (for example, through gaining acceptance for their form of practice from health insurers or corporates), or align with the interests of the state (in the form of practice in public institutions), seek to dominate supply and exclude others – thus collaboration is only favoured by those with power to award contracts to supply.

The integration of the interests of coaching and the market or the state could result in the prioritizing of certain forms of knowledge over others. The market may favour short-term, cost-effective interventions which might demonstrate value to the client, but primarily to the fee-paying manager. In this scenario, the state will also favour approaches that are legitimized by evidence-based practice. There are those who see this route as detrimental to the interests of both clients and coaching as a profession.

It could be argued that the practice of some specific types of coaching is divisive, because of the ways in which priority is given to certain forms of knowledge over others, asserting that these represent the 'truth'. These separate approaches create regimes that lead to forms of knowledge, competences and values that are impervious to other ideas and create isolation between different practitioners in the field. Thus coaches come to work, think and act within narrow areas of practice set by others because they have internalized what Foucault (1983) would call 'regimes of truth'. There can be seen in the behaviour of some organizations an attempt to dominate based on a limited set of ideas rather than an attempt to enrich the field through collaboration.

The Global Convention on Coaching

The Global Convention on Coaching (GCC), subsequently renamed the Global Coaching Community, was established in 2007 with the explicit aim of promoting consultation and exploration of areas such as the professionalization of coaching. Ten working groups were formed by the GCC to develop white papers on key aspects of the possible future of coaching worldwide. These white papers were presented and debated at a GCC Convention held in

Dublin on 7–11 July 2008. The result was the Dublin Declaration on Coaching (GCC, 2008), which recommended:

1. the establishment of a common understanding of the profession through creation of a shared core code of ethics, standards of practice, and educational guidelines;
2. acknowledgement and affirmation of the multi-disciplinary roots and nature of coaching as a unique synthesis of a range of disciplines that creates a new and distinctive value to individuals, organisations and society;
3. using coaching to respond to a world beset by challenges with no predetermined answers by using coaching to create a space wherein new solutions can emerge; and
4. moving beyond self-interest to address the critical issues identified by the 10 working groups in an ongoing dialogue. (GCC, 2008: 5)

Significantly, a number of those consulted throughout the GCC process want to draw upon a much wider range of evidence to inform coaching practice than has traditionally been the case. In doing so they are contesting the power that professional coaching bodies are seeking. They argue that many forms of evidence should inform the work of coaches including more implicit or 'intuitive' knowledge, as well as greater creativity in our practice.

Another group want to emphasize relationships with clients as the primary basis on which coaches should think about their identity as a profession. While they accept the claim that our solutions to human problems are grounded in evidence, they want to recognize that we have to understand how they are shaped through social networks. Lane and Corrie (2006) have looked at how such networks operate, and argue that an expert cannot exist without a lay public recognizing and engaging the badge of expertise. The lay public is expert in other ways to which we have often failed to give sufficient credence and this, they argue, has limited professional understanding. For example, by failing to legitimize clients' stories (or rather, by requiring clients to conform to our way of telling them), we have come to favour technical solutions that do not challenge those in authority. In so doing, we are not recognizing how we might become part of the problem, rather than the solution. We fix problems defined by those in power rather than really hear the voice of the client (see Corrie & Lane, 2009, for a more detailed account of the use of the client's voice). Also, the coach becomes a part of the organizational system and unable to see the real issues as defined by the client. The use of fixed-agenda coaching determined by a sponsor following a 360° feedback process is an example of this problem-fixing approach (Jarvis, Lane, & Fillery-Travis, 2006).

A further example of this hegemony is the way in which the client, in some approaches to coaching, is asked to provide data in the format required by the client's coaching process or methodology. This situation is evidenced by the number of textbooks in the field which point to a step-by-step process in which the client is asked questions in a specific order and maybe even in a specific way – the assumption of the 'miracle coaching question' being a case in point.

Many practitioners working in diverse and complex settings have adopted a more broadly-based definition of coaching and argue that this should lead us into a reconceptualization of what it means at the current time to embrace a 'coaching' identity. The members of the working and consultation groups and those present at the GCC in Dublin raised many different questions. It was generally felt that the recommendations of the Dublin process were focused and action-oriented; the entire process identified five key areas for immediate attention: research, ethics, coach education and development, standards of competence and supervision.

Profession or occupation?

Common concerns of GCC participants around the professional status of coaching focused on whether it should become a profession or remain an occupation. Not all coaching is facilitated by a 'professional coach'; the 'coach' might be engaged in another profession, e.g. a teacher coaching a colleague, a nurse coaching a trainee, or a line manager coaching another manager or employee. Coaching in this context is part of continuous professional development, where everybody in an organization or company can potentially be coach or coachee, and where employees acquire coaching competencies through specific coaching training programmes (see Law, Ireland, & Hussain, 2007). Thus coaching might be seen as a dialogical tool for continuous professional development rather than as a professional area of practice.

So, although coaching draws on multiple disciplines and is used by many types of people in many environments, it is not necessarily the case that everyone in the coaching community wants to see the creation of a profession. An occupation can be defined as (1) an activity that serves as one's regular source of livelihood; a vocation; or (2) the principal activity in your life that one practises to earn money. To have an occupation does not – by its definition – require a special education to be able to handle the vocational tasks at hand.

On the other hand, if a profession is deemed desirable it means that a number of specific criteria such as those outlined by Bennett (2006) have to be fulfilled. It might be necessary to go further and consider the narrower position of state-regulated professions, as defined by DBVC (2007), if coaches really want to legitimize their practice. This is probably a step too far for coaching, but voluntary agreements exist currently for many bodies in the field. They share some minimal commitment to standards covering:

- voluntary commitment to possible professional standards and code of ethics
- vocational training in coaching (competence- or skills-based, rather than based on an agreed knowledge base)
- voluntary organizations making some minimal degree of commitment to safeguarding the interests of the field, including coaches and clients.

Individually, many of the nascent professional bodies in the field go beyond this.

Professionalism rather than a profession

It might be a long and, in the traditional sense, possibly a never-ending path to establish the coaching profession. It might be more fruitful to make explicit that coaching has some of its roots in different disciplines and professions (for example, HR management, psychology, organizational systems, social work, education, counselling); but that coaching expertise is further enhanced by vocational training and further education in the field of coaching – enterprises led by institutions of higher education, coach training bodies and in-house courses that can ensure that the training received is based on research and on a high degree of theoretical and empirical evidence. The existing bodies in the field which have made commitments to research-led models (WABC in the USA and the EMCC in the UK/Europe among others) also represent part of that drive towards professionalism.

In respect of professionalism, the Dublin meeting of the GCC concluded as follows:

(a) Coaching is an emerging profession.
(b) Coaching draws on multiple disciplines, which in combination create its own knowledge base and professional practice. The multiple disciplines and knowledge bases include learning theories, adult development, behavioural/social sciences, leadership and management sciences, communication techniques.
(c) Coaching in its broadest form is also a process or technique increasingly used by different types of people in many environments and may not always be formally recognized as such.
(d) The quality of the coaching engagement is dependent on the standard, consistency and rigour of the education, development, ethics and core competencies of the emerging profession.

As such a number of questions emerge:

(a) As things stand, there are no barriers to entry; anyone can call themselves a coach and there is a community which likes that freedom.
(b) The integration of 'coaching' into the wider community, particularly as a style of communication, does not mean that everyone is a 'professional' coach.
(c) Will other professions and associations see a coaching profession as a threat?
(d) Do all parts of the coaching community want to see the creation of a coaching profession?
(e) Will the politics of the coaching community get in the way of creating a profession?

The ICRF and research on coaching

The ICRF has worked to promote the value of research, critical self-reflective practice and the development of a coaching knowledge base. As part of this process, a group of internationally recognized researchers, coach practitioners and other coaching stakeholders gathered in September 2008 at Harvard University to foster progress and community in coaching research. These ICRF 'thought leaders' developed a set of 100 research proposals which could be accessed by stakeholders worldwide, with the aim of prompting new coaching studies among researchers and graduate students to advance coaching as an evidence-based discipline (Kauffman, Russell, & Bush, 2008).

While there have been other calls for further research in coaching, the ICRF proposals serve as a particularly interesting reference point as they were generated through a multi-disciplinary forum of experts in coaching representing many regions, disciplines, roles and perspectives. A recent review of progress in research on the major focus areas covered by the ICRF proposals has highlighted the impressive volume and scope of coaching research being undertaken around the world. A survey of primary, evidence-based research into best-practice coaching published in English-language, peer-reviewed journals during the period January 2008 to June 2012 found no less than 263 relevant articles, in more than 80 journals covering a wide range of fields including coaching, coaching psychology, other psychology, medicine, business and management, human resources, and education and training. The focus areas most commonly addressed were coaching processes (88 articles) and coaching outcomes (46 articles), with fewer studies focusing on coach education and training (12 articles) and issues related to the professional development of coaching as a discipline (12 articles) (Stern & Stout-Rostron, 2013).

Should practitioners do research?

The concept of primary, evidence-based research into best-practice coaching has been a key feature of the debate for coaching to be an evidence-based discipline (Cavanagh & Grant, 2006). This raises the question of the role of coaches as scientist practitioners. While coaching as reflective practice has been well accepted and the need for evidence-based practice is also largely accepted is it incumbent on practitioners to contribute to the profession through research from practice? The concept of practitioners as scientists has its origins in clinical psychology but has since extended to all areas of professional psychology practice. Yet it has been argued that while this is an ideal it is rarely achieved in practice with practitioners contributing very little to the literature in published refereed journals (Lane & Corrie, 2006). However, if a broader view of contribution is adopted to include publication in a wider range of sources, contributions to quality reviews and to work-based projects, then it is clear, as Lane and Corrie (2006) argue, that the scientist-practitioner model has more merit. Woolfe (2012) has also made the point in relation to counselling psychology that it is this broader view of the scientist-practitioner that should be adopted. It certainly fits coaching more adequately. Seen from this broader perspective there are ways in which coaches at all levels can contribute to the development of the profession.

WABC Professional Standards Task Force

During 2009–2011 the WABC led an initiative to develop international professional standards for business coaching. The purpose was to outline a well-researched, relevant set of principles that inform the 'real world' practice of business coaching. The standards are intended to:

- Define the essence of business coaching practice.
- Educate clients, peers and the public about what business coaches do.
- Help clients understand what they can expect from business coaches.
- Distinguish business coaching from other types of coaching.

WABC has engaged in research for these core standards and principles, covering the definition of business coaching, business coaching competences, a proposed code of ethics and programmes for credentialing members and accrediting training providers. As a result, the WABC Professional Standards Task Force has:

- Formulated a definition of business coaching and an internationally agreed set of competences for business coaching.
- Created rigorous membership standards for the WABC.
- Developed a code of 'business ethics' and integrity for business coaches.

- Developed an international certification programme.
- Provided an international accreditation programme for business coaching training providers.
- Established ongoing research into business coaching.

Australian standards on coaching in organizations

In Australia, a united effort during 2009–2011 by no less than 26 bodies participating in a Coaching Guideline Working Group has produced a comprehensive draft handbook on coaching standards. Key stakeholder organizations involved in the Working Group include coaches, coaching agencies, buyers of coaching, coach training organizations, universities and government bodies. The project was a completely independent initiative, rather than an attempt by government to impose regulations, prompted by a call from the Australian marketplace for increased clarity and standards of practice by the coaching industry. The Working Group was coordinated by the HR & Employment Committee of Standards Australia, an independent non-profit organization recognized by the Australian government.

The standards are intended to identify key issues to be aware of when purchasing, delivering and administering coaching services, including the education and business development of coaches. The draft handbook covers (Standards Australia, 2011):

- key coaching terms and definitions
- the current context of coaching in organizations
- guidelines for coaching services (including relationships, contracting, confidentiality, standards of practice, supervision and roles)
- types of coaching and coaching competences for each type
- training guidelines
- ethical standards
- purchasing and management of coaching engagements.

Concerns and questions

A variety of questions and concerns have arisen throughout the GCC process that require shared dialogue, research, recommendations and action to be taken. If coaching is to emerge as a discipline with a professional future, a wide variety of difficult conversations need to take place in such forums as the GCC and other professional body events, where stakeholders can share their expertise and work collaboratively.

It has been recommended as a result of the GCC process that we need empirical evidence that coaching can make a difference on an individual, organizational and societal level. There still remains a lack of clarity and consensus as to what is professional coaching, what makes for an effective and reputable coach, whether coaching should in effect become a profession and if coaching works (Fillery-Travis & Lane, 2006). Globally, research needs to be conducted to determine what competences are necessary for the education and development of coaches worldwide, and what will be a definition of coaching that the global community will accept. Clearly, academic researchers and coach practitioners are addressing these issues in evidence-based research, although such studies are still focused predominantly on processes and outcomes of coaching rather than the professionalization of the discipline per se (Stern & Stout-Rostron, 2013).

One substantial concern is whether the international coaching bodies are committed to working together, and in collaboration with coach education and development organizations, and with other coaching stakeholders to define and regulate the profession. Thinking about Germany, where coaching is a major industry, but where there are more than two dozen associations that include coaching and comparable activities (like consulting, mentoring, supervision) in their association name, there seems to be a long way ahead before we have one powerful and united voice for the profession of coaching (Frank Bresser, 2009) Other concerns relate to the role of supervision in the education and development of coaches; the distinctions between the curricula across different levels of coach education and practice; and whether a universal ethical code can be developed with the various professional bodies being willing to adapt a code that reaches across borders.

It is important that there is some kind of synthesis between the professional coaching bodies, the educational institutions developing academic and practitioner programmes, and the organizations who are currently buying coaching interventions. In seeking to clarify what is coaching, and what role practitioners, academics and all stakeholders have to play, the dialogue has begun. The progress made in initiatives such as the WABC Professional Standards Task Force and the Coaching Guidelines Working Group in Australia are encouraging indications of what can be achieved by stakeholders collaborating together around the world. The new EMCC/ICF/AC alliance may provide a format to further elaborate this debate.

There are serious issues of power and diversity which may impact on how and which initiatives are taken forward. What are the issues of power that we need to address in order to be willing to listen to each other and how can we use the dialogue process to do so? The successful professional development of coaching is going to take commitment, perseverance and a willingness to let go of power, control, ego and territoriality. Although we live and work in a diverse world, we still mistrust differences. In the coaching community, there is the beginning of dialogue, events and collaboration to understand the status of coaching within each country and culture and an understanding that our common needs are similar. It is only through a continuation of concerted dialogue that we can begin to shift the status quo and move coaching towards becoming a more rigorous field.

We are still a fair distance from becoming a profession. The current status of coaching is reliant on self-regulation through various professional bodies such as the ICF, EMCC, WABC, AC and Coaches and Mentors of South Africa (COMENSA). Self-regulation is supported by their underlying principles and values, voluntary codes of ethics, recommended standards of competence, complaints procedures and other guidelines. Despite these recommended guidelines, most practitioners do not, for example, carry liability insurance as do such other professions as medicine and psychology. In this regard, it is important to remember that the Dublin Declaration on Coaching recommends 'regulating ourselves' before someone else does: 'In the absence of us defining ourselves the market will do it for us' (GCC, 2008: 9).

EVALUATION

While we take the view that it is an appropriate aim to strive for more professionalism in the field of coaching, we should be aware of a number of obstacles or conditions that hinder the establishment of coaching as a profession in the traditional sense. We would argue that it might not even be in the best interests of coaching or its clients to pursue the traditional route to legitimization. The concept of a 'profession' is under attack and it may be that coach practitioners need to think about different forms of association, perhaps along the following lines:

1. Coaching is a beneficial and useful enterprise as part of other professions.
2. The concept of profession has changed. In that sense, it might not even be realistic to establish coaching as a profession in a traditional sense.
3. The professionalism of coaches can be developed through interdisciplinary efforts based on research and evidence-based practice.
4. To be able to work professionally as a coach means to be aware of specific antinomies and tensions in the coaching process.
5. Voluntary bodies in collaboration can begin to define new models of association that sit outside of traditional professions which retain their virtues but avoid their vices.

FURTHER READING

Jarvis, J., Lane, D.A., & Fillery-Travis, A. (2006). *The case for coaching: Making evidence based decisions on coaching.* Wimbledon: Chartered Institute of Personnel and Development.

Law, H., Ireland, S., & Hussain, Z. (2007). *The psychology of coaching, mentoring and learning.* Chichester: John Wiley.

Lo, M-C. M. (2004). The professions: Prodigal daughters of modernity. In J. Adams, E.S. Clemens, & A.S. Orloff (Eds), *Remaking modernity: Politics, history, and sociology* (pp. 381–406). Durham, NC: Duke University Press.

Spence, G.B. (2007). Further development of evidence-based coaching: Lessons from the rise and fall of the human potential movement. *Australian Psychologist*, 42(4): 255–65.

DISCUSSION QUESTIONS

• What should be the benefits of the professionalization of coaching to clients of coaching services?
• Should coaching, as an emerging professional discipline, be regulated by nationally-based professional associations, or by an overarching, international body?
• How important are the distinctions between coaching services delivered by coaching psychologists and coaching services delivered by non-psychologist coaches to the definition and professionalization of coaching?

REFERENCES

Bennett, J.L. (2006). An agenda for coaching-related research: A challenge for researchers. *Coaching Psychology Journal: Practice and Research*, 58(4): 240–9.

Berglas, S. (2002). The very real dangers of executive coaching. *Harvard Business Review,* June: 87–92.

Frank Bresser Consulting Group (2009). *Global Coaching Survey 2008/09*, accessed 20 July 2013 from www.frank-bresser-consulting.com/globalcoachingsurvey09-report.pdf.

Cavanagh, M.J.M & Grant, A.M. (2006) Coaching psychology and the scientist-practitioner model (pp. 146–57). In D.A. Lane & S. Corrie, *The modern scientist-practitioner: A guide to practice in psychology*. Hove: Routledge.

Corrie, S. (2009). *The art of inspired living: Coach yourself with positive psychology.* London: Karnac Books.

Corrie, S. & Lane, D.A. (2009). *Constructing stories, telling tales: Case formulation in psychology.* London: Karnac Books.

Deutscher Bundesverband Coaching (Federal Association of Coaching in Germany – DBVC) (Ed.). (2007). *Leitlinien und Empfehlungen für die Entwicklung von Coaching als Profession* [Guidelines and recommendations for the development of coaching as a profession]. Osnabrück: DBVC.

Drake, D.B. (2007). The art of thinking narratively: Implications for coaching psychology and practice. *Australian Psychologist*, 42(4): 283–94.

Drake, D.B. (2009). What story are you in? Four elements of a narrative approach to formulation in coaching. In D. Corrie & D.A. Lane (Eds), *Constructing stories, telling tales: Case formulation in psychology*. London: Karnac Books.

Fillery-Travis, A. & Lane, D. (2006). How to develop your research interests. In S. Palmer & R. Bor (Eds), *The practitioner's handbook: A guide for counsellors, psychotherapists and counselling psychologists*. London: Sage.

Foucault, M. (1983). The subject and power. In H. Dreyfus & P. Rabinow (Eds), *Michel Foucault: Beyond structuralism and hermeneutics*. Chicago, IL: University of Chicago Press.

Global Coaching Community (GCC). (2008). *Dublin declaration on coaching*. Paper presented at the Global Convention on Coaching, Dublin, August.

Jarvis, J., Lane, D.A., & Fillery-Travis, A. (2006). *The case for coaching: Making evidence based decisions on coaching*. Wimbledon: Chartered Institute of Personnel and Development.

Johnson, T.J. (1995). Governmentality and the institutionalization of expertise. In T. Johnson, G. Larkin, & M. Saks (Eds), *Health professions and the state in Europe* (pp. 7–24). New York: Routledge.

Kauffman, C.M., Russell, S.G., & Bush, M.W. (Eds) (2008). *100 Coaching Research Proposal Abstracts*. International Coaching Research Forum. Cambridge, MA: The Coaching & Positive Psychology Initiative, McLean Hospital, Harvard Medical School and The Foundation of Coaching.

Lane, D.A. & Corrie, S. (2006). *The modern scientist-practitioner: A guide to practice in psychology*. Hove: Routledge.

Larson, M.S. (1977). *The rise of professionalism: A sociological analysis*. Berkeley, CA: University of California Press.

Law, H., Ireland, S., & Hussain, Z. (2007). *The psychology of coaching, mentoring and learning*. Chichester: John Wiley.

Lo, M-C. M. (2004). The professions: Prodigal daughters of modernity. In J. Adams, E.S. Clemens, & A.S. Orloff (Eds), *Remaking modernity: Politics, history, and sociology* (pp. 381–406). Durham, NC: Duke University Press.

Spence, G.B. (2007). Further development of evidence-based coaching: Lessons from the rise and fall of the human potential movement. *Australian Psychologist*, 42(4): 255–65.

Standards Australia (2011). *Coaching in organizations*. Draft handbook produced by Coaching Guideline Working Group HB41 of Standards Australia HR & Employment Committee MB 9. Sydney: Standards Australia.

Stern, L. & Stout-Rostron, S. (2013). What progress has been made in coaching research in relation to 16 ICRF Focus Areas from 2008 to 2012? *Coaching: An International Journal of Theory, Research and Practice* (forthcoming).

Woolfe, R. (2012) Risorgimento: A history of counselling psychology in britain. *Counselling Psychology Review*, 27(4): 72–8.

27

Coaching Supervision

Peter Hawkins

At the core of continuing professional development is continual personal development, where our own development is weaved through every aspect of our practice. When this happens every coachee becomes a teacher, every piece of feedback an opportunity for new learning, producing practices that support the balanced cycle of action, reflection, new understanding and new practice. Elsewhere (Hawkins, 2006, 2011a; Hawkins & Smith, 2006, 2013) I have shown why I believe that having supervision is a fundamental aspect of continuing personal and professional development for coaches, mentors and consultants. Supervision provides a protected and disciplined space in which the coach can reflect on particular client situations and relationships, the reactivity and patterns they evoke in them and, by transforming these live in supervision, can profoundly benefit the coachee, the client organization and their own professional practice.

Coaching and mentoring have been areas of enormous growth in the last twenty years. The 2007 International Coach Federation coaching survey estimated that the coaching industry generated $1.5 billion dollars in revenue worldwide and Carr (2005) estimated the number of coaches worldwide to be approaching 30,000. Coaching has become a significant and regular part of most leadership development activities and approximately 70% of companies surveyed in the UK and North America are investing in coaching (The Chartered Institute of Personnel and Development (CIPD), 2011; Hawkins, 2012).

Despite this, coaching supervision was noticeable by its absence in the first 20 years of the growth of this new profession, but at the turn of the century it began to be advocated by a number of key writers (see Downey, 1999; Flaherty, 1999). In the early part of the twenty-first century very few coaches were receiving supervision and those who did so were approaching supervisors trained in psychotherapy or counselling. While there is much we can learn from these and other people professions where quality supervision has been practised for longer than coaching, there are also dangers as outlined below.

It was not until 2003 that the first specific training was offered for coaching supervisors and 2006 that the first book on coaching supervision was published (Hawkins and Smith, 2006). Since the first edition of this book, there has been a significant growth in coaching supervision, particularly in the UK, where it has been endorsed by most of the major professional coaching bodies and where there has been a number of new significant publications (Bachkirova, Jackson, & Clutterbuck, 2011; Passmore, 2011; de Hahn, 2012; Hawkins & Smith, 2013).

In carrying out research into supervision for CIPD in the UK, we explored the reasons for the lack of development of coaching supervision (Hawkins & Schwenk, 2006). In interviews and focus groups with experienced coaches we were given a number of different explanations:

1. lack of clarity about what supervision involves
2. lack of well-trained supervisors
3. lack of commitment to personal development as it makes us vulnerable
4. lack of discipline among coaches
5. addiction to being in the role of the person enabling others, rather than receiving enablement.

Probably all of these have some degree of truth and a full answer needs to include these and other factors. In the absence of a body of good theories, trainings and practitioners, many coaches have turned to counsellors, psychologists and psychotherapists for supervision or supervisory models.

There is much that the helping professions can learn from each other, but it is also important to recognize the difference between the fundamental work of each professional group and hence the dangers of over-applying the theories and models of one group to the work of another. One of the dangers of a coach visiting a counsellor or counselling psychologist for supervision is that a supervisor's professional focus may tend towards understanding the psychology of the coachee. Depending on their orientation the supervisor might also focus on the relationship of coach and coachee and may have a tendency to focus more on pathology than on health! The biggest danger is when a fundamental orientation that is more interested in individuals than organizations tips over into an unrecognized tendency to see individuals as victims of 'bad' or 'unfeeling' organizations. At worst this can create a classic drama triangle of 'organization as persecutor; coachee as victim and coach as rescuer'. One of the key challenges of coaching supervision is for it to develop its own approach and methodology for supervision, which, while learning from what has been developed elsewhere, can address the challenge of coaching having multiple stakeholders.

Since writing the first edition of this chapter, supervision models have been developed for a great variety of coaching situations, which include: supervising teams of coaches (Morel, 2011); internal coaching communities (Maxwell, 2011; Hawkins, 2012); team coaches (Hawkins, 2011a); mentors (Merrick & Stokes, 2011); peer supervision (Bachkirova & Jackson, 2011; Moyes, 2011); and e-supervision (Hay, 2011).

COACHING SUPERVISION RESEARCH

The research for the CIPD mentioned above (Hawkins & Schwenk, 2006) focused on a number of key questions:

What is coaching supervision?

Why should HR professionals be interested in it?

What do HR professionals need to know about coaching supervision?

What does good practice look like?

How can supervision help coaching to be more effective?

The research was conducted through a variety of methods: a web survey, where we had responses from over 500 individual coaches and over 120 organizations; four focus groups in various parts of the UK, which included both buyers of coaching and experienced providers; and six best-practice case studies of organizations that had committed to incorporating supervision into both their internal and external coaching provision.

What we found was that:

Coaching supervision was much advocated but poorly practised.

According to the surveys, 88% of organizers of coaching and 86% of coaches believed that coaches should have regular ongoing supervision of their coaching.

Only 44% of coaches receive regular ongoing supervision and only 23% of organizations provided regular ongoing coaching supervision.

Of the coaches receiving supervision only 58% had started within the last two years.

Many of those who were receiving supervision were consulting with supervisors of counselling or psychotherapy and some with peers without supervision training.

There was a shortage of training courses in coaching supervision.

This was the first research in the field of coaching supervision.

There was an absence of specific models and methodologies for coaching supervision.

WHAT IS SUPERVISION?

In 2006 and 2013, Hawkins and Smith defined supervision as 'the process by which a coach with the help of a supervisor, can attend to understanding better both the client system and themselves as part of the client-coach system, and by so doing transform their work and develop their craft' (Hawkins & Smith, 2006, 2013).

To this could be added: 'Supervision also does this by attending to the transformation of the relationship between the supervisor and coach and to the wider contexts in which the work is happening'.

We believe that coaching supervision has three elements:

1. coaching the coach on their coaching
2. mentoring the coach on their development in the profession
3. providing an external perspective to ensure quality of practice.

This three-function model parallels the three functions that Kadushin put forward for social work supervision in the 1970s and that Proctor espoused for counselling supervision in the 1980s. Kadushin (1992) talked of the 'managerial, educative and supportive' aspects of supervision and Proctor (1988) of supervision being 'normative, formative and restorative'.

Having worked with these two models for many years we have found both to be rather confined to their own fields and so have developed our own model that defines the three main functions as developmental, resourcing and qualitative. Kadushin focuses on the role of the supervisor, Proctor on the supervisee benefit and our new distinctions on the process in which both supervisor and supervisee are engaged.

ROLE AND PURPOSE OF SUPERVISION

I believe that the role and purpose of the supervision of coaches is to build strongly upon the work carried out in the field of supervision by those in the helping professions, but some important changes are necessary in order to really support the executive coaching agenda.

Supervision is a key element in both the training process for coaches and for their lifetime continuing professional development. In training it is the process of rigorous supervision that helps the trainee link the theory and skills they learn on courses to the real-time experience of working with coachees. On workshops we can absorb models and develop competencies, but these do not by themselves produce an excellent coach. Supervision provides the reflective container for the trainee to turn their competencies into capabilities and to develop their personal and coaching capacities.

Importantly, supervision is there to serve not only the profession, but also the developmental needs of the coach/supervisee, the individual coachees that the coach is coaching and the client organizations that employ the coach.

Some key outcomes on which supervision should be focused include:

provision of the key part of continuous professional development and action learning of the coach or mentor (D)

help for the coach or mentor to develop their internal supervisor and become a better reflective practitioner (D)

provision of a supportive space for the coach or mentor to process what they have absorbed from their clients and their clients' systems (R)

help to keep the coach and mentor honest and courageous, attending to what they are: not seeing, not hearing, not allowing themselves to feel, or not saying (Q)

a chance to look at where and how the coach or mentor may need to refer the client on for more specialized help (Q).

Table 27.1   Three main functions of supervision

Hawkins and Smith (2006)	Proctor (1988)	Kadushin (1992)
Developmental	Formative	Educational
Resourcing	Restorative	Supportive
Qualitative	Normative	Managerial

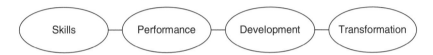

Figure 27.1   Coaching continuum (Hawkins & Smith, 2006, 2013)

Bracketed letters indicate how these outcomes link back to the three functions of Qualitative (Q), Developmental (D) and Resourcing (R) – see Table 27.1.

STAGES IN A SUPERVISION SESSION

The five-stage coaching model CLEAR (*Contract, Listen, Explore, Action, Review*) that was discussed in Chapter 16 can also be applied to the stages of supervision, or coaching the coach.

In this model the supervisor starts by *Contracting* with the supervisee on both the boundaries and focus of the work. Then the supervisor *listens* to the issues that the coach wishes to bring, listening not only to the content, but also to the feelings and the ways of framing the story that the coach is using. Before moving on, it is important that supervisors let the coach know that they have not only heard the story, but have 'got' what it feels like to be in their situation. Only then is it useful to move on to the next stage, to *Explore* with the coach what is happening in the dynamics of both the coaching relationship and also in the live supervisory relationship, before facilitating the coach to explore new *Action*. Finally, *Review* the process and what has been agreed about next steps.

This model can be developed and utilized differently depending on the nature of the coaching. In Hawkins and Smith (2006, 2013) we outlined a continuum of coaching (see Figure 27.1).

We argued that the form of supervision being utilized needs to match the coaching approach, thus performance coaches need performance supervision and transformational coaching needs transformational supervision. To illustrate this I have put below the different types of interventions that may be made by a supervisor at each of the CLEAR stages, depending on whether they were doing performance or transformational supervision (see Table 27.2).

Campone (2011) provides a very useful reflective practice model that deepens the CLEAR stages. After contracting Campone's model starts with 'research in action' – reflecting on what happened in recent coaching. This is followed by 'naming and reconfiguring mental models' – which is a form of exploring, that ensures the exploration engages with all four levels of

Table 27.2 The CLEAR model

Performance coaching	Transformational coaching
C. What do you want to focus on?	**C.** What would success look like from this session?
L. Tell me about the situation?	**L.** What I am sensing from your story is …
E. What else might you try?	**E.** What is the wildest thing you could do?
A. So what are you going to do and when?	**A.** Imagine I am that person and rehearse your opening line.
R. When will we meet to review it?	**R.** My appreciation is … My encouragement is …

engagement (see Chapter 16 on Transformational Coaching) and helps the coach shift his/her assumptions and mental frames. The third step is 'enacting the changes' which is a form of action stage that includes 'fast-forward rehearsals' (also discussed in Chapter 16). Both de Hahn (2012) and Clutterbuck (2011) provide useful frameworks for showing that the supervisory process starts before the supervisory meeting and continues after the supervision session has concluded. De Hahn (2012: 93) also provides a very useful framework for various ways a supervisee can bring their reflections into the session (memory, written case notes, audio or video recordings etc.)

Contracting for supervision

All forms of supervision relationship need to begin with a clear contract, which is created and formed by both parties, and also reflects the expectations of the organizations and professions involved. Supervision contracts need to include:

(a) practicalities, such as times, frequency and place; anything that might be allowed to interrupt or postpone the session; and clarification of any payment involved
(b) boundaries, including how supervision is different from coaching or counselling; and any confidentiality arrangements
(c) working alliance – how the relationship needs to work for the supervisee to get the most benefit from the supervision
(d) the session format – how the process will work
(e) the organizational and professional context – who else the supervision needs to serve, including the organization that employs the coach, their coachees and their organization; the professional bodies to which the coach belongs; and anyone who might accredit the coach.

THE SEVEN-EYED COACHING MODEL

In 1985 a more in-depth model of supervision was created (Hawkins, 1985), which later became known as the seven-eyed supervision model. This has been used across many different people professions and in many countries around the world (Hawkins & Shohet, 2012). Since 1995, with colleagues at Bath Consultancy Group, the model has been further developed for the world

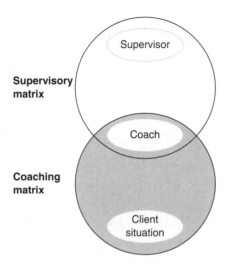

Figure 27.2   The seven-eyed model of coaching supervision

of coaching, mentoring and organizational consultancy (Hawkins, 1995; Hawkins & Smith, 2006, 2013). It is based on a systems understanding of the ways things connect, interrelate and drive behaviour. It points out the way in which the systemic context of the coachee can be mirrored in the coaching relationship and how the dynamics of the coaching relationship can be mirrored in the supervisory relationship (see Figure 27.2). Munro-Turner (2011) and Congram (2011) have both built on this model and usefully posit that there are three worlds in play in coaching supervision – the supervisory relationship, the coaching relationship and the coachee's relational world at work. The purpose of the model is to provide a complete range of different areas in supervision that can be focused on and the range of styles necessary. These seven areas of potential focus can be useful to both supervisor and supervisee in reviewing the supervision they give and receive and help them discover ways in which they can expand their supervision practice (see Figure 27.3).

1. The coachee's system

Here the focus is on the coachee and the content of the issues they have brought to the coaching as well as the wider issues of the coachee's organization. It includes not only the problem with which the coachee and the client organization want help, but also how the issues are being presented and framed.

Mode one skill. The supervisor's skill in this mode is to help the coach return accurately to what actually happened with the coachee – what they saw, what they heard and what they felt – and to try and separate this actual data from their preconceptions, assumptions and interpretations. It is useful for the coach to be helped to take notice of what happened at the boundaries of their time with the coachee, including their arrival and departure, for it is often at the boundaries that the richest unconscious material is most active.

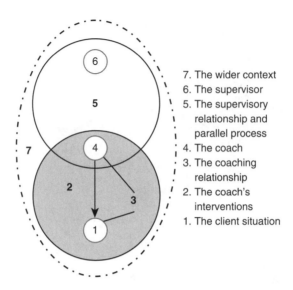

Figure 27.3   The seven modes of coaching supervision

2. The coach's interventions

Here the focus is on any interventions the coach may have made and alternative choices that might have been used. Focus may, for example, be on a situation in which the coach is about to intervene and explore possible options, including the likely impact of each.

Mode two skill. Often coaches will ask for help with an impasse they have arrived at in facilitating the change process. They will often present this impasse in the form of an 'either/ or', such as: 'Should I collude with this situation or confront the issue?' The skill of the supervisor is to avoid the trap of debating the either/or options and instead enable the coach to realize how they are limiting their choices to two polarized possibilities. They could facilitate a shared brainstorming session that frees up energy and enables the creation of new options. The benefits and difficulties of these new options can be explored and some possible interventions tried out in role-play.

3. The relationship between the coach and the coachee

Here the focus is neither solely on the coachee and their system, nor on the coach, but on the relationship that they are creating together.

Mode three skill. The supervisor has to facilitate a situation where the coach can stand outside the coach/coachee relationship to see it afresh and from a new angle. The Chinese have a proverb: the last to know about the sea are the fish, because they are constantly immersed within it.

In this way the supervisor is helping the coach to be a flying fish, so they can see the water in which they normally swim.

4. The coach

Here the focus is on the coach, highlighting both what is being re-stimulated in them by the coachee's material and the dynamics of the client system and themselves as an instrument for registering what is happening beneath the surface of the coaching relationship.

Mode four skill. In this mode the supervisor helps the coach to work through any re-stimulation of their own feelings that may have been triggered by working with this client. Having done this the coach can be helped to explore how this may be very useful data for understanding what the coachee and the client system are experiencing but are unable to directly articulate. The coach can then explore how their own blocks may be preventing them from facilitating the coachee and their system to change, and what needs to shift in them to enable a shift in the coachee and the client organization.

5. The supervisory relationship

Here the focus is on the live relationship between the supervisor and the coach. The focus needs to include what the coach has unconsciously absorbed from the coachee system and how that may be being played out in the relationship with the supervisor. The coach can inadvertently treat the supervisor in the way their coachee treated them.

Mode five skill. Here the supervisor needs to be able to attend not only to what they are being told about the coaching system, but also to what is happening in the relationship in the room. This includes both the real relationship and supervisory relationship, as well as the 'parallel process' (Hawkins & Smith, 2013). The supervisor can offer their tentative reflections on the impact of the coaching relationship on the supervisory relationship to illuminate the coaching dynamic. When done skilfully this process can help the coach bridge the gap between their conscious understanding of the coaching relationship and the emotional impact it has had upon them.

6. The supervisor self-reflection

The focus for mode six is the supervisor's 'here and now' experience while with the coach and what can be learnt about the coach/coachee/client relationship from the supervisor's response to the coach and the material they present.

Mode six skill. In this mode the supervisor has to attend, not only to the presented material and the impact on the 'here and now' relationship, but also their own internal processes. The supervisor can discover the presence of unconscious material related to the coaching relation-ship by attending to and reflecting on their own feelings, thoughts and fantasies while listening to the presentation of the coaching situation. These can be tentatively commented on and made available as possible indicators of what lies buried in the relationship with the coachee. The additional skill is to explore the means of sharing this with the coach in a non-judgemental and speculative way.

7. The wider context

The focus of mode seven is on the organizational, social, cultural, ethical and contractual context in which the coaching is taking place. This includes being aware of the wider group of stakeholders in the process that is being focused upon. This may include the client organization and its stakeholders, the coach's organization and its stakeholders, and the organization or professional network of the supervisor. Bolman and Deal (2008) provide a very useful model for looking at the organizational context through four different frames (structural, human resources, political and symbolic).

Mode seven skill. The supervisor has to be able to bring a whole systems perspective to the understanding of how the systemic context is affecting not only the behaviour, mind-sets, emotional ground and motivations of the coach and coachee, but also themselves (see Hawkins, 2011b). The skill is to attend appropriately to the needs of the critical stakeholders in the wider systems and to understand how the culture of the systemic context might be creating illusions, delusions and collusions in the coach and supervisor. To attend to mode seven also requires a high level of transcultural competence (Hawkins & Shohet, 2012; Hawkins & Smith, 2006, 2013).

Using all seven modes

In talking with both supervisors and coaches who have gone to others in search of help in exploring coaching situations, we have discovered that different supervisors are often stuck in the groove of predominantly using one of the seven modes of working. Some focus entirely on the situation out there with the coachee and adopt a pose of pseudo-objectivity (mode one). Others see their job as coming up with better interventions than the coach managed to produce (mode two). This can often leave the coach feeling inadequate or determined to show that these suggested interventions are as useless as the ones they had previously tried. Other coaches have reported taking up a problem with a coachee and having left supervision feeling that the problem was entirely due to their own shortcomings (mode four).

'Single-eyed vision', which focuses on only one aspect of the process, will always lead to partial and limited perspectives. This model suggests a way of engaging in an exploration that looks at the same situation from many different perspectives and can thus create a critical subjectivity, where subjective awareness from one perspective is tested against other subjective data.

Each mode of supervision can be carried out in a skilful and elegant manner or ineffectively, but no matter how skilful one is in one mode, the skill will prove inadequate without the ability to move from mode to mode.

The most common order for moving through the modes is to start with mode one, talking about specific coaching situations, then to move into modes three and four to explore what is happening both in the coaching relationship and for the coach/supervisee. This may well lead to exploring the here and now relationship in the room between the coach and the supervisor (modes five and six) and/or bring into awareness the wider context (mode seven). Finally, having gained new insights and created a shift in the supervisory matrix, the attention may turn back to mode two, to explore what different interventions the coach might use in their next session to create the necessary shift in the coaching matrix. The coach might even try out some of these interventions in what is termed a 'fast-forward rehearsal' (see Chapter 16). From our experience we have learnt that if the change starts to happen live in the supervision, it is far more likely to happen back in the coaching.

The model has also been used as a way of empowering the coach, who is the customer of the supervision, to enable feedback on the help they are being given and to request a change in focus. It can be used as a framework for a joint review of the supervision process by the coach and supervisor.

TRAINING AS A SUPERVISOR

In 2002, the debate about the need for supervision in coaching began to change. Some of the professional coaching bodies, particularly in the UK but also in the USA, started to argue that all coaches should receive supervision from trained and qualified supervisors. In response, Bath Consultancy Group led the way in the development of a certified training programme in the supervision of coaches and mentors.

Our starting belief was that these professions had much in common with other helping professions when it came to supervision, but were also significantly different, particularly as their work was focused primarily on an individual client. In contrast, work-based coaches and mentors always have a minimum of three clients:

1. the coachee
2. the organization they work in and for
3. the relationship between them and their organization.

Our second belief is that learning to be a supervisor is best undertaken through cycles of action learning, not by sitting in a classroom. Thus the training involves a great deal of supervision practice in threes, comprising a supervisor, supervisee and shadow supervisor, who gives feedback to the supervisor, sometimes at the end of the practice session and sometimes in the middle, in structured 'time-outs'. The trainee supervisors, as well as undertaking the modules, receive 10 hours of supervision from an experienced supervisor on 50 hours of supervision practice and two tutorials to help them maximize their individual learning.

In the Bath Consultancy Group we are constantly learning from each cohort of new trainees about the fascinating craft of supervising coaches and the lifelong journey to develop this craft. Increasingly, we are reminded that at the heart of being a good coach or a good coaching supervisor is not academic knowledge, a collection of theories and models, or an armoury of tools and techniques, but constant dedication to developing one's human capacity to be fully present for another, acting with what we term 'ruthless compassion'. For it is the ruthless compassion we can bring, not only to our client, but also to the work they do in the world and to our craft, that ultimately allows the fears and anxieties that pervade so many work situations to be overcome and for our clients to find new strength to act courageously.

EVALUATION

It is important that supervision is not seen as an activity carried out by a supervisor, supposedly with super vision! Rather, it should be seen as a joint activity between coach and supervisor that: ensures that the quality of practice; constantly develops the capacity and capability of the coach; and makes sure they are resourcing themselves adequately for the work they are undertaking.

It is important that supervision is not just a process for experienced supervisors to pass on their way of practising to other coaches. In Hawkins and Shohet (2006, 2012) the way in which supervision needs to play an important role in facilitating a learning profession is described. It is argued that:

> For too long we have reduced the concept of supervision to a cultural socialization process where the elders of the professional community shape the practice, behaviours, understanding, perceptions, feelings and motivations of the apprentices and noviciates.
>
> This approach to supervision can restrict the learning to that of the supervisee learning what has already been discovered by the supervisor and more senior members of the coaching profession. This in turn can lead to the profession becoming more constrained in well-established practices, rather than constantly refreshing itself from the regular new challenges both that clients bring to coaches and coaches bring to their supervisor. (Hawkins & Shohet, 2006: 205)

and we go on to advocate that:

> If we are to create learning professions that constantly renew their cultures, then supervision needs to become the learning lungs that assist the professional body in its learning, development and cultural evolution. This entails not only focusing on both the supervisee and supervisor learning, but providing a dialogical container in which new learning can emerge in the space between the supervisor and supervisee. Supervision needs to be practised in a way that allows learning to emerge in the interaction between the three unique areas of experience that are brought into relationship:
>
> - The client situation and context
> - The supervisee's experience and understanding
> - The supervisor's experience and understanding
>
> Too often we have seen supervision reduced to the exchange of pre-existent 'thoughts' and knowledge. The supervisee tells their supervisor what they already have thought and know about their client, and the supervisor shares their pre-existent knowledge about similar clients. (Hawkins & Shohet, 2012: 238)

Supervision needs to be a place of co-creative and generative thinking where new learning is being forged for clients, coach and supervisor and for the profession.

ACKNOWLEDGEMENTS

The author would like to acknowledge contributions from colleagues and fellow authors Nick Smith and Gil Schwenk in the writing of this chapter. The author can be contacted at peter.hawkins@bathconsultancygroup.com.

FURTHER READING

The principal books focusing specifically on coaching supervision are:

Bachkirova, T., Jackson, P., & Clutterbuck, D. (Eds) (2011). *Supervision in mentoring and coaching: Theory and practice*. Maidenhead: Open University Press.

De Haan, E. (2012). *Supervision in action*. Maidenhead: Open University Press/McGraw-Hill.

Hawkins, P. & Smith, N. (2013). *Coaching, mentoring and organizational consultancy: Supervision and development* (2nd ed.). Maidenhead: McGraw-Hill/Open University Press.

Passmore, J. (Ed.) (2011). *Supervision in coaching*. London: Kogan Page.

DISCUSSION QUESTIONS

- How would you define supervision, who and what it serves and the value it creates?
- How would you contract for and build a collaborative partnership between the supervisor and supervisee?
- How would you evaluate the benefits of supervision for the client and his/her organization?

REFERENCES

Bachkirova, T., Jackson, P., & Clutterbuck, D. (2011). *Supervision in mentoring and coaching: Theory and practice*. Maidenhead: Open University Press.

Bachkirova, T. & Jackson, P. (2011). Peer supervision for coaching and mentoring. In Bachkirova, T., Jackson, P., & Clutterbuck, D. (Eds), *Supervision in mentoring and coaching: Theory and practice*. Maidenhead: Open University Press.

Berglas, B. (2000). The very real dangers of executive coaching. *Harvard Business Review,* June: 86–92.

Bolman, L. & Deal, T. (2008). *Reframing organizations: Artistry, choice and leadership* (4th ed.). San Francisco, CA: Jossey-Bass.

Campone, F. (2011). The reflective coaching practitioner model. In Passmore, J. (Ed.), *Excellence in coaching: The industry guide*. London: Kogan Page.

Carr, R. (2005). *Coaching statistics, facts, guesses, conventional wisdom and the state of the industry*. Victoria, British Columbia: Peer Resources.

Chartered Institute of Personnel and Development CIPD (2011). *The coaching climate report*. London: CIPD.

Clutterbuck, D. (2011). Using the seven conversations in supervision. In Bachkirova, T., Jackson, P., & Clutterbuck, D. (Eds), *Supervision in mentoring and coaching: Theory and practice*. Maidenhead: Open University Press.

Congram, S. (2011). The use of gestalt approaches in supervision. In Bachkirova, T., Jackson, P., & Clutterbuck, D. (Eds), *Supervision in mentoring and coaching: Theory and practice*. Maidenhead: Open University Press.

De Haan, E. (2012). *Supervision in action*. Maidenhead: Open University Press/McGraw-Hill.

Downey, M. (1999). *Effective coaching*. London: Orion Publishing Group.

Flaherty, J. (1999). *Coaching: Evoking excellence in others*. Woburn, MA: Butterworth-Heinemann.

Hawkins, P. (1985). Humanistic psychotherapy supervision. A conceptual framework: Self and society. *European Journal of Humanistic Psychology, 13*(2): 69–77.

Hawkins, P. (1995). *Shadow consultancy*. Bath: Bath Consultancy Group.

Hawkins, P. (2006). Coaching supervision. In Passmore, J. (Ed.), *Excellence in coaching: The industry guide*. London: Kogan Page.

Hawkins, P. (2011a). *Leadership team coaching: Developing collective transformational leadership*. London: Kogan Page.

Hawkins, P. (2011b). Systemic coaching supervision. In Bachkirova, T., Jackson, P., & Clutterbuck, D. (Eds), *Supervision in mentoring and coaching: Theory and practice*. Maidenhead: Open University Press.

Hawkins, P. (2012). *Creating a coaching culture*. Maidenhead: McGraw-Hill.

Hawkins P. & Schwenk, G. (2006). *Coaching supervision*. London: CIPD Change Agenda.

Hawkins, P. & Shohet, R. (2006 & 2012). *Supervision in the helping profession* (3rd ed. and 4th ed.). Maidenhead: McGraw-Hill Open University Press.

Hawkins, P. & Smith, N. (2006 & 2013). *Coaching, mentoring and organizational consultancy: Supervision and development* (1st ed. and 2nd ed.). Maidenhead: McGraw-Hill Open University Press.

Hay, J. (2011). E-Supervision: application, benefits and considerations. In Bachkirova, T., Jackson, P., & Clutterbuck, D. (Eds), *Supervision in mentoring and coaching: Theory and practice*. Maidenhead: Open University Press.

Kadushin, A. (1992). *Supervision in social work*. New York: Columbia University Press.

Maxwell, A. (2011). Supervising the internal coach. In Bachkirova, T., Jackson, P., & and Clutterbuck, D. (Eds), *Supervision in mentoring and coaching: Theory and practice*. Maidenhead: Open University Press

Merrick, L & Stokes, P. (2011). Supervision in mentoring programmes. In Bachkirova, T., Jackson, P., & Clutterbuck, D. (Eds), *Supervision in mentoring and coaching: Theory and practice*. Maidenhead: Open University Press.

Morel, M. (2011). A French model of supervision: Supervising a 'several-to-several' coaching journey. In Bachkirova, T., Jackson, P., & Clutterbuck, D. (Eds), *Supervision in mentoring and coaching: Theory and practice*. Maidenhead: Open University Press.

Moyes, B. (2011). Self-Supervision using a peer-group model. In Passmore, J. (Ed.), *Excellence in coaching: The industry guide*. London: Kogan Page.

Munro-Turner, M. (2011). The three worlds four territories model of supervision. In Bachkirova, T., Jackson, P., & Clutterbuck, D. (Eds), *Supervision in mentoring and coaching: Theory and practice*. Maidenhead: Open University Press.

Proctor, B. (1988). *Supervision: A working alliance* (videotape training manual). St Leonards-on-Sea, East Sussex: Alexia Publications.

28

Coaching and Mental Health

Michael Cavanagh and Andrew Buckley

Coaching is used by organizations and individuals for a range of purposes including skills acquisition, performance enhancement, the development of leadership and personal functioning. While these tasks often involve the remediation of unhelpful patterns of thought and behaviour (Standards Australia, 2011), coaching is not therapy. The dominant position among coaches maintains that coaching is targeted toward working with clients from non-clinical populations, whereas therapy is designed to address the needs of people suffering from diagnosable conditions such as personality disorders, substance abuse, depression, anxiety and other mood disorders (Buckley, 2007; Grant, 2005).

However, both experience and a growing body of research, tells us that such simple distinctions are problematic. The boundary between clinical and non-clinical is imprecise and fluid. In reality, coaches are likely to be regularly faced with coachees exhibiting some form of mental health difficulty. Epidemiological studies suggest that up to 45% of people in the general population will suffer from some diagnosable mental health problem at some point in their life (Australian Bureau of Statistics, 2008) and that 10–15% of the population suffer from some form of personality disorder (Svrakic et al., 2002). Furthermore, professionals and managers – the greatest users of organizational coaching – exhibit higher rates of stress, anxiety and depression than skilled, semi-skilled and unskilled individuals (Eaton, Anthony, Mandel, & Garrisson, 1990).

Coaches are not trained to be mental health diagnosticians and should not seek to offer diagnostic advice to clients. Nevertheless, professional practice obliges coaches to take seriously the task of determining the limits of their practice. When it comes to the boundaries between psycho-pathology and the normal range of human functioning, this can be difficult. When is a person simply sad and when are they depressed? When is the worry an executive feels over delivering a key presentation just the normal butterflies associated with public speaking and when is it a symptom of a more pervasive case of social phobia? Clutterbuck suggests as coaches we 'need to be aware of the boundaries that it is dangerous to cross' (Clutterbuck, 2007: 19); and 'the coach does need the ability to be able to judge when not to coach' (Buckley, 2007: 20).

This chapter is about the recognition and management of individuals for whom mental state issues mean that coaching is likely to prove ineffective, inappropriate or potentially harmful. Starting with an exploration of mental ill health in its broadest sense, this chapter goes on to explore warning signs that may indicate a problem. This is followed by a discussion of the law, ethics and practicalities that coaches need to consider before deciding on the most appropriate action.

We use case studies to highlight ways that coachees could behave and to raise questions for the coach. None of these examples show clear signs of mental illness but illustrate the more borderline cases that may occur as part of anyone's coaching practice.

MENTAL ILL HEALTH AND THE COACHEE POPULATION

The extent to which individuals suffer temporary and more permanent mental health problems has become clearer over recent years. The fact that 'mental illness accounts for over a third of the burden of illness in Britain' (Centre for Economic Performance (CEP), 2006: 3) highlights just how widespread are the problems. Mental ill health occurs in our workplaces, communities and families. The view that it mental illness only happens to 'them'; those 'poor souls' that need hospitalization or have 'inadequate personalities', is mistaken.

Even when one considers current morbidity due to mental health issues (as opposed to life-time morbidity), the figures are large. One in six employees suffer problems at any one time (Sainsbury Centre for Mental Health (SCMH), 2007). Issues range from the less common, but severe and enduring, conditions such as schizophrenia and bipolar affective disorder at less than 1 in 100 people of working age, to the very common and often transitory problems of depression and anxiety affecting up to 20% of the population.

Evidence highlights that problems are by no means contained just within those employees who take sickness absence (Johns, 2010). In what is becoming known as 'presenteeism', employees attend work but struggle with a physical or mental health issue. Presenteeism accounts for a higher cost to business than the costs associated with employees taking formal sickness absence (Johns, 2010; Collins & Cartwright, 2012). It is also more of an issue among executive, technical and managerial grades than other staff (SCMH, 2007).

Information on the extent of mental illness or psychopathology among coachees is limited. Green, Oades and Grant (2005) found that over 23% of applicants for a life coaching pro-gramme in Australia had clinically elevated scores of symptoms of mental health problems pre-coaching. This is similar to the findings of Spence and Grant (2007), where 25% of participants in a life coaching programme had elevated scores. The results of these and other studies suggest that coachees, in both life coaching and occupational settings are as likely to be experiencing mental health problems as the general population (see Grant, 2007 for a summary of the available research).

As mentioned above, when faced with a client with potential mental health issues, the coach's task is not diagnosis. Rather, the coach's task is to answer the questions 'Can my coaching help?', 'What are my limitations with this issue?' and 'What is in the best interest of the client?' before deciding what to do. Diagnosis, treatment and exploration of underlying issues is the province of mental health specialists and is best avoided. Coaches whose background is in psychology or the psychological therapies may have the skills, training and experience to be able to come to an informed decision as to what is wrong and may be well placed to offer effective 'therapy', but should still ask the question 'can my coaching help?' rather than 'can I help?'

Buckley (2007: 21) articulates four capacities that enable the coach to ethically, professionally and effectively to manage these clients:

1. Awareness that some people will have temporary, or more permanent, mental health issues that will prove to be barriers to effective coaching. For the coach to know that an inability to be able to offer help is no reflection on competence as a coach but an acceptance of the range of people likely to be seen.
2. An ability to recognize the signs that may suggest a possible mental health issue. The capacity to explore these signs with the client so that premature judgements are not taken.
3. Thorough knowledge of legalities and ethics at a national level as well as an ability to make informed judgements in view of the coach's own level of training and experience and any specific contractual arrangements that may be in place.
4. A willingness to make choices around coaching as an appropriate solution and to be able to offer alternatives to those client's in need. Choice of the best course of action may not be straightforward and all the factors need to be considered before a decision is made.

UNDERSTANDING MENTAL ILL HEALTH

There are two major approaches to identifying and understanding mental illness. The first is a the categorical approach, as embodied in diagnostic systems such as the World Health Organization's' International Classification of Diseases (ICD-10), or the American Psychiatric Association's Diagnostic and statistical Manual of Mental Disorders (DSM IV-TR). Categorical approaches use closely defined constellations of symptoms to decide whether a person meets criteria for a particular disorder. The use of these diagnostic systems requires significant training and is beyond the remit of coaching and this chapter. Nevertheless, some understanding of the disorders and their symptoms is an important resource in informing our understanding as coaches.

The second major approach to understanding mental illness is the dimensional or psychosocial approach (see Kessler, 2002; Lopez et al., 2007; Sperry, 2007). Dimensional approaches view psychopathology, not as simply absent or present, but as more usefully represented as falling along dimensions that stretch from normal or healthy expression of a symptom, to

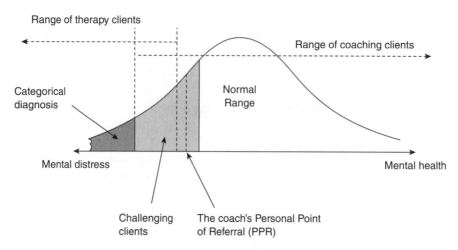

Figure 28.1   The dimensional approach to assessing mental health (adapted from Cavanagh, 2005)

unhealthy or disordered (see Figure 28.1). Again, it is not the task of the coach to provide the client with a dimensional diagnosis. Rather, a dimensional perspective better enables the coach to assess whether they have reached the limits of their own skills and abilities (i.e., their own personal point of referral) and referral to another professional is warranted. The dimensional approach also assists the coach in assessing whether coaching should be continued, delayed or terminated (see Figure 28.1). For a fuller discussion of this approach see Standards Australia (2011).

Dimensional approaches also honour the changing nature of mental health in illness in the individual. UK-based consultant psychiatrist Mike Nowers says 'mental illnesses lie on a spectrum between health and illness and an individual may slide from health into illness over a period of time and in a way that may be hard to identify' (as quoted in Buckley & Buckley, 2006: x).

Case Study 1

A coach is pleased to be put in contact with a Chief Executive (CE) and there is an optimistic telephone conversation.

During the first meeting, the coachee appears flat and tired and shows little interest in coaching. During the next session, everything seems a struggle for the CE. The coach mentions what has been noticed and asks how long it has been like this. There is a trigger point, a personal loss with which the CE is trying to come to terms.

The coach is able to help the CE to work out a temporary plan and coaching is delayed to enable the CE to come to terms with the loss.

When the coach and coachee meet next, some months later, the CE appears completely different and coaching continues in a very positive way towards a successful outcome.

In this example, coaching is delayed until the coachee is able to benefit from the experience. Coaching through the period needed to come to terms with the loss would have been questionable from a contractual perspective, as real coaching could not take place and ethically any help needed may have been more appropriately met by another type of 'helping-by-talking', such as a psychological therapist.

No one is immune from suffering mental health problems; issues, distress and clear illness can appear as if from nowhere. Most people will understand that an event in life can lead to distress and changes in outlook and behaviour. The CE in Case Study 1 is an example; the loss mentioned could be the death of someone close; changes in how he sees himself due to age; or even the realization that personal aspirations can no longer be met. The key is the trigger event that offers a cause for the suffering.

Case Study 2

John has been responsible for the IT needs of a fast-growing company for several years. He seemed the obvious choice to develop a team as the company grew in size. The CEO was convinced of the benefits of coaching and organized a coach to help John in his new role.

The coach found that John would talk passionately and knowledgably about the IT infrastructure but not about his new team. The sense was that the team was just there to do tasks that John did not have time for. John appears to be managing the growing needs of the IT department by working longer hours and getting more frustrated. Coaching could help with this through discussions of delegation and team working. John gets visibly upset, as the IT system is not working well and, although he has the skills to fix the problems, he cannot manage the workload. He says that only he can do the tasks; he has no trust in his team members. Although John was highly capable of managing the IT needs of a small company he is not able to manage a team and has become very distressed as this became more evident.

Coaching has proved unable to help John with the contracted task, that of transitioning to manager. From the organization's perspective a positive coaching outcome could be to recognize this and to take steps to manage the business needs of the IT team. John may gain insight and realization that managing people is not for him. Should he choose to try to address this then it is likely that a therapeutic way of working would be indicated.

There are many similarities to Case Study 1 in the problems faced by John, the IT manager, in Case Study 2. Again, there is a trigger event; his 'environment' at work changed from dealing with the IT system to facilitating the system management. Coaching to support a change in work focus has proved ineffective. Any underlying cause is unclear and likely to remain so for the coach.

Mike Nowers suggests,

It is the context within which people are living their lives that is the key. How their individual personalities can manage the pressures and stresses of everyday living and the occurrence of negative or sometimes seemingly positive life events will dictate whether and when people cross the threshold from health into mental illness. (as quoted in Buckley & Buckley, 2006: xi)

The variable nature of mental health and the effect of environmental changes is one of the reasons why a mental health problem is so difficult to predict and often to identify.

For the coach, understanding mental ill health, mental illness and other terms such as psychopathology is more than deciding if a coachee has a mental illness. An ability to recognize unusual signs and relate these to an individual's circumstances is the task when deciding how to answer the question 'is my coaching appropriate?'

RECOGNIZING MENTAL HEALTH ISSUES

Table 28.1 lists the signs of mental ill health and is based upon a mental state examination that could be conducted by a mental health specialist. None of these signs or symptoms will demonstrate, unequivocally, that the coachee has a mental health problem; rather, it is the accumulation of signs and linked behaviour that would lead the clinician to diagnose a mental illness. When taken in isolation many of these signs form part of normal behaviour for all of us at one time or another.

Table 28.1   Warning signs of mental ill-health

Appearance	Is there anything unexpected with respect to dress and personal care?
	Are there any clues in how the coachee moves, or doesn't?
	Is there any unusual body language?
Behaviour	Is there any agitation or nervousness?
	Is the coachee lethargic or uninterested?
	Repetitive behaviours can be a sign of problems
	Is there incongruence between what is being discussed and expressions and body language?
Mood	Overly optimistic or pessimistic – especially if this doesn't correlate with other information
	Does the coachee appear fixed emotionally or inactive, possibly apathetic?
Thoughts	Any preoccupations or fixations?
	Are thoughts, as expressed, reasonably rational or are there some signs of irrationality, possibly delusions
Perception	Are there any signs that the coachee is not experiencing the world 'normally'?
Intellect	Any changes in intellect over time?
	Does the coachee appear as expected intellectually?
	Are there any signs that the coachee is 'not here' today, not present and not taking part in the session?
Insight	Can the client offer an explanation for these unusual signs?
	Does the explanation or how the client attributes the unusual signs seem reasonable?

Once puzzling behaviours have been noticed, reflecting on all that is known of the coachee can give helpful clues as to whether referral may be warranted. Cavanagh (2005: 26) suggest five questions that can assist the coach in this decision making:

How long has the client's distress or dysfunction been going on? If there is a persistent pattern of distress or dysfunction over a long period of time, then one should consider the need to consult a mental health specialist.

How extreme are the behaviours or responses of the client? If the client's behaviours and responses (at the behavioural, emotional, cognitive, or physiological level) appear to fall outside the range expected of an average person, it may indicate the presence of psychopathology.

How pervasive are the distresses and patterns of dysfunctional behaviour? Is the problem limited to a circumscribed situation or aspect of the person's life, or does it seem to be operating in multiple areas and at multiple times?

How defensive is the person? Does the person actively seek to avoid addressing the unhelpful behaviours? Do they deny the existence of problems in the face of significant evidence to the contrary? Do they become overly aggressive, defensive or passive when appropriately challenged by the coach? Such responses may indicate that there is something going on for the client that is deep seated or particularly threatening at a psychological level.

How resistant to change are the dysfunctional patterns of behaviour, thinking or emotions? Do the negative or unhelpful patterns persist despite the client's attempts to address them? This may indicate that the person specialist help in overcoming the unhelpful patterns of behaviour.

Identifying any changes in behaviour, thoughts or feelings is central to the recognition of a mental health problem and may present as a challenge to the coach. Friends, family and work colleagues have the advantage of knowing someone over a period of time and in different situations, whereas the coach will usually have only limited knowledge of what could be considered usual behaviour for the coachee.

Once the coach has noticed something unusual or possibly worrying, thinking through all that is known of the coachee is an important step. Unless the coachee's behaviour is so worrying that immediate action is needed, time spent reflecting on the situation, ideally with a supervisor, and exploring the background with the coachee, before deciding what to do, may be time well spent. While seemingly bizarre behaviour may indicate mental illness, it may also be nothing more than an unusual personality or a transitory aberration. Reflection and focused listening to the client time can help one to avoid jumping to conclusions, or deciding on a 'diagnosis' or explanation based on a fragment of evidence. The goal is to consider what may be happening for the client rather than to ignore the behaviours before continuing coaching.

Exploring emerging concerns with the coachee enables the coach to be in a much clearer position to decide the next step and is as important as knowledge of the signs of mental ill health. The answers to questions help to complete a picture. How this impacts on the future of any coaching depends, though, on several other factors, such as the coaching context, the contract and the specific skills of the coach, as well as the wishes of the coachee.

THE COACHING CONTEXT

The next part of the decision-making journey towards answering the question 'can my coaching help?' or 'should my coaching continue?' looks at the factors and views to be considered as part of the wider context. Coaching typically involves multiple stakeholders; the coachee, the coach and the systems within which they are operating. These systems include, but are not limited to, society, the coaching profession, the coachee's workplace and family. The ethical, practical and legal management of these boundaries is particularly important when the coach suspects, or is told by the coachee, that significant mental illness is present.

At a legal level, society influences the boundaries between coaching and other activities, between the coach and other professionals, through both the general understanding of what coaching is and is not, and any laws currently in place. It is beyond the scope of this chapter to detail the laws in individual countries. It is, however, imperative that the individual coach has an understanding of the legal framework in which they work. Of most relevance will be those laws pertaining to the status of coaching in relationship with other 'helping-by-talking' activities such as counselling, psychotherapy and the psychologies. The legal status of the psychological therapies has real relevance and potential impact on, with whom and under what circumstances the coach may work.

The codes of ethics and good practice of professional membership organizations such as the Association for Coaching, the International Coach Federation and the European Mentoring and Coaching Council are relevant to those who may be coached. Membership of one of these bodies implies acceptance of these codes and, while they will have no legally binding implications, complaints about malpractice could result. Linked to this is the provision of indemnity insurance. The insurance provider will have insured the activity of coaching and the onus is on an individual coach to show both that coaching (and not another activity) was undertaken and to show that the client was suitable to be coached within the competences of the coach and the laws and practices in force.

The rights and obligations of third parties to the coaching also need to be appropriately considered. For example, should the coachee maintain an overwhelming focus on personal issues over the course of a business coaching engagement, the organization paying for the coaching may well consider this a poor use of resources. If the coachee shows signs of a possible mental health issue, or has a history of mental illness, then it is possible there may be legal implications around the duty of care owed to an employee. Misusing coaching as a more socially acceptable route to help an employee who would be best placed by seeing a therapist does have legal implications. Many of these difficulties can be avoided or lessened by clear contracting at the beginning of the coaching engagement. Contracts and agreements should make explicit the focus and allowable content of coaching and what should occur should mental health issues (including serious workplace stress) arise in the course of coaching.

In making such agreements, it should be remembered that disclosures involving suspected mental health issues, to employers or other third parties, may have serious material and reputational consequences for the coachee – this includes disclosing that coaching is being terminated or delayed, or that the coachee is being referred for assessment or treatment. Neither is always clear that a sponsoring organization has a right to such personal information. The management of these boundaries is complex. However, clear contracting and establishing explicit agreements regarding limits to confidentiality prior to commencement of coaching can greatly help in managing these boundaries. (For a fuller discussion of these issues, see Standards Australia, 2011.)

So far, the contextual considerations around the advisability of starting or continuing coaching have focused on those cases where the system suggests coaching should not continue. One other possible conflict is the potential coachee who has little, if any, understanding of what coaching is. Should an individual approach a coach for help with a psychological problem or mental illness that is likely to be outside the legal and social norms of what coaching is, then the coach is advised not to offer coaching and should suggest a more appropriate route to help, such as a visit to the individual's family doctor in the first instance.

As in any profession, the range of skills and experience of individual coaches varies widely and there will be times when it is the competency of the coach that decides the best thing to do next. A skilled coach, possibly with a therapeutic background, may be able to continue with a coachee who has some specific problem areas that can be avoided. Knowing how to avoid this 'can of worms' requires training and experience. Inadvertently opening up deep-seated psychological problems may cause considerable hardship for the coachee. It is difficult to pack away psychological problems once they have been exposed. Time available also plays a part in these decisions. If the coaching contract is for only three or four sessions then there is a greater need to avoid issues than if there were a much longer expected relationship when it would be considered reasonable that the coachee could work around or through any problem areas.

WHAT TO DO?

The options available are:

Delay coaching – put coaching on hold for a period to see if the coachee is able to resolve any problems. Functional suffering, such as grieving a loss, may well pass and the coachee could benefit from coaching in a few weeks or months.

Continue coaching – perhaps with extra care. Most likely appropriate if the focus of any mental health issue is clearly separate from the coaching focus. Coaching may also be possible while the coachee receives treatment or support from a mental health specialist, although this often requires discussion between the coach, therapist and coachee to delineate the role and scope of coaching. First and above any coaching goals must come the overall health of the coachee.

Stop coaching – if no clear benefit to the coachee of continued coaching can be seen, the safest option is to draw a line under any coaching once mental ill health is suspected.

The Standards Australia guideline for coaching in organizations was created via an extensive consultation process involving coach service providers, coaching professional bodies, Psychological Associations, universities, coach training providers and purchasers of coaching from the public and private sectors. It provides a set of five practical criteria for deciding whether coaching should be allowed to commence or continue with a client who displays mental health difficulties. The guideline suggests that coaching should only be commenced or continued if *each* of the five following conditions are present (Standards Australia, 2011: 75):

1. The coach has met his or her duty of care to refer to an appropriately qualified mental health professional if he or she suspects the presence of an undiagnosed or untreated mental illness.
2. The coach has reasonably determined that the client's mental health problem will not interfere with the client's ability to identify, set and work toward appropriate goals.
3. The coaching does not contradict or interfere with any therapy or treatment being undertaken by the client. This may require consultation between the coach, coachee and any mental health professional/s involved.
4. The coach is able to recognize and work within the limits of their training and competence with respect to mental health issues.
5. The coachee is likely to gain benefit from entering into the coaching relationship.

Table 28.2 provides some helpful questions to further explore these criteria and decide 'what next?' Whether or not the decision is taken that coaching is inappropriate, the coach may need to offer some support to the coachee to find appropriate help. This ranges from suggesting a visit to the family doctor, suggesting therapy as more appropriate and, in rare and extreme cases, taking action on behalf of the coachee, such as calling an ambulance or emergency services. Supervision may provide the coach with the opportunity to clarify any suspicions and to reflect on courses of action before any decision and discussion takes place with the coachee.

The ethics of coaching is discussed in its wider context elsewhere in this Handbook as well as by de Jong (2006) and Buckley and Buckley (2006). An understanding of the ethics and good practice of coaching, irrespective of membership of, and agreement to any codes from, coaching organizations, is important for any coach. The efficacy of any coaching will be viewed with these standards in mind. One of the most important ethical considerations for the coach when considering whether to offer coaching to someone is non-malfeasance – a term which means a commitment to taking actions that do not harm the coachee. This suggests that a cautious approach will be best when a coach meets anyone with possible mental health problems.

Table 28.2 Deciding 'what next?'

Can the expected focus of coaching be seen as clearly separate from the issues giving concern?
If the coachee's problems seem separate from the coaching focus, continuing may be appropriate.
If all of the coachee's life seems affected by the issues, then stop.
Are the coachee's problems likely to pass?
Functional suffering will often pass; consider continuing.
If long term or a recurring pattern, stop.
Has the coachee received appropriate help elsewhere?
If the coachee is supported elsewhere, then consider continuing.
Emotional support is not the province of coaching; if the coachee is unsupported, then stop.

How emotionally resilient or robust does the coachee appear?

An emotionally robust person may be able to benefit from coaching while struggling through problems in part of their life; consider continuing.

A coachee who struggles emotionally is less likely to benefit from coaching; stop.

How self-aware of the issues is the client?

Self-awareness is linked to emotional resilience; a self-aware coachee may be able to separate coaching from their issues; consider continuing.

An inability on the part of the coachee to recognize issues and problems probably precludes coaching as a sensible approach; stop.

Issues in others can have personal impact on any of us.

If, as coach, you are affected by the coachee's issues, then stop.

Case Study 3

Mike phones a coach whose number he has been given by his wife. He says he has to change his behaviour, as he has become quite aggressive and angry with both his wife and daughter. His daughter has left home to live with a boyfriend who 'is a waster'. Mike was made redundant some months ago and is spending more and more time in the bar, where he says he can relax and unwind.

Mike appears upset at how his life has changed and seems keen to try to make some changes.

He misses an appointment and then phones to say he still wants to see the coach, even though his wife has left and gone to stay with her mother. He is tearful on the phone and the coach wonders if he has been drinking, even though it is morning.

Mike's life is unravelling in many ways and he probably needs professional support. If he refuses to accept this view and wants to continue seeing the coach s/he would be best advised to refuse. Help cannot be forced on anyone; inappropriate help may well do more harm than good.

Mike in Case Study 3 may not be showing clear signs of mental illness yet, but he is experiencing real difficulties. What is normally meant by coaching could cause harm in this example. So much of his life has changed and there is a hint that his choice of behaviour, in increasingly using alcohol to mask feelings and problems, may be a contributory factor. It may appear harsh to refuse to support someone who is so obviously struggling, but there is a real risk of doing more harm by continuing.

EVALUATION

For the coach, understanding when not to coach is a vital skill. It is important for the coach as well as for the coachee, who may be encouraged to seek more appropriate help; 'after all most people who suffer from a mental illness will make a full recovery with appropriate diagnosis, management and treatment' (Buckley & Buckley 2006: xii). Effective management of the boundary between psychologically 'healthy' coachees and those with problems is equally important for any purchaser of coaching services, for the ongoing professionalism of the coaching industry and for relationships, both legal and professional, with others who work in the 'helping-by-talking' professions.

If one in four or five coachees have elevated levels of psychological distress, then hopefully it can be seen how important it is that all coaches are appropriately trained in the recognition and management of mental health and psychological problems. As the coach training industry continues to mature and coach training standards become increasingly available, we believe that specific training in the recognition of those coachees with psychological problems or mental illness will become the norm. Developing training that meets the needs of individual coaches, including those with a background in psychology or psychological therapies, may present challenges. The most obvious type of training may be an adaptation of the diagnostic model as used in medicine and much of psychology. This would present challenges, due to the length of training needed for the coach to gain an understanding of this complex area. There is a growing body of evidence suggesting that short courses in the recognition of mental illnesses following this medical model may be problematic for the non-medical professional (Kitchener & Jorm, 2004; Moor et al., 2007; Read, 2007).

Although there are advantages of being aware of the categorical approach to diagnosis (Cavanagh, 2005: 23), the dimensional or psychosocial understanding of mental health and illness is critically important for the coach. As most coaches are not trained diagnosticians, the primary question the coach faces is not, '*is the coachee suffering from a diagnosable disorder?*', nor even, '*is the coachee mentally ill?*' Rather, the coach's primary question needs to be, 'Is my coaching in the best interest of the coachee, and if not, is referral to another professional indicated?'

FURTHER READING

Buckley, A. & Buckley, C. (2006). *A guide to coaching and mental health: The recognition and management of psychological issues.* London: Routledge.

Cavanagh, M., Grant, A.M., & Kemp, T. (Eds) (2005). *Evidence-based coaching, Vol. 1: Theory, research and practice from the behavioural sciences* (pp. 21–36). Bowen Hills, QLD: Australian Academic Press.

Standards Australia (2011). *Handbook of organisational coaching.* Sydney: Standards Australia.

DISCUSSION QUESTIONS

- How can I better inform myself to notice mental health issues in coaching?
- What is my personal point of referral? How do I identify my skills and limitations in dealing with mental health issues?
- How can supervision be of use in managing mental health issues that arise in coaching?

REFERENCES

Australian Bureau of Statistics (2008). *National survey of mental health and wellbeing: Summary of results, 2007*, retrieved April 2013 from www.abs.gov.au/ausstats/abs@.nsf/latestproducts/4326.0main%20features32007?opendocument& tab name=summary&prodno=4326.0&issue=2007&num=&view=.

Buckley, A. (2007). The mental health boundary in relationship to coaching and other activities. *International Journal of Evidence Based Coaching and Mentoring*, Special Issue, *Summer*: 17–23.

Buckley, A. & Buckley, C. (2006). *A guide to coaching and mental health: The recognition and management of psychological issues*. London: Routledge.

Cavanagh, M. (2005). Mental-health issues and challenging clients in executive coaching. In M. Cavanagh, A.M. Grant & T. Kemp (Eds), *Evidence-based coaching, Vol. 1: Theory, research and practice from the behavioural sciences* (pp. 21–36). Bowen Hills, QLD: Australian Academic Press.

Centre for Economic Performance (CEP) (2006). *The depression report: A new deal for depression and anxiety disorders*. London: London School of Economics.

Clutterbuck, D. (2007). *Coaching the team at work*. London: Nicholas Brealey.

Collins, A. & Cartwright, S. (2012). Why come into work ill? Individual and organizational factors underlying presenteeism. *Employee Relations, 34*(4): 429–42.

de Jong, A. (2006). Coaching ethics: Integrity in the moment of choice. In J. Passmore (Ed.), *Excellence in coaching, the industry guide* (pp. 191–202). London: Kogan Page.

Eaton, W.W., Anthony, J.D., Mandel, W., Garrison. R., (1990). Occupations and the prevalence of major depressive disorder. *Journal of Occupational Medicine, 32*, 1079–1087.

Grant, A.M. (2005). What is evidence-based executive, workplace and life coaching? In M. Cavanagh, A.M. Grant & T. Kemp (Eds), *Evidence-based coaching, Vol. 1: Theory, research and practice from the behavioural sciences* (pp. 1–12). Bowen Hills, QLD: Australian Academic Press.

Grant, A.M. (2007). A model of goal striving and mental health for coaching populations. *International Coaching Psychology Review, 2*(3): 248–62.

Green, S., Oades, L., & Grant, A.M. (2005). An evaluation of a life-coaching group programme: Initial findings from a waitlist control study. In M. Cavanagh, A.M. Grant & T. Kemp (Eds), *Evidence-based coaching, Vol. 1: Theory, research and practice from the behavioural sciences* (pp. 127–41). Bowen Hills, QLD: Australian Academic Press.

Johns, G. (2010). Presenteeism in the workplace: A review and research agenda. *Journal of Organizational Behavior, 31*: 519–42.

Kessler, R.C. (2002). The categorical versus dimensional assessment controversy in the sociology of mental illness. *Journal of Health and Social Behavior, 43*(2): 171–88.

Kitchener, B.A. & Jorm, A.F. (2004). Mental health first aid in a workplace setting: A randomized controlled trial. *BMC Psychiatry, 4*: 23.

Lopez, M.F., Compton, W.M., Grant, B.F., & Brieling, J.P (2007). Dimensional approaches in diagnostic classification: a critical appraisal. *International Journal of Methods in Psychiatric Research, 16*(S1): S6–S7.

Moor, S., Maguire, A., McQueen, H., Wells, E.J., Elton, R., Wrate, R., & Blair, C. (2007). Improving the recognition of depression in adolescence: Can we teach the teachers? *Journal of Adolescence, 30*: 81–95.

Read, J. (2007). Why promoting biological ideology increases prejudice against people labelled schizophrenic. *Australian Psychologist, 42*(2): 118–28.

Sainsbury Centre for Mental Health (SCMH) (2007). *Mental health at work: Developing the business case*. Policy Paper 8, retrieved June 2008 from www.scmh.org.uk.

Spence, G. & Grant, A.M. (2007). Professional and peer life coaching and the enhancement of goal striving and well-being: An exploratory study. *Journal of Positive Psychology, 2*(3): 185–94.

Sperry, L. (2006). *Cognitive behavior therapy of DSM-IV-TR personality disorders: Highly effective interventions for the most common personality disorders* (2nd ed.). New York: Routledge.

Standards Australia (2011). *Handbook of organisational coaching*. Sydney: Standards Australia.

Svrakic, D., Draganic, S., Hill, K., Bayon, C., Przybeck, T., & Cloninger, C. (2002). Temperament, character and personality disorders: etiologic, diagnostic and treatment issues. *Acta Psychiatrica Scandinavica, 106*: 189–95.

29

Continuing Professional Development for Coaches

Dianne Stober

Since 2000, conversations regarding what is required for a professional practice of coaching have expanded from discussions within informal networks of individuals to global dialogues among coaching bodies and other stakeholder groups. While coaching is still emerging as a profession and consensus is lacking among the coaching community, developments have occurred in options for education and training, efforts continue to delineate what are the requisite bodies of knowledge and initial forays have been made in identifying coaching competencies. Given the lack of coherence at this point in time, one suggestion has been to adopt an evidence-based practice philosophy as a guide for professional development. This calls on coaches to integrate the best available knowledge with their own expertise in the service of individual coachees and their contexts.

This chapter explores the challenges for coaches' professional development going forward from this current scenario.

Initial challenges for professional development

Coaching has emerged over the past 25 years into silos of communities and information has proliferated from approaches to established practice in fields as diverse as psychology, management and education to grassroots approaches to personal development such as life coaching. These networks have varied from organized interest groups within professional associations, such as the British and Australian Psychological Societies, to topics of interest within divisions of other associations like the Academy of Management and the American Psychological

Association, the National Education Association and many others, to coaching-specific organizations such as the International Coach Federation (ICF), the European Mentoring and Coaching Council (EMCC), the Worldwide Association of Business Coaches (WABC), the International Association of Coaches (IAC) and many others. While this rapid development of various organizations and groups is a reflection of the interest in coaching, this same development means that there are a multitude of simultaneous challenges to a coherent view of professional development.

Probably the biggest challenge lies in the fact that coaching is not as yet an established profession. Coaching, as an emerging profession, is still in the early stages of defining itself. In particular, there are a number of criteria that distinguish a profession that have not yet been fulfilled in coaching, although progress has been made. Some of these criteria include (Bennett, 2006):

- minimum levels of education and training required to become proficient; accepted competencies and skill sets
- practice grounded in identified bodies of knowledge and avenues of communication and idea exchange
- an agreed set of ethical standards by which coaching can self-discipline practice, including avenues of enforcement
- widely accepted professional organizations that represent the profession and those practising it
- systems for evaluating merit or certifying competence that are widely accepted and allow for further development of the profession
- external recognition of coaching's professional status by those served and the general public.

Several of these criteria directly relate to the challenges facing professional development in coaching. The education and training required for practice, the competencies needed and grounding in the bodies of knowledge which comprise the profession all have direct ties to professional development. We will look at each of these criteria in terms of professional development in turn.

A second challenge is how the various stakeholders view professional development itself. Some professions, such as psychology, management and education, have communities that have developed a speciality or focus in coaching. These professions have established structures for development through continuing training and education, supervision and outlets such as peer-reviewed journals and conferences that serve as recognized forums for discussion of new areas of practice like coaching. Generally speaking, there are assumptions within these professions that newer practices will be developed through the formulation of theory and practice and then tested through research methods. Coaching, as a new area of practice, is developing within the established structures of these professions.

Meanwhile, grassroots coaching organizations that have sprung up outside established professions and academic circles have recognized the need for standards of professional development and have begun developing programmes and criteria of their own. Some of these organizations have professionals from various backgrounds involved in their development, who bring with them previous history of what constitutes professional development. However, while undoubtedly the development of training and ethical standards, along with standards of qualification, are informed by various professionals' educational histories, many grassroots organizations take a somewhat *tabula rasa* approach to professional development. What it means to be a coach has been founded on common sense and observed experience rather than tightly tied to existing theories or empirical data.

As a result of these varied approaches to coaching, at this point in time we still have a chaotic and uneven landscape of professional development. We have different established professions with their own particular views of coaching as a subset of their discipline, others formulating coaching as a cross-disciplinary endeavour, and industry organizations proposing coaching as a unique and distinct arena of practice. These different approaches result in different pictures of what a coaching professional needs in terms of development.

Areas of focus for professional development

There a several areas within professional development that warrant special focus, both at the individual level and at the professional community level. For individual coaches, it is important to assess where they might need to seek additional experience, skills, or knowledge. For the coaching community, there is a distinct need to focus on those areas which are not agreed upon nor fully developed.

Education and training as professional development

The landscape of coach education and training is a diverse terrain. If we include initial education and training as an important part of the professional development of individuals as coaches, as yet there is no widely agreed upon body of knowledge, set of skills or core competencies that would reflect what is required to educate a coach. This means there is no established clarity or consensus about what constitutes the initial professional development of coaches, much less what would entail continuing professional development of practising coaches. There are industry training organizations of widely varying quality; programmes within graduate schools of business, psychology, education, etc. offering everything from individual courses to continuing education certificates to specializations within doctoral programmes; special interest groups within existing professions that offer workshops, conferences and publications; and coaching-specific associations that offer various certifications in coaching. The plethora of options, groups, claims made and territory staked out can be an overwhelming and difficult wilderness to navigate for the individual coach seeking education, training and ongoing development.

Industry training organizations. One option for training and professional development in coaching lies within the various industry training organizations. A typical Google search (in 2013) of coach training organizations yields 11,800,000 hits. Types of training run the gamut from workshop intensives that teach coaching skills to programmes with multiple courses over many months. Some are face-to-face and many have a distance-based aspect whether online or via teleconferencing. The background of those providing the training may vary from those who base their expertise in work and life experience to those who have PhDs in fields that overlap with coaching.

As coaching has grown towards a potential profession, an uncomfortable question arises in a 'live and let live' context regarding education and training. At this point, there are so many different training programmes, certifications and such a lack of consensus about what even defines coaching that it begs the question of what the educational requirements should be for a coach. In looking at this issue, there is an underlying question of scope of practice. Are we talking about someone who applies coaching skills within a particular context, whether it is managers who use coaching as part of their management approach, or teachers who coach students, or healthcare professionals who apply coaching skills to supporting patients making positive health behaviour change? Or are these individuals who work with others coming for coaching as the main service? In the former, coaching skills training may be the primary need in order to use coaching as a tool within the practice of another profession or occupation. In the latter, there is a fundamental question of what knowledge is required for the professional practice of coaching. For those who are practising as coaching professionals, skills training is not enough (Drake & Stober, 2007). Professional coaches should ground their practice in theoretical and research knowledge.

Graduate schools. Another source of education, training and professional development is higher educational institutions. As coaching has continued to develop, colleges and universities have entered the coaching education arena. In 2006, the Graduate School Alliance in Executive Coaching identified 123 colleges and universities providing a variety of types of coaching education within the United States alone (Starr, 2006). Overlapping somewhat with coach training organizations, some of the university programmes focus more on coaching skills; others are full-blown programmes linked with graduate degrees with specializations in coaching. Those that are linked with existing degrees tend to have explicit requirements for the study of relevant theoretical and empirical bodies of knowledge along with supervised experiences of coaching practice. Because higher education institutions have been through recognized accreditation processes for education, they tend to have more uniform requirements for coursework and practicum experiences. Graduate programmes also require some education and training in research methods, which brings us to another key issue in professional development for coaches.

The question of research competency for coaches

As coach education and training has taken root within academic circles at the graduate level and more research on coaching has been undertaken, the issue of research competency arises. One of the hallmarks of a profession includes establishing a body of knowledge (Bennett, 2006). Much of the coaching-specific research continues to be conducted within universities by graduate students. These students are often housed within departments such as psychology or organizational development that have areas of overlap with an emerging discipline of coaching. As these students move on to other academic positions or out into practice and continue research, they will continue to grow and develop a coaching-specific literature and body of knowledge. A challenge will be whether these efforts remain splintered among many different disciplines, or whether they coalesce into a coherent and distinct discipline of coaching.

Returning to the development of individual coaches, an important distinction is that between formal and informal research. While coaches are often encouraged to 'do their own research' in terms of assessing progress with clients with questions regarding outcomes that coachees are realizing, this is not to be confused with formal research. With access to tools such as Survey Monkey, it can be tempting to put together a list of questions, which, while potentially valuable in gathering feedback, most likely will not constitute an assessment with validity or reliability. Formal research requires an explicit methodology, whether that is a qualitative or quantitative method. Such methodologies require a particular set of knowledge, skills and abilities.

However, this does not mean that all coaches must be empirical researchers. Rather than insisting that all coaching practitioners must be trained to do original research, a scholar–practitioner approach would enable coaches to critically evaluate and apply evidence to their practice with coachees. The goal of such an approach is to give coaches enough grounding to become critical consumers of research (Stober, 2005). In order to be a critical consumer, coaches need to have a basic understanding of research methods and analysis. Being able to assess whether a particular piece of research has been conducted well and whether the results have been interpreted fairly is the aim of a scholar–practitioner model. As an example, let us assume that a journal article reported results that suggested that a certain approach to goal setting was highly effective in facilitating high potential coachees transitioning from lower ranks of leadership to the executive level within organizations. The coaching intervention was given to fifteen coachees and results for five different assessments were analysed. A scholar– practitioner might be quite sceptical of the results based only on this description, as there would probably be serious questions raised as to the adequacy of the sample size in drawing conclusions about the results, especially if this was intended as a quantitative study. Without a basic understanding of research, there can be a temptation to assume that because a piece of research has been published, then the research is valid. For an excellent critical review of previous research and a discussion of the various types of research used to study coaching, see Passmore and Fillery-Travis (2011) in the Further Reading section.

Having an adequate understanding of research methods enables professional coaches to assess what are accurate and fair applications of research results to practise and within what contexts. Would it be legitimate to apply a life coaching approach to values setting that was found to be effective for early career coachees to a sample of college students? A coach who can read such a research report and recognize points of overlap between the two types of coachees and any critical areas of difference is likely to be able to assess more effectively the validity of applying the results from one group to another.

In terms of professional development and research competency, a scholar–practitioner model will serve coaches well. This means that coaches who may not have a background that includes education in research methods will want to obtain some additional education and those that do will need to apply those skills to coaching-specific research. It may be uncomfortable to say that learning coaching skills is not enough, but if coaching is ever to meet the qualifications of a true profession and for coaches to be recognized as practising a true profession (vs. acting in a professional manner), being a critical evaluator of what is good coaching research is a must.

Grounding coaching in existing bodies of knowledge and professional development

One of the areas with both high points and gaps is the grounding of coaching in existing bodies of knowledge. Within a number of fields, notably psychology, management and education, there have been concerted efforts to tie coaching practice directly to knowledge of human growth, development and interaction. This volume, along with a number of others (e.g. Peltier, 2009; Skiffington & Zeus, 2003; Stober & Grant, 2006; Palmer & Whybrow, 2007; Cox, 2013) reflects development in linking coaching to bodies of knowledge. There are also a growing number of journals, special issues and literature reviews that have been devoted explicitly to coaching. Coaching-specific journals include the *International Coaching Psychology Review*; *Coaching: An International Journal of Theory, Research, and Practice*; the *International Journal of Evidence-based Coaching and Mentoring*; and the *International Journal of Coaching in Organizations*. Other journals that have had special issues on coaching or an ongoing stream of articles on coaching include the *Consulting Psychology Journal: Practice and Research*; the *Academy of Management Review*; and the *Journal for Supervision and Curriculum Development*.

Along with developments in producing explicit links between coaching and existing bodies of knowledge, attention is being paid to what bodies of knowledge are required for coaching professionals. For example, the Graduate School Alliance for Executive Coaching in North America has developed a comprehensive set of guidelines for academic programmes (see www.gsaec.org/curriculum.html). These guidelines include the following broad bases of knowledge for executive coaches: (1) individual differences and development; (2) interpersonal dynamics and communication; (3) group and inter-group dynamics; (4) organizational systems and dynamics; (5) social systems and dynamics; (6) change management; (7) adult learning; (8) coaching theory and principles. Within each of these areas, there are many theories and approaches for coaches to understand and with which to become familiar.

Given that many coaches are coming from a particular background of expertise and knowledge, whether it be from psychology, healthcare, management, or other professions, it is important that they take stock of where gaps in their knowledge base might lie. For example, someone who is a clinical psychologist and seeking to practise as an executive coach might need to seek out ways to develop their knowledge and skills relating to organizations or business. Likewise, someone coming from a corporate background would probably need to obtain expertise in psychological theories and practice as they pertain to coaching. Until there is agreement (and regulation) within the coaching industry regarding which knowledge bases with which professionals must have familiarity, it is up to individuals to come to decisions about their own development and what is required for competent practice.

It will be helpful to outline a few questions that can aid in that decision process:

- What type of coaching is the goal?
- What knowledge bases are relevant for ethical practice in this area?

- Out of those knowledge bases, which have I mastered and which require further study in order to be mastered?
- Where can I obtain exposure and education to bases of knowledge with which I lack familiarity?
- Do I need to seek formal education or training in these areas? Or in supervision?

In answering these questions, coaches and potential coaches are able to outline what gaps exist in their background and what education or training they need to seek out. However, until the coaching industry has developed consensus regarding what bases of knowledge are needed for professional, ethical practice, wide variation will remain in this area among the various coaching associations, coach training organizations, academic programmes, and related professional associations.

Competencies for coaching

Central to the question of what education and training for coaches is required is the clarification of what coaching competencies are needed. Calls for competencies have been made over the past decade and as yet there are no generally agreed upon competency models (Brotman, Liberi, & Wasylyshyn, 1998; Ennis et al., 2005; Bennett, 2006). A number of coaching industry associations have listed competencies that are linked to their credentialing criteria, including the ICF, the EMCC and the WABC (see organization websites for full descriptions). There are commonalities among the various competency descriptions that generally fall within the following:

- ethical standards which promote 'do no harm' and respect for the coachee
- effective establishment of the coaching relationship and its boundaries, including building trust, rapport, effective communication
- effective promotion of growth and change for the coachee including increased awareness, reaching goals, leveraging strengths, etc.
- continuing education and skill development by the coach linked to the area of practice within coaching (e.g. business coaching, life coaching, executive coaching).

Implications for professional development of coaches. The various competencies listed within coaching organizations have yet to be researched or systematically evaluated, so, as with many other areas of professional development in coaching, it is up to the individual to assess the face validity of these competency areas. Similar to the questions regarding bodies of knowledge, it is important for the individual coach to assess the range of intended practice of coaching, what competencies they already have and how they might seek further development for competencies they may not yet have mastered. Specific educational or training courses may fit the bill and, in other situations, seeking out a supervisor might enable a coach to further develop their professional identity.

In looking at the professional development realities of an emerging profession of coaching, it is clear that the varied options for education and training and lack of agreement on required bodies of knowledge and coaching competencies complicate any straightforward approach to coach development. At this point, a model of how coaches could implement a scholar–practitioner philosophy may at least give the individual coach a point of focus in their professional development.

The call for evidence-based coaching

An initial step forward towards a profession lies in agreeing a philosophy of practice and therefore an understanding of what contributes to the professional development of coaches. If establishing coaching as a profession requires a specified body of knowledge and minimum levels of education and training, then the professional development of coaches, both initially and continuing, will need to be grounded in that knowledge. Evidence-based practice (EBP) is a philosophy of practice that can provide a guide to the professional development of coaches as we strive to bring both structure and flexibility to the emerging profession. EBP grew out of a recognition within the field of medicine that there was research that had implications for clinical practice, but that much of that research was never taken up by practitioners and used with patients. For coaching, EBP offers great potential for how coaches can learn from the development of other professions. So what does EBP actually mean? EBP, in medicine, is: 'the conscientious, explicit, and judicious use of current best evidence in making decisions about the care of individual patients, [which] means integrating individual clinical expertise with the best available external clinical evidence from systematic research' (Sackett, Haynes, Guyatt, & Tugwell, 1996: 71).

Sackett et al. (1996) go on to say that neither individual practitioner expertise nor external evidence is enough. Research evidence gives us new knowledge, yet it is the practitioner who needs to decide how and when that evidence applies. And without the input of new evidence, practitioners miss out on knowledge that can improve their skills or indicate a particular approach is no longer valid. As discussed earlier, this has implications for the need for coaches to have a basic understanding of research in order to critically evaluate and apply research evidence. However, EBP is not about dry, academic texts and journals; rather EBP is an approach 'where "artful" practice and "scientific" evidence meet' (Stober, Wildflower, & Drake, 2006: 1).

The benefit of using an EBP framework is that it can provide an overarching guide to the coach as he or she works with each individual coachee. Regardless of approach or orientation of the coach, EBP can help guide how coaches structure and think about the coachee, the relationship and indeed themselves in that context. This is done by paying attention to the integration of three main components of an evidence-based approach: (1) best available knowledge; (2) the coach's expertise; and (3) the individual coachee's preferences, personality, values, etc. If coaches pay attention to each of these areas and look to add to their knowledge and expertise in a reflective manner, using EBP will support continuous professional development.

Best available knowledge. Without stipulated bases of knowledge for competent coaching, it is important for coaches to look at what background knowledge they have from previous work and what knowledge they still need to seek out. Professional development for coaches means being familiar with the coaching-specific literature while also knowing relevant literature from other established disciplines. Much of the coaching-specific evidence is exploratory or descriptive (Passmore & Fillery-Travis, 2011; Stober, 2005). These approaches are sources of hypotheses and can inform theory development; however, they do not demonstrate cause and effect nor explain underlying mechanisms at work. While coaching-specific evidence is still in early stages of explanatory research, there is quite a bit of evidence to be found in related disciplines that is applicable. We can extrapolate evidence from other practices aimed at growth and development, such as humanistic approaches (Stober, 2006); cognitive–behavioural approaches (Costa & Garmston, 2002; Edwards, 2003; Auerbach, 2006; Peterson, 2006); developmental theory (Berger, 2006); adult learning (Cox, 2006); psychoanalytic theories (Kilburg, 2003; Allcorn, 2006; Orenstein, 2007); systems approaches (O'Neill, 2000; Cavanagh, 2006); and goal-setting research (Grant, 2006), among many others.

As a result, in terms of professional development, coaches will have the significant task of casting a wide net across related fields in order to gain disparate knowledge that is relevant to coaching practice. As education and training guidelines for coaching continue to develop, this task is likely to become more codified and circumscribed within educational programmes. Along with the need to identify relevant knowledge, coaches may also need to seek out education regarding research methods and develop skills in critically evaluating relevant research in order to identify that best available knowledge. An EBP approach does not mean that coaches blindly follow any particular published evidence, theory, or practice; rather, coaches are able to apply critical thinking skills to what knowledge is relevant, useful and applicable to practise (Grant & Stober, 2006).

The coach's expertise. Along with acquiring relevant bases of knowledge and identifying the best available, professional practice also means coaches need to be able to apply that knowledge of evidence appropriately. We have already discussed the lack of agreed competencies for coaching and have laid out broad areas of competency that seem to be represented by various coaching associations. Beyond mastering the necessary skills for delivering coaching, the EBP approach can help coaches become more expert; they will be able to draw upon the depth and breadth of their accumulated knowledge and use themselves as effective instruments of change and to apply that knowledge within the fluid environment of various coaching conversations and contexts. Given the wide range of backgrounds different coaches bring to their practice, it is paramount that they pay attention to the sources of information and knowledge upon which they can draw. It is also important in the development of coaches that awareness of the limits of skill and practice is sharp and that coaches do not go beyond those boundaries while seeking to gain the expertise that might be needed.

An EBP approach is an integrative approach, urging coaches to blend the best available knowledge with their own expertise and background in the service of their coachees. This requires a deep appreciation for each individual coachee and the selection of appropriate methods and models that fit the particular context. Next we turn to the third component of an EBP approach.

Individual coachee preferences and characteristics. Given that each client has a unique personality, situation and goals, EBP requires the coach to pull together the best available knowledge and his or her own expertise within the particular context of that coachee. Each client's values, outlook, expectations and situation must be considered if coaching is to be effective. Thus coaches will also need to assess a variety of characteristics of each coachee such as age, developmental stage, sociocultural contexts (e.g. gender, culture, socioeconomic status, etc.), current environmental factors such as job and career status, individual and personality factors and expectations for coaching (Stober et al., 2006). The implication for professional development is that coaches will seek to develop structures and frameworks for gathering and evaluating important characteristics of the coachees with whom they work. Developing competencies in conceptualizing coaching contexts is vital for effective coaching. Some questions to consider include:

- Do I have a structure or protocol for gathering important characteristics of coachees?
- What assessments would generally be most helpful and which in particular individual contexts?
- How can the collected knowledge be integrated with knowledge and expertise?

In terms of professional development within the coaching industry as a whole, an EBP approach gives grounding for education and training and for ongoing development of practising coaches. There is a wide range of coach training programmes; some base training primarily on skills development and some also emphasize the need for grounding in bodies of knowledge that inform the practice of coaching. There are professional development needs and opportunities for these organizations and for individual coaches wherever they might be along this EBP continuum. For coaches and training organizations that have focused primarily on skills development, there is a huge professional development opportunity to seek out the connections between 'what we do' and the theory and evidence that provides the 'why we do what we do'. For training organizations, there is a need for honest assessment of whether current programmes adequately educate coaching professionals in bodies of knowledge. Likewise, coaching programmes need to evaluate how robust their education and training is in terms of assisting individual coaches to assess their own expertise and to develop effective frameworks for evaluating the individual coachee's characteristics and context. By taking an EBP approach to education and training, we have the possibility of integrating relevant evidence and expertise from various root disciplines of coaching and moving into an era of synthesis and solidification of what constitutes the practice and profession of coaching.

EVALUATION

At this point in the emergence of coaching as a potential profession, what constitutes professional development is as varied as the wide range of coaching organizations, stakeholders, and education and training programmes. Until there is agreement on what is required for educating and training coaching professionals, what the requisite bodies of knowledge are, and establishing a distinct coaching-specific literature, professional development will continue to remain a fuzzy area. In addition, what is considered acceptable continuing education and ethical standards of practice remains within individual stakeholder associations rather than at a profession or industry-wide level. However, individual coaches certainly can evaluate the state of practice and look for opportunities to address any gaps in their own development. An evidence-based approach can guide coaches in this endeavour by outlining three broad areas of concern: their familiarity with the best available knowledge, their awareness of their own expertise and the boundaries of that expertise, and their ability to assess the individual characteristics of each coachee. If coaches work towards integrating these three key components, their own continuing professional development will surely grow.

FURTHER READING

Passmore, J. & Fillery-Travis, A. (2011). A critical review of executive coaching research: A decade of progress and what's to come. *Coaching: An International Journal of Theory, Research, and Practice, 4*(2): 70–88. (This is a *must* read for a comprehensive overview of published research on coaching, a discussion of types and limitations of research methods used and an outline of needed research over the next decade.)

DISCUSSION QUESTIONS

- In assessing yourself, what bodies of knowledge would support your continued development as a coach? Where can you learn more in these areas?
- Considering the various statements of professional conduct and competencies among professional coaching associations, professional associations in psychology, management, etc., and various educational and training programmes, what differences and commonalities do you see? Do you see any areas of development for yourself based on your assessment of the state of coaching?
- Taking a look at your coaching process, are there any areas that you can further develop from an EBP perspective? Additional training or knowledge? Additional structure or processes in your practice?
- How would regular peer supervision and case consultation help you continue your professional development?

REFERENCES

Allcorn, S. (2006). Psychoanalytically informed executive coaching. In D.S. Stober & A.M. Grant (Eds), *Evidence based coaching handbook: Putting best practices to work for your clients* (pp. 129–52). New York: Wiley.

Auerbach, J.E. (2006). Cognitive coaching. In D.S. Stober & A.M. Grant (Eds), *Evidence based coaching handbook: Putting best practices to work for your clients* (pp. 103–28). New York: Wiley.

Bennett, J.L. (2006). An agenda for coaching-related research: A challenge for researchers. *Consulting Psychology Journal: Practice and Research, 58*: 240–9.

Berger, J.G. (2006). Adult development theory and executive coaching practice. In D.S. Stober & A.M. Grant (Eds), *Evidence based coaching handbook: Putting best practices to work for your clients* (pp. 77–102). New York: Wiley.

Brotman, L.E., Liberi, W.P., & Wasylyshyn, K.M. (1998). Executive coaching: The need for standards of competence. *Consulting Psychology Journal: Practice and Research, 50*: 40–6.

Cavanagh, M. (2006). Coaching from a systemic perspective: A complex adaptive conversation. In D.S. Stober & A.M. Grant (Eds), *Evidence based coaching handbook: Putting best practices to work for your clients* (pp. 313–54). New York: Wiley.

Costa, A.L. & Garmston, R.J. (2002). *Cognitive coaching: A foundation for Renaissance schools* (2nd ed.). Norwood, MA: Christopher-Gordon.

Cox, E. (2006). An adult learning approach to coaching. In D.S. Stober & A.M. Grant (Eds), *Evidence based coaching handbook: Putting best practices to work for your clients* (pp. 193–218). New York: Wiley.

Cox, E. (2013). *Coaching understood: A pragmatic inquiry into the coaching process*. London: Sage.

Drake, D. & Stober, D.R. (2007). The rise of the post-professional: Lessons learned in thinking about coaching as an evidence-based practice. In M. Cavanagh, A. Grant, & T. Kemp (Eds), *Evidence-based coaching (Vol. 2): Cross-disciplinary perspectives*. Sydney, NSW: Australian Academic Press.

Edwards, J. (2003). Cognitive coaching: Research on outcomes and recommendations for implementation. In I.F. Stein & L.A. Belsten (Eds), *Proceedings of the 1st ICF Coaching Research Symposium* (pp. 20–32). Mooresville, NC: International Coach Federation.

Ennis, S., Goodman, R., Hodgetts, W., Hunt, J.M., Mansfield, R., Otto, J., et al. (2005). *Core competencies of the executive coach*. Retrieved 8 September 2008 from www.theexecutivecoachingforum/ECFCompetencyModel1905.pdf.

Grant, A.M. (2006). An integrative goal-focused approach to executive coaching. In D.S. Stober & A.M. Grant (Eds), *Evidence based coaching handbook: Putting best practices to work for your clients* (pp. 153–92). New York: Wiley.

Grant, A.M. & Stober, D.R. (2006). Introduction. In D.S. Stober & A.M. Grant (Eds), *Evidence based coaching handbook: Putting best practices to work for your clients* (pp. 1–14). New York: Wiley.

Kilburg, R.R. (2003). *Executive coaching: Developing managerial wisdom in a world of chaos.* Washington, DC: American Psychological Association.

O'Neill, M.B. (2000). *Executive coaching with backbone and heart: A systems approach to engaging leaders with their challenges.* San Francisco, CA: Jossey-Bass.

Orenstein, R.L. (2007). *Multidimensional executive coaching.* New York: Springer.

Palmer, S. & Whybrow, A. (2007). *Handbook of coaching psychology.* New York: Routledge.

Passmore, J. & Fillery-Travis, A. (2011). A critical review of executive coaching research: A decade of progress and what's to come. *Coaching: An International Journal of Theory, Research, and Practice, 4*(2): 70–88.

Peltier, B. (2009). *The psychology of executive coaching: Theory and application.* (2nd ed.) New York: Brunner-Routledge.

Peterson, D.B. (2006). People are complex and the world is messy: A behavior-based approach to executive coaching. In D.S. Stober & A.M. Grant (Eds), *Evidence based coaching handbook: Putting best practices to work for your clients* (pp. 51–76). New York: Wiley.

Sackett, D.L., Haynes, R.B., Guyatt, G.H., & Tugwell, P. (1996). Evidence-based medicine: What it is and what it isn't. *British Medical Journal, 13*: 71–2.

Skiffington, S. & Zeus, P. (2003). *Behavioral coaching: How to build sustainable personal and organizational strength.* Sydney, NSW: McGraw-Hill.

Starr, L.M. (2006). *Academic guidelines distribution project.* Retrieved 6 September 2008 from www.gsaec.org/ research. html.

Stober, D.R. (2005). Approaches to research on executive and organizational coaching outcomes. *International Journal of Coaching in Organizations, 3*: 6–13.

Stober, D.R. (2006). Coaching from the humanistic perspective. In D.S. Stober & A.M. Grant (Eds), *Evidence based coaching handbook: Putting best practices to work for your clients* (pp. 17–50). New York: Wiley.

Stober, D.R. & Grant, A.M. (2006). *Evidence based coaching handbook: Putting best practices to work for your clients.* New York: Wiley.

Stober, D.R., Wildflower, L. & Drake, D. (2006). Evidence-based practice: A potential approach for effective coaching. *International Journal of Evidence Based Coaching and Mentoring, 4*(1): 1–8.

30

Ethics in Coaching

Diane Brennan and Leni Wildflower

The issue of ethical standards is critical in any profession. Coaching is no exception. The increasing success of coaching since 1995 in North America, Europe, Australia, Asia and, more recently, Africa, has prompted a rapid growth of coaching programmes and coaches entering the field worldwide (PricewaterhouseCoopers (PwC), 2012). With this success comes a measure of notoriety. Coaching has grown widely in acceptance in business and professional organizations, and there are few barriers to individuals wishing to establish themselves as coaches: coaching operates independently of oversight by any one professional body or government.

Various professional coaching bodies, however, have established standards of ethical practice for their members, including:

European Mentoring and Coaching Council (EMCC)

International Coach Federation (ICF)

Association for Coaching (AC)

Association for Professional Executive Coaching and Supervision (APECS)

International Association of Coaching (IAC)

Worldwide Association of Business Coaches (WABC).

In addition to the various coaching bodies, the British Psychological Society (BPS), Australian Psychological Society (APS) and the American Psychological Association (APA) have established special interest groups in coaching psychology.

These bodies work independently, but there are commonalities across the codes that will be explored in this chapter. Each provides a code of ethics and a complaints process to encourage compliance with professional standards and ethical practice among its membership. The opportunity to join and be held accountable for ethical conduct builds public confidence for practitioners in this relatively young emerging profession (Garlo & Prior, 2003).

Considering the PricewaterhouseCoopers estimate of 47,500 coaches worldwide in the International Coach Federation Global Coaching Study (PwC, 2012), a conservative estimate of perhaps 65% of coaches could belong to one or more of the professional bodies. Those who do are assumed to demonstrate commitment to some definition of ethical practice.

This chapter includes a discussion and comparison of the ethical standards of coaching, psychological, law and education organizations, and a discussion of the ethical issues that currently face professional coaches including contracting, confidentiality, conflict of interest, dual and multiple relationships and boundary management. The issues will be considered for independent coaches as well as for those who are employed within organizations.

EVOLUTION OF ETHICS IN COACHING

A code of ethics provides foundational guidelines in relation to what to expect from those in the profession (Gert, 1988). Ethical codes are standards of conduct that define the essentials of honourable behaviour within the particular field or organization. Upon joining, a member of a professional body agrees to abide by the organization's' code and acknowledgement of the code creates a feeling of community and mutual obligation among the members toward each other and the overall profession (Khurana & Nohria, 2008). For example, physicians, psychologists, counsellors, lawyers, teachers and Human Resources professionals all follow a code of conduct and meet the standards established for their particular profession. Acknowledging the code demonstrates commitment to high standards of practice for those they serve.

In relation to coaching, de Jong considers sound ethics to be the essence and underpinning of good coaching (de Jong, 2006). Coaching pioneers such as Thomas Leonard and Laura Whitworth (Brennan, 2008) came from various professions including accounting, finance, psychology, law, management and education, and also saw the need for an ethical framework early on in the development of the field (Garlo & Prior, 2003).

Looking at codes of ethics across various disciplines, the common themes are:

1. Do no harm: Do not cause needless injury or harm to others.
2. Duty of care: Act in ways that promote the welfare of other people.

3. Know your limits: Practise within your scope of competence.
4. Respect the interests of the client.
5. Respect the law.

COMPARISON OF COACHING CODES

The ethical codes from organizations, including ICF, EMCC, AC, APECS, IAC and WABC, are strikingly similar. Even what appear at first as differences tend to reveal themselves, on closer inspection, as regroupings of familiar principles – variations in taxonomy rather than content. For example, the EMCC code of ethics references competence, context, boundary management, integrity and professionalism, while ICF describes professional conduct at large, conduct with clients, conflicts of interest and confidentiality. The similarities are not surprising, given that some of these codes have been modelled on others and all of them derive from a limited number of common sources. On the other hand, such bodies as have taken the trouble to draw up new codes for coaching have clearly been motivated to look afresh, and with conscientious attention, at the ethical pressures that an individual in this emerging profession is likely to encounter. We can rule out careless or uncritical borrowing.

The degree of similarity in the resulting formulations is a reminder of the extent to which these codes are based not only on earlier professional codes drawn up by other professional groups such as psychologists and medics but, beyond them, on more basic societal codes. They spring, in other words, from a deeper source (Weiner, 2006). The major areas of professional concern expressed in these codes, which include not exploiting positions of power or status, avoiding conflicts of interest and keeping confidences, could be applied directly to people in general as they function in work and in relationships. These codes seem to give expression to an emerging consensus of what constitutes conscientious behaviour that goes beyond the limits of coaching or any other specialized activity. The consensus underlying these modern codes is aspirational, pragmatic and humane, concerning itself with the ways in which our behaviour impacts other people.

These values are expressed with particular thoroughness and attempted precision in professional codes of ethics for several reasons. First, it is in the nature of being a professional that one functions with a particular level of consciousness of the effect of one's behaviour. Second, professional bodies have the power, to a greater or lesser extent, to enforce high standards of behaviour on a group of individuals who have chosen to abide by a particular code, in return for which they can enjoy the status and benefits of membership.

Coaching here is in a significantly different position from medicine, where qualifications and membership are far more tightly defined, and removing someone from the profession, though difficult, is possible. In coaching, standards of behaviour are largely self-imposed. Even in this unregulated environment, however, the existence of a code is crucial, serving as a set of descriptors against which a client or colleague can measure a coach's performance, or as a system of prompts for self-evaluation.

Codes of ethics in coaching, based though they are on the codes of older more established professions, also tend to differ in emphasis, tilting somewhat in their overall effect towards the positive and balancing prohibition with exhortation. At the same time they focus more attention on the subtle psychological interaction between coach and client which is both the context of the work and a significant part of its content and, in doing so, they emphasize the autonomy and dignity of the client.

In the nuanced exchanges that form the basis of the coaching relationship, codes of ethics, however elaborate and however strictly enforced, will never be sufficient. The coach will always be called upon, by the nature of the work, to be acutely conscious of its ethical dimension.

In July 2008, the Global Convention on Coaching (GCC), a gathering of individuals representing some 40 countries around the world, came together to continue a dialogue about the future of coaching. Ethics was one of the ten topics covered in the dialogue process. Key findings and recommendations from the GCC were published in a summary document (GCC, 2008) and confirmed:

1. After twelve months of open discussions worldwide, it has become evident that a strong code of ethics is of paramount importance.
2. The code underpins the emergence of coaching as a profession, its status, education and development and core competencies.
3. A strong code will help sustain the profession. It is also evident that such a code needs accountability mechanisms.

The common elements among the existing codes point the way towards a shared code of conduct for the emerging profession. ICF and EMCC filed a joint initiative with the European Union for a common code of conduct as the benchmark standard for the coaching and mentoring industry. The code's goal is to establish a benchmark for ethics and good practice in coaching and mentoring. It forms the basis for the development of self-regulation for the coaching and mentoring profession. It is drafted with regard to European law and registered on the dedicated European Union database which lists self-regulation initiatives in Europe (2011). More recently, AC, EMCC and ICF created the Global Coaching & Mentoring Alliance designed to advance the profession. The formal agreement that declares, 'As a collective of global professional coaching and mentoring bodies we seek to build alliances, a cooperative spirit, purpose and initiatives where we can partner to make a difference to the emerging profession and society as a whole.' The Alliance is reviewing other professional coaching organizations to extend joining invitations (2012).

ETHICAL BEHAVIOUR IN A COACHING RELATIONSHIP

Ethical codes, though they attempt to define a set of behaviours, are necessarily limited. The process of abstracting moral principles leaves out the tacit frameworks that inform one's self-understanding, sense of self-worth and sense of moral behaviour (Taylor, 1989). It is a fair assumption that most coaches act within the code of ethics drawn up by their coaching organization: they do not explicitly cross boundaries between the personal and the professional; they do not knowingly lie to clients; and they do not become sexually involved with them. But what about transgressions that are sufficiently subtle that they might not even be recognized by the coach responsible for them?

One of the areas of ethical concern often stated by respected coaches is the concern over competence. In an effort to win over clients, coaches may promise unrealistic outcomes. They might assume that they can help create changes or provide insights for clients which are beyond their level of ability.

In a profession where the very act of engagement has emotional and moral ramifications, it is more necessary and more difficult to describe correct ethical behaviour. It is in precisely this zone of subtle moral judgement that the most important dimension of an ethical practice lies. It is also where adult development and moral competencies overlap with ethical guidelines. Unfortunately, behaviour at this level cannot be legislated for, or controlled with consequences for infractions. In every coaching situation, we must count on the coach's impulse not only to 'do no harm', but to work conscientiously towards positive results for the client.

Circumstances where unethical behaviour might pass under the radar of a code of ethics might include situations where the coach:

1. misrepresents his or her ability to deliver an outcome in order to keep a client or, more innocently, to make the client feel better
2. becomes emotionally involved in the client's issues and indirectly or inadvertently manipulates the client in order to meet his or her own needs
3. retains a client who loves being coached but makes no progress in his/her coaching work.

The aspiration to act ethically cannot be separated from the ability of individuals to separate themselves from others and to have developed a sophisticated level of moral reasoning. Professional practice as a coach requires ongoing commitment to ethics with continuous awareness and learning in the process.

ETHICAL ISSUES

The coaching organizations with established codes of ethics and standards also have complaint processes should concerns arise. These provide for self-monitoring in a field that has no overarching system of monitoring or regulation. They are not intended to remediate damage caused to clients, but rather to steer the future actions of the coach.

The complaint processes, while distinct within the framework of each organization's operation, consistently include a request for a written complaint with the identification of the individual initiating the concern. The processes are complex and intended to provide an independent and objective review of the situation. If the coach is found to have breached the code of ethics, remedies or sanctions are determined in accordance with the seriousness of the breach. Remedies might be mentoring, supervision and/or additional education specific to the area of concern. Sanctions may include a loss of certification in or membership of the organization.

During an ethics presentation at its annual international conference in 2006, the ICF summarized the situations generating the most frequent inquiries. Four categories were identified: contracting, confidentiality, misrepresentation and conflict of interest.

1. Contracting

Contracting issues included concerns about compensation, where a coach might require a percentage of the client's increase in gross profit in addition to the coaching fee. This type of arrangement is not uncommon in consulting. Tying the coach's compensation to the client's outcome, however, creates an attachment that is contrary to the foundational competencies in coaching and could be viewed as exploiting the client.

In some parts of the world it is not uncommon for coaches to request payment for services in advance. This can cause concern if a client ends a coaching relationship prematurely. The coach is responsible for ensuring there is a clear agreement that defines services and financial terms that are in alignment with area business practices. It is the responsibility of coaches to be aware of differences that may be relevant within their region.

Other inquiries reported around compensation involve coaches receiving income from affiliate relationships and referrals to other services, programmes or products. While it may seem profitable to engage in these types of relationships to generate revenue, it is important to investigate fully and determine if they are indeed fit for the business and are acceptable practice in the particular area of the world. Any relationships of this type need to be clearly disclosed.

2. Confidentiality/boundary management

The confidential nature of the relationship between coach and client forms the basis for trust within the relationship. Brock states that the expectation for confidentiality in coaching is to 'Respect confidentiality of all client information (including company and/or client name) except as authoried by client or required by law' (2006). The question of a breach in confidentiality can arise among coaches as they share stories or examples of work with clients. However, sharing an anonymized coaching situation with a supervisor or coaching group as part of reflective practice (Hay, 2007) is encouraged and is beneficial for ongoing professional development and learning. Concern arises when a coach uses a client's name without permission or describes a situation in a manner that promotes the coach and disregards the client.

Coaches working in organizations, either internally as employees, or externally as contractors, face an added dimension of complexity around confidentiality. Organizations funding coaching for an individual or team often require, at least initially, a periodic report on the value of the coaching experience. The organization is often referred to as the 'sponsor' of the coaching. Sponsors with a formal coaching programme or past experience with coaching generally understand the importance of a clear agreement to define the reporting process at the beginning of the relationship. To avoid an unintentional breach of confidentiality, the coach should not be in a position to prepare or present a report on the client's progress. The coach can support the client in this process, although the communication is best done by the client.

Boundary management is important to note here. Coaching clients are healthy and whole in their lives. They are coming to coaching to move forward in their goals and development. Clients may be unknown prior to beginning the coaching relationship or they may be acquaintances, business associates, colleagues, friends and sometimes even family. Coach and client may develop a friendship over time. It is important to have a clear coaching relationship and not allow personal bias to influence professional actions. Blurring the lines between coach and friend, family, colleague, etc., creates a potential for ethical concern and poor outcome. It is critical to stay mindful of the ethical responsibility to the client and to maintain confidentiality, objectivity and equal partnership. Should there be any concerns, the coach has a responsibility to raise the issue, act in the best interest of the client and, if necessary, end the coaching relationship.

Coaches working within organizations may have the opportunity to work with individuals and teams crossing lines throughout the company. The confidential space created between client and coach allows for openness and honesty that may not occur anywhere else in the individual's life. It is not uncommon for the coach to hear sensitive and personal information about the individual, or about others within the organization or the organization itself. With the privilege of coaching comes great responsibility to maintain client confidentiality.

3. Misrepresentation

The desire to attain a competitive edge in the market place can drive coaches to embellish their qualifications, credentials or value to the client.

They might also be tempted to extend their activities beyond coaching. Coaches come from a variety of backgrounds and bring a wealth of knowledge and expertise from previous professions. It is advisable for coaches to acknowledge these areas of expertise and to be clear on what coaching is and what it offers. What separates coaching from other professional services is the belief in the client's resourcefulness and potential. Consulting or training should be identified as distinct activities.

Another area where concerns of misrepresentation arise is with marketing and presentation materials. Members of the coaching community are generous and supportive of individuals entering the emerging profession. The international composition of the community creates opportunity for ideas and materials to be shared around the world. However, just as in any other profession, coaches need to respect copyright law, ask permission for use of materials and acknowledge creators.

4. Conflict of interest

The success of coaching has prompted many to enter the market in various ways. There are new training programmes, products and services marketed to coaches daily. In turn, coaches market these products to clients. There is little to measure one programme, product or service against another or to ensure that all truly bring value to the buyer. It is up to the coach involved in these types of arrangements to stay aware and 'not knowingly exploit any aspect of the coach–client relationship for personal, professional or monetary advantage or benefit' (ICF, 2005).

Brock (2006) succinctly summarizes the responsibility of the coach: 'Seek to avoid conflicts between my interests and the interests of my clients; whenever any actual conflict of interest or the potential for a conflict arises, I will openly disclose it and fully discuss with my client how to deal with it in whatever way best serves my client'.

Additional areas that are of importance as we consider ethical issues include: dual and multiple relationships, competence and self-management.

5. Dual and multiple relationships

Brickey (2002) defines the dual relationship as one where the relationship with someone has more than one role or interest. Relative to coaching, this may be a client who is also a colleague, the spouse of a friend or the cousin of another client, etc. Thinking further, the client may additionally be the coach's accountant, lawyer or physician. Successfully navigating dual or multiple relationships depends on: full disclosure of any conflict of interest; clearly defined roles, responsibilities and boundaries; a client-focused approach; reflective practice; and supervision (Zur & Anderson, 2006).

6. Competence

Competence is defined in Human Resources terms as meeting the standard requirement to properly perform a particular job. Competence in coaching includes a combination of knowledge, skills and behaviour. While there is not a universally accepted measure of competence, what is held consistent among coach professionals is the support for coach-specific education, skill development, practice and ongoing professional development. In the absence of a universal standard, anyone can call themselves a coach and they do. Proliferation of the open field poses the possibility of damaging the reputation of coaching.

Coaches need to be conscious of their own limits, understand the requirements of coaching competence, be coached on their coaching and engage in reflective practice for ongoing professional development. They should not try to be all-encompassing or fit to what the client needs. Even if they have a background in psychology or counselling, it is best to stay out of the counselling realm when contracted to coach with the client (Rogers, 2004). In coaching situations where counselling appears to be needed, the issue should be raised with the client and an offer of referral made.

7. Self-management

Self-management as defined here is recognizing bias, preconceived ideas, initial impressions, opinions or stereotypes that can influence the ability to be fully focused and present with the client.

Distractions can occur in any coaching relationship, though within the corporate environment the internal coach faces this challenge with more intensity. A coach may have knowledge of the client's reputation within the company or through coaching with the client's peers before the coaching partnership began (Rogers, 2004 update). The coach needs to recognize any bias and to self-manage in order to be focused and present with the client. If coaches cannot achieve the level of self-management to fully support the client, they should remove themselves from the engagement and assist the client in finding another coach. Firing oneself as a coach, whether within a company or in a private coaching business, is sometimes necessary in the service of the client.

The role of the coach is to facilitate the client's learning to find his/her own answers. There may be times when the coach strategizes or brainstorms with the client or offers an idea for consideration. The idea is not the client's solution but rather one possibility. If the client's expectation is that the coach will have the solution to their concern, perhaps the client does not understand the coaching relationship. If coaches feel they need to offer advice to give value to the client, they may need to step back to examine the relationship with the client and their own understanding of coaching.

THE FUTURE: AN ETHICAL COACHING COMMUNITY

Coaching is a powerful process that is increasingly evolving in research, understanding of theories, practice and professional qualification (Brennan, 2008). Coaches have a responsibility to engage as professionals and to recognize their responsibility and contribution to their clients, colleagues and society as a whole. The Canadian Psychological Association (CPA) provides definition and language to describe the responsibility that applies to the professional coach and the coaching community:

> Every discipline that has relatively autonomous control over its entry requirements, training, development of knowledge, standards, methods, and practices does so only within the context of a contract with the society in which it functions. This social contract is based on attitudes of mutual respect and trust, with society granting support for the autonomy of a discipline in exchange for a commitment by the discipline to do everything it can to assure that its members act ethically in conducting the affairs of the discipline within society. (CPA, 2000: Preamble)

As critical as practising ethical behaviour within a coaching relationship is the ability of coaches to create, maintain and foster an ethical community of coaches. Ethical behaviour among coaches would include the practice of sharing information and best practices; being open to new knowledge; respecting diversity and cultural difference and collaborating with a range of coaches and organizations to help strengthen the profession as a whole.

Many coaching organizations and training schools are run as businesses and have to succeed in a competitive market place. But in conflict with the economic pressure to compete is the professional impetus to co-operate. It is clear that coaching will only progress towards full professional status if the many parties involved find common ground. This will involve a shared understanding that the communal benefits of a free exchange of ideas and knowledge and a willingness to refer clients outweigh the dangers of giving up areas of control and sources of income. It will require a degree of mutual trust that is not so different from the trust that as coaches we ask of our clients.

If, as suggested by Kohlberg (1981), we assume that ethical behaviour depends on a level of individual maturity then the work of the developmental theorists is important to consider.

According to Robert Kegan, individuals pass through developmental stages throughout their lives (Kegan, 1982, 1994). As they move to higher stages, their ability to make meaning in life becomes more complex and multifaceted:

- At stage 3, people are 'other dependent'. They are able to see themselves as part of something larger than themselves, but cannot resolve conflicting viewpoints of others or between themselves and others.
- At stage 4, people are able to own their own work and make their own decisions, and are internally motivated. They are able to see different points of view, yet are ultimately driven by their own sense of mission and values.
- At stage 5, people are capable of seeing their own and others' points of view simultaneously. They are able to view an issue from multiple perspectives.

Kegan's and Kohlberg's models share several qualities. In both, one must progress through each successive stage. It is not possible to skip over a developmental stage. Furthermore, individuals seldom regress into less complex stages.

The ability to understand others in more complex terms is a critical component of ethical behaviour (Laske, 2006: 11). An important outcome of a coach functioning at a higher stage of development is the nuanced ability to view the client's situation and to act ethically in service of the client.

Kegan and Kohlberg provide two theoretical lenses through which to view moral and ethical development. There are many others. What we learn from these theories is that the acquisition of values and ethical behaviour is, at least in part, a developmentally driven process and not something handed to people from parents, churches or schools. How we respond to a moral or ethical dilemma is a function of a range of complex factors. Understanding our own and others' moral behaviour is an intricate process.

Ethical behaviour among coaches might include the following:

1. Recommending a competing coach training school to a prospective student, when one's own school is not a good match for that individual.
2. Recommending a competing coach or coaching organization to a prospective client, who would benefit from a specific area of expertise.
3. Competing coach training schools offering to hold joint or collaborative conferences or seminars.
4. Reaching out to coaches with different coaching methods with an offer to share ideas, knowledge and new research.

EVALUATION

There is a growing movement in America, Europe and around the world, to form a coherent identity for the practice of coaching in order to move it towards full professional status. An agreed ethical framework governing the relationship between the coach and the client would be an essential element of this new professional identity. Adopting the code of conduct (2011) is a step toward support of a common benchmark. In an age where greed and corrupt behaviour seem too prevalent we have a chance not only to put coaching itself on a firm ethical footing but to model standards of ethical behaviour for society as a whole.

This process challenges us to go beyond the isolation of individual organizations and strengthen the foundation for the future development of the profession. It requires a coming together of a community of coaches who all share a level of trust and respect in their dealings with each other. Only when coaching can move beyond preconceived notions and limitations and integrate into the fabric of society will its potential to make a sustainable and measurable impact be realized.

CASE STUDIES AND DISCUSSION QUESTIONS

Case 1

When coaching within an organization, we are often involved with the client who is participating in coaching, the client's line manager, and often a representative from the organization sponsoring the coaching (Human Resources, Talent Management, Organizational Development). Managing the expectations and conversations with the various stakeholders in the coaching relationship can be complex and potentially introduce an unintended ethical breach.

Consider the case of Owen, a mid-level leader in a technology organization. Owen's line manager recommended coaching and supports his development. Owen selected his coach, Julie, after interviewing several coaches presented by his Human Resources representative. Julie is on the coaching panel for the organization, and she works with people in different areas and levels of leadership.

Owen and Julie started out fabulously in their coaching. He is excited to be engaged in this process. His initial conversations included concerns about his supervisor and the impact stress is having on him and his work.

One day as Julie was leaving the organization she said hello to her Human Resources contact who just happened to be talking to Dave (Owen's line manager). Julie was introduced to Dave as the coach who is working with Owen. Dave was happy to meet her and immediately asked when she thought Owen would be making some improvement. Julie froze, thinking 'now what?'

Questions

- What is Julie's responsibility to the sponsoring organization? To the client?
- How can she answer Dave's question without violating Owen's confidentiality?
- What could be done to prevent this type of dilemma?

Guidelines for ethical interaction

Establishing clear expectations and agreements with the client and the sponsor are a priority in maintaining ethical practice. It is best to have these conversations at the beginning of the coaching assignment. However, if as in Julie's case that did not happen, it is not too late to go back and have clarifying conversations with the client and reassure him in relation to support and the confidentiality of the agreement. A coach will also want to let him know that there is a responsibility to the organization and a structure that supports him in communicating updates, measures of progress or problems with his line manager and HR if requested as sponsors of the coaching. Involving the client in establishing the meeting and supporting him to be accountable for updates allows him to potentially strengthen communications with his supervisor and takes the coach out of the middle.

Sustainable, significant change in the client's inner systems can often only happen if there is corresponding and supporting change in the systems around them. Creating clarity – especially about the responsibilities of each of the people in the system – can head off many of the problems relating to unmatched expectations. Had Julie met Dave with Owen as they began their coaching, she would not have cause to feel unprepared. In this case Julie might respond with what she knows. One response might be, 'I'm pleased to meet you Dave. I am happy to be working with Owen.' As the conversation continues, Julie might add, 'It sounds like it is important for you to have updates on how the coaching is going. There are also some things I'd like you to consider as we continue the coaching. Can I follow up with you to schedule a call or a meeting time?' This allows Julie to stay true to ethical conduct and it engages Dave in considering how he can support the client.

Case 2

Robert, a professional coach for over ten years, has worked with hundreds of clients in many different areas. Robert has an excellent reputation as a coach. He is a likeable fellow and easily makes friends. In fact, several of his clients are also his friends. Robert is careful to keep the coaching relationship separate from the friendship setting clear boundaries and agreements with each client and has not had any difficulty managing this.

In an effort to increase his income and diversify his business, Robert started selling health and nutrition products advertised to support weight and stress management. Robert believes in these products and finds them effective in his own life. In his enthusiasm to support others in receiving the benefits, Robert begins introducing the products to his clients and sometimes encourages them to become agents for the product under his relationship with the company. One client asks if this is a pyramid scheme. Robert is surprised by the question and insists it is not. The client stays quiet and wonders about the appropriateness of his coach offering such products and encouraging a relationship where the coach makes money from the individual's purchases, contacts, or potential sales. He achieved a lot with Robert as his coach, but he is uncomfortable with the change he sees in Robert and the tension he feels between them. Robert seems not to notice the concern.

Questions

- How should the boundary be managed between client and friend, relative, or other relationships?
- Where is the boundary around selling products to a client?
- Who is there for support if there is a question of 'boundary creep'?

Guidelines for ethical interaction

As a new coach our friends and family are often part of our support network. Perhaps the coach asks a friend or family member to be a pro bono client as he begins his coach training. As he progresses, other friends or family members may contact him to serve as their coach because they trust and value him. When engaging with friends and family as a coach, be sure to set clear expectations, boundaries and agreements. The coach and client must have the foresight and confidence to speak any concern with each other. The coach bears primary responsibility here to stay aware of the relationship and to not allow tension or concern to go unaddressed.

In our example, Robert is a personable individual. He is coaching friends and family members and some of his clients have also become his friends. Remember, any of these 'clients' can talk about their work or encounter with Robert as a coach, but Robert is bound to confidentiality as his ethical responsibility. A breach of this boundary in any conversation is not acceptable.

Robert is very excited about the results he has experienced with his new product and he sees the potential to help others. His helping others also translates into additional revenue for him. In this case, Robert's products are not directly related to his core business. In fact, Robert has two separate businesses. He needs to keep them separate and not push the products onto his clients, especially not within a coaching session.

Case 3

Stephanie is an excellent personal coach. She has worked with hundreds of women over her 30-year coaching career. She is certified and regularly takes workshops to maintain her credential and keep her coaching fresh. She has several clients with whom she has had long working relationships. One client in particular, Judith, has been seeing Stephanie for over three years. Judith loves the sessions, is anxious to continue and has an income that would afford her an endless commitment to coaching. On the other hand, she can't find time to do her homework, hasn't got round to making any of the changes in her life that she always talks about making and seems to be going around the same issues over and over. In short, after three years of coaching, she has made little progress.

Questions

- What is Stephanie's responsibility in this situation?
- How might Stephanie confront Judith on the issue of progress?
- When is it ethically responsible to end a coaching situation?

Guidelines for interaction

While a willing, enthusiastic fee-paying client is a gift, the coach has an ethical responsibility to take some action when a client is merely treading water. It may be that the coach can hold the client more firmly to the terms of the coaching engagement. Or it may be time to signal the end of the engagement Some coaching situations don't work out, for whatever reason. When this becomes clear, it is the responsibility of the coach to bring the relationship to a close.

Managing ourselves ethically, in whatever situation, is our ongoing responsibility as coaches. A coaching supervisor can help one gain objectivity and perspective to stay on track. Another resource for questions on ethics is a professional coaching body. The professional bodies such as the AC, EMCC, ICF and others have ethics complaint processes. They track concerns and they can assist with questions. The codes of ethics are available on the respective websites. However, every coach should be a member of the professional body to ask questions or for access to additional ethics resources.

FURTHER READING

Passmore, J. (Ed.). (2011). *Supervision in coaching: Supervision, ethics and continuous professional development.* London: Kogan Page.

REFERENCES

Brennan, D. (2008). Coaching in the US: Trends and challenges. *Coaching: An International Journal of Theory, Research and Practice, 1*(2). 186–191.

Brickey, M. (2002). *Dual relations: Can coaches be pragmatic?* Division 42 Professional Practice, Spring. www.division42.org/MembersArea/IPfiles/IPSprg_2002/articles/prof_practice/duel_relations.html.

Brock, V. (2006). Where do we align our ethical code? Learning from other professions. *Choice, 4*(3), 42–5.

Canadian Psychological Association (CPA) (2000). Retrieved June 2009 from http://ethics.iit.edu/codes/coe/can.psychological.assoc.2000.html#intro.

de Jong, A. (2010). Coaching ethics: Integrity in the moment of choice. In J. Passmore (Ed.), *Excellence in coaching* (pp. 204–14). London: Association for Coaching.

European Economic and Social Committee (2011). *The professional charter for coaching and mentoring,* International Coach Federation and European Mentoring and Coaching Council, June 2011. Web 09 December 2013. www.eesc.europa.eu/self-and-coregulation/documents/codes/private/142-private-act.pdf.

Garlo, D.M. & Prior, D.M. (2003). Committing to an ethical framework: A powerful choice. *Choice, 1*(1), 30–3.

Gert, B. (1988). *Morality: A new justification of the moral rules.* New York: Oxford University Press.

Global Convention on Coaching (GCC) (2008). *Dublin declaration and appendices.* International Coach Federation Research Portal, www.coachfederation.org.

Hay, J. (2007). *Reflective practice and supervision for coaches.* New York: Open University Press.

International Coach Federation (2010) *Ethics code.* Web 20 January 2013. www.coachfederation.org/about-icf/ethics/icf-code-of-ethics/.

Kegan, R. (1982). *The evolving self: Problem and process in human development.* Cambridge, MA: Harvard University Press.

Kegan, R. (1994). *In over our heads: The mental demands of modern life.* Cambridge, MA: Harvard University Press.

Khurana, R. & Nohria, N. (2008). It's time to make management a true profession. *Harvard Business Review,* October: 70–7.

Kohlberg, L. (1981). *Essays on moral development (Vol. 1): The philosophy of moral development.* San Francisco, CA: Harper and Row.

Laske, O. (2006). Why does your maturity matter? *Choice, 4*(3), 10–12.

Partnership leads to creation of the Global Coaching and Mentoring Alliance. International Coach Federation, European Mentoring and Coaching Council, Association for Coaching, November 2012. Web 18 January 2013. www.coachfederation. org/about-icf/press-room/.

PricewaterhouseCoopers (PwC) (2012). *International Coach Federation Global Coaching Study.* Lexington, KY: International Coach Federation. www.coachfederation.org.

Rogers, J. (2004). *Coaching skills: A handbook* (ch. 7, pp. 163–8). New York: Open University Press.

Rubenstein, D. (2006). Cracking the code: Unveiling the mystery – beta test and walk away with the new ICF ethics education program. *Paper presented at the International Coach Federation Annual Conference,* St. Louis, Missouri, November.

Taylor, C. (1989). *Sources of the self: The making of modern identity.* Cambridge, MA: Harvard University Press.

Weiner, K.C. (2006). Foundations of professional ethics. In P. Williams & S.K. Anderson (Eds), *Law and ethics in coaching: How to solve and avoid difficult problems in your practice* (pp. 21–38). Hoboken, NJ: John Wiley & Sons.

Zur, O. & Anderson, S.K. (2006). Multiple-role relationships in coaching. In P. Williams & S.K. Anderson (Eds), *Law and ethics in coaching: How to solve and avoid difficult problems in your practice* (pp. 126–9). Hoboken, NJ: John Wiley & Sons.

PROFESSIONAL BODIES' CODES OF ETHICS CONSULTED (RETRIEVED JANUARY 2013)

American Psychological Association (APA) www.apa.org

Association for Coaching (AC) www.associationforcoaching.com

Association for Professional Executive Coaching and Supervision (APECS) www.apecs.org

Australian Psychological Society (APS) www.psychology.org.au

British Psychological Society (BPS) www.bps.org.uk

European Mentoring and Coaching Council (EMCC) www.emccouncil.org

International Association of Coaching (IAC) www.certifiedcoach.org

International Coach Federation (ICF) www.coachfederation.org

Worldwide Association of Business Coaches (WABC) www.wabccoaches.com

31

Researching Coaching

Annette Fillery-Travis and Elaine Cox

Research into the activity of coaching has been gradually increasing over the last two decades and there is now a developing evidence base for the subject. In addition there are academic journals dedicated to coaching, as well as a growing number of subject-specific journals that publish on the topic. Much of the research to date has been practitioner led and is focused on exploring how coaching works in certain, mainly organizational, situations or on distinguishing coaching from other applied helping and/or learning approaches in an attempt to carve a distinct niche for coaching.

However, there are still many gaps in the coaching research and the development of the academic debates necessary to grow the profession is slow. This is partly because coaching is multi-disciplinary and little funding is available to support collaborations between university departments, corporate sponsors, practitioners and professional bodies in order to begin to create interdisciplinary discussion and research into coaching itself. So there is a strong need within the discipline for coherent, well-managed programmes of research that can add to the body of academic knowledge. Such research would, of course, need to take account of the cross-disciplinary nature of coaching in order to provide a greater understanding of complex dilemmas impacting on the field and it might include investigating the contributions of different disciplines and exploring new theories, paradigms and methods of research. This necessarily means that research into coaching is either published in the coaching journals or is somewhat marginalized in journals from the disciplinary source. The task of supporting an interdisciplinary research agenda requires coaches and researchers to be aware of the challenge and to work across the separate disciplines, championing interdisciplinary collaboration and integrating ideas from different subject areas.

Our chapter begins by giving a short overview of recent research on coaching in order to draw out implications for research design. This allows for discussion of a number of methodological and other issues and leads to exploration of how what we perceive as a major gap might begin to be addressed through the use of some little used research methods. We conclude with some thoughts on the way ahead for coaching research. Our aim is to broaden researcher and practitioner perspectives on what is possible in order to encourage further research and debate.

Overview of current coaching research

Whilst undertaking a review of the literature we were struck, like many commentators, by the growth in the number of publications of coaching research in the last decade. We cannot discuss in detail the work and concepts contained in over seven hundred scholarly articles and dissertations recently estimated to be available from the literature (Grant, 2010). Instead we must look to some general themes to allow us to make sense and meaning from this wealth of information: our focus specifically will be to explore how knowledge is developing to serve practitioners in the field.

The most recent reviews (Fillery-Travis & Passmore, 2011; Grant, 2013; Grant & Cavanagh, 2007; Passmore & Gibbes, 2007) have all been concerned with the overall development of the coaching research base, the type of studies reported and the quality of the evidence produced. Specifically they lament the paucity of empirical studies and the small number of rigorous studies, especially those that use a randomized controlled trial design. Some authors even identify this perceived deficit as holding back progress in the professional practice of coaching (Orenstein, 2006). Before we discuss methodological issues in detail we will look at what research is currently available and how it has emerged. First, we consider what the literature has to say concerning what happens as a result of coaching by looking at *outcome studies*, and then we move to explore what actually happens *in* the coaching sessions and the factors which are important to their design and conduct, through reviewing *process studies*.

Outcome studies – what is the outcome of coaching and whose outcome is it?

The large growth in the market for coaching has been a significant driver for outcomes research and the development of appropriate evidence for efficacy (Bennett, 2006). Specifically, buyers of coaching are asking what outcomes should be expected from coaching and what is the return on investment? The first attempts at an answer were through practitioner case studies with measures such as client satisfaction surveys. These commonly identified high levels of satisfaction (>90%) (Fillery-Travis & Lane, 2006) and large estimates of the return on investment figures; in one case greater than 400% (McGovern et al., 2001). Grant (2013) identified 234 outcome studies that had been published between 2000 and 2011.

Recently some randomized uncontrolled and controlled trials (RCTs) have been undertaken, but the numbers of such studies are small. Of the 518 scholarly articles and dissertations published in the last five years (Grant, 2010) only 186 were empirical studies and of these only 11 are of a randomized controlled design seeking to test the hypothesis that some performance indicator had improved as a result of coaching (Clutterbuck, 2001). The significance of this shift in methodology to RCTs is that this type of study design is generally considered the 'gold standard', providing generalizable and reliable results (Clutterbuck et al., 2001). But at first glance these 11 studies are not persuasive in terms of workplace coaching. Predominantly they focus on an educational setting (MBA students or college students) or supporting a medical outcome (doctors' professional development or health coaching). Indeed the medical arena has developed a dominance in outcomes research as they explore the effectiveness of motivational interviewing (DiLillo, Siegfried, & Smith West, 2003) as a particular mode of coaching for change, influencing health and well-being. Design of studies in this context is relatively straightforward with specific, quantifiable and objective end points (for example, reduction in weight, blood pressure or substance misuse). In 2011 alone there were 197 papers cited within PubMed examining the application of motivational interviewing in supporting behaviour change in, for example, families of asthma sufferers (Garbutt, Highstein, Yan, & Strunk, 2012) and obesity management (Pearson, Irwin, Morrow, & Hall, 2012). In support of this work interviewing skill effectiveness measures for clinicians have been developed (Torres et al., 2012) to allow consistent practice and comparison within research studies.

In workplace coaching, however, Grant (2010) identified only two studies which met the criteria for randomized controlled trials (a PhD dissertation by Deviney, 1994, looking at multi-rater feedback to measure the impact of coaching on supervisor behaviour and Duijts, van den Brandt & Swaen (2008) looking at sickness leave reduction). Neither of these studies identified significant improvement on the primary measure but significant change was noted in areas such as general well-being. De Haan (2011) argues that it is only when the studies are less controlled that statistically significant effects are seen. Levenson (2009), for example, reviewed outcome studies looking at behaviour change, perceived effectiveness and 'hard' performance measures. These criteria were selected on the basis that they were progressing along the 'line of sight' from the clients' own performance to a measure of the organizational impact of such performance. In general there was a positive association for the first two elements although the effect lessened as the 'hard' measures were considered. Examples are Evers, Brouwers and Tomic's (2006) and Orenstein's (2005) measurement of leadership behaviours and Wasylyshyn, Gronsky and Haas's (2006) consideration of improvement in emotional competence of high potential employees. It is interesting to note that so far there are only a few studies looking at the impact of coaching specifically upon women (Starman, 2007).

The instruments most commonly used to collect information on perceived effectiveness are customized surveys involving multi-rater feedback (Kombarakaran, Yang, Baker, & Fernandes, 2008; Smither, London, Flautt, Vargas, & Kucine, 2003; Thach, 2002) although Nowack (2009) provides a word of caution about the potential negative impact of the use of these surveys on emotions and sustained behaviour change. The use of more validated instruments such as leadership style assessments, as used by Duijts et al (2008), and goal attainment scaling (Prywes, 2012), is rare, however.

An example of a study using the 'hard' measures of productivity is that of Olivero, Bane and Kopelman (1997) who identified a positive impact on productivity of public sector managers of the use of coaching in addition to training-only provision in a management development programme. Trying to formalize such measures into a return on investment figure, however, is inherently difficult in human interventions as there are a significant number of factors of potential impact which are un-quantified or unknown. A relatively recent paper by De Meuse, Dai and Lee (2009), however, has undertaken the first meta-analysis study. The paper drew on a limited range of studies, six in total – Evers et al. (2006), Luthans and Peterson (2003), Peterson (1993), Smither et al. (2003), Togel and Nicholson (2005) and Wolfred (2003) – and identifies a return on investment (ROI) of 1.27. However, with such a large range of variation it suggests that we will need to wait until there are over one hundred such studies available for comparison before statistically significant conclusions can be drawn. The literature into what organizations can expect from coaching in terms of outcomes, their specificity and impact is still in its infancy as it relies upon us being able to determine what will work for the many in most situations.

A major stumbling block to the design of RCTs is that we do not, as yet, know what needs to be controlled, what measures are relevant and validated or how to structure a coaching intervention for consistency across many given its unique focus on the individual. It can be argued that this range of unknowns is a contributor to the relatively low impact measured in RCTs to date compared to the fulsome descriptions of change consistently obtained from qualitative studies.

It is perhaps not surprising then that researchers are seeking to simplify the environment and get some control on factors by measuring a specified outcome of coaching in a defined group, e.g. improving medical doctors' diagnostic skills in one medical condition. The results may be more robust from a methodological viewpoint but perhaps less directly relevant to workplace coaching. Grant (2013) has also argued that financial ROI is an unreliable and insufficient measure of coaching outcomes and that an over-emphasis on financial returns can restrict coaches' and organizations' awareness of the full range of positive outcomes possible through coaching and even increase job-related stress and anxiety. He suggests the well-being and engagement framework (WBEF) and goal attainment could give a richer overview of coaching outcomes than financial ROI.

So, if we return to the question of whom the outcomes are for and consider individual clients, then we see that we also need to research the 'helpfulness' of the intervention (de Haan, Culpin, & Curd, 2011) and the nature of the intervention itself (Cox, 2012). In the next section we look at this issue by considering how research has focused on the process of coaching.

Process studies

One of the difficulties involved in the design and comparison of outcome studies, including RCTs, is the multitude of factors that affect the outcomes by having an impact on the *process* of coaching. Thus the bulk of methodologies and approaches chosen by researchers tend to reflect the aim of exploring the phenomenon of coaching as a whole. Researchers often favour the collection of qualitative data allowing an exploration of the richness of what is a multidimensional process through, for example, in-depth case analyses using mixed methods, or through action research studies of their own practice (for example, McLaughlin, 2013;

Cook, 2013). The aim of such studies is to discover factors influencing the process of coaching through open exploration of the phenomenon. One of us clustered the potential factors operating in the coaching interaction in to the following way: (a) coach attributes, (b) client attributes, (c) the coaching practice itself and (d) context (Fillery-Travis & Lane, 2006).

Coach attributes have generally been considered in terms of competencies such as interpersonal skills, communication skills and instrumental support for external coaches (Dingman, 2004; Morgan, Harkins, & Goldsmith, 2006) and relationship building, empowering, facilitating and courageous leading for manager coaches (Ellinger & Bostrom, 1998; Ellinger, 2003; Ellinger, Hamlin, & Beattie, 2008; Graham, Wedman, & Kester, 1993; Wenzel, 2001). Wheeler (1978), in particular, has investigated, through case study, how the adoption of such behaviours by manager coaches contributes to organizational goal achievement.

The attributes of the coachee have also been explored; specifically the need for an absence of any performance issues or psychopathology but also the coachee's readiness for change either for leadership (Carey, Philippon, & Cummings, 2011), or through adherence and interest in their own development (Seamons, 2006; Wasylyshyn, 2003). As mentioned issues of gender are relatively under researched with only a small number of process studies looking at diversity (Passmore, 2008; Ruderman & Ohlott, 2005), the same is also true of coaching of members of sexual minorities (Rocco, Landorf, & Delgado, 2009).

There has, as yet, been no comprehensive study of the individual components of the coaching process although three elements are readily identified from the literature as impactful: (1) the coach–client relationship, (2) duration of the process and (3) an identification of both purpose and model of practice. The coach–client relationship is a strong voice within the literature with contributions from de Haan particularly, using critical incident methodology (de Haan & Stewart, 2011; de Haan, 2008a, 2008b). Research in this area is also reviewed by Baron and Morin (2009) in their field study of the relationship and its complimentarity with the concept of the 'working alliance'. This coherence is also noted more generally (Berry, Ashby, Gnilka, & Matheny, 2011; Cox, 2010; Kampa-Kokesch, 2002). Baron, Morin and Morin (2011) go on to explore this relationship further in relation to self-efficacy using a pre-post test study design of 30 coachees and their internal coaches. Such studies of relationship have also included manager-as-coach interactions (Gregory & Levy, 2011). All agree on the pivotal role of the relationship and indeed how it can outweigh factors such as the model of coaching itself (de Haan, Culpin, & Curd, 2011).

The duration of the coaching relationship and the process of its ending (Cox, 2010) is often assumed within studies with a seemingly arbitrary selection of length of coaching (ranging from one phone call to 12 months of structured work). There are a few longitudinal studies exploring either the sustainability of behaviour change after coaching (Grant, Green, & Rynsaardt, 2010) or the duration of coaching for optimal impact (Grant, 2003), which found significant change after 6 months but diminishing return at 12 months. Both studies were small scale and are not generalizable.

There is also a significant part of the literature describing, if not testing, coaching models and a few studies comparing those in a specific field or context. For example, coaching models for leadership development are reviewed in Carey et al. (2011). However, there is still a strong case for delineation of the theoretical orientation of coaching when reporting a study as it is not clear what the impact of a diverse range of models has or will have on outcomes and process (Spence & Oades, 2011).

What constitutes appropriate evidence and to whom is also a critical question. It is a common dilemma that the more relevant to practice the research is the more difficult it is to design an academically rigorous enquiry. The number of factors that need to be taken into account in the 'real world' will often confound the most elegant design. This relevance/rigour debate should not be an either/or debate but more like a spectrum within which we should be clear how we place our research designs and how we discuss them so practitioners can clearly identify where 'trade offs' have occurred and how they impact the usefulness or 'actionability' of the results. As Grant (2013: 33) confirms 'well-conducted qualitative research into coaching can provide important insights that are simply not possible with quantitative approaches'.

The evolution of coaching research

Above we have discussed how in the coaching field there is an evolving empirical literature that uses a multitude of research approaches and produces many forms of evidence concerning the outcomes and the process of coaching. We would like to suggest that research is developing as we might expect for an emerging field. This has already been noted by Grant, Passmore, Cavanagh, and Parker (2010) who compared coaching research to the research literature of Human Resources Management (HRM). Specifically, as with coaching, HRM practice is described as: outstripping theory, having a perceived lack of a research base, drawing from a range of related disciplines and participating in 'territory' disputes as it explores its contribution in organizational contexts. We have also looked at the history of counselling research as being a close comparator as it has the added similarity of dealing mainly with one-to-one interactions; led by the agenda of the client and looking to effect behaviour change (Hill & Corbett, 1993).

The first research in the counselling field from the 1950s was naturalistic process research seeking to answer the question 'what is happening in a counselling session?' This was overtaken by outcomes research as counselling sought to justify the investment in it (driven by the post-WWII need for therapy), process research then went into the laboratory to be conducted under controlled conditions (analogue research) and finally came out into practice again through the use of case studies and qualitative methods to explore practice as performed.

We suggest coaching is undergoing a similar journey as practitioners have initially sought to establish a defined field of practice through sharing their own experience and that of their clients, in case studies and other small-scale enquiries. This work appealed to other coaches keen to develop their own professional tool kits. The criterion for such evidence was relevance and resonance with their practice plus efficacy for their client base. As coaching grew in popularity, and with it the financial investment by organizations, there was a real driver for outcomes and ROI research appropriate to warrant large-scale investment by organizations. We see a corresponding increase in the quantifiable and generalizable nature of the evidence sought and with it the scale and controlled nature of the studies. Other factors at play here are the original disciplines of researchers and hence how they view the criteria for quality of evidence. Psychologists, for example, have a rich tradition of quantitative studies seeking generalizable evidence whereas educationalists have a mixed tradition of both qualitative and quantitative studies, as do management and HRM.

However, only if studies are clear about how their findings are applicable in practice, through rigorous reporting of each element of the design and research activity, can practitioners invest in changing their own practice to embrace the results. The development of such pragmatic reporting would enable practitioners to take evidence through the complete research cycle by 'testing' it within their practice and then contributing to knowledge by reporting innovations and requirements in the field of practice (Cox, 2011). Following a pragmatic approach apparent truths are 'tested' against practice or action and the evidence from application then 'mapped' back to relevant theoretical origins, asking: 'was the recommendation made by the original theory "true" and in what ways should it be modified to meet particular needs?' Such practice-based evidence would complement and enhance research and drive a pragmatic development of the body of coaching knowledge whose criteria for inclusion is robustness in the field of practice and the field of enquiry.

We suggest that researchers and practitioners alike need to take responsibility for their published research, ensuring it contributes to current debates and the literature *as whole* and designing studies within a theoretical framework to enable comparison with other studies. Such considerations apply as veraciously to smaller studies using qualitative data collection and analysis as they do to quantitative studies. Indeed the issues of potential rigour are just as challenging. Greater coherence and synergy can be achieved by gaining better agreement on the measures we use. Robustness can be enhanced by gathering multiple perspectives; for example, coach, coachee, reports, managers – as well as using several measures self-reports, behavioural or assessments. We also need to clearly identify the theoretical bases and techniques used within any coaching study and the researcher's adherence to it.

Addressing a gap in coaching research

In this section we now consider whether the two realms of outcomes and process research as presented earlier are a complete story of coaching or whether we are missing a perspective in our exploration of coaching.

From looking at the range of outcome and process research it can be seen that the focus of has been on:

- the context – often using organizational case studies
- the benefits and outcomes of coaching
- how coaching achieves certain outcomes for the client
- the qualities, abilities or skills of the coach
- the improvement of coaching practice and models.

However, the research is relatively silent on a critical part of coaching practice – the intervention or what happens within the coaching relationship itself. Current studies have concentrated upon building a theory of how coaching is used, its utility and payback and even how coaching can be improved for different purposes. For example, studies focus on how coaching works in different contexts and with different groups of people, there are attempts to discover how coaching can change behaviours and attitudes and how coaching can help people achieve goals (their own and those of their organization). There are also studies that look at the motivations and reactions of coaches and clients but in general they stop short of investigating the interaction itself. There is almost no research that focuses on the coaching interaction as a learning intervention with the power to generate powerful changes in thinking.

Using the metaphor of an iceberg we can show how existing research has focused – above and below the 'waterline' of coaching, but not at the waterline, i.e. not at the point of intervention itself. In Figure 31.1, the waterline is the point at which the current consciousness of the client and coach come together and interact. They both bring their own values, beliefs and motivations, and it is important to study those, and they are operating in particular cultures and societal settings, and these are vital to study also. But coaching research also needs to focus specifically on what the two people are actually doing together. However, in the research there is little to inform our understanding of the coaching interaction. In de Haan's (2008) study of critical moments in coaching the findings have the potential to get close to 'waterline' activity, but the research stops short of exploring moments in detail. In Cox (2013) the focus is on these issues, but the discussion is conceptual and not followed up with research.

Figure 31.1   The coaching interaction – a neglected area of research

So, researchers have begun to explore: contexts of coaching; behaviour change and measurable behaviours; changes in attitudes, preferences of the client and some elements of process. But rarely has anyone looked at the interaction – the part of the coaching process where the choices, goals and plans are actually discussed and made. The focus on the interaction is glaringly missing from a recent summary of the progress made in coaching research between 2008 and 2012 (Stern and Stout-Rostron, 2013). As suggested, some research looks at the relationship and addresses how coaches and clients interact with each other. But the coaching activity itself, the interaction of the dyad including the elements of listening, questioning, clarifying, reflecting, challenging and thinking have simply not yet been researched.

Figure 31.2 illustrates a range of activities that take place during coaching and which, it could be argued, need more study. As a profession, for example, we need to find out more about how and when coaches use questions as well as their influence on the client; we need to explore how the coach listens and how reflection and thinking are encouraged. In researching these elements of coaching we might also examine how they differ from their use in other helping approaches such as counselling and mentoring.

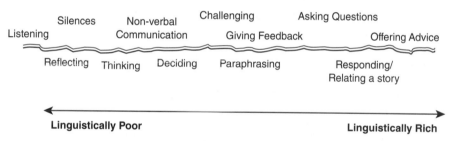

Figure 31.2   Interactions in the coaching process

Research methods to explore the coaching 'waterline'

Having established that there is more research to be done in this area, we now move to explore what methods we might use to inform studies of the interaction. Sommer and Sommer (2010: 12) have suggested that in social science four techniques – observation, experiment, questionnaire and interview – account for more than 90% of the articles in the journals. However, although observation is well-suited for researching what people do in public, experiments help decide between alternative explanations or approaches to a phenomenon, action research is appropriate for developing new models and questionnaires and interviews are acceptable for finding out peoples' attitudes and perspectives, researching a private, confidential, interpersonal interaction is difficult. We may need new methodologies in order to help us explore exactly what happens in the coaching interaction.

In fact, what we have termed the 'waterline' area of coaching is probably not researched because it is quite challenging methodologically and ethically. It may involve some form of interruption to coaching sessions, which could be an anathema to the researcher and the participants. It could be obtrusive and it may be time-consuming. However, this should not discourage researchers when they are in pursuit of the reality of coaching. It may just be that we need new research strategies in order to research at the dyad interface.

In Figure 31.2 we also show how the varieties of interaction in coaching can be placed on a continuum from those that are linguistically rich – such as asking questions, responding or giving feedback, to those that are linguistically poor – like listening, reflecting, silence, thinking and deciding.

These linguistic distinctions suggest that we need at least two different approaches to research. Methods for uncovering what happens in the linguistically 'rich' end of the spectrum might involve recordings and videos of speech and interaction during the coaching session followed by the use of conversation or discourse analysis approaches. Such analysis usually only involves the researcher in interpreting the data. At the linguistically 'poor' end of the spectrum research will require self-observation methods, which involve the participants in reporting (and possibly analysing) their own practice, often in situ.

Two methods that we consider appropriate for researching the 'linguistically poor' interactions are Systematic Self-Observation (Rodriguez, & Ryave, 2001) and the Experience Sampling Method (Hektner, Schmidt, & Csikszentmihalyi, 2006). These methods could also augment linguistic methods and enrich a study.

Examples of research designs that could incorporate these methods might be:

- using experience sampling as part of a Grounded Theory study to contribute towards a theory of phenomena, such as questioning
- using individual Case Studies and systematic self-observation to explore listening or video vignettes to examine non-verbal communication
- using phenomenological approaches to describe coach and client experiences of paraphrasing
- designing an Action Research study to explore silence, reflectivity or non-verbal behaviours with co-researchers over time.

Research is still needed about peripheral phenomena, such as outcomes, the coaching context, the models and the emotional or perceptual changes in clients, but the elements of coaching that are constructed at the point of the interaction also need urgent attention from researchers. We hope that these ideas will prompt further research.

The way ahead for coaching research

In this chapter we have highlighted how research, by necessity, has lagged behind practice as coaches were faced with working in ambiguous and uncharted territories. But coaching research has now reached a level of maturity where it has something meaningful to say to practitioners about their practice and can help inform them as to what constitutes effective and ethical coaching. Maintaining the dialogue between practice and research is critical to producing a robust body of evidence. Coaching journals such as the *International Journal of Evidence Based Practice*; *Coaching: An International Journal of Theory, Research and Practice*; *International*

Journal of Mentoring and Coaching; *Mentoring and Tutoring*; and the *International Coaching Psychology Review* all publish practitioner-based research and are excellent sources of evidence-based practice.

However, the role of research gatekeepers, such as universities, journal editors and funding bodies, may need to be monitored. As mentioned earlier there is a growing number of coaching journals that currently publish a range of quantitative and qualitative research, but a problem may arise as those journals mature and seek a more elite status that they cease to acknowledge the value of publishing exploratory, qualitative studies. Then a difficult situation arises for an applied field like coaching. A disjunct occurs between theory and practice. Papers with a clear exploratory stance and some practical application can sometimes be rejected by journals on the grounds that they do not have a large enough sample size or that they have not used a control group. Similarly universities may only support research by academics who produce papers for the elite journals, while funding bodies are notoriously only interested in large-scale, quantitative studies, rather than practitioner-based research.

Our review of the coaching literature further suggested that current research can be categorized as either outcome or process studies and that broadly outcome studies tended to use quantitative methods, although few were RCTs and process studies used a more qualitative approach. To overcome this lack we consider that the enhancement larger quantitative studies will only occur from genuine dialogue with the smaller qualitative studies that are exploring coaching and allowing factors and variables to emerge from practice. Similarly the results of RCTs require challenge out in the field of practice. Research is not an end in itself but a way of constructing an evidence base for practice.

Whilst considering the evolution of coaching research and the tendency to focus on outcomes and process, we noticed a gap in the research. Little has been done to explore the interactions between coach and coachee *in vivo*. We believe that significant research is needed in this area in order to justify the practice of coaching.

If we look at what could usefully be the focus of research in the future, as well as exploring elements of the interaction in order to understand what constitutes coaching, there also appears to be a significant need to test the entire model of coaching. Specifically coaching suffers from the same issue as therapy – our clients are not uniform. Addressing this 'uniformity myth' we might adjust the oft-cited comment by Paul (1967: 11) to relate to the coaching context: '*what* coaching, delivered by *whom,* is most effective for *this* client with *that* specific issue and under *which* set of circumstances?'

Getting to grips with such a range of variables in order to study coaching is a mighty task and one which requires a range of methodological approaches. However, the diversity of the approaches will add to the depth of our understanding of coaching only if they are fully reported in terms of the research activity. For example, it should be clearly identified what kind of coaching was carried out, from what theoretical perspective, in what manner and to what purpose. Otherwise we are in danger of comparing apples with pears from a research process perspective. This further requires practitioners to be aware of coaching models and philosophies so that they can generate and contribute to rigorous debate.

FURTHER READING

Three useful reviews of coaching research:

Stern, L. & Stout-Rostron, S. (2013). What progress has been made in coaching research in relation to 16 ICRF focus areas from 2008–2012? *Coaching: An International Journal of Theory, Research and Practice, 6*(1), 72–96.
Grant, A., Passmore, J., Cavanagh, M., & Parker, H. (2010). The state of play in coaching today: A comprehensive review of the field. *International Review of Industrial and Organizational Psychology, 25*, 125–67.
Grant, A. (2013). The efficacy of coaching, in Passmore, J., Peterson, D., & Freire, T. (Eds), *The Wiley-Blackwell handbook of the psychology of coaching and mentoring*. Chichester: Wiley-Blackwell, pp. 15–39.

DISCUSSION QUESTIONS

- From the perspective of the development of a coaching profession, what is the most important area that coaching research should focus on?
- How could practitioners undertake rigorous research on their own practice and then report and share their findings?

REFERENCES

Baron, L. & Morin, L. (2009). The coach–coachee relationship in executive coaching: A field study. *Human Resource Development Review, 20*(1), 85–106.
Bennett, J. L. (2006). An agenda for coaching-related research: A challenge for researchers. *Consulting Psychology Journal: Practice and Research, 58*(4), 240–9.
Berry, R. M., Ashby, J. S., Gnilka, P. B., & Matheny, K. B. (2011). A comparison of face-to-face and distance coaching practices: Coaches' perceptions of the role of the working alliance in problem resolution. *Consulting Psychology Journal: Practice and Research, 63*(4), 243–53.
Carey, W., Philippon, D. J., & Cummings, G. G. (2011). Coaching models for leadership development: An integrative review. *Journal of Leadership Studies, 5*(1), 51–69. doi: 10.1002/jls.20204
Clutterbuck, D. (2001). *Everyone needs a mentor: fostering talent at work*. London: Chartered Institute of Personnel and Development.
Cook, J. (2013). Coaching: an expensive conversation or a return on investment. *International Journal of Evidence Based Coaching and Mentoring*. Special Issue No. 7, 115–24.
Cox, E. (2010). Last things first: ending well in the coaching relationship, in Palmer, S. & McDowell, A. (Eds) *The coaching relationship: Putting people first: The interactional aspects of coaching*. London: Routledge, pp. 159–181.
Cox, E. (2011). Coaching philosophy, eclecticism and postitivism: A commentary. *Annual Review of High Performance Coaching and Consulting.*
Cox, E. (2013). *Coaching understood: A pragmatic inquiry into the coaching process*. London: Sage.
de Haan, E. (2008a). I doubt therefore I coach: Critical moments in coaching practice. *Consulting Psychology Journal: Practice and Research, 60*(1), 91–105.
de Haan, E. (2008b). I struggle and emerge: critical moments of experienced coaches. *Consulting Psychology Journal: Practice and Research, 60*(1), 106–31.
de Haan, E. & Stewart, S. (2011). *Relational coaching: journeys towards mastering one-to-one learning*. John Wiley & Sons.
de Haan, E., Culpin, V., & Curd, J. (2011). Executive coaching in practice: What determines helpfulness for clients of coaching? *Personnel Review, 40*(1), 24–44.
De Meuse, K., Dai, G., & Lee, R. (2009). Does Executive Coaching Work: A Meta analysis study. *Coaching: An International Journal of Theory. practice and research, 2*(2), 117–34.

DiLillo, V., Siegfried, N. J., & Smith West, D. (2003). Incorporating motivational interviewing into behavioral obesity treatment. *Cognitive and Behavioral Practice, 10*(2), 120.

Dingman, M. E. (2004). *The effects of executive coaching on job-related attitudes.* Unpublished doctoral dissertation, Regent University, Virginia Beach, VA.

Duijts, S., van den Brandt, P., & Swaen, G. (2008). The compatibiity between characteristics of employees at risk for sickness absense and componetns of a preventative coaching intervention. *International Journal of Evidence Based Coaching and Mentoring, 5*(1), 30–41.

Ellinger A. D. (2003). Antecedents and consequences of coaching behaviour. *Performance Improvement Quarterly, 16*(1), 5–28.

Ellinger, A. & Bostrom, R. (1998). Managerial coaching behaviours in learning organisations. *Journal of Management Development, 18*(9), 752–71.

Ellinger, A. D., Hamlin, R. G., & Beattie, R. S. (2008). Behavioural indicators of ineffective managerial coaching. *Journal of European Industrial Training, 32*(4), 240–57.

Evers, W. J., Brouwers, A., & Tomic, W. (2006). A quasi-experimental study on management coaching effectiveness. *Consulting Psychology Journal: Practice and Research, 58*(3), 174–82. doi: http://dx.doi.org/10.1037/1065-9293.58.3.174

Fillery-Travis, A. & Lane, D. (2006). Does coaching work or are we asking the wrong question? *International Coaching Psychology Review, 1*(1), 23–36.

Fillery-Travis, A. & Passmore, J. (2011). A critical review of executive coaching research: A decade of progress and what's to come. *Coaching: An International Journal of Theory, Research and Practice,* 70–88.

Franke, R. H. & Kaul, J. D. (1978). The Hawthorne experiments: First statistical interpretation. *American Sociological Review, 43*, 623–43.

Garbutt, J. M., Highstein, G., Yan, Y., & Strunk, R. C. (2012). Partner randomized controlled trial: Study protocol and coaching intervention. *BMC Pediatrics, 12*, 42.

Graham, S, Wedman, J. F., & Kester, B. G. (1993). Manager coaching skills: Development and application. *Performance Improvement Quarterly, 6*(1), 2–13.

Grant, A. M. (2003). The impact of life coaching on goal attainment, metacognition and mental health. *Social Behaviour and Personality, 31*, 253–64.

Grant, A. (2013). The efficacy of coaching, in Passmore, J., Peterson, D., & Freire, T. (Eds), *The Wiley-Blackwell handbook of the psychology of coaching and mentoring.* Chichester: Wiley-Blackwell, pp. 15–39.

Grant, A. M. & Cavanagh, M. J. (2007). Evidence-based coaching: Flourishing or languishing? *Australian Psychologist, 42*(4), 239–54.

Grant, A. M., Green, L., & Rynsaardt, J. (2010). Developmental coaching for high school teachers: Executive coaching goes to school. *Consulting Psychology Journal: Practice and Research, 62*(3), 151–68.

Grant, A. M., Passmore, J., Cavanagh, M. J., & Parker, H. (2010). The state of play in coaching today: A comprehensive review of the field. *International Review of Industrial and Organizational Psychology, 25*, 125–67.

Gregory, J. B. & Levy, P. E. (2011). It's not me, it's you: A multilevel examination of variables that impact employee coaching relationships. *Consulting Psychology Journal: Practice and Research, 63*(2), 67–88. doi: http://dx.doi.org/10.1037/a0024152

Hegstad, C. D. & Wentling, R. M. (2005). Organisational antecedents and moderators that impact on the efectiveness of exemplary formal mentoring prgrams in Fortune 500 companies in the United States. *Human Resource Development International, 8*(4), 467–87.

Hektner, J., Schmidt, J., & Csikszentmihalyi, M. (2006). *Experience sampling method: Measuring the quality of everyday life.* Thousand Oaks, CA: Sage.

Hill, C. E. & Corbett, M. M. (1993). A perspective on the history of process and outcome research in counseling psychology. *Journal of Counseling Psychology, 40*(1), 3–24.

Kampa-Kokesch, S. (2002). Executive coaching as an individually tailored consultation intervention: Does it increase leadership? *Dissertation Abstracts International: Section B: The Sciences and Engineering, 62*(7-B), 3408.

Kombarakaran, F. A., Yang, J. A., Baker, M. N., & Fernandes, P. B. (2008). Executive coaching: It works! *Consulting Psychology Journal: Practice and Research, 60*(1), 78–90. doi: http://dx.doi.org/10.1037/1065-9293.60.1.78

Levenson, A. (2009). Measuring and maximizing the business impact of executive coaching. *Consulting Psychology Journal: Practice and Research, 61*(2), 103–21. doi: http://dx.doi.org/10.1037/a0015438

Luthans, F. & Peterson, S. J. (2003). 360-degree feedback with systematic coaching: Empirical analysis suggests a winning combination. *Human Resource Management, 42*(3), 243–56.

McGovern, J, Lindemann, M, Vergara, M, Murphy, S, Barker, L., & Warrenfeltz, R. (2001). Maximizing the impact of executive coaching. *Manchester Review, 6*(1), 1–9.

McLaughlin, M. (2013) Coaching for brave leadership. *International Journal of Evidence Based Coaching and Mentoring,* Special Issue No 7, 125–39.

Morgan, H., Harkins, P., & Goldsmith, M. (2006). The right coach, in Gallos, J. V (Ed.), *Organization development. A Jossey-Bass reader.* Chichester: Wiley.

Nowack, K. M. (2009) Leveraging multirater feedback to facilitate successful behavioral change. *Consulting Psychology Journal: Practice and Research, 61*(4), 280–97.

Olivero, G., Bane, K. D., & Kopelman, R. E. (1997). Executive coaching as a transfer of training tool: Effects on productivity in a public agency. *Public Personnel Management, 26*(4), 461–69.

Orenstein, R. L. (2006). Measuring executive coaching efficacy? The answer was right here all the time. *Consulting Psychology Journal: Practice and Research, 58*(2), 106.

Passmore, J. (2008). *Diversity in coaching: Working with gender, culture, race an age.* London: Kogan Page.

Passmore, J. & Gibbes, C. (2007). The state of executive coaching research: What does the current literature tell us and what's next for coaching research? *International Coaching Psychology Review, 2*(2), 116–28.

Pearson, E. S., Irwin, J. D., Morrow, D., & Hall, C. R. (2012). The CHANGE program: Comparing an interactive versus prescriptive obesity intervention on university students' self-esteem and quality of life. *Applied Psychological Health and Well Being, 4*(3), 369–89.

Peterson, D. B. (1993). Measuring change: A psychometric approach to evaluating individual coaching outcomes. *Paper presented at the Annual Conference of the Society for Industrial and Organizational Psychology*, San Francisco, CA.

Prywes, Y. (2012). *Examining the influence of goal attainment scaling on changes in goal attainment in a coaching versus non-coaching context.* Columbia University.

Rocco, T. S., Landorf, H., & Delgado, A. (2009). Framing the issue/framing the question: A proposed framework for organizational perspectives on sexual minorities. *Advances in Developing Human Resources, 11*(1), 7–23. doi: 10.1177/1523422308328528

Rodriguez, N. & Ryave, A. (2002) *Systematic self-observation*. Thousand Oaks, CA: Sage.

Ruderman, M. N. & Ohlott, P. J. (2005). Leading roles: What coaches of women need to know. *Leadership in Action, 25*(3), 3–9.

Seamons, B. L. (2006). *The most effective factors in executive coaching engagements according to the coach, the client, and the client's boss.* Saybrook Graduate School And Research Center, USA.

Smither, J. W., London, M., Flautt, R., Vargas, Y., & Kucine, I. (2003). Can working with an executive coach improve multisource feedback ratings over time? A quasi-experimental field study. *Personnel Psychology, 56*(1), 23, 23–44.

Spence, G. & Oades, L. (2011). Coaching with self-determination in mind: Using theory to advance evidence-based coaching practice. *International Journal of Evidence Based Coaching and Mentoring, 9*(2), 37–55.

Starman, J. (2007). *The impact of executive coaching on job performance from the perspective of executive women.* Unpublished doctoral dissertation, Capella University. Minneapolis, MN.

Stern, L. & Stout-Rostron, S. (2013). What progress has been made in coaching research in relation to 16 ICRF focus areas from 2008–2012? *Coaching: An International Journal of Theory, Research and Practice, 6*(1), 72–96.

Thach, E. C. (2002). The impact of executive coaching and 360 feedback on leadership effectiveness. *Leadership and Organization Development Journal, 23*(4), 205–214.

Togel, G. & Nicholson, N. (2005). *Multisource feedback, coaching and leadership development: Gender homophily in caoching dyads.* Paper presented at the Academy of Management.

Torres, L. A., Navarro, M. C., Fontcuberta, J. M., Brun, N. B., Ortiz, J. C., Fontan, J. B., & Rodriguez, J. M. (2012). Is the scale for measuring motivational interviewing skills a valid and reliable instrument for measuring the primary care professionals motivational skills?: EVEM study protocol. *BMC Family Practice, 13*(1), 112.

Wasylyshyn, K. M. (2003). Executive coaching: An outcome study. *Consulting Psychology Journal: Practice and Research, 55*(2), 94–106.

Wasylyshyn, K. M., Gronsky, B., & Haas, J. (2006). Tigers, stripes, and behavior change: Survey results of a commissioned coaching program. *Consulting Psychology Journal: Practice and Research, 58*(2), 65–81. doi: http://dx.doi.org/10.1037/1065-9293.58.2.65

Wenzel, L. H. (2001). *Understanding managerial coaching: The role of manager attributes and skills in effective coaching.* Colorado State University.

Wolfred, T. (2003). *Executive coaching project: Evaluation of findings.* San Franciso, CA: CompassPoint Non-profit Services.

Conclusion

Tatiana Bachkirova, David Clutterbuck
and Elaine Cox

To conclude this book we want to address some issues that became apparent to us when considering the spectrum of approaches, genres and contexts of coaching that have been presented as building blocks for the growing knowledge base of coaching. In the book we have brought together the theories and influences on coaching that form the picture of the field as we, the editors, see it – from a particular perspective and at a particular point in time. Our intention was to be the most inclusive we could be in terms of the theoretical perspectives, contexts, genres and professional issues that can currently be identified in the coaching field. That is why further chapters on Research in Coaching and Health Coaching were added to this second edition. Although it could be argued that the range of approaches in the book is still a selection and many other traditions and applications of coaching are not represented we believe the book covers the most distinct and influential trends in this area of knowledge that currently exist.

The intention to be inclusive has the result that the approaches and positions of our chapter authors are underpinned by different philosophies and different views on the world as a whole and human nature in particular. One of these philosophies is clearly identified as modern positivism – a worldview based on the assumption that physical and social reality are governed by general laws that can be objectively described and scientific method is the best way for discovering them. In relation to coaching, this paradigm emphasizes the importance of clear goals, the value of techniques and assessments, and behaviours of the coach that are attributed to the effectiveness of coaching.

Other authors approached their chapters from the position of postmodern constructionism – a worldview based on the assumption that reality is not objectively knowable, but rather constructed by individuals and groups as a result of particular beliefs and cultural, historical or social contexts. According to this philosophy, knowledge of reality is relative and depends on the position of the observer. In coaching, this paradigm is manifested through attention to the meaning that is constructed in the session and in the process of building relationship, attention to discourses that shape clients' goals and an opportunity to reconstruct the self of the client in an open dialogue of equal partners.

Identifying these philosophies and the differences between them may help readers to see why significant disagreements exist in evaluating what good coaching is, how coaching competences are assessed and what contributes to the knowledge base of coaching. For example, what is considered as justification of knowledge or evidence of good practice according to one philosophy may not be seen as such in another. This also might leave readers confused in evaluating the value of each approach and also curious about overarching principles that would allow them to do this evaluation.

Although we are not proposing such principles, it might be argued that an alternative philosophical paradigm of pragmatism can be useful for the coaching field at this stage of development. The pragmatic stance is not concerned with 'truth' of particular approach or with how each perspective corresponds to reality. The pragmatic truth lies in the usefulness of the approach helping us to solve particular problems and achieve particular goals, similar to the way many coaches approach their coaching engagements. From this position we hope that readers will take something useful from each perspective of this book.

BUILDING YOUR OWN MODEL

We also hope that the range of perspectives presented in this book will help the readers to create (or recreate) their own model of coaching. The value of having a personal theory or model is that it allows practitioners to examine their practice, to be aware of what is important for them, to know what they ultimately want to achieve in their work and the means they use in this process. We hope that this book provides sufficient input to enable readers to identify or to construct their own model of coaching practice.

Building on Lane and Corrie (2006), we suggest that a personal model of coaching practice may include three essential elements:

> A philosophy that underpins coaching practice: How practitioners see human nature and the world? What is important for them?
>
> The main purpose of coaching: What is it for? What is the coach trying to achieve?
>
> A coherent process: What tools, methods and procedures are needed and appropriate for working towards this purpose and are congruent with this philosophy?

We believe that a personal model should start from a philosophy, that is, a coherent framework that encompasses our own worldview and what is important for us in the way we practise. It also includes a rationale for why this framework is as it is, in the context relevant to our particular practice. The task of creating this element of the model would be well served by gaining a good understanding of the traditions and approaches discussed in this book. For example, a coach's philosophy may fit perfectly with one of the approaches or traditions introduced in Section I of the book. In this case, it is quite possible that what that coach tries to achieve in his/her practice will be identical or closely aligned with the main goals and tasks of this approach. The process described in this approach could also fit with the procedures that are followed and with the tools that are used. If coaches already have a model of their coaching practice, then the book may offer ways of questioning or confirming it from different perspectives. Sometimes coaches may discover that their values resonate with two or more approaches and this may require them to explore if these philosophies are compatible and what implications any tension between them may have on their practice.

Our experience shows, however, that often coaches do not have an explicit model of their practice. Sometimes this is a reflection of the pragmatic stance that coaches take towards their role of helping clients to achieve their goals, without recognition that it is not really a value-free position. Sometimes they explain the lack of an explicit model by defending the flexibility of their approach and the fact that they change the model according to the needs of the client or appropriateness of the situation. Such flexibility, however justified, may cover a reluctance to explore potential frameworks and their own underlying values and intentions, leaving the coach without a clear rationale for why they do what they do. A clear rationale does not mean a rigid position. It indicates a current state of reasonable consistency from which coaches might choose to increase awareness and to experiment in enhancing their practice.

EXPERIMENTING WITH COACHING INTERVENTIONS

Given that the knowledge base for coaching is still emerging, it is valuable for coaches to experiment with, both the techniques and their own learning processes while developing their coaching approach. Some existing traditions in coaching (for example, Gestalt) actively encourage experimentation; others (for example, clean language, or GROW) tend to lead the practitioner towards a relatively fixed logic and process. However, even in the latter case, coaches may seek opportunities to expand their skills through experimentation.

It is important to say that we are not advocating that coaches should create mixed tradition approaches. The 'depth versus breadth' debate about comparing single theory-based approaches (for example, transactional analysis or cognitive–behavioural) and those, which draw upon a more eclectic portfolio of philosophies and theories, is still ongoing. On the one hand, it could be argued that using techniques and procedures from one school of knowledge enables the coach to operate at a greater depth of understanding with a consistent rationale for practice as discussed above. This consistency of the approach then develops the routines of the client's experience, so that they can work *with* the coach in the application of process. It can equally be argued that a single-theory approach is incompatible with the variety of needs and receptivity of the client; that a wider portfolio of potential responses and methods from the coach offers greater flexibility to design approaches specific to the individual. From this latter perspective, the single-theory coach might be seen as more coach-centred (as opposed to client-centred), because the coach's assumptions about the issues and process of solution create a boundary to the coaching conversation. At the other extreme, excessive breadth – knowing a little about a lot of approaches – may be equally questionable if the coach is only able to use these at a relatively superficial level. It is also a bigger challenge in this case for the coach to build a coherent model of practice if they adapt many traditions, which could also be philosophically incompatible.

There are no simple conclusions to draw from this debate, but we believe in the value of a well-formulated model of coaching that may incorporate one, two or more theoretical perspectives that do not clash in terms of their main assumptions. Such a foundation could withstand a pull in a different direction from the inspiring variety of other well-supported perspectives on coaching. It would be able to support 'a managed eclecticism' in terms of the tools, techniques and knowledge that other approaches offer.

At a more pragmatic level, there are some useful basic suggestions for situations that call for the use of tools and techniques that are not embedded in any one perspective or approach to coaching (Megginson & Clutterbuck, 2005):

> Use only what you know from the inside: practice first – if necessary on yourself.
>
> Use them within a loose model of helping.
>
> Have many, so that you are not offering a solution in search of a problem.
>
> Make explicit the intention of the coach in using the technique – apply them *with* the client, not *to* the client.

OUR FINAL REFLECTION ON THIS EDITION

What we have presented here is a shared body of theoretical and contextual knowledge built on the research and experience of a large number of experts in the field. It was a privilege and a challenge to work with a book of such scope and with so many recognized, experienced professionals who generously shared their knowledge and ideas for coaching practice. Also, it was an opportunity to put into practice our view of the field as a matrix – the only structure that made sense for us in trying to capture and conceptualize the diversity of the coaching field.

Although we are aware that much more needs to be done to create a solid knowledge base for coaching, working on this book made us aware again of how vast is the pool of knowledge that is potentially useful for coaching and how wide is the range of ideas brought to coaching from other disciplines. It made us very hopeful about the future of coaching to see how rigorous and sometimes ingenious we as coaches are at distilling from the immensely wide and deep subject areas of knowledge the focused and practical ways necessary for understanding and enriching the coaching process for the benefit of our clients.

In a sense, there cannot be a conclusion to this Handbook, as the need for a second edition attests, because the variety of chapters on approaches, genres and contexts that we have brought together here can only ever be a partial picture of the field of coaching. Indeed, even with new chapters added, there will almost certainly be a variety of new approaches and new applications. Similarly, the professional issues that are discussed are constantly shifting in nature and emphasis. For example, the role of coaching supervision was relatively marginal in development of the field at the time of the first edition. Now supervision is accepted as an important element of being a coaching practitioner. The area of knowledge about coaching supervision is also growing supported by many new publications and existence of the international conference that promotes new research and scholarly debate about issues of practice.

As a natural consequence of continuous development of the coaching field we can say that coaches who care about their model of coaching practice will be wise to constantly reform, refine, re-examine and rebuild that model. If integration of old and new approaches is their ambition we hope that creating this integration will never reach an end, but rather become an ongoing and meaningful process.

REFERENCES

Lane, D.A. & Corrie, S. (2006). *The modern scientist-practitioner: A guide to practice in psychology*. Hove: Routledge.
Megginson, D. & Clutterbuck, D. (2005). *Techniques for coaching and mentoring*. Oxford: Butterworth-Heinemann.

Index

Page references to Figures or Tables will be in *italics*